## HISTORICAL DICTIONARIES
## OF WAR, REVOLUTION, AND CIVIL UNREST
Jon Woronoff, Series Editor

# Historical Dictionary of the Zulu Wars

John Laband

*Historical Dictionaries of War,
Revolution, and Civil Unrest, No. 37*

The Scarecrow Press, Inc.
Lanham, Maryland • Toronto • Oxford
2009

# SCARECROW PRESS, INC.

Published in the United States of America
by Scarecrow Press, Inc.
A wholly owned subsidiary of
The Rowman & Littlefield Publishing Group, Inc.
4501 Forbes Boulevard, Suite 200, Lanham, Maryland 20706
www.scarecrowpress.com

Estover Road
Plymouth PL6 7PY
United Kingdom

British Library Cataloguing in Publication Information Available

**Library of Congress Cataloging-in-Publication Data**

Laband, John, 1947–
  Historical dictionary of the Zulu wars / John Laband.
    p. cm. — (Historical dictionaries of war, revolution, and civil
unrest ; no. 37)
  Includes bibliographical references.
  ISBN 978-0-8108-6078-0 (cloth : alk. paper)
  ISBN 978-0-8108-6300-2 (ebook)
  1. Zululand (South Africa)—History, Military—19th century—Dictionaries.
2. Zulu (African people)—Wars—Dictionaries. 3. South Africa—History,
Military—19th century—Dictionaries. I. Title.
  DT2400.Z85L317 2009
  968.04'403—dc22                                                2008049635

∞ ™ The paper used in this publication meets the minimum requirements of
American National Standard for Information Sciences—Permanence of Paper
for Printed Library Materials, ANSI/NISO Z39.48-1992.
Manufactured in the United States of America.

# Contents

# Editor's Foreword

If you like your wars nice and neat, one side against the other, or just the "good guys" beating the "bad guys," this is not the book for you. In its simplest form, the Zulu Wars can be regarded as a three-way struggle between the Zulus, the Boers, and the British, in various combinations and at various times from 1838 to 1888. But the Zulus were also divided among themselves and lapsed into several civil wars during this period. The Boers were also not very well unified, not being one single political entity. The British, of course, were a single force and had the advantage in soldiers, weapons, wealth, and backing. So of course the Boers beat the Zulus, then the British beat the Boers and the Zulus. But eventually the Boers overcame the British and created a state dominated by the Afrikaners, which in the fullness of time was decolonized and run by the Zulus and others in the modern state of South Africa.

Given the rather confusing and changing situation, a historical dictionary such as this is extremely valuable. It provides the background—first in an extensive chronology and next in a comprehensive stand-alone introduction—that places the historical events in context. The dictionary then examines the various people, places, and events; skirmishes and battles; military units and formations; and equipment and logistics. The bibliography is particularly important because it collects most relevant literature written by eyewitnesses and distant observers in English, as well as Afrikaans and sometimes Zulu.

The author is not related directly to any of the three participants, which is a definite advantage. John Laband studied at the University of Cambridge in England and the University of Natal in South Africa, and he is currently a professor of history at Wilfrid Laurier University in Waterloo, Ontario, Canada. He is also an associate of the Laurier Centre for Military Strategic and Disarmament Studies, and he has written about the Zulu Wars extensively, including several books and numerous articles. He has also shown increasing interest in the Zulu people themselves, having coedited *Zulu Identities: Being Zulu, Past and Present*. This *Historical Dictionary of the Zulu Wars* thus benefits from Professor Laband's considerable knowledge and experience as well as his desire to bring greater fairness and balance to an area in which this is sometimes lacking.

Jon Woronoff
Series Editor

# Acknowledgments

A historical dictionary covering 50 years of conflict in 19th-century Zululand and its neighboring states must owe an enormous debt to scholars who have researched not only the Zulu kingdom but also colonial Natal and the Cape, the Boer republics, the Ndebele, Tsonga, Swazi, Pedi, Sotho, Griqua, and Mpondo polities, and the British military and empire. Two fellow historians with whom I have collaborated in the past, Ian Knight and Paul Thompson, were as generous as ever with their advice and assistance, and in compiling this dictionary I have been especially dependent on their expert publications. I received valuable assistance from my doctoral student Heiko Stang in compiling the bibliography, and from Brian Scribner and Owen Cooke in researching Boer and British biographical entries. Brian Henderson, director of the Wilfrid Laurier University Press, and Eveline Escoto, administrative assistant to the History department at Wilfrid Laurier University, kindly assisted me in preparing the maps and illustrations for publication. Jon Woronoff, series editor, exercised great forbearance during the book's long gestation and lent a steadying hand. I must also thank Wilfrid Laurier University for granting me a course release and sabbatical leave, which were essential for completing this book. My colleagues in the Department of History and the Laurier Centre for Military Strategic and Disarmament Studies were unfailingly supportive. Fenella, as always, sustained me while I wrestled with yet another manuscript.

# Reader's Notes

There is no settled terminology for either the various conflicts in Zululand between 1838 and 1888 or the progressive dismemberments of the Zulu kingdom. In the interests of consistency, concision, and clarity, variant terms have been eliminated from the text. This has meant deciding which particular form should be adopted throughout when variants exist, and establishing new terms where none is commonly in use. Thus the British invasion of 1879 is called the Anglo-Zulu War, and the Zulu uprising of 1888 the uSuthu Rebellion. The Boer invasion of 1838 is termed the Voortrekker-Zulu War to parallel the war of 1879. Civil war wracked Zululand in 1840, 1856, and 1883–1884. The issues behind these wars diverged, but for convenience they are termed the 1st, 2nd, and 3rd Zulu Civil Wars. Zululand was partitioned in 1879, 1882, and 1884 in very different circumstances on each occasion, but as with the civil wars, it is expedient to refer to them as the 1st, 2nd, and 3rd Partitions of Zululand.

In accordance with modern orthographic practice, Zulu words are alphabetized by the root word and not the prefix, thus iKlwa, and not Iklwa (stabbing spear). Entries in the dictionary that include a number, such as that of a regiment, battalion, or battery, are alphabetized under the name of the military formation, for example "Natal Native Contingent, 1st Battalion" or "Royal Artillery, H Battery, 4th Brigade." The same goes for field formations, such as "Column, No. 1" or "South African Field Force, 1st Division." Events such as numbered invasions, wars, or partitions are alphabetized under the name of the event, such as "Anglo-Zulu War, 1st Invasion" or "Zulu Civil War, 1st."

Zulu terms and their plurals regularly employed in the dictionary are listed in the glossary with an English translation. The same applies to terms in Afrikaans. In most cases, Zulu terms are employed in the dictionary entries rather than the English translation in order to avoid a misleading gloss. For example, in referring to the Zulu hierarchy of power, *inKosi* is preferred to *chief* because the latter carries connotations of a paid African functionary of the colonial state. Yet because the same term is used to mean a king, to avoid confusion I have used the English term *king* to describe Zulu rulers, rather than *inKosi*. Other Zulu terms, like *iButho*, or age-grade regiment, refer to a specific Zulu institution that has no direct counterpart in English, so it is preferable to stick to the Zulu term rather than fumble for an inexact counterpart in English. Afrikaans terms usually allow for more precise translation, and many employed in the dictionary, such as *veld* or *laager*, have entered common English usage in South Africa and Great Britain, though not always elsewhere. For this reason, they are also listed in the glossary.

Zulu and other Africans of the period included in the dictionary did not employ surnames but called themselves *ka* (son of) in Zulu, *wa* in Swazi, and *woa* in Pedi: thus King Cetshwayo kaMpande. They are consequently entered in the dictionary under their first name. In a number of cases, the name of the father is not known, because in a society without writing, much depends on patchy oral transmission. While it is often possible to note when a Zulu individual died, the date of birth can mostly be only approximated, although knowledge of the *iButho* to which the person belonged narrows the date to within a span of only a few years. Some of the white colonials (and one or two British officers) have also slipped between the records, and diligent efforts have failed to come up with all the salient dates of their lives and careers.

The colonial term *tribe* is not used to describe the adherents of an *inKosi* who, although offering him their allegiance, were potentially free to transfer it to another. Thus, political units must always be considered in terms of the number of people accepting the rule of an individual rather than in terms of geographical boundaries. Kingdoms could migrate, picking up adherents as they went, and like the Ndebele, they could move the enormous distance from Zululand to modern-day Zimbabwe. It was not unusual, therefore, for King Dingane kaSenzangakhona to attempt to move the Zulu kingdom north in 1839 at the expense of the Swazi when threatened by the Voortrekkers settling to the south.

In biographical entries, an individual's changing rank and titles are noted, but when such individuals are mentioned in entries on other topics, they are accorded the rank or title carried at the time. Thus, while it is Brevet Colonel Evelyn Wood who commanded at Khambula, it is Brigadier-General Wood who fought at Ulundi. The dates in biographical entries given after campaigns in which the subjects fought refer to the dates of their service rather than to the full extent of the campaigns, although in many cases these coincided. When describing the uniforms of units, common features appear under various DRESS entries in the dictionary, and only specific differences are noted in the individual entries. With British infantry regiments, for example, only the color of the facings is mentioned, as uniforms were otherwise standard, whereas the very distinctive uniforms of cavalry regiments are detailed in each case.

Throughout the dictionary, entries are listed in alphabetical order and are cross-referenced to indicate additional information. When a term that has its own entry is mentioned in another dictionary entry, it appears in **bold**. Some entries are simply cross-references to other entries and thus contain nothing more than a *see* reference. There are *see also* references at the end of some entries.

Women were inextricably woven into the fabric of Zulu and Boer military culture and society, and as civilians, many women suffered the full impact of war. Specific entries are not devoted to individual women except for such prominent figures as Harriette Colenso, but women are mentioned in many entries, and cross-referencing has been provided.

In this dictionary covering two major invasions of Zululand, three civil wars, and a rebellion, it was not possible for me to include every single skirmish and every individual involved in events. I had to exercise judgment and exclude potential entries on many secondary players. The task of selection was made easier by the knowledge that many biographical registers are in print where such information can be readily found (see the bibliography for references). Furthermore, I had to balance the need to include biographical information that could be found elsewhere against the desire to provide contextual information that elucidated events in Zululand.

# Acronyms and Abbreviations

| | |
|---|---|
| CDD | Colonial Defensive District |
| DEIC | Dutch East India Company |
| GOC | General officer commanding |
| HMS | Her Majesty's Ship |
| INC | Ixopo Native Contingent |
| NCO | Noncommissioned officer |
| NMP | Natal Mounted Police |
| NMR | Newcastle Mounted Rifles |
| NNC | Natal Native Contingent |
| OFS | Orange Free State |
| RE | Royal Engineers |
| RML | Rifled muzzle-loader |
| RTC | Reserve Territory Carbineers |
| SAR | South African Republic |
| ZP | Zululand Police |
| VOC | Vereenigde Oostindische Compagnie |

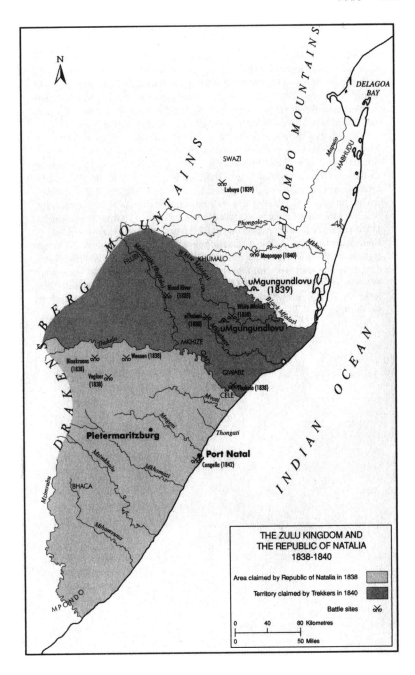

N

DELAGOA
BAY

SWAZI

Lubuya (1839)

L I B O M B O   M O U N T A I N S

Mepupo

MABHUDU

Phongolo

Mkhuze

M O U N T A I N S

KHUMALO

Magongqo (1840)

Mzinyathi (Buffalo)

HLUBI

White Mfolozi

Blood River
(1838)

uMgungundlovu
(1839)

B E R G

White Mfolozi
(1838)

Black Mfolozi

eThaleni
(1838)

uMgungundlovu

Mvoti

MKHIZE

Thukela

OPATI

Weenen (1838)

Blaaukrans
(1838)

Vegloer
(1838)

QWABE

Thukela (1838)

CELE

Mvoti

Mngeni

Thongati

Pietermaritzburg

Mzimvubu

Mambulu

Mkhomazi

Port Natal
Congella (1842)

BHACA

I N D I A N   O C E A N

Mthamvuna

M P O N D O

D R A K E N S B E R G

THE ZULU KINGDOM AND
THE REPUBLIC OF NATALIA
1838-1840

Area claimed by Republic of Natalia in 1838

Territory claimed by Trekkers in 1840

Battle sites

0     40     80 Kilometres

0          50 Miles

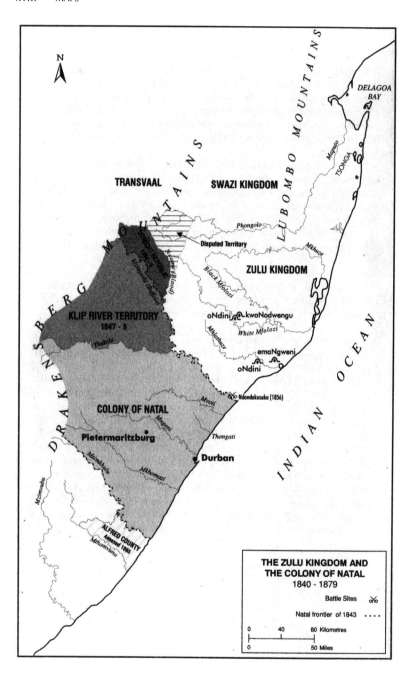

N

TRANSVAAL

SWAZI KINGDOM

DELAGOA BAY

LUBOMBO MOUNTAINS

Phongolo

Disputed Territory

Mkhuze

Maputo

TSONGA

ZULU KINGDOM

Black Mfolozi

Mfolozi

Uithkeane (Blood)
1838

Mkomane (Blood)

Monte (Blood)

KLIP RIVER TERRITORY
1847 - 8

Thukela

oNdini

kwaNodwengu

White Mfolozi

Mhlathuze

emaNgweni

oNdini

Ndondakusuka (1856)

COLONY OF NATAL

Mvoti

Mngeni

Pietermaritzburg

Thongati

Mzimkhulu

Mkhomazi

Durban

DRAKENSBERG MOUNTAINS

INDIAN OCEAN

Mzimvubu

ALFRED COUNTY
Annexed 1865

Mthamvuna

THE ZULU KINGDOM AND
THE COLONY OF NATAL
1840 - 1879

Battle Sites

Natal frontier of 1843   - - - -

0        40        80 Kilometres

0                    50 Miles

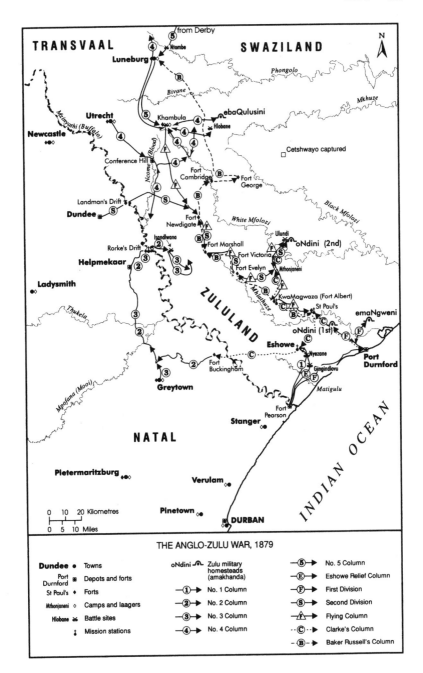

THE ANGLO-ZULU WAR, 1879

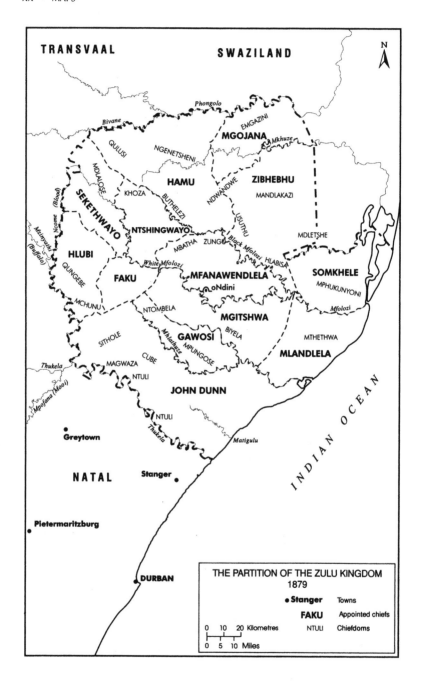

TRANSVAAL

SWAZILAND

N

*Phongolo*

*Bivane*

EMGAZINI

QULUSI

**MGOJANA**

*Mkhuze*

NGENETSHENI

MDLAQEBE

**HAMU**

NDWANDWE

**ZIBHEBHU**

KHOZA

BUTHELEZI

MANDLAKAZI

*Ncome (Blood)*

**SEKETHWAYO**

USUTHU

MDLETSHE

*Mzinyathi (Buffalo)*

**NTSHINGWAYO**

MBATHA

ZUNGU

*Black Mfolozi*

HLABISA

**HLUBI**

*White Mfolozi*

**MFANAWENDLELA**

**SOMKHELE**

QUNGEBE

**FAKU**

oNdini

MPHUKUNYONI

MCHUNU

NTOMBELA

*Mfolozi*

SITHOLE

**MGITSHWA**

BIYELA

MTHETHWA

*Mhlathuze*

**GAWOSI**

CUBE

MAGWAZA

MPUNGOSE

**MLANDLELA**

*Thukela*

NTULI

*Mpofana (Mooi)*

**JOHN DUNN**

NTULI

**Greytown**

*Thukela*

*Matigulu*

**NATAL**

**Stanger**

INDIAN OCEAN

**Pietermaritzburg**

**DURBAN**

THE PARTITION OF THE ZULU KINGDOM
1879

● **Stanger**     Towns

**FAKU**     Appointed chiefs

NTULI     Chiefdoms

0  10  20 Kilometres

0  5  10 Miles

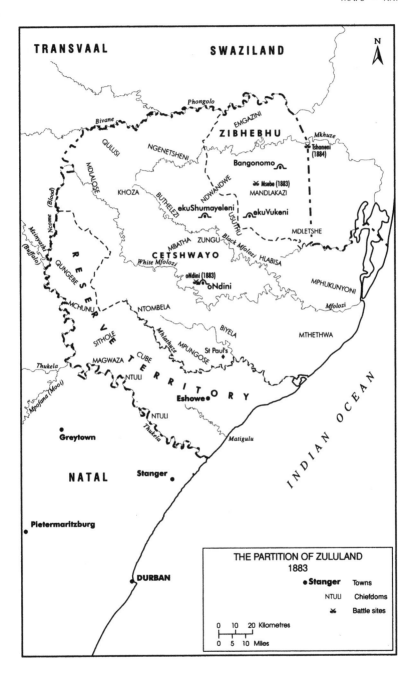

THE PARTITION OF ZULULAND
1883

• **Stanger**    Towns

NTULI    Chiefdoms

✣    Battle sites

0    10    20 Kilometres

0    5    10 Miles

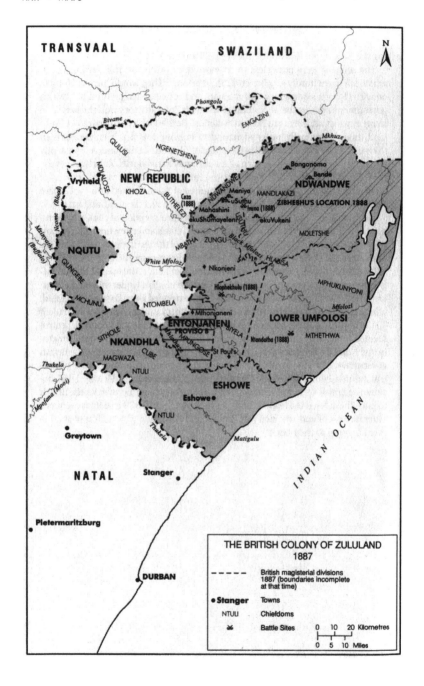

TRANSVAAL

SWAZILAND

N

*Phongolo*

*Bivane*

QUILISI

EMGAZINI

NGENETSHENI

*Mkhuze*

*Ncome (Blood)*

NDLOSE

KHOZA

**NEW REPUBLIC**

Vryheld

BUTHELEZI

Ceza (1888)

NDWANDWE

Meniya

ekuSuthu

Iwna (1888)

Bangonomo

Bande

**NDWANDWE**

MANDLAKAZI

**ZIBHEBHU'S LOCATION 1888**

*Mainywini (Buffalo)*

Mahashini

ekuShumayeleni

ekuVukeni

QUNGEBE

**NQUTU**

MBATHA

ZUNGU

*Black Mfolozi*

HLABISA

MDLETSHE

*White Mfolozi*

Nkonjeni

MPHUKUNYONI

MCHUNU

NTOMBELA

Hlophekhulu (1888)

*Mfolozi*

Mthonjaneni

**LOWER UMFOLOSI**

*Thukela*

SITHOLE

**ENTONJANENI**

PROVISO B

MAPINGOSE

BIYELA

Ntondotha (1888)

MTHETHWA

**NKANDHLA**

CUBE

MAGWAZA

St Paul's

NTULI

**ESHOWE**

Eshowe

*Mpofana (Mooi)*

NTULI

*Thukela*

Greytown

*Matigulu*

INDIAN OCEAN

**NATAL**

Stanger

Pietermaritzburg

DURBAN

---

**THE BRITISH COLONY OF ZULULAND**
**1887**

- - - - -  British magisterial divisions
1887 (boundaries incomplete
at that time)

● **Stanger**  Towns

NTULI  Chiefdoms

✕  Battle Sites

0   10   20 Kilometres

0   5   10 Miles

# Chronology

## THE ZULU KINGDOM AND THE PORT NATAL SETTLERS

**1816** Shaka succeeds his father, *inKosi* Senzangakhona kaJama, to the Zulu chieftainship and begins to consolidate the Zulu kingdom through the conquest or enforced submission of neighboring chiefdoms.

**1824** **May:** First British hunter-traders from the Cape settle at Port Natal. **August:** King Shaka recognizes the Port Natal settlers as tributary chiefs.

**1826** **September:** Port Natal traders with firearms support the Zulu in finally crushing their great rivals, the Ndwandwe, at the battle of the izinDolowane Hills.

**1827** Armed party from Port Natal under James King assists Shaka in subduing the Bheje people.

**1828** **August:** British at the Cape Colony warn Shaka that any further Zulu expansion southward would be sharply resisted. **24 September:** Shaka is assassinated at his kwaDukuza *iKhanda* (administrative center) and is succeeded by his half-brother, Dingane kaSenzangakhona.

**1831** **April:** King Dingane punishes the Port Natal settlers for insubordination.

## THE GREAT TREK AND THE VOORTREKKER-ZULU WAR

**1834** Beginning of the Great Trek, the migration of Dutch-speaking settlers from the Cape (Voortrekkers) into the South African interior.

**1835 March:** Scouting trek under Pieter Uys reports that Zulu territory would make an excellent place to settle. **13 July:** Dingane proclaims Captain Allen Gardiner, the first Christian missionary in Zululand, chief over all the territory between the Thukela and Mzimkhulu rivers, including Port Natal.

**1836 16 October:** At Vegkop, just south of the Vaal River, laagered (encamped) Voortrekkers under Andries Potgieter repel an Ndebele attack.

**1837 17 January:** Voortrekkers under Potgieter and Gert Maritz defeat Ndebele at Mosega. **Late January:** Mercenaries from Port Natal (Durban) under John Cane assist Dingane in raiding the Swazi kingdom. **June–September:** Zulu army unsuccessfully raids Ndebele. **19 October:** Pieter Retief arrives in Port Natal and opens good relations with the British settlers. **November:** The Voortrekkers laager in Zululand. **4–13 November:** Voortrekkers under Potgieter and Piet Uys defeat Ndebele at eGabeni and they flee north across the Limpopo River. **5 November:** Retief visits Dingane at his uMgungundlovu *iKhanda* and receives permission to settle in Zululand. In return, he agrees to recover Zulu cattle raided by Sekonyela of the Mokotleng Tlokwa. **December:** Retief leads a commando (militia unit) over the Drakensberg against Sekonyela.

**1838 January:** Retief successful in recovering the Zulu cattle from Sekonyela. **3 February:** Retief and his following arrive at uMgungundlovu with the cattle. **4 February:** Dingane puts his mark to a dubious document ceding to the Voortrekkers the lands between the Thukela and Mzimvubu rivers. **6 February:** Dingane orders the execution of Retief and his party. **16–18 February:** Zulu army overruns many Voortrekker encampments along the Bloukrans and Bushman rivers (the region later known as *Weenen*, or Weeping) before being driven off. **March:** Voortrekkers and Port Natal settlers agree on a joint offensive against Dingane. Port Natal forces under John Cane raid the Zulu at Ntunjambili near the middle Thukela River. **10 April:** Zulu under Nzobo kaSobadli ambush and defeat Boer commando (*Vlugkommando*) led by Pieter Uys and Andries Pretorius at eThaleni in central Zululand. **17 April:** Zulu under *umNtwana* Mpande kaSenzangakhona rout the Grand Army of Natal under Robert Biggar at Ndondakusuka on the lower Thukela. **24**

**April–3 May:** Zulu comprehensively sack Port Natal. **13–15 August:** Voortrekkers in the Gatsrand laager under Johan Hendrik (Hans Dons) de Lange repel main Zulu army under *inKosi* Ndlela kaSompisi in the battle of Veglaer. **October:** Boers lay out township of Pietermaritzburg. **26 November:** Voortrekkers at Sooilaer elect Andries Pretorius their chief commandant. **27 November:** *Wenkommando* under Pretorius commences its advances into Zululand. **3 December:** Port Natal contingent joins *Wenkommando*. **4 December:** First British occupation of Port Natal. **9 December:** Voortrekkers make a covenant with God at Danskraal on the Wasbankspruit in return for victory over the Zulu. **16 December:** The laagered *Wenkommando* routs main Zulu army under Ndlela and Nzobo at Blood (Ncome) River. **20 December:** *Wenkommando* reaches uMgungundlovu, which Dingane has ordered beforehand to be burned. **26 December:** *Wenkommando* encamps on the Mthonjaneni Heights. **27 December:** Boer commando under Karel Landman and Port Natal forces under Alexander Biggar raid the White Mfolozi valley and are ambushed and routed by the Zulu. **28 December:** Boer commando burns three *amaKhanda* in the emaKhosini valley.

**1839** **2–8 January:** *Wenkommando* returns to the Sooilaer. **January:** Voortrekkers begin settling in Pietermaritzburg, to be their capital. **25 March:** Peace concluded between the Boers and Zulu, permitting the former to live unmolested south of the Thukela River.

## THE 1ST ZULU CIVIL WAR

**1839** **June–July:** Dingane tries to reestablish his kingdom to the north, but the Swazi defeat his forces at Lubuye and force them to withdraw. **September:** "Breaking of the rope": Mpande flees to the Republic of Natalia with his adherents. **27 October:** Mpande strikes alliance with the Boers to attack Dingane. In return for being made king, he agrees to cede to the Boers the lands south of the Thukela as well as St. Lucia Bay. **24 December:** British evacuate Port Natal.

**1840** **4 January:** Boers repudiate their treaty of 25 March 1839 with Dingane. **14 January:** Opening of joint campaign by Mpande and Boers under Pretorius against Dingane. **29 January:** Mpande's army under Nongalaza kaNondela defeats Dingane's forces under Ndlela at the battle of the Maqongqo hills in northern Zululand, and Dingane flees to the Lubombo Mountains. **8 February:** Boer commando withdraws. **10 February:** Boers recognize Mpande as Zulu king. **14 February:** In amendment to the treaty of 27 October 1839, Mpande further cedes Boers all the lands between the Thukela and Black Mfolozi rivers. **March (?):** Dingane, now a refugee with the Nyawo people, is put to death by a Swazi patrol.

## ZULULAND BETWEEN THE BRITISH AND THE BOERS AND THE 2ND ZULU CIVIL WAR

**1842  4 May:** Second British occupation of Port Natal. **23 May:** Boers repulse British in a skirmish at Congella. **24 May–25 June:** Boers besiege the British garrison in Port Natal. **25 June:** British garrison is relieved. **5 July:** *Volksraad* of the Republic of Natalia submits to British authority.

**1843  12 May:** District of Port Natal annexed as a British dependency. **June:** "Crossing of Mawa": refugees from Mpande's rule flee to Natal. **5 October:** Mpande and the British in Natal recognize their respective sovereignties with the Thukela and Mzinyathi rivers as the border.

**1844  31 May:** District of Natal annexed to the Cape Colony.

**1847  January:** Klip River Insurrection: Boers "buy" land between Thukela and Mzinyathi rivers and proclaim independence.

**1848  January:** British exert their authority and suppress independent Klip River. **3 February:** Proclamation of the Orange River Sovereignty extends British authority over the Boers settled between the Orange and Vaal rivers.

**1852  17 January:** Sand River Convention between Britain and the Transvaal Boers recognizes the latter's independence as the South African Republic (SAR).

**1854  23 February:** Bloemfontein Convention between Britain and the Transorangia Boers recognizes the latter's independence as the Orange Free State (OFS). **September:** Mpande cedes the land between the Mzinyathi and Ncome rivers to Boers, who proclaim the Utrecht Republic.

**1856  15 July:** Natal becomes a separate colony of the British Crown. **2 December:** At the battle of Ndondakusuka on the lower Thukela, *umNtwana* Cetshwayo kaMpande leads his uSuthu to a crushing victory over the iziGqoza of his brother, *umNtwana* Mbuyazi kaMpande, and his white-hunter ally from Natal, John Dunn. His victory in the 2nd Zulu Civil War secures Cetshwayo's right of succession to the Zulu throne.

**1859  6 December:** Utrecht Republic absorbed as a district into the SAR.

**1861  March:** Treaty of Waaihoek: Boers hand exiled royal rivals over to Cetshwayo in return for indeterminate land claims east of the Ncome River, thus creating the problem of the "Disputed Territory." **May:** Theophilus Shepstone, Natal secretary for native affairs, recognizes Cetshwayo as Mpande's co-ruler. **June–August:** Invasion scare in Natal as Zulu mobilize against Boer incursions into Zululand.

**1868  12 March:** British annexation of Sotho kingdom.

**1869**  Diamond rush begins near the confluence of the Orange and Vaal rivers just west of the Orange Free State. **June:** SAR allots farms east of the Ncome to Boer settlers.

**1871  August:** Basutoland annexed to the Cape. **October:** British annexation of Griqualand West and the diamond diggings.

**1872  September or October:** Mpande dies.

**1873  August:** King Cetshwayo's Zulu coronation. **1 September:** Shepstone "crowns" Cetshwayo, who agrees to the "coronation laws." **29 October–31 December:** Suppression by Natal colonial forces of a "rebellion" led by *inKosi* Langalibalele kaMthimkhulu of the Hlubi people.

**1875  25 May:** SAR proclamation claiming the Zulu territory "ceded" in 1861, plus a slice of territory south of the Phongolo River between Zululand and Swaziland. **June:** Natal prohibits the direct sale of firearms to Zululand.

**1876   May:** SAR goes to war with the Pedi people on its northeastern border. **2 August:** Boers fail to take Pedi stronghold, and SAR abandons campaign.

## CONFEDERATION, THE ANGLO-ZULU WAR, AND THE 1ST PARTITION OF ZULULAND

**1876   August:** London Conference on South African Affairs promotes confederation.

**1877   27 February:** Sir Bartle Frere appointed governor of the Cape and high commissioner for South Africa with the task of confederating the subcontinent under the Crown. **12 April:** Shepstone annexes the SAR as the British Transvaal Territory. **18 October:** Unsuccessful meeting at Conference Hill between Shepstone and Zulu delegation to resolve the issue of the Disputed Territory. **10 August:** Permissive Federation Bill receives royal assent as the South Africa Act of 1877. **August:** 9th Cape Frontier War breaks out. **November:** abaQulusi *iButho* (regiment) asserts Zulu territorial claim north of the Phongolo of land inhabited by the Luneburg settlers. **8 December:** Henry Bulwer offers Natal's mediation in the Zulu–Transvaal border dispute. **25 December:** Fighting between two rival *amaButho* at the *umKhosi* (first-fruits ceremony) exposes fissures between Zulu ruling elite.

**1878   16 February:** Britain and Portugal prohibit sale of firearms and ammunition to Africans. **4 March:** Lieutenant-General Thesiger (later Lord Chelmsford) takes up his command as general officer commanding in South Africa. **17 March:** Boundary Commission meets at Rorke's Drift. **5 March:** British in the Transvaal reopen campaign against Pedi. **April–May:** Failed uprising in Griqualand West against British rule. **15 July:** Boundary Commission submits report favorable to Zulu claims. **28 July:** Sihayo "incident" on the Natal–Zululand border alarms settlers. **August:** Conclusion of 9th Cape Frontier War. **9 August:** Thesiger sets up headquarters in Pietermaritzburg. **31 August:** Thesiger annexes Port St. John's. **September:** Provocative hunts by Zulu *amaButho* opposite Natal border; abaQulusi order Luneburg settlers to leave. **10 September:** Thesiger persuades Natal government to raise large field force of African levies (troops) to guard the frontier with Zululand. **17 September:** Deighton and Smith "incident" on the Natal–Zululand border. **7 October:** British suspend unsuccessful campaign against Pedi. Swazi freebooter Mbilini waMswati (allied to Cetshwayo) raids Luneburg area. **19 October:** British troops move up from Utrecht to Luneburg to protect settlers. **October:** Temporary mustering of the *amaButho* in the Mahlabathini Plain. **6 November:** *UmNtwana* Hamu kaNzibe informs British of intention to defect if war should break out. **13 November:** Zulu messengers to Natal convey Cetshwayo's desire for peace. **23 November:** Issue of regulations for raising the Natal Native Contingent (NNC) in Natal. **26 November:** Natal divided into Colonial Defensive Districts. Natal Mounted Volunteers called out for active service. **11 December:** John Shepstone delivers the boundary award and the British ultimatum to Zulu deputation at the Lower Thukela. NNC called into service. **13 December:** British military preparations for the invasion of Zululand completed. **20 December:** African Border Guards and part-time reserve levies organized for the defense of the Natal border. **22 December:** Zulu deputation reports to Cetshwayo with the terms of the ultimatum. **31 December:** John Dunn, Cetshwayo's white chief, deserts to Natal with adherents.

**1879   6 January:** No. 4 Column under Colonel Wood crosses the Ncome River into Zulu territory. **8 January:** Zulu *amaButho* muster for the *umKhosi* in the Mahlabathini Plain. **9 January:** No. 3 Column under Colonel Glyn concentrates at Rorke's Drift. **10 January:** Public meeting at Wonderfontein of irreconcilable Transvaal Boers decides on policy of noncooperation with British. Bemba, a Mdlalose *inDuna* (officer), surrenders to Wood. **11 January:** No. 3 Column under Chelmsford's effective command invades Zululand at Rorke's Drift. Natal Defensive Districts along Zululand border placed under military command. **11–13 January:** Wood raids toward Rorke's Drift with a flying column. **12 January:** No. 1 Column under Colonel Pearson invades Zululand at Fort Pearson. No. 3 Column wins skirmish at kwaSogekle. **15 January:** Zulu force prevents *inKosi* Sekethwayo kaNhlaka of the Mdlalose from surrendering to Wood. No. 2 Column under Colonel Durnford divided: part to remain at Middle Drift and rest under Durnford to reinforce No. 3 Column. **17 January:** Zulu army marches out from the kwaNodwengu *iKhanda*. **18 January:** Zulu army splits: smaller force under *inKosi* Godide kaNdlela moves against No. 1 Column; larger force under *inKosi* Ntshingwayo kaMahole and *inKosi*

Mavumengwana kaNdlela moves against No. 3 Column. **20 January:** No. 4 Column crosses White Mfolozi. Thinta, a Mdlalose *inDuna*, surrenders to Wood. AbaQulusi repulse Colonel Buller and mounted men of No. 4 Column at Zungwini Mountain. No. 3 Column encamps at Isandlwana. Main Zulu army encamps by Siphezi Mountain. **21 January:** No. 1 Column burns undefended kwaGingindlovu *iKhanda*. Reconnaissance in force under Major Dartnell moves out of Isandlwana camp. **21–22 January:** Main Zulu army moves undetected by British to Ngwebeni valley. **22 January:** Chelmsford moves out of camp to reinforce reconnaissance force that Dartnell believes is threatened by Zulu forces. Durnford reinforces garrison left in Isandlwana camp with part of No. 2 Column. Main Zulu army overruns Isandlwana camp. Chelmsford returns too late to save it. No. 1 Column fights through Zulu ambush at Nyezane River. Wood disperses Zulu on Zungwini. **22–23 January:** Garrison at No. 3 Column's depot at Rorke's Drift repulses the Zulu reserve under *inKosi* Dabulamanzi kaMpande. **23 January:** No. 1 Column reaches Eshowe mission station and begins to fortify it. Remnants of No. 3 Column retire to Natal. No. 4 Column retires toward Khambula Hill on learning of Isandlwana. **27–29 January:** Court of Enquiry convened by Chelmsford looks into the loss at Isandlwana. **January–February:** Colonists take refuge in their laagers on learning of Isandlwana. **26 January:** No. 5 Column under Colonel Rowlands (which had remained in garrison at Derby and Luneburg) raids the Kubheka in Ntombe River valley. **30 January:** Pearson decides to hold fast at Eshowe with British troops and sends the NNC and mounted men back to Natal. Zulu under Dabulamanzi blockade Eshowe. **1 February:** No. 4 Column forms an entrenched camp at Khambula. Patrol under Buller burns the ebaQulusini *iKhanda*. **10 February:** Buller raids abaQulusi on Hlobane Mountain. **10–11 February:** The Kubheka, Mbilini's adherents, and abaQulusi ravage farms and mission stations in the Ntombe valley. **15 February:** Buller raids the Kubheka in the Ntombe valley and Rowlands attacks the abaQulusi on Talaku Mountain. **16 February:** British government agrees to Chelmsford's urgent request for reinforcements. **26 February:** No. 5 Column attached to Wood's command. **February–March:** British reinforcements and colonial troops from the Cape arrive in Natal. **1 March:** Raid by Eshowe garrison burns eSiqwakeni *iKhanda*. Zulu peace emissaries arrive at Middle Drift. **10 March:** Hamu and his Ngenetsheni adherents, pursued by Cetshwayo's forces, defect to Wood. **Mid-March:** Cetshwayo summons his councilors to oNdini to discuss prosecution of the war. **12 March:** At the Ntombe drift, Mbilini's forces overwhelm convoy of No. 5 Column under Captain Moriarty on way from Derby to Luneburg. **22 March:** Zulu army reassembles at oNdini. **23 March:** Eshowe Relief Column under Chelmsford concentrates at Fort Pearson. Zulu peace emissaries arrive at Fort Eshowe. **24–28 March:** Zulu army under *inKosi* Mnyamana kaNgqengelele marches against Wood at Khambula. **24 March:** British border demonstration under Major Twentyman along Thukela at Middle Drift. **25 March:** Buller raids Kubheka in Ntombe valley. **27 March:** British demonstration under Captain Lucas along lower Thukela. **28 March:** Zulu peace emissaries arrive at Middle Drift. Force under Wood trying to clear Hlobane of abaQulusi and Mbilini's followers trapped by arrival of main Zulu army and routed. **29 March:** Wood routs the Zulu army attacking Khambula. Eshowe Relief Column advances into Zululand. **2 April:** Zulu army concentrated near Eshowe under *inKosi* Somopho kaZikhala attacks the Eshowe Relief Column's laager at Gingindlovu and is routed. **2–3 April:** Twentyman raids Zululand at Middle Drift. **3 April:** Eshowe garrison evacuated to Thukela and fort abandoned. AbaQulusi and Mbilini's followers evacuate Hlobane. **4 April:** Frere orders that Zulu peace feelers must not delay military operations. **5 April:** Mbilini killed in skirmish and local Zulu resistance withers in the northwest. **9 April:** Rorke's Drift garrison raids up the Batshe River to Isandlwana. **12 April:** Frere meets Boer leaders at Hennopsrivier and unsuccessfully offers the Transvaal self-government within British confederation. **13 April:** Eshowe Relief Column becomes the 2nd Brigade of the 1st Division, South African Field Force, concentrating on the lower Thukela under Major-General Crealock. No. 4 and 5 Columns restyled Wood's Flying Column. **April–June:** 1st Division concentrates supplies and builds force in preparation for advance up Zululand coast. **Mid-April:** 2nd Division, South African Field Force, under Major-General Newdigate begins concentrating at Dundee. **21 April:** *UmNtwana* Makwendu kaMpande surrenders to 1st Division. **2 May:** 2nd Division masses at entrenched camp at Landman's Drift on the Mzinyathi River. **5 May:** Wood's Flying Column begins its march toward oNdini. **13–21 May:** Mounted patrols from 2nd Division clear path of division's advance of any Zulu presence. **15 May:** Zulu peace emissaries arrive at Fort Chelmsford on the coast. **20 May:** Twentyman raids Zululand at Middle Drift. **21 May:** Reconnaissance in force by 2nd Division begins the burial of the British dead at Isandlwana. **26 May:** British government subordinates Chelmsford's command to General Wolseley. **28 May:** Lucas raids Zululand at lower Thukela. Zulu peace emissaries arrive at Fort Chelmsford. **31 May:** 2nd Division crosses Ncome River at Koppie Alleen into Zululand. **1 June:** Prince Eugène Louis Napoleon Bonaparte of France (an observer on Chelmsford's staff) killed at the Tshotshosi River on patrol. **3 June:** 2nd Division and Wood's Flying Column effect junction at the Tshotshosi River under Chelmsford's overall command. **4 June:** Zulu peace emissaries arrive at Wood's camp at the Nondwini River. **5 June:** Mounted men of 2nd Division and Wood's Flying Column skirmish unsuccessfully with Zulu irregulars at Zungeni Mountain and withdraw. **7–17 June:** Chelmsford's columns halt at Ntinini River to escort convoys of supplies. Zulu raiders sweep Luneburg district with assistance of disaffected Transvaal Boers. **14 June:** Buller raids north to Ntabankulu Mountain. **16 June:** Chelmsford lays down easy terms for surrender of Zulu chiefs but retains stringent conditions for Cetshwayo himself. Chelmsford learns informally of Wolseley's appointment. **18 June:** Joint advance of 2nd Division and Wood's Flying Column recommences. **20 June:** Buller skirmishes with Zulu in Mphembheni valley. **23–26 June:** Mounted patrols from 1st Division raid between the Ngoye Hills and the coast. **24 June:** Wolseley arrives in Cape Town. **25 June:** 1st Division crosses Mhlathuze River and starts Fort Napoleon. Zulu peace emissaries arrive at Fort Pearson. Zulu raiders cross Thukela and ravage valley below Ntunjambili in Natal. **26 June:** Wood leads patrol into the emaKhosini valley and burns nine *amaKhanda* and the sacred *iNkatha* (symbolic grass coil). **27 June:** Zulu peace emissaries arrive near Mthonjaneni. **29 June:** Chelmsford's columns laager on Mthonjaneni Heights overlooking Mahlabathini Plain. **30 June:** Zulu peace emissaries arrive at Fort Napoleon. Zulu peace emissaries come into Mthonjaneni camp. Chelmsford gives Cetshwayo until 3 July to comply with conditions. **1 July:** 1st Division encamps at Port Durnford where it is supplied by sea and by convoys from Fort Chelmsford. **2 July:** Chelmsford forms laager on south bank of the White Mfolozi. Cetshwayo makes last, futile attempt to negotiate a peace. **2–4 July:** Wolseley unable to land through heavy surf at Port Durnford. **3 July:** Zulu ambush and repel Buller's mounted reconnaissance from the White Mfolozi camp toward oNdini. **4 July:** British under Chelmsford rout the Zulu at the battle of Ulundi and burn all the *amaKhanda* in the Mahlabathini Plain. Cetshwayo flees north and Zulu army disperses home. Chelmsford withdraws to his base on Mthonjaneni. Mounted patrol from 1st Division burns emaNgweni *iKhanda*. More local *amaKhosi* make their submission at Port Durnford. **5 July:** Major coastal *amaKhosi* surrender at 1st Division camp at the lower drift of the Mhlathuze. Chelmsford resigns his command. **6 July:** Mounted patrol from 1st Division burns old oNdini *iKhanda*. **7 July:** Buller raids south to kwaMagwaza. Wolseley rides into Port Durnford from Durban. **9 July:** Chelmsford receives formal notice of Wolseley's appointment. Wood's Flying Column starts to withdraw south toward Natal. **10 July:** 2nd Division withdraws the way it had come to Natal. **12 July:** Dabulamanzi surrenders. **19 July:** Wolseley receives formal submission of coastal *amaKhosi* at lower drift of Mhlathuze near burned emaNgweni and states his terms. **23 July:** 1st Division broken up. Elements form Clarke's Column to reoccupy the Mahlabathini Plain. **26 July:** Wolseley issues instructions for inducing Zulu chiefs to surrender. Cetshwayo's messengers reach kwaMagwaza seeking terms. Baker Russell's Column (made up of elements of Wood's Flying Column) begins final pacification of northwestern Zululand. 2nd Division is broken up. **31 July:** Wood's Flying Column broken up. **August:** African levies and contingents mustered out. **10 August:** Wolseley encamps at kwaSishwili, close to the destroyed oNdini. Cetshwayo's final message reaches Wolseley. Colonel Villiers's Column moves south from Derby with Swazi forces and Hamu's fighting men to support Baker Russell's Column. **14 August:** Mnyamana sues for terms from Wolseley on behalf of Cetshwayo. **15 August:** Sekethwayo surrenders to Baker Russell at Fort Cambridge. **14–26 August:** Zulu chiefs of central and northern Zululand, including Mnyamana and Zibhebhu, submit to Wolseley. **20 August:** Chiefs of southwestern Zululand submit to Natal official, Francis Fynn, at Rorke's Drift. **25 August:** Villiers's Column reaches Luneburg. **28 August:** Cetshwayo betrayed and captured at kwaDwasa in the Ngome Forest by patrol under Major Marter. **1 September:** At kwaSishwili, Wolseley imposes his settlement (the 1st Partition of Zululand) on defeated Zulu chiefs. He abolishes the Zulu monarchy and divides former kingdom into 13 independent chiefdoms under appointed chiefs to be supervised by a British Resident.

AbaQulusi surrender to Baker Russell as his column approaches Luneburg. **4 September:** Cetshwayo taken off by sea at Port Durnford for exile at the Cape. **4–8 September:** Baker Russell's Column and Luneburg garrison break last of Kubheka resistance in the Ntombe valley. **5 September:** Clarke's Column begins its march from kwaSishwili to Middle Drift to enforce submission of southern Zulu chiefs. **8 September:** Villiers's Column disbanded. **10 September:** Baker Russell's Column ordered to Transvaal for renewed operations against the Pedi. British posts along the Zulu border abandoned. **21 September:** Final Zulu submissions to Clarke's Column at Middle Drift. **September–December:** Wolseley crushes Pedi resistance in the Transvaal.

## THE 2ND AND 3RD PARTITIONS OF ZULULAND AND THE 3RD ZULU CIVIL WAR

**1880**   **May:** First uSuthu deputation to Pietermaritzburg pleading for restoration of Cetshwayo. **September:** Outbreak of the "Gun War" in Basutoland against Cape rule. **13 December:** Transvaal Boers meeting at Paardekraal reconstitute the republican government and proclaim martial law. **18 December:** The British administration in the Transvaal acts to put down the Transvaal Rebellion by force.

**1881**   **15 March:** British and Boer forces in the Transvaal agree to an armistice. **3 August:** Pretoria Convention signed conceding Transvaal independence under nebulous British "suzerainty." **31 August:** Major-General Wood (acting high commissioner) meets representatives of the contending Zulu factions at Nhlazatshe Mountain and confirms the British will uphold the 1st Partition of Zululand.

**1882**   **April:** Second unsuccessful uSuthu deputation to Pietermaritzburg. **September–October:** Factional clashes in northwestern Zululand. **August:** Cetshwayo permitted to travel to England to plead his cause with the British government. **11 December:** Cetshwayo agrees to his restoration to the central portion of his former kingdom. Northeastern Zululand remains under the collaborationist Mandlakazi chief Zibhebhu. The Reserve Territory is created between the Thukela and Mhlathuze rivers and is put under British protection to be administered by Natal officials.

**1883  10 January:** Cetshwayo lands at Port Durnford. **January–March:** Fighting breaks out between the uSuthu and their opponents in northern Zululand. **30 March:** Zibhebhu with white mercenaries under Johan Colenbrander routs the uSuthu army at the Msebe River. **1 April–20 July:** Fighting continues between the uSuthu and their opponents in northern Zululand. **April:** Creation of paramilitary police force, the Reserve Territory Carbineers, with its headquarters in Eshowe. **21 July:** Zibhebhu and Hamu crush the uSuthu in dawn attack at oNdini and kill most of the leadership; uSuthu scatter and Cetshwayo flees. **August:** Cetshwayo takes refuge in the Nkandla Forest in the Reserve Territory. **August–September:** Zibhebhu and Hamu raid central and coastal Zululand. **19 September:** Boers from the SAR begin to occupy northwestern Zululand. **20 September:** The Etshowe Column, drawn from the British garrison in Natal, moves into the Reserve Territory to support the African levies, raised by Melmoth Osborn, the resident commissioner, maintain order. **24 September:** Zibhebhu threatens the Reserve Territory. **29 September:** Etshowe Column occupies Eshowe and builds Fort Curtis. **15 October:** Cetshwayo takes refuge with the British in Eshowe. **September–December**: Chaotic fighting continues across Zululand.

**1884  January–February:** Fighting continues, particularly in northern Zululand, with Zibhebhu ascendant over the uSuthu. **8 February:** Cetshwayo dies, possibly by poison, and is succeeded by his minor son Dinuzulu kaCetshwayo under the guardianship of his uncles. **February–March:** Fighting in the coastal region between the uSuthu and the Mthethwa. **29 April:** Hamu and his Ngenetsheni scatter the uSuthu concentrating in the Ngome Forest in northern Zululand. **May:** uSuthu forces in southwestern Zululand resume struggle against the Mandlakazi and Zulu loyal to the British. Osborn raises African levies to defend the Reserve Territory from the uSuthu. **2 May:** Dinuzulu meets Boers at Hlobane Mountain to negotiate an alliance. **10 May:** uSuthu under Dabulamanzi defeat Osborn's forces in the eastern Nkandla Forest. **20 May:** Hlubi's "Basutos" recruited to fight uSuthu in the western Reserve Territory. **21 May:** Boers of the Committee of Dinuzulu's Volunteers proclaim Dinuzulu king of the Zulu and promise him military assistance against Zibhebhu in return for land in Zululand. **22–23 May:** Basutos worst uSuthu forces in the Nkandla Forest. **27**

**May:** British troops from the Natal garrison reinforce the military posts in the Reserve Territory. **1 June:** Basutos and African levies defeat uSuthu under Dabulamanzi in the Nkandla Forest. **5 June:** Boers and uSuthu rout Zibhebhu at Tshaneni Mountain in northeastern Zululand. **June–August:** Boers and uSuthu ravage Mandlakazi territory. British garrison at Fort Northampton aids Basutos against uSuthu still resisting in the Nkandla Forest. **3 July:** uSuthu attack loyalists in the Nkandla Forest. **7 July:** British troops from Eshowe make reconnaissance in force toward the Nkandla and erect Fort Yolland. **11 August:** Osborn begins negotiating surrender of the uSuthu in the Nkandla. **16 August:** Dinuzulu cedes 2,710,000 acres of northwestern Zululand to the Boers for the establishment of the New Republic. Boers also extend a "protectorate" over the rest of Zululand north of the Reserve Territory (Eastern Zululand). **August:** New Republic Boers occupy the farms they have allocated themselves and reduce Zulu living there to labor tenants. **7 September:** Osborn grants Zibhebhu and Mandlakazi refuge in the Reserve Territory. **9 September:** uSuthu in Nkandla submit to British. **21 December:** Britain asserts its claims to St. Lucia Bay to forestall the SAR and Germany.

**1885   26 October:** New Republic proclaims a boundary that extends to the coast.

**1886   29 April:** Under British pressure, New Republic modifies its boundary line. **22 October:** Britain recognizes New Republic in return for abandoning its claim to Eastern Zululand and for ceding Proviso B, a block of territory in central Zululand where the Boers are allowed to retain ownership of the farms they have laid out.

**1887   25 January:** Boundary Commission defines the borders of the New Republic.

## THE BRITISH ANNEXATION OF THE COLONY OF ZULULAND AND THE USUTHU REBELLION

**1887   5 February:** Osborn informs uSuthu leadership that British protection has been extended over Eastern Zululand. **February:** Hamu dies. **19 May:** Reserve Territory, Eastern Zululand, and Proviso B annexed as the British Colony of Zululand and put under white magistrates. Reserve Territory Carbineers restyled the Zululand Police. **22 August:** British troops moved up to Nkonjeni in the new Ndwandwe District in support of the civil authorities being defied by the uSuthu leadership concentrated there, and other Zululand bases reinforced by the Natal garrison. **November:** British repatriate Zibhebhu and Mandlakazi to the Ndwandwe District to help overawe the uSuthu, who respond with hostility to their presence.

**1888 January:** Large location assigned Zibhebhu inflames the uSuthu further. More troops moved up temporarily to Ndwandwe contain the situation. **15 February:** Dinuzulu unsuccessfully seeks assistance from New Republic. **March–April:** AbaQulusi supporters of Dinuzulu start mustering on Ceza Mountain on the border of northwestern Zululand and the New Republic. **26 April:** Attempt by the Zululand Police to arrest uSuthu ringleaders at Dinuzulu's oSuthu homestead resisted by force. **May:** uSuthu under Dinuzulu join abaQulusi on Ceza and raid Zulu loyalists and white traders. **31 May:** Zibhebhu reinforces the Ivuna magistracy held by the Zululand Police. **2 June:** Zululand Police, assisted by British troops, repulsed when they attempt to arrest uSuthu leaders on Ceza. **June:** uSuthu on Ceza and Boer freebooters in control of much of northern Zululand. Usuthu forces under *umNtwana* Shingana kaMpande concentrate on Hlophekhulu Mountain in central Zululand. Zibhebhu raids his uSuthu neighbors from Ivuna. **6 June:** Reinforcements dispatched to Zululand from the Natal garrison. African auxiliaries raised in the Eshowe and Nkandhla Districts of Zululand. **23 June:** uSuthu from Ceza, under Dinuzulu, rout Zibhebhu at Ivuna but avoid attacking the magistrate's fort. **24 June:** Ivuna garrison and Mandlakazi survivors evacuated to British base at Nkonjeni. British abandon Zululand north of the Black Mfolozi River. **28 June:** Lieutenant-General Smyth, the general officer commanding in South Africa, arrives in Eshowe to take command. **30 June:** In battle of Ntondotha, coastal uSuthu unsuccessfully attack Fort Andries in the Lower Umfolosi District. **2 July:** British troops and African auxiliaries under Colonel Stabb storm Hlophekhulu and restore British control in central Zululand. **6 July:** Formation of Eshowe Column under Major McKean at Kongella Camp to relieve Fort Andries. Usuthu in northeastern Zululand, assisted by Boer freebooters, begin ravaging Zibhebhu's abandoned territory. **9 July:** Eshowe Column relieves Fort Andries and replaces it with Fort McKean. **11–13 July:** Eshowe Column returns to Eshowe, burning deserted uSuthu homesteads on the march. **Mid-July:** Disaffected African levies desert at Nkonjeni and go out of control at Mfule. **20 July:** New Republic is incorporated into the SAR as the Vryheid District. **25 July:** Coastal Column under McKean joins Dunn's Native Levy at the lower Mhlathuze drift to enforce uSuthu submissions along the coast. British reinforcements concentrate at Nkonjeni for final push to reestablish civil authority in Zululand. **28 July:** Coastal Column encamps at Camp Umfolosi and ravages surrounding uSuthu territory. **30 July:** Submission of *inKosi* Somkhele kaMalanda and other coastal uSuthu chiefs. **1 August:** Smyth moves his headquarters from Eshowe to Nkonjeni. **1–6 August:** Dunn's Levy collects cattle fines along coast. **2 August:** Coastal Column commences its march into Ndwandwe District. **6 August:** Coastal Column reaches Ivuna. **6–7 August:** Dinuzulu disbands uSuthu on Ceza and seeks refuge in SAR. **7 August:** Colonel Martin's Flying Column from Nkonjeni arrives at Ivuna. **8 August:** Dunn's Levy returns to Eshowe District. **8–20 August:** Mutinous Mounted Basutos at Ivuna raid loyal Zulu for supplies. **11–12 August:** Patrols from Nkonjeni clash with uSuthu at Dlebe Mountain and violate SAR territory. **18–30 August:** Joint column (Coastal Column and Flying Column) marches from Ivuna to Eshowe, subduing last pockets of resistance. **19 August:** Zibhebhu attacks and repels uSuthu ravaging his district. **23 August:** Mounted Basutos and African levies disbanded. **27 August:** Civil magistrate and Zululand Police reoccupy Ivuna magistracy. **10 September:** uSuthu in northeastern Zululand raid Zibhebhu. **30 September:** Smyth orders all advanced posts in Ndwandwe be abandoned, with troops either to be redistributed to garrisons at Entonjaneni or Eshowe or to return to Natal. **2 November:** Zululand garrison reduced to its normal level. **15 November:** Dinuzulu surrenders to the civil authorities in Pietermaritzburg. **17 November:** British authorities arrest Zibhebhu and remove him from the Ndwandwe District.

**1889    13 February–27 April:** Special Court of Commission in Eshowe finds Dinuzulu and other uSuthu ringleaders guilty of high treason and sentences them to imprisonment on St. Helena. **1 August:** Governor of Zululand decrees that Zibhebhu may not return to Ndwandwe.

**1895  30 May:** Tongaland (Amaputaland) annexed as a British protectorate. **15 July:** District of Ingwavuma incorporated into the Colony of Zululand.

**1897  24 December:** Tongaland incorporated into the Colony of Zululand. **30 December:** Colony of Zululand annexed to Natal and administered as a province of Natal until the Union of South Africa on 31 May 1910.

**1898  January:** Dinuzulu and Zibhebhu brought back to Zululand as part of a general settlement to restore stability. Dinuzulu's status reduced from king to "government inDuna" of the uSuthu location.

**1903  27 January:** Following defeat in the Anglo-Boer War (1899–1902), former SAR cedes the northern districts of Vryheid, Utrecht, and Paulpietersburg to Natal, thus bringing all the constituent parts of the former Zulu kingdom under Natal's administration.

**1906  31 January:** White occupation of Zululand commences in accordance with the findings of the Zululand Lands Delimitation Committee of 1902–1904. **February–August:** Zulu Uprising of 1906 (Bhambatha Rebellion).

**1910  31 May:** Colony of Natal becomes a province of the Union of South Africa.

# Introduction

The term "Zulu Wars" is very imprecise, there being no single, generally accepted understanding of what it encompasses. Most often it is sloppily applied to the Anglo-Zulu War of 1879, but to do so is to ignore the many other wars fought in Zululand during the course of the 19th and early 20th centuries. Yet where should the lines of definition be drawn? For the purposes of this historical dictionary they embrace the extended confrontation between the Zulu kingdom and the advancing forces of colonialism and imperialism that began with the Voortrekker invasion of 1838 and ended in 1888 with the failure of resistance to newly imposed British rule. Excluded are the Zulu campaigns of the 1820s and early 1830s against neighboring African polities before the coming of the Voortrekkers, as well as the much later participation of Zulu people as British subjects in the Anglo-Boer (South African) War of 1899–1902. A more problematical case is that of the Zulu Uprising of 1906 (Bhambatha Rebellion) that flared up in both the colony of Natal and in what was by then its province of Zululand. Yet, unlike the traditionalist uSuthu Rebellion of 1888 that yearned back to the freshly extinguished Zulu kingdom, the 1906 uprising was a different phenomenon in which oppressed African subjects of the established colonial state were developing new forms of resistance. The Zulu Wars, then, are the story of initial Zulu resistance to conquest by the steadily encroaching Boers and British, and of the civil wars triggered in the consequently destabilized Zulu kingdom that made it increasingly vulnerable to partition between its colonial neighbors.

## ZULULAND: THE LAND AND ITS PEOPLE

Because it began as an expanding conquest state in the early 1820s, and was later contained and then fragmented and incorporated by its Boer and British neighbors, the boundaries of Zululand were in constant flux during the 19th century. Nevertheless, the core of the kingdom always lay between the Mzinyathi River to the west and the Indian Ocean to the east, the Thukela River to the south, and the Phongolo River to the north. At its heart was the valley of the White Mfolozi River, where the Zulu kingdom arose and where many of its kings were buried. Today this region comprises the northern half of the South African province of KwaZulu-Natal, bounded to the north by the states of Swaziland and Mozambique.

Unlike mountainous Swaziland and Lesotho to the north and west, where the people were protected from conquerors by their difficult and broken terrain, the Zulu lived mainly in open and well-watered country suitable for stock farming and agriculture. These advantages later made their land fatally attractive to white settlers. The river systems rise in the great chain of the Drakensberg Mountains to the west, and with their steep-sided, sinuous tributaries, they have incised wide, deep, open valleys through the countryside. During much of the year, the riverbeds are nearly empty, but during the summer rainy season, they are often in torrent. When they reach the coastal plain, the rivers become sluggish, and their mouths are closed by sandbars that produce lagoons and marshes. The humid subtropical coastal plain, with its heavy rainfall, rises a few miles inland to well-watered, boldly modeled hills. Farther inland, as the rains borne off the Indian Ocean decrease, the terrain changes. The undulating countryside of the midlands that swells in gentle, rounded ridges is broken across by great, forested spurs of the Drakensberg that thrust out toward the coast. Between the foothills of the Drakensberg and the midlands stretch high, dry, open plains dotted with solitary, abruptly rising, flat-topped mountains, their rocky coronets full of caves. Wild game once abounded in great variety and in unimaginable numbers, but already by the 1870s, the fauna was diminishing rapidly, especially elephant, hippopotamus, and buffalo, which were the prime targets of commercial hunting and trading pursued by Zululand's settler neighbors.

Human habitation in the regions extends back 500,000 years to the Early Stone Age. The hunter-gatherers of the Later Stone Age from about 30,000 years ago lived in rock shelters and temporary camps while they followed the game as it migrated seasonally between the Drakensberg and the coast. Between 2,000 and 1,500 years ago, Iron Age people entered the region down the east coast of Africa and gradually displaced the original inhabitants. Physically they were the direct ancestors of the present black population, and they developed their own distinctive Nguni-speaking culture. They lived in small settlements, cultivating small, scattered fields (by the early 19th century, Indian maize with its superior yield had supplanted sorghum and millet as the staple crop) and keeping domestic stock. Indeed, the Zulu were essentially pastoralists, and the grasslands of Zululand were ideal for raising cattle.

Vegetation types are constantly being affected by climate change and human activity, and at the beginning of the 19th century, the low-lying alluvial plain was still extensively covered with bush, and not with sugarcane as it is today. In-between the bush flourished the luxuriant sourveld grasses that are good for cattle only after the spring rains, for once sourveld matures, it ceases to be nutritious. Inland, with less rain and a more temperate climate, there were progressively less bush and wider tracts of grassland. The great river valleys, with their low rainfall, sheltered savanna or lowveld vegetation, with its scattered thorntrees and grassy understory. These grasses are "sweet," and provide excellent grazing for cattle, even in the dry winter months. Fortunately there was sufficient surface water from the many streams rising in the forest-covered hills to support the great herds. Between the sweetveld and sourveld regions were belts of mixed veld that can be grazed for about half the year. Ideally, herds had to be free to move to take advantage of both the spring sourveld grazing and the sweetveld in the winter. The tsetse fly, which in many parts of Africa injects the trypanosome parasite into cattle with devastating effect, was usually confined to the deepest valleys or to the northeastern margins of Zululand.

During the period of the Zulu kingdom, the people lived in scattered family _imiZi_, or homesteads, each a tiny, circular village of grass beehive-shaped huts supported by its own grazing and agricultural land. By the 1870s, somewhere around 300,000 people were living in about 22,000 _imiZi_ and keeping at least 300,000 cattle, 200,000 goats, and

40,000 African sheep. Positioned at strategic points about the kingdom were also some two dozen huge *amaKhanda*, or royal military and administrative centers, of an average of 500 huts each, where *amaButho*, or regiments of warriors (about 29,000 men when fully mobilized), were periodically stationed to serve their king in peace and war.

## THE RISE OF THE ZULU KINGDOM

Until the late 18th century, there were no large chiefdoms in the region that would become the Zulu kingdom. Then a process of political centralization and expansion began that historians once explained by pointing to sharpening competition at a time of recurring drought for limited resources, especially for suitable winter and summer pastures for cattle. More recently, the emphasis has fallen on the effects of the expanding international trade in ivory and (more controversially) slaves carried on by Europeans from Delagoa Bay and across the Orange River from the Cape Colony. Either way, the little chiefdoms of the future Zululand were compelled to strengthen themselves and undergo social and political adjustments in order to compete and survive. These involved most notably the emergence of *amaButho* under the tighter authority of their chiefs, who employed them as instruments of internal control and as armies against external enemies. To keep them fed and rewarded necessitated raids against neighboring chiefdoms, which added to the growing cycle of violence.

By the end of the 18th century, three major chiefdoms had begun to emerge in the region: the Mabhudu-Tsonga in what is now southern Mozambique; the Ndwandwe to the southwest of them, between the Mkhuze and Black Mfolozi rivers; and the Mthethwa to the south of the Ndwandwe, between the lower Mfolozi and Mhlathuze rivers. In the late 1810s, intensifying warfare between these three rival chiefdoms caused their weaker neighbors to migrate out of harm's way and to spark destructive conflicts in the South African interior still known commonly (although the concept is under revision by historians) as the *mfecane*, or "the crushing."

The Mthethwa paramountcy encouraged some of its tributary chiefdoms to expand their own military potential to help obstruct Ndwandwe ambitions. One of these vassals was the obscure Zulu chiefdom in the valley of the middle White Mfolozi River, ruled over by *inKosi* Senzangakhona kaJama. In about 1817, the Ndwandwe defeated the Mthethwa and shattered their political hegemony in central and southern Zululand. The little Zulu chiefdom nevertheless continued to defy the Ndwandwe because, since about 1816, they had been ruled by Shaka, a son of Senzangakhona's who had overthrown his legitimate heir. A leader of extraordinary abilities, Shaka had become a renowned general in the Mthethwa service, and he now increased the size of his little Zulu army, improved its military capability through rigorous training, and schooled it in effective strategic and tactical maneuvers. Most likely, Shaka would first have learned these among the Mthethwa, although he certainly improved upon them. Shaka allied his growing military weight with the exercise of ruthless but extremely skillful diplomacy to consolidate his position over the entire region between the White Mfolozi and the Thukela to the south. Smaller chiefdoms who prudently submitted to him provided additional manpower for the Zulu *amaButho* in return for his protection. Larger neighboring chiefdoms like the Ndwandwe were faced with the unpalatable options of resistance, flight, or submission.

By the mid-1820s, Shaka had extended his sway north to the Phongolo River, west into the foothills of the Drakensberg, and as far south as the Mzimkhulu River. Yet distance and difficult terrain were imposing a natural limit on the extent of the territory that Shaka could effectively control. By the later 1820s, his armies had increasingly to confine themselves to frequent raids and the extraction of tribute from subordinate chiefdoms along the margins of the central Zulu domain.

## THE IMPINGING COLONIAL WORLD AND INTERNAL STRESSES

In 1824, the establishment at Port Natal (later Durban) of a tiny settlement of British hunters and traders connected Zululand to all the apparent material advantages and many insidious dangers of the colonial world. Shaka treated the Port Natal adventurers as client chiefs under his suzerainty because he saw that they were more accessible suppliers of exotic goods than the distant Portuguese traders at Delagoa Bay, and that they could serve as intermediaries with the Cape Colony to the south, where the British were growing apprehensive of Zulu armies operating near their borders. He also prized them as mercenaries with battle-winning firearms, and with their assistance he conclusively crushed and dispersed the Ndwandwe in 1826.

Yet all was not well in the new Zulu kingdom. Disaffected groups among the recently conquered chiefdoms and ambitious Zulu notables were persistently plotting Shaka's overthrow. There was discontent among many of his subjects because of his increasingly cruel and arbitrary rule, and most dangerously, the *amaButho* were growing resistant to interminable and ever less rewarding military campaigns. On 24 September 1828, disaffection coalesced, and Shaka fell to assassins in a well-laid coup. His half-brother *umNtwana* Dingane kaSenzangakhona seized the throne, eliminated his co-conspirators and almost all his rivals in the royal house, replaced Shaka's high officials with his own, and made concessions pleasing to the *amaButho*. He accepted that the kingdom was overextended, and he returned the center of gravity of the Zulu kingdom to the White Mfolozi valley, largely relinquishing direct rule over the territory south of the Thukela. There the settlement at Port Natal was growing in size and local influence, although the settlers remained in an uneasy tributary relationship with Dingane. Relations between the two almost broke down on several occasions during the 1830s, but self-interest on both sides averted a final rupture.

## THE VOORTREKKER-ZULU WAR

In October 1837, the Voortrekkers from the Cape Colony, migrating on the Great Trek into the South African interior in search of new lands to settle free from British rule, entered Zululand from the west over the Drakensberg. Dingane realized they posed a formidable challenge, and his worst suspicions were realized when they began negotiating for the cession to them of all the lands owing allegiance to the Zulu south of the Thukela River. Deeply apprehensive of the military reputation the Boers had recently earned in crushing the powerful Ndebele kingdom on the highveld, Dingane and his advisers decided they could only defeat them through a surprise attack. So when a Voortrekker deputation under Pieter Retief visited Dingane at his capital, uMgungundlovu, he executed them on 6 February 1838 and dispatched his armies to obliterate the rest of the invaders in their scattered encampments in the foothills of the Drakensberg. Despite suffering many casualties between 16 and 18 February, the Voortrekkers in their wagon laagers (encampments) succeeded in repulsing the Zulu. The Boers soon attempted to strike back, but on 10 April at eThaleni Hill, the Zulu ambushed and routed their mounted commando (militia). Port Natal settlers and their African auxiliaries, who advanced north against the Zulu in support of the Boers with whom they had struck an alliance, were likewise routed at Ndondakusuka on 17 April, and the Zulu went on to sack Port Natal. The main Zulu army then attacked the well-prepared Boer position at Veglaer but was thrown back in a three-day battle (13–15 August), which handed the initiative back to the Voortrekkers.

These encounters suggested several military lessons that were to hold good throughout the Zulu Wars. Zulu tactics were to envelop their foes with the two "horns" of their army, and then to bring up the "chest" to finish them off in hand-to-hand combat with the stabbing spear. Even though colonial forces held the overwhelming technological advantage with their firearms, standard Zulu tactics could be successful if the colonists were caught scattered in a running battle in the open field, when firearms could not be used to full effect. On the other hand, the Zulu could not succeed against all-round defensive positions such as wagon-laagers and forts from which impenetrable firepower could be concentrated. Both lessons were confirmed when, in a fresh offensive, a Voortrekker commando advanced on uMgungundlovu and decisively routed the Zulu army on 16 December 1838 from its laager at the Ncome River, but it was then worsted in a running skirmish in the valley of the White Mfolozi on 27 December.

Nevertheless, the Boers had sufficiently mangled Dingane's army for him to cede them the territory they wanted south of the Thukela on 25 March 1839. They proclaimed the Republic of Natalia, with its capital at the recently founded village of Pietermaritzburg, and commenced dividing the land into farms. Apprehensive of the new Boer republic to the south, Dingane attempted to shift his power base north across the Phongolo River into southern Swaziland. After some initial successes, in the winter of 1839 the Zulu army was soundly defeated by the Swazi at Lubuye and forced to withdraw. This reverse, coming on top his defeat at the hands of the Boers, fatally compromised Dingane's authority.

## THE 1ST ZULU CIVIL WAR AND
## THE BRITISH ANNEXATION OF NATAL

In September 1839, Dingane's half-brother *umNtwana* Mpande ka-Senzangakhona, fearing the king intended to execute him as a potential rival, defected to the Republic of Natalia with a large following and made common cause with the Voortrekkers against Dingane. In January 1840, Mpande's army advanced north, supported by a Boer commando, and on 29 January routed Dingane's forces at the Maqongqo Hills. Dingane fled northeast toward the Lubombo Mountains, where he sought refuge among the Nyawo people, who soon collaborated with a Swazi patrol to kill him. On 10 February 1840, the Boers recognized Mpande as the new Zulu king in return for his giving them extensive concessions of territory as far north as the Black Mfolozi River.

The feeble yet unrealistically aggressive Republic of Natalia seemed set to destabilize all of southeastern Africa. To prevent this, the British at the Cape intervened in a long-drawn-out process between 1842 and 1856 to annex Natalia as a British colony. Boers who could not stomach British rule in Natal trekked away to the highveld. On 5 October 1843, the British recognized the independence of the Zulu kingdom and agreed on the Thukela and Mzinyathi rivers as the boundary between it and Natal.

## THE 2ND ZULU CIVIL WAR AND THE DISPUTED TERRITORY

The Zulu kingdom under Mpande was wedged between British Natal to the south and southwest, the newly established Boer South African Republic to the northwest, and the Swazi kingdom to the north. The latter was the only salient still open for raids by the *amaButho* to win the booty on which the military system depended. Mpande's armies repeatedly campaigned there in the 1840s and early 1850s, but the British deprecated these disturbances to the regional balance, and Mpande gradually desisted. An astute ruler, he accepted that it was necessary to cultivate the British, particularly in order to counteract the land-hungry Boers, who were repeatedly trying to thrust into northwestern Zululand. He thus did his best to foster good relations with the Natal authorities, permitting traders and hunters into his kingdom and, after 1850, missionaries.

The matter of the royal succession, however, continued to destabilize the kingdom. In polygynous Zulu society, custom made clear
who should be a ruler's heir, but Shaka and his two successors were
all usurpers who gained the throne through assassination or civil war.
Shaka and Dingane had sought to postpone the issue through siring
no legitimate offspring, but Mpande had many sons. He attempted to
secure his own position by playing one off against another, but this fostered a civil war for the succession between his favorite son, *umNtwana*
Mbuyazi, and *umNtwana* Cetshwayo, whose claim was the stronger.
The issue was decided on 2 December 1856 when Cetshwayo's uSuthu
faction obliterated Mbuyazi and his iziGqoza faction at the ferocious
battle of Ndondakusuka. Thereafter Mpande had no alternative but to
share his authority with his overmighty undisputed heir.

Unfortunately, Zulu dynastic politics also involved relations with the
Boers and British. While Mpande lived, Cetshwayo courted the Boers to
strengthen his dynastic position against his pro-British father. In March
1861, Cetshwayo recognized indeterminate Boer land claims east of
the Ncome River in return for their support. Though he subsequently
repudiated this agreement, the damage was done. The Boers henceforth
persisted in asserting their land rights in northwestern Zululand, in what
became known as the Disputed Territory.

## CONFEDERATION AND THE ANGLO-ZULU WAR

Mpande died in September 1872, having managed, despite all perils,
to maintain the integrity of his kingdom. King Cetshwayo, no less than
his father, was confronted on the one hand by white neighbors greedy
to carve out farms in Zululand, and on the other by ambitious great
chiefs who were using their developing trading contacts with the colonial world that brought them wealth and firearms to aggrandize their
local power. He responded by strengthening royal authority, primarily
through strictly enforcing its mainstay, the *iButho* system, which had
grown lax during the latter part of Mpande's reign. On the diplomatic
front, he continued his father's successful policy of fostering good relations with the British to counteract the more overt menace presented by
the Boers.

Through no fault of Cetshwayo's, the situation changed drastically when, in the later 1870s, the British began pursuing a policy of

confederation in southern Africa. In the interests of imperial strategy, financial saving, and economic opportunity, they planned to bring all the white-ruled states in the region under their single authority. One of the major building blocks in the new structure was the South African Republic, which the British annexed in April 1877 as the Transvaal Territory. To help placate their reluctant new Boer subjects, it was necessary for the Transvaal authorities to support Boer claims to the Disputed Territory and jettison their previous support for Cetshwayo. In any case, the British sought to neutralize independent and militarily powerful black states like the Zulu kingdom that were perceived as a potential threat to the confederation process. Finding to his dismay that his old ally had changed sides, Cetshwayo was compelled to negotiate fruitlessly while the British moved inexorably toward a military confrontation aimed at conclusively knitting together the threads of confederation. Finally, the British issued an ultimatum requiring him to abolish the *iButho* system and make other concessions that would disrupt the political, social, and economic structure of his kingdom and place it under British supervision. Cetshwayo did not respond. Thus, on 11 January 1879, British and colonial forces invaded Zululand.

The intention of the British commander, Lieutenant-General Lord Chelmsford, was that three invading columns would converge on oNdini, Cetshwayo's capital, forcing a decisive battle and a quick end to the war. Chelmsford presumed that the fully mobilized Zulu armies of 29,000 men, who clung to their traditional fighting methods and made poor use of whatever firearms they possessed, would be no match for modern breech-loading rifles, artillery, and Gatling guns. However, the British advance became bogged down by inadequate transport and supply, and its strategy was drastically dislocated on 22 January when the main Zulu army annihilated part of the British No. 3 Column at Isandlwana. The Zulu failure that same night to capture the British depot at Rorke's Drift did not change the strategic picture, nor did the success on the same day of the British No. 1 Column in fighting its way through a Zulu ambush at Nyezane. Chelmsford was forced to retire to Natal to regroup, eventually building up a total force of nearly 17,000 troops (7,000 of whom were African) and raising over 8,000 African levies to defend the borders of Natal. Meanwhile, while No. 1 Column remained blockaded at Fort Eshowe, No. 4 Column based at Khambula in northwestern Zululand made the British presence felt through constant mounted raids.

Zulu lack of commissariat arrangements and their need for ritual purification after battle meant they were unable to mount a sustained campaign and press their advantage. Besides, Cetshwayo reopened negotiations, presuming that the Zulu success at Isandlwana would persuade the British to withdraw, not realizing that their humiliation would impel them to fight until complete victory had been attained. The Zulu were ready for a second round of combat by March, when their main army marched against the troublesome No. 4 Column. On the way, the Zulu overwhelmed a large British mounted patrol on Hlobane Mountain on 28 March. The following day, the Zulu attacked the fort and laager at Khambula in the most hard-fought and decisive battle of the war. The eventual rout of the Zulu army permanently broke its morale. To compound this defeat, on 2 April, Chelmsford's Eshowe Relief Column, secure in its laager at Gingindlovu, broke a smaller Zulu army blockading Fort Eshowe and evacuated the garrison.

The lessons of the Voortrekker-Zulu War of 1838 had been reconfirmed. Rorke's Drift, Khambula, and Gingingdlovu proved that the Zulu were helpless against concentrated firepower from behind all-round defenses. But Isandlwana and Hlobane showed how they could be successful in a battle of maneuver in the open if the British were foolish enough to give them the opportunity.

Chelmsford launched his second invasion in May. While the 1st Division, South African Field Force, moved cumbersomely up the coastal plain, the 2nd Division advanced into the Zulu heartland from the northwest in cooperation with Wood's Flying Column. The joint force, drawn up as an impenetrable infantry square, conclusively routed the Zulu army at Ulundi on 4 July. Realizing even before Ulundi that the war was lost, many *amaKhosi* scrambled to submit on easy terms to the British. Any lingering Zulu resistance was ended by September with the sending in of two flying columns to secure submissions, and with the capture of the fugitive Cetshwayo, who was exiled to Cape Town.

## THE 1ST AND 2ND PARTITIONS OF ZULULAND

The British did not annex the defeated Zulu kingdom, for it was not their intention to burden themselves with its administration. It was sufficient to ensure that the Zulu would never again pose a military threat to their colonial neighbors. To that end, on 1 September 1879 a settlement was imposed on the Zulu *amaKhosi* whereby the monarchy was abolished, and with it its main prop, the *iButho* system. The former kingdom was partitioned into 13 independent chiefdoms under appointed chiefs, most of whom could be relied on out of self-interest to ensure that there would be no resurgence of the centralized Zulu monarchy.

The 1st Partition of Zululand soon broke down. Growing strife between the pro-royalist faction (uSuthu) and their opponents persuaded the British in December 1882 to restore the exiled Cetshwayo to the central part of his former kingdom. To ensure that he would pose no threat to his colonial neighbors, the 2nd Partition of Zululand hemmed Cetshwayo's territory in from two sides. To the northeast was an independent chiefdom under *inKosi* Zibhebhu kaMaphitha of the Mandlakazi people, who had proved himself a reliable British collaborator and inveterate enemy of the royal house. To the south was the Reserve Territory created between the Mhlathuze and Thukela rivers and placed under British protection and administration to act as a buffer between Natal and Cetshwayo.

## THE 3RD ZULU CIVIL WAR AND THE 3RD PARTITION OF ZULULAND

War rapidly broke out between the uSuthu and the Mandlakazi and their Ngenetsheni allies in northwestern Zululand. At the outset of the 3rd Zulu Civil War, the uSuthu invaded Zibhebhu's territory, but on 30 March 1883 at Msebe, the Mandlakazi ambushed and completely routed them. Zibhebhu then counterattacked and, after a night march, surprised and routed the uSuthu at oNdini on 21 July 1883. The uSuthu were scattered, most of their leadership killed, and Cetshwayo fled to the Reserve Territory, where he died on 8 February 1884.

Cetshwayo's young heir, King Dinuzulu kaCetshwayo, was helpless against continuing Mandlakazi attacks and British antagonism and turned to the neighboring Boers for military assistance. With their essential firepower, he crushed Zibhebhu at Tshaneni on 5 June 1884 and drove him into the Reserve Territory. Yet Boer aid came with a steep price. On 16 August 1884 in the 3rd Partition of Zululand, Dinuzulu ceded them the northwestern two-thirds of Zululand outside the Reserve Territory. This territory (with somewhat reduced boundaries recognized by the British on 22 October 1886) became the short-lived New Republic and was absorbed into the South African Republic on 20 July 1888 as the Vryheid District. The Zulu living in this territory—and they included some of the royal house's staunchest supporters, like the abaQulusi—found themselves reduced overnight to labor tenants on the farms the Boers allocated themselves.

## THE BRITISH ANNEXATION OF ZULULAND AND THE USUTHU REBELLION

Britain, fearing the intervention of rival imperial powers in this chaotic region, on 19 May 1887 annexed the Reserve Territory and the rump of Zululand outside the New Republic as the British Colony of Zululand. Dinuzulu and many of the uSuthu found it difficult to cooperate with the new colonial administration. To curb him, in late 1887 the Zululand officials restored the collaborationist Zibhebhu to his enlarged former chiefdom. His return sparked renewed unrest, and by April 1888 the uSuthu were in open rebellion, defying the paramilitary Zululand Police, the regular troops of the Zululand garrison, their Mandlakazi allies, and other African auxiliaries. On 2 June, the uSuthu repulsed a British force at Ceza Mountain, their principal fastness, and went on to rout Zibhebhu's forces at Ivuna on 23 June. The discomforted British withdrew south of the Black Mfolozi River to regroup and reinforce. They swiftly took the offensive and on 2 July drove the uSuthu from Hlophekhulu Mountain in central Zululand. On 9 July, they relieved Fort Andries, which was under siege in the southeast. Between July and September, British flying columns traversed the disaffected areas north of the Black Mfolozi and along the coast, securing uSuthu submissions.

## THE PACIFICATION OF ZULULAND

The ringleaders of the uSuthu Rebellion were tried for high treason at Eshowe and found guilty in April 1889. Dinuzulu and two of his uncles were removed to St. Helena to serve their sentences. A chastened Zululand administration then set about pacifying the colony and disentangling the land claims of the rival factions that remained a potent cause of unrest. It was believed that the return of Dinuzulu would help restore stability, but his restoration was strenuously opposed by the Natal colonists, who insisted that it be coupled with the throwing open of Zululand to white settlement. Eventually, a deal was struck with the British government. On 30 December 1897, the Colony of Zululand (including British-ruled Ingwavuma and Tongaland) were annexed to Natal as the Province of Zululand. As a result of the findings of the Zululand Lands Delimitation Commission of 1902–1904, two-fifths of the best land in Zululand were set aside, beginning from 31 January 1906, for white occupation. The Zulu occupiers of the land at the time either became labor tenants on the white farms or were removed to the remaining three-fifths of Zululand that had been declared African reserves. Thus, the young men of Zululand, who in their *amaButho* had once served their king, became rural labor tenants or migrant laborers in the mines and in the towns of a white-ruled, industrializing South Africa.

# The Dictionary

## – A –

**ACCOUTREMENTS, AFRICAN LEVIES.** African infantry levies (troops) in British service in **Zululand** between 1879 and 1888 were each issued a blanket to be carried in bandolier fashion over the left shoulder. A cooking pot was supplied for every 10 men.

**ACCOUTREMENTS, BRITISH FORCES.** The set of accoutrements of the Valise pattern introduced in 1871 consisted of a black water-proofed canvas sack (or valise) supported in the small of the back by shoulder straps. These were attached to a waist belt, to which were attached three ammunition pouches holding 70 rounds of ammunition. The rolled greatcoat and mess tin were secured above the valise. **Mounted infantry** replaced ammunition pouches with a bandolier. Accoutrements for the **Naval Brigade** were of brown leather.

**ACCOUTREMENTS, COLONIAL FORCES.** Standard equipment for the **Natal Mounted Volunteers** included a white canvas haversack over the right shoulder, a brown leather shoulder belt with ammunition pouch attached over the left shoulder, two bandoliers of ammunition (one worn around the waist and the other over the left shoulder), and a revolver in a brown leather holster on a strap worn over the right shoulder. **Irregular cavalry** units carried a valise, saddlebags, patrol tin, and blanket on their **horses**.

**ADDISON, RICHARD HALLOWES (1857–1921).** Addison began his career in the **Natal** civil service and served during the **Anglo-Zulu War** in the **Stanger Mounted Rifles**, seeing action at

1

**Nyezane**. Commissioned second-in-command of the **Reserve Territory Carbineers** in 1883, during the 3rd **Zulu Civil War** he was present at the battle of the **Nkandla Forest**. In June 1887, he was appointed resident commissioner of the Ndwandwe District in the British Colony of **Zululand**, where the **uSuthu** were concentrated and members of the royal house had their *imiZi*. His openly partisan mishandling of the uSuthu, combined with unwavering support of *inKosi* **Zibhebhu kaMaphitha** whom the British returned to his location in Ndwandwe in November 1887 as a counterweight to the uSuthu, were material in driving King **Dinuzulu kaMpande** into revolt. During the **uSuthu Rebellion**, Addison was present at **Ceza**, **Ivuna**, and **Hlophekhulu** as the representative of the civil power. His questionable conduct toward the uSuthu led to an official censure in December 1889. His services as political adviser to the Natal forces during the **Zulu Uprising of 1906** (Bhambatha Rebellion) revitalized his career, and he retired as chief native commissioner for Natal and Zululand (1913–1916).

**ADDISON'S HORSE.** During the last stage of the **uSuthu Rebellion**, Captain Charles B. Addison recruited 150 men from the Christian African community of Edendale outside **Pietermaritzburg**, many of whom had served in the **Anglo-Zulu War** as the **Edendale Horse**. Paid for out of the funds of the British Colony of **Zululand** and mustered as **mounted infantry**, they were issued **carbines** or **rifles** (not necessarily of the latest model) and dressed in an assortment of blue or khaki frocks, usually with buff trousers and riding boots or puttees. They wore brown slouch hats with a red puggaree around the hatband and carried their ammunition in leather bandoliers. They reinforced the **Zululand garrison** at **Nkonjeni** in August 1888 and were disbanded at the end of the month.

*AGTERRYER.* Black, acculturated servants in Boer households were an inseparable part of the **commando** (militia) system in the **Cape** from its beginnings in the late 17th century, and they continued to be so when the institution moved inland in the 1830s with the **Great Trek**. These *agterryers*, or "after-riders," drove the wagons, herded the draught animals and **horses**, slaughtered livestock, cooked, and looked after the sick and wounded. They also guarded ammunition and sometimes took a direct military role, accompanying their masters on punitive expeditions and helping defend **laagers** against attack. Because their ubiquity on campaign was so much taken for granted, there is often little reference to them in the sources, and their presence on the battlefield must frequently be inferred.

**AIVUNA CAMP.** In late July 1888 during the **uSuthu Rebellion**, the British established this temporary post across the Black Mfolozi River as a forward base for mounted reconnaissance by **Martin's Flying Column** into uSuthu-held territory. It also served as the column's base in early August 1888 for joint operations with the **Coastal Column**.

**ALEXANDRA MOUNTED RIFLES.** One of the 10 corps of **Natal Mounted Volunteers** who were called out in November 1878 for active service in the **Anglo-Zulu War**, it was formed in 1865. In December 1878, its 20 troopers joined No. 1 **Column** at **Fort Pearson** and remained there on convoy duty while the column advanced into **Zululand**. Until mustered out in July 1879, it joined other units of the Natal Mounted Volunteers in patrolling the **Natal** border along the lines of communication between **Fort Pearson**, **Stanger,** and **Ntunjambili** in **Colonial Defensive Districts** VI and VII and participated in cross-border raids. Its uniform introduced in 1874 was of thick khaki cloth, the first uniform of that color recorded to have been issued in South Africa. The helmet was white with a white metal spike.

**AMABOMA CORPS.** Previously stationed during the **Anglo-Zulu War** near **Pietermaritzburg** in **Colonial Defensive District** No. III as a reserve to the **Border Guard**, this unit of about 70 Bomvu people under their *inKosi*, Siphandla, were transferred in April 1879 from colonial to military command and were attached to the **Cavalry Brigade** of the 2nd Division, **South African Field Force**. They advanced with the brigade as far as **Fort Newdigate** and **Fort Marshall**, where they remained in garrison, undertaking scouting, escort, and dispatch-riding duties until the withdrawal of the 2nd Division from **Zululand**. They were disbanded in August.

**AMANGWANI SCOUTS.** Previously stationed during the **Anglo-Zulu War** near **Pietermaritzburg** in **Colonial Defensive District** No. III as a reserve to the **Border Guard**, this unit of some 40 Ngwane people under their *inKosi*, Pusha, were transferred in April 1879 from colonial to military command and were attached to the **Cavalry Brigade** of the 2nd Division, **South African Field Force**. They advanced with the brigade as far as **Fort Newdigate** and **Fort Marshall**, where they remained in garrison, undertaking scouting, escort, and dispatch-riding duties until the withdrawal of the 1st Division from **Zululand**. They were disbanded in August.

**AMMUNITION BOX CONTROVERSY.** The myth has persisted that the British lost the battle of **Isandlwana** in the **Anglo-Zulu War** because the boxes containing the ammunition for the **Martini-Henry** rifles could not be opened quickly enough. These ammunition boxes were stoutly constructed of wood, reinforced by two copper bands, with a sliding lid secured by a single two-inch brass screw. They were therefore simple to open, though the introduction in 1881 of a split-pin fastening made for even quicker release. The firing-line at Isandlwana ran out of ammunition because it was positioned up to half a mile from the camp, and no proper ammunition carts were available to bring up more. To compound the problem, no system of runners had been organized before the battle to carry ammunition, and the quartermaster distributing it was overly conscious of his duty to account for every round issued. Certainly, there seems to have been a reluctance to hand out ammunition to African troops.

**ANGLO-BOER (SOUTH AFRICAN) WAR (1899–1902).** In order to assert its paramountcy over South Africa, Great Britain fueled a long-building crisis with the independent Boer states of the **South African Republic** and **Orange Free State** until they were provoked into declaring war in October 1899. Despite humiliating initial setbacks, by October 1900 Britain and contingents from its empire had won the conventional phase of the war and occupied the two republics. Boer diehards then initiated the guerrilla phase that took a terrible toll on civilians during British counterinsurgency operations. The Boers finally capitulated on 31 May 1902, and in 1910 their former republics became part of the Union of South Africa.

**ANGLO-ZULU WAR (1879).** The Anglo-Zulu War is described in terms of the 1st Invasion and 2nd Invasion. The 1st Invasion, 6 January–5 April 1879, encompassed the initial advance in January 1879 of the three invading British columns into **Zululand**; the battles of **Isandlwana**, **Rorke's Drift**, and **Nyezane**; the blockade of **Fort Eshowe**; the period of regrouping, skirmishing, and border raiding from February to March; and the turning point from mid-March to early April when the Zulu were crushed at **Khambula** and **Gingindlovu** and Eshowe was relieved. The 2nd Invasion, 6 April–8 July 1879, encompassed the period when reinforcements pursued the war to its conclusion at the battle of **Ulundi**.

On 11 January 1879, imperial and colonial British forces under Lieutenant-General Lord **Chelmsford** invaded Zululand. In the 1st Invasion, three columns were to converge on **oNdini**, King **Cetshwayo kaMpande**'s capital, forcing a decisive battle and a quick end to the war. Instead, the British advance became bogged down by inadequate transport and supply. Its strategy was drastically dislocated on 22 January when the main Zulu army under *amaKhosi* **Ntshingwayo kaMahole** and **Mavumengwana kaNdlela** outmaneuvered, divided, and annihilated the British No. 3 **Column** at Isandlwana. The Zulu failure that same night to capture No. 3 Column's depot at Rorke's Drift did not change the strategic picture, nor did the success at Nyezane of the British No. 1 Column under Colonel **Charles Knight Pearson** in fighting its way (also on 22 January) through a Zulu ambush led by *inKosi* **Godide kaNdlela**. Chelmsford was forced to retire to **Natal** to regroup, eventually building up a total force of nearly 17,000 troops (7,000 of whom were African) and raising over 8,000 African levies (troops) to defend the borders of Natal. Meanwhile, Pearson remained blockaded at Fort Eshowe, and it was left to Brevet Colonel **Henry Evelyn Wood** and No. 4 Column based at Khambula in northwestern Zululand to make the British presence felt through constant mounted raids.

The inadequacy of Zulu **logistics** and their need for **ritual** purification after battle meant they were unable to mount a sustained campaign and press their advantage. Besides, Cetshwayo reopened **negotiations** presuming that the Zulu success at Isandlwana would persuade the British to withdraw, not realizing that their humiliation would impel the British to fight until complete victory was attained.

The Zulu were ready for a second round of hostilities by March, when the main army under *inKosi* **Mnyamana kaNgqengelele** marched against the troublesome No. 4 Column. On the way, the Zulu overwhelmed a large British mounted patrol on **Hlobane Mountain** on 28 March. The following day, the Zulu attacked the fort and laager at Khambula in the most hard-fought and decisive battle of the war. The eventual rout of the Zulu army permanently broke its morale. To compound this defeat, on 2 April Chelmsford's **Eshowe Relief Column**, secure in its wagon laager at Gingindlovu, broke a smaller Zulu army under **Somopho kaZikhala** and evacuated the Eshowe garrison. Rorke's Drift, Khambula, and Gingindlovu proved that the Zulu were helpless against concentrated firepower from behind all-around defenses, but Isandlwana showed how they could outflank the British if given the opportunity, and Hlobane demonstrated how they could be successful in a running battle in the open.

Chelmsford launched his 2nd Invasion of the Anglo-Zulu War in May. While the 1st Division, **South African Field Force**, under Major-General **Henry Hope Crealock** moved cumbrously up the coastal plain, the 2nd Division (accompanied by Chelmsford and his staff) advanced into the Zulu heartland from the northwest in cooperation with **Wood's Flying Column**. The joint columns devastated the countryside along their lines of march in order to break the Zulu spirit of resistance, and they persuaded many to surrender rather than face the loss of their homes and livestock. On 4 July, the joint force under Chelmsford's command, drawn up as an impenetrable infantry **square** at the battle of Ulundi, conclusively routed the Zulu army under *umNtwana* **Ziwedu kaMpande**, which then dispersed.

General **Garnet Joseph Wolseley**, who replaced Chelmsford, broke up the two British divisions and formed two flying columns to complete the pacification of Zululand. **Baker Russell's Column** subdued the last Zulu resistance in northwestern Zululand by 8 September, and **Clarke's Column** secured the **submission** of southern Zululand by 21 September. Meanwhile, any possibility of organized resistance ended with the capture of the fugitive Cetshwayo on 28 August. The Zulu leaders formally surrendered to Wolseley on 1 September and accepted the 1st Partition of Zululand, which abolished the kingdom and broke it into 13 independent chiefdoms under appointed chiefs.

**ARMY HOSPITAL CORPS.** In 1873, when medical care in the British army was brought under control of the **Army Medical Department**, the Army Hospital Corps was formed to provide trained orderlies. During the **Anglo-Zulu War**, when not nearly enough medical personnel was available, even when reinforcements were brought in after **Isandlwana**, small detachments of orderlies were assigned to base hospitals and attached in the 1st Invasion of the war to the various columns, and in the 2nd Invasion to particular units. They were consequently present at all the major engagements of the campaign. The uniform was blue with scarlet piping. During the Anglo-Zulu War, the corps was armed with **Martini-Henry rifles**. *See also* BEARER CORPS.

**ARMY MEDICAL DEPARTMENT.** The Army Medical Department dated from 1873, when the existing regimental system of medical officers was abolished and the department assumed responsibility for trained surgeons of officer rank, station hospitals, and the **Army Hospital Corps**. During the **Anglo-Zulu War**, Surgeon-General John Woolfreys broke his limited personnel into small detachments with each column in the 1st Invasion, and personnel were present at all engagements, and then at **Gingindlovu** with the **Eshowe Relief Column**. During the 2nd Invasion of the war, they were attached to specific units and were present at **Ulundi**. Personnel, assisted by a number of volunteer civilian doctors, were in charge of the convalescent station at Pinetown, the base hospitals in **Durban**, **Pietermaritzburg**, **Ladysmith**, **Newcastle**, and **Utrecht**, the hospital at **Fort Pearson**, and the field hospitals with the forces operating in **Zululand**. Tunic facings were black.

**ARMY REFORM, BRITISH.** In the 19th century, the professional British army (there was no conscription) was a self-contained, conservative, and authoritarian institution. It played an essential role in imperial defense; between 1814 and 1914, it waged more overseas campaigns than any other colonial power's military except for that of France. From the 1840s, the British government made various attempts to improve the effectiveness of the army while at the same time attempting to make the colonies more self-reliant militarily through raising and training settler volunteer units supported by auxiliaries drawn from the indigenous population. The hope was that the colonies would bear more of the cost of their own defense and so reduce the need for garrisons of British troops stationed overseas. The **Cardwell Reforms** and the related **Childers Reforms** addressed these objectives but failed to raise the number or quality of recruits, to make pay competitive, or materially to improve the conditions of service life. Moreover, the mounting demands during the 1870s and 1880s for imperial defense (of which the **Zululand** campaigns were an instance) required a stronger military presence abroad than the reformers envisaged, and exposed the continuing inability of colonial forces to take full responsibility for their own security.

**ARMY SERVICE CORPS.** The Army Service Corps was formed in 1869 with the amalgamation of the other ranks of the Military Train, Commissariat Staff Corps, Military Store Staff Corps, and the Purveyor Branch of the **Army Hospital Corps**. It was officered by the **Commissariat and Transport Department** and the Ordnance Store Department. Detached personnel were with **No. 3 Column** in the 1st Invasion of the **Anglo-Zulu War** and were present at **Isandlwana**. Two companies of the corps were among the reinforcements brought in after Isandlwana. During the 2nd Invasion of the war, they were attached to the 2nd Division, **South African Field Force**, and also assisted **Wood's Flying Column** once the two field formations came together in early June for their joint advance. The corps performed poorly during the Zululand campaign, and in 1881 it was abolished and replaced by the **Commissariat and Transport Corps**. The blue tunic had blue facings and white piping.

**ARTILLERY, BRITISH.** British field batteries in the later 19th century were normally equipped with 9-pounder rifled muzzle-loader (RML) field guns sighted between 1,690 and 2,740 yards. However, these were not employed in the **Anglo-Zulu War** until reinforcements were brought in for the 2nd Invasion. The 7-pounder RML Mark IV steel mountain gun, with a maximum range of 3,200 yards, was fitted with a low-slung colonial carriage and narrow track, pulled by three mules, and was considered more mobile and better suited to local conditions than 9-pounders. Consequently, after the Anglo-Zulu War, the British continued to deploy 7-pounders during the

3rd **Zulu Civil War** and the **uSuthu Rebellion**, even though they never had cause to fire them in action. On the demerit side, 7-pounders capsized easily in rough ground, and their low muzzle velocity and the small bursting charge of the shells they fired rendered their destructive power relatively ineffective. Case-shot, or canister, could only be employed at ranges of less than 280 yards.

The **Naval Brigade** from **HMS** *Active* landed in **Natal** in November 1878 with two 12-pounder Armstrong RML guns but left them at **Fort Pearson** when they advanced into **Zululand**. The guns were never fired during the Anglo-Zulu War.

The **Durban Volunteer Artillery** deployed two 6-pounder rifled breech-loading Armstrong guns in the Anglo-Zulu War for the defense of **Durban** but never fired them in action.

**ARTILLERY, VOORTREKKER.** At **Ncome**, the Boers placed two, possibly three, small 2.5-inch muzzle-loading brass cannons on improvised carriages at openings in their laager's wagon wall. They were most likely modified swivel guns of the sort used primarily aboard ships as short-range antipersonnel ordnance. Their effective range was several hundred yards, and they fired grapeshot and a variety of small, hard projectiles such as stones or metal pot legs. In 1842, one of these cannon, nicknamed "Ou Grietjie," was used again in the Boer siege of the British in **Smith's Camp** at Port Natal (**Durban**).

**ARTISTS.** *See* SPECIAL ARTISTS.

**ASHANTI RING.** *See* WOLSELEY, SIR GARNET JOSEPH.

**AWARDS.** During the **Anglo-Zulu War**, only two decorations for gallantry and one campaign medal could be awarded British troops. The Victoria Cross, established in 1856 for all ranks of the armed forces, was the supreme award for conspicuous bravery in action. There was no provision in 1879 for the posthumous award of the Victoria Cross, but this was authorized in 1907. The medal for Distinguished Conduct in the Field was instituted in 1854 for other ranks only. All those troops involved in one or more of the campaigns in South Africa between 25 September 1877 and 2 December 1879 were eligible for the South Africa Medal. The date bar fixed to the medal specified the campaign. No medal was issued for operations in **Zululand** during the 1880s.

## – B –

**BAKER RUSSELL'S COLUMN.** On 26 July 1879, General **Sir Garnet Joseph Wolseley** put Brevet Lieutenant-Colonel **Baker Creed Russell** in command of the reduced **Wood's Flying Column** that was required for the pacification of northwestern **Zululand** in the last stage of the **Anglo-Zulu War**. Baker Russell's Column left **St. Paul's** on 26 July for **Fort Cambridge**, which it reached on 5 August. The column then moved across the **White Mfolozi** to construct **Fort George** on 10 August. Between 13 and 25 August, patrols were sent out as far as the headwaters of the Black Mfolozi, and the **Mdlalose** surrendered. On 25 August, the column moved north to **Hlobane Mountain**, and between 1 and 4 September proceeded to **Luneburg**, accepting piecemeal **submissions** from the **abaQulusi** as it went. At Luneburg, the column cooperated with the garrison and **Villiers's Column**, which had advanced from Derby to attack the **Kubheka** on 4, 5, and 8 September in their caves in the Ntombe valley and secure their submission. On 10 September, the column was ordered to Lydenburg in the Transvaal to join in renewed operations against the **Pedi** that concluded successfully in November. *See also* CIVILIANS IN WARTIME ZULULAND.

**BAKER'S HORSE.** Commandant Francis James Baker, a former soldier, came out to the **Cape** in 1877 and during the 9th **Cape Frontier War** raised a unit of **irregular cavalry** that was disbanded in December 1878. After **Isandlwana**, he raised a new unit of about 140 men in the **Eastern Cape** for the **Anglo-Zulu War**. They wore yellow or brown corduroy uniforms and the customary wideawake hat. In late March 1879, Baker's Horse joined No. 4 **Column**. A squadron fought at **Hlobane** with Lieutenant-Colonel **Redvers Henry Buller**'s force and also at **Khambula**. As part of **Wood's Flying Column** in the 2nd Invasion of the Anglo-Zulu War, a squadron took part in the skirmish at **Zungeni**, and two squadrons participated in the **White**

**Mfolozi reconnaissance in force** and fought at **Ulundi**. With the breakup of Wood's Flying Column in late July, the unit returned to the Cape and disbanded in August.

**BALTE SPRUIT LAAGER.** Boers built a stonework **laager** at Balte Spruit in the **Utrecht District** of the **South African Republic** in the 1870s, and they took refuge there twice in 1877 for fear of Zulu attack related to the **Disputed Territory**. In December 1878, No. 4 **Column** established a depot there and improved the laager, also building a square stone redoubt with two opposing bastions. During the **Anglo-Zulu War**, Balte Spruit continued as No. 4 Column's advanced depot after it moved forward on 4 January 1879 into **Zululand**. It was held by a small garrison.

*iBANDLA. See* POLITICAL ORGANIZATION, ZULU.

**BANGONOMO** *iBUTHO.* In*Kosi* **Zibhebhu kaMaphitha** raised this **Mandlakazi** *iButho* in his chiefdom after the 1st Partition of **Zululand**, in resumption of the prerogatives of the great *amaKhosi* before the era of **Shaka**. He named it after his **Bangonomo** *umuZi*. During the 3rd **Zulu Civil War**, the Bangonomo *iButho* participated in the victories at **Msebe** and **oNdini**, but it was defeated at **Tshaneni**. During the **uSuthu Rebellion**, it formed the Mandlakazi right horn at **Ivuna** but was routed by the **uSuthu**.

**BANGONOMO** *umuZi.* The primary *umuZi* in northeastern **Zululand** of *inKosi* **Zibhebhu kaMaphitha**, Bangonomo was his preferred place for rallying his forces for the various campaigns of the 3rd **Zulu Civil War**, and it was his base during the **uSuthu Rebellion**. On 6 July 1888, the pro-uSuthu **Mdletshe** and **Hlabisa** people burned Bangonomo while Zibhebhu and his forces were under British protection at **Nkonjeni**.

**BARROW, PERCY HARRY STANLEY (1848–1886).** Captain Barrow went to South Africa on special service in March 1878 to form a **mounted infantry** squadron during the 9th **Cape Frontier War**. During the **Anglo-Zulu War**, he served first with No. 1 **Column** in command of No. 2 Squadron, Mounted Infantry, and fought at

**Nyezane**. He then served with the **Eshowe Relief Column** and at **Gingindlovu** led the mounted pursuit and was wounded. During the 2nd Invasion of the Anglo-Zulu War, he commanded the mounted troops of the 1st Division, **South African Field Force**, and subsequently the mounted infantry with **Clarke's Column**. In 1884, Lieutenant-Colonel Barrow was severely wounded at El Teb in the Suakin campaign while in command of the 19th Hussars; he never fully recovered.

**BASUTO SPECIAL POLICE.** *See* MOUNTED BASUTOS.

**BASUTOLAND.** In the 1820s, King Moshoeshoe I (c. 1786–1870) consolidated the chiefdoms of the mountainous country of Lesotho and ruled them as king from his stronghold of Thabu Bosiu, or "mountain of the night." From the late 1830s, his kingdom was threatened from the west by the **Voortrekkers** in a series of wars, and in 1868 Moshoeshoe appealed to the British for help. They took his kingdom under their protection, and the boundary between the **Orange Free State** and the Basutoland Protectorate was defined by the Treaty of Aliwal (1869). In 1871, the protectorate was annexed to the **Cape Colony**, and in 1879 Moorosi of the Phuti people rose up unsuccessfully against its administration. The Cape then attempted to disarm the protectorate and sparked off the Gun War of 1880–1881. The Cape's inability to pacify Basutoland led to the resumption in 1884 of a Crown protectorate over the Territory of Basutoland. On 4 October 1966, the kingdom of Lesotho attained full independence. *See also* SOTHO BORDER WITH NATAL IN 1879.

**BATTLE-AXE, ZULU.** A few *amaButho* (regiments) might wield a crescent-bladed battle-axe of **Swazi** or **Pedi** origin (*isiZenze*), instead of some other form of striking weapon. More usually, the battle-axe was carried by Zulu men of status as a ceremonial rather than fighting weapon.

**BAYONETS, BRITISH.** The **Martini-Henry rifle** was fitted with a triangular socket bayonet, 22 inches long, which had been universal issue since 1876. Although the "lunger" gave formidable reach in hand-to-hand combat, its blade was of poor quality and often bent or broke. The 1871-pattern sword bayonet was carried by infantry sergeants. The **Royal Artillery** adopted a saw-backed bayonet in 1875 that was 18 inches long. Men of the **Army Service Corps** carried the 1870-pattern Elcho bayonet with a saw-backed blade 21 inches long and a swelling spear point. A cutlass bayonet was issued to the **Naval Brigade**.

**ekuBAZENI** *iKHANDA*. In the late 1840s, *umNtwana* **Cetshwayo kaMpande** established this *iKhanda* in the Vuna valley in northern **Zululand**, close to the first **kwaGqikazi** *iKhanda*, as the center for his growing **uSuthu** faction in the coming succession crisis, and it was his base in the 2nd **Zulu Civil War**. It remained a powerful node of uSuthu support during the 3rd Zulu Civil War and during the **uSuthu Rebellion**. On 25 April 1888, the **Zululand Police** raided it to collect **cattle** fines that **Richard Hallowes Addison**, the resident magistrate of Ndwandwe District, had levied against the uSuthu leaders for their contumacy.

**BEARER CORPS.** During the **Anglo-Zulu War**, there were not enough orderlies in the **Army Hospital Corps** to adequately staff base and field hospitals. Thus, African auxiliaries were recruited during the 2nd Invasion of the Anglo-Zulu War to help bring in the wounded to field hospitals and to the convalescent facilities in **Natal**. The wounded were transported in hammocks slung between poles that two bearers supported on their shoulders. Bearers were present at **Ulundi**.

*BEESKOMMANDO.* The *Beeskommando*, or Cattle Commando, was the name derisively given to the Boer **commando** (militia) under **Andries Wilhelmus Jacobus Pretorius** that supported the Zulu army of *umNtwana* **Mpande kaSenzangakhona** during the 1st **Zulu Civil War**. The commando set out on 17 January 1840 and gave up the campaign on 6 February. It had done no fighting, but it had captured some 36,000 Zulu **cattle**.

**BEGAMUZA CAMP.** During the **uSuthu Rebellion**, Lieutenant-General **Henry Augustus Smyth** established the Begamuza Camp on 29 July 1888 as an intermediate post between his main base at

Nkonjeni and his forward base at **Aivuna**. With the departure of **Martin's Flying Column** and the **Coastal Column** from **Ivuna** on 18 August 1888, the Begamuza Camp was abandoned in favor of the **Ceza Camp**.

**BENDE STRONGHOLD.** *InKosi* **Zibhebhu kaMaphitha**'s impregnable Bende stronghold, established on a hill of that name, was 10 miles southeast of his **Bangonomo** *iKhanda* in northeastern **Zululand**. Zibhebhu periodically retired to Bende when hard pressed in the 3rd **Zulu Civil War**. In July 1888, the **uSuthu** failed to capture it, even though it was held by only a small garrison of **Mandlakazi**.

**BESTER'S LAAGER.** A square stone encampment constructed by a farmer in the late 1850s, Bester's **laager** was considered in late 1878 as a defensive post for local settlers in **Colonial Defensive District No. II**, but it was never used in the **Anglo-Zulu War** because of its defensive weaknesses.

*isiBHALO. See* NATAL NATIVE CONTINGENT (INFANTRY); NATAL NATIVE PIONEER CORPS.

**BHAMBATHA REBELLION.** *See* ZULU UPRISING (1906).

**BHEJANA kaNOMAGEJE (c. 1860–?).** Bhejana was enrolled in the **uFalaza** *iButho* and was an *inDuna* (official) of the **emaNgweni** people. He strongly supported King **Cetshwayo kaMpande** after the 2nd Partition of **Zululand**. During the 3rd **Zulu Civil War**, he was an **uSuthu** commander at the battle of **oNdini**. After Cetshwayo's death, he continued the pro-uSuthu struggle on the coast against *inKosi* Sokwetshata kaMlandlela of the **Mthethwa**, under whose father he had been reluctantly placed in the 1st Partition of Zululand. During the **uSuthu Rebellion**, Bhejana joined with **Somopho kaZikhala**, the senior *inDuna* of the emaNgweni, in operating against Andries Pretorius, the resident magistrate of the Lower Umfolosi District, and attacked **Fort Andries** in the battle of **Ntondotha**. The **Eshowe Column** ravaged his territory in July 1888, and Bhejane took refuge in the Yome bush in the northern coastal district, moving on to the **Dukuduku stronghold**

when the joint **Coastal Column** and **Martin's Flying Column** passed through in August 1888. He did not surrender until 1890, when the High Court of Zululand sentenced him to three years' imprisonment.

**BIGGAR, ALEXANDER HARVEY (1781–1838).** Born in Ireland, Biggar served as an officer in the British army and was an 1820 settler in the **Eastern Cape**. He failed at farming and moved to Port Natal (**Durban**) in 1836. Elected commandant of the Port Natal Volunteers, he identified with the Voortrekkers in the **Voortrekker-Zulu War**. His two sons were killed fighting with the Boers against the Zulu, and to avenge them he joined the *Wenkommando* in October 1838 with a force of Port Natal Africans. He fought at **Ncome** and was later killed in the battle of the **White Mfolozi**. *See also* BIGGAR, ROBERT.

**BIGGAR, ROBERT (1812–1838).** The eldest son of **Alexander Harvey Biggar**, Robert grew up in the **Eastern Cape** and settled in Port Natal (**Durban**) in 1834 as a trader, when he had many contacts with King Dingane kaMpande. During the **Voortrekker-Zulu War**, he led the Grand Army of Natal that was routed at the battle of the **Thukela**, where he was killed.

**BIYELA PEOPLE.** In the 1st Partition of **Zululand**, General **Sir Garnet Joseph Wolseley** appointed *inKosi* Mgitshwa kaMvundlana of the Biyela people in south-central Zululand as one of the 13 chiefs. In 1883, the Biyela supported the anti-**uSuthu** faction in the first phase of the 3rd **Zulu Civil War**, but a section under Somhlolo ka-Mkhosana, whose father had died at **Isandlwana** in the **Anglo-Zulu War**, was an uSuthu supporter. In July 1884, he drove the rest of the Biyela into the **Reserve Territory**. During the **uSuthu Rebellion**, Somhlolo, now the Biyela regent, reinforced *umNtwana* **Shingana kaMpande** on **Hlophekhulu**. The Biyela were encamped to the east of the mountain when the British stormed it, and they were put to flight by the **Eshowe Levy**. *See also* CIVILIANS IN WARTIME ZULULAND.

**BLOOD RIVER, BATTLE OF.** *See* NCOME, BATTLE OF.

**BLOUKRANS MASSACRE (1838).** On 6 February 1838, King **Dingane kaSenzangakhona** ordered the execution at his **uMgungundlovu** *iKhanda* of **Pieter Retief** and his party of Voortrekkers, who had been negotiating with him to secure land in the **Zulu kingdom** on which to settle. That same day, Dingane's *amaButho* (warriors) set out to the southwest in the first campaign of the **Voortrekker-Zulu War** to surprise and kill the rest of the Voortrekkers in their encampments in the valleys of the Bloukrans and Bushman's rivers in the foothills of the **Drakensberg**. Because no Zulu attack was anticipated, the encampments were widely scattered, many had made no preparations for defense by forming wagon **laagers**, and many of the men were away hunting or helping newly arriving parties of Voortrekkers over the mountains.

The chest and right horn of the Zulu army began their attack before midnight on 16 February on the Voortrekker camps along the Bloukrans and its tributaries (later named by the Boers the Great and Little Moord, or Murder, rivers). The camps were rapidly overrun, but the arrival of fugitives and the sight of flames granted some time to the Boers in the camps to the west to prepare their defense. The Zulu, involved in unaccustomed night fighting and laden with booty, lost cohesion and control among the widely scattered encampments. They broke into small groups, and the impetus of their attack petered out beyond the Little Moord River. Some of the fugitives took refuge in the laagers (the largest being the Doornkop laager that held the family of Pieter Retief) beyond the Bloukrans River, which the Zulu had not reached.

The attack of the Zulu left horn was less successful than that of the right. **Gerrit Maritz** and **Johan Hendrik (Hans Dons) de Lange** had established proper laagers where many Voortrekkers rallied and threw back the Zulu attack, while Commandant Johannes Jacobus Janse van Rensburg made a successful stand on a hillock (the Rensburgkoppie) behind his camp. On the afternoon of 17 February, the Boers launched a mounted counterattack from their laagers. They inflicted casualties on the exhausted Zulu, who retreated, driving 25,000 **cattle** and thousands of sheep and **horses** before them. At dawn on 18 February, Maritz led out a commando of 50 men in pursuit from his Saailaer camp, but they could not prevent the Zulu from crossing the swollen Thukela River with their booty.

The Boers bitterly called the region of devastation Weenen, or Weeping. Apart from destroyed wagons and property and captured livestock, the Voortrekkers lost 40 Boer men, 56 Boer women, 185 children, and some 250 colored servants. The number of Zulu dead is unknown, although the Boers believed it amounted to perhaps as many as 500. Though damaged, the Boers had not been eliminated, and they were now implacably thirsting for revenge. *See also* COMMANDO SYSTEM, BOER; STRATEGY, ZULU; TACTICS UP TO 1879, ZULU.

**BOER REPUBLICS.** *See* KLIP RIVER REPUBLIC; NEW REPUBLIC; ORANGE FREE STATE; UTRECHT DISTRICT; SOUTH AFRICAN REPUBLIC.

**BOER WAR, 1ST (TRANSVAAL REBELLION, 1880–1881).** On 12 April 1877, Great Britain annexed the **South African Republic** (SAR) as the Transvaal Territory. On 13 December 1880, the Transvaal Boers rebelled against British rule. They then ambushed a British column and besieged the small British garrisons scattered across the Transvaal. When the Natal Field Force attempted to relieve the garrisons from neighboring **Natal**, the Boers defeated it at the border in three successive engagements, culminating in the humiliating British debacle on Majuba on 27 February 1881. The two sides agreed to an armistice on 15 March. On 3 August, they signed the Pretoria Convention, conceding the independence of the SAR under nebulous British "suzerainty."

**BOERS AND THE ZULULAND CAMPAIGN OF 1884.** The **Boers** from the **South African Republic** took frequent advantage of the 3rd **Zulu Civil War** to raid Zulu livestock. In May–June 1884, they intervened militarily in support of the **uSuthu** against the **Ngenetsheni** and **Mandlakazi**. A Boer **commando** (militia) of 100–120 mounted men from the **South African Republic** under **Lukas Johannes Meyer** and about 20 mounted volunteers from **Luneburg** under Adolf Schiel were crucial to the uSuthu victory at **Tshaneni.**

**imBOKODWEBOMVU *iBUTHO.*** A Zulu *iButho* (age-grade regiment) formed in 1886 by King **Dinuzulu kaCetshwayo** of youths born in 1861–1865, the imBokodwebomvu was a military formation of the **uSuthu** faction. In the **uSuthu Rebellion**, it fought as part of the uSuthu right horn at **Ceza** and the chest at **Ivuna**.

**BONAPARTE, PRINCE (EUGÈNE) LOUIS NAPOLEON (1856– 1879).** The only son and heir of exiled French Emperor Napoleon III, who died in 1873, the Prince Imperial was the Bonapartist pretender to the French throne. He graduated in 1875 from the Royal Military Academy, Woolwich, but as a foreigner he could not take a British commission. He nevertheless craved active service to prove his Napoleonic military credentials. In 1879, he was permitted to join the British forces in the **Anglo-Zulu War** as a spectator and was attached as an extra aide-de-camp to Lieutenant-General Lord **Chelmsford**'s staff during the 2nd Invasion of the war. Chelmsford attached him to the Quartermaster-General's Department to map the road ahead of the 2nd Division, **South African Field Force**. The prince was killed when his patrol was ambushed on 1 June 1879 near the **Tshotshosi River**. His body was transported on the **HMS** *Boadicea* and then **HMS** *Orontes* for eventual burial in England.

**BORDER GUARD, NATAL.** Since there were not enough units of the **Natal Volunteer Corps** and other settler volunteers available to defend the **Natal** border during the **Anglo-Zulu War**, and because the **Natal Native Contingent** was intended for service in **Zululand**, the Natal government agreed in December 1878 to raise and maintain levies (troops) furnished on a quota basis from African chiefs in **Colonial Defensive Districts** I, VI, and VII. The government could not afford a large standing force, and the local economy could not survive the loss of more of its labor force, so the designated levies were to assemble and take the field under white levy leaders only when a Zulu raid threatened. The government provided for small standing reserves of Border Guards to be stationed at designated strategic points, ready to move to any threatened stretch of frontier. River Guards were posted at strategic drifts across the Thukela and Mzinyati rivers. During the course of the war, the Border Guard was augmented by additional levies from Colonial Defensive Districts II, IV, and V. In March, early April, and late May, Lieutenant-General Lord **Chelmsford** ordered the Border Guard to raid **Zululand** to create diversions in favor of the operations of the **Eshowe Relief Column** and the 2nd Division, **South African Field Force**. These orders brought Chelmsford into conflict with **Sir Henry Gascoyne Bulwer**, the Lieutenant-Governor of Natal, who envisaged the colonial levies as acting in an entirely defensive capacity. Their lack of military effectiveness was conclusively exposed during the successful Zulu raid at **Middle Drift** in July. *See also* CIVIL–MILITARY RELATIONS.

**BOUNDARIES AND COLONIAL CONTROL IN ZULULAND.** Basic to the civil strife in **Zululand** during the 3rd **Zulu Civil War** and the **uSuthu Rebellion** was the way in which the territorial boundaries imposed in the 1st, 2nd, and 3rd Partitions of Zululand disregarded the territorially complex patterns of authority and loyalty in existing Zulu chiefdoms. All too often, the *imiZi* (homesteads) of adherents of different chiefs were intermingled, making it impossible for boundary commissioners to draw clean boundary lines that would follow easily recognizable topographical features. The solution (going back to the 1st Partition) was to decree that where people were excluded from their old chief's territory by the new boundaries, they had the option of moving back across the line to their former chief or tendering their allegiance to the new one. This was a recipe for an infinite number of disputes, especially when the boundaries were repeatedly redrawn, forcing many Zulu to reconsider their allegiances. *InKosi* **Zibhebhu kaMaphitha**'s territory was redefined five times between 1879 and 1890, for example. The British also manipulated boundaries as an instrument of control. By favoring the territorial claims of loyal collaborators at the expense of uncooperative chiefs, they perpetuated local divisions, thereby weakening concerted opposition.

**BOUNDARY AWARD.** Since King **Mpande kaSenzangakhona**'s reign, the British, in order to foil attempts by the Boers of the **South African Republic** to extend their territory to the sea and gain a port, had always supported the Zulu in their claims to the **Disputed Territory**. However, when the British annexed the Transvaal Territory in April 1877 and needed to court Boer opinion, their policy underwent a turnabout. A meeting at **Conference Hill** on 18 October 1877 between Zulu and British representatives failed to resolve the dispute, and the angry Zulu saw that the British were now supporting the Boer claims. **Sir Bartle Frere**, the British high commissioner, who believed an independent Zulu kingdom stood in the way of his **confederation** plans, supposed the impasse gave him the necessary justification for the military solution he sought.

At this crucial moment, the lieutenant-governor of Natal, **Sir Henry Gascoyne Bulwer**, who feared the effects on **Natal** of a war with **Zululand**, offered to mediate. King **Cetshwayo kaMpande** accepted Bulwer's proposal for a Boundary Commission, and Frere, although thwarted, could not refuse. The commission, made up from Natal officials, duly began its sittings at **Rorke's Drift** on 17 March 1878, and Frere received its scrupulous report on 15 July. Its findings did not affect the disputed area north of the Phongolo River, which had been excluded from its purview. It rejected Zulu claims of sovereignty that extended west over the **Utrecht** and **Wakkerstroom** districts of the Transvaal. It did recognize the Transvaal's rights to the land between the Mzinyathi and Ncome rivers (effectively the Utrecht District) but, crucially, not to the territory east of the Ncome, where some Boers had settled. Frere realized he could not make the report public without fatally alienating the Boers of the Transvaal. He held it back until 11 December, when it was delivered directly before his **ultimatum** to the Zulu king and its import thereby negated.

**BREAKING OF THE ROPE.** In September 1839, *umNtwana* **Mpande kaSenzangakhona**, fearing that his half-brother King **Dingane kaSenzangakhona** intended to execute him, fled across the Thukela River to the sanctuary of the Republic of **Natalia** with 17,000 adherents and 25,000 **cattle**. Safe in Boer territory, Mpande entered into an alliance with the Boers that culminated in the 1st **Zulu Civil War** and Dingane's overthrow. The Zulu called Mpande's defection "the breaking of the rope that held the nation together."

**BREVET RANK.** Officers in the British army held substantive rank in their regiment based on seniority, but between the ranks of captain and lieutenant-colonel, they could concurrently hold a rank one higher in the army as a reward for distinguished service in the field, when serving in a staff appointment, or when it became necessary on campaign to make them eligible to hold a more senior command.

**BROMHEAD, GONVILLE (1845–1892).** A lieutenant in the 24th (2nd Warwickshire) **Regiment** during the **Anglo-Zulu War**, Bromhead was left in command of a detachment of the regiment at the depot at **Rorke's Drift** when No. 3 **Column** advanced to encamp at **Isandlwana**. He was awarded the Victoria Cross for his gallant defense of the post during the battle of Rorke's Drift. During the advance of the 2nd Division, **South African Field Force**, he commanded detachments in garrison at **Dundee, Landman's Drift**, and Koppie Alleen (**Fort Whitehead**). He subsequently served in the Burma campaign (1886–1888) and died of fever while still a major.

**BUFFALO BORDER GUARD.** One of the 10 corps of **Natal Mounted Volunteers** who were called out in November 1878 for active service in the **Anglo-Zulu War**, it was formed in 1873. The corps of 40 troopers joined No. 3 **Column** at **Helpmekaar** in December 1878. The majority advanced with the column in the 1st Invasion of the war, though a few men declined to do so and remained in **Natal** patrolling the **border**. The corps with No. 3 Column took part in the skirmish at **kwaSogekle** on 12 January. Two-thirds of the corps were absent with Major **John George Dartnell**'s reconnaissance in force when the remainder left in the camp at **Isandlwana** suffered heavy casualties in the Zulu attack. The corps retired with No. 3 Column to Natal, where it garrisoned its headquarters at **Fort Pine** between February and July 1879 while engaged in patrol work, cross-border raids, escort duty, and dispatch riding. Its uniform was of black cloth with black braiding and white metal buttons, black riding-boots, and a white helmet with a spike.

**kwaBULAWAYO *iKHANDA*.** In 1824, King **Shaka kaSenzangakhona** established the first *iKhanda* of this name on the coastal plain between the Mhlathuze and lower Thukela rivers. It contained perhaps as many as 1,400 huts. King **Cetshwayo kaMpande** later reestablished it in the **Mahlabathini Plain**, and it was burned by the British in the **Anglo-Zulu War** following the battle of **Ulundi**.

**BULLER, REDVERS HENRY (1839–1908).** Commissioned in 1858, Buller served in the 2nd China (Opium) War (1860), the Red River Expedition (1870), the 2nd Asante War (1873–1874), and 9th **Cape**

**Frontier War** (1878), when he became a brevet lieutenant-colonel. Now an established member of **Sir Garnet Joseph Wolseley's** Ashanti Ring, he was on special service during the **Anglo-Zulu War** when he commanded the mounted troops in No. 4 **Column** and **Wood's Flying Column.** He saw action in numerous skirmishes, including at **Zungeni** and the **White Mfolozi reconnaissance in force**, and he fought in the general actions at **Hlobane** (where he won the Victoria Cross), **Khambula,** and **Ulundi.** He served in the 1st **Boer War** (1881) with the local rank of major-general, and in the Egyptian campaign of 1882, after which he was knighted. He saw service again in the Suakin campaign in 1884 and the Gordon Relief Expedition of 1884–1885. Between 1887 and 1897, he was at the War Office as quartermaster-general and then as adjutant-general. He was promoted to general in 1896. In October 1899, he was appointed commander-in-chief in South Africa in the first stage of the **Anglo-Boer (South African) War,** but he was replaced in January 1900 by Field Marshal Lord Roberts after a series of reverses on the **Natal** front. Buller continued in command of the Natal Army until October 1900. He retired from the army in 1906.

**BULWER, SIR HENRY ERNEST GASCOYNE (1836–1914).** Before serving in **Natal** as lieutenant-governor (September 1875 to April 1880), Bulwer had been official resident in the Ionian Islands (1860–1864), treasurer and receiver-general of Trinidad (1866), administrator of the government of Dominica and the Leeward Islands (1867–1869), and governor of Labuan and consul-general for Borneo (1871–1875). In Natal, his overriding concern was for the peace and security of the colony, and he did his best to avert war with **Zululand**, intervening to set up the Boundary Commission of 1878. During the **Anglo-Zulu War,** he came into conflict with Lieutenant-General Lord **Chelmsford** over the parameters of civil and military authority, and he opposed Chelmsford's cross-border raids for fear of Zulu retaliation. Bulwer returned to Natal in March 1882 as governor. He opposed the restoration of King **Cetshwayo kaMpande** to Zululand as endangering Natal's security, but with the 2nd Partition of Zululand, he was appointed in 1883 special commissioner for Zulu affairs. He was unable to influence the course of the 3rd **Zulu Civil War**, though he did his best to restrain the territorial ambitions of the **New Republic** following the 3rd Partition of Zululand. He left Natal in October 1885 and ended his career as high commissioner for Cyprus, retiring in 1892.

**BURGHER'S LAAGER.** *See* PIVAAN LAAGER.

**BUTHELEZI PEOPLE.** The *amaKhosi* (chiefs) of the Buthelezi people in north-central **Zululand** had served the Zulu kings in the highest positions of state since the time of King **Shaka kaSenzanga-khona**. In the 3rd **Zulu Civil War**, the Buthelezi remained stalwart **uSuthu** supporters. The uSuthu army crushed at **Msebe** mustered in their territory, and their contingent was in the vanguard at the battle. In May 1883, they were prominent in the inconclusive campaign against *umNtwana* **Hamu kaNzibe**'s stronghold on the Phongolo River, and against *inKosi* **Zibhebhu kaMaphitha** in July. They were among the uSuthu force that arrived too late to intervene at **oNdini**. In the aftermath of the uSuthu defeat, they were severely harried in August and September 1883 by the **Mandlakazi** and **Ngenetsheni**. On 29 April 1884, the Ngenetsheni defeated them in central Zulu-land. In 1887, **Mnyamana kaNgqengelele**, the Buthelezi *inKosi*, decided not to contest British rule in the colony of Zululand, so when King **Dinuzulu kaCetshwayo** unleashed the **uSuthu Rebellion**, he targeted the Buthelezi for their disloyalty to the uSuthu cause. In May 1888, the uSuthu raided the Buthelezi from their base on **Ceza**, and the Buthelezi took refuge with the British at **Nkonjeni**. On 24 June, the uSuthu on **Hlophekhulu** raided them at Nkonjeni. Only in late August did the Buthelezi feel secure enough to return home. *See also* CIVILIANS IN WARTIME ZULULAND.

***iBUTHO*, STRUCTURE AND SIZE OF.** The Zulu military system was made up of regimental groups called *amaButho*. Each *iButho* was divided up into a number of sections, or *amaViyo*. An *iViyo* consisted of men of the same age group, drawn from a particular locality, who had been formed into the section or company during their days as cadets at one of the district *amaKhanda* (administrative centers). Each *iButho* was commanded by an *inDuna* (officer) appointed by the king. An *inDuna* might also be an *inKosi* (hereditary chief) or *umNtwana* (prince). Under him were a second in command and two experienced wing officers, all of an older generation than the men they led. There were also a number of junior officers, at least two to each *iViyo*, chosen by their contemporaries for their natural leadership in their days as cadets.

It was customary to express the size of an *iButho* in terms of the number of *amaViyo* that constituted it. Yet it is not possible to specify the strength of an *iViyo*, as this depended on the degree of royal favor involved, as did the number of *amaViyo* constituting any particular *iButho*. An *iViyo* could be 40–60 men, though in prize *amaButho*, the number could reach 100 or more. An *iButho* could consequently muster between several hundred and a few thousand men. Older *amaButho* that the king was not keeping up to strength would be smaller through natural attrition. The partially revived *amaButho* of the period of the 3rd **Zulu Civil War** and the **uSuthu Rebellion** were also small. It is particularly difficult to compute the size of an *iButho* in complex campaigns like the **Anglo-Zulu War** because elements of the same *iButho* could be engaged simultaneously in different theaters. *See also iBUTHO* SYSTEM DURING THE ZULU KINGDOM; *iBUTHO* SYSTEM IN THE 1880s; *iBUTHO* SYSTEM, SERVICE IN; POLITICAL ORGANIZATION, ZULU.

*iBUTHO* **SYSTEM DURING THE ZULU KINGDOM.** The Zulu military system was an instrument both of internal control and external defense that allowed the king to exercise real economic and social control over all his subjects, men and women. It diverted their productive and military potential away from their own *imiZi* (family homesteads), localities, and *amaKhosi* (hereditary chiefs) to the service of the state, for it operated as a system of taxation where labor was substituted for money or goods. It was built on the institution of age-set units called *amaButho* that seem to have developed from the ancient practice among the Nguni-speaking people of southern Africa of banding together youths of similar age in circumcision sets. By the early 19th century, among the chiefdoms that would later be incorporated into the **Zulu kingdom**, the function of these *amaButho* was moving beyond initiation into organizing youths to perform economic and military services. In the 1820s King **Shaka kaSenzangakhona** brought this evolving *iButho* system into its fully developed form as an instrument for integrating the members of conquered chiefdoms into the new kingdom under its sole ruler, and weaning them away from regional loyalties to their original *ama-Khosi*. The system persisted, with modifications, as the central pillar of the Zulu state until the fall of the kingdom in the **Anglo-Zulu War**. It survived in attenuated form during the period of the 3rd **Zulu Civil War** and **uSuthu Rebellion**.

Zulu boys between the ages of 14 and 18 would gather at *ama-Khanda*, or administrative centers, where they might serve for two to three years as cadets, herding **cattle**, working the fields (more usually a woman's task in Zulu society), and practicing military skills. Once enough boys of an age group were congregated at a district *iKhanda*, they would be brought before the king at his main *iKhanda*, or "great place," at the time of the *umKhosi*, or first-fruits festival. The king then formed them into an *iButho* with orders to build a new *iKhanda*, often bearing the name he had given the *iButho*. Sometimes, a new *iButho* was incorporated into an old one whose strength the king wished to maintain and was quartered with it in its existing *iKhanda*.

Not all *amaButho* were made up from cadets from every part of the kingdom. The **abaQulusi** in northwestern **Zululand** and the **emaNgweni** along the coast had each developed out of an *iKhanda* founded to establish royal authority in the locality, and each formed a separate *iButho* composed only of men living in the region they dominated.

Women were fully part of the *iButho* system in that they constituted the major agricultural labor force in Zululand and produced food to feed their male relatives when they were away from home serving the king. Girls were also formed into *amaButho*, primarily for the purpose of regulating marriage. At intervals, the king gave members of a female *iButho* leave to marry middle-aged men from a male *iButho* who had received royal permission to put on the *isiCoco*, or headring. By delaying permission for a male *iButho* to marry and set up his own *imiZi* as an *umNumzane* (married headman), the king was prolonging the period in which the man would be regarded as a youth in Zulu society and thus would remain more firmly under the authority of his elders when providing labor and military service.

The 1st Partition of Zululand at the close of the **Anglo-Zulu War** also suppressed the *iButho* system along with the monarchy. It would be temporarily and incompletely revived following King **Cetshwayo kaMpande**'s short-lived restoration after the 2nd Partition of Zululand. *See also* *iBUTHO* SYSTEM IN THE 1880s; *iBUTHO* SYSTEM, SERVICE IN; *iBUTHO*, STRUCTURE AND SIZE OF; POLITICAL ORGANIZATION, ZULU.

*iBUTHO* **SYSTEM IN THE 1880s.** When the British government agreed to the 2nd Partition of **Zululand** and the restoration of King **Cetshwayo kaMpande**, it was on condition (insisted upon by **Natal**, which feared Zulu military potential) that he would not revitalize or even permit the existence of the *iButho* system in his territory. This prohibition made it difficult for Cetshwayo to reassert his authority or defend himself in the 3rd **Zulu Civil War**. Cetshwayo made a half-hearted attempt to revive the *iButho* system, but with the abolition of the monarchy in the 1st Partition of Zululand, Cetshwayo's rivals, notably *inKosi* **Zibhebhu kaMaphitha** and *umNtwana* **Hamu kaN-zibe**, had resumed the ancient prerogative of chiefs raising their own *amaButho*. Thus, many members of the *amaButho* who had survived the **Anglo-Zulu War** no longer remained loyal to the royal cause and had given their allegiance to their local *amaKhosi* instead of to the monarch. Consequently, in the 3rd Zulu Civil War, when Cetshwayo tried to muster his old *amaButho*, only a limited number heeded his summons. When he tried to raise a new *iButho*, the **uFalaza**, he found he could only recruit young men from his own territory and not from throughout the kingdom as formerly. His *amaButho* thus no longer performed their previous function of bringing all Zulu men into the king's service; they functioned merely as military units of the royalist **uSuthu** faction. Cetshwayo's crushing defeat at **oNdini** scattered his partially reconstituted *amaButho*, and almost all his loyal, if elderly, commanders died in the rout.

Cetshwayo's successor, King **Dinuzulu kaMpande**, employed his royal prerogative to form a new *iButho*, the **imBokodwebomvu**, but like the uFalaza, it was really nothing more than a military formation of the uSuthu faction. In fact, during the 3rd Zulu Civil War and the **uSuthu Rebellion**, the uSuthu drew their military strength far more from territorially based irregulars like the **abaQulusi**, or contingents under their own *amaKhosi*, than from the imperfectly reconstituted *amaButho*. The fact that the *iViyo*, or company, replaced the *iButho* as the tactical unit of Zulu forces operating in the field underlined the profound change that had taken place in Zulu military organization and scale since the defeat to the royal armies in the Anglo-Zulu War. *See also iBUTHO* SYSTEM DURING THE ZULU KINGDOM; IRREGULARS, ZULU; POLITICAL ORGANIZATION, ZULU.

*iBUTHO* **SYSTEM, SERVICE IN.** When the *iButho* system was functioning fully during the heyday of the Zulu kingdom, young men congregated at the district **amaKhanda** as cadets before being formed into *amaButho*, and married men assembled there for short periods of two to five months, often with their wives. Unmarried *amaButho* served at the central *amaKhanda* for seven to eight months immediately after their initial formation, and thereafter for a few months a year when they served the king. All the *amaButho*, married and unmarried, gathered at the central *amaKhanda* for national ceremonies like the **umKhosi**, or when they were mobilized to go on campaign.

While serving at an *iKhanda*, an *iButho* kept it in repair, herded and milked the royal **cattle** attached to it, and cultivated the king's land. Daily dancing and praise-singing doubled as military exercises. The men were supposed to be provisioned through the king's bounty, but they were mainly dependent on food provided from home by their women.

Sometimes the king would call up a few *amaButho* for special tasks: building a new *iKhanda* in a region where he wished to assert his authority (like in the **Disputed Territory**); repairing an *iKhanda* damaged by fire; participating in great hunts; supplying him with exotic foodstuffs and items for apparel from the margins of the kingdom; and collecting tribute from outlying subject people like the **Tsonga**. The *amaButho* also served as an instrument of internal control, collecting cattle fines from offenders against the king, or "eating them up" by destroying their *imiZi* and executing them and their dependents. The cattle and commodities which the *amaButho* accumulated for the king on their forays—particularly on full-scale campaigns against an external enemy like the **Swazi** or **Ndebele**—provided a vital source of royal power, because by redistributing them to the *amaButho* or to the great men of the kingdom, the king ensured their loyalty. In the 1880s, when the *iButho* system was imperfectly revived after its abolition at the end of the **Anglo-Zulu War**, these services continued to be patchily performed on a much reduced scale. *See also iBUTHO* SYSTEM DURING THE ZULU KINGDOM; POLITICAL ORGANIZATION, ZULU.

## – C –

**CAMBRIDGE, PRINCE GEORGE WILLIAM FREDERICK CHARLES, 2ND DUKE OF (1819–1904).** Cambridge entered the British army in 1837 and succeeded his father, the 7th son of King George III, as 2nd Duke in 1850. In the Crimean War, he commanded the 1st (Guards) Division in 1854 and was present at the Alma, Balaclava, and Inkerman. In 1856, he was promoted general and appointed general commanding-in-chief of the British Army, a post he held until 1895. In 1862, he was made field marshal. He found it difficult to countenance the **army reforms** instituted by **Edward Cardwell** in 1870–1873 because he believed they would render the overseas battalions less effective, and he resented the subordination of his post to the secretary of state for war. As the spokesman for the more conservative elements in the army, he was also suspicious and dismissive of the reforming General **Sir Garnet Wolseley** and his Ashanti Ring of like-minded officers. *See also* CARDWELL REFORMS.

**CAMP KONGELLA.** On 6 July 1888, during the **uSuthu Rebellion**, Major **Alexander Chalmers McKean** formed the **Eshowe Column** in a camp close by the Hermannsburg mission station at Kongella on the south bank of the Mhlathuze River before marching to the relief of **Fort Andries**.

**CAMP UMFOLOSI.** Between 28 July and 2 August 1888, during the **uSuthu Rebellion**, the **Coastal Column** encamped on the northern bank of the Mfolozi River and sent out patrols to enforce **submissions** of the **uSuthu**. *InKosi* **Somkhele kaMalanda** and various **Mphukunyoni** *izinDuna* (headmen) surrendered there on 30 July 1888.

**CAMP UMLALAZI.** On 23 July 1888, during the **uSuthu Rebellion**, Major **Alexander Chalmers McKean** formed the **Coastal Column** in a camp on the south bank of the Mhlathuze River on the **Zululand** coast, preparatory to advancing to **Ivuna** and forcing the **submission** of the coastal **uSuthu**.

**CANE, JOHN (c. 1800–1838).** Born in London, Cane arrived in Port Natal (**Durban**) in 1824 as one of the first hunter-traders to settle there. He was among the white **mercenaries** who aided King **Shaka kaSenzangakhona** against the Khumalo people in the campaign of 1827. In 1828, Shaka sent him on a mission that proved unsuccessful to open relations with the government of the **Cape**. King **Dingane kaSenzangakhona** employed him for the same purpose in 1830, and Cane's fresh failure led to fractious relations with Dingane. In 1837, Cane led a contingent from Port Natal to assist Dingane in raiding the **Swazi**. He welcomed the arrival of the Voortrekkers in 1837, and in the **Voortrekker-Zulu War**, he led the Port Natal raid at **Ntunjambili**. He was killed at the battle of the **Thukela**.

**CAPE COLONY.** In 1652, the Dutch East India Company (Vereenigde Oostindische Compagnie, or VOC) established a refreshment station on the way to the East Indies at the southern tip of Africa. In a series of frontier conflicts, the growing settler community gradually spread out over the interior from the initial settlement at **Cape Town** at the expense of the indigenous population. During the wars with revolutionary France, Great Britain first occupied the Cape in 1795 but in 1803 made it over to the Batavian Republic (to which the VOC had ceded its territories in 1798) in terms of the Treaty of Amiens. On the resumption of hostilities with Napoleonic France, the British occupied the Cape for the second time in 1806. By the Anglo-Dutch Treaty (London Convention) of 13 August 1814 between the United Provinces and Great Britain, the Cape was ceded to Britain. The Cape Colony achieved responsible government in 1872. In 1910, the colony became a province in the Union of South Africa. *See also* CAPE FRONTIER WARS; EASTERN CAPE; GREAT TREK.

**CAPE FRONTIER WARS.** The Dutch settlers at the Cape of Good Hope had a long history of frontier conflict. Their nearly a century and a half of endemic warfare was inherited by the British, who first occupied the **Cape Colony** in 1795. The most powerful resistance to white intrusion was conducted by the Xhosa people, who lived on the margins of the eastern frontier. Their nation consisted of a number of chiefdoms acknowledging a shadowy paramount chief but often deeply divided among themselves. Early in the 19th century, they took to **firearms** and guerrilla warfare as the best means in their broken terrain of resisting encroaching white settlement. The Cape eastern frontier gave the British army its first South African lessons in irregular, bush warfare and taught it that the way to defeat the Xhosa was by destroying the logistical base that sustained them, rather than by trying to beat them in conventional operations and set-piece battles. Dutch forces engaged the Xhosa in the 1st (1779–1781) and 2nd (1789–1793) of the nine Cape Frontier Wars. The British and Xhosa fought seven of the wars: 3rd (1799–1803); 4th (1811–1812); 5th (1818–1819); 6th (1834–1835); 7th (1846–1847); 8th (1850–1853); and 9th (1877–1878). The last of these bitter conflicts ended in final Xhosa defeat.

**CAPE TOWN.** Founded on 6 April 1652 on the northern end of the Cape Peninsula under Table Mountain as a way station for the ships of Dutch East India Company (Vereenigde Oostindische Compagnie, or VOC), Cape Town was the first European settlement in southern Africa. It was the administrative center while the Cape of Good Hope was under the rule of the VOC, and after 1814 it became the capital of the British **Cape Colony**. During the 19th century, it remained a strategically vital coaling station and naval base. Later in the century it was overtaken as the biggest city in South Africa by the gold-mining town of Johannesburg in the **South African Republic**.

**CAPE TOWN CASTLE.** After his defeat in the **Anglo-Zulu War**, the British sent King **Cetshwayo kaMpande** in exile to the Cape, where he was imprisoned between September 1879 and February 1881 in the Flagstaff Bastion of the Cape Town Castle (Castle of Good Hope). This fortress with five bastions was built between 1666 and 1679 by the Dutch East India Company (Vereenigde Oostindische Compagnie) to guard their settlement at **Cape Town**.

**CARBINES.** In 1877, the British cavalry adopted the **Martini-Henry** carbine, sighted up to 1,000 yards, as a secondary weapon to the **sword** or **lance**. It was replaced in 1892 by the Martini-Metford carbine. **Mounted infantry** in the **Anglo-Zulu War** carried the .450-caliber Swinburn-Henry carbine. In the 3rd **Zulu Civil War** and the **uSuthu Rebellion**, they were issued the Martini-Henry carbine. The standard weapon of the **Natal Volunteer Corps** was the .450-caliber Swinburn-Henry carbine, which replaced the Snider carbine in 1877, although because of shortages many of the **irregular** mounted units raised in the Anglo-Zulu War continued to be issued with Snider carbines.

**CARBUTT'S BORDER RANGERS.** On the eve of the **Anglo-Zulu War**, Captain Thomas Carbutt, a farmer near **Ladysmith** with previous military experience in the Natal Frontier Guard that had been disbanded in 1876, began to recruit volunteers from among the local settler community for the defense of **Colonial Defensive District No. I.** His 30 men wore their everyday clothes and carried their own weapons. After **Isandlwana**, they patrolled the vulnerable border along the Mzinyathi River from their base at the **Ladysmith laager**. In recognition of this valuable service, the unit was regularized on 15 March and maintained and equipped thereafter by the military. They continued to patrol the border and took part in the patrol of 21 May that began the burial of the British dead at Isandlwana. They disbanded in late July. *See also* BORDER GUARD, NATAL.

**CARDWELL, EDWARD (1813–1886).** Cardwell first entered parliament in 1842 and in 1868 was appointed secretary of state for war in William Ewart Gladstone's first Liberal ministry. Between 1870 and 1873, he instituted wide-ranging army reforms, reorganizing the War Office, abolishing purchase of commissions, and introducing linked battalions to promote recruitment and build up a reserve. The **Cardwell Reforms** were controversial at the time and did not achieve all that was hoped of them, although they did lay the basis for a more efficient and professional army. Cardwell did not hold office again after the fall of Gladstone's ministry in 1874 and was raised to the peerage as the 1st Viscount Cardwell of Ellerbeck.

**CARDWELL REFORMS.** The wide-ranging British army reforms carried out under **Edward Cardwell**, secretary of state for war (1868–1874), directly affected the army's conduct of the **Anglo-Zulu War**. For the sake of economy and efficiency, Cardwell reduced Britain's military presence overseas by accelerating the withdrawal of troops from colonies of settlement and by scaling down garrisons elsewhere, except in India. The introduction of short service in 1870, whereby recruits spent six years in the regular army and six in the reserve, was designed to create a large reservoir of trained reservists, reduce unhealthy service abroad, and save money. The Localization Bill of 1872 created 69 brigade districts in Britain (usually conforming to an existing county) with two linked battalions attached to each depot. The intention was to tie infantry battalions to specific geographical regions in order to foster local loyalties and to encourage recruitment. The battalions alternated in recruiting at home and serving abroad with the intention of ensuring that the empire was guarded only by seasoned troops. In 1871, the purchase of commissions was abolished and promotion opened to merit in order to encourage the development of a professional officer corps.

In practice, the system did not work. In the officer corps a large private income was still necessary in all except the technical corps, so it still remained a conservative social elite. Recruits to the rank and file still came mainly from the poorest and least educated elements of society, and the army had to lower physical standards to find enough recruits to meet the large turnover of men caused by short-term enlistment. Since the reserve was not to be called up except in the event of a national emergency, colonial campaigns (such as the Anglo-Zulu War) could only be provided for by attracting special service officers, calling upon regular and reserve units for volunteers, and draining standing garrisons. As colonial commitments increased in the later 19th century, a growing number of home-based and imperfectly trained battalions was required to serve overseas. Thus, at the time of the Anglo-Zulu War, 82 battalions were abroad, and only 59 at home depots. Short-term enlistment meant that experienced soldiers left the ranks earlier, with the consequence that the number of younger, inexperienced men rose proportionately. Thus in 1879, many of the draftees sent out to **Zululand**, and some fresh battalions too, were militarily unsatisfactory: young, inadequately trained, unused to combat conditions, and susceptible to disease. *See also* ARMY REFORM, BRITISH; CHILDERS REFORMS; MILITARY ORGANIZATION, BRITISH.

**CAREY, JAHLEEL BRENTON (1847–1883).** Carey was educated mainly in France and was first commissioned in 1865, serving in

Honduras in 1867. During the Franco-Prussian War (1870–1871), he served with distinction with the English Ambulance Service. In 1878, he attended Staff College. He was promoted to captain, went on special service to the **Anglo-Zulu War**, and was mentioned in dispatches for his excellent conduct during the loss of the troopship *Clyde*. Serving with the 2nd Division, **South African Field Force**, and attached to the staff of the acting quartermaster-general planning the invasion route, Carey accompanied **Prince Louis Napoleon Bonaparte** on patrol on 1 June, and was ambushed in the **Tshotshosi skirmish**. For his questionable part in the affair, he was tried by general court-martial on 12 June, found guilty of misbehaving before the enemy, and ordered back to England. There he found much public support, and on a technicality the findings of the court-martial were not confirmed. Carey rejoined his regiment in India, but his reputation and promising career were ruined. He died of peritonitis in February 1883.

**CARNARVON, HENRY HOWARD MOLYNEUX, 4TH EARL OF (1831–1890).** Carnarvon, who became the 4th Earl of Carnarvon in 1849, pursued a political career in Britain's Conservative Party. He was the secretary of state for colonies in 1866–1867, when he guided through the British North America Bill (1867) that brought the federal dominion of Canada into being. Carnarvon was again colonial secretary in 1874–1878, when he promoted a **confederation** in South Africa along the lines of the Canadian federation. In March 1877, he sent **Sir Bartle Frere** to South Africa as high commissioner to implement confederation. Carnarvon resigned from the cabinet in January 1878 over the Eastern Question (the Turco-Russian crisis). Except for a short period as lord lieutenant of Ireland (1885–1886), his political career was at an end.

**CARRIER CORPS.** In July 1879, General **Sir Garnet Joseph Wolseley**, who had successfully used African carriers in the 2nd Asante War (1873–1874), ordered the formation of a corps of carriers in **Zululand** drawn from the disarmed Natal **Border Guard** and African levies (troops) with the 1st Division, **South African Field Force**, to replace what he considered the inefficient and expensive **ox-wagon** system of **transport** being used in the **Anglo-Zulu War**. During late

July and early August, 2,000 carriers brought up supplies from **Port Durnford** to **St. Paul's** for **Baker Russell's Column**. They each carried loads of about 50 lbs. for an average of 10 miles a day, then returned the same day unloaded. The unarmed carriers were liable to panics and found working conditions harsh. Many deserted and had to be replaced by Zulu recruited locally. The cost of maintaining carriers proved four times higher than ox-wagon transport, and the military decided not to rely on carriers in Zululand again.

**CARRINGTON'S LEVY.** In the final stages of the **uSuthu Rebellion**, Lieutenant-General Henry Augustus Smyth brought in Colonel Frederick Carrington, in command of the Bechuanaland Border Police (1885–1893), to instill order and discipline into the demoralized African levies (troops) under his command. Carrington created a force of 1,760 comprising *inKosi* **Zibhebhu kaMaphitha** and 200 of his **Mandlakazi** who had taken refuge at **Nkonjeni** after the battle of **Ivuna**, 150 of Yamela's men (the remnants of the **Eshowe Levy** that had deserted on 14 July 1888), and fresh recruits. Carrington's Levy made up **Martin's Flying Column**, which joined the **Coastal Column** at Ivuna on 7 August for their joint march back to the coast. On 23 August, the levy made a night march to the Nhlati Hills to disperse *inKosi* **Somopho kaZikhala**'s followers, and on 25 August it reconnoitered the deserted **Dukuduku stronghold**.

**CATTLE, ZULU.** Iron Age Bantu speakers introduced domestic cattle into southern Africa about 2,000 years ago. The cattle may have stemmed from the humpless, long-horned *Bos taurus* originally domesticated in either Egypt or West Africa, with a strong admixture of the humped, short-horned *Bos indicus* first domesticated in the Near East about 7,000 years ago and then introduced to Africa via the Horn and east coast. "Sanga" is the term widely used today for African indigenous breeds of cattle and includes strains such as the Nguni found in **Zululand**. Cattle were susceptible to Redwater fever and Ngana, two wasting diseases caused by parasites injected into the bloodstream by the bite, respectively, of ticks and tsetse flies.

The Zulu were essentially pastoralists, and the Zulu language contains hundreds of terms by which to identify the distinctive shapes of cattle horns, the presence or absence of a hump, colorings, and markings. Favorite oxen had praise names and were trained to respond to whistled commands. The paramount importance of cattle in Zulu life was symbolized by the position of the cattle-fold, or *isiBaya*, in the center of every ***umuZi*** (homestead). All ceremonies and rituals were performed there, and the ***amaDlozi*** (ancestral spirits) summoned and propitiated when cattle were sacrificed to them there. While in theory all cattle belonged to the nation and, by extension, to the king, in fact cattle were part of the *umuZi* unit, and individuals' private control over their own cattle was practically complete.

Prized as the prime indicator of wealth in a society that had little other means of storing it, cattle constituted ***iLobolo***, or bridewealth, which was exchanged for a wife on marriage. Cattle provided food (especially milk), their hides were used for clothing, and their dung was a vital source of fuel and construction material for *izinDlu* (huts). The capture of cattle was thus a prime objective of every military campaign and the indicator of its success. Cattle taken in war were technically the sole property of the king, who gave away large numbers to *amaKhosi* and favorites, and to reward and feed his ***amaButho***. Having sufficient disposable cattle was therefore essential if the king were to bind his *amaKhosi* and ***amaButho*** to him, and in a circular process this necessitated sustaining an army to go out on campaign to acquire them. In the custom known as *ukusisa*, the king would also entrust his royal cattle for a time to *amaKhanda* (royal military centers) or *imiZi*, granting them the right to make use of the cattle (e.g., for milk, dung, or offspring) before having to return them.

**CAVALRY BRIGADE.** On 8 April 1879 during the **Anglo-Zulu War**, the Cavalry Brigade, consisting of the 1st (King's) **Dragoon Guards** and the 17th (Duke of Cambridge's Own) **Lancers** (1,247 men) under the command of Major-General **Frederick Marshall**, was attached to the 2nd Division, **South African Field Force**, and directed to join it in northern **Natal**. The Cavalry Brigade saw action throughout the entire 2nd Invasion of the war, and it fought at **Zungeni** and **Ulundi**.

**CETSHWAYO kaMPANDE (c. 1832–1884).** In 1839, King **Mpande kaSenzangakhona** identified Cetshwayo as his heir. Cetshwayo was enrolled in the **uThulwana** *iButho* and took part in the **Swazi**

campaign of 1852. He was a popular *umNtwana* (prince) and gathered a faction around him, known as the **uSuthu**. Mpande began to fear his power and favored other sons for the succession, notably *umNtwana* **Mbuyazi kaMpande**. The issue was decided when Cetshwayo defeated Mbuyazi in the 2nd **Zulu Civil War** and other surviving claimants fled into exile. In May 1861, Mpande recognized Cetshwayo as his heir, and thereafter he exercised most of his father's royal prerogatives until he succeeded him on his death in 1872.

During his reign, Cetshwayo tried to consolidate royal power that had been subverted by the leading *amaKhosi* and to revitalize the *iButho* **system** that was its basis. He maintained Mpande's policy of fostering good relations with the British as a counterweight to the **South African Republic**'s territorial claims in **Zululand**. After the annexation of the Transvaal in 1877, however, British policy toward Zululand turned hostile, and Cetshwayo's efforts to stave off the **Anglo-Zulu War** through **negotiation** were rendered futile.

Cetshwayo's strategy in the Anglo-Zulu War was to defend his country stoutly and then to try to negotiate further from a position of military success. Military defeat wrecked this policy. The British captured the fugitive king on 28 August 1879 at the remote **kwa-Dwasa** *umuZi* in the Ngome Forest and sent him into exile in **Cape Town**. His many supporters agitated for his restoration to bring stability in Zululand after the 1st Partition, and in August 1882 he visited London to argue his case. The 2nd Partition of Zululand was the consequence, but many in Zululand who had benefited from the suppression of the monarchy in the 1st Partition resisted his restoration. The 3rd **Zulu Civil War** broke out immediately on his return, and by July 1883 Cetshwayo was a refugee in the **Nkandla Forest** in the **Reserve Territory**. In October, he sought shelter with the British at **Eshowe**. Cetshwayo died suddenly on 8 February 1884, possibly of poison. He was buried deep in the Nkandla Forest near the *umuZi* of Luhungu of the Shezi people, whose descendants still watch over his grave.

**CEZA CAMP.** In the final stages of the suppression of the **uSuthu Rebellion**, the British abandoned the **Nsukazi Fort** and the **Begamuza Camp** on 18 August 1888 for a small fort built at Peter Louw's store close to **Ceza** Mountain. The move was aimed at preventing the **uSuthu** from regrouping on the mountain. The garrison was withdrawn in late September 1888, when all the advanced posts in Ndwandwe District in the colony of **Zululand** were given up.

**CEZA MOUNTAIN, BATTLE OF (1888).** This small engagement was the last time Zulu forces defeated the British in **Zululand**. At the outset of the **uSuthu Rebellion**, the resident magistrate of Ndwandwe, **Richard Hallowes Addison**, resolved to arrest the **uSuthu** ringleaders on Ceza Mountain. Since this was still a civil matter, the troops supporting the operation could only take action if Addison called on them to do so.

On 2 June 1888, Addison, 67 **Zululand Police** under Commandant **George Mansel**, and 600 of **Mnyamana's Auxiliaries**, supported by 84 of the 6th (Inniskilling) **Dragoons** and 80 **mounted infantry** under Major **Edward Graham Pennefather**, halted near Ceza. The 2,000 uSuthu under King **Dinuzulu kaCetshwayo** formed up on the slopes and started marching to the flat summit that was just across the border with the **New Republic**. Fearing that the uSuthu would consequently soon be out of British jurisdiction, Mansel pushed ahead with a small party of Zululand Police to execute the warrants. They encountered some Zulu in the thick bush, and on hearing firing, the rest of the uSuthu came streaming back down the mountain in traditional battle formation. Realizing the Zululand Police would be cut off by the encircling horns, Addison called on Pennefather's soldiers to extricate them. The auxiliaries were caught up in the chaotic retreat, and the Zulu followed closely, skirmishing along their flanks. Pennefather and his mounted men formed into two ranks and charged the Zulu, who then gave up further attempts to surround and cut off the British but continued to harry them down to the Black Mfolozi River. The British crossed the river and re-formed at the **Nsukazi laager**.

Two British soldiers died in the affray and an unknown number of uSuthu, though it could not have been very large. The ignominious retreat of the British was a devastating blow to their prestige in Zululand and greatly encouraged the uSuthu in their continued resistance. *See also* CEZA MOUNTAIN STRONGHOLD; CIVIL–MILITARY RELATIONS; TACTICS, AFRICAN INFANTRY LEVIES; TACTICS, BRITISH INFANTRY; TACTICS, BRITISH MOUNTED TROOPS; TACTICS IN 1880s, ZULU.

**CEZA MOUNTAIN STRONGHOLD.** Ceza is a looming, flat-topped mountain rising above the Sikhwebezi River basin in northwestern **Zululand**, and it was a traditional place of refuge. In 1888, the border between British Zululand and the **New Republic** bisected the mountain and put all but its eastern slopes under Boer rule. This ambiguous border made it an ideal place for King **Dinuzulu kaCetshwayo** to concentrate the **uSuthu** in May 1888 during the **uSuthu Rebellion**, and it put him in close touch with the **abaQulusi** in the New Republic. On 2 June, his followers repulsed the British in the battle of Ceza Mountain. On the British withdrawal to **Nkonjeni**, they began raiding Zulu loyalists and white storekeepers along the Sikhwebezi. Dinuzulu led his men on a night march from Ceza on 22–23 June to defeat the **Mandlakazi** in the battle of **Ivuna**. Once the British regained control of central Zululand in July after capturing **Hlophekhulu**, the uSuthu on Ceza were put on the defensive and began to disperse. By August, those remaining there with Dinuzulu were mainly only the abaQulusi. On 6–7 August, Dinuzulu disbanded the last of the uSuthu on Ceza and left to take refuge in the **South African Republic**. *See also* CEZA MOUNTAIN, BATTLE OF; STRATEGY, ZULU.

**CHARD, JOHN ROUSE MERRIOTT (1847–1897).** During the **Anglo-Zulu War**, Lieutenant Chard joined No. 5 Company, **Royal Engineers**, and was the senior officer present at the battle of **Rorke's Drift**. He was awarded the Victoria Cross. He accompanied the advance of the 2nd Division, **South African Field Force**, in the 2nd Invasion of the war, and he rose to lieutenant-colonel in a career that saw no further campaigns.

**CHELMSFORD, SIR FREDERIC AUGUSTUS THESIGER, 2ND BARON (1827–1905).** Commissioned in 1844, Chelmsford served in the Crimean War (1855–1856) and the Indian Mutiny (1858). For the next 16 years, he filled staff appointments in India, rising to adjutant-general (1869–1874), and served as deputy adjutant-general of the Abyssinian Expeditionary Force (1868). He returned to England in 1874 and was promoted to major-general in 1877. In March 1878, he took up his command as general officer commanding in South Africa, with the local rank of lieutenant-general. He brought the 9th

**Cape Frontier War** to an end by August 1878 and was knighted. He then set up his headquarters in **Pietermaritzburg** to prepare for the **Anglo-Zulu War**. In October 1878, he succeeded as the 2nd Baron Chelmsford.

In January 1879, Chelmsford accompanied No. 3 **Column** into **Zululand**, but the 1st Invasion of the Anglo-Zulu War was derailed at **Isandlwana**, and he had to retire to **Natal** to defend the colony and build up reinforcements for a renewed offensive. He cleared the way by leading the **Eshowe Relief Column** to victory at **Gingindlovu** and evacuating the **Eshowe** garrison. He then accompanied the 2nd Division, **South African Field Force**, during the 2nd Invasion of the war, advancing with excessive caution. The failure of the 1st Invasion, followed by Chelmsford's temporary loss of nerve and his protracted dispute with **Sir Henry Ernest Gascoyne Bulwe**r over the parameters of military and civil command, caused the British government to lose faith in his abilities. In May, General **Sir Garnet Joseph Wolseley** was appointed to supersede him, but Chelmsford only learned of his appointment on 16 June. This knowledge spurred him on to fight the battle of **Ulundi** before Wolseley could arrive in the field.

Having (to his mind) vindicated his generalship, Chelmsford resigned his command on 9 July and returned to England. There his conduct of the Zululand campaign came under much adverse scrutiny, and he was never again offered an active command. He became a full general in 1888 and was placed on the retired list in 1893.

**CHILDERS REFORMS.** The British army reforms carried out under Hugh Culling Eardley Childers (1827–1896), secretary of state for war (1880–1882), brought the earlier **Cardwell Reforms** to a logical conclusion by permanently linking regular battalions within specific geographical areas in Great Britain. The reforms came into effect on 1 June 1881. Each regiment consisted in future of two regular or "line" battalions and two militia battalions (except in Ireland, which was to have three militia battalions instead of two). The restructuring was achieved by giving the first 25 numbered line regiments two battalions, while the remainder were amalgamated in pairs to form the two battalions of the new regiments. The old regimental numbers and county affiliations were changed to territorial titles, and the county militia regiments were renamed. In addition, the various corps of rifle volunteers were designated as volunteer battalions and affiliated to the new regiments. Each of the new regiments and their affiliates was linked by headquarters location and territorial name to its regimental district. This structure survived until 1948. *See also* ARMY REFORM, BRITISH; MILITARY ORGANIZATION, BRITISH.

**CITY GUARD, PIETERMARITZBURG.** This was a force of white male citizens of **Pietermaritzburg** with elected officers who volunteered in November 1878 for the defense of the city during the coming **Anglo-Zulu War**. After **Isandlwana**, the City Guard was assigned to help defend the **Pietermaritzburg laager** and was also employed to maintain order in the city. By April, as the threat of Zulu attack receded, it ceased to patrol the streets and finally stood down later in the month.

*CITY OF PARIS. See* HMS *TAMAR*.

**CIVIL–MILITARY RELATIONS.** In the British Empire of the late 19th century, the respective spheres of authority of the civil and military powers were not always clearly defined. In **Zululand** during the **Anglo-Zulu War** and the **uSuthu Rebellion**, disputes between these spheres threatened the efficient conduct of military operations.

The lieutenant-governor of **Natal** (governor from 1882) had, in his capacity as supreme chief over the native population, the right to extract *isiBhalo*, or compulsory labor and military service. This gave him the right to raise African levies (troops) in time of war. From 1882, he was also the special commissioner for Zulu affairs, becoming the governor of the Colony of Zululand in 1887, and this gave him the authority to raise levies in British-ruled Zululand. However, as governor, he was subordinate to the British high commissioner for South Africa, who answered to the Colonial Office. The high commissioner was also commander-in-chief, with claim to exercise control over all military planning and operations. This did not sit well with the general officer commanding in South Africa (GOC), who was responsible to the War Office and the Horse Guards.

At the outset of the Anglo-Zulu War, **Sir Henry Gascoyne Bulwer**, the lieutenant-governor of Natal, ceded the command of the **Natal Native Contingent** (NNC) and mounted African levies to the command of Lieutenant-General Lord **Chelmsford** but retained control of the **Border Guard**. Chelmsford believed in "active defense" and in March 1879 required the border levies to assist his operations in Zululand by making diversionary raids into Zululand. Bulwer believed such raids would only exacerbate the situation along the vulnerable Natal border, and he attempted to forbid the border levies to participate in cross-border raids. The increasingly acrimonious dispute between Chelmsford and Bulwer embroiled the high commissioner and then the British government. The government put an end to it by superseding both men with General **Sir Garnet Joseph Wolseley**, entrusting him with supreme military and civil authority in southeast South Africa. On 19 May 1879, the government also laid down the principle that command of all the forces operating in the field must rest with the general in command.

Despite this clear cabinet decision, during the **uSuthu Rebellion** a fresh dispute arose over the parameters of civil and military authority. **Sir Arthur Elibank Havelock**, the governor of both Natal and Zululand, believed that to hand the suppression of the revolt over to the military would be an admission that his civil administration had failed. He therefore desired that the troops act only in support of the civil authorities on their request. The GOC, Lieutenant-General **Henry Augustus Smyth**, strenuously objected to the subordination of the military to the civil authorities, as he believed this arrangement would hamper effective operations by the military, not least because Havelock insisted on interfering with his plans. By the beginning of July 1888, they had reached a compromise, though not (as had also happened previously in 1879) without first involving the secretaries of state for the colonies and war in their dispute. It was agreed that Smyth would have command over the British regulars and any African levies organized along military lines, as the NNC had been. The civil authorities would command the **Zululand Police** and African auxiliaries provided they were deployed in close cooperation with Smyth's forces. The civil authorities would remain responsible for enforcing the law and arresting rebels but could call on the military to provide support.

This renewed dispute over divided command concerned the British government, and in November 1888 it revised the *Colonial Office Rules and Regulations* to specify that once full hostilities in a colony had broken out, the GOC assumed entire operational authority over the troops stationed in a colony, and that the governor must restrict himself to the civil sphere. *See also* CIVILIANS IN WARTIME ZULULAND.

**CIVILIANS IN WARTIME ZULULAND.** During the wars of 19th-century **Zululand**, noncombatants died of violence, starvation, exposure, and deprivation, sometimes in greater numbers than fighting men. If they dwelled along the line of march of even a friendly Zulu army, people were always vulnerable as inadequately supplied *amaButho* (regiments) demolished their *imiZi* (homesteads) for firewood, stripped their vegetable gardens, consumed their grain stores, and drove off their livestock. If the army were hostile, as in the three **Zulu Civil Wars**, then the devastation was intended to drive the people off their land. Taking refuge from attackers in a mountain or forest fastness brought with it great hardship and real danger of starvation. Civilians also suffered directly in the fighting when a ruler and his adherents came under attack while migrating. Then noncombatants had no choice but to stand by and watch, hoping their men won the day. If not, they faced being butchered. The women and children of King **Dingane kaSenzangakhona** were slaughtered when he lost the battle of the **Maqongqo Hills** in the 1st Zulu Civil War. In the 2nd Zulu Civil War, the greatest known slaughter of civilians in the kingdom's history took place when the families of the defeated **iziGqoza** were massacred in the rout after the battle of **Ndondakusuka**. In the 3rd Zulu Civil War, at the battle of **oNdini**, the victorious **Mandlakazi** slaughtered the civilians during the rout of the **uSuthu** and killed most of the surviving leadership of the former **Zulu kingdom**. The uSuthu later took their revenge on the Mandlakazi noncombatants after the battle of **Tshaneni**.

During the **Anglo-Zulu War** and the **uSuthu Rebellion**, the British conducted operations according to the principles of **small wars** and deliberately targeted civilians' property to induce **submission** to British control. According to the not always complete evidence, in 1879 they destroyed over 200 *imiZi* and about an equal number in 1888, besides driving off at least 14,000 **cattle** in 1879 alone. Because military operations were limited in their extent and impact, it would seem that less than 10 percent of Zulu livestock was captured and an even smaller percentage of *imiZi* destroyed. And while the

British certainly waged war on civilians' property and livelihood, causing them much sorrow and hardship, with a very few, specific exceptions they never deliberately killed civilians but allowed them to escape or encouraged them to submit.

During the uSuthu Rebellion, **uSuthu** raiders attacked and killed a few of the small number of white traders who had been allowed since the British annexation of the Colony of Zululand to set up their stores. *See also* LOGISTICS, ZULU.

**CLARKE, CHARLES MANSFIELD (1839–1932).** Commissioned in 1856, Clarke saw action in the Indian Mutiny (1858) and in the 3rd New Zealand War (1861–1867). In May 1878, Lieutenant-Colonel Clarke was appointed to command the 57th (West Middlesex) **Regiment**, and served with it during the **Anglo-Zulu War** in the **Eshowe Relief Column** and at **Gingindlovu**. He was given command of the 2nd Brigade, 1st Division, **South African Field Force**, in the 2nd Invasion of the Anglo-Zulu War. When the 1st Division was broken up in July 1879, he commanded **Clarke's Column** in the pacification of **Zululand**. Appointed brevet colonel, he served as commandant-general of colonial forces in the **Cape** before returning to England in 1884. He then held a series of home commands and staff positions and commanded the forces in Madras (1893–1898). He was knighted in 1896 and succeeded as 3rd baronet in 1899. He retired from the army a lieutenant-general and was appointed governor of Malta (1903–1907).

**CLARKE'S COLUMN.** In July 1879 during the final stages of the **Anglo-Zulu War**, General **Sir Garnet Joseph Wolseley** broke up the 1st Division, **South African Field Force**, and formed a column under Brevet Colonel **Charles Mansfield Clarke** out of the units not sent back to **Natal**. The column's mission was to reoccupy the **Mahlabathini Plain** and enforce Zulu compliance with Wolseley's peace terms. Clarke's Column marched on 24 July, and on 7 August it built **Fort Victoria** at the foot of the **Mthonjaneni** Heights. On 10 August, it escorted Wolseley to his camp at **kwaSishwili**, where between 14 and 26 August most of the important Zulu *amaKhosi* **submitted**. Patrols were sent out to capture King **Cetshwayo ka-Mpande**, who on 31 August passed through the camp on his way to exile. On 1 September, the *amaKhosi* accepted Wolseley's terms for the 1st Partition of **Zululand**, and on 5 September the column left for Natal by way of **St. Paul's**, eNtumeni, and **Middle Drift**, which it reached on 20 September. On the way through the inaccessible border region, Clarke sent out patrols to confiscate **firearms**, levy **cattle** fines, and enforce the submission of *amaKhosi* who had not formally surrendered. Between 12 and 21 September, the *amaKhosi* reluctantly did so against the wishes of their younger *amaButho*, who wanted to continue the struggle.

**CLIFFORD, HENRY HUGH (1826–1883).** Clifford was commissioned in 1846 and saw much action in South Africa, serving in the 7th **Cape Frontier War** (1846–1847), against the Boers in 1848 during the annexation of the Orange River Sovereignty, and against the **Sotho** in 1852. In the Crimean War (1854–1855), he fought at the Alma and Inkerman and was awarded the Victoria Cross. He next served in the 2nd China (Opium) War (1857–1858). Back in England, he had a long period of service on the staff and came to the favorable attention of the Duke of **Cambridge**. In 1877, he was promoted to major-general. In April 1879, during the **Anglo-Zulu War**, Clifford was sent out to **Natal** on special service, and with Cambridge's support was appointed inspector-general of line of communication and base, with the task of reorganizing army **transport** and repairing strained **civil–military relations**. He was also appointed Lieutenant-General Lord **Chelmsford**'s second-in-command and during the 2nd Invasion of the Anglo-Zulu War was left in charge of the base in Natal and all forces stationed in the colony. Relations were strained between him and Chelmsford, and Clifford resented that his authority ceased at the **Zululand** border. Clifford was knighted after the war and retired from the army in 1882.

**CLYDE.** A steamer of 1,480 tons built in 1870, the *Clyde* was owned by Temperleys, Carter, and Drake. The ship was carrying 541 officers and men as drafts for the 1st Battalion, 24th (2nd Warwickshire) **Regiment**, to replace the battalion's losses at **Isandlwana** in the **Anglo-Zulu War**, when it was shipwrecked on 3 April 1879 on Dyer Island, three miles off the **Cape** shore, about 70 miles southeast of

Simon's Town. The troops were rescued and taken on to **Durban** by the **HMS** *Tamar*.

**COASTAL COLUMN.** On 23 July 1888, during the **uSuthu Rebellion**, Major **Alexander Chalmers McKean** formed a column of 312 British regulars and 180 **Mounted Basutos** at the **Umlalazi Camp**. On 25 July, the column joined with **Dunn's Native Levy** accompanied by Charles R. Saunders, the resident magistrate of Eshowe, who represented the civil authorities in the Colony of **Zululand** to whom the **uSuthu** were to **submit**. The column advanced on 28 July, burning *imiZi* as it went. On 30 July, the coastal *amaKhosi* surrendered at **Camp Umfolosi**, and on 1 August the Coastal Column proceeded inland to the Ndwandwe District, except for Dunn's Native Levy, which was assigned to collect **cattle** fines before returning to **Natal**. The Coastal Column reached **Ivuna** on 6 August, where it was joined by **Martin's Flying Column**. The uSuthu still on **Ceza Mountain** dispersed, and on 18 August the two columns marched back to the coast, dispersing the few remaining pockets of resistance on the way. They reached **Eshowe** on 30 August. *See also* CIVILIANS IN WARTIME ZULULAND; CIVIL–MILITARY RELATIONS.

*isiCOCO.* The *isiCoco*, or headring, was a circlet of tendons or fibers sewn into the hair of a Zulu man. It was coated with beeswax or gum, and then greased and polished. It was the Zulu king's prerogative to permit his *amaButho* (warriors) to assume the *isiCoco* that denoted attainment of ritual manhood and the right to marry and set up an *umuZi* (homestead) as an *umNumzane* (headman). Even after the **Anglo-Zulu War** and the subsequent fading away of the *iButho* system, no Zulu male in the 1880s was prepared to jettison this prized and visible indication of his mature status in the community—even if it did not sit well with a hat.

**COGHILL, NEVILL JOSIAH AYLMER (1852–1879).** Lieutenant Coghill joined the 24th (2nd Warwickshire) **Regiment** in 1873 and proceeded with it to the **Cape** in 1875, where he was appointed aide-de-camp to the commander-in-chief, South Africa, and served in the 9th **Cape Frontier War**. In 1878, he rejoined his regiment for the coming **Anglo-Zulu War** and served as staff officer to Colonel **Richard Thomas Glyn**, the commander of No. 3 **Column**. A knee injury kept Coghill in camp at **Isandlwana** on 22 January 1879, and he escaped the battle on horseback down the **Fugitives' Trail**. He was killed on the Natal bank of the Mzinyathi River after he had turned back to assist Lieutenant **Teignmouth Melvill**, who was attempting to carry the queen's **color** of the 1st Battalion, 24th Regiment, to safety. In 1907, Coghill was posthumously awarded the Victoria Cross.

**COLENBRANDER, JOHANNES WILHELM (1857–1918).** Born in **Natal,** Colenbrander served with the **Stanger Mounted Rifles** in the **Anglo-Zulu War** and fought at **Nyezane**. In the last stages of the war, he acted as **John Dunn**'s secretary and was entrusted with the **negotiations** for *inKosi* **Zibhebhu kaMaphitha**'s surrender. Colenbrander earned Zibhebhu's trust and he stayed on in **Zululand** as his secretary, resident trader, and gun-runner. During the 3rd **Zulu Civil War**, he and the small party of white **mercenaries** he commanded played an active role in the fighting on the **Mandlakazi** side and contributed to the victory at **Msebe**. He was away in Natal recruiting more mercenaries when Zibhebhu was defeated at **Tshaneni**. Colenbrander lost all his cattle and trade goods in the debacle. He moved to **Swaziland**, where he continued trading, and was one of the early settlers of Rhodesia.

**COLENSO, HARRIETTE (1847–1932).** For many years, Harriette Colenso collaborated closely with her father, Bishop **John William Colenso**, in the cause of Africans in colonial **Natal** and, after the **Anglo-Zulu War**, in support of the Zulu royal house. On Colenso's death, his mantle fell on her. She steadfastly advocated King **Dinuzulu kaCetshwayo**'s cause as King **Cetshwayo kaMpande**'s successor, and in her writings she excoriated colonial officials and their Zulu collaborators whom she blamed for the 3rd **Zulu Civil War** and the **uSuthu Rebellion**. She played a prominent part in organizing the defense of Dinuzulu and others accused before the **Special Court of Commission for Zululand** after the failed rebellion. When these efforts were unsuccessful, she spent many years after 1889 in Britain, campaigning and pamphleteering to secure Dinuzulu's pardon. When Dinuzulu, who had returned to **Zululand** in 1898, was arraigned in 1907 for his alleged role in the **Zulu Uprising of 1906** (Bhambatha Rebellion), she once again rallied his legal defense, but without success.

**COLENSO, JOHN WILLIAM (1814–1883).** Consecrated in 1853 the first Anglican bishop of **Natal**, Colenso confronted difficulties in converting the Zulu. When he questioned the literal interpretation of the Bible, the ecclesiastical courts found him guilty of heresy in 1863 and excommunicated him, but in 1865 the civil courts allowed him to retain his bishopric. A religious schism opened up in the Anglican community of Natal when the rival Bishop of Maritzburg was consecrated in 1869. Always a controversialist, Colenso forfeited support among the colonists by steadfastly championing Africans against the oppressive colonial administration, particularly during the **Langalibalele Rebellion** in 1873. Colenso was known by Africans as "Sobantu" or "Father of the People." He protested against the **Anglo-Zulu War**, which he believed the British had unjustly and unnecessarily provoked, and this brought him into conflict with the military authorities as well as the colonists. After the war, he vehemently took up the cause of the exiled King **Cetshwayo kaMpande** and agitated successfully for his restoration in the 2nd Partition of **Zululand**.

**COLONIAL CAMPAIGNS, BRITISH.** *See* SMALL WARS.

**COLONIAL DEFENSIVE DISTRICTS, NATAL.** On 10 September 1878, Lieutenant-General Lord **Chelmsford** attended a meeting of the Natal Executive Council's Defense Committee and persuaded it to take appropriate security measures for the colony during the coming **Anglo-Zulu War**. **Natal** was accordingly divided on 26 November 1878 into seven Colonial Defensive Districts (CDDs), with **Pietermaritzburg** and **Durban** forming two subdistricts. The district commanders were named on 3 December. Each was to have command of the colonial forces in his district, as well as of all the public **laagers** and government arms and ammunition. He was to be responsible for the defense of his district until such time as it was placed under direct military command. On 11 January 1879, Chelmsford subordinated the commanders of the crucial districts bordering

**Zululand** (CDDs I, VI, and VII) to the British officers commanding imperial bases and lines of supply. *See also* CIVIL–MILITARY RELATIONS.

**COLORS, BRITISH.** British regiments were proud of their individuality and traditions, and during the 19th century, the colors, or identifying flags, assumed great symbolic significance. They were made of silk, measured 3 feet, 9 inches by 3 feet, and were attached to a pike of 8 feet, 7 inches that was topped by the lion or crown of England. The colors were normally transported furled in a brass-capped black leather case. Each British regiment of infantry carried two colors: the sovereign's color that was the gold-fringed Union Flag with the regimental number, and the individual regimental color that was inscribed with its battle honors (the names of the campaigns and battles in which it had taken honorable part). The colors were carried unfurled into battle by the two junior officers of the battalion, escorted by a color party, to encourage the men or to serve as a rallying point in defense. The last time a British regiment did so was on 28 January 1881, when the 58th (Rutlandshire) **Regiment** fought at the battle of Laing's Nek in the 1st **Boer War**. When a regiment's colors became thin and frayed, they were laid up in a church or cathedral and new ones were presented. *See also* ISANDLWANA, SAVING THE COLORS AT.

**COLUMN, NO. 1.** On 12 January 1879 during the 1st Invasion of the **Anglo-Zulu War**, No. 1 Column of 4,750 men under Colonel **Charles Knight Pearson**, drawing its supplies through Stanger and **Durban**, crossed the Thukela River below **Fort Pearson** and built **Fort Tenedos** on the Zulu bank. On 18 January, the column, escorting 130 wagons, began its advance in two supporting divisions on **Eshowe**, where it intended to use the abandoned mission station as a depot for its advance on the second **oNdini** *iKhanda*. It fought through a Zulu ambush at **Nyezane** on 22 January and reached Eshowe the following day. Learning on 27 January of **Isandlwana** and the retreat of No. 3 Column, Pearson decided to hold fast at Eshowe to divert the Zulu from invading **Natal**. On 30 January, he sent the men of the **Natal Mounted Volunteers**, the **Natal Native Contingent**, and **oxen** back to Natal, and the Zulu then blockaded the fort.

Pearson's lack of initiative and mounted men meant that he contented himself with improving the fortifications of **Fort Eshowe**, and he made only one punitive raid on 1 March against the **eSiqwakeni** *iKhanda*. The Eshowe garrison grew increasingly short of supplies before it was relieved by the **Eshowe Relief Column** on 3 April. It was evacuated to Natal the following day, and on 13 April became the 1st Brigade, 1st Division, **South African Field Force**, for the 2nd Invasion of the Anglo-Zulu War.

**COLUMN, NO. 2.** For the 1st Invasion of the **Anglo-Zulu War**, the 3,871 African levies (troops) of No. 2 Column under Brevet Colonel **Anthony William Durnford** were positioned at **Ntunjambili** (Kranskop) in **Colonial Defensive District** No. VII. On 15 January 1879, Lieutenant-General Lord **Chelmsford** ordered two of the three infantry battalions of the 1st Regiment, **Natal Native Contingent**, to remain at Ntunjambili to guard the **Natal** middle border against local Zulu **irregulars** concentrated in the **Nkandla Forest**. He sent Durnford, the men of the **Natal Native Horse**, a **rocket** battery, and the rest of the contingent to reinforce No. 3 Column. On 22 January, Durnford was ordered up from **Rorke's Drift** to reinforce the camp at **Isandlwana**. He was killed in the battle and the troops with him suffered heavy casualties. The detached Natal Native Contingent that had not yet reached Rorke's Drift halted in Natal to defend the border in Colonial Defensive District No. I. No. 2 Column ceased to exist; in the succeeding months, its surviving units were reassigned to new field formations.

**COLUMN, NO. 3.** For the 1st Invasion of the **Anglo-Zulu War**, No. 3 Column of 4,709 men under Colonel **Richard Thomas Glyn**, accompanied by Lieutenant-General Lord **Chelmsford** and his staff, was concentrated at **Rorke's Drift** on 9 January 1879, leaving garrisons along its line of supply through **Helpmekaar**, **Greytown**, **Ladysmith**, and **Durban**. It began its advance into **Zululand** on 11 January. The next day, it won a skirmish at **kwaSogekle** in the valley of the Batshe River. Heavy rains and poor tracks delayed its advance, and it was only on 20 January that the column halted at **Isandlwana Mountain**. The camp was not fortified, as it was intended only as temporary, while patrols were sent out to find a suitable site for the next camp on the road to the second **oNdini** *iKhanda*. On 21 January, Chelmsford sent out a reconnaissance in force to locate the Zulu army. In the early hours of 22 January, he moved troops out of the camp to reinforce it, leaving the camp with a much reduced garrison. In the course of the day, the camp was reinforced by elements of No. 2 Column, but the main Zulu army overwhelmed the defenders. The Zulu reserve went on to attack the small British garrison left at **Rorke's Drift** but was repulsed. That night, Chelmsford brought his forces back to the camp after the Zulu had withdrawn, and they marched out early on 23 January to relieve Rorke's Drift, narrowly avoiding contact with the retiring Zulu. On 24 January, the remnants of the column broke up, leaving strong garrisons at Rorke's Drift and Helpmekaar to bar the anticipated Zulu invasion of **Natal**.

**COLUMN, NO. 4.** For the 1st Invasion of the **Anglo-Zulu War**, No. 4 Column of 2,278 men under Brevet Colonel **Henry Evelyn Wood** assembled in early January 1879 near **Balte Spruit**, drawing its supplies from **Newcastle** and **Utrecht**. On 6 January, the column advanced across the Ncome River to encamp at Bemba's Kop. Wood led a flying column between 11 and 13 January to within 12 miles of **Rorke's Drift** in support of No. 3 Column, capturing much livestock. On 18 January, the column resumed its advance and on 20 January halted across the **White Mfolozi** River at **Fort Tinta**. On the same day, the **abaQulusi** and **Mbilini waMswati**'s adherents repulsed a mounted patrol under Lieutenant-Colonel **Redvers Henry Buller** on **Zungwini Mountain**. In retaliation, Wood led out the column on 22 January and dispersed the Zulu on Zungwini, capturing much livestock. On 24 January, the column broke up another Zulu concentration between Zungwini and Ntendeka Mountain. News of **Isandlwana** reached Wood that same day and he withdrew his column to **Khambula**, where he formed an entrenched camp on 31 January, relocating it along the ridge in February and again in April for sanitation and firewood.

Thanks to Wood's energy and the number of experienced **irregular cavalry** at his disposal, the column retained the ascendancy in northwestern **Zululand**. On 1 February, a mounted patrol under Buller destroyed the **ebaQulusini** *iKhanda*. On 10 February, it raided **Hlobane Mountain**, where many Zulu had taken refuge.

Great numbers of livestock were captured, and many Zulu began moving eastward out of range of Wood's raids. On 15 February, Buller raided the **Kubheka** people in the Ntombe valley, who had been harassing **Luneburg** and its environs, but he did not succeed in subduing them entirely. On 24 March, the main Zulu army began its march to confront Wood at Khambula. On the way, it succeeded on 28 March in helping local irregulars cut off and severely maul a large British raiding party of mounted men and African auxiliaries on Hlobane. The British survivors fell back on Khambula, where the Zulu attack was severely repulsed the following day. With the rout of the Zulu army, the local Zulu irregulars largely dispersed. On 13 April, Wood's forces were restyled **Wood's Flying Column** for the 2nd Invasion of the Anglo-Zulu War. *See also* CIVILIANS IN WARTIME ZULULAND.

**COLUMN, NO. 5.** During the 1st Invasion of the **Anglo-Zulu War**, No. 5 Column of 1,565 men under Colonel **Hugh Rowlands** remained in garrison on the Phongolo River frontier to protect the left flank of No. 4 Column from **Pedi** and Zulu **irregulars** and did not advance beyond its posts at Derby and **Luneburg**. A mounted patrol from Luneburg on 26 January 1879 worsted the **Kubheka** in the Ntombe valley, and another from Derby on 15 February repulsed the **abaQulusi** at Talaku Mountain. Neither raid did much to stop the activities of local irregulars, and the British lines of supply remained vulnerable to attack. On 12 March, **Mbilini waMswati**'s forces overwhelmed a convoy from Derby to Luneburg when it halted at the Ntombe Drift. On 26 February, No. 5 Column, which had reached Luneburg on 19 February, was attached to Brevet Colonel **Henry Evelyn Wood**'s command when Rowlands returned to **Pretoria** to deal with the disaffected Boers of the Transvaal. *See also* NTOMBE, ACTION AT.

*COMET.* The *Comet* was a 120 ton brig that had been trading gunpowder and general goods since 1836 with Port Natal (**Durban**) and other places on the east coast of Africa between Algoa Bay and **Delagoa Bay**. On 29 March 1838 during the **Voortrekker-Zulu War**, it anchored in Durban Bay under its master, William Thomas Haddon, and was still there on 17 April, when the Zulu crushed the

Grand Army of Natal at the battle of **Thukela** and advanced on Port Natal. Survivors gave warning to the white settlers, who took refuge on board the *Comet*, leaving their black adherents on shore. The Zulu swept into Port Natal on 24 April and sacked the settlement for nine days while the settlers looked on helplessly from the *Comet*. On 12 May, the *Comet* sailed first to Delagoa Bay with all but a few of the refugees on board, and then on to Algoa Bay, where it discharged its passengers on 23 June.

**COMMANDANT, BOER.** The Boer commandant (*kommandant*) who led a **commando** (militia) was elected by open, popular vote. He was invariably a prominent and wealthy person who already controlled clients and armed retainers and was able to exert pressure on the electors.

**COMMANDO SYSTEM, BOER.** The Boer commando (militia) system was formalized in 1715 on the **Cape** frontier when the Dutch East India Company sought a mobile mode of defense against African raiding. It became a central feature of Boer society and persisted in the Cape after 1806 when British rule was established. The Voortrekkers perpetuated it when they left the Cape in the 1830s for the interior of South Africa and institutionalized it once they established their republics on the highveld.

Every able-bodied burgher between 16 and 60 was required to serve without payment in time of need. He was expected to provide his own weapons and ammunition, his own **horse** and saddlery, and rations for about a week. He was accompanied on campaign by black servants (*agterryers*). He had no uniform and wore ordinary clothes. There was no structured military training or parade-ground drill. **Commandants** and **field cornets** were popularly elected, and these officers often had to struggle to exert control over their independent-minded and outspoken men. There was no punishment for desertion, and burghers often left a commando if they disagreed with the plans adopted at the war council, which was open to all.

On commando, Boers fought as **mounted infantry**, often dismounting in action for better firepower (their horses were trained to stand without being held) and retired in alternate ranks if it became necessary to disengage. In hostile territory, the lightly encumbered and mobile Boer commando made unexpected, rapid thrusts against the enemy from the secure base provided by its wagon **laager**, and commando members scouted, pillaged, and skirmished. As members of a citizen militia made up from a very small population, they were unwilling to take unnecessary casualties. They consequently avoided hand-to-hand combat and saw no shame in retreating if necessary.

**COMMISSARIAT AND TRANSPORT CORPS, BRITISH.** In 1881, the **Army Service Corps**, which had performed poorly during the **Anglo-Zulu War**, was replaced by the Commissariat and Transport Corps. The new corps was amalgamated in December 1888 into the new Army Service Corps.

**COMMISSARIAT AND TRANSPORT DEPARTMENT, BRITISH**. During the army reforms of 1876, the Control Department that had been created in 1870 was broken into the Commissariat and Transport Department and the **Ordnance Store Department**. The success of the **Anglo-Zulu War** campaign depended on effective logistical arrangements, but the Commissariat and Transport Department proved unequal to the task. Lieutenant-General Lord **Chelmsford** augmented the overstretched and inefficient officers in the department with inadequately trained regular staff officers. Their inexperience in purchasing methods, compounded by antagonist relations with the colonial officials on whose cooperation they should have depended, drastically drove up the costs of securing draught animals and vehicles from the colonists. It was consequently only with the greatest difficulty that the department assembled sufficient **transport** for the invasion of **Zululand**. In 1881, it was replaced by the reformed Commissariat and Transport Staff. Tunic facings were blue.

**CONFEDERATION, SOUTHERN AFRICAN.** Successive British governments throughout the 19th century debated the merits of formal and informal empire in southern Africa, sometimes seeking to assert political paramountcy over the region, only to withdraw again. In the 1870s, British imperial planners were seeking to consolidate rather than expand the British Empire. Southern Africa's traditional significance had always been its strategic position on the sea routes to India, and it was essential for Britain to maintain its ports and coaling stations there. What was new in the 1870s was southern Africa's growing economic potential set off by the burgeoning mineral revolution initiated by the **Kimberley diamond fields** and the associated increasing demands for productive land and a dependable supply of cheap wage-laborers. The combination of traditional strategic concerns and new economic considerations required that Britain consolidate her paramountcy in southern Africa. Yet the region was economically and politically fragmented into the British colonies of the **Cape**, **Natal** and other lesser possessions, the two Boer republics of the interior, and several surviving independent African polities, of which the **Zulu kingdom** was the most powerful. Moreover, conflict between settlers and African states was endemic and debilitating.

The Earl of **Carnarvon**, colonial secretary from 1874 to 1878, believed that the creation of a comprehensive political structure, funded by the region's improving economy, would serve Britain's imperial interests best. If all the white-ruled states of southern Africa were brought into a confederation under a streamlined administration fostering a settled environment and vibrant economy, then South Africa would be able to afford its own armed forces and the existing expensive British garrison would no longer be necessary. A successful confederation might also be the launching pad for future British economic and political expansion into the interior of Africa.

The major obstacle to confederation was the security risk posed by neighboring independent African kingdoms. It was thus necessary to impose some form of British supremacy over them. What made the fulfillment of this requirement essential was the reluctance of the Cape—the largest and most prosperous piece in the structure—to commit itself to confederation until it was assured it would not entail fresh costly wars with neighboring Africans. As his proconsul to implement this delicate mission, Carnarvon appointed the experienced **Sir Bartle Frere** as high commissioner for South Africa.

Frere was used to acting on his own initiative. Arriving in South Africa in March 1877, he acted swiftly. He secured the northern component of confederation with the annexation of the **South African Republic** in April 1877 as the Transvaal Territory and undertook to bring the republic's mismanaged and unresolved conflict with the **Pedi** to a successful conclusion. Frere also executed a series of further strategic annexations aimed at stabilizing the Cape's eastern frontier and securing the remaining potential ports along the southern African coast.

**Sir Michael Hicks Beach** replaced Carnarvon as colonial secretary in February 1878 and was happy to leave the consummation of confederation in Frere's hands. One major hurdle was the Zulu kingdom, which was believed to be the inspiration behind an African conspiracy to overthrow white supremacy in the subcontinent, and whose *iButho* military system was perceived as a standing threat to its neighbors. To reconcile Boer public opinion to annexation, it was necessary to intervene against the Zulu on the side of the Transvaal in the bitterly divisive issue of control of the **Disputed Territory**. The report on 15 July 1878 of the **Boundary** Commission, which partially upheld Zulu territorial claims, caused Frere to fear that if he made it public, the consequent alienation of Boer opinion would result in a rebellion in the Transvaal that might lead to widespread hostilities in southern Africa. It was thus more urgent than ever to break Zulu power. Frere was convinced that a swift military campaign would do so, and during 1878 he drove the **ultimatum** crisis to an open breach with the Zulu kingdom. Unfortunately for Frere, his military experts had gravely miscalculated, and the **Anglo-Zulu War** of 1879 turned into a major campaign. Frere was disgraced, the Transvaal was not reconciled to British rule, British prestige in southern Africa was damaged, and the cause of confederation was temporarily abandoned, not to be fully resurrected for nearly 20 years.

**CONFERENCE HILL FORTIFICATIONS.** In early February 1879, during the **Anglo-Zulu War**, a detachment of No. 4 **Column** took up position at Conference Hill in the **Utrecht District** of the Transvaal to guard stores. In May 1879, the 2nd Division, **South African Field Force**, established its forward depot there for the 2nd Invasion of the war and built a fort and twin redoubts below the hill to protect the stores. When in late May reconnaissance patrols established that the more direct route to the second **oNdini** *iKhanda* was farther south via Koppie Alleen, the stores were transferred there from Conference Hill. *See also* FORT NAPOLEON; FORT WHITEHEAD.

**CONFERENCE HILL MEETING.** Conference Hill is a prominent little hill on the west bank of the Ncome River. On 18 October 1877, **Theophilus Shepstone**, the administrator of the Transvaal, met representatives of the Zulu nation to discuss the **Disputed Territory**. The British had formerly always supported the Zulu, but now that they ruled the Transvaal, they changed their position. When Shepstone championed the Boer claims, the Zulu leaders were astounded and enraged, and the meeting broke down in recriminations. For **Sir Bartle Frere**, the high commissioner, who was engineering a military solution to the Zulu question to further the cause of **confederation**, this incident provided a useful casus belli.

**CONGELLA, BATTLE OF (1842).** The Boers had established a settlement at Congella in 1840 half a mile up Durban Bay west of Port Natal (**Durban**). On 4 May 1842, Captain Thomas Smith raised the Union Flag at Port Natal, and the Boers of the Republic of **Natalia** decided to resist British annexation. Smith led out 133 men from **Smith's Camp** on 23 May in what he intended as a surprise attack on the Boers at Congella. About 30 Boers, however, under the command of **Andries Wilhelmus Jacobus Pretorius**, were waiting for them in ambush among the mangrove trees of the bay. The British column fell back in confusion, reaching their camp on 24 May. The British lost 18 dead and some ammunition wagons and guns; the Boers suffered no losses. *See also* CAMP KONGELLA.

**CONVOYS.** *See* TRANSPORT CONVOYS, BRITISH.

**CORONATION LAWS.** One of **Cetshwayo kaMpande**'s first initiatives as king was to secure the support of the colonial government of **Natal** against his powerful rivals within the **Zulu kingdom**. Early in 1873, he invited a Natal deputation to visit him to discuss matters of common concern, and **Theophilus Shepstone**, the ambitious secretary for native affairs, saw it as an opportunity to expand British influence in **Zululand**. Cetshwayo had been crowned in August according to Zulu ritual, but on 1 September 1873 Shepstone staged a coronation ceremony at Cetshwayo's **emLambongwenya** *iKhanda* that he claimed imposed Zulu suzerainty over the Zulu kingdom. He also proclaimed a set of "coronation laws" that Cetshwayo assented to. Cetshwayo understood the laws as restricting the independent power of his *amaKhosi* (chiefs) and restoring the exclusive power over life and death into his hands, but British officials interpreted them as restricting the king's right to execute his subjects. Cetshwayo's apparent noncompliance with these coronation laws was exploited by **Bartle Frere** in 1878 as an important justification for unleashing the **Anglo-Zulu War**.

**CORRESPONDENTS.** *See* SPECIAL CORRESPONDENTS.

**COW-TAIL DECORATIONS, ZULU.** *See imiSHOKOBEZI.*

**CREALOCK, HENRY HOPE (1831–1891).** Henry Hope Crealock saw action in the Crimean War (1854–1855), the first stage of the 2nd China (Opium) War (1857–1858), the Indian Mutiny (1858–1859), and the second stage of the 2nd China (Opium) War (1860). He was promoted to major-general in 1870 and from 1874 to 1877 was deputy quartermaster-general in Ireland. On special service during the **Anglo-Zulu War**, he took command of the 1st Division, **South African Field Force**, from its formation in April 1879 until the end of the campaign. Hampered by a shortage of **wagons** and by many rivers to cross, "Crealock's Crawlers," as his force became known, made slow progress up the coast, establishing fortified depots and a landing place for supplies at **Port Durnford**, and forcing Zulu **submissions**. Crealock retired from the army in 1884.

**CREALOCK, JOHN NORTH (1836–1895).** John North Crealock served in the Indian Mutiny (1858–1859) and between 1870 and 1878 held a series of staff appointments. In February 1878, he was appointed assistant military secretary, Cape of Good Hope, to Lieutenant-General Frederic Augustus Thesiger (later Lord **Chelmsford**). In recognition for his services in the 9th **Cape Frontier War**, Crealock was made brevet lieutenant-colonel and continued on Chelmsford's personal staff during the **Anglo-Zulu War**, being promoted to military secretary in May 1879. He served as senior staff officer to the **Eshowe Relief Column** and was slightly wounded at **Gingindlovu**. He was present at **Ulundi** and returned with Chelmsford to England in July. He retired in 1895 as a major-general in India.

Although privately critical of Chelmsford's generalship, Crealock was suspected of wielding undue influence over the general and in deflecting criticism from him after **Isandlwana**. Crealock's water-color paintings and sketches are an invaluable record of his campaigns in South Africa.

**CUBE PEOPLE.** *See* MANZIPHAMBANA STRONGHOLD; NANDLA FOREST.

**CURTIS, FRANCIS GEORGE SAVAGE (1836–1906).** Curtis was commissioned in 1854 and served in the Crimean War (1855–1856), the Indian Mutiny (1857–1858), and the 1st **Boer War** (1881). Promoted to lieutenant-colonel in 1879 and colonel in 1883, he commanded the 6th (Inniskilling Dragoons) between 1883 and 1886 when they formed part of the **Natal garrison**. In January 1883, when he was deputy adjutant- and quartermaster-general in South Africa, Curtis commanded the guard of honor that escorted the restored King **Cetshwayo kaMpande** to his new territory after the 2nd Partition of **Zululand**. During the 3rd **Zulu Civil War**, Curtis commanded the cavalry with the **Etshowe Column** and in July 1884 pushed forward the troops to **Fort Yolland** to threaten the **uSuthu** in the **Nkandla Forest**. He then served with the Bechuanaland Expedition (1884–1885). In 1888, he served as Lieutenant-General **Henry Augustus Smyth**'s chief of the staff during the **uSuthu Rebellion**. In 1889, he was appointed colonel on the staff in South Africa. He retired in 1893.

**CUTLASS, NAVAL.** The 1871 pattern cutlass carried by the **Naval Brigade** in the **Anglo-Zulu War** had a bowl guard with two cast-iron sides and a 26-inch blade in a brown leather scabbard with steel mounts.

## – D –

**ekuDABUKENI** *iKHANDA*. This was one of the nine *amaKhanda* in the **emaKhosini valley** burned on 26 June 1879 by **Wood's Flying Column** in the 2nd Invasion of the **Anglo-Zulu War**.

**DABULAMANZI kaMPANDE (c. 1839–1886).** Like his half-brother **Cetshwayo kaMpande**, *umNtwana* Dabulamanzi was enrolled in the **uThulwana** *iButho*. During the 2nd **Zulu Civil War**, he strongly supported Cetshwayo who, when he became king, appointed Dabulamanzi an *inDuna* of the **esiQwakeni** *iKhanda* (military center) near Dabulamanzi's **eZuluwini** *umuZi* (homestead). Dabulamanzi developed close contacts with colonial hunters and traders in southeastern **Zululand**. During the **Anglo-Zulu War**, he was with the uncommitted Zulu reserve at **Isandlwana**, and although he held no official command, he asserted his royal status to lead the unsuccessful assault on **Rorke's Drift**. Retiring in disgrace to eZuluwini, he coordinated the Zulu blockade of **Fort Eshowe** and led the Zulu right horn at the battle of **Gingindlovu**.

Placed under **John Dunn** in the 1st Partition of Zululand, he was active in agitating for Cetshwayo's restoration. During the 3rd Zulu Civil War, he was one of Cetshwayo's commanders. Defeated at **Msebe** and again at **oNdini**, he vigorously carried on the struggle from the **Reserve Territory**. On 10 May 1884, he repulsed **Melmoth Osborn**'s forces at the battle of the **Nkandla Forest**. He was instrumental in arranging the alliance between King **Dinuzulu kaCetshwayo** and the Boer **mercenaries** known as **Dinuzulu's Volunteers** in 1884, but he later fell out with the Boers over their exorbitant land claims. They shot him in a scuffle on 22 September 1886.

**DARKE, HENRY GROSVENOR (?–1905).** A Welsh adventurer, Darke formed a trading partnership with **Johannes Wilhelm Colenbrander** in *inKosi* **Zibhebhu kaMaphitha**'s territory in 1880, after the 1st Partition of **Zululand**. He played an active role in the 3rd **Zulu Civil War** and was among the white **mercenaries** fighting for Zibhebhu at **oNdini** and **Tshaneni**. He escaped to **Natal** after Tshaneni but lost all his property in **Zululand**. In 1886, he moved to **Swaziland** to continue trading; he left for England in 1899.

**DARTNELL, JOHN GEORGE (1838–1913).** Commissioned in 1855, Dartnell served in the Indian Mutiny (1857–1858). In 1869, he resigned his commission as brevet major and settled in **Natal**. He was appointed commandant of the **Natal Mounted Police** (NMP) in 1874 and inspector of the **Natal Volunteer Corps**. During the **Anglo-Zulu**

**War**, he was on Lieutenant-General Lord **Chelmsford**'s head-quarters staff during the 1st Invasion of the **Anglo-Zulu War** and commanded the NMP and **Natal Mounted Volunteers** with No. 3 **Column**. He was away skirmishing during the battle of **Isandlwana**. From December 1878 to July 1879, he was commandant of **Colonial Defensive District** No. I. He served in **Basutoland** during the "Gun War" (1880), in the 1st **Boer War** (1880–1881), in the **Anglo-Boer (South African) War** (1899–1902), and in the **Zulu Uprising of 1906** (Bhambatha Rebellion). He was appointed chief commissioner of the reconstituted Natal Police in 1894, was knighted in 1901, and retired in 1903.

**DEAD, ZULU TREATMENT OF.** Friends or relatives of Zulu killed on campaign had the obligation, if circumstances permitted, to dispose of their corpses decently in dongas, antbear holes, or grain-pits of abandoned *imiZi* (homesteads). Otherwise, the Zulu dead were left where they had fallen, covered if possible by a **shield**. The Zulu left the enemy dead unburied, to be devoured by wild animals. On occasion, such as after the battles of **Rorke's Drift**, **Gingindlovu**, and **Khambula** in the **Anglo-Zulu War**, the British buried the Zulu dead in mass graves, but only because they presented a health hazard to their camp. They left them where they had fallen after **Ulundi**.

**DEIGHTON AND SMITH BORDER INCIDENT.** By late 1878, with the **Anglo-Zulu War** looming, the situation was very tense along the border between **Natal** and **Zululand**. On 17 September, W. H. Deighton and David Smith of the Natal Colonial Engineers Department went down into the valley of the Thukela River to inspect a wagon **road** being built down to the river that marked the border. The Zulu believed the road was intended to facilitate a British invasion, and a small party of men roughed up the two officials when they strayed onto an island in the middle of the river the Zulu considered their territory. The incident provoked outrage in colonial Natal, and **Bartle Frere** seized on it as another justification for the war he was fomenting to bring about **confederation**. *See also* NATAL–ZU-LULAND BOUNDARY; SIHAYO'S SONS, CROSS-BORDER INCIDENT BY.

**DELAGOA BAY.** The Portuguese discovered Delagoa Bay and natural harbor on the southeast coast of Africa in 1502, and in 1544 the trader Lourenço Marques explored its environs. Control of the bay was long contested. The Dutch East India Company maintained a fort and factory there between 1720 and 1730. In 1787, the Portuguese built a fort around which the settlement of Lourenço Marques began to grow. King **Dingane kaSenzangakhona** sent an army in 1833 to overawe the Portuguese. In 1823 and in 1861, the British asserted their control of the bay, as did the **South African Republic** (SAR) in 1868. In 1869, the SAR acknowledged Portuguese sovereignty over the bay, as did the British in 1875 after French arbitration. Delagoa Bay was important as a trade outlet, initially for ivory and slaves, but by the later 19th century for the diamonds and gold of the interior.

**DE LANGE, JOHAN HENDRIK (HANS DONS) (1799–1861).** A farmer from the Grahamstown District of the **Eastern Cape**, de Lange was nicknamed Hans Dons, "Orphan Fluff," after his sparse beard. In 1830, he hunted and explored in the South African interior, and he was a member of **Petrus Lafras Uys**'s scouting commission (*kommissietrek*) in 1834 to Port Natal (**Durban**) to ascertain the region's suitability for settlement. De Lange was a supporter of the trek idea and strongly influenced his neighbors in the Cape to join his party of Voortrekkers in mid-1837. He joined up with **Pieter Retief**'s party in crossing the **Drakensberg** into **Zululand** in November 1837. As a veteran of the **Cape Frontier Wars**, he put his faith in the defensibility of the **wagon laager**. During the **Voortrekker-Zulu War**, his wagon laager survived the **Bloukrans Massacre**. He was a member of the *Vlugkommando* defeated at **eThaleni**, but he soon showed himself to be one of the Voortrekkers' ablest commanders and an expert scout. He played a leading part at **Veglaer**, fought at **Ncome** as a member of the *Wenkommando*, and saved the ambushed commando at the battle of the **White Mfolozi**. After the British annexation of **Natal**, he was one of the Boer farmers who tried in 1847 to set up the abortive **Klip River Republic**. He was farming in British northern Natal when in December 1860 he shot and killed an African in circumstances that were never properly clarified. He was found guilty of murder and executed on 26 March 1861.

**izinDIBI.** Boys over 14 years of age who were still too young to be formed into an **iButho** (regiment) accompanied the Zulu army as izinDibi, or carriers. They were attached to amaKhosi (chiefs) and principal izinDuna (officers), for whom they carried items such as mats, headrests, and tobacco. They also drove the **cattle** required for the army's consumption. See also LOGISTICS, ZULU.

**DINGANE kaSENZANGAKHONA (c. 1795–1840).** In 1828, Dingane assassinated his half-brother King **Shaka kaSenzangakhona** and seized the crown of the **Zulu kingdom**. Dingane immediately eliminated his co-conspirators and royal rivals and moved the focus of royal power back to central **Zululand** from the recently conquered and tenuously controlled lands south of the Thukela River where Shaka had established his capital. Dingane maintained Shaka's uneasy relationship with the settlers at Port Natal (**Durban**) in order to ensure the supply of desirable trade goods, and he attacked the Portuguese at **Delagoa Bay** in 1833 to assert his control over them. During his reign, he continued to raid his neighbors, notably the **Swazi** in 1836 and 1837, and the **Ndebele** in 1837. The arrival of the Voortrekkers in his kingdom in late 1837 presented a mortal threat, and his initial response was to attempt to eliminate them through treachery and surprise attack. This failed, and despite some successes against the Boers and their allies from Port Natal, he was defeated in the **Voortrekker-Zulu War** and had to negotiate a temporary settlement. Defeat by the Swazi in 1839 prevented him from relocating his kingdom northward, and his suspicions of his half-brother umNtwana **Mpande kaSenzangakhona** led to the latter striking an alliance with the Boers and defeating Dingane in the 1st **Zulu Civil War**. Dingane fled to Nyawo territory on the slopes of the Lubombo Mountains. His reluctant hosts and a Swazi patrol killed him in his eSankoleni umuZi, where he is buried.

**DINUZULU kaCETSHWAYO (1868–1913).** Dinuzulu was the heir of King **Cetshwayo kaMpande**. Before his flight at the end of the **Anglo-Zulu War**, Cetshwayo appointed inKosi **Zibhebhu ka-Maphitha** Dinuzulu's guardian, but when it became apparent after the 1st Partition of **Zululand** that Zibhebhu was determined to keep the royal house in submission, Dinuzulu escaped to the guardianship of his uncle *umNtwana* **Ndabuko ka Mpande**. After the **uSuthu** defeat at the **oNdini** *iKhanda* during the 3rd **Zulu Civil War**, he fled to the sanctuary of the **Nkandla Forest**. On Cetshwayo's sudden death in 1884, Dinuzulu's uncles rallied around him to prevent a disputed succession. Dinuzulu entered into negotiations with the Boers, who proclaimed him king on 21 May 1884 and aided him against his enemies in return for a huge grant of land in the 3rd Partition of Zululand.

Dinuzulu led the uSuthu forces at the battle of **Tshaneni**, but he could not protect his people from escalating land claims by the Boers of the **New Republic**, and he could not prevent them from imposing a "protectorate" over him. Consequently, he welcomed British intervention and acquiesced in their annexation of the Colony of Zululand in 1887, but he soon bitterly resented the imposition of their administration. During the **uSuthu Rebellion**, he assumed a prominent part in the planning of military operations and fought in the front line at the battles of **Ceza** and **Ivuna**. In early August 1888, acknowledging that the British had regained control of Zululand, he fled to the South African Republic for sanctuary but surrendered to the British in November. He stood trial in **Eshowe** between February and April 1889, was found guilty of high treason and public violence, and was sentenced to 10 years' imprisonment, to be served on St. Helena.

In January 1898, Dinuzulu was returned to Zululand as part of a general settlement to restore stability. He came back not as king, but as a "government *inDuna*" (official). Nevertheless, he was perceived by many Zulu as their rightful ruler, and during the **Anglo-Boer (South African) War**, the British reluctantly exploited his status to raise Zulu levies (troops) to help defend Zululand from Boer incursions. In 1908, he was controversially arraigned for being implicated in the **Zulu Uprising of 1906** (Bhambatha Rebellion), stripped of his remaining powers, and imprisoned. In 1910, the government of the new Union of South Africa commuted his sentence to exile on the farm Rietvlei in the Transvaal Province, where he died on 18 October 1913. He was buried in the **emaKhosini valley** among his royal ancestors.

**DINUZULU'S CORONATION.** On 20 May 1884 Dinuzulu's uncles **Ndabuko kaMpande, Ziwedu kaMpande,** and **Shingana kaMpande**

installed him as king by traditional Zulu ritual. The following day he was "crowned" by the Boer **Committee of Dinuzulu's Volunteers** at their **Nyathi Hill laager**.

**DINUZULU'S VOLUNTEERS, COMMITTEE OF.** On 2 May 1884 Boers from the **Wakkerstroom** and **Utrecht** districts of the **South African Republic** and from further afield, who were taking advantage of the chaos in the 3rd **Zulu Civil War** to infiltrate the northwest of the country, met King **Dinuzulu kaCetshwayo**, who was seeking military aid against his enemies at the **Hlobane laager**. Calling themselves the Committee of Dinuzulu's Volunteers, on 21 May the leading Boers from among the 350 gathered at their **laager** at **Nyathi Hill** crowned Dinuzulu king at an improvised ceremony in the presence of 9,000 **uSuthu**. In return for their recognition and promise of military aid, Dinuzulu promised to cede them about a third of **Zululand**. *See also* DINUZULU'S CORONATION; NEW REPUBLIC.

**DISEMBOWELMENT.** *See* RITUAL DURING BATTLE, ZULU.

**DISPUTED TERRITORY.** The valleys of the Mkhondo, Ntombe, Phongolo, and Bivane rivers in northwestern **Zululand**, as well as the lands stretching east of the Ncome River in central Zululand, are open and grassy and an ideal region for grazing if the free seasonal movement of **cattle** is secured between winter and summer pastures. The cattle-keeping peoples of the region—Zulu, **Swazi** north of the Phongolo, and Boers of the **South African Republic** (SAR)—all desired to control this valuable territory. In the mid-19th century, it became a cockpit of competing claims. Particularly assertive were the Boers of the SAR, who were trying to push toward the sea to secure a port.

By the treaty of Waaihoek in March 1861 with *umNtwana* **Cetshwayo kaMpande**, who was trying to consolidate his claim to the Zulu throne, the SAR agreed to hand over fugitive rivals for the succession in return for indeterminate land claims east of the Ncome River. Cetshwayo repudiated the treaty in June 1861, but Boers moved into the territory anyway. In August, King **Mpande kaSenzangakhona** agreed to honor Cetshwayo's land concession. In late 1864, the Boers asserted their land rights by beaconing off a boundary line between their farms east of the Ncome and what they decided was Zulu territory. Cetshwayo ordered the beacons to be torn down, but the Boers were not to be put off. In June 1869, the SAR began to allot farms east of the Ncome to Boer settlers. On 25 May 1875, the SAR issued a proclamation claiming Zulu territory "ceded" in 1861, plus a slice of territory south of the Phongolo River between Zululand and Swaziland. The **Boundary Award** stated in July 1878 that the Boers had no legitimate claim to the lands east of the Ncome, but the **Anglo-Zulu War** negated this ruling. The 1st Partition of Zululand finalized the matter by drawing the boundary of western and northern Zululand up the Ncome from its confluence with the Mzinyathi to the Bivane's confluence with the Phongolo, and then along that river to the sea. *See also* ZULU INVASION SCARE (1861).

**DISTINGUISHED CONDUCT MEDAL.** *See* AWARDS.

**uDLAMBEDLU** *iBUTHO*. King **Dingane kaSenzangakhona** formed this *iButho* around 1829 of youths born about 1809. The **shield** was white with black or red spots. During the **Voortrekker-Zulu War**, the uDlambedlu formed part of the Zulu left horn at **Ncome**, and it ambushed and pursued the defeated Boers at the battle of the **White Mfolozi**. It fought on *umNtwana* **Cetshwayo kaMpande**'s side at **Ndondakusuka** in the 2nd **Zulu Civil War**, when it formed the right horn. In the **Anglo-Zulu War**, most of its members remained in reserve at the second **oNdini** *iKhanda*, though small local elements fought in the battle of **Nyezane**. At the time of the battle of **Ulundi**, it was guarding Cetshwayo at the **kwaMbonambi** *iKhanda*.

**oDLAMBEDLWINI** *iKHANDA*. This was one of the nine *amaKhanda* in the **emaKhosini valley** burned on 26 June 1879 by **Wood's Flying Column** during the 2nd Invasion of the **Anglo-Zulu War**.

**uDLANGEZWA** *iBUTHO*. King **Shaka kaSenzangakhona** formed this *iButho* around 1823 of youths born about 1802. The **shield** was black with many white patches. In the **Voortrekker-Zulu War**, it formed part of the Zulu chest at **Ncome**.

**DLEBE MOUNTAIN.** On 11 August 1888, Captain Robert Stephenson Smyth Baden-Powell (the future founder of the Boy Scout movement), nephew and aide-de-camp of Lieutenant-General **Henry Augustus Smyth** during the **uSuthu Rebellion**, led a punitive expedition from **Nkonjeni** to Dlebe Mountain on the border of **Zulu-land** and the **South African Republic** (SAR), where some **uSuthu** had clashed with British scouts the previous day. He inadvertently crossed the frontier into the territory of the SAR and compounded his mapping error by attacking loyalist **Buthelezi** refugees on Dlebe, killing 12 civilians.

**uDLOKO *iBUTHO*.** King **Mpande kaSenzangakhona** formed this *iButho* around 1858 of youths born about 1838. The **shield** was red with white patches or plain white. It was part of the chest in *umNtwana* **Cetshwayo kaMpande**'s army at the battle of **Ndonda-kusuka** in the 2nd **Zulu Civil War**. In the **Anglo-Zulu War**, it was part of the uncommitted reserve at **Isandlwana**, but it went on to attack **Rorke's Drift**. At **Khambula**, it fought with the Zulu chest. At **Ulundi**, it attacked the east side of the British infantry **square**. At **oNdini** in the 3rd Zulu Civil War, elements made up part of the **uSuthu** chest.

*amaDLOZI*. For the Zulu, good fortune in an enterprise depended on the approval of the *amaDlozi*, or ancestral spirits, who lived under the ground and were interested in every aspect of their descendants' lives. Because the spirits maintained the status they had enjoyed while alive, it was essential before proceeding on campaign to secure the favor of the *amaDlozi* of the king's royal forebears, since they were concerned with the welfare of the entire Zulu nation. Before it marched away to war, the army propitiated the royal *amaDlozi* with a generous sacrifice of royal **cattle** so they would accompany the *amaButho* (regiments) and deploy their powers against the enemy. *See also* umKHOSI; *iNKATHA*.

*inDLU*. The basic dwelling place for every Zulu was the hut, or *inDlu*. Whether forming an *umuZi* (family homestead) or an *iKhanda* (administrative center), all *izinDlu* were alike in basic construction and furnishings, but those of the great were distinguished by size, choice of materials, and workmanship. *IzinDlu* in 19th-century **Zululand** were circular and domed. They were constructed from thousands of curved intersecting saplings and sticks, like wicker work, tied together with grass where they crossed. The average hut was three yards in diameter, but those occupied by *amaKhosi* (kings or chiefs) were double that size, with several poles (rather than a single central one) supporting the structure. A neat thatch of long, tall grass covered the huts. The floor, made of a mixture of the earth from antheaps compressed with cow dung, was polished to a blackish, dark green, glossy smoothness. The hearth was a circular cavity in the center of the floor with a raised edge, and pots were placed on the three cooking stones. There was no chimney. The right-hand side of the hut was reserved for men and the left for women. At the back was a special area, the *umSamo*, where the ***amaDlozi*** were thought to dwell and where weapons, food, and prized implements were kept. During the day, the sleeping mats, headrests, baskets, and other items were hung on the walls. *IzinDlu* had to be frequently repaired, as the materials from which they were built fell easy prey to the depredations of insects, fire, and weather. They were easily destroyed in war, but the simplicity of their construction meant that they could be quickly reconstructed. *See also* CIVILIANS IN WARTIME ZULULAND.

**DOORNHOEK CAMP.** On 15 May 1879, the four corps of **Natal Mounted Volunteers** who had been serving during the **Anglo-Zulu War** with the **Eshowe Relief Column** moved to Doornhoek from **Potspruit**, their previous camp in **Colonial Defensive District** No. VII. They remained at Doornhoek until 26 July 1879, when they returned home and mustered out.

**DRAGOONS, 6TH (INNISKILLING).** The regiment was ordered out to South Africa in February 1881 to reinforce the Natal Field Force in the 1st **Boer War** and constituted part of the **Natal garrison** until 1890. The Dragoons formed part of Major-General **Evelyn Wood**'s escort at the meeting with the Zulu leaders at **Nhlazatshe Mountain** in 1881 and the guard of honor for King **Cetshwayo kaMpande** on his restoration in 1883 following the 2nd Partition of **Zululand**. In September 1883, during the 3rd **Zulu Civil War**, a squadron made up part of the **Etshowe Column** sent to support the colonial administration in the **Reserve Territory** and was stationed at **Fort Curtis**. In July 1884, it made up part of a reconnaissance in force toward the **Nkandla Forest**, where the **uSuthu** were operating, and erected **Fort Yolland**. On 14 August, a detachment was sent to garrison **Fort Northampton**. With the **submission** of the uSuthu in the Nkandla Forest, the Dragoons returned to **Fort Napier** in November 1884.

During the **uSuthu Rebellion**, a troop of the Dragoons was stationed in October 1887 at **Entonjaneni** and a squadron at **Nkonjeni** to support **Richard Hallowes Addison**, the resident magistrate of the Ndwandwe District of the Colony of Zululand, against the uSuthu. In June 1888, a squadron covered the retreat of the civil authorities repulsed on **Ceza Mountain**. In June, reinforcements from the Natal garrison brought the strength of the dragoons in Zululand up to three squadrons. A squadron was among the British forces that stormed **Hlophekhulu Mountain** in July, and another was with the supporting troops on **Lumbe Mountain**. A squadron served temporarily with the **Coastal Column** between 23 July and 3 August before rejoining the others at Nkonjeni. With the suppression of the uSuthu rebels, the **Zululand garrison** was reduced to its normal level, which included one squadron of Dragoons stationed at Entonjaneni.

The uniform consisted of a scarlet tunic with yellow facings, dark blue breeches with a yellow stripe, and white accoutrements. In Zululand, the steel helmet with white plumes was replaced by a white sun helmet.

**DRAGOON GUARDS, 1ST (THE KING'S).** Sent out as reinforcements for the 2nd Invasion of the **Anglo-Zulu War**, the regiment under the command of Colonel H. Alexander made up half the **Cavalry Brigade** attached to the 2nd Division, **South African Field Force**. It was employed in reconnoitering into **Zululand** in advance of the division. In May 1879, the regiment took part in the patrol to **Isandlwana** to bury the British dead. A squadron took part in the skirmish at **Zungeni**. Detachments were stationed at **Rorke's Drift**, **Conference Hill**, and **Fort Newdigate**, where they escorted convoys and raided the surrounding countryside. A troop fought at **Ulundi**. Detachments then served with **Clarke's Column** and **Baker Russell's Column** and played a part in the capture of King **Cetshwayo kaMpande**.

The uniform consisted of a scarlet tunic with blue facings, dark blue breeches with a yellow stripe, and white accoutrements. In Zululand, the brass helmet with red plumes was replaced by a white sun helmet.

**DRAKENSBERG.** The principal mountain range in southern Africa, the Drakensberg stretches for over 600 miles separating the coastal lands of the east from the highveld of the interior. Its tallest peaks are nearly 12,000 feet high. The headwaters of the main rivers of **Natal** and **Zululand** rise in the Drakensberg. The name means "Dragon's Mountain" in Afrikaans. The Zulu call the mountains uKhahlamba, or "Barrier of Spears." A limited number of difficult passes cross the Drakensberg, connecting the highveld with the coast.

**DRESS, AFRICAN LEVIES.** The African levies (troops) raised by the Port Natal (**Durban**) settlers for the Grand Army of Natal in the **Voortrekker-Zulu War** wore white calico to distinguish them from their Zulu adversaries. The African infantry formations raised by the **Natal** government during the **Anglo-Zulu War** and the **Zululand** authorities during the 3rd **Civil War** and **uSuthu Rebellion** likewise wore civilian dress that consisted of little more than the traditional Zulu loin cover sometimes augmented with items of European clothing like jackets or hats. The levies were distinguished from African noncombatants and hostile Zulu by a colored cloth twisted around the head or arm. During the Anglo-Zulu War, the color of the cloth was predominantly red, as it always was in Zululand in the 1880s. With the reorganization of the **Natal Native Contingent** for the 2nd Invasion of the Anglo-Zulu War, scarlet tunics were issued to all battalions. Some also received white trousers, but the men found them uncomfortable and refused to wear them. The **Natal Native Pioneer Corps** wore similar uniforms from the outset of the Anglo-Zulu War.

White mounted officers provided their own clothing, usually military-style blue patrol jackets or corduroy breeches, although noncommissioned officers (NCOs) received brown or yellow uniforms. Officers and NCOs wore red puggarees around their headgear. Mounted levies received uniforms of yellow or brown corduroy and broad-brimmed felt hats with a puggaree. Boots were issued, but in the Anglo-Zulu War only the **Edendale Horse** elected to wear them, as the men preferred to ride barefoot with only the big toe in the stirrup iron. *See also individual units.*

**DRESS, BOER MEN.** Boer men wore civilian clothes on campaign, although by the 1860s some **commandos** (militias) identified themselves by wearing colored puggarees around their hats. Frontier costume for men at the time of the **Great Trek** was full of variety, but because clothes were expected to last and were usually home-made, they were normally decades behind the latest metropolitan fashion. Men wore short jackets and waistcoats made of moleskin or corduroy (though poorer men wore leather clothes) which were black, green, brown, or dark yellow. Trousers were of the *klapbroek* type, with a front flap that buttoned, and they were held up by a belt or braces. Weekday shirts were of wool and overcoats of woolly duf-fel. Boots were often worn without stockings. Broad-brimmed straw hats were popular, as were high-crowned felt hats with brims of vary-ing width. A few men at the time of the Great Trek adopted the more dandyish, pale-colored, bell top hat. Every man would have *kisklere*, or Sunday-best clothes: linen shirt, broadcloth coat, and cashmere trousers for the well-off, corduroy for the rest. Many had fancy silk waistcoats. By the 1860s, the short jacket was being replaced by a full-skirted coat, but fashion otherwise changed little.

**DRESS, BOER WOMEN.** Boer women wore plain and sober clothing. Dresses could be made of every material from silk to woolly baize and usually had a turned-over collar, fairly wide sleeves fastened at the wrist, and flounces at the bottom of the skirt. Women never wore their hair loose but parted it in the middle and fastened it into a bun. Over it they wore a *kappie*, a big, intricately tucked and em-broidered sunbonnet made ordinarily of white linen but sometimes of dull-colored merino or silk. To protect their complexions further, women often wore light goatskin masks when on trek. Most women had shawls of wool or silk.

**DRESS, BRITISH ARMY.** No specifically tropical uniform was is-sued to the British soldier, with the exception of those stationed in India. Uniforms on active service were not replaced and thus became tattered and stained. The standard overseas issue in the 1870s and 1880s for infantry was the single-breasted unlined frock with five brass buttons; Rifles wore dark green. With the **Childers Reforms** of 1881, the traditional different-colored facings of the old infantry regiments in the **Anglo-Zulu War** were replaced by national ones worn on cuffs and on the collar: white for English and Welsh regi-ments, yellow for Scottish, and green for Irish. Trousers were dark blue with a scarlet welt down the outside seam for infantry. They were tucked into black leather leggings. Officers wore either scarlet frocks of the plain tunic color or the blue patrol jackets introduced in 1866 and preferred in the field. On campaign, they often adopted a strange assortment of jackets and caps. Highland regiments wore kilts and their officers trews.

The **Royal Engineers** and **Royal Marine Light Infantry** wore a uniform similar to that of the infantry. The **Royal Artillery** and **Royal Marine Artillery** wore dark blue tunics with scarlet collars, and blue trousers with a wide red stripe. **Mounted infantry** retained their regimental tunic but replaced their blue trousers with brown cord riding-breeches. Cavalry uniforms, individual to different regiments, were in dashing combinations of scarlet, blue, and white.

Headgear was the light cork sun helmet, covered in white canvas, which was adopted for overseas service in 1877 to replace the blue helmet worn in Europe by infantry, or the ostentatious headgear of the cavalry. It was normally dyed brown with tea when on campaign and the shiny brass shako-plate removed. *See also individual units.*

**DRESS, IMPERIAL MOUNTED UNITS RAISED LOCALLY.** Experienced units of imperial mounted troops in South Africa were properly turned out in uniform. Standard headgear was a wideawake (soft-brimmed felt hat) with a red puggaree. Boer **commandos** (militias) in British service dressed in their everyday clothes. *See also individual units.*

**DRESS, NATAL MOUNTED POLICE.** The quasi-military **Natal Mounted Police** wore tight-fitting black cord tunics trimmed with black braid and fastened with five brass buttons. Their black breeches were tucked into black calf-high boots fastened with six buckled straps. Their white helmets had a dark band, brass spike, and brass monogrammed badge.

**DRESS, NATAL VOLUNTEER UNITS.** Inconsistent attempts at uniforms based on European patterns were made by the **Natal Volunteers Corps** and **Natal Native Horse**, though some of the better-established units were properly turned out. *See also individual units.*

**DRESS, NAVAL BRIGADE.** Sailors of the Naval Brigade wore a blue frock and trousers with leather-bound tan canvas gaiters. Officers wore a double-breasted blue frock coat or a single-breasted five-buttoned blue tunic with blue or white trousers and white canvas leggings. Headgear was a blue foreign service helmet, blue cap or broad-brimmed straw sennet hat for sailors, or peaked cap with white cover for officers.

**DRESS, ZULU MEN.** The ceremonial dress of the *amaButho* (regiments) that distinguished them one from another was lavish and intricate and contained many rare and fragile feather and skin items supplied through the king's favor. By the 1870s, when hunting had depleted these materials, dress became simpler. Basic dress consisted of white cow tails fastened around the neck, below the knees, and above the elbows (*imiShokobezi*). The loin cover evolved by the period of the **Anglo-Zulu War** to become a bunch of tails in the front and an oblong of cowhide behind. The most valuable and distinctive items were reserved for the headdress. The king and Zulu notables wore the same festival dress as did ordinary *amaButho*, their status marked by the costliness or profusion of the materials used.

On campaign, most of this precious costume was discarded except for the loin cover and some distinctive elements of headdress. *IzinDibi*, youths serving as carriers for the army, wore only a loin cover of strips of skin or tails in front and a back flap of leather. Men of status retained more of their festival attire as an indication of rank, as did older, more conservative *amaButho*. During the 3rd **Zulu Civil War** and the **uSuthu Rebellion**, almost all of the showy regalia was abandoned, though distinctive headdress feathers, for example, might still identify different *amaButho*. In the 1880s, members of the **uSuthu** faction wore the *imiShokobezi* as a sign of their allegiance to the royal cause. This was a period of transition in **Zululand**, so traditional dress jostled with articles of Western apparel like wideawake hats, tweed jackets, braided coats, trousers, and gaiters. Most Zulu still preferred not to wear shoes or boots. *See also individual units.*

**DRESS, ZULU WOMEN.** For Zulu women, who accompanied the *amaButho* on campaign for a few days carrying supplies, dress was minimal. Unmarried young women wore an oblong piece of beadwork or leaves as a frontal covering, or a fringed waistband of skin. Married women wore a short leather skirt, and a skin concealed their breasts until the birth of their first child, or when pregnant. Hair dressing varied from district to district, although that for married women was uniformly more intricate than that of unmarried women. Ornaments of imported beads, copper, or brass were favored by young women at the time of courting though were not worn much when married.

**DRUMMOND, THE HONORABLE WILLIAM (1845–1879).** The second son of the 9th Viscount Strathallan, Drummond went adventuring in southern Africa as a hunter between 1868 and 1872, when he learned Zulu. He returned to **Natal** in 1876 or 1877 and earned his living as a hunter. During the **Anglo-Zulu War**, he was appointed to Lieutenant-General Lord **Chelmsford**'s headquarters staff. He was put in charge of the Intelligence Department of the **Eshowe Relief Column** and then acted as interpreter and guide for the 2nd Division, **South African Field Force**. He was killed in the **oNdini** *iKhanda* during the pursuit after **Ulundi**.

**uDUDUDU** *iBUTHO*. King **Mpande kaSenzangakhona** formed this *iButho* around 1859 from youths born about 1839. The **shield** was black with white markings. During the **Anglo-Zulu War**, it formed part of the right horn at **Isandlwana**. Small local elements fought at **Nyezane**. It was part of the chest at **Khambula** and attacked the north side of the British infantry **square** at **Ulundi**. In the 3rd **Zulu Civil War**, it was stationed near **oNdini** at the **kwaNodwengu** *iKhanda* and was caught up in the **uSuthu** rout before it could come into action.

**DUKUDUKU STRONGHOLD.** Dukuduku was the stronghold of **Somkhele kaMalanda** in the thickly forested and swampy terrain of the northern **Zululand** coastal plain. Somkhele was a pro-**uSuthu** *inKosi* (chief) of the **Mphukunyoni** people. In August 1883, during the 3rd **Zulu Civil War**, the Mphukunyoni took refuge at Dukuduku after *inKosi* **Zibhebhu kaMaphitha**'s victory at **oNdini** when the **Mandlakazi** and their allies, the **Mthethwa**, raided their territory. During the **uSuthu Rebellion**, when in mid-1888 the Mphukunyoni again felt threatened by the Mandlakazi and the Mthethwa, they temporarily took refuge at Dukuduku once more. On the approach of the **Coastal Column** in July 1888, the Mphukunyoni and **emaNgweni** fell back on the stronghold but decided not to defend it, to the relief of Major **Alexander Chalmers McKean**, who feared his column was not strong enough to attack it without the support of gunboats on **St. Lucia Bay**. *See also* CIVILIANS IN WARTIME ZULULAND.

**kwaDUKUZA *iKHANDA*.** In late 1826, King **Shaka kaSenzangakhona** established the first *iKhanda* of this name near the lower Mvoti River, only 45 miles from Port Natal (**Durban**), to assert his authority in the southern marches of his kingdom. He was assassinated at kwaDukuza on 24 September 1828 and buried there. King **Dingane kaSenzangakhona** later reestablished the *iKhanda* in the **emaKhosini valley**, close to the *umuZi* of his father, *inKosi* **Senzangakhona kaJama**, and his grandfather, *inKosi* Jama kaNdaba. It was intended as a spirit home for Shaka, whose shade thereafter dwelled in the company of his ancestors. It was one of the nine *amaKhanda* burned in the emaKhosini valley on 26 June 1879 by **Wood's Flying Column** during the 2nd Invasion of the **Anglo-Zulu War**.

*inDUNA. See* POLITICAL ORGANIZATION, ZULU.

**DUNN, JOHN ROBERT (1834–1895).** Dunn entered **Zululand** as a trader and hunter in 1853. Even though he fought for the **iziGqoza** in the 2nd **Zulu Civil War**, he succeeded in gaining King **Cetshwayo kaMpande**'s confidence and became his adviser and supplier of **firearms**. Cetshwayo rewarded him with a large chiefdom in southeastern Zululand. In 1878, Dunn strongly advised Cetshwayo against war with Britain; when accused of treachery by the members of the *iBandla* (royal council), he crossed over to **Natal** in December 1878 with his adherents. During the **Anglo-Zulu War**, Dunn threw in his lot with the British. He rode with the **Eshowe Relief Column** to organize reconnaissance and to advise on **laager** procedures, and he was present at **Gingindlovu**. He then joined the 1st Division, **South African Field Force**, in command of the **Native Foot Scouts**, and he played an important role in **negotiating** the **submission** of the coastal chiefs. He advised General **Garnet Joseph Wolseley** in devising the 1st Partition of Zululand and was rewarded with a large chiefdom in southeastern Zululand. In the 2nd Partition, Dunn's chiefdom was incorporated into the **Reserve Territory**, but he continued to cooperate loyally with the British authorities. During the 3rd **Zulu Civil War**, he raised levies (troops) in 1884 to defend the Reserve Territory against **uSuthu** attacks down the coast. During the **uSuthu Rebellion**, he raised **Dunn's Native Levy**. Until his death, he lived as a "white chief" at his Mangethe and Moyeni homesteads, the quintessential "transfrontiersman." He was survived by 23 Zulu wives and 79 children.

**DUNN'S NATIVE LEVY.** During the final stages of the **uSuthu Rebellion**, **John Dunn** raised a levy to assist the British. On 6 July 1888, 1,500 men of Dunn's Levy joined the **Eshowe Column** in its operations while 500 more remained as border guards south of the Mhlathuze River. On 25 July, 2,400 of Dunn's Levy joined the **Coastal Column** in its pacification operations and proceeded as far north as **Camp Umfolozi**. From there, in early August, they collected the **cattle** fines imposed on the surrendered **uSuthu** along the coast. They were armed with their traditional **spears** and **shields**, though a few carried obsolete muzzle-loading **firearms**.

**DUNDEE.** By the 1860s, the plentiful coal outcrops in northern **Natal** were being mined, and by 1878 a tiny hamlet had sprung up on the farm Dundee for the few resident artisans who had been attracted by the workings. The laying out of a proper township began only in 1882. In May 1879, during the 2nd Invasion of the **Anglo-Zulu War**, Dundee, which fell into **Colonial Defensive District** No. I, became the depot for the 2nd Division, **South African Field Force**, and **Fort Jones** was built to protect the stores accumulating there.

**DURBAN.** The first permanent white settlement in southeast Africa was established at Port Natal in 1824 by white hunter-traders from the **Cape**. In August 1824, they opened communications with King **Shaka kaSenzangakhona**, who allowed them to occupy and exercise authority over the land surrounding Port Natal as tributary *amaKhosi*. After 1832, other traders from the Cape joined them, and by 1838 the population of whites had increased to about 40. King

**Dingane kaSenzangakhona** was uncertain how best to deal with these intruders in his realm, and crises in relations occurred in 1831 and in 1833, when the traders temporarily fled Port Natal for fear of Zulu attack. In 1835, a township was laid out on the north side of the bay, and Port Natal was officially renamed Durban, though it continued to be known as Port Natal for years afterward.

The Port Natal traders allied with the Voortrekkers in 1837 and fought on their side in the **Voortrekker-Zulu War**. After the disastrous defeat at the battle of **Thukela**, the remaining whites took refuge on the brig *Comet* anchored in the bay. On 24 April 1838, the Zulu army swept down on the settlement and put it to sack for nine days. The returning settlers had to rebuild the village from scratch. On 16 May 1838, the Voortrekkers annexed Port Natal to the Republic of **Natalia** and started laying out their rival settlement of **Congella** on the bay half a mile to the west. Concerned that the policies of the Republic of Natalia would adversely affect the stability of the eastern frontier of the Cape Colony, the Cape government sent a detachment of the 72nd **Regiment** (Duke of Albany's Own Highlanders) under Major Samuel Charters to occupy Port Natal. They arrived on 4 December 1838 and built **Fort Victoria** on the point. The British garrison withdrew on 24 December 1839 once it seemed the Republic of Natalia's relations with its African neighbors had normalized.

When it became apparent that the Republic of Natalia's policies continued to pose a threat to the Cape, a detachment of the 27th (Inniskilling) Regiment and **Royal Artillery** under Captain Thomas Charleton Smith was sent overland from the Cape to occupy **Natal**. The British troops took possession of Port Natal on 4 May 1842, and the Boers decided to resist. On 23 May, they defeated the British in a night skirmish at Congella and besieged them in **Smith's Camp** until the British were relieved on 25 June 1842 by five companies of the 25th Regiment (King's Own Borderers) under Lieutenant-Colonel Josias Cloete, which arrived by sea. The Boers withdrew and capitulated on 5 July 1842.

With the establishment of British rule in Natal, new British settlers clustered particularly in Durban, which became the new colony's trading, banking, manufacturing, and commercial center and the terminus by the late 1860s of the lucrative Overberg trade to the **Kimberley diamond fields**, **Orange Free State**, and **South African**

**Republic**. By 1878, its population stood at 5,300 whites and 3,500 Africans. During the **Anglo-Zulu War**, almost all of the men and material for the British campaign passed through its port. *See also* DURBAN HARBOR.

**DURBAN HARBOR.** Although 19th-century **Durban** possessed in its bay a perfect natural harbor essential for the success of the **Natal** economy, it remained inaccessible to most oceangoing vessels because of the notorious sandbar across its entrance between the Point in the north and the Bluff in the south. Not until 1881 were proper measures taken to remove this obstacle through the gradual construction of breakwaters, and to make the bay more accessible to larger ships through effective dredging. At the time of the **Anglo-Zulu War**, all but smaller ships with a shallow draft had to remain in the outer anchorage, and men, **horses**, and supplies had to be brought through the surf to shore by lighter. *See also* LOGISTICS, BRITISH.

**DURBAN MOUNTED RESERVE.** In late November 1878, Harry Escombe, a **Durban** lawyer, organized the Durban Mounted Reserve from 40 volunteers in the town to take the place of the **Natal Mounted Volunteers** who had taken the field in the **Anglo-Zulu War**. On the news of **Isandlwana**, the unit initially moved north to the Mdloti River to give warning of Zulu attack. In early February 1879, it moved back closer to Durban and took up position at Kennedy's Drift across the Mngeni River. It remained there until 3 March, when the unit was dissolved.

**DURBAN MOUNTED RIFLES.** Formed in 1873, the Durban Mounted Rifles was one of the 10 corps of **Natal Mounted Volunteers** called out in November 1878 for active service in the **Anglo-Zulu War**. In December 1878, the corps of about 30 troopers joined No. 1 **Column** at **Fort Pearson**. It advanced with the column but was absent on convoy duty during the battle of **Nyezane**. On 28 January, it returned from **Fort Eshowe** to **Natal** with the other mounted men of the column. Until the corps was mustered out in July, it served by patrolling the border along the lines of communication between Fort Pearson, **Stanger**, and **Ntunjambili** (Kranskop) in **Colonial Defensive Districts** VI and VII, and it participated in cross-border raids. A number of its men volunteered for service in the **Natal Volunteer Guides**. Its uniform was of dark blue cloth with black facings and scarlet piping, black trouser stripes, and a white helmet with a spike.

**DURBAN REDOUBT ("OLD FORT").** The 27th (Inniskilling) **Regiment** that relieved **Smith's Camp** north of **Durban** on 25 June 1842 from siege by the Boers swept away the entrenched wagon **laager** and replaced it with a proper fort that commanded the northern approaches to the port. They constructed a square of wattle and daub barracks surrounded by an earthwork wall with two flanking bastions. By 1845, the earthworks were increased in height, and a brick magazine was built. In 1858, brick barracks were erected, and British troops continued to garrison the fort until 1897. *See also* DURBAN TOWN LAAGER.

**DURBAN TOWN LAAGER.** In the panic after **Isandlwana** during the **Anglo-Zulu War**, the townspeople of **Durban** clamored for the town to be entirely encircled by fortifications. Instead, the military decided to follow the principles for the defense of an open town, which required holding key buildings not linked by continuous barricades. Accordingly, substantial edifices like the court house, market house, jail, and various shops and warehouses were prepared for defense by storing ammunition inside, loopholing walls and doors, and sandbagging parapets. The British garrison of Durban, units of the **Natal Volunteer Corps** and the **Durban Town Guard** (incorporating the Natal Coast **Rifle Association**), were assigned to defend the fortified buildings and the civilians who took refuge inside. By April 1879, all fears of a Zulu invasion had passed and these defensive arrangements were abandoned. *See also* DURBAN REDOUBT; POINT LAAGER; WESTERN VLEI REDOUBT.

**DURBAN VOLUNTEER ARTILLERY.** The single artillery corps of the **Natal Volunteer Corps** was not initially mobilized with other colonial units for the **Anglo-Zulu War**. After **Isandlwana**, when **Durban** seemed in danger of Zulu attack, the corps of 75 men with two guns was posted until the end of February 1879 at the Eastern

Vlei near the **Durban Redoubt**, and then at the **Point laager** until it was disbanded on 12 March.

**DURNFORD, ANTHONY WILLIAM (1830–1879).** Commissioned into the **Royal Engineers** in 1848, Durnford was posted to Ceylon in 1851 and also served in Malta, Gibraltar, Ireland, and England. He was promoted to major and posted to **Natal** in 1872. He served during the **Langalibalele Rebellion** of 1873, when he was much blamed by the colonists for the debacle at the Bushman's River Pass. Promoted to lieutenant-colonel in 1873, between 1873 and 1875 he acted as colonial engineer for Natal. In 1878, he sat on the Zululand Boundary Commission. Durnford was promoted to brevet colonel in December 1878 and raised and commanded the 1st Regiment of the **Natal Native Contingent**. For the 1st Invasion of the **Anglo-Zulu War**, he was given command of No. 2 **Column**. On 22 January 1879, he reinforced the camp of No. 3 Column at **Isandlwana** with part of his force. He was killed in the battle, and subsequently much of the blame for the defeat was fastened on him by Lieutenant-General Lord **Chelmsford** and his staff, who were determined to make him the scapegoat.

**DUTCH BURGHERS.** *See* TRANSVAAL BURGHER FORCE.

**kwaDWASA *umuZI*.** On 28 August 1879, at the very end of the **Anglo-Zulu War**, a mounted patrol from **Clarke's Column** led by Major Richard James Coombe Marter captured the fugitive King **Cetshwayo kaMpande** at this *umuZi* (homestead) deep in the Ngome Forest in northern **Zululand**.

## – E –

**EASTERN CAPE.** The settlers of the far-flung eastern frontier regions of the **Cape Colony** had a long tradition of resenting the political supremacy of distant **Cape Town** and developed a culture of separatism fostered by their particular concern with security issues during the **Cape Frontier Wars**. For a time the British responded administratively to this particularism by appointing a commissioner-general of the eastern districts between 1827 and 1833, and a lieutenant-governor of the Eastern Cape between 1836 and 1847. It was from this region of disaffected frontier farmers that the Voortrekkers were mainly drawn.

**EASTERN ZULULAND.** On 16 August 1884, when King **Dinuzulu kaCetshwayo** ceded northwestern **Zululand** for the establishment of the **New Republic**, he also agreed that the Boers would extend a protectorate over the rest of Zululand north of the **Reserve Territory**, to be known as Eastern Zululand. Now no more than a nominal king in the hands of the Boers, Dinuzulu could do nothing to protect his people as the Boers fanned out into Eastern Zululand, making further extensive land claims in 1885 and 1886. Driven from their lands, the **uSuthu** took refuge in their fastnesses or began to resist, bringing on themselves savage Boer retaliation. As part of the price for British recognition on 22 October 1886, the New Republic dropped all claims to a protectorate over Eastern Zululand.

**ECKERSLEY, JOHN.** A white trader in **Zululand**, in January 1880 Eckersley joined **Johannes Wilhelm Colenbrander** in *inKosi* **Zibhebhu kaMaphitha**'s chiefdom. Until 1883, he acted as secretary for both Zibhebhu and *umNtwana* **Hamu kaNzibe** in their correspondence with the **Natal** authorities. In the 3rd **Zulu Civil War**, he fought at **Msebe** and **oNdini** as one of the white **mercenaries** with Zibhebhu's forces.

**EDENDALE HORSE.** In December 1878, the African Christians of the Wesleyan mission community at Edendale outside **Pietermaritzburg** raised an excellent troop of well-disciplined **irregular cavalry** for the **Natal Native Mounted Contingent**. During the **Anglo-Zulu War**, they formed part of No. 2 **Column** and fought at **Isandlwana**. In the reorganization of February 1879, they became a troop in the **Natal Native Horse** and joined No. 4 Column, subsequently **Wood's Flying Column**, and fought at **Hlobane**, **Khambula**, and as part of the **White Mfolozi reconnaissance in force**. With the breakup of Wood's Flying Column in late July, they returned home and were disbanded.

**ENTONJANENI CAMP.** On 22 August 1887, British troops of the **Zululand garrison** moved forward from **Eshowe** to a camp on the **Mthonjaneni** Heights to secure the line of communications to the Ndwandwe District of the new British colony of **Zululand**, where the **uSuthu** were disaffected, and to ensure swift military intervention if required. There they built a large, circular, earthwork fort and smaller, supporting earthworks. In early June 1888, following the outbreak of the **uSuthu Rebellion**, reinforcements from the **Natal garrison** moved up to the Entonjaneni Camp. During the rest of June and July, small detachments remained there while the main body of troops moved forward to the **Nkonjeni** Camp. When after the suppression of the rebellion the Zululand garrison was reduced in November 1888 to its normal levels, Entonjaneni remained its forward base.

**ENTONJANENI LEVY.** Raised in late June 1888 during the **uSuthu Rebellion**, the 500 men of the Entonjaneni Levy under John Locke Knight, the resident magistrate of the Entonjaneni District in British **Zululand**, were with the forces on **Lumbe Mountain** that supported the British assault on **Hlophekhulu Mountain**. On 18 July, they went out of control at Knight's magisterial post at Mfule, burning the *imiZi* of "loyal" Zulu and rustling 300 head of **cattle**. They were armed with their traditional **spears** and **shields**, though a few carried obsolete muzzle-loading **firearms**.

**ERMELO FORT (DÖHNE'S LAAGER).** This square, stonework **laager** with two opposing bastions in **Colonial Defensive District** No. I was begun in January 1878 on the initiative of the local settlers, and in late 1878 arrangements were made for its defense. In the **Anglo-Zulu War**, it was briefly used by some farmers during their flight out of the district in the panic after **Isandlwana**.

**ESHOWE.** In 1860, *umNtwana* **Cetshwayo kaMpande** built an *umuZi*, eziQwaqeni, on the site of the future town of Eshowe. In 1861, **Ommund Christiansen Oftebro**, the superintendent of the Norwegian Mission Society, established his mission station, kwa-Mondi, in the vicinity. He abandoned kwaMondi in March 1878 when relations with Cetshwayo deteriorated. During the **Anglo-Zulu War**, No. 1 **Column** occupied the buildings between January and April 1879 and built **Fort Eshowe**. On the British withdrawal in April, the Zulu burned the mission buildings. In 1883, **Melmoth Osborn**, the resident commissioner of the **Reserve Territory**, established his post close by. When **Zululand** was annexed as a British colony in May 1887, Eshowe became the seat of the administration and the headquarters of the British **Zululand garrison** and the **Zululand Police**. By the 1890s, about 100 white civilians lived there in dwellings made of wood and iron.

**ESHOWE COLUMN.** On 6 July 1888, during the **uSuthu Rebellion**, Major **Alexander Chalmers McKean** formed a column at **Camp Kongella** to relieve **Fort Andries**, which was under **uSuthu** attack. The Eshowe Column consisted of 251 British regulars drawn from **Nkonjeni** and **Eshowe**, 180 **Mounted Basutos**, and about 1,500 men of **Dunn's Native Levy**. The column advanced on 7 July, brushing aside some weak uSuthu resistance, and relieved Fort Andries on 9 July. While Fort Andries was being replaced with the better-built **Fort McKean**, Dunn's Native Levy raided the surrounding countryside. On 11 July, the column began its return in three divisions: the British troops kept to the road, the Mounted Basutos scoured the countryside to the southwest, and Dunn's levies ranged between the two detachments. The column encountered no resistance on the way but burned 180 deserted *imiZi*. It reached Eshowe on 13 July. *See also* CIVILIANS IN WARTIME ZULULAND.

**ESHOWE LEVY.** Raised in June 1888 during the **uSuthu Rebellion** from Zulu living in the Eshowe District of the British colony of **Zululand**, and paid for by the Zululand administration, the African Eshowe Levy was placed under white leaders and was subject to some military discipline. Stationed at **Nkonjeni**, 1,000 of the levy took part in the storming of **Hlophekhulu Mountain**, but on 14 July all but 150 of them deserted. In August, this remnant was incorporated into **Carrington's Levy** and took part in the operations of **Martin's Flying Column**. They were armed with their traditional **spears** and **shields**, though a few carried obsolete muzzle-loading **firearms**.

**ESHOWE RELIEF COLUMN.** Before Lieutenant-General Lord **Chelmsford** could renew his offensive after the failure of the 1st Invasion of the **Anglo-Zulu War**, it was necessary to relieve No. 1 **Column**, beleaguered in **Fort Eshowe**. On 23 March 1879, Chelmsford took command of the Eshowe Relief Column of 5,670 men assembled at **Fort Pearson**. While forces stationed along the Thukela and Mzinyathi rivers in **Colonial Defensive Districts** VI and VII mounted demonstrations to divert Zulu attention, the column began its advance into **Zululand** on 29 March. To rectify the deficiencies that had led to the **Isandlwana** disaster, Chelmsford organized effective forward reconnaissance and followed regular laagering procedures on the march. The Zulu army attacked the column's entrenched **laager** at **Gingindlovu** on 2 April and was routed. The column relieved Eshowe the next day, and while the garrison withdrew on 4 April, a patrol destroyed the **eZuluwini** *umuZi* nearby. The column formed a new entrenched camp a mile south of the Gingindlovu laager on 6 April, and on 13 April it became the 2nd Brigade of the 1st Division, **South African Field Force**, that was preparing to advance up the Zulu coast during the 2nd Invasion of the Anglo-Zulu War.

**ESTCOURT LAAGER.** In early January 1879, shortly before the outbreak of the **Anglo-Zulu War**, the **Natal** government proclaimed the **laager** outside the village of Estcourt in **Colonial Defensive District** No. II as the central defensive post for the settlers of the region. It consisted of a blockhouse (**Fort Durnford**) erected in 1874 for the **Natal Mounted Police**, three associated loopholed guardhouses, and a stables block built in 1876. The buildings were connected in 1878 by an eight-foot-high stone wall to form a large enclosure. During the **Anglo-Zulu War**, the laager was further strengthened (which included leveling a small hill that overlooked it), and it was stocked with arms and ammunition. It was recognized, however, that the laager was far too big for defense by the Weenen County **Rifle Association** and the small number of settlers expected to take refuge there. It continued to be used as barracks for the Natal Mounted Police until 1900.

**ETSHOWE COLUMN.** In September 1883, the officer in command of **Natal**, Colonel W. D. Bond, became alarmed at the course of the 3rd

**Zulu Civil War** and resolved to send troops of the **Natal garrison** to **Eshowe** to support **Melmoth Osborn**, the resident commissioner of the **Reserve Territory**. The Etshowe Column of 529 British regulars under Lieutenant-Colonel W. G. Montgomery assembled at **Fort Pearson** and began its advance on 20 September, reaching Eshowe on 29 September. When Montgomery died of a snake bite, he was succeeded on 25 September by Lieutenant-Colonel R. J. Hawthorne, who commenced **Fort Curtis** outside Eshowe, which the column garrisoned. In May 1884, troops from Fort Curtis built **Fort Chater** to support **Osborn's Levies** operating against the **uSuthu** in the **Nkandla Forest**. The deteriorating situation in the Reserve Territory required that the Etshowe Column be reinforced, and by 27 May the troops garrisoning Fort Curtis were brought up to 800 men under the command of Colonel **Francis George Savage Curtis**.

**EUPHORBIA HILL REDOUBT.** This small, earthwork redoubt close to **Fort Pearson** was where the **Naval Brigade** encamped during the **Anglo-Zulu War**.

## – F –

**FAIRLIE'S SWAZI.** This small force of African levies (troops) raised in the Transvaal served in the **Anglo-Zulu War** with No. 5 **Column**. It took part in the raid of 15 February against the **abaQulusi** on Talaku Mountain. It seems that once No. 5 Column was attached in late February to Brevet Colonel **Henry Evelyn Wood**'s command they were incorporated into **Wood's Irregulars**.

**uFALAZA *iBUTHO*.** Formed by King **Cetshwayo kaMpande** in 1877 from youths born in 1856–1858, this *iButho* (regiment) was then called uMsizi. It took no part in the **Anglo-Zulu War**, but when Cetshwayo was restored in 1883 after the 2nd Partition of **Zululand**, he exercised his former authority to reconstitute and rename the *iButho*. Since the uFalaza was raised only from young men in Cetshwayo's truncated territory and not from the entire kingdom as formerly, it was in effect a military unit of the **uSuthu** faction, and it took an active role in the 3rd **Zulu Civil War**. On 24 June 1883, it was beaten back by the **Ngenetsheni** supported by the **Mandlakazi** when it raided *umNtwana* **Hamu kaNzibe**'s stronghold on Ngotshe Mountain. On 4 July, the uFalaza was part of an uSuthu force that defeated the Mandlakazi in a skirmish at the Dlomodlomo Hills in northern Zululand. At **oNdini**, it formed the uSuthu left horn and was routed. It formed part of the uSuthu army at the victory at **Tshaneni** in 1884. In victorious engagements in the **uSuthu Rebellion**, it fought on the uSuthu right horn at **Ceza**, and on the right of the chest at **Ivuna**.

**FIELD CORNET.** The primary duties of a field cornet (or *veldkornet*) were to ensure that the burghers in his ward or district were combat ready, to muster them in wartime into the local **commando** (militia), and to commandeer transport and supplies. On campaign, he acted as a subordinate officer to the **commandant** (*kommandant*). He was an elected official, but because the vote was not secret, influential local notables invariably secured nomination.

**FIREARMS, BOER.** The Voortrekkers in the 1830s and 1840s normally carried a *voorlaaier*, or muzzle-loading **musket**, known as a *snaphaan* when it was a flintlock. Flints were preferred because **percussion caps** were difficult to come by in the interior of South Africa. Single- or double-barreled fowling pieces firing buckshot were in common use, as were heavier muskets of various calibers, including the heavy elephant gun. Generically known as *Sannas*, these flintlock muskets were tolerably accurate only up to about 80 yards, and the rate of fire was no more than four shots a minute at best. Nevertheless, they proved most effective in breaking up a massed attack on a wagon **laager** because the Boers fired and loaded in rotation, keeping up a constant wall of fire. Boers carried their powder in an ox or buffalo horn sawn off at the tip and fitted with a measure. It was attached to the waist belt. Buckshot slugs were set in cylinders of hard fat or sewn into oiled buckskin bags, *loopers*, that slid easily down the barrel and would explode at about 40 yards. *Loopers*, musket balls, and wadding were carried in the pockets of a broad leather bandolier.

By the 1840s, the Boers of the interior of South Africa began increasingly to adopt percussion-cap muskets and **rifles** in place of their old flintlocks, and powder-horns were replaced by cartouche pouches and belts with cap pouches. By the 1870s, most were armed with breech-loading rifles and **carbines** and carried their cartridges in leather bandoliers or in pouches sewn onto their waistcoats.

Voortrekkers occasionally carried muzzle-loading flintlock pistols, but they were inaccurate and ineffective except at very short range.

**FIREARMS, ZULU.** In the **Voortrekker-Zulu War**, some Zulu had firearms captured in successful engagements, but they lacked skill in effective use. In the 1st **Zulu Civil War**, neither side apparently made use of them, though in the 2nd Zulu Civil War, the **iziGqoza** were supported at **Ndondakusuka** by the **iziNqobo** with their firearms. From the 1860s, firearms began entering **Zululand** through **Delagoa Bay** and **Natal**. By 1878, there were about 12,000 inferior, obsolete weapons like muzzle-loading flintlock **muskets**, as well as some 7,500 **percussion-cap** and 500 breech-loading **rifles** reserved for men of higher status. In recognition of the power and prestige conferred by firearms, the king always attempted to regulate their distribution to favored individuals and *amaButho*. Most Zulu preferred to rely on their traditional weapons and **tactics**, and tended to employ firearms as secondary weapons in place of throwing-**spears**, to be cast aside when hand-to-hand fighting ensued. Muskets were in any case inferior, inaccurate weapons, especially when gunpowder was of poor quality, the improvised bullets of irregular shape, and *amaButho* untrained in their effective use. Marksmanship was consequently very poor, with Zulu firing while out of range or shooting high.

By the 1870s, several hundred Zulu were familiar with modern firearms through contact with white hunters, traders, and adventurers in Zululand. They made effective snipers during the **Anglo-Zulu War** and made good use of **Martini-Henry rifles** captured from the British. Most of these rifles were surrendered to the British at the end of the war. During the 3rd Zulu Civil War and the **uSuthu Rebellion**, firearms were more in evidence, especially among the **Mandlakazi** faction that had closer contacts with Europeans than the **uSuthu**. Nevertheless, modern rifles were still in the minority on both sides, and most Zulu firearms continued to be muzzle-loaders.

**FORBES, ARCHIBALD (1838–1900).** In 1867, Forbes left the British cavalry to pursue journalism. From 1870, he was a **special**

**correspondent** to the *Daily News*, reporting on the Franco-Prussian, Carlist, Serbian, Russo-Turkish, and Afghan wars. During the **Anglo-Zulu War**, he reported critically on the advance of the 2nd Division, **South African Field Force**, and relations between him and Lieutenant-General Lord **Chelmsford**'s staff became strained. His "ride of death" brought the news of **Ulundi** to the public ahead of Chelmsford's official dispatch, and Chelmsford was instrumental in denying him the South Africa Medal for the exploit. In retaliation, Forbes published damaging attacks on Chelmsford's generalship. Having established himself as the leading special correspondent of his time, Forbes covered no more campaigns but lectured and wrote reminiscences.

**FORT ALBERT.** During the **Anglo-Zulu War**, **Wood's Flying Column**, on withdrawing after **Ulundi**, built this earthwork fort on 11–12 July 1879 close by the Anglican **kwaMagwaza mission** in **Zululand** to secure its line of supply to the coast. The small garrison it left behind was relieved when **Baker Russell's Column** passed through on 27 July 1879. This was withdrawn in turn when the column reached the Transvaal in early September 1879. During the **uSuthu Rebellion**, a small detachment of British troops from the **Natal garrison** reoccupied the fort between June and September 1888.

**FORT AMIEL.** In June 1877, the British built this stone-walled fort, which commanded the village of **Newcastle**, as a base for troops involved in the annexation of the Transvaal. During the **Anglo-Zulu War**, the fort, now in **Colonial Defensive District** No. I, served as a rear depot and hospital for No. 4 **Column**. The fort continued in use by the British during the 1st **Boer War** (1880–1881) and the **Anglo-Boer (South African) War** (1899–1902), when it was greatly extended.

**FORT ANDRIES.** In June 1888, during the **uSuthu Rebellion**, Andries Pretorius, the resident magistrate of the Lower Umfolosi District in the British colony of **Zululand**, hurriedly threw up two small earthworks flanking his magistracy office built on the lower slopes of **Ntondotha** Hill. He and the garrison of 40 **Zululand Police**, aided by **Mthethwa** auxiliaries, beat off an **uSuthu** attack on 30

June 1888 in the battle of Ntondotha. The **Eshowe Column** relieved the post on 9 July.

**FORT ARGYLL.** In the last stages of the **Anglo-Zulu War**, the 91st **Regiment** (Princess Louise's Argyllshire Highlanders) with the 1st Division, **South African Field Force**, built this earthwork fort as an advance post commanding the drift across the Mhlathuze River and garrisoned it between 24 July and 14 September 1879.

**FORT AYR.** During the advance of **Wood's Flying Column** in the 2nd Invasion of the **Anglo-Zulu War**, detachments were sent on 26 April 1879 to cut wood for fuel on the Doornberg, where they built this earthwork fort. They were followed on 8 May by detachments from the 2nd Division, **South African Field Force**, that improved the fortifications and formed a wagon **laager** as well. By 29 May, all troops had left the Doornberg.

**FORT BENGOUGH.** This fort in **Colonial Defensive District** No. I, with loopholed, rough stone walls 15 feet high, was built during the **Anglo-Zulu War** in the fortnight after **Isandlwana** by the 2nd Battalion, **Natal Native Contingent** (NNC), on the road between **Greytown** and **Helpmekaar**. The central, square section was the magazine. The white officers camped in one of the flanking sections, and their black troops in the other and in huts below the fort. The NNC actively patrolled the vicinity until they left the fort in May 1879 to join the 2nd Division, **South African Field Force**, for the 2nd Invasion of the Anglo-Zulu War. Some of the local **Border Guard** may have partially occupied the fort after they had gone.

**FORT BUCKINGHAM.** In July 1861, during the **Zulu Invasion Scare**, troops of the **Natal garrison** built this earthwork fort on the escarpment overlooking the middle Thukela River. In 1863, when it was reconstructed and garrisoned, it consisted of a collection of wattle-and-daub huts surrounded by a sod parapet and palisade bastions. It was abandoned after 1868 and was in ruins by 1878. During the **Anglo-Zulu War**, troops operating in **Colonial Defensive District** No. VII occasionally used it as an outpost but never reoccupied it. The fort was altered in September 1901 during the **Anglo-Boer**

(South African) War by Natal colonial units anticipating a Boer raid, and again during the Zulu Uprising of 1906.

FORT CAMBRIDGE. These two earthwork redoubts were thrown up on 26 July 1879 during the Anglo-Zulu War, and Baker Russell's Column encamped there from 5 to 9 August, sending out patrols to enforce Zulu submissions. When the column continued its advance, it left a garrison to secure the area until the British evacuated Zululand in September 1879.

FORT CHATER. In May 1883 during the 3rd Zulu Civil War, the uSuthu repulsed the local forces raised by Melmoth Osborn, the resident commissioner of the Reserve Territory, in the battle of the Nkandla Forest. Osborn's men fell back on Fort Chater, an earthwork hastily thrown up by British troops of the Natal garrison stationed at Fort Curtis. Fort Chater was close to Entumeni, a Norwegian mission station, and barred the way to Eshowe, the seat of Osborn's administration, against the uSuthu in the Nkandla. During mid-1884, British troops reinforced the African levies holding this strategic post. The uSuthu in the Nkandla submitted in early September 1884, and the British garrison of Fort Chater was reduced. The fort was abandoned in May 1887 when the Reserve Territory became part of the colony of Zululand.

FORT CHELMSFORD. During the Anglo-Zulu War, men of the 2nd Brigade, 1st Division, South African Field Force, began this earthwork fort on 25 June 1879 as an advanced post and depot along the line of the division's advance. It was garrisoned by detachments of the 1st Division until early August 1879.

FORT CHERRY. This large, irregularly shaped earthwork fort in Colonial Defensive District No. VII was hastily constructed during the Anglo-Zulu War in the panic after Isandlwana, and it was strengthened thereafter. It was garrisoned by the 1st and 3rd Battalions of the Natal Native Contingent until the end of September 1879. D'Almaine's fortified farmhouse on the hill close by was used by the garrison as a storehouse.

**FORT CLERY.** During November 1878, the detachment of the 90th **Regiment** (Perthshire Volunteers Light Infantry) from the **Utrecht** garrison that had been garrisoning the **Luneburg laager** since October built this military earthwork fort nearby for their own use. During the **Anglo-Zulu War,** succeeding detachments of No. 4 and No. 5 **Columns** relieved each other at the fort until July 1879.

**FORT CREALOCK.** Men of the 1st Brigade, 1st Division, **South African Field Force,** began this earthwork fort on 23 April 1879 as an advanced post and depot along the line of the division's advance during the 2nd Invasion of the **Anglo-Zulu War**. It was garrisoned by detachments of the 1st Division until early August 1879.

**FORT CROSS.** In July 1861 during the **Zulu Invasion Scare**, a slight defensive work was thrown up at Balcomb's farm in **Natal** on a strategically placed hill overlooking the Thukela valley. On about 10 May 1879 during the **Anglo-Zulu War**, a detachment of the **Ixopo Native Contingent** (INC) encamped at Balcomb's, and in late June or early July, following the Zulu raid at **Middle Drift** in **Colonial Defensive District** No. VII, they constructed a rectangular earthwork fort with two opposing bastions in order to protect their camp. Fort Cross was garrisoned by the INC until they were withdrawn on 26 August 1879.

**FORT CURTIS.** Constructed in October 1883 by the **Etshowe Column** as the **Natal garrison**'s headquarters in the **Reserve Territory** close to the **Eshowe** Mission Station, this fort consisted of a permanent earthwork lunette commanding a timber stockade riveted with sods and surrounded by a ditch and barbed-wire entanglements. With the surrender of the **uSuthu** in the **Nkandla Forest** in September 1884 during the 3rd **Zulu Civil War**, the garrison was reduced. In August 1887, the **Zululand garrison** was again increased because of uSuthu disaffection with the British annexation of **Zululand**. During the **uSuthu Rebellion** of 1888, the fort remained the British base for operations in Zululand. When the Zululand garrison was reduced to its normal level in November 1888, nearly half the remaining British troops were concentrated there.

**FORT DURNFORD.** In the period of alarm following the **Langal-ibalele Rebellion** of 1873 in **Natal**, the Natal government decided in 1874 to build a permanent fort overlooking the village of Estcourt. Designed by Lieutenant-Colonel **Anthony William Durnford**, the acting colonial engineer, the blockhouse was two stories high, with two flanking towers and water storage tanks in the basement. A detachment of **Natal Mounted Police** was stationed there. In 1878, it was linked by stone walls to stables and blockhouses to form the **Estcourt laager**. The Natal Mounted Police continued to be stationed there until 1900.

**FORT ESHOWE.** After fighting through a Zulu ambush at **Nyezane** during the **Anglo-Zulu War**, No. 1 **Column** halted at the abandoned Norwegian mission station at **Eshowe** and between 23 and 30 January 1879 built this earthwork fort there. The church was turned into a hospital and the other buildings given over to stores. On news of **Isandlwana**, Colonel **Charles Knight Pearson** decided to hold fast at Eshowe with the infantry, and he sent his mounted men, African levies, and oxen back to **Natal**. The Zulu blockaded the garrison until it was relieved on 3 April 1879 by the **Eshowe Relief Column**. The fort was abandoned on 4 April. A small detachment of the 1st Division, **South African Field Force**, was briefly stationed there between mid-July and early August 1879.

**FORT EVELYN.** Men of the 2nd Division, **South African Field Force**, built this stone fort on 22–23 June 1879 during the **Anglo-Zulu War** at their camp along their line of supply and communication back to **Fort Marshall**. The depot was abandoned after **Baker Russell's Column** passed through in late July 1879 on its way to the Transvaal.

**FORT FROOM.** In May 1879 during the **Anglo-Zulu War**, a detachment of the 94th **Regiment** relieved the garrison of **Greytown** in **Colonial Defensive District** No. VII and replaced the existing military earthwork, **Fort Moore**, with Fort Froom. The detachment of the 94th Regiment was replaced in August 1879 by a detachment of the 99th (Duke of Edinburgh's Lanarkshire) Regiment that now formed part of the permanent British garrison of **Natal**.

**FORT GEORGE.** These two earthwork supporting redoubts were built on 10 August 1879 during the last stages of the **Anglo-Zulu War** by **Baker Russell's Column** as a forward base while it probed across the Black Mfolozi River from **Fort Cambridge**, sending out patrols to secure Zulu **submissions**. The column continued its advance on 25 August 1879, leaving a garrison at Fort George that was withdrawn in September 1879.

**FORT JONES.** This earthwork fort was built in early May 1879 during the **Anglo-Zulu War** to protect the main supply depot of the 2nd Division, **South African Field Force**, at the little settlement of **Dundee** in **Colonial Defensive District** No. I. It enclosed the three galvanized iron commissariat sheds that were moved there from **Helpmekaar** when that fort ceased in April 1879 to be an important depot with the mounting of the 2nd Invasion of the Anglo-Zulu War. Fort Jones was garrisoned until July 1879 by detachments of the 2nd Division.

**FORT KHAMBULA.** During the **Anglo-Zulu War**, No. 4 **Column** built a small redoubt between 11 and 13 February 1879 to command its entrenched camp, begun on 27 January and relocated higher up the Khambula spur on 11 February. Effective patrols from Khambula maintained the British initiative in northwestern **Zululand** after the failure of the 1st Invasion of the Anglo-Zulu War. The fort played a key role in the defense of the British position during the battle of **Khambula**. It was abandoned when **Wood's Flying Column** began its advance on 5 May 1879 during the 2nd Invasion of the war.

**FORT LAWRENCE.** This earthwork fort was built on 8 May 1879 during the **Anglo-Zulu War** at the Widow Potgieter's farm in the **Disputed Territory** by a detachment of the 2nd Battalion, 4th (King's Own Royal) **Regiment**, that had been distributed in reserve among posts to the rear of the 2nd Division, **South African Field Force**, and **Wood's Flying Column** during the 2nd Invasion of the war. It is likely the detachment garrisoned Fort Lawrence until September 1879.

**FORT LIDDLE.** In early July 1879 during the **Anglo-Zulu War**, following the Zulu raid at **Middle Drift** in **Colonial Defensive District**

No. VII, a detachment of the **Ixopo Native Contingent** (INC) constructed this rectangular earthwork fort with two opposing bastions in order to bolster the frontier defenses. The fort was garrisoned until the INC was withdrawn on 26 August 1879.

**FORT LUCAS.** In May 1879, Captain George Lucas, commandant of **Colonial Defensive District** No. VI, built this earthwork fort as headquarters for his **Border Guard** during the **Anglo-Zulu War.**

**FORT MARSHALL.** On 18 June 1879 during the 2nd Invasion of the **Anglo-Zulu War**, the 2nd Division, **South African Field Force**, and **Wood's Flying Column** built this earthwork fort on their line of communications back to **Fort Newdigate**. It consisted of three connected five-sided enclosures. It was garrisoned by various detachments, including cavalry, to protect the line forward. The 2nd Division was formally broken up nearby on 26 July 1879 after its withdrawal after the battle of **Ulundi**, although the garrison was maintained until convoys could bring out unconsumed supplies. The depot was abandoned in early August 1879 after **Baker Russell's Column** passed through on its way to the Transvaal.

**FORT MCKEAN.** On 9 July 1888 during the **uSuthu Rebellion**, the **Eshowe Column** relieved **Fort Andries** and the magistracy in the Lower Umfolosi District in the Colony of **Zululand**. It replaced the fort with a more professionally constructed military earthwork called Fort McKean that was temporarily garrisoned by **Mounted Basutos**. When in late July 1888 the Mounted Basutos joined the advance of the **Coastal Column**, they left a small detachment of **Zululand Police** to defend the fort.

**FORT MELVILL.** Built in the **Anglo-Zulu War** between March and May 1879 by detachments of the former No. 3 **Column** broken up after **Isandlwana**, this stone-walled fort overlooked the Mzinyathi River at Rorke's Drift. It superseded the fortified mission station, **Rorke's Drift Fort**, whose stores and troops were transferred to the new fort. Fort Melvill was garrisoned until early September 1879.

**FORT MIZPAH.** *See* UVOTI LAAGER.

**FORT MONTGOMERY.** Men of the 1st Battalion, **Natal Native Contingent** (NNC), threw up this earthwork fort to secure **Middle Drift** across the Thukela River during the border demonstrations from 25 March to 11 April 1879 undertaken during the **Anglo-Zulu War** by the forces in **Colonial Defensive District** No. VII to co-ordinate with the advance of the **Eshowe Relief Column**. The fort was then left unoccupied until after the Zulu raid at Middle Drift on 25 June 1879. A detachment of the NNC was sent to garrison and strengthen the fort on 30 June, and it probably remained there until the NNC was disbanded at the end of September 1879.

**FORT MOORE.** In January 1879, a detachment of the 2nd Battalion, 4th (King's Own Royal) **Regiment**, which during the **Anglo-Zulu War** formed the British garrison of **Greytown** in **Colonial Defensive District** No. VII, built this earthwork adjoining the civilian **Greytown laager**. The garrison was relieved in May 1879, and **Fort Froom** was erected in Fort Moore's place.

**FORT NAPIER.** The Fort Napier military station was the headquarters of the permanent British **Natal garrison** from 1 September 1843 until 12 August 1914. The fort was begun in September 1843 on a hill commanding **Pietermaritzburg** from the west. By 1845, it consisted of a rectangle of brick barracks, whose windowless outer walls were loopholed for defense, flanked by two stone bastions at opposite corners with guns on revolving platforms. During the **Zulu Invasion Scare of 1861** when most of the garrison was deployed on the **Zululand** border, the alarmed citizens of Pietermaritzburg moved close to the fort, and units of the **Natal Volunteer Corps** manned the redoubts. A new building program was begun in August 1876 because facilities and accommodation in the fort were reported lacking, and because growing tensions in southern Africa indicated that better defenses were required. A 10-foot-deep trench with corresponding earthwork walls was built to enclose the barracks and other buildings. Stone redoubts and gun emplacements were built at various angles of the new earthworks, and the main roadways to the fort were protected by drawbridges. In the panic after **Isandlwana** during the **Anglo-Zulu War**, plans were made for the white women and children of Pietermaritzburg to take shelter in the fort with the soldiers of the garrison while the men of the town were to defend the **Pietermaritzburg laager**.

**FORT NAPOLEON.** During the 2nd Invasion of the **Anglo-Zulu War**, as part of the **Conference Hill fortifications**, the 1st Division, **South African Field Force**, started this square, earthwork redoubt on 25 June 1879 to cover the pontoon bridge across the Mlalazi River.

**FORT NEWDIGATE.** On 6 June 1879 during the **Anglo-Zulu War**, the 2nd Division, **South African Field Force**, built this stone-walled fort on its line of supply and communication back to **Fort Warwick**. **Wood's Flying Column** joined the 2nd Division there on 18 June for their joint advance in the 2nd Invasion of the war. Various detachments, including cavalry, garrisoned the fort and depot to maintain communications. On its withdrawal after **Ulundi**, the 2nd Division halted there on 18 July. Until **Baker Russell's Column** passed through in early August 1879 on its way to the Transvaal, the garrison was maintained to ensure unconsumed supplies were brought out of **Zululand**.

**FORT NOLELA.** *See* FORT ULUNDI.

**FORT NORTHAMPTON.** In June 1884 during the 3rd **Zulu Civil War**, troops of the **Natal garrison** built and garrisoned Fort Northampton in the **Reserve Territory**, just north across the Mzinyathi River from **Rorke's Drift**, to provide a military point of entry for supporting operations against the **uSuthu** in the **Reserve Territory** to the west of the **Nkandla Forest**. It consisted of a dry-stone parapet and mealie-bag traverses. A small garrison remained after the **submission** of the uSuthu in September 1884, but it was withdrawn in May 1887 when the Reserve Territory became part of the British colony of **Zululand**.

**FORT PEARSON.** In November 1878, detachments of No. 1 **Column** built and garrisoned this earthwork fort and two small redoubts to command the lower drift over the Thukela River. During the **Anglo-Zulu War**, Fort Pearson acted as the base and main supply depot for No. 1 Column in January 1879, the **Eshowe Relief Column** in March, and the 1st Division, **South African Field Force**, in April. During April and May, the fort was strengthened to cover the pont (rope-hauled ferry) and pontoon bridge constructed across the lower Thukela. Its garrison was withdrawn in September 1879. The fort was briefly used again in late September 1883 during the 3rd **Zulu Civil War** when the **Etshowe Column** concentrated there preparatory to advancing into the **Reserve Territory**.

**FORT PIET UYS.** During the **Anglo-Zulu War**, **Baker Russell's Column** built the stonework fort in August 1879 below **Hlobane Mountain** to forestall **abaQulusi** resistance and to protect the stores brought up from **Fort Cambridge**, its previous base. When it resumed its advance on 1 September, the column left a small garrison there until it reached the Transvaal in the second week of September 1879.

**FORT PINE.** Begun in 1878 by the **Natal** government in **Colonial Defensive District** No. I, this solid fort with loopholed stone walls 14 feet high and two opposed bastions was originally intended as a post for the **Natal Mounted Police**, but the **Buffalo Border Guard** made it their headquarters instead. After **Isandlwana** during the **Anglo-Zulu War**, it was entirely filled with panicked refugees from the locality. They did not finally leave until May 1879. Units of the **Natal Mounted Volunteers** garrisoned the fort from early February until July 1879 and regularly patrolled the surrounding countryside.

**FORT RICHARDS.** This earthwork fort was begun on 1 July 1879 during the **Anglo-Zulu War** by men of the 1st Brigade, 1st Division, **South African Field Force**, to command the landing place and camp at **Port Durnford**. It was apparently never completed.

**FORT SCOTT.** This fort was built in 1857 on the northern **Natal** coastal plain by the **Natal garrison** as a defense against possible Zulu incursions. It was abandoned by the 1870s.

**FORT TENEDOS.** Between 13 and 17 January 1879 during the **Anglo-Zulu War**, No. 1 **Column** built and garrisoned this earthwork fort on the Zulu bank of the Thukela River across from **Fort Pearson**. It was abandoned in July 1879 with the withdrawal of the 1st Division, **South African Field Force**, from **Zululand**.

**FORT TINTA.** On 21 January 1879 during the **Anglo-Zulu War**, the advancing No. 4 **Column** built and garrisoned this stone fort overlooking Tinta's Drift across the **White Mfolozi**. From this base, the column sent out strong patrols on 22 January against **Mbilini waMswati** on **Hlobane Mountain**, and on 24 January against the **ebaQulusini** *iKhanda*. On learning of **Isandlwana**, the column fell back on 26 January 1879 to a fortified camp at **Khambula**, and Fort Tinta was abandoned.

**FORT ULUNDI (FORT NOLELA).** On 2 July 1879 during the **Anglo-Zulu War**, men of the 2nd Division, **South African Field Force**, built this little stonework fort on the hill commanding the double **laager** constructed on the banks of the White Mfolozi by men of the 2nd Division and **Wood's Flying Column**. It was from this camp that Colonel **Redvers Henry Buller** made his **White Mfolozi reconnaissance in force** on 3 July. During the battle of **Ulundi**, a garrison of 622 men under Colonel William Bellairs held the fort while the rest of the British were committed in the **Mahlabathini Plain**. A Zulu force some 5,000 strong approached, crossed the White Mfolozi River, and came to within 500 yards of the fort and laager. The Zulu did not press their attack; they soon melted away to join the battle in the plain. The British force routed the Zulu and returned to their camp on the White Mfolozi. The following day, the joint force retired to the **Mthonjaneni laager**, abandoning Fort Ulundi.

**FORT VICTORIA, DURBAN.** On 4 December 1838, a detachment of the 72nd **Regiment** (Duke of Albany's Own Highlanders) from the **Cape** under Major Samuel Charters occupied Port Natal (**Durban**) and established a fortified camp on the Point commanding the anchorage and entrance to the bay. During the course of the year, a stockade of mangrove trees was erected that enclosed barracks, officers' huts, a magazine, a hospital, and sheds and marquees for commissariat stores. The stockade was commanded by an earthwork redoubt and gun emplacements. The garrison of Fort Victoria withdrew from Port Natal on 24 December 1839. The British reoccupied Port Natal on 4 May 1842, establishing **Smith's Camp** at the Eastern Vlei north of the town and garrisoning Fort Victoria with only a small force. Following the British repulse at **Congella** on 23 May 1842, the Boers surprised Fort Victoria on 26 May, quickly enforced its surrender, and seized the stores and weapons.

**FORT VICTORIA, ZULULAND.** Once he had assumed command of operations in early July 1879, General **Sir Garnet Joseph Wolseley** decided it was necessary to reoccupy the **Mahlabathini Plain** to ensure the **submission** of the major Zulu *amaKhosi* and terminate the **Anglo-Zulu War**. On the breakup of the 2nd Division, **South African Field Force**, on 26 July and the formation of **Clarke's Column**, the 58th (Rutlandshire) **Regiment** advanced to the foot of the **Mthonjaneni** Heights, where on 7 August it built this rectangular earthwork fort to secure the column's line of supply and communication to **Port Durnford**. Companies of the regiment were detached to other garrisons until only one remained at Fort Victoria; it marched back to **Natal** on 26 August.

**FORT WARWICK.** In June 1879 during the 2nd Invasion of the **Anglo-Zulu War**, a detachment of the 2nd Division, **South African Field Force**, threw up this small earthwork fort on the advancing division's line of communication back to **Fort Whitehead**.

**FORT WHITEHEAD.** The 2nd Division, **South African Field Force**, advanced to Koppie Alleen in late May 1879 during the **Anglo-Zulu War** and formed a depot there on the west bank of the Ncome River. The depot replaced **Conference Hill** to the north as the division's forward base for the 2nd Invasion of the war because reconnaissance had established that it was on a more direct route to the second **oNdini** *iKhanda*. Stores were relocated from Conference Hill to the new depot, and two supporting earthwork redoubts were begun on 28 May to guard it. A small detachment garrisoned Fort Whitehead until late July 1879, when the 2nd Division was broken up.

**FORT WILLIAMSON.** Begun in 1861 during the **Zulu Invasion Scare** to guard the lower drift across the Thukela River, this earthwork fort was in disrepair by 1870, and it was not reoccupied during the **Anglo-Zulu War**.

**FORT YOLLAND.** In July 1884 during the 3rd **Zulu Civil War**, Lieutenant-Colonel **Francis George Savage Curtis**, in command of the British troops in the **Reserve Territory**, erected the earthwork Fort Yolland as a forward base from **Fort Chater** for operations against the **uSuthu** in the **Nkandla Forest**. By September, the uSuthu had **submitted**, and in November the British garrison was withdrawn from Fort Yolland and replaced by the **Reserve Territory Carbineers**. The fort was abandoned in May 1887 when the Reserve Territory became part of the colony of **Zululand**.

**FORTIFICATIONS IN NATAL AND ZULULAND.** In **Natal** and **Zululand**, stone or earthwork fortifications erected by British forces or the colonial government were never very elaborate because the Zulu had no **artillery** or scaling ladders. Nor were they able to support close or prolonged sieges because of their own problems of supply and discipline. All that was required for defense was a closed work a few yards high, surrounded by a ditch and possibly an abatis of felled trees and bushes, with a clear, all-around field of fire extending over several hundred yards. The ground had to be sufficiently level and drained for encampment, and easy access to good water, grazing, and fuel were essential. *See also individual fortifications.*

**FRERE, SIR (HENRY) BARTLE EDWARD (1815–1884).** Frere enjoyed a distinguished career as an administrator in India. He was political resident to the rajah of Satara (1847–1850), chief commissioner of Sind (1851–1859), member of the Council of the Governor-General (1859–1862), and governor of Bombay (1862–1867). He retired from India in 1867 to take up a seat on the Indian Council in London. In 1872–1873, he was sent on a special mission to curb the slave trade in Zanzibar. He was created a baronet in 1876.

Believing fervently in extending the benefits of empire, Frere took up the challenge of effecting the **confederation** of South Africa when in March 1877 he was appointed governor of the **Cape** and high commissioner for South Africa. He was also commander-in-chief and could employ the military forces in South Africa to achieve his objective of creating a new dominion along the lines of Canada, with himself as the first governor-general. Frere unleashed the **Anglo-Zulu War** in the belief that a quick military victory would eliminate the **Zulu kingdom** as an obstacle to his plans. The war proved disastrous, drawn out, and expensive. The government censured Frere and in May 1879 split the high commission in two, appointing General **Sir Garnet Joseph Wolseley** as high commissioner in the southeast. Wolseley consequently took the responsibility for the 1st Partition of **Zululand** out of Frere's hands. The new Liberal government recalled Frere in August 1880, and his stellar career ended in disappointment and humiliation.

**FRONTIER LIGHT HORSE.** The Frontier Light Horse was first raised in 1877 from rough recruits in the **Eastern Cape** for service in the 9th **Cape Frontier War**. Lieutenant Frederick Carrington and then Major **Redvers Henry Buller** formed it into a tough and efficient unit. At the conclusion of the 9th Cape Frontier War, the unit marched to the Transvaal Territory, where it took part in the campaign against the **Pedi** before joining No. 4 **Column** for the **Anglo-Zulu War**. Along with other units of **irregular cavalry** with the column, it patrolled and raided northwestern **Zululand**. Two squadrons fought at **Hlobane** with Lieutenant-Colonel Buller's force and then at **Khambula**. As part of **Wood's Flying Column**, a squadron took part in the skirmish at **Zungeni**, and two squadrons participated in the **White Mfolozi reconnaissance in force** and fought at **Ulundi**. After the breakup of Wood's Flying Column in late July, they joined **Baker Russell's Column** and were disbanded in September. They had no specific uniform, though generally the men wore yellow or buff corduroy with black trimmings and a wideawake hat with a red puggaree.

**FUGITIVES' DRIFT.** *See* SOTHONDOSE'S DRIFT.

**FUGITIVES' TRAIL.** When the Zulu army enveloped the British camp at **Isandlwana** during the **Anglo-Zulu War**, the Zulu right horn poured into the valley behind the mountain. Forming in long lines between the camp and Mzinyathi River, they cut the British retreat along the road to **Rorke's Drift**. However, before the Zulu left horn could complete their encirclement, some mounted men and African levies (troops) on foot fled through the gap south-southeast of Isandlwana and led the way down what came to be known as the Fugitives' Trail to **Sothondose's Drift** downstream of Rorke's Drift. But the going was difficult, and the pursuing Zulu caught up with even the mounted men. The Zulu ran along with those in retreat, shooting and stabbing. The two 7-pounder guns overturned in a stony donga and were abandoned. In addition to those killed along the trail, some drowned in the swollen Mzinyathi as they attempted to cross under Zulu fire, or died on the **Natal** bank where the local **Qungebe** people cut them off. Some of the British regulars attempted a fighting withdrawal through the gap in the Zulu encirclement down the Fugitives' Trail. Shepherded on their left by the Zulu who held the ridge parallel to their line of retreat, and bounded on their right by steep dongas, groups of up to half-company strength were systematically cut off and killed. No group got farther than the far bank of the Manzimnyama stream, a third of the way down to the Mzinyathi.

**FYNN, HENRY FRANCIS, JR. (1846–1915).** The son of one of the early pioneers in **Natal**, Fynn was fluent in Zulu. He rose through the ranks of the Natal civil service to the post of resident magistrate of the Umsinga Division in 1876. In 1878, he acted as interpreter to the **Boundary Commission**. During the **Anglo-Zulu War**, he was appointed in January 1879 as Lieutenant-General Lord **Chelmsford**'s personal interpreter and political adviser and accompanied No. 3 **Column** into **Zululand**. He was away with Chelmsford during **Isandlwana**. After Chelmsford retreated to Natal, Fynn resumed his magisterial duties in Umsinga and raised a **Border Guard** for the defense of the division. In August 1879, he negotiated the surrender of the Zulu *amaKhosi* along the Mzinyathi border. On 12 January 1883, following the 2nd Partition of Zululand, Fynn was appointed British resident with King **Cetshwayo kaMpande**, whom Fynn had known since 1873. Fynn enjoyed a close friendship with Cetshwayo that inclined him to empathize with the restored king during the 3rd **Zulu Civil War**. But Fynn had no armed forces with which to intervene, and as the representative of the British government, he was expected to remain neutral. Cetshwayo regarded this as a betrayal. After **oNdini**, Fynn stayed with Cetshwayo in the **Nkandla Forest**

until 16 October 1883, when the fugitive king finally took refuge with the British in **Eshowe**. Fynn resumed his post at Umsinga, retiring in 1897.

**FYNNEY, FREDERICK BERNARD (c. 1840–1888).** Fynney was **Natal** government interpreter (1876–1877) and administrator of native law and special border agent, Lower Tugela Division (1878–1879). During the **Anglo-Zulu War**, he was also in command of the **Border Police** in **Colonial Defensive District** No. VI with responsibility for passing on intelligence of events in **Zululand** to the military authorities. He compiled the booklet *The Zulu Army and Zulu Headmen* (1878), which proved very influential in forming British perceptions of Zulu political organization and military capability.

## – G –

**GATLING GUN.** The American inventor Richard Jordan Gatling (1818–1903) took out a patent in 1862 for this early version of the machine gun. It came into service with the British army in 1871 and was first employed in the 2nd Asante War of 1873–1874. The British deployed a Gatling gun in combat in the open field at **Nyezane** during the **Anglo-Zulu War**, but the guns were regarded primarily as defensive weapons to be sited at prepared, all-around positions, and they were deployed in that way at **Gingindlovu** and **Ulundi**. During the 3rd **Zulu Civil War** and **uSuthu Rebellion**, they were incorporated into fortified positions but were never fired in action.

The Gatling gun was mounted on a carrier similar to that of a field gun. It could fire 200 boxer .250 rounds a minute from 10 rifle barrels (which limited overheating) rotated around a fixed central axis by a manually operated crank. The bullets were fed by gravity from a revolving upright case holding 40 cartridges, which was replaced after every four revolutions. Though highly effective up to 1,000 yards, the Gatling gun proved unreliable because of its tendency to jam, as occurred at Ulundi.

**eGAZINI PEOPLE.** The eGazini people of northwestern **Zululand** were **uSuthu** supporters in the 3rd **Zulu Civil War**. They made up part of the uSuthu army arranged in territorial units of **irregulars**

under their own *amaKhosi* that was defeated at **Msebe**. They participated in offensives in northern Zululand against the **Ngenetsheni** until the uSuthu defeat at **oNdini** put them on the defensive. *See also* CIVILIANS IN WARTIME ZULULAND.

**emGAZINI PEOPLE.** The emGazini people of northeastern **Zululand** were strong **uSuthu** supporters assigned in the 1st Partition of **Zululand** to the north of the chiefdom made over to their foe, *inkosi* **Zibhebhu kaMaphitha**. During the 3rd **Zulu Civil War** they made up the left horn of the uSuthu army routed at **Msebe**. In April 1888 during the **uSuthu Rebellion** emGazini **irregulars** rallied to King **Dinuzulu kaCetshwayo** on **Ceza**. They were part of the uSuthu chest at the battle of Ceza and of the right horn at **Ivuna**. With the crushing of the rebellion, they began to disperse home in late July. *See also* CIVILIANS IN WARTIME ZULULAND.

**emaGEBENI.** *See* VEGLAER, BATTLE OF.

**GINGINDLOVU, BATTLE OF (1879).** On 1 April 1879 during the **Anglo-Zulu War**, the **Eshowe Relief Column** under Lieutenant-General Lord **Chelmsford**, consisting of 3,240 British troops, 150 white mounted troops, 130 African mounted troops, 2,000 African levies, and 150 African scouts, marched to within a mile of the Nyezane River, just south of the burned-out **kwaGingindlovu** *iKhanda*. On a slight knoll, **John Dunn** selected the site for a wagon **laager** made about 130 yards square to accommodate the African levies and the livestock. It was surrounded by a shelter trench 15 yards in front of the wagons.

That night, Zulu forces that had been blockading **Fort Eshowe** concentrated in the vicinity of the laager. They numbered between 10,000 and 11,000 men (3,000 of them **Tsonga irregulars)** and were under the overall command of **Somopho kaZikhala**. On 2 April, they advanced to the attack, one column from across the Nyezane and another from the Misi Hill to the west. The British troops manned the laager's shelter trench two deep, and the African levies, 300 horses, and 2,280 oxen remained inside the laager. Its corners were strengthened by 9-pounder guns, **Gatling guns**, and **rocket tubes**. Marksmen were stationed on top of the wagons.

The Zulu were deployed in open order, and their skirmishers drove in the British pickets and mounted scouts. Once their two columns had enveloped the laager in a crescent that left only its eastern side free, the Zulu made repeated attempts to break through the concentrated British fire, which was not as effective as it might have been on account of the inexperience of many of the raw British troops. Chelmsford ordered a mounted sortie that proved premature and had to withdraw under the determined Zulu assault that, under the leadership of *umNtwana* **Dabulamanzi kaMpande**, particularly threatened the laager's southern face. The Zulu onslaught faltered again, and Chelmsford ordered out another mounted sortie that caused the Zulu to retreat. The British horsemen turned the Zulu withdrawal into a rout and kept up the pursuit for nearly two miles. The African levies advanced out of the laager to mop up behind the horsemen, killing all the Zulu wounded. Zulu reserves on the hills beyond the Nyezane retreated when they saw their army in flight. Fire from the 9-pounders dispersed those Zulu who tried to rally on Misi Hill. The British killed were two white officers, seven white troops, and five black troops. Nearly 500 Zulu were buried within 500 yards of the laager, and many hundreds more were found along the Zulu line of flight. It seems probable that the Zulu lost close to 1,200 men.

Chelmsford advanced the next day and relieved and evacuated the **Eshowe garrison**, clearing the way for the commencement of the 2nd Invasion of the Anglo-Zulu War. *See also* TACTICS, AFRICAN INFANTRY LEVIES; TACTICS, BRITISH INFANTRY; TACTICS, BRITISH MOUNTED TROOPS; TACTICS UP TO 1879, ZULU.

**GINGINDLOVU CAMP.** On 6 April 1879, the **Eshowe Relief Column**, when retiring after the relief of **Eshowe** during the **Anglo-Zulu War**, formed a new entrenched camp a mile to the south of the **Gingindlovu laager**. The force that had been left guarding the latter moved to the new camp on 7 April. The troops there were redesignated the 1st Brigade, 1st Division, **South African Field Force**. They left the Gingindlovu Camp on 21 April 1879 to help guard convoys and build forts along the 1st Division's line of advance during the 2nd Invasion of the Anglo-Zulu War.

**kwaGINGINDLOVU** *iKHANDA.* This small *iKhanda* of about 60 huts was established by King **Cetshwayo kaMpande** to assert his authority in the southern coastal plain of **Zululand**. In October 1878, Zulu forces mustered there to monitor that sector against possible

British attack. In January 1879, during the opening phase of the **Anglo-Zulu War**, the secondary Zulu army under *inKosi* **Godide kaNdlela** marched to confront the British No. 1 **Column** but found that the British had already burned it on 21 January. Local members of the *amaButho* associated with the burned kwaGingindlovu played their part in the blockade of **Fort Eshowe**. On 1 April, the **Eshowe Relief Column** laagered just south of its ruins, and the battle the following day was named after it.

**GINGINDLOVU LAAGER.** *See* GINGINDLOVU, BATTLE OF.

**GLYN, RICHARD THOMAS (1831–1900).** Glyn saw service in the Crimean War (1855–1856) and the Indian Mutiny (1857–1858). In 1872, he was promoted to colonel. He was posted to the **Cape** in 1875, where he served throughout the 9th **Cape Frontier War** (1877–1878). During the **Anglo-Zulu War**, he was given the command of No. 3 **Column**, but Lieutenant-General Lord **Chelmsford**, who accompanied the column, allowed him little independence of action. During the battle of **Isandlwana**, Glyn was absent with part of his force on a reconnaissance in force. He subsequently was in command of the garrison at **Rorke's Drift**, where he suffered a temporary breakdown. In May 1879, he took up command of the 1st Brigade, 2nd Division, **South African Field Force**, and he was present at **Ulundi** in command of the Infantry Brigade. He was promoted to major-general in 1882 and knighted. He retired from the army in 1887.

**GODIDE kaNDLELA (c. 1820–1883).** The son of *inKosi* **Ndlela kaSompisi**, who was King **Dingane kaSenzangakhona**'s chief *inDuna*, Godide was enrolled with the **iziNyosi** *iButho* and succeeded Ndlela as *inKosi* of the **Ntuli** people. Already an *isiKhulu* (important hereditary chief) under King **Mpande kaSenzangakhona**, Godide continued in favor under King **Cetshwayo kaMpande** and was the senior *inDuna* of the **uMxhapho** *iButho*. During the **Anglo-Zulu War**, he commanded the army defeated at **Nyezane** and retired home to the middle border in disgrace. He finally surrendered to **Clarke's Column** in August 1879. In the 1st Partition of **Zululand**, he was placed under **John Dunn** and was active in appealing for Cetshwayo's restoration. During the 3rd **Zulu Civil War**, he joined the **uSuthu** forces with his adherents and was killed at **oNdini**.

**kwaGQIKAZI** *iKHANDA*. In the early 1840s, King **Mpande kaSenzangakhona** established the first *iKhanda* of this name in the Vuna valley in northern **Zululand** to assert royal authority there. It was later reestablished in the **Mahlabathini Plain** and was burned by the British on 4 July 1879 following the battle of **Ulundi**. Its influence continued in northern Zululand, where the people originally attached to it remained stalwart **uSuthu** supporters during the 3rd **Zulu Civil War** and **uSuthu Rebellion**.

**iziGQOZA FACTION.** In the escalating succession dispute that culminated in the 2nd **Zulu Civil War**, the supporters of *umNtwana* **Mbuyazi kaMpande** (whose claims King **Mpande kaSenzangakhona** was promoting to offset those of *umNtwana* **Cetshwayo kaMpande**) came to be called the iziGqoza, or "those who drop down like water from a roof," signifying the steady trickle of support for Mbuyazi's cause. In November 1856, Mpande allocated the iziGqoza land in southeastern **Zululand** in an attempt to separate them from Cetshwayo's rival **uSuthu** faction in northern Zululand. But Cetshwayo mobilized his forces and crushed the iziGqoza at **Ndondakusuka**. He drove defeated fighting men and noncombatants alike into the swollen Thukela River in a massacre that obliterated the iziGqoza faction. *See also* CIVILIANS IN WARTIME ZULULAND.

**GRAND ARMY OF NATAL.** *See* THUKELA, BATTLE OF (1838).

**GREAT TREK.** When Great Britain formally annexed the **Cape Colony** from the Dutch in 1814, some 27,000 white colonists already lived there. These Cape colonists, derived from Dutch, Flemish, German, and French Huguenot settlers, were already beginning to develop a sense of their own "Afrikaner" identity. Between 1834 and 1840, some 15,000 of them trekked north across the Orange River into the interior of South Africa in a series of settler parties, taking with them all their portable possessions and livestock as well as black dependents and servants in numbers equal to their own. The "Great Trek," as this migration came to be called, has been subject to many interpretations. It was in part a revolt against the British government of the Cape that, while emancipating slaves and intent on establishing the idea of the equality of the races before the law, was unable to provide the settlers of the frontier with security against their black neighbors and the land and labor they required. The trek was also a continuation of a long tradition among individual white stock farmers and hunters of the Cape frontier to trek into the interior in search of grazing and game. And the recent dislocations in the hinterland (including the rise of the Zulu, **Ndebele**, and **Sotho** kingdoms), which caused the temporary depopulation of whole regions, gave these pastoralists the inviting impression of an "empty" land.

The Voortrekkers, or pioneers, as they are known today, called themselves "emigrant farmers." Modern Afrikaner nationalists argue that they had a sense of a national mission and were determined to establish their independent republics as far away as possible from British interference. They also wanted to grasp new economic possibilities following the extension of the frontier. In the interior, they displaced or incorporated the peoples living there (as had other indigenous states like the Ndebele) and replicated their loose-knit, patriarchal society as it had been before the British had interfered with their master–servant arrangements and their dominance over the black majority. Once settled in the interior, they also hoped to free themselves from the British colonial commercial network on which they still reluctantly depended for many essential commodities. They could do so only by gaining access to traders and ports on the east coast of Africa beyond the sphere of British control, like **Delagoa Bay** or **St. Lucia Bay**, and this brought their nascent republics into conflict with African states in the way, primarily the Zulu and **Swazi**.

Disunity and dissension bedeviled the Voortrekkers regarding both the direction the trek should take and its command. Several groups made for the highveld, where by the early 1850s they had established the independent republics of the **Orange Free State** and **South African Republic**. Other groups crossed the **Drakensberg** into the **Zulu kingdom** and founded their short-lived Republic of **Natalia**. For the British, the Great Trek (which the Cape authorities had failed to impede) threatened to create further instability and warfare in the interior with likely repercussions on the volatile Cape frontier. Until British victory in the **Anglo-Boer (South African) War** over the Boer republics solved this problem, the dilemma over how best to assert British control in southern Africa beyond its colonial frontiers

dominated British policy in the subcontinent. *See also* CONFED-
ERATION, SOUTH AFRICAN.

**GREYTOWN.** The township of Greytown was laid out in 1850 as the
administrative center of Umvoti County in the British Colony of **Natal**, where many Boers had remained after British annexation of their
Republic of **Natalia**. At the time of the **Anglo-Zulu War**, Greytown
was a thriving place with a rectangular grid of streets on the Boer
model, and with a population of 1,500 white inhabitants.

**GREYTOWN LAAGER.** In 1854, the **Natal** government erected a
loopholed, stone-walled **laager** in **Greytown** for the white settlers of
the district to be defended by the Umvoti **Rifle Association**. During
1877 and 1878, the laager was strengthened and improved. During
the **Anglo-Zulu War**, the settlers of Greytown and the surrounding
region in **Colonial Defensive District** No. VII took refuge there in
the panic after **Isandlwana**, and some lingered until after the relief of
**Eshowe** in early April 1879. On 2 February, a false alarm filled the
laager, and many temporarily resorted there again after the Zulu raid
at **Middle Drift** on 25 June 1879.

**GRIQUA AND MPONDO BORDERS WITH NATAL IN 1879.** In
**Natal**'s two southernmost **Colonial Defensive Districts**, Nos. IV
and V, with their tiny settler populations, there was some anxiety
in 1879 that their African neighbors over the border might use the
opportunity of the **Anglo-Zulu War** to make hostile incursions.
However, to the south of District IV, the Griqua of East Griqualand
(which had been administered by the **Cape** since 1873 and would be
annexed later in 1879) did not act. Nor did the **Mpondo** people south
of District V. King **Cetshwayo kaMpande** maintained some diplomatic contact with the Mpondo, but they were riven by succession
disputes, and the area was effectively under informal Cape control.

**GRIQUA PEOPLE.** *See* GRIQUA AND MPONDO BORDERS
WITH NATAL IN 1879.

**izinGULUBE iBUTHO.** King **Mpande kaSenzangakhona** formed
this *iButho* around 1844 from youths born about 1824. The **shield**

was white with black or red spots. It apparently was incorporated with the **uDlambedlu** *iButho* to maintain the latter's strength. It formed part of the **uSuthu** center at **Ndondakusuka** in the 2nd **Zulu Civil War**. A small contingent fought at **Nyezane** in the **Anglo-Zulu War**.

**iziGULUTSHANE** *iBUTHO*. King **Dingane kaSenzangakhona** formed this *iButho* around 1833 from youths born about 1815. The **shield** was black with white spots. In the **Voortrekker-Zulu War**, it fought at **eThaleni** and at **Ncome**, where it was part of the Zulu right horn.

**ezinGWEGWENI** *iKHANDA*. This was one of the nine *amaKhanda* in the **emaKhosini valley** burned on 26 June 1879 by **Wood's Flying Column** during the 2nd Invasion of the **Anglo-Zulu War**.

*inGXOTHA*. The most prestigious ornament the Zulu king could confer on his favorites, men and women alike, or on those who had performed distinguished service, was the *inGxotha*, or brass armband, which reached from wrist to elbow. It was split along its length for easy removal, since it was most uncomfortable to wear.

## – H –

**HAMU kaNZIBE (c. 1834–1887)**. *UmNtwana* Hamu was enrolled in the **uThulwana** *iButho*. He was King **Mpande kaSenzangakhona**'s eldest son, but through the *ukuvuza* custom he was heir not to his biological father but to Mpande's full brother, Nzibe, the senior son of Senzangakhona kaJama, who had died in 1828 and for whose spirit Mpande was "raising seed." Hamu ruled over the **Ngenetsheni people** in northwestern **Zululand** and maintained royal state at **kwaMfemfe**, his chief *umuZi*. During the 2nd **Zulu Civil War**, he fought on *umNtwana* **Cetshwayo kaMpande**'s side, but he coveted the throne and became increasingly resistant to Cetshwayo's authority. In the 1860s, the white trader **Herbert Nunn** became an adviser and supplied Hamu with **firearms** and trade goods.

A leading *isiKhulu* (hereditary chief), Hamu was prominent in the *iBandla* (royal council) on the eve of the **Anglo-Zulu War** in advocating peace and the surrender of *inKosi* **Sihayo kaXongo**'s sons to the British. During the war, Hamu feared his enemies in Zululand and, with the help of Nunn, defected to the British in March 1879 in the hope they would recognize him as king. They did not, but they rewarded him with a large chiefdom in the 1st Partition of Zululand.

After the 2nd Partition of Zululand, Hamu was placed in the restored Cetshwayo's territory and rejected his authority. Throughout the 3rd Zulu Civil War, Hamu fought against the **uSuthu**, particularly the neighboring **Buthelezi** and **abaQulusi** people, taking refuge when occasionally worsted in his strongholds near the Phongolo River. His Ngenetsheni fought at **oNdini** and joined in harrying the uSuthu. After King **Dinuzulu kaCetshwayo** struck his alliance with the Boers in May 1884, they forced Hamu to surrender in June. With the 3rd Partition of Zululand, his chiefdom was incorporated into the **New Republic**. *See also* MFEMFE *iBUTHO*.

**HARDING LAAGER.** This earthwork laager abutting the magistrate's office was erected during 1878 on the orders of the **Natal** government at the tiny village of Harding in **Colonial Defensive District No. V**. It was supplied with weapons and ammunition for the local **Rifle Association** and the detachment of **Natal Mounted Police** stationed in the village. The district was never threatened during the **Anglo-Zulu War** by its neighbors along the **Griqua and Mpondo borders**, so the laager was never manned.

**HAVELOCK, SIR ARTHUR ELIBANK (1844–1908).** Previously governor of Sierra Leone and the West African Settlements (1881) and governor of Trinidad (1884), and knighted in 1884, Havelock came to **Natal** as governor in 1886. On 19 May 1887 as an economy measure on the part of the Colonial Office, he was concurrently appointed governor of the new British Colony of **Zululand**. Havelock was a proven administrator of humanity and sense. His mistake was to accept the advice of **Sir Theophilus Shepstone** and his disciples among the Zululand officials, for it led him to confrontations with King **Dinuzulu kaCetshwayo** and the **uSuthu**. By the time he realized these policies were flawed and biased, it was too late, and the **uSuthu Rebellion** had broken out. Loath to admit that his civil administration had failed, Havelock was initially reluctant to call in military aid. When he did, he clashed with Lieutenant-General **Henry August Smyth** over the parameters of civil and military authority. He left South Africa in 1889 and served successively as governor of Ceylon, Madras, and Tasmania. *See also* CIVIL–MILITARY RELATIONS.

**HEADRING, ZULU.** *See isiCOCO.*

**HELIOGRAPH.** The heliograph was a simple instrument for instantaneous optical communication. It sent its signals by reflecting sunlight toward the recipient with a mirror mounted on a tripod, the beam being keyed on and off with a shutter or tilting mirror, thereby transmitting Morse code at the rate of up to 12 words per minute, depending on the skill of the operator. Visibility depended on the clearness of the sky and the size of the mirrors used, though under good conditions a flash could be seen from 30 miles away with the naked eye and up to 50 miles away with a telescope.

British commanders employed the Mance pattern heliograph, devised in 1869, throughout the **Anglo-Zulu War**, 3rd **Zulu Civil War**, and **uSuthu Rebellion**. Magistrates in British **Zululand** used the heliograph during the uSuthu Rebellion to relay messages from their magisterial posts to **Eshowe**, where the telegraph line ended.

**HELPMEKAAR FORT.** In early December 1878, during the buildup to the **Anglo-Zulu War**, the main depot for No. 3 **Column** was established on the heights at Helpmekaar in **Colonial Defensive District** No. I overlooking the valley of the Mzinyathi River. Three galvanized iron sheds and large huts were erected to hold the accumulating stores. No. 3 Column concentrated there in early January 1879 and moved down to **Rorke's Drift** by 9 January. The garrison left at Helpmekaar formed a strongly entrenched wagon **laager** around the stores on the night of **Isandlwana**. During the following weeks, the laager was supplemented by a strong earthwork fort that surrounded the galvanized iron commissariat sheds, the marquees protecting commissariat stores, and a hospital. Helpmekaar ceased to be an important depot with the mounting of the 2nd Invasion of the

Anglo-Zulu War. In April 1879, the bulk of its stores were transferred to **Fort Jones**. The fort at Helpmekaar continued to be garrisoned until the military post was finally broken up on 25 October 1879.

**HEMULANA kaMBANGEZELI.** A member of the Sibiya people, Hemulana was *inKosi* **Mnyamana kaNgqengelele**'s *inDuna* and one of King **Dinuzulu kaCetshwayo**'s most influential councilors. In the 3rd **Zulu Civil War**, Hemulana fought at **Msebe**, where three of his sons were killed. During the **uSuthu Rebellion**, he was a commander at **Ceza** and concerted the successful **uSuthu** strategy at **Ivuna**, where he again commanded.

**HERMANNSBURG LAAGER (FORT AHRENS).** In 1878, local Boer farmers in **Colonial Defensive District** No. VII of **Natal** subscribed to build this square, stone-walled **laager** with two opposing bastions. They took shelter there with their families from the outbreak of the **Anglo-Zulu War** in January 1879 until mid-April. They furnished a small mounted force that used the laager as their headquarters and base for patrols of the vicinity.

*HERNEUTERMES.* All Boer men, when hunting or on trek in hostile territory, carried a large sheath knife with a steel blade 7–18 inches long with a guard modeled on that of the Bowie knife. It was known as a *herneutermes* after the first of them made by the Hernhutters, or Moravian Brethren, at their mission station at Genadendal in the Western **Cape**. On 6 February 1838, when King **Dingane kaSenzangakhona** ordered the execution of **Pieter Retief** and his comrades at **uMgungundlovu**, many of the Boers, who had left their **firearms** at the gate of the *iKhanda* as protocol required, desperately fought back with their *herneutermesse* but were overpowered and killed.

**HICKS BEACH, SIR MICHAEL EDWARD (1837–1916).** Hicks Beach, who succeeded as 9th baronet in 1854, was a Conservative politician and entered Parliament in 1864. As colonial secretary (1878–1880), he inherited the plans of his predecessor, the Earl of **Carnarvon**, to push ahead with the **confederation** of South Africa. Hicks Beach was not committed to the cause of confederation and was more concerned over his government's desire to avoid costly imperial adventures and looming war in Afghanistan. Nevertheless, he proved unable to restrain **Bartle Frere**, the high commissioner in South Africa, from forcing the **Anglo-Zulu War** in order to cement confederation. In subsequent years, Hicks Beach held cabinet posts in three Conservative administrations and on his retirement from Parliament in 1906 was created 1st Viscount St. Aldwyn.

**iHLABA *iBUTHO*.** King **Dingane kaSenzangakhona** formed this *iButho* around 1837 from youths born about 1817. The **shield** was black with white spots. In the **Voortrekker-Zulu War**, it fought with the Zulu right horn at **Ncome**.

**HLABISA PEOPLE.** The pro-**uSuthu** Hlabisa people under *inKosi* Mthumbu kaMbopha were assigned by the 1st Partition of **Zululand** to the south of *inKosi* **Zibhebhu kaMaphitha**'s chiefdom and resented his rule. In June 1888 during the **uSuthu Rebellion**, when Zibhebhu was encamped at **Ivuna** with his fighting men, the Hlabisa and the **Mdletshe** people took advantage of his absence to raid **Mandlakazi** territory. After Zibhebhu's defeat at Ivuna, on 6 June the Hlabisa and the Mdletshe burned **Bangonomo**, his main *umuZi*, and went on to ravage his territory until early August, assisted by opportunistic Boers from the **South African Republic**. On 19 August, Zibhebhu struck back at the Hlabisa and Mdletshe, who withdrew toward **St. Lucia Bay** and then retaliated on 10 September. The raiding and counterraiding did not end until the British arrested Zibhebhu on 17 November 1888 and banished him from his location. *See also* CIVILIANS IN WARTIME ZULULAND.

**HLOBANE, BATTLE OF (1879).** During the **Anglo-Zulu War**, **Hlobane Mountain** was the central defensive position for the **abaQulusi people** in northwestern **Zululand** and the base for *umNtwana* **Mbilini waMswati**, the most effective leader of **irregulars** in the region. It thus formed an important military objective for Brevet Colonel **Henry Evelyn Wood** in command of No. 4 **Column** encamped at **Khambula**. To attack it would create a diversion in favor of the **Eshowe Relief Column** then beginning its advance in southeastern Zululand. Hlobane was also a tempting source for booty in the form of **cattle**, as the local Zulu had concentrated their herds there for safety.

For this raiding expedition, Wood employed only his **mounted** units, supported by African auxiliaries. They were to attack the mountain in a pincer movement. Lieutenant-Colonel **Redvers Henry Buller**'s force of 675 officers and men would go up the steep path on the eastern side of the mountain and capture cattle, while Lieutenant-Colonel **John Cecil Russell**'s force of 640 officers and men would ascend the mountain on its western side by way of Ntendeka Mountain, which was joined to Hlobane by a rocky ridge called the Devil's Pass. Wood would operate freely with his own mounted escort. What he did not know was the main Zulu army under *inKosi* **Mnyamana kaNgqengelele** had left **oNdini** on 24 March and was marching toward his camp.

Buller's force scaled the eastern slopes of Hlobane early in the morning of 28 March. Fighting through a heavy cross-fire from Zulu irregulars, it gained the summit. Wood's small party followed in its wake but suffered heavy casualties and withdrew south around the mountain toward Ntendeka. On the summit, Buller's force drove west under sniping Zulu fire across the mountain to the Devil's Pass, rounding up about 2,000 cattle as they went. When Russell's force on Ntendeka, also busy rounding up cattle, saw the Zulu army advancing across the plain from the southeast, Buller was alerted and prepared to descend with his booty by the way he had come. But the Zulu irregulars under Mbilini's command, reinforced from Mashongololo Mountain to the east, did their best to bar his path.

Buller decided to retire instead over the western side of Hlobane, but Russell's force was no longer there to support him. Alarmed at the approach of the Zulu army, Russell had withdrawn to the foot of Ntendeka, and Wood ordered him to fall back farther to Zungwini Nek, some four miles to the west. Buller's men scrambled down the precipitous Devil's Pass, harried by the Zulu and suffering many casualties. They rallied on Ntendeka and were then pursued toward Zungwini. Once the Zulu irregulars gave up the chase, Russell withdrew to Khambula with his and Buller's exhausted men. Most of the African auxiliaries were cut off in the rout, but the survivors succeeded in retaining 300 head of captured cattle.

The main Zulu army did not allow itself to be diverted from its march on Khambula, but it detached elements from its right horn to intercept British fugitives in the plain to the south of Hlobane and Ntendeka. A force of irregular horse ordered to return to Khambula that way collided with the detached Zulu *amaButho* and turned about in an attempt to escape north over the steep Itentyeka Nek between Hlobane and Mashongololo. The horsemen were intercepted by Zulu irregulars and very few broke through to reach Khambula across the plain north of Hlobane. Up to 2,000 Zulu were engaged in the battle, and their losses are unknown. Among the British, 15 officers and 79 men were killed, and well over 100 African auxiliaries. It was fortunate for Wood's reputation that his decisive victory at Khambula the following day blunted criticism of his badly bungled raid on Hlobane.

Many British exhibited considerable bravery in the rout, and the Victoria Cross was awarded to Buller of the 60th Rifles (King's Royal Rifle Corps); Major William Knox-Leet, 1st Battalion, 13th (1st Somersetshire) Prince Albert's Light Infantry; Lieutenant Edward Stevenson Browne, 1st Battalion, 24th (2nd Warwickshire) Regiment; and Lieutenant Henry Lysons and Private Edmund John Fowler of the 90th Regiment (Perthshire Volunteers Light Infantry). Corporal W. D. Vinnicombe and Trooper R. Brown of the Frontier Light Horse received the Distinguished Conduct Medal. *See also* TACTICS, AFRICAN INFANTRY LEVIES; TACTICS, BRITISH INFANTRY; TACTICS, BRITISH MOUNTED TROOPS; TACTICS UP TO 1879, ZULU.

**HLOBANE LAAGER.** On 2 May 1884, the Committee of **Dinuzulu's Volunteers**, a Boer **mercenary** group, met King **Dinuzulu kaCetshwayo** at their Hlobane **laager** to begin negotiating a military alliance. The Boers were victorious at **Tshaneni** on 5 June, ravaged the territory of the defeated **Mandlakazi** and **Ngenetsheni**, and in mid-July concentrated again in the Hlobane laager preparatory to setting up the **New Republic**.

**HLOBANE MOUNTAIN.** Hlobane is a huge, flat-topped mountain in northwestern **Zululand**. Its steep slopes culminate in a belt of sheer cliffs full of caves. Only a few viable paths lead to the summit, where springs make for good grazing for livestock. Its defensibility made it an ideal refuge for the **abaQulusi people**, whose *iKhanda*, **ebaQulusini**, was only five miles away to the northeast. During the **Anglo-Zulu War** when patrols sent out by No. 4 **Column** broke up abaQulusi concentrations on 22 and 24 January 1879 at **Zungwini Mountain** a few miles to the west, the Zulu retired up Hlobane. On 10 February, a patrol led by Lieutenant-Colonel **Redvers Henry Buller** raided Hlobane and captured many cattle. The next raid on Hlobane on 27–28 March almost ended in disaster when the British were caught up the mountain by abaQulusi irregulars and detachments from the Zulu army advancing on **Khambula**. On 29 August, **Baker Russell's Column** camped beneath Hlobane to enforce the surrender of the abaQulusi. During the 3rd **Zulu Civil War**, the abaQulusi periodically took refuge there, especially after the **uSuthu** defeat at **oNdini**. *See also* HLOBANE, BATTLE OF.

**HLOPHEKHULU MOUNTAIN.** This mountain is on the north bank of the White Mfolozi River in central **Zululand**, and its thickly wooded southeastern face falls precipitously to the river. A traditional Zulu stronghold, during the **uSuthu Rebellion** it was held by *umNtwana* **Shingana kaMpande** until stormed by the British in 1888. *See also* HLOPHEKHULU MOUNTAIN, BATTLE OF; NONKWENKWEZIYEZULU STRONGHOLD.

**HLOPHEKHULU MOUNTAIN, BATTLE OF (1888).** In June 1888 during the **uSuthu Rebellion**, *umNtwana* **Shingana kaMpande** assembled a force of uSuthu on **Hlophekhulu Mountain** in central **Zululand** in support of King **Dinuzulu kaCetshwayo**'s men on **Ceza Mountain** and raided British loyalists in the vicinity as well as the British lines of communication. In late June, *inKosi* Ngobozana's Mpungose people began to reinforce Shingana's men, bringing their number up to about 1,100. On 28 June, Lieutenant-General **Henry Augustus Smyth** assumed command of the British troops in Zululand and determined to clear Hlophekhulu of the **uSuthu** and Mpungose.

On the morning of 2 July 1888, British **Dragoons** and **Mounted Infantry** and 141 **Mounted Basutos** from the British camp at

**Nkonjeni** under the command of Colonel **Henry Sparke Stabb**, representing the military authority, supported 87 **Zululand Police** under Commandant **George Mansel**, representing the civil government of Zululand. Accompanied by the resident magistrate of Ndwandwe, **Richard Hallowes Addison**, with a warrant for Singana's arrest, they successfully stormed the mountain in skirmishing order. They were supported on the flanks by 1,400 African auxiliaries and levies that also drove off some **Biyela** people under *inKosi* **Somopho kaZikhala** camped close to the mountain. The **uSuthu** dislodged from the crest of Hlophekhulu were forced down to a narrow strip of land between the mountain and the White Mfolozi River, where their families and **cattle** were sheltering. In the hand-to-hand fighting and general rout, the uSuthu lost their cattle to their pursuers and abandoned the mountain entirely. The uSuthu casualties were heavy, with between 200 and 300 killed. The British lost two white officers, five of the African mounted men, and 55 of the African levies. The capture of Hlophekhulu restored British control in central Zululand and secured their lines of supply to Nkonjeni. This was the last major engagement of the uSuthu Rebellion. *See also* STRATEGY, BRITISH; STRATEGY, ZULU; TACTICS, AFRICAN INFANTRY LEVIES; TACTICS, BRITISH INFANTRY; TACTICS, BRITISH MOUNTED TROOPS; TACTICS IN 1880s, ZULU.

**HLUBI kaMOTA MOLIFE.** Hlubi kaMota Molife and his Sotho-speaking Tlokwa adherents migrated over the **Drakensberg** in 1867 to the Weenen-Estcourt area in northwestern **Natal**. Over the years, they proved loyal allies of the colonial authorities, and Hlubi repeatedly raised military units of good quality, which he personally led on campaign. They supported the Natal government during the **Langalibalele Rebellion**, and again during the **Anglo-Zulu War**. In the 1st Partition of **Zululand**, Hlubi was appointed chief of the strategic territory at the confluence of the Thukela and Mzinyathi rivers. As a result of the 2nd Partition of Zululand, Hlubi's territory fell into the **Reserve Territory**. His men continued loyally to support the British during the 3rd **Zulu Civil War**, as they did again during the **uSuthu Rebellion**. *See also* HLUBI'S TROOP (MOUNTED BASUTOS); MOUNTED BASUTOS.

**HLUBI PEOPLE.** *See* LANGALIBALELE REBELLION.

**HLUBI'S TROOP (MOUNTED BASUTOS).** *InKosi* **Hlubi kaMota Molife** of the Tlokwa people had served effectively with Major **Anthony William Durnford** during the **Langalibalele Rebellion** in 1873, and in December 1878 he raised a troop of **irregular** horse from his adherents for the **Natal Native Mounted Contingent**. During the **Anglo-Zulu War**, it formed part of No. 2 **Column** and fought at **Isandlwana**. In the reorganization of February 1879, it became a troop in the **Natal Native Horse** and joined No. 4 **Column**, subsequently **Wood's Flying Column**. It fought at **Hlobane** and **Khambula**, the reconnaissance in force across the White Mfolozi and Ulundi. With the breakup of Wood's Flying Column in late July, the troop returned home and was disbanded.

**HMS *ACTIVE*.** A 3,078-ton, 270-foot corvette built of iron and sheathed wood and completed in 1873, the *Active* was stationed at the Cape of Good Hope during the **Anglo-Zulu War**. On 19 November 1878, it landed a **Naval Brigade** at **Durban** under Commander Captain H. J. F. Campbell consisting of 170 sailors and **Royal Marine Light Infantry**.

**HMS *BOADICEA*.** A 3,913-ton, iron-built corvette completed in 1877 during the **Anglo-Zulu War**, on March 1879 the *Boadicea* landed a **Naval Brigade** of 200 men under Captain T. W. Richards at **Durban**. On 11 June, the body of **Prince Louis Napoleon Bonaparte**, who had been killed at the **Tshotshosi River**, was embarked on her for conveyance to **Cape Town**. *See also* HMS *ORONTES*.

**HMS *ORONTES*.** A troopship that had landed drafts in **Durban** on 4 June 1879 for all the British battalions and regiments fighting in the **Anglo-Zulu War**, the *Orontes* was specially prepared in **Cape Town** to take on the body of **Prince Louis Napoleon Bonaparte** from **HMS *Boadicea*** on 15 June for conveyance to England for burial. The *Orontes* anchored at Spithead on 10 July, and the coffin was transferred to the Admiralty yacht *Enchantress*. The prince was buried in the mortuary chapel at Chislehurst on 12 July.

**HMS *SHAH*.** Completed in 1873, this 5,700-ton frigate was built of iron and cased in teak. On learning of **Isandlwana** during the **Anglo-Zulu War**, it sailed from St. Helena with No. 8 Battery, 7th Brigade, **Royal Artillery**, and a company of the 88th **Regiment** (Connaught Rangers). The *Shah* arrived in **Durban** on 6 March 1879 and with these reinforcements also landed a **Naval Brigade** of 400 men under Commander J. Brackenbury. Later in the Anglo-Zulu War, the *Shah* with General **Garnet Joseph Wolseley** and his staff aboard was forced to remain at the anchorage off **Port Durnford** during 2 and 3 July 1879 because they could not be landed through the heavy surf. The ship returned to Durban the next day, and Wolseley was forced to join the 1st Division, **South African Field Force**, by land.

**HMS *TAMAR*.** This 4,857-ton, iron-built troopship was built in 1863. During the **Anglo-Zulu War**, it brought the 57th (West Middlesex) **Regiment** from Ceylon to **Durban** on 11 March 1879. When the *City of Paris* ran aground entering Simon's Bay on 23 March, the 2nd Battalion, 21st Regiment (Royal Scots Fusiliers), was transferred to the *Tamar*. On the way to Durban with them, the *Tamar* rescued the shipwrecked troops on the *Clyde*.

**HMS *TENEDOS*.** This 1,755-ton corvette was built of wood in 1870. On the eve of the **Anglo-Zulu War**, it sailed from the North American and West Indies station and on 6 January 1879 landed reinforcements at **Durban** for a **Naval Brigade** consisting of 50 sailors and **Royal Marine Light Infantry**.

**HORSES.** Horses were not indigenous to southern Africa. The Boers and other South African colonials generally rode the Cape Horse or *Boereperd*, a distinct breed that was a cross between horses imported to the **Cape** from Europe and Indonesia during the rule of the Dutch East India Company. They were accustomed to the local terrain, could survive by grazing the veld, and had overcome the endemic horse (or stallion) sickness, a disease caused by the trypanosome parasite injected by the bite of the tsetse fly. An even hardier variant of horse was the Basuto Pony. These tough little horses were ideal for patrolling and skirmishing and were used by Boer **commandos**

(militia) and by all units of British **irregular cavalry**, as well as by **mounted infantry**.

British cavalry chargers found it very difficult to adjust to local conditions in **Zululand**. Not only did they have to recoup after the long sea voyage, but they would not graze and had to be fed on special forage out of the nose-bags they were accustomed to. They also found it difficult going in the local terrain and were very susceptible to horse sickness. Nevertheless, they were schooled to charge in battle with superb discipline. During the **Anglo-Zulu War**, they showed their worth at **Ulundi**.

The Zulu first began to acquire horses in the 1860s from white traders. Their price made horses more of a status symbol for rich *amaKhosi* (especially those with developed trading contacts with **Natal**) than a viable addition to the Zulu military. During the **Anglo-Zulu War**, some leaders regularly went mounted, and *inKosi* **Zibhebhu kaMaphitha** skillfully deployed small bodies of horsemen as scouts and skirmishers, most notably against the British **White Mfolozi reconnaissance in force**. Zibhebhu used mounted riflemen to great effect during the 3rd **Zulu Civil War** in conjunction with white mounted **mercenaries**. *See also* QUARTER IN BATTLE; TACTICS, BRITISH MOUNTED TROOPS; TACTICS IN 1880s, ZULU.

**HOSPITALS IN ANGLO-ZULU WAR.** *See* ARMY HOSPITAL CORPS; ARMY MEDICAL DEPARTMENT; BEARER CORPS; NURSES, BRITISH.

**HOWICK LAAGER.** During the **Anglo-Zulu War**, on learning of **Isandlwana**, townspeople of the village of Howick in **Colonial Defensive District** No. III in the **Natal** midlands built this stone **laager** adjoining Ford's Hotel to defend the government armory. It was never used.

**HULETT'S STOCKADE.** In late 1878, J. Liege Hulett, a prominent sugar planter on the **Natal** north coast, set about fortifying his estate at Kearsney in **Colonial Defensive District** No. VI with temporary works as a place of refuge for local farmers and their indentured Indian laborers during the coming **Anglo-Zulu War**. The Natal government saw Hulett's stockade as a place to which the **Border Guard** might fall back if attacked by the Zulu but did not supply it with arms or ammunition. It never came under threat during the war.

– I –

**IRREGULAR CAVALRY (IRREGULAR HORSE).** During 19th-century campaigns in southern Africa, mounted troops were necessary for reconnaissance, vedette (sentinel) duties, patrols, and raids. Regular cavalry was most effective when shock action turned the enemy's retreat into a rout, but irregular cavalry was generally more useful because they operated as **mounted infantry**, combining the horseman's speed and range with the infantryman's firepower. They fought dismounted except when in pursuit. During the **Anglo-Zulu War**, units of irregular horse maintained by the military authorities (as opposed to the **Natal Mounted Volunteers** maintained by the colonial government) were raised from white colonials (including many foreign nationals) living in the **Cape** and Transvaal. Most of these troopers were already well practiced as mounted infantry. African units of irregular horse (the **Natal Native Mounted Contingent** and the **Natal Native Horse**) were also raised in **Natal** for the Anglo-Zulu War. During the 3rd **Zulu Civil War** and the **uSuthu Rebellion**, units of African irregular horse were again raised for service in **Zululand**.

**IRREGULARS, ZULU.** During the time of the **Zulu kingdom**, irregulars, not incorporated into the *iButho* system, usually supported a Zulu army operating in their locality, and they sometimes took full part in the battle. For example, during the reign of King **Shaka kaSenzangakhona**, the iziYendane (who were tributary people from south of the Thukela River or from the western marches of the Zulu kingdom, and who were not part of a regular *iButho*) guarded the royal **cattle** posts and often took part in fighting. During the **Anglo-Zulu War**, the **Kubheka** people, **Mbilini waMswati**'s adherents, and **abaQulusi** irregulars played a major part in the campaign in northwestern **Zululand**. On the coast, thousands of **Tsonga** irregulars took part in the blockade of **Eshowe** and the battle of **Gingindlovu**.

During the 3rd **Zulu Civil War** and the **uSuthu Rebellion**, when the *iButho* system had largely broken down, regular *amaButho* were increasingly replaced by territorially based irregulars like the abaQulusi or **emGazini**, or by the local followings of particular *amaKhosi*.

**ISANDLWANA, BATTLE OF (1879).** The battle of Isandlwana in the **Anglo-Zulu War** was the greatest Zulu victory over the forces of colonialism. It was also one of the heaviest defeats suffered by British troops during the **small wars** of the Victorian era. Early in the morning of 22 January 1879, Lieutenant-General Lord **Chelmsford** marched out of the camp of No. 3 **Column** at the eastern base of **Isandlwana Mountain** to support a force under Major **John George Dartnell** operating about 10 miles to the southeast. This left a depleted garrison under Lieutenant-Colonel **Henry Burmester Pulleine** to hold the camp.

Later that morning, when a Zulu force was reported approaching, Pulleine recalled most of the pickets and formed up the troops in front of the camp. After an hour, when no attack seemed to threaten, the troops fell out, and Brevet Colonel **Anthony William Durnford** reinforced the camp on Chelmsford's order with 500 men from No. 2 **Column**, bringing the garrison up to 67 officers and 1,707 men (about half of whom were African levies). Durnford assumed command of the camp and moved out northeastward to intercept a Zulu force reportedly threatening Chelmsford's rear. About midday, one of his mounted patrols stumbled upon the Zulu army of nearly 24,000 men under *inKosi* **Ntshingwayo kaMahole** and *inKosi* **Mavumengwana kaNdlela** concealed in the Ngwebeni valley only nine miles from the camp, which they had reached undetected by British patrols in the early hours of 22 January.

Without **ritual preparation**, and in relative disorder, most of the Zulu army were stung into action and began their advance on the camp along the Nyoni ridge. A strong reserve of about 3,000 men kept its discipline and followed at a distance on the Zulu right flank. The British formed an extended skirmishing line about half a mile in advance of the camp, both to command the dead ground and to support Durnford's horsemen and other detached units as they fell back before the Zulu. The Zulu chest was pinned down by British fire, but the horns extended to outflank the British line and raced around to enter the rear of the camp.

Realizing they were being enveloped, the British fell back on their camp, losing all cohesion in hand-to-hand fighting with the Zulu. Though harried, a few mounted men, including Lieutenant **Teignmouth Melvill**, who was attempting to save the queen's **color** of the 24th (2nd Warwickshire) **Regiment**, broke southwestward through the Zulu encirclement to escape over the Mzinyathi River at **Sothondose's Drift**. The Zulu were soon in command of the camp. Many of the British infantry conducted a fighting retreat in the same direction as the mounted fugitives but were all cut off and killed before they reached the Manzimnyama stream 1.5 miles away. The Zulu pillaged the camp and retired at nightfall when Chelmsford and his force finally marched back in battle order. No fewer than 1,000 Zulu died in the battle. The British and colonial troops lost 52 officers and 739 men, and the **Natal Native Contingent** lost 67 white noncommissioned officers and close to 500 men.

Private Samuel Wassall of the 80th Regiment (Staffordshire Volunteers) was awarded the Victoria Cross. There was no provision in 1879 for the medal's posthumous award, but in 1907 the regulation was changed and the families of Melvill and Lieutenant **Nevill Josiah Aylmer Coghill**, both of the 1st Battalion of the 24th Regiment, were sent the decoration. *See also* ISANDLWANA CAMPAIGN (1879); TACTICS, AFRICAN INFANTRY LEVIES; TACTICS, BRITISH INFANTRY; TACTICS, BRITISH MOUNTED TROOPS; TACTICS UP TO 1879, ZULU.

**ISANDLWANA, BURIAL OF BRITISH DEAD AT.** For several months, the bodies of the **British troops** killed at **Isandlwana** in the **Anglo-Zulu War** lay unburied where they had fallen, much to the indignation of British soldiers and colonists alike. Major Wilsone Black, who was stationed at **Rorke's Drift**, led two hurried patrols to the battlefield on 14 March and 15 May 1879, but his men were too few in number to carry out burials or defend themselves against possible Zulu attack. Pressure mounted on Lieutenant-General Lord **Chelmsford** to send a larger force to Isandlwana to perform the task, but the general was not prepared to take the risk before he had sufficient cavalry for prior reconnaissance. British reinforcements continued to come in for the 2nd Invasion of the war, and on 19 May, Chelmsford dispatched a force from **Landman's Drift** consisting of the **Cavalry Brigade** under Major-General **Frederick Marshall** and five companies of the 2nd Battalion, 24th (2nd Warwickshire) **Regiment**. On 21 May, the force reached Isandlwana and, without any Zulu interference, went about its gruesome task of burying soldiers in shallow graves marked by cairns. It retired that night to Rorke's Drift with 40 unbroken wagons found on the battlefield.

Colonel **Richard Thomas Glyn** of the 24th Regiment had requested that the corpses of the men of his regiment be left undisturbed until they could be buried by their comrades in the presence of both battalions. Marshall honored the request, but it was not until 20 June that detachments of the 24th Regiment could be released from garrison duty at Rorke's Drift to begin to perform the burial with the assistance of other troops stationed there. Over the next few months, patrols continued to find and bury bodies, also reburying in seemly fashion some of those hastily interred in May and June. Only in March 1880 could a party of the 60th Regiment (King's Royal Rifle Corps) report that the task had been completed.

**ISANDLWANA CAMPAIGN (1879).** On 20 January 1879 during the opening days of the **Anglo-Zulu War**, the invading British No. 3 **Column** encamped at **Isandlwana Mountain**. The position was difficult to defend, but as Lieutenant-General Lord **Chelmsford** considered the camp only temporary, no attempt was made to fortify it. The same day, the Zulu army bivouacked at Siphezi Mountain, nearly 13 miles east of Isandlwana, but the British remained unaware of their presence. Chelmsford believed that a local Zulu force to the southeast under *inKosi* **Matshana kaMondisa** posed a threat to his line of supply. On 21 January, he accordingly sent out 150 colonial mounted troopers and about 1,600 men of the **Natal Native Contingent** (NNC) under Major **John George Dartnell** to reconnoiter. Matshana retired eastward before them, and that night Dartnell bivouacked on the Hlazakazi Heights about 10 miles from the camp. That same night, the main Zulu army moved northwest in small, undetected detachments to the Ngwebeni valley, about nine miles northeast of Isandlwana.

About midnight, there was a panic among the NNC on Hlazakazi, and Dartnell requested support. Chelmsford moved out of camp early on 22 January with about half the garrison under Colonel **Richard Thomas Glyn** to reinforce Dartnell. During the morning, Matshana's men skirmished with the British on the Phindo Heights and withdrew steadily northeast toward Siphezi, drawing the British after them, away from the camp and its depleted garrison under Lieutenant-Colonel **Henry Burmester Pulleine**.

Chelmsford received a message from Pulleine that the Zulu were advancing on the camp, but the general and his staff thought the camp could be in no danger, so they rode off to reconnoiter the column's next campsite near the Mangeni River. Chelmsford was out of communication, and further messages that the camp was under attack failed to find him or were discounted. When Chelmsford finally moved back toward Isandlwana to investigate, he learned that the camp had fallen. He ordered all the troops operating in the area to concentrate, which they eventually were able to do three miles east of Isandlwana. Chelmsford advanced on the camp in the dark in battle formation, and the Zulu looting it retired to their bivouac in the Ngwebeni valley. Chelmsford's men bivouacked among the dead at Isandlwana and withdrew before light next morning toward **Rorke's Drift** to regroup in **Natal**. *See also* ISANDLWANA, BATTLE OF (1879).

**ISANDLWANA MOUNTAIN.** In the Zulu language, Isandlwana means "something like a little house," which is how the Zulu perceived the distinctive mountain in southern **Zululand** at the base of which the Zulu army overran the camp of No. 3 **Column** during the **Anglo-Zulu War**. To the British, the mountain resembled the sphinx that, by sinister chance, was portrayed on the badge of the 24th (2nd Warwickshire) **Regiment** garrisoning the camp. *See also* ISANDLWANA, BATTLE OF (1879).

**ISANDLWANA, SAVING THE BRITISH COLORS AT.** To lose a **color** (regimental flag) to the enemy was the ultimate disgrace for a British regiment. When No. 3 **Column** invaded **Zululand** in the **Anglo-Zulu War**, the 24th (2nd Warwickshire) **Regiment** left its green regimental color (with its 12 battle honors) at **Helpmekaar**

and marched with the queen's color only. The color was in the camp during the battle of **Isandlwana**. Lieutenant-Colonel **Henry Burmester Pulleine**, who was in charge of the stricken camp, apparently instructed the adjutant of the 1st Battalion, 24th Regiment, Lieutenant **Teignmouth Melvill**, to save the queen's color. Melvill, who was mounted, carried the color down the **Fugitives' Trail** as far as the swollen Mzinyathi River, where he was swept downstream under Zulu fire. He lost his grip on the color and it was carried away. Melvill reached the **Natal** bank with the aid of Lieutenant **Nevill Josiah Aylmer Coghill**, but both were overtaken and killed by the Zulu. On 4 February, Major Wilsone Black of the 2nd Battalion, 24th Regiment, accompanied by a few of the mounted officers of the disbanded 3rd Regiment, **Natal Native Contingent**, stationed at **Rorke's Drift**, patrolled down the Natal bank of the Mzinyathi River from Rorke's Drift and found not only the bodies of Melvill and Coghill but also the lost color wedged into rocks in the river. The following morning the color was trooped in front of an emotional general parade at Helpmekaar, where two companies of the 1st Battalion, 24th Regiment, were in garrison. Battle honors were not usually awarded for defeats, but on this occasion Queen Victoria, who later inspected the recovered color, made an exception.

**IVUNA (NDUNU HILL), BATTLE OF (1888).** British authority in northern parts of the Colony of **Zululand** collapsed following the debacle on **Ceza Mountain** during the uSuthu Rebellion. The **uSuthu** under King **Dinuzulu kaCetshwayo** were consequently able to raid their opponents with impunity from their fastness on Ceza. They resolved to attack their archenemy, *inKosi* **Zibhebhu kaMaphitha**, who had been encamped since 31 May 1888 with about 800 of his **Mandlakazi** forces on Ndunu Hill in support of the resident magistrate of Ndwandwe District, **Richard Hallowes Addison**. The Mandlakazi camp was 900 yards east of the **Ivuna Fort**, held by only 50 **Zululand Police**. Huddled for protection from uSuthu raids 900 yards south of the fort next to the Mbile stream were *umNtwana* **Ziwedu kaMpande**'s adherents with their **cattle**.

On the night of 22 June 1888, about 4,000 uSuthu led by Dinuzulu conducted a night march from Ceza and soon after daybreak on 23

June took the Mandlakazi by surprise. The uSuthu attacked in traditional formation, their horns outflanking the outnumbered Mandlakazi, with the right horn cutting off their retreat to the fort. The uSuthu deliberately did not attack the fort, but the Zululand Police inside did its best to support the Mandlakazi with covering fire. The uSuthu pursued the routed Mandlakazi for five miles to the Mona River, rounding up all their cattle and those of Ziwedu's adherents, who were hiding along the Mbile's banks. The uSuthu then retired to Ceza with their booty. A mounted patrol of the Zululand Police succeeded in recapturing several hundred cattle. Nearly 300 Mandlakazi and seven of Ziwedu's adherents died in the battle, with between 25 and 30 uSuthu, some by fire from the fort. Believing Ivuna now to be untenable, on 24 June the British evacuated the magistrate, garrison, and Mandlakazi survivors to **Nkonjeni**. *See also* CIVILIANS IN WARTIME ZULULAND; TACTICS IN 1880s, ZULU.

**IVUNA CAMP.** During January 1888 and again in mid-May, British cavalry moved forward temporarily from their base at **Nkonjeni** to a camp near the **Ivuna Fort** to overawe the disaffected **uSuthu** and dissuade them from taking up their arms against the British administration. *See also* DRAGOONS, 6TH (INNISKILLING).

**IVUNA FORT.** The magisterial post of the Ndwandwe District of British **Zululand** at Ivuna consisted of the magistrate's office, a **heliograph** station, and the adjoining fort. The circular earthwork fort with its loopholed, sandbagged parapet surrounded by a ditch was constructed in late 1887 and early 1888. Inside were huts for the small garrison of **Zululand Police** and a mess house for the white officers. During the **uSuthu Rebellion**, when on 23 June 1888 the **uSuthu** routed the **Mandlakazi** camped nearby on Ndunu Hill in the battle of Ivuna, they avoided attacking the fort, even though fired upon. British troops from **Nkonjeni** evacuated the fort the following day. On 7 August 1888, the **Coastal Column** and **Martin's Flying Column** rendezvoused at the abandoned Ivuna Fort preparatory to their joint advance to the coast on 18 August. On 27 August 1888, the magistrate, **Richard Hallowes Addison**, reoccupied the post with the Zululand Police.

**IXOPO LAAGER.** There were plans in late 1878 to build a sod **laager** at Stuartstown, the seat of the Ixopo magistracy in **Natal Colonial Defensive District** No. IV, but nothing had been done by the time of **Isandlwana** during the **Anglo-Zulu War**. An earthwork was then hastily thrown up at the magistrate's office and the Wesleyan chapel, but it was never manned because no attack by the neighboring Griqua materialized.

**IXOPO MOUNTED RIFLES.** This was the only corps of the **Natal Mounted Volunteers** that was not called out for active service in the **Anglo-Zulu War**. Instead, it remained in **Colonial Defensive District** No. IV to protect the southern border of **Natal** against a possible attack by the Griqua, which never occurred.

**IXOPO NATIVE CONTINGENT.** By February 1879 during the **Anglo-Zulu War**, the **Natal** colonial authorities had raised all the African levies they could from **Colonial Defensive Districts** I, VII, and VI and had to augment them with levies drawn from districts to the south. The Ixopo Native Contingent was raised in District IV and consisted of about 500 mounted men and about 800 infantry led by white officers under the command of Captain R.W.I. Walker. In March, it was stationed at strategic defensive positions in District VII above the Thukela valley. In May, it constructed and garrisoned the **Wolf Trap Fort**, and it took part in the transborder raid of 20 May. In June, after the Zulu raid at **Middle Drift**, it built and garrisoned **Fort Cross** and **Fort Liddle**. In late August, it returned home and was disbanded. Throughout its service, its discipline and morale were poor. It was issued with a number of **rifles**, was organized along traditional lines instead of British military ones, and was identified by a gray band with an orange stripe worn around the arm.

## – J –

**JANTZE'S (JANTJE'S) NATIVE HORSE.** Chief Mqundana (Jantze) of the Ximba people in southwestern Natal had supported the Boers of the Republic of **Natalia** against King **Dingane kaSenzan-**

**gakhona** and had served with Major **Anthony William Durnford** during the **Langalibalele Rebellion**. He was eager to participate in the **Anglo-Zulu War**, and his troop of **irregular** horse was mustered into the **Natal Native Mounted Contingent** and attached in December 1878 to No. 2 **Column**. They remained at **Ntunjambili** (Kranskop) in **Colonial Defensive District** No. VII when the rest of the Mounted Contingent reinforced No. 3 Column at **Isandlwana**, and they formed part of the garrison at **Fort Cherry**. A second troop was raised in early March, and the squadron joined the **Eshowe Relief Column** and fought at **Gingindlovu**. After the relief of **Eshowe**, the squadron joined the 1st Division, **South African Field Force**, in its advance to **Port Durnford**. On the breakup of the 2nd Division in late July, it served with **Clarke's Column** during its march back to **Natal** and was disbanded in September.

## – K –

**KAFFRARIAN RIFLES.** Commandant Felix Schermbrucker, who had originally come to the **Cape** in 1856 with the British German Legion, raised a force of **irregulars** and African levies in the 9th **Cape Frontier War**. In October 1878, Lieutenant-General Lord **Chelmsford** requested Schermbrucker to raise a force of infantry volunteers from the **Eastern Cape**, the majority of them of German stock. They joined No. 4 **Column** in December and proceeded to **Luneburg**, where they garrisoned the **laager** and **Fort Clery**. Brevet Colonel **Henry Evelyn Wood** was short of mounted men for his column, and in February 1879 marched Schermbrucker's 40 men to the **Khambula** camp, where they were mounted. Part of the unit fought at **Hlobane** in Lieutenant-Colonel **John Cecil Russell**'s force and then at Khambula. On 30 April, their period of service expired, and most of the men returned home. Schermbrucker returned to Luneburg with the few men who remained to help protect the region. The unit was then known as Schermbrucker's Horse, and it disbanded in September. The uniform was of black corduroy with a white puggaree around the wideawake hat. The unit was armed with **Martini-Henry rifles**.

**oKATHONGWENI STRONGHOLD.** This was the stronghold in the **Nkandla Forest** of the pro-**uSuthu** *inKosi* **Godide kaNdlela** of the **Ntuli**. On 22 May 1884, during the 3rd **Zulu Civil War**, the **Mounted Basutos** drove out the Ntuli in the campaign to reassert the colonial administration's control over the **Reserve Territory**.

**KHAKI UNIFORM, BRITISH.** The British began to adopt khaki for uniforms in India during the Indian Mutiny of 1857–1859, though its reception throughout the army was slow and reluctant. In South Africa, after the military disasters in the 1st **Boer War** against the rebel Boer marksmen, the British army was committed to fighting in future in khaki. Operations in **Zululand** during the 3rd **Zulu Civil War** and the **uSuthu Rebellion** proved the exception, as it was believed that with the memory of the **Anglo-Zulu War** fresh in Zulu minds, the moral effect of wearing scarlet would outweigh the negligible danger from indifferent Zulu marksmen. In the event, the British troops skirmishing in Zululand in 1888 were the last in the British army to fight in scarlet. In 1897, khaki was adopted as service wear on all overseas postings. *See also* DRESS, BRITISH ARMY.

**KHAMBULA, BATTLE OF (1879).** The fortified base at Khambula of No. 4 **Column**, operating during the **Anglo-Zulu War** in northwestern **Zululand** under Brevet Colonel **Henry Evelyn Wood**, consisted of a wagon **laager** connected to an earthwork redoubt (**Fort Khambula**) and a smaller **cattle** laager. At midday on 29 March 1879, the advancing Zulu army of about 20,000 men (the veterans of the Zulu victory at **Isandlwana** supported by the **abaQulusi** *iButho* and local **irregulars**) under the command of *inKosi* **Mnyamana kaNgqengelele** halted four miles southeast of the camp that was held by 2,086 troops, 132 of them African. Aware of the danger of attacking entrenched positions, King **Cetshwayo kaMpande** had instructed Mnyamana to draw the British into the open by threatening their line of supply, but the younger *amaButho* insisted on an immediate, direct assault. The Zulu army deployed with the intention of enveloping Khambula, but the right horn began an unsupported advance from the north, drawn on by mounted troops sent forward by Wood, and was repulsed. The Zulu were consequently unable to complete their envelopment of the camp, whose northern and western salients remained unthreatened, thus enabling the British to concentrate against the main Zulu attack which unfolded from the south.

The Zulu drove the British from the cattle laager and threatened the wagon laager. Several British companies then sortied and drove the Zulu back at bayonet point, and the Zulu abandoned their assault from the south. Over the next two hours, they renewed the attack, first from the east and then from the northeast, but were repeatedly beaten back. When the Zulu attack slackened off, British infantry sortied once more, supported by the mounted troops. The exhausted Zulu were unable to rally, and their retirement turned into a rout. The mounted troops relentlessly pursued them eastward until night fell. The British lost 28 killed, the Zulu over 1,000. The fighting spirit of the Zulu army never recovered from this crushing defeat that marked the turning point in the war.

Sergeant-Major Learda, Natal Native Horse, and Sergeant E. Quigley and Private A. Page of the 1st Battalion, 13th (1st Somersetshire) Prince Albert's Light Infantry, were awarded the Distinguished Conduct Medal. *See also* TACTICS, BRITISH INFANTRY; TACTICS, BRITISH MOUNTED TROOPS; TACTICS UP TO 1879, ZULU.

**KHAMBULA CAMP.** *See* FORT KHAMBULA.

*iKHANDA.* The *amaKhanda*, or military homesteads, scattered across **Zululand** served as the centers of royal authority in the far-flung districts of the kingdom and were presided over by representatives of the king in the form of members of the royal family or trusted *izinDuna* (royal officers). When serving the king, an *iButho* (regiment) was stationed at an *iKhanda*. These homesteads ranged from one at **oNdini** with nearly 1,500 *izinDlu* (huts) to small ones a tenth that size. Because of the materials of construction, *amaKhanda* were very susceptible to damage by fire. All were similar in layout. At the upper end was the *isiGodlo*, or royal enclosure, where the king or the king's representative lived, with the members of his or her household. From either side of the *isiGodlo* swept two wings of huts, or *izinHlangothi*, housing the *amaButho* and surrounding the large, elliptical parade ground. At the upper end of the parade ground, in front of the *isiGodlo*, was a **cattle** enclosure, or *isiBaya*, sacred to the king. There his councilors would consult, and he would perform the required rituals or ceremonies.

Nearly half the *amaKhanda* were concentrated in the valley of the White Mfolozi River in the heart of the kingdom; the rest were widely dispersed as regional centers of royal influence and mobilization points for cadets and local elements of the *amaButho*. As centers of royal power, they were always prime military objectives of enemies, whether in the **Voortrekker-Zulu War** or the **Anglo-Zulu War**. In 1838, the Zulu themselves set fire to three major *amaKhanda* in the **emaKhosini valley** to forestall the advancing Boers. In 1879, the British burned all 13 central *amaKhanda* and 10 of the 14 regional ones. On his restoration following the 2nd Partition of Zululand, King **Cetshwayo kaMpande** started rebuilding the *amaKhanda* in the **Mahlabathini Plain**, though on a smaller scale. They were still incomplete when they were destroyed again in 1883 during the 3rd **Zulu Civil War** and were never revived.

**uKHANDEMPEMVU *iBUTHO*.** *See* uMCIJO *iBUTHO*.

**kwaKHANDEMPEMVU *iKHANDA*.** This *iKhanda* was in the **Mahlabathini Plain**, where the **uMcijo *iButho*** was stationed. It was one of the *amaKhanda* burned by the British following the battle of **Ulundi** in the **Anglo-Zulu War**.

**kwaKHANGELA *iKHANDA*.** Originally established by King **Dingane kaSenzangakhona**, this was one of the nine *amaKhanda* in the **emaKhosini valley** burned on 26 June 1879 by **Wood's Flying Column** during the 2nd Invasion of the **Anglo-Zulu War**.

**emaKHENI *iKHANDA*.** In the 18th century, Ndaba kaPhunga, the *inKosi* of the then obscure Zulu people, built an *umuZi* (homestead) in the **emaKhosini valley**. It was used by his grandson, *inKosi* Senzangakhona kaJama, whose son, King **Mpande kaSenzangakhona**, rebuilt it as an *iKhanda*. Its name meant the "Perfumery" because it was here the king and his household were periodically anointed with sweet herbs. In August 1873, **Cetshwayo kaMpande** was proclaimed king there by the Zulu people prior to **Theophilus Shepstone**'s coronation of him. EmaKheni was one of the nine *amaKhanda* in the emaKhosini valley burned on 26 June 1879 by **Wood's Flying Column** during the 2nd Invasion of the **Anglo-Zulu War**.

**esiKHLEBHENI** *iKHANDA*. *InKosi* Senzangakhona kaJama built this *iKhanda* close to the **kwaNobamba** *umuZi* of his father, *inKosi* Jama kaNdaba, in the **emaKhosini valley**. It is still hallowed as the place where Senzangakhona was buried. This *iKhanda* was restored by his royal successors and presided over by Langazana, Senzangakhona's fourth wife. King **Dingane kaSenzangakhona** placed the *iNkatha* there for safekeeping. It was one of the nine *amaKhanda* in the emaKhosini valley burned on 26 June 1879 by **Wood's Flying Column** during the 2nd Invasion of the **Anglo-Zulu War**. Men of the **uNokhenke** and **uMxhapho** *amaButho* stationed there retired when they came under fire from Wood's 9-pounder guns. They abandoned the *iNkatha* to the flames, and its loss was an enormous symbolic blow to the Zulu.

**uKHOKHOTHI** *iBUTHO*. King **Dingane kaSenzangakhona** formed this *iButho* around 1838 from youths born about 1818. At **Ncome** during the **Voortrekker-Zulu War**, the inexperienced *iButho* was armed only with **knobbed sticks** and was kept in reserve east of the Ncome River, waiting to be deployed if the Zulu attack on the Boer **laager** succeeded. In 1841, King **Mpande kaSenzangakhona** incorporated it with the **iNdabakawombe** *iButho*.

*umKHOSI*. The Zulu king was the great rainmaker, and the fruitfulness of the crops depended on him. At crucial times of the agricultural years, he was strengthened with ritual medicines to ensure a good harvest. For the Zulu, one of the most important rituals was the *umKhosi*, or national first-fruits ceremony, celebrated annually at the king's principal *iKhanda* in late December or early January when the full moon was about to wane. All the *amaButho* gathered at the district *amaKhanda* before proceeding to the king's "great place" for the ceremonies. The *amaDlozi* (ancestral spirits) were invoked through sacrifice and their favor courted. The king, his *amaButho*, and his people were ritually purified, strengthened against evil influences, and bound together anew, and mystical confusion was sent out among their enemies. The ceremonies would conclude after three days with a grand review of the *amaButho* in their festival attire, followed by the proclamation of the laws the king and the *iBandla* (royal council) had decided on.

**emaKHOSINI VALLEY.** The "Valley of the Kings" is south across the White Mfolozi River from the **Mahlabathini Plain** and is the most sacred spot in **Zululand**. The residences of the *amaKhosi* (chiefs) who preceded Shaka were built there, and they were constantly renewed during the period of the **Zulu kingdom**. During the reigns of **Dingane kaSenzangakhona**, **Mpande kaSenzangakhona**, and **Cetshwayo kaMpande**, the symbol of the nation, the *iNkatha* (sacred grass coil), was stored there in the **esiKhlebheni** *iKhanda*. The Zulu rulers Zulu, Nkosinkulu, Mageba, Phunga, Ndaba, Jama, Senzangakhona, and **Dinuzulu kaCetshwayo** are buried there.

*isiKHULU. See* POLITICAL ORGANIZATION, ZULU.

**umKHULUTSHANE** *iBUTHO*. King **Dingane kaSenzangakhona** formed this *iButho* around 1833 from youths born about 1813. In the **Voortrekker-Zulu War**, it fought at **eThaleni** and Ncome, where it formed part of the right horn.

**KIMBERLEY DIAMOND FIELDS.** In 1866, diamonds were discovered at the confluence of the Vaal and Orange rivers, and a diamond rush followed. Britain annexed the territory in 1871 as Griqualand West, and the central site of the diggings was named in June 1873 after the secretary of state for colonies, John Wodehouse, 1st Earl Kimberley. By the late 1870s, Kimberley was second only to **Cape Town** as the biggest town in the subcontinent, and the diggings attracted thousands of migrant African laborers like the **Pedi**, who often used their pay to buy **firearms**. Because of the *iButho* system, no men were allowed to leave the **Zulu kingdom** to work at the diamond diggings until after the **Anglo-Zulu War**.

**KLIP RIVER REPUBLIC.** After the British annexation of **Natal**, there were Boers living in the wedge of territory between the Thukela and Mzinyathi rivers who wished neither to trek to the highveld nor to accept British rule. In January 1847, Andries Spies bought the territory from King **Mpande kaSenzangakhona**, but in terms of the boundary treaty with Britain of October 1843, it was no longer his to sell. Under British pressure, Mpande repudiated his agreement with Spies in July 1847, and in January 1848 the British asserted their authority over the territory, putting an end to the "Klip River Insurrection." *See also* LADYSMITH; NATAL-ZULULAND BOUNDARY, 1843.

**KNIGHT'S LEVY.** *See* ENTONJANENI LEVY.

**KNOBBED STICK, ZULU.** For close fighting, some *amaButho* carried a heavy wooden knobbed stick, or *iWisa* (also called a "knobkerrie" in English and Afrikaans). It was also used to put badly wounded comrades out of their misery, or for execution. Lighter versions were employed during ceremonial dancing displays.

**KOPPIE ALLEEN.** *See* FORT WHITEHEAD.

***inKOSI.*** *See* POLITICAL ORGANIZATION, ZULU.

**KRANSKOP.** *See* NTUNJAMBILI.

**KUBHEKA PEOPLE.** The Kubheka people north of the Phongolo River in the **Disputed Territory** were what remained of various chiefdoms conquered by **Shaka kaSenzangakhona** and **Dingane kaSenzangakhona** whom King **Mpande kaSenzangakhona** had allowed to settle in the Ntombe River valley. In the **Anglo-Zulu War**, their *inKosi*, Manyonyoba kaMaqondo, owed King **Cetshwayo kaMpande** allegiance, and they took the field against the British with the **abaQulusi** and other **irregulars** of the region. On 26 January 1879, a mounted patrol from **Luneburg** worsted the Kubheka, captured much livestock, and forced them to take refuge in their caves along the steep hillsides of the Ntombe River. On 10–11 February, the Kubheka hit back with the aid of the abaQulusi and **Mbilini waMswati**'s adherents, and they ravaged the Luneburg farmlands. On 15 February, Lieutenant-Colonel **Redvers Henry Buller** of No. 4 **Column** raided the Kubheka caves in retaliation but did not succeed in fully subduing them. On 25 March, a patrol from No. 4 Column again attacked the Ntombe valley inconclusively. During the 2nd Invasion of the Anglo-Zulu War, once **Wood's Flying Column** began its march from **Khambula**, leaving only small garrisons behind, the Kubheka and other people in the region were emboldened to raid the Luneburg district thoroughly between 7 and 21 June. On 4, 5, and 8 September, **Baker Russell's Column** and the Luneburg garrison attacked the Kubheka in their caves in the Ntombe valley, blowing up some of the caves with women and children inside. Kubheka resistance collapsed, and Manyonyoba surrendered on 22 September. *See also* CIVILIANS IN WARTIME ZULULAND.

**KWAMAGWAZA (kwaMAGWAZA) FORT.** *See* FORT ALBERT.

**KWAMAGWAZA MISSION.** *See* kwaMAGWAZA MISSION.

## – L –

**LAAGER, BOER WAGON.** For defensive purposes and as a secure base for their **commandos** (militias) on campaign, the Boers of the **Cape** developed the wagon laager (encampment) and took the concept with them on the **Great Trek**. Wagons were drawn into a circle, rough triangle, or whatever shape best suited the terrain and natural features that might impede the enemy's advance. The wagons were lashed together, end to end, with the shaft of each wagon fitting under the chassis of the next. Branches from thorn trees or wooden hurdles (*veghekke* or "fighting gates") filled the gaps, and oxskins were stretched over the wheels. Noncombatants and livestock sheltered inside the laager. The defenders were positioned between each wagon and ideally fired in ordered rotation to keep up an uninterrupted rate of fire, supported sometimes by small cannon. Once they had broken the enemy's attack, the defenders sallied out on their **horses** to turn the enemy's retreat into a rout.

**LAAGER, BRITISH MARCH.** After their unlaagered camp was overwhelmed at **Isandlwana** during the **Anglo-Zulu War**, the

British thereafter formed march laagers at every halt, which were a modification of the Boer wagon **laager**. The wagons were parked in echelon because it took too much time to maneuver them end to end, as was Boer practice. Formations of three mutually supporting laagers were preferred, but when a single square or oblong laager was formed, it was divided into compartments for livestock, soldiers, and headquarters. With a large force and a moderate convoy of wagons, the practice was to man a shelter trench two deep outside the wagon laager, into which the livestock was corralled with enough space between trench and wagons for the ammunition and African auxiliaries. With a small force and large convoy, a smaller perimeter was desirable to concentrate firepower, so the wagons themselves were manned. Some men fired through the spaces left between the spokes of the wagon wheels that had been packed with earth from the surrounding trench, and others fired from the wagons. It was always the practice to clear the bush and burn the grass around the laager to prevent the enemy using them as cover or setting them alight to endanger the wagons. If **mounted** troops were available, it was usual for them to sally out in a counterattack once the enemy's assault faltered. *See also individual British camps and laagers.*

**LAAGER, PERMANENT SETTLER.** During the second half of the 19th century in **Natal**, settler committees or the colonial government erected permanent fortifications in time of peace against possible future danger, and usually termed them "laagers." Large enough to accommodate the white settler families of the vicinity with their African retainers, wagons, and some livestock, they usually took the form of square enclosures built of dressed stone and mortar about 10 feet high, with bastions at opposite corners. Sometimes they were added to existing government buildings like magistrate's offices or jails. *See also individual colonial forts and laagers.*

**LADYSMITH.** The village of Ladysmith was proclaimed on 20 June 1850 as the administrative center of Klip River County in northern **Natal**. This was the region where dissident Boers had proclaimed their short-lived **Klip River Republic**. By the late 1870s, the village was well established, with a population of about 250 white settlers.

**LADYSMITH LAAGER.** A **laager**, begun in 1861, whose walls linked together the magistracy buildings in **Ladysmith**, was in disrepair by 1878 when the **Natal** government gave orders for it to be renovated. On 23 February 1879, during the **Anglo-Zulu War**, it was designated a place of security for white settlers of **Colonial Defensive District** No. I in the event of a Zulu invasion. Although never threatened, the laager was manned by the Ladysmith Town Guard (incorporating the Klip River **Rifle Association**) and African levies until the end of May 1879. A detachment of the 2nd Division, **South African Field Force**, was stationed there from April until September 1879, when the laager operated as its rear base for the 2nd Invasion of the Anglo-Zulu War.

**emLAMBONGWENYA** *iKHANDA*. This *iKhanda* in the **Mahlabathini Plain** was the home of King **Mpande kaSenzangakhona**'s mother, Songiya. **Cetshwayo kaMpande** was crowned there as king by **Theophilus Shepstone** on 1 September 1871. After the battle of **Ulundi** in the **Anglo-Zulu War**, the British burned it along with all the other *amaKhanda* in the plain. *See also* CORONATION LAWS.

**LANCE.** The lance was a close-quarter cavalry shock weapon favored in pursuit. The lance used by the 17th (Duke of Cambridge's Own) **Lancers** in the **Anglo-Zulu War** was of the 1868 pattern, with a nine-foot bamboo pole and triangular steel head.

**LANCERS, 17TH (DUKE OF CAMBRIDGE'S OWN).** Sent out as reinforcements for the 2nd invasion of the **Anglo-Zulu War**, the regiment under the command of Colonel Drury Curzon Drury-Lowe made up half the **Cavalry Brigade** attached to the 2nd Division, **South African Field Force**. During the advance, a detachment was based at **Fort Marshall** to protect the line forward. In May, the regiment took part in the patrol to **Isandlwana** to bury the British dead. A squadron saw action in the skirmish at **Zungeni**, and two squadrons participated in Brigadier-General **Henry Evelyn Wood**'s raid on the **emaKhosini valley**. At **Ulundi**, the regiment played a key part in the mounted pursuit. The regiment embarked in September for England.

The uniform consisted of a double-breasted dark blue tunic with white facings (in marching order, the white plastron front was reversed to show the blue side), dark blue breeches with a white stripe, and white accoutrements. In **Zululand**, the lancer's helmet with a white plume was replaced by a white sun helmet.

**LANDING-PLACES, ZULULAND.** The **Zululand** coast offers no secure anchorages or harbors. The only practicable landing place the British identified during the **Anglo-Zulu War** was the open sandy beach at **Port Durnford**. Supplies and personnel were brought to shore in 40-foot surf-boats from ships anchored out to sea beyond the heavy surf. In northern **Zululand**, the shallow **St. Lucia Bay** provided a reasonable holding ground for anchoring, provided the wind was not blowing a gale from the south.

**LANDMAN, KAREL PIETER (1796–1875).** Landman was a prosperous stock farmer from the Uitenhage District of the **Eastern Cape** who in late 1837 led his party of Voortrekkers into the interior. They crossed over the **Drakensberg** in February 1838 soon after the **Bloukrans Massacre**. Although a cautious leader, Landman was also experienced in Cape frontier warfare. He was a member of the *Vlugkommando* and successfully defended the rearguard in the retreat at **eThaleni**. In May 1838, he occupied Port Natal (**Durban**) for the Voortrekkers and ensured the flow of necessary supplies. He was second in command of the *Wenkommando* and fought at **Ncome**. He almost led his force to disaster when ambushed by the Zulu at the battle of the **White Mfolozi**. He played an active role in the Volksraad of the Republic of **Natalia**. When the British occupied Port Natal in May 1842, Landman refused to take up arms against them and retired to farm in the **Natal** midlands.

**LANDMAN'S DRIFT.** This area on the west bank of the Mzinyathi River in **Colonial Defensive District** No. I is where the 2nd Division, **South African Field Force**, massed in May 1879 during the 2nd Invasion of the **Anglo-Zulu War**, constructing a depot and three earthwork forts to guard the stores. They were garrisoned by small detachments of the 2nd Division until September 1879.

**LANGALIBALELE REBELLION (1873).** In late 1873, relations broke down between Langalibalele kaMthimkhulu (1818–1889), the powerful *inKosi* of the Hlubi people who had lived in the foothills of the **Drakensberg** since 1849, and the **Natal** colonial government over the registration of **firearms**. Rather than suffer punishment, Langalibalele resolved to lead his people over the Drakensberg and out of Natal. Major **Anthony William Durnford**, with a small force of **Natal Mounted Volunteers** and **Mounted Basutos**, tried to intercept them on 4 November 1873 at the Bushman's River Pass and was routed. The Natal government severely punished those Hlubi who remained in Natal, and Langalibalele was later captured and exiled for life to the **Cape**, where in 1881–1882 he shared his captivity with the deposed King **Cetshwayo kaMpande**.

**LEE-METFORD MARK I RIFLES.** Introduced in 1888, this bolt-action **rifle** was the first magazine rifle adopted by the British army, although it was not yet in use in **Zululand** during the **uSuthu Rebellion**.

**LESOTHO.** *See* BASUTOLAND.

*iLOBOLO*. When a Zulu man married, he handed over **cattle** or goods to his wife's family to formalize the transaction and to compensate them for the loss of a productive member of their *umuZi* (homestead). Members of an *iButho* (regiment) given permission by the king to assume the *isiCoco* (headring) and take a wife from a designated female *iButho* had to pay *iLobolo*, usually about three cattle, though the number varied according to the period and the status of the recipient.

**LOGISTICS, BRITISH.** The British knew that the basis for any successful campaign in **Zululand** depended on the accumulation of the necessary supplies and ammunition and on the organization of sufficient **transport** to carry them to the front. During the **Anglo-Zulu War**, transport eventually required 748 colonial **horses**, 4,635 mules, 27,125 **oxen**, 641 horse- and mule-carriages, 1,770 ox wagons, 796 ox carts, and 4,080 conductors and *voorlopers*. The inefficient and inexperienced **Commissariat and Transport Department** and **Army**

**Service Corps** barely proved adequate to the task. Many items were first brought to **Durban** by sea and then off-loaded by lighter across the harbor bar and stockpiled. Convoys loaded with ammunition, baggage, camping equipment, and rations then had to cover great distances over rudimentary tracks, across drifts (fordable points in a river) and dongas (dry riverbeds). Transport was also required for **artillery** and **rocket** batteries, engineering and signaling equipment, **medical** stores, camp kitchens, and shoeing smithies. Fodder had to be carried for cavalry mounts and for mules that could not subsist entirely on grazing, as could oxen and colonial horses. Depots for reserve supplies were established at intervals between the rear supply bases and forts or other forward encampments.

The scale of British operations in Zululand during the 3rd **Zulu Civil War** and the **uSuthu Rebellion** was considerably smaller than in the Anglo-Zulu War, and the pressure much less on the reformed Commissariat and Transport Staff and **Commissariat and Transport Corps**. In any case, the logistical lessons of 1879 were taken to heart by the British operating in Zululand during the 1880s. The nature of the required transport had not changed, but there was a better understanding of how to employ it effectively. Fortified depots along the main lines of communication were established early. Tracks in Zululand were improving, and better knowledge of the country meant the best routes were selected. Nevertheless, tracks were still often impassable during the rainy season, and there were no bridges across the many dongas and rivers. In such conditions, transport still regularly broke down, making it difficult to bring up supplies. *See also* LANDING-PLACES, ZULULAND.

**LOGISTICS, ZULU.** The Zulu had no wheeled vehicles or draught animals. They marched to war carrying their supplies or living off the countryside. Until it reached enemy territory, a Zulu army marched in one great column, the ***amaButho*** ordered in terms of status, the most prestigious in the lead. Every man carried his **shield** rolled up on his back and had with him rations in a skin bag. *IzinDibi*, youths serving as carriers for men of status, accompanied the army, moving in the rear or a mile off its flanks; they also drove the **cattle** to feed the army. Some of the men of importance were also accompanied by young women carrying beer, corn, and milk; when these supplies were exhausted, the young women returned to their homes, as did *izinDibi* who could not keep up. Then even the *izinDuna* (officers) would have to carry their belongings.

A Zulu army on the march rapidly consumed its supplies and rations. To spare its own civilian population, it slaughtered the cattle it brought with it and camped whenever it could at ***amaKhanda*** where there were stores of food. In enemy territory, an army foraged mercilessly, but even on its own soil it was usually forced to raid the grain and cattle of its own civilians. In turn, civilians did their best to remove their precious supplies from their ***imiZi*** before an army passed through. Sometimes a hungry army advanced in skirmishing order, driving wild game to the center to kill for food. Lack of water, especially in the dry months, and insufficient wood for cooking and warmth added greatly to an army's privations.

Whether victorious or not, a Zulu army could not stay in the field after combat. There were the wounded to bring home and purification **rituals** to observe. Also, all supplies in the area of operations would have been consumed. If the enemy could not swiftly be brought to combat, a Zulu army had to be content with ravaging the enemy's territory and then retiring with its booty.

There was a change during the 3rd **Zulu Civil War** and the **uSuthu Rebellion** when contending Zulu forces made use of natural fastnesses to defend themselves from attack and subsisted by raiding the surrounding countryside for supplies. They could do so for as long as their enemies did not ravage around their strongholds and deny them supplies. *See also* CIVILIANS IN WARTIME ZULULAND; STRATEGY, ZULU.

**LONGCAST, HENRY WILLIAM (1850–1909).** The orphaned Longcast was brought up at the Rev. **Robert Robertson**'s Anglican mission at **kwaMagwaza** in **Zululand**. In 1870, he married a Zulu convert to Christianity, thus compromising his position in settler society. In November 1878, he was appointed to Lieutenant-General Lord **Chelmsford**'s headquarters staff as interpreter and guide, remaining with him throughout the **Anglo-Zulu War**. He was present at **Gingindlovu** and **Ulundi**. In July 1879, he joined General **Sir Garnet Joseph Wolseley**'s staff in the same capacity. Longcast played an essential part in the search for the fugitive King **Cetshwayo kaMpande**. In September 1879, he accompanied the captive king to the **Cape** and remained with him until January 1881. He then returned to kwaMagwaza. After the 2nd Partition of Zululand, the restored Cetshwayo granted him land nearby as a reward for his services. In the 3rd Partition of Zululand, kwaMagwaza fell under Boer control in **Proviso B**, and Longcast and his family took refuge at the eThalaneni mission in the **Reserve Territory**. They remained there in poverty until his death. The British, who gained control of Proviso B in 1886, refused to recognize the land grant Cetshwayo had made him.

**LONSDALE'S HORSE (MOUNTED RIFLES).** Commandant Rupert LaTrobe Lonsdale had commanded Mfengu levies during the 9th **Cape Frontier War**. During the first stage of the **Anglo-Zulu War**, he was given command of the 3rd Regiment, **Natal Native Contingent**. In the reorganization of forces after **Isandlwana**, Lieutenant-General Lord **Chelmsford** ordered him to the **Cape** to recruit a unit of mounted **irregulars**. He raised four troops, three of which joined the 1st Division, **South African Field Force**, and advanced with it to **Port Durnford**. On the breakup of the 1st Division in late July, two troops joined **Clarke's Column** and one **Baker Russell's Column**. The latter took part in the final operations against the **Kubheka** in the Ntombe caves on 5 and 8 September. The unit mustered out in September. Uniforms were of yellow or brown corduroy.

**LUBUYA, BATTLE OF (1839).** Apprehensive about the future of the Zulu kingdom after his defeat in the **Voortrekker-Zulu War** and his cession of territory and livestock to the Boers in March 1839, King **Dingane kaSenzangakhona** planned to secure his position by carving a new kingdom out of the southern parts of the **Swazi** domain north of the Phongolo River. In the winter of 1839, he mobilized his remaining military resources and, as a preliminary to conquest, dispatched four *amaButho* under Klwana kaNgqengelele to build a strategic *iKhanda* called Mbelebele on the Nguthumeni ridge north of the sources of the Ngwavuma River in Swazi territory. Usually the Swazi retired to their mountain fastnesses when raided by the Zulu, but realizing that this time the Zulu intended conquest, they met them in battle under Mngayi Fakudze in the valley of the Lubuya stream. After a hard fight, the Zulu were forced to withdraw, leaving two *amaButho* dead in the field behind them. Dingane hurried two further *amaButho* north to sustain the faltering campaign, but continued Swazi resistance resulted in his abandoning it in failure. The battle not only secured the Swazi from Zulu conquest but destroyed what remained of Dingane's reputation and led to the 1st **Zulu Civil War** that dethroned him. *See also* STRATEGY, ZULU; TACTICS UP TO 1879, ZULU.

**LUMBE MOUNTAIN.** This mountain in central **Zululand** is three miles to the southeast of **Hlophekhulu Mountain** across the White Mfolozi River. During the **uSuthu Rebellion** when the British stormed Hlophekhulu on 2 July 1888 and dislodged the **uSuthu** holding it, a supporting force of 205 British troops, two mountain **guns**, and 500 African levies under the command of Lieutenant-Colonel Albert Froom were stationed in support on Lumbe. They had been encamped there since 30 June to deter any uSuthu raids in that direction from Hlophekhulu.

**LUNEBURG LAAGER.** In 1869, King **Mpande kaSenzangakhona** permitted a community of German settlers of the Hermannsburg Mission Society to establish the tiny settlement of Luneburg deep within the **Disputed Territory** claimed by the Zulu. The settlers built a stone-walled **laager** around their church, and they took refuge there twice in November 1877 and once again in May 1878 for fear of Zulu attack. A further scare in October 1878 resulted in a detachment of troops being sent from the **Utrecht** garrison in the Transvaal to protect the settlers. The troops arrived on 19 October 1878, strengthened the laager, and fortified the adjoining cemetery. During the **Anglo-Zulu War**, succeeding garrisons of detachments from No. 4 and No. 5 **Columns** manned the laager until July 1879. In early January 1879, the settlers took refuge in the laager, and in February, March, and again in April there were fears of a Zulu attack. Settler apprehensions were only fully allayed in late September 1879 with the final Zulu **submissions**.

# – M –

**MABENGE HILLS LAAGER.** Following the victory at **Tshaneni** during the 3rd **Zulu Civil War**, the Boers concentrated at their **Hlo-**

bane laager. Fresh arrivals of white adventurers and landgrabbers, attracted by the possibility of sharing in the spoils of victory, swelled their numbers to nearly 800. To accommodate them, a new and larger laager was set up nearby at the Mabenge Hills on 20 July. King Dinuzulu kaCetshwayo met them there on 16 August and granted them the land to form the New Republic.

MABHUDU-TSONGA CHIEFDOM. Relations between the Zulu and the Mabhudu-Tsonga, the dominant chiefdom across the trade route from the Portuguese at Delagoa Bay to Zululand, had been strained since the 1860s as both tried to control the lucrative trade and smaller chiefdoms of the region. The Mabhudu-Tsonga paid tribute to the Zulu but were content to see a diminution of their power. During the Anglo-Zulu War, the Zulu feared the Mabhudu-Tsonga would aid the British if they attempted a seaborne invasion from St. Lucia Bay or Delagoa Bay. In May 1879, King Cetshwayo kaMpande ordered the Mabhudu-Tsonga to come to his aid, but the regent, Muhena, listened instead to H. E. O'Neill, the British consul at Zanzibar, who persuaded him to support the British. When a fugitive after Ulundi, Cetshwayo did not seek refuge with the Tsonga chiefdoms, as he expected they would kill him or capture him for the British.

MACLEOD, NORMAN MAGNUS (1839–1929). MacLeod arrived in Natal in 1873 and earned his living as a hunter and government official. In October 1878, he was appointed border agent to the Swazi and civil and political assistant to Brevet Colonel Henry Evelyn Wood at Utrecht. In November 1878 and repeatedly during the Anglo-Zulu War until August 1879, he made visits to King Mbandzeni waMswati and persuaded the Swazi not to join the Zulu but to remain British allies, though he could not induce them to intervene actively in the war until Zulu defeat was assured. As a justice of the peace, he also dealt competently with the Boers of the Utrecht, Wakkerstroom, and Lydenburg districts of the Transvaal, who were not reconciled to British rule and were cooperating with the Zulu in the Disputed Territory. After the Anglo-Zulu War, he raised Swazi auxiliaries for the renewed campaign against the Pedi in late 1879. He returned to Britain in 1880 and in 1895 became Chief of the Clan MacLeod of MacLeod.

**MAFUNZI'S MOUNTED NATIVES. Natal** Chief Hemuhemu of the Funzi people in **Colonial Defensive District** No. III called out his fighting men in February 1879 for a mounted unit some 70 strong that mustered in **Pietermaritzburg** and was originally called the Umlaas Corps. Although well mounted, the men were armed with **spears** and were issued only a few **firearms**. They served with the **Eshowe Relief Column** and fought at **Gingindlovu**. They then served with the 1st Division, **South African Field Force**; after it was broken up, they joined **Clarke's Column** in its march back to Natal. They disbanded in September.

**kwaMAGWAZA FORT.** *See* FORT ALBERT.

**kwaMAGWAZA MISSION.** The Rev. **Robert Robertson** founded the Anglican mission station at kwaMagwaza in 1860. Robertson abandoned the mission in August 1877, and the Zulu destroyed it during the **Anglo-Zulu War**. He abandoned it again in 1884 during the 3rd **Zulu Civil War**. *See also* FORT ALBERT.

**MAHASHINI** *umuZI.* This was one of *umNtwana* **Ndabuko ka-Mpande**'s *imiZi* in the Vuna valley, where the **uSuthu** were concentrated. During the **uSuthu Rebellion**, it was plundered between 6 and 9 June 1888 by the **Mandlakazi** while they were encamped on Ndunu Hill close by the **Ivuna Fort**.

**MAHLABATHINI PLAIN.** Overlooked from the south across the White Mfolozi River by the **Mthonjaneni** Heights, the Mahlabathini Plain was in the heart of the Zulu kingdom. King **Mpande kaSenzangakhona** established his principal *amaKhanda* there (his predecessor's had been in the **emaKhosini valley**), and King **Cetshwayo kaMpande** followed suit. The British burned all the *amaKhanda* in the plain during the **Anglo-Zulu War**. After the 2nd Partition of **Zululand**, Cetshwayo started rebuilding many of them on a smaller scale, but all were destroyed in the 3rd **Zulu Civil War**.

**MALAKOFF TOWER.** As a precaution against a Zulu incursion, in 1857 James Saunders, a prosperous sugar planter on the **Natal** north coast, erected a square, loopholed tower on a hill on the south bank of the Tongate River overlooking his estate. By 1878, the tower was in ruins and was not used in the **Anglo-Zulu War**.

**MANDLAKAZI.** In 1819, *inKosi* Maphitha kaSojiyisa of the Mandlakazi, who was closely related to the Zulu kings, was named by King **Shaka kaSenzangakhona** as his viceroy of the territories in northeastern **Zululand** newly conquered from the Ndwandwe. Maphitha's son *inKosi* **Zibhebhu kaMaphitha** continued to carry equal weight in the kingdom, and it was vital for *umNtwana* **Cetshwayo kaMpande** in the 2nd **Zulu Civil War** to bring the Mandlakazi into the **uSuthu** camp. During the **Anglo-Zulu War**, they fought loyally against the British. As a result of the 1st and 2nd Partitions of **Zululand**, they formed the core of Zibhebhu's chiefdom and fought relentlessly against the uSuthu in the 3rd Zulu Civil War. Following their defeat at **Tshaneni**, they took refuge in 1884 in the **Reserve Territory** and only returned home in November 1887, when the administration of the British colony of Zululand assigned Zibhebhu a new location in the Ndwandwe District. During the **uSuthu Rebellion**, they steadfastly supported the British and used the opportunity to harry the uSuthu in their territory.

**MANSEL, GEORGE.** Mansel joined the **Natal Mounted Police** in 1874. During the **Anglo-Zulu War**, he survived **Isandlwana**. He was the commandant of the **Reserve Territory Carbineers** (RTC) from 1883 to 1887 and during the 3rd **Zulu Civil War** commanded at the battle of the **Nkandla Forest**. He continued in command when the RTC were renamed the **Zululand Police** on the British annexation of **Zululand** in May 1887. During the **uSuthu Rebellion**, he fought at **Ceza** and **Hlophekhulu**. On Zululand becoming a province of **Natal** in December 1897, he was made assistant commissioner of the Natal Police, eventually rising to chief commissioner.

**MANYONYOBA kaMAQONDO.** *See* KUBHEKA PEOPLE.

**MANZIPHAMBANA STRONGHOLD.** This traditional stronghold of the Cube people, deep in the **Nkandla Forest**, was where they successfully defended themselves against King **Shaka kaSenzangakhona** in the days of their *inKosi* Dlaba. During the 3rd **Zulu Civil**

**War**, when King **Cetshwayo kaMpande** escaped in July 1883 after the battle of **oNdini**, this is where Cube warriors initially conducted him for safety.

**MAQONGQO HIILS, BATTLE OF (1840).** In September 1839, *umNtwana* **Mpande kaSenzangakhona**, fearing that his half-brother King **Dingane kaSenzangakhona** intended to kill him, fled across the Thukela River with 17,000 of his adherents and 25,000 **cattle** to seek refuge with the Boers of the Republic of **Natalia**. On 27 October 1839, Mpande struck an alliance with the Boers for a combined attack on Dingane. The Boers would establish Mpande as the Zulu king, and in return Mpande would cede them **St. Lucia Bay** and much cattle. The campaign opened on 14 January 1840. Mpande's army led by *inKosi* **Nongalaza kaNondela** advanced into **Zululand** along the coast, making for Dingane's new **uMgungundlovu** *iKhanda* at the Vuna River in northern Zululand. Mpande marched with the Boer *Beeskommando* of 308 armed men, 500 *agterryers* (African servants), and 50 **wagons** under Commandant-General **Andries Wilhelmus Jacobus Pretorius** that followed the path of the Boers' 1838 campaign across the Mzinyathi and Ncome rivers.

Dingane made futile diplomatic efforts to halt the invasion. Realizing he had to stand and fight, he withdrew 30 miles north from uMgungundlovu to Magudu Mountain, which dominates the plain eight miles south of the Phongolo River. His army, under veteran general *inKosi* **Ndlela kaSompisi**, took up a defensive position a mile to the southwest of Magudu on a group of rounded knolls in the open plain known as the Maqongqo Hills.

The *Beeskommando*, which was treating the campaign as a hunting expedition and was more concerned to capture cattle than to fight, had only just passed the **Ncome** battlefield on 29 January when Mpande's forces clashed with Dingane's 100 miles away to the north. It would have been more prudent for Nongalaza to have waited for the Boer commando to arrive with their invincible **firearms**, but Mpande wished to win the battle without their aid to loosen their political hold over him.

Each side at the Maqongqo Hills fielded about 5,000 men, who faced each other armed with **spears** and **shields** and arrayed in traditional chest and horns formation. The morale of Nongalaza's men was higher, but even so the battle was fiercely contested and the issue long hung in doubt. Ndlela's men started to take heavy casualties, and increasing numbers began to go over to the enemy. These defections decided the day, and Ndlela's army withdrew. Nongalaza's forces, who had also suffered considerable casualties, were reluctant to pursue the enemy with any vigor. They did finish off the wounded and killed women of Dingane's household who did not manage to escape. Dingane fled across the Phongolo with only a few followers, but not before ordering Ndlela's execution. His defeated *amaButho* dispersed home. The *Beeskommando* made contact with Nongalaza on 6 February, but in heavy rain and with horse sickness ravaging their **horses**, they decided to call off the campaign and returned home with 36,000 captured cattle. On 10 February, in their camp on the south bank of the Black Mfolozi River, they proclaimed Mpande king. *See also* TACTICS UP TO 1879, ZULU.

**MARITZ, GERRIT (1797–1838).** Maritz was a prosperous wagon-maker, businessman, and administrator from the town of Graaff-Reinet in the **Eastern Cape**. In September 1836, he led a party of Voortrekkers into the interior, where in January 1837 they reinforced the Voortrekkers under **Andries Hendrik Potgieter** in their confrontation with the **Ndebele**. Maritz decided not to stay on the highveld. His party joined **Pieter Retief**'s over the **Drakensberg** in November 1837 and established their Saailaer **laager** on a horseshoe bend of the Bushman's River. Maritz was dubious about attempting to treat with King **Dingane kaSenzangakhona** and would not support Pieter Retief's ill-fated efforts to do so. During the **Bloukrans Massacre**, Saailaer proved a bulwark against the Zulu attack.

After fighting in the **Veglaer** battle in August, Maritz moved from the Doornkop laager to the Sooilaer ("Sod laager"), between the Little Thukela River and Loskop. In the winter of 1838, disease struck the Voortrekkers in their laagers, and Maritz died on 23 September at Sooilaer.

**MARITZBURG RIFLES.** This was one of the three infantry corps in the **Natal Volunteer Corps**. It was not initially mobilized for service in the **Anglo-Zulu War**, but in the panic after **Isandlwana**, it helped defend the **Pietermaritzburg laager** and mounted guard until the end of February 1879.

**MARSHALL, FREDERICK (1829–1900).** Commissioned in 1849, Marshall saw service in the Crimean War (1855). He was commanding officer of the 2nd Life Guards from 1864 to 1873 and was promoted major-general in 1877. During the **Anglo-Zulu War**, he proceeded to **Natal** in February 1879 to command the **Cavalry Brigade** attached to the 2nd Division, **South African Field Force**, during the 2nd Invasion of the war. He commanded at the burial of the dead at **Isandlwana** in May and at the unsuccessful skirmish at **Zungeni**. When the Cavalry Brigade was disbanded in July, General **Garnet Joseph Wolseley** placed him in command of advanced posts and lines of communication. He was promoted to lieutenant-general in 1884 and knighted in 1897.

**MARTIN, RICHARD EDWARD ROWLEY (1847–1907).** Commissioned in 1867, Martin served in the 1st **Boer War** (1881). He was promoted to lieutenant-colonel in 1886. In 1887, he was in command of the cavalry of the British **Zululand garrison** in the Colony of **Zululand**, based at **Nkonjeni**. In January 1888, he patrolled forward to support the civil authorities at **Ivuna** against the disaffected **uSuthu**. In August 1888, during the final stage of the **uSuthu Rebellion**, Martin led **Martin's Flying Column** from Nkonjeni to **Eshowe** in a joint march with the **Coastal Column** in order to eliminate the last pockets of uSuthu resistance. In 1889, he assumed command of the 6th (Inniskilling) **Dragoons** and was promoted colonel in 1890. He was commandant-general of the British South Africa Company's police during operations in South Africa in 1897 and was knighted in 1898.

**MARTIN'S FLYING COLUMN.** In the final stages of the **uSuthu Rebellion**, Lieutenant-Colonel **Richard Edward Rowley Martin**, the officer commanding the 6th (Inniskilling) **Dragoons** stationed at **Nkonjeni**, formed a flying column consisting of 1,760 African levies (troops). It joined the **Coastal Column** at **Ivuna** on 7 August, and on 18 August marched back with it along the coast to **Eshowe** (which it reached on 30 August), dispersing the last few pockets of **uSuthu** resistance.

**MARTINI-HENRY MARK II RIFLE.** British infantry had carried the single-shot Martini-Henry Mark II **rifle** since 1874, when it replaced the Snider Enfield rifle, and continued to do so in **Zululand** through 1888. It weighed 9 lbs. and fired a .450-caliber, hardened-lead bullet of 1.1 ounces, with a muzzle velocity of 375 yards per second. A lever behind the trigger guard, when lowered, dropped the breech block, allowing the center-fire Boxer cartridge to be inserted into the chamber. The cartridge, which was covered with paper, was difficult to insert, and the thin rolled-brass case often became stuck when the chamber was fouled and heated by the black gunpowder propellant. Fouling also lodged easily in the rifled barrel with its seven deep, square-cut grooves. This significantly increased the already severe recoil, made the barrel too hot to touch, and affected accuracy, since the bullet would no longer spin properly.

The Martini-Henry lead bullet flattened on impact, causing massive tissue damage and splintering the bone lengthways. Its effect nevertheless depended on range and volume of fire. At close range (100–300 yards), two minutes' fire at six shots per minute would only be 10 percent effective against a mass attack; at medium range (300–700 yards), effectiveness would decrease to 5 percent for four minutes' fire at six shots per minute; at long range (700–1,400 yards), the effectiveness of six shots per minute over seven minutes would fall to 2 percent. At point-blank range (below 100 yards), a wall of fire could be impenetrable for a charging enemy if the troops were sufficiently concentrated. Thus a company of 100 men in close order, two deep, with a frontage of 40 yards, could maintain the necessary volume of 12 shots a minute per yard. Yet, as was demonstrated at **Isandlwana** during the **Anglo-Zulu War**, even at point-blank range, a skirmishing line with regulation intervals of at least four paces and as many as 10 could not develop the volume of fire necessary to deter a determined charge.

**kwaMATIWANE.** In 1829, *inKosi* Matiwane kaMasumpa of the Ngwane people returned a suppliant to the **Zulu kingdom** after the destruction of his migrating people by the forces of the **Cape Colony**. King **Dingane kaSenzangakhona** did not trust him and ordered his execution on a small rocky hill across the Mkumbane stream, 500 yards from the main entrance of his **uMgungundlovu** *iKhanda*. On

6 February 1838, an *amaButho*, on Dingane's signal, dragged **Pieter Retief** and his companions to this hill of execution and clubbed them to death.

**MATSHANA kaMONDISA.** Matshana was the *inKosi* of the section of the Sithole people living south of the Mzinyathi River in a region that fell first into the Republic of **Natalia** and then British **Natal**. In 1858, Matshana ran afoul of the colonial authorities and fled to **Zululand**, where **Cetshwayo kaMpande** appointed him *inKosi* of the section of the Sithole living at the confluence of the Mzinyathi and Mangeni rivers and gave him two of his sisters in marriage. But King Cetshwayo's advisers mistrusted Matshana's connections with Natal, and at the outbreak of the **Anglo-Zulu War**, they were reluctant to entrust him with an important military command. So instead of joining the Zulu army marching to confront the No. 3 **Column**, he and his fighting men remained in his own district to the southeast of **Isandlwana** and skirmished with the British on 21–22 January 1879. The war thereafter largely passed him and his people by and he **submitted** on 20 August. In the 1st Partition of **Zululand**, Matshana's chiefdom fell under **John Dunn**; in the 2nd Partition it became part of the **Reserve Territory**. During the 3rd **Zulu Civil War**, Matshana's levy supported the **Mounted Basutos** in 1884 against the u**Suthu** in the **Nkandla Forest**. He managed to remain aloof during the **uSuthu Rebellion** but was not so fortunate during the **Zulu Uprising of 1906** (Bhambatha Rebellion), when many of his younger adherents supported the rebels. He was afterward tried for sedition but acquitted.

**MAVUMENGWANA kaNDLELA (c. 1830–c. 1893).** The younger brother of *inKosi* **Godide kaNdlela**, Mavumengwana was *inKosi* of a lesser section of the **Ntuli** people. During the 1st **Zulu Civil War**, he vacillated in his support of *umNtwana* **Mpande kaSenzangakhona**, but on Mpande becoming king he grew in royal favor. He was enrolled in the **uThulwana** *iButho* and became a close associate of *umNtwana* **Cetshwayo kaMpande**, serving with him in the **Swazi** campaign of 1847 and supporting him in the 2nd Zulu Civil War. During Cetshwayo's reign, Mavumengwana was one of the greatest men in the kingdom, a prominent member of the *iBandla* (royal council), and principal *inDuna* of the uThulwana. In the crisis before the **Anglo-Zulu War**, he was a leading member of the peace party in the *iBandla*. Nevertheless, Cetshwayo appointed him joint commander of the army in the **Isandlwana** campaign. After Isandlwana, Mavumengwana returned to his chiefdom and together with *umNtwana* **Dabulamanzi kaMpande** took command of the forces blockading the British in **Fort Eshowe**. At the battle of **Gingindlovu**, he held a lesser command, and after the defeat he returned home. By May 1879, Cetshwayo was losing confidence in his loyalty, but Mavumengwana did not surrender to the British until August. In the 1st Partition of **Zululand**, he was placed under **John Dunn**. After the 2nd Partition of Zululand, when his chiefdom fell into the **Reserve Territory**, he did not actively support Cetshwayo in the 3rd **Zulu Civil War**.

**MAWA, CROSSING OF.** *See* SOTHONDOSE'S DRIFT.

**MBILINI waMSWATI (c. 1843–1879).** Mbilini was a favorite son of King Mswati waSobhuza of the **Swazi**, but he lost the succession struggle in 1865. He fled to **Zululand** and put himself under the protection of *umNtwana* **Cetshwayo kaMpande**, who saw how he could use him to assert Zulu control in the **Disputed Territory**. From his *umuZi* at Tafelberg a dozen miles northeast of **Luneburg**, Mbilini built up a personal following and forged close relations with the nearby **Kubheka** and **abaQulusi** people. He raided Swazi and Transvaal Boers alike and threatened the Luneburg settlers. In 1877, he established a new *umuZi* at **Hlobane** out of range of Boer retaliation. During the **Anglo-Zulu War**, he employed his superior skills as a guerrilla leader against the British No. 4 **Column**. He engaged its forces at **Zungwini** and Hlobane in January 1879, raided the Luneburg settlement in February, overran a convoy from Derby at the **Ntombe** action in early March, and defeated the British at the battle of Hlobane later that month. After the battle of **Khambula**, the British asserted their ascendancy in the region and killed Mbilini in a skirmish on 5 April. *See also* MORIARTY, DAVID BARRY.

**uMBONAMBI *iBUTHO*.** King **Mpande kaSenzangakhona** formed this *iButho* around 1863 from youths born about 1843. The **shield**

was black, or black with white spots or speckles. In the **Anglo-Zulu War**, it fought at **Isandlwana**, where it was on the left horn and was the first into the British camp. It also fought at **Gingindlovu**, where elements had been barracked at the original **oNdini** *iKhanda* to maintain the blockade of **Fort Eshowe**; at **Khambula**, where it fought on the left of the Zulu chest; and at **Ulundi**, where it attacked the southeastern corner of the British infantry **square**. A tiny detachment was also involved in the skirmish at the **Tshotshosi** River. During the 3rd **Zulu Civil War**, elements were present at the battle of oNdini, where they formed part of the **uSuthu** chest.

**kwaMBONAMBI** *iKHANDA*. This *iKhanda* in the **Mahlabathini Plain** was one of King **Cetshwayo kaMpande**'s favorite residences. On the morning of 4 July 1879 during the **Anglo-Zulu War**, when he learned that Lieutenant-General Lord **Chelmsford**'s forces had crossed the White Mfolozi River, Cetshwayo moved to kwaMbonambi from the **emLambongwenya** *iKhanda*, and he was there throughout the battle of **Ulundi**. When his lookouts informed him the battle was lost, he fled northward. Later that day, the British burned kwaMbonambi.

**iMBUBE** *iBUTHO*. King **Mpande kaSenzangakhona** formed this *iButho* around 1857 from youths born about 1837. The **shield** was black with white spots. The iMbube was apparently incorporated into the **uDududu** *iButho*. In the **Anglo-Zulu War**, it fought at **Isandlwana** on the right horn and at **Khambula** as part of the chest. At **Ulundi**, it attacked the southeast corner of the British infantry **square**. At the battle of **oNdini** during the 3rd **Zulu Civil War**, it was stationed nearby, at the **kwaNodwengu** *iKhanda*, and was caught up in the **uSuthu** rout before it could come into action.

**MBUYAZI kaMPANDE (c. 1832–1856).** A son of King **Mpande kaSenzangakhona**, *umNtwana* Mbuyazi was a rival of *umNtwana* **Cetshwayo kaMpande** for the succession, and for a time he was favored by the king. Supporters of Mbuyazi came to be called the *iziGqoza*, or "those who drop down like water from a roof," signifying the steady trickle of support for Mbuyazi's cause. But Cetshwayo was popular and gathered a faction around him, known as the **uSuthu**.

The issue was decided when Cetshwayo defeated Mbuyazi in the 2nd **Zulu Civil War**, crushing the iziGqoza at **Ndondakusuka**.

**uMCIJO** *iBUTHO*. King **Mpande kaSenzangakhona** formed this *iButho* around 1867 from youths born about 1848. The shield was black or dark brown with white markings down one side, or black with a white patch across the center. In the **Anglo-Zulu War**, it fought as part of the chest at **Isandlwana**, and elements stationed at the original **oNdini** *iKhanda* fought at **Gingindlovu**. At **Hlobane**, elements were detached from the main army marching on **Khambula** to cut off the British retreat. At Khambula, it formed the left horn, and at **Ulundi** it attacked the northwestern side of the British infantry square. In the 3rd **Zulu Civil War**, elements made up part of the **uSuthu** right horn at the battle of oNdini.

**MCKEAN, ALEXANDER CHALMERS (1852–?).** Commissioned in 1871, McKean served in the 1st **Boer War** (1881) and was promoted to major in 1883. In 1886, he was detached from his garrison duties at **Fort Napier** to serve on the boundary commission that reported back on 25 January 1887 on the borders of the **New Republic**. He then served as subcommissioner for the Nqutu District in the **Reserve Territory**, becoming the resident magistrate when in May 1887 Nqutu became part of the colony of **Zululand**. During the **uSuthu Rebellion**, McKean raised a force of **Mounted Basutos** in his district in June 1887 and led them in the storming of **Hlophekhulu**. In early July, he formed and led the **Eshowe Column** in the relief of **Fort Andries**. Later in July, he formed the **Coastal Column** for pacification operations concluded in late August. In October 1888, he was promoted to brevet lieutenant-colonel and left South Africa to become assistant military secretary in Malta. He was promoted to brevet colonel in 1894 and retired in 1898. During World War I, he served as a base commandant.

**MDLALOSE PEOPLE.** During the **Anglo-Zulu War**, the Mdlalose people of northwestern **Zululand** bore the brunt of raiding by No. 4 **Column** and took to their places of refuge in the hills. By late August 1879, they had **submitted** to the British and in the 1st Partition of Zululand were placed under *inKosi* **Ntshingwayo kaMahole**. In the

2nd Partition of Zululand, they were included in the restored King **Cetshwayo kaMpande**'s territory, and they rallied to the **uSuthu** cause in the 3rd **Zulu Civil War**. Their contingent was among the uSuthu forces routed at **Msebe**. In May–July 1883, they were involved in operations against the **Ngenetsheni** in the north, but after the uSuthu defeat at **oNdini**, many fled to the **Reserve Territory** for safety. In June 1884, they participated in the successful fighting against the **Mandlakazi**, but with the 3rd Partition of Zululand, they found themselves within the borders of the **New Republic** and reduced to labor tenants on the Boer farms. *See also* CIVILIANS IN WARTIME ZULULAND.

**MDLETSHE PEOPLE.** In the 1st Partition of **Zululand**, the pro-**uSuthu** Mdletshe people under *inKosi* Nkhowana kaMfuzi were assigned to the southeast of *inKosi* **Zibhebhu kaMaphitha**'s chiefdom. They remained under his oppressive rule after the 2nd Partition of Zululand and were placed under it again when the authorities of British Zululand restored him to his chiefdom in 1887. During the **uSuthu Rebellion**, while Zibhebhu was encamped at **Ivuna**, they took advantage of his absence to raid the **Mandlakazi**, who retaliated. After Zibhebhu's defeat at Ivuna, the Mdletshe burned **Bangonomo**, his main *umuZi*, and with the **Hlabisa** people ravaged his territory, assisted by opportunistic Boers from the **South African Republic**. In mid-August, Zibhebhu struck back at the Mdletshe and Hlabisa, who withdrew toward **St. Lucia Bay** before retaliating. The raiding and counterraiding did not end until the British arrested Zibhebhu on 17 November 1888 and banished him from his chiefdom. *See also* CIVILIANS IN WARTIME ZULULAND.

**MEDICAL ATTENTION, BOER.** In case of illness, the Boers of the interior had for decades depended on their own folk-medicine and herbal remedies derived from 17th-century European practices and from the medicinal knowledge of local Africans. Some brought patent medicines with them on trek from the **Cape**, or bought medical ingredients from peddlers, or *smouse*. Women usually took on the role of amateur doctor and nurse for their families.

**MEDICAL ATTENTION, BRITISH.** By the 1870s, orderlies and bandsmen in the British army brought the wounded to field hospitals, where injuries were treated and dressed by trained medical personnel. Litters or mule-drawn ambulance wagons with springs were then used to take the wounded to base hospitals to convalesce. Standards of battlefield surgery had improved, but the real killers were infection and disease, and the causes for these were imperfectly understood. Typhoid and other gastrointestinal bacterial infections carried by water or food polluted with human feces continued to present the greatest risk to the health of men in camp. In the **Anglo-Zulu War**, more British soldiers died of disease than were wounded in action, by a ratio of three to two; the number invalided out through disease was greater than the number wounded, by a ratio of nearly six to one. *See also* ARMY HOSPITAL CORPS; ARMY MEDICAL DEPARTMENT; BEARER CORPS; NURSES, BRITISH.

**MEDICAL ATTENTION, ZULU.** For uncomplicated flesh wounds, Zulu *izinYanga*, or traditional healers, administered a poultice to prevent inflammation and encourage healing. The poultices were made from leaves of the ubuHlungwana herb (*Wadelia natalensis*) or the powdered bulb of the uGodide (*Jatropha hirsuta*). Open wounds were tied up with grass. Fractures were set with splints, and certain herbs, particularly the powdered root of the uMathunga (*Cyrtanthus obliquus*), were rubbed into incisions made at the point of the breakage. Some *izinYanga* had the ability to open skulls crushed by blows and remove harmful bloodclots, and some could successfully amputate limbs. However, the Zulu had no effective means of dealing with the splintered bones and massive tissue damage and internal injuries inflicted by modern bullets. Those wounded by **rifle** fire in the 2nd **Zulu Civil War**, the **Anglo-Zulu War**, the 3rd **Zulu Civil War**, and the **uSuthu Rebellion** seldom survived the march home, and had scant chance of recovery if they did.

**MEHLOKAZULU kaSIHAYO (c. 1854–1906).** The senior son of *inKosi* **Sihayo kaXongo** of the **Qungebe** people, Mehlokazulu was a favorite *iNceku* (personal attendant) of King **Cetshwayo kaMpande**

and a junior *inDuna* of the **iNgobamakhosi** *iButho*. In July 1878, several of **Sihayo's sons**, led by Mehlokazulu, raided across the border from **Zululand** into **Natal**, provoking a crisis. But Cetshwayo would not surrender Mehlokazulu to the Natal authorities and instead put him under the protection of **Mbilini waMswati**. During the **Anglo-Zulu War**, Mehlokazulu fought at **Isandlwana**, **Khambula**, and **Ulundi**. After the war, he was handed over to the authorities in Natal for trial but was released by October 1879. In the 1st Partition of Zululand, Mehlokazulu and his family were placed under **Hlubi ka-Mota Molife** and lost all local influence. During the 3rd **Zulu Civil War**, he was active in securing Boer support for the **uSuthu** cause. He took advantage during the **uSuthu Rebellion** of Hlubi's absence fighting with the British to attack his *imiZi* (homesteads). After the suppression of the rebellion, the Zululand authorities, in their attempt to reconcile the warring factions, recognized Mehlokazulu in 1893 as the *inKosi* of the Qungebe. He was drawn into the **Zulu Uprising of 1906** (Bhambatha Rebellion) against the colonial authorities and was killed at the battle of Mome Gorge on 10 June 1906.

**MELVILL, TEIGNMOUTH (1842–1879).** Commissioned in 1865, Lieutenant Melvill was appointed adjutant of the 1st Battalion, 24th (2nd Warwickshire) **Regiment** in 1873. In 1875, he proceeded to the **Cape** with his battalion and served throughout the 9th **Cape Frontier War** (1877–1878). During the **Anglo-Zulu War**, he was present at the storming of **kwaSogekle** and remained in camp with the **Isandlwana** garrison when the rest of No. 3 **Column** went out on its reconnaissance in force. At the climax of the battle, Melvill attempted to save the queen's **color** by riding down the **Fugitives' Trail**. He lost the color in the swollen Mzinyathi River, and he and Lieutenant **Neville Josiah Aylmer Coghill,** who had turned back to assist him, were killed on the **Natal** bank. In 1907, Melvill was posthumously awarded the Victoria Cross.

**MENIYA** *umuZI.* Meniya was *umNtwana* **Ndabuko kaMpande**'s principal *umuZi* in the Vuna valley, where the **uSuthu** were concentrated. At the outset of the **uSuthu Rebellion**, it was raided on 25 April 1888 by the **Zululand Police**, who were collecting **cattle**

fines that **Richard Hallowes Addison**, the resident magistrate of the Ndwandwe District, had imposed against the uSuthu leaders.

**MERCENARIES.** Among the mercenaries active in southern Africa were white frontiersmen with the latest **firearms** and **horses** operating as **mounted infantry**. They early became an important military adjunct to Zulu armies. In the 1820s, King **Shaka kaSenzangakhona** used Port Natal (**Durban**) mercenaries in various campaigns. During the 2nd **Zulu Civil War**, **John Dunn**'s well-armed **iziNqobo** played a vital part at **Ndondakusuka**. In the chaotic conditions of the 3rd Zulu Civil War, mercenaries were particularly evident among the **Mandlakazi** forces, and their intervention was crucial at **Msebe**. They suffered defeat at **Tshaneni** at the hands of the **uSuthu** and the Boer mercenaries of **Dinuzulu's Volunteers**, who were supporting the uSuthu in return for land and booty. Also functioning as a mercenary force was the *Beeskommnado* that operated in conjunction with *umNtwana* **Mpande kaSenzangakhona**'s forces in the 1st Zulu Civil War. *See also* CANE, JOHN; COLENBRANDER, JOHANNES WILHELM; DARKE, HENRY GROSVENOR; ECKERSLEY, JOHN.

**MEYER, LUKAS JOHANNES (1846–1902).** A field cornet in the **Utrecht District** of the **South African Republic** (SAR) from 1872, Meyer strongly opposed the British annexation of the Transvaal in 1877. He was wounded in the 1st **Boer War** (1880–1881). After the SAR regained its independence in August 1881, he was appointed magistrate of the Utrecht District from 1882 to 1884. In April 1884, he joined the group of **mercenaries** known as **Dinuzulu's Volunteers** and was present when the Boers proclaimed **Dinuzulu kaCetshwayo** king on 21 May 1884. The following day, he was elected commandant of the Boer **commando** (militia) that played the decisive role in the battle of **Tshaneni**. He was elected president and commandant-general of the **New Republic** when it was proclaimed on 16 August 1884 and retained those posts until it was absorbed into the SAR on 20 July 1888. In 1893, Meyer was an elected member for Utrecht in the *volksraad* of the SAR and in 1899 became chair of the *volksraad*. During the **Anglo-Boer (South African) War**, he was an only moderately successful commander, took no part in the guerrilla phase of the conflict, and worked for a negotiated peace.

**MFEMFE *iBUTHO*.** This was an **Ngenetsheni** *iButho* raised by *umNtwana* **Hamu kaNzibe** after the 1st Partition of **Zululand** in resumption of the prerogatives of the great *amaKhosi* preceding **Shaka**. It was named after **kwaMfemfe**, one of his principal *imiZi*. The Mfemfe *iButho* fought the **uSuthu** throughout the 3rd **Zulu Civil War**, and it was part of *inKosi* **Zibhebhu kaMaphitha**'s army at **oNdini**.

**kwaMFEMFE *umuZI*.** *UmNtwana* **Hamu kaNzibe**'s "great place" was at kwaMfemfe in northwestern **Zululand.** Here he kept his own *isiGodlo* (private enclosure) in royal style and challenged King **Cetshwayo kaMpande**'s authority. It remained his seat when he was appointed one of the 13 chiefs in the 1st Partition of Zululand. During the 3rd **Zulu Civil War**, it was the main **Ngenetsheni** military base for operations against the **uSuthu** and gave its name to the **Mfemfe** *iButho*.

**uMGUNGUNDLOVU *iKHANDA*.** In 1829, King **Dingane kaSenzangakhona** began the first *iKhanda* of this name in the **emaKhosini valley** in the heart of the **Zulu kingdom**; *uMgungundlovu* means "the place that encloses the elephant" or king, and it was Dingane's great place. It consisted of 1,400–1,700 huts. **Pieter Retief** and a small party of Voortrekkers came there on 5 November 1837 to negotiate with Dingane, and they returned with a larger party on 3 February 1838. The next day, they signed a treaty with Dingane. But before they could leave on 6 February, Dingane ordered their execution, and they were killed at **kwaMatiwane**, a nearby hill. On 20 December 1838, after its victory at **Ncome**, the *Wenkommando* reached uMgungundlovu, which they found deserted and in flames. Before he withdrew north, Dingane had ordered it and two neighboring *amaKhanda* set on fire.

Dingane moved the focus of his kingdom north and in early 1839 began building a second, smaller uMgungundlovu in the valley of the Hluhluwe River. Malaria was prevalent, and Dingane then moved the *iKhanda* to a site on higher, healthier ground, just south of where the

Vuna River runs into the Black Mfolozi. There he set about rebuilding his authority. But in January 1840, his brother *umNtwana* **Mpande kaSenzangakhona** along with Boer allies invaded **Zululand** during the 1st **Zulu Civil War**. Dingane fell back from uMgungundlovu to the **Maqongqo Hills**, where he was defeated. With his flight and death, the third and last uMgungundlovu was abandoned.

**MIDDLE DRIFT, RAID AT (1879).** On 25 June 1879 during the **Anglo-Zulu War**, the Zulu mounted an extensive raid across the Thukela River at Middle Drift into **Natal** in retaliation for raids into **Zululand** in April and May by colonial troops stationed along the border. The colonial and imperial border forces had intelligence of an impending Zulu raid but were nevertheless taken by surprise when it occurred. The Zulu forces were commanded by Bheje and Solinye, two *izinDuna* of the Ngcolosi people of the Natal side of the Thukela valley, who had defected to the Zulu in November 1878.

Under cover of early morning mist, a party of about 500 local Zulu under Bheje crossed in the vicinity of the hot springs above Middle Drift, brushed aside ineffective resistance by the **Special Border Police**, and ravaged the valley as far as the foot of **Ntunjambili**. There they were met by another force of 500 men under Solinye, who had crossed at Domba's Drift below Middle Drift and likewise disposed of feeble resistance by the River Guard, devastating the valley as they went. The two groups then joined and ravaged all the country back to Middle Drift, where they crossed into Zululand with 678 **cattle**, 771 goats, and about 40 prisoners, leaving behind them 73 burned *imiZi*, destroyed food stores, and about 30 of the Natal border population dead. Some of the scattered Special Border Police and river guards were able to rally and harry the retiring Zulu, recovering some livestock. But the Zulu were gone before the **Natal Native Contingent** in garrison at **Fort Cherry** could be prepared for action. The arrangements for the defense of the Natal border against a Zulu raid had been tested and found sadly wanting. *See also* CIVIL–MILITARY RELATIONS; CIVILIANS IN WARTIME ZULULAND; STRATEGY, ZULU.

**MILITARY INTELLIGENCE, BRITISH.** During the **Anglo-Zulu War**, inadequate and inaccurate maps forced British commanders to rely on mounted reconnaissance patrols to provide information about the terrain to be traversed and to locate military objectives. Information extracted from captured Zulu, volunteered by informants (usually Christian converts), or collected by spies was inevitably problematic and required expert evaluation. But the professional accumulation and analysis of intelligence was not adequately addressed in the late Victorian army, despite the establishment in 1858 of the Staff College at Camberley in Surrey. Moreover, the conservative Lieutenant-General Lord **Chelmsford**, in command of operations, was reluctant to establish a staff along modern lines. He was content to depend on regular officers without specialist staff training, and on civilians who claimed some knowledge of **Zululand**. But his staff fatally underrated the fighting capability of the Zulu, despite Chelmsford's attempts to supply his officers with information gleaned from settler observers about Zulu military organization and fighting methods.

General **Sir Garnet Joseph Wolseley**, with his "advanced" military notions, took over command in July 1879 and insisted on appointing trained staff officers. They were too late to make an appreciable difference in the conduct of the Anglo-Zulu War, but their assiduous map-making and intelligence-gathering was of service to the British in Zululand during the 3rd **Zulu Civil War** and the **uSuthu Rebellion**, as were the reports submitted by officers on the conduct of the 1879 campaign. During the 1880s, the British had a continuous presence in Zululand and were able to gather intelligence about everything from the state of the roads to Zulu politics. The nature of internecine Zulu strife and the number of active collaborators meant that intelligence was much more freely available than in 1879. The widespread use of the **telegraph** also greatly speeded up the dissemination of intelligence. *See also* ARMY REFORM, BRITISH.

**MILITARY INTELLIGENCE, ZULU.** The Zulu had an absolute edge over their Boer or British adversaries when it came to intelligence gathering. It had always been standard procedure for the Zulu armies to send out considerable numbers of spies and scouts to keep their enemies under close observation and to report on their movements. In the major campaigns of the **Voortrekker-Zulu War** and **Anglo-Zulu War**, they had the advantage of knowing the terrain and having the support of the civilian population, which was more than ready to volunteer information of hostile activity. Moreover, the Boers and British found it difficult to differentiate between their African levies, civilians, and spies posing as deserters or seeking employment as camp servants, and they suspected with good reason that Zulu envoys were also spying out their military dispositions. They consequently took stern measures against presumed spies, and they sent out mounted patrols to screen their movements from observation. These precautions were ineffective and could never prevent the Zulu from possessing considerable knowledge of their movements and dispositions. During the Anglo-Zulu War, Zulu spies were collecting intelligence as far afield as **Natal,** the Transvaal, and **Delagoa Bay**.

**MILITARY ORGANIZATION, BRITISH.** At the time of the **Anglo-Zulu War** and the campaigns in **Zululand** during the 1880s, a regiment of regular cavalry on overseas service consisted of eight troops (the standard tactical unit)—or four squadrons—nominally made up of 27 officers and 607 men, including a farrier and trumpeter for each troop. A battery of six guns was the **Royal Artillery**'s usual tactical unit, but it was often broken up into three divisions of two guns, each worked by two officers and 45 men. The standard infantry tactical unit was the battalion. On service, each battalion comprised a headquarters and eight companies, nominally made up of 30 officers and 866 men, though the establishment in the field was often considerably lower. A squadron of **mounted infantry** consisted of three officers and 110 men.

**MILITARY SYSTEM, ZULU.** *See iBUTHO* SYSTEM DURING THE ZULU KINGDOM; *iBUTHO* SYSTEM IN THE 1880s.

*uMNYAMA*. The Zulu believed that their world overlapped with the world of the *amaDlozi*, or ancestral spirits. This was expressed by a mystical force, *uMnyama*, which was darkness or evil influence, and was represented by the color black. It could be contagious in its most virulent forms. Because such pollution was a mystical rather than organic illness, it could be cured only by symbolic medicines. Death by violence, expressed as *umkhoka*, was an especially powerful form of *uMnyama*, as the killer was polluted. *See also* RITUAL

DURING BATTLE, ZULU; RITUAL PREPARATION BEFORE WAR, ZULU.

**MNYAMANA kaNGQENGELELE (c. 1813–1892).** King **Shaka kaSenzangakhona** made Ngqengelele kaMvulana, Mnyamana's father, *inKosi* of the **Buthelezi** people and his *iNceku* (personal attendant) and principal *inDuna* (official). King **Mpande kaSenzangakhona** appointed Mnyamana, who was enrolled in the uMkhulutshane *iButho*, to succeed to the chiefdom and in 1854 appointed him senior *inDuna* of the **uThulwana *iButho***, in which eight of Mpande's sons were enrolled. He supported *umNtwana* **Cetshwayo kaMpande** in the 2nd **Zulu Civil War**, and on his accession King Cetshwayo made him his chief *inDuna*. Mnyamana was rich in **cattle**, and as a man of peace, he strongly urged against war with the British. Nevertheless, he did his duty in the **Anglo-Zulu War** and exercised overall command at **Khambula**. In mid-August 1879, Mnyamana negotiated his surrender with General **Sir Garnet Joseph Wolseley** but declined to be appointed a chief in the 1st Partition of **Zululand**.

Mnyamana was prominent in appealing for Cetshwayo's restoration. As an ardent **uSuthu** partisan during the 3rd **Zulu Civil War**, he led the Buthelezi repeatedly against the neighboring **Ngenetsheni**. After **oNdini**, he brought together the remnants of the uSuthu forces in the Ngome forest in northern Zululand, where they continued to resist until the end of 1883. After Cetshwayo's death, he counseled King **Dinuzulu kaMpande** against making an alliance with the Boers that would cost the Zulu land, as indeed occurred with the proclamation of the **New Republic**. Always a political realist, Mnyamana acquiesced in the British annexation of Zululand in 1887 to prevent further turmoil. He and his adherents were consequently targeted by Dinuzulu's forces during the **uSuthu Rebellion**, during which they took refuge with the British at **Nkonjeni** and formed **Mnyamana's Auxiliaries** to assist in quelling the rebellion.

**MNYAMANA'S AUXILIARIES.** In May 1888, during the **uSuthu Rebellion**, *inKosi* **Mnyamana kaNgqengelele** and his **Buthelezi** adherents took refuge with the British at the **Nkonjeni** camp after being raided by the **uSuthu** from **Ceza Mountain**. **Richard Hallowes Addison**, the resident magistrate of Ndwandwe District, raised a force of

600 Buthelezi, who became known as Mnyamana's Auxiliaries, for the unsuccessful attempt to arrest the uSuthu leaders on Ceza. Later in June, they were among the force from Nkonjeni that evacuated the garrison from **Ivuna** after the defeat of its **Mandlakazi** allies. They then took part in the successful attack against the uSuthu on **Hlophekhulu Mountain**. By late July, the uSuthu threat had dissipated and the Buthelezi dispersed to their homes. They were armed with their traditional **spears** and **shields**, though a few carried obsolete **muzzle-loading firearms**.

**MORIARTY, DAVID BARRY (1837–1879).** Commissioned in 1857, Moriarty served in the Mediterranean, the Channel Islands, Ireland, and India, where he fought in the Hazara campaign (1868). In 1870, he was promoted to captain and joined the 80th **Regiment** (Staffordshire Volunteers) in 1876, proceeding with it to South Africa, where he was stationed at **Newcastle** and then at **Utrecht**. In August 1878, he took part in the campaign against the **Pedi**. During the **Anglo-Zulu War**, he was stationed at Derby under Brevet Colonel **Henry Evelyn Wood**'s command on convoy duties. He was in command of the convoy that **Mbilini waMswati** overran in its encampment at the **Ntombe River** and was killed in hand-to-hand fighting.

**MOUNTED BASUTOS.** In the 1st Partition of **Zululand**, **Hlubi kaMota Molife** of the Tlokwa was appointed one of the 13 chiefs. Over the next decade, he and his **mounted infantry** (and some infantry as well) repeatedly rallied to the British call for military assistance. They were paid for out of the funds of the Zululand administration (whether **Reserve Territory** or **colony**) and were dressed in an assortment of blue or khaki frocks, usually with buff trousers and riding boots or puttees, and wore brown slouch hats with a red puggaree (scarf) around the hatband. Issued with **carbines** or **rifles**, they carried their ammunition in leather bandoliers.

During the 3rd **Zulu Civil War**, the Mounted Basutos escorted the fugitive King **Cetshwayo kaMpande** to **Eshowe** in October 1883. In May 1884, 127 Mounted Basutos supported by infantry levies were deployed by Andries Pretorius, the subcommissioner of Nqutu in the Reserve Territory, to repel the **uSuthu** concentrating against the district from the north. In late May and early June, the Basutos were successfully redeployed in the western **Nkandla Forest** against the uSuthu concentrated there. During the **uSuthu Rebellion**, the Mounted Basutos were raised once again in June 1888, and 200 were stationed at **Nkonjeni**. A squadron of 140 men took part in the storming of **Hlophekhulu**. In July, they were redeployed to the coast, and 180 Mounted Basutos made up part of the **Eshowe Column** in the relief of **Fort Andries**, and subsequently of the **Coastal Column** during its pacification operations during August. In mid-August, when the Coastal Column was at **Ivuna**, the Mounted Basutos, who were dissatisfied because of lack of supplies and forage, lost discipline and raided all around. They were disbanded by 23 August.

**MOUNTED BURGHER FORCE.** This irregular body of volunteers, first raised in **Natal** in 1863, was based on the Boer **commando** (militia) system and was favored by the Dutch-speaking settlers of the rural areas of the colony. They were bound to respond when called out for service by the local **field cornet** of each ward into which the counties of Natal were divided. They supplied all their own equipment and found the formal, British-style discipline adopted by the **Natal Volunteer Corps** uncongenial. As they were not required to serve more than 20 miles from their own county, let alone outside the borders of Natal, they stood on the defensive during the **Anglo-Zulu War** and prepared to defend citizen **laagers** against Zulu attacks that never materialized.

**MOUNTED INFANTRY.** Experience gained during the 1870s prompted the British in South Africa to emulate the Boer **commando** (militia) concept of mounted infantry as an effective response to local conditions and as a useful substitute for regular cavalry in **small wars**. The major difference between cavalry and mounted infantry was that the latter would do the work of reconnaissance, screening, advance guard, sentry, and escort duty but would not be required to take part in a charge, which was left to the cavalry. The success during the **Anglo-Zulu War** in deploying a mounted infantry force detached from regular infantry was recognized, and after 1881 all infantry battalions in South Africa were required to train one company in mounted infantry work. During the 1880s, the British always deployed mounted infantry in operation in **Zululand** and after 1887 maintained two companies as part of the **Zululand garrison**. *See also individual units*; DRESS, BRITISH ARMY.

**MOUNTED INFANTRY MUSTERED FROM 2ND BATTALION, NORTHAMPTONSHIRE REGIMENT.** During the 3rd **Zulu Civil War**, a company of **mounted infantry** mustered from the battalion in garrison at **Fort Napier** was stationed at **Fort Northampton** in the **Reserve Territory** from September 1884 until the end of the year.

**MOUNTED INFANTRY MUSTERED FROM 1ST BATTALION, PRINCE OF WALES'S (NORTH STAFFORDSHIRE REGIMENT).** In October 1887, following the British annexation of the Colony of **Zululand**, a company of **mounted infantry** mustered from the battalion in garrison at **Fort Napier** was posted to **Nkonjeni** in support of the civil authorities in the Ndwandwe District. During the **uSuthu Rebellion**, it took part in the unsuccessful assault on **Ceza**, and a detachment was part of the force that captured **Hlophekhulu**. It was disbanded in November 1888 when the **Zululand garrison** was reduced to its normal level.

**MOUNTED INFANTRY MUSTERED FROM 1ST BATTALION, ROYAL SCOTS (LOTHIAN REGIMENT).** In September 1888, during the final stages of the **uSuthu Rebellion**, two companies of **mounted infantry** were mustered from the battalion stationed in **Zululand** at **Fort Curtis**. One was moved forward to **Entonjaneni** and the other remained at Fort Curtis. On the withdrawal of the battalion in November to **Natal** where it was in garrison, the two companies of mounted infantry remained behind as part of the **Zululand garrison**.

**MOUNTED INFANTRY MUSTERED FROM 1ST BATTALION, ROYAL INNISKILLING FUSILIERS.** In October 1887, soon after the annexation of the Colony of **Zululand**, a company of **mounted infantry** mustered from the battalion in garrison at **Fort Napier** was stationed at **Entonjaneni**. During the **uSuthu Rebellion**, it moved forward to **Nkonjeni** in April 1888. It was part of the force repulsed at **Ceza** and was with the force on **Lumbe Mountain** supporting the assault on **Hlophekhulu Mountain**. Between July and August, it joined the **Eshowe Column** and then the **Coastal Column** in their pacification operations. It was withdrawn to **Natal** when the **Zululand garrison** was reduced to its normal level in November.

**MOUNTED INFANTRY MUSTERED FROM 1ST BATTALION, WELSH REGIMENT.** During the 3rd **Zulu Civil War**, a company of **mounted infantry** was mustered from the battalion in garrison at **Fort Napier** and joined the **Etshowe Column** in September 1883. It remained in garrison at **Fort Curtis** until February 1884.

**MOUNTED INFANTRY, NO. 1 AND 2 SQUADRONS.** On the eve of the **Anglo-Zulu War**, there were no regular British cavalry in South Africa, but two squadrons of mounted infantry were available. They had been formed during the 9th **Cape Frontier War** from various infantry regiments and mounted on regulation cavalry saddles on **horses** bought in **South Africa**. Each was armed with a Swinburn-Henry **carbine** and a bowie knife that attached to the muzzle. By the end of the war, the 2nd Squadron also had **swords**.

In early January 1879, No. 1 Squadron joined No. 3 **Column**. Most of the unit was away with the reconnaissance in force during the battle of **Isandlwana**, though 30 remained in camp as vedettes (sentinels). The depleted squadron retired with the remnants of No. 3 Column to **Natal**. No. 1 Squadron stayed in garrison at **Helpmekaar** until it left in mid-March to join No. 4 Column at **Khambula**. During the rout on **Hlobane**, it was with Lieutenant-Colonel **John Cecil Russell**'s force and fought the next day at Khambula, where it took part in the pursuit. It advanced with **Wood's Flying Column** during the 2nd Invasion of the **Anglo-Zulu War** and took part in the **White Mfolozi reconnaissance in force** and in the battle of **Ulundi**. With the breakup of Wood's Flying Column in late July, it joined **Baker Russell's Column** in its march to the Transvaal.

No. 2 Squadron joined the 1st Division, No. 1 Column, and fought at **Nyezane**. On receiving the news of Isandlwana, the squadron was sent back from **Eshowe** to **Natal** with all the other mounted forces in No. 1 Column. It then formed part of the **Eshowe Relief Column** and fought at **Gingindlovu**. After the relief of Eshowe, it joined the 2nd Brigade, 1st Division, **South African Field Force** and advanced with it to **Port Durnford**. With the breakup of the 1st Division in late July, it was attached to **Clarke's Column**. In August, detachments were engaged in the pursuit and capture of King **Cetshwayo kaMpande**. It mustered out in October.

**MPANDE kaSENZANGAKHONA (c. 1798–1872).** *UmNtwana* Mpande kaSenzangakhona was spared by his half-brother King **Dingane kaMpande** when he seized the Zulu throne in 1828 and eliminated his other rivals. Mpande wisely kept a low profile during Dingane's reign, but when Dingane was defeated in the **Voortrekker-Zulu War** and turned against potential rivals, he fled in September 1839 to take sanctuary in the Republic of **Natalia**. He struck an alliance with the Boers in the 1st **Zulu Civil War** whereby they recognized him as Zulu king in return for land. When the British imposed their rule over **Natal**, Mpande came to an agreement with them in 1843 over the boundaries of **Zululand**. Mpande's policy was to remain on good terms with the British in order to foster trading relations and to check the claims of the Boers of the **South African Republic** to the **Disputed Territory**. To those ends, he encouraged a missionary presence from 1850 and curtailed disruptive Zulu campaigns against their African neighbors, particularly the **Swazi**. As he grew older, Mpande was threatened by impatient heirs to the throne, and the peace of the kingdom was shattered in the 2nd **Zulu Civil War**, when *umNtwana* **Cetshwayo kaMpande** defeated his major rivals. The succession was finally settled in May 1861 when Mpande recognized Cetshwayo as his heir and effective co-ruler. Thereafter his powers as king diminished steadily, and he died in September or October 1872; his death was kept secret until a smooth succession was secured. Mpande was buried at his **kwaNodwengu** *iKhanda*.

**MPHUKUNYONI PEOPLE.** The Mphukunyoni people under *inKosi* **Somkhele kaMalanda** dominated the remote northern coastal plain of **Zululand**. In the 1st Partition of Zululand, Somkhele was appointed one of the 13 chiefs. After the 2nd Partition of Zululand, his chiefdom fell into King **Cetshwayo kaMpande**'s territory, and the Mphukunyoni strongly espoused the **uSuthu** cause. During the 3rd **Zulu Civil War**, they and the **Mandlakazi** repeatedly raided each other. In March 1884, the Mphukunyoni beat off an attack by *inKosi* **Zibhebhu kaMaphitha**'s coastal allies, the **Mthethwa**, and threatened the **Reserve Territory**. During the **uSuthu Rebellion**, the Mphukunyoni again rallied to the uSuthu cause and on 30 June unsuccessfully attacked the British magistrate at **Fort Andries** in the battle of **Ntondotha**. On 30 July 1888, Somkhele and the Mphukunyoni surrendered to the **Coastal Column**. *See also* CIVILIANS IN WARTIME ZULULAND; DUKUDUKU STRONGHOLD.

**MPONDO PEOPLE.** *See* GRIQUA AND MPONDO BORDERS WITH NATAL IN 1879.

**iMPUNGA *iBUTHO*.** *See* uMXHAPHO *iBUTHO*.

**MPUNGOSE PEOPLE.** *See* HLOPHEKHULU MOUNTAIN, BATTLE OF (1888).

**MSEBE, BATTLE OF (1883).** In late March 1883 during the 3rd **Zulu Civil War**, the **uSuthu** decided to muster an army to invade the territory of *inKosi* **Zibhebhu kaMaphitha** to eliminate the threat he was posing to the restored King **Cetshwayo kaMpande**. On 29 March, the uSuthu army of 5,000 under the command of *inKosi* Makhoba kaMaphitha, organized into divisions according to allegiance to *inKosi* rather than by *iButho*, began its march toward **Bangonomo**, Zibhebhu's chief *umuZi*. Zibhebhu had only 1,500 **Mandlakazi** to face them, but they were well disciplined and many were mounted riflemen. They were bolstered by five or six white **mercenaries** under **Johannes Wilhelm Colenbrander**.

On the early morning of 30 March, the uSuthu advanced carelessly into the shallow valley of the Msebe stream, their ranks disordered and crowded with noncombatant *izinDibi* (carriers). The Mandlakazi were concealed in the long grass in traditional chest and horns formation, with the mounted riflemen on the right horn. When they unleashed their ambush, they surprised and outflanked the leading uSuthu contingents and put them to flight. The long column of uSuthu marching behind them put up a token resistance before joining the desperate rout. The pursuit lasted until sunset, with the mounted Mandlakazi ranging at will among the stampeding uSuthu, shooting their leaders. Makhoba and many uSuthu of high lineage were killed,

The interior of a Zulu *umuZi* close to the Thukela River. Illustration courtesy of John Laband.

"An attack of Zulu Warriors." Note the combination of traditional weapons and firearms. Illustration courtesy of John Laband.

Men of the uNokhenke *iButho* photographed c. 1879 dressed for the hunt or war. Photo courtesy of the Cecil Renaud Library, University of KwaZulu-Natal, Pietermaritzburg.

The Border Guard stationed at White Rock Drift across the lower Thukela River in Colonial Defensive District No. VI during the Anglo-Zulu War. Photo courtesy of John Laband.

The final repulse of the Zulu at the battle of Gingindlovu during the Anglo-Zulu War. Illustration courtesy of John Laband.

Officers of Wood's Flying Column during the Anglo-Zulu War. Brigadier-General Evelyn Wood is seated center. Lieutenant-Colonel Redvers Buller is on the chair to his left and Lieutenant Henry Lysons on the ground at his feet. Both won the Victoria Cross at Hlobane. Captain Lord William Beresford, who won the Victoria Cross in the reconnaissance in force across the White Mfolozi, is standing behind, second from left. Photo courtesy of the *Witness* Collection, Pietermaritzburg.

The burning of oNdini after the battle of Ulundi during the Anglo-Zulu War. Illustration courtesy of John Laband.

King Cetshwayo kaMpande in European dress photographed c. 1882 while in captivity. Photo C. 245 courtesy of the Western Cape Provincial Archives.

The unveiling of the Anglo-Zulu War memorial in Pietermaritzburg on 11 October 1883. A contingent of the 2nd Battalion, Northamptonshire Regiment, then forming part of the Natal garrison, is drawn up with backs to the camera. The volunteer Maritzburg Rifles are arrayed at right angles to them. Photo C. 111 courtesy of the KwaZulu-Natal Archives (Pietermaritzburg Repository).

King Cetshwayo kaMpande receiving a delegation from his relatives on the Mthonjaneni Heights a few days before his installation on 29 January 1883 following the 2nd Partition of Zululand. Illustration courtesy of John Laband.

*InKosi* Zibhebhu ka-Maphitha of the Mandlakazi standing center. Photo C. 740 courtesy of the KwaZulu-Natal Archives (Pietermaritzburg Repository).

Fort Curtis constructed in October 1883 by the men of the Eshowe Column. The timber stockade, which was commanded by an earthwork lunette, is shown in the photograph with men of the garrison and a 7-pounder gun. Photo INIL 7583 courtesy of the National Library of South Africa (Cape Town campus).

Boers of the Committee of Dinuzulu's Volunteers proclaim Dinuzulu kaCetshwayo king of the Zulu on 21 May 1884 at their laager at Nyathi Hill before a gathering of about 9,000 uSuthu. Illustration C. 4785 courtesy of the KwaZulu-Natal Archives (Pietermaritzburg Repository).

Men of the Reserve Territory Carbineers with their commander, Commandant George Mansel, standing center. His second in command, Lieutenant Richard Addison, stands on the far left with his dog. Photo C. 5055 courtesy of the Kwa-Zulu-Natal Archives (Pietermaritzburg Repository).

Chief Hlubi kaMota Molife sitting in the center with his Mounted Basutos drawn up behind him and his sergeant to his right. To his left (with the terrier) sits Major Alexander McKean, the commander of the Eshowe Column during the uSuthu Rebellion. Photo INIL 932 courtesy of the National Library of South Africa (Cape Town campus).

*UmNtwana* Shingana kaMpande, who during the uSuthu Rebellion defied the British from Hlophekhulu Mountain. Photo C. 874 courtesy of the Kwa-Zulu-Natal Archives (Pietermaritzburg Repository).

along with well over 1,000 of their men. The Mandlakazi lost only 10 men. The comprehensive rout of their army disrupted uSuthu strategy and forced them to build up fresh forces before resuming the conflict. *See also* STRATEGY, ZULU; TACTICS IN 1880s, ZULU.

**MTHETHWA PEOPLE.** Mlandlela kaMbiya, *inKosi* of the Mthethwa on the coastal plain, surrendered in good time during the **Anglo-Zulu War** and in the 1st Partition of **Zululand** was appointed one of the 13 chiefs. His had been one of the great chiefdoms preceding **Shaka**, and the Mthethwa resented Zulu overlordship. In the 2nd Partition of Zululand, they were unwillingly assigned to King **Cetshwayo kaMpande**'s territory. Under Mlandlela's son, Sokwetshatha ka-Mlandlela, they stoutly resisted Cetshwayo's authority in the 3rd **Zulu Civil War** and allied themselves with *inKosi* **Zibhebhu ka-Maphitha**. In February and March 1884, they attacked the **Mphu-kunyoni** who supported the **uSuthu**, but when the Mphukunyoni counterattacked in late March, the Mthethwa had to seek temporary refuge in the **Reserve Territory**. During the **uSuthu Rebellion**, the Mthethwa came to the defense of the British magistrate at **Fort Andries** and helped defend the post against an uSuthu assault in the battle of **Ntondotha**. On 5 July, an attempt by Mthethwa levies to open a way between the fort and **Eshowe** ended in their being routed by the uSuthu and losing 40 men.

**MTHONJANENI LAAGER.** On 29 June 1879 during the 2nd Invasion of the **Anglo-Zulu War**, the 2nd Division, **South African Field Force**, and **Wood's Flying Column** halted on the Mthonjaneni Heights overlooking the valley of the White Mfolozi River and built three **laagers** surrounded by a breastwork. When the joint force resumed its advance on **oNdini** on 30 June, it left a garrison at Mthonjaneni consisting of small detachments from every unit in the two forces. After the battle of **Ulundi**, the 2nd Division returned to the camp on Mthonjaneni on 5 July, **Wood's Flying Column** joining them the next day. Violent rain between 6 and 8 July prevented any further movement, but on 9 July the joint force recommenced its withdrawal, and the laager was broken up. *See also* ENTONJANENI CAMP.

**MUNHLA HILL CAMP. Wood's Flying Column** constructed this redoubt and lunette when it encamped at Munhla Hill between 25 May and 1 June 1879 during the **Anglo-Zulu War**. The column was advancing from **Khambula** by way of its camp at **Wolf Hill** to join with the 2nd Division, **South African Field Force**, for their advance on **oNdini**.

**MUSKETS.** The .750 caliber, 60-inch long, muzzle-loading flintlock-action Land Pattern Musket and its derivatives were in service with the British army from 1722 to 1838. The flintlock musket was then superseded by the percussion-lock smoothbore musket, which in turn gave way in the early 1850s to the rifled musket. Huge stocks of decommissioned muskets were bought up by arms dealers, who sold them to unsophisticated markets, especially in Africa. Tens of thousands entered **Zululand** from **Delagoa Bay** and **Natal** in the decades before the **Anglo-Zulu War**. These muskets had no sights, and their accuracy was low. Effective range was no more than 100 yards, and the rate of fire was generally about three rounds a minute. The musket was commonly known as the "Brown Bess" or "Tower musket," after the mark of the Tower of London system that subcontracted manufacture to many gunsmiths.

**uMXHAPHO** *iBUTHO*. King **Mpande kaSenzangakhona** formed this *iButho* around 1861 of youths born about 1841. It carried **shields** of any color. In the **Anglo-Zulu War**, it formed the crack unit of the Zulu army at **Nyezane** and fought on the left horn. Smaller elements formed part of the Zulu chest at **Isandlwana**. The day before the battle of **Ulundi**, it played a prominent part in the ambush of the British of the **White Mfolozi reconnaissance in force**. At Ulundi, it attacked the northeast corner of the British infantry **square**. In the 3rd **Zulu Civil War**, elements made up part of the **uSuthu** chest at **oNdini**.

– N –

*NATAL.* During the **Anglo-Zulu War**, the transport steamer *Natal* anchored off **Port Durnford** on 11 July 1879 and remained there until 4 September, when the captured King **Cetshwayo kaMpande** came on board from a surf-boat with the small party that was to share his exile. These included his long-standing companion and adviser Mkhosana kaZangqana, four young women of the royal household, and three male attendants. The *Natal* arrived in **Cape Town** on 14 September, and the king and his party were transferred to the **Cape Town Castle**.

**NATAL, BRITISH COLONY OF.** On 5 July 1842, the *volksraad* of the Republic of **Natalia** submitted to British authority, though a period of shared rule continued until October 1845. The "District of Port Natal" was annexed as a British dependency on 12 May 1843. On 31 May 1844, the district was annexed to the **Cape Colony**, being constituted on 30 April 1845 as a separate administrative district. The first lieutenant-governor of Natal, appointed by the governor of the Cape, took the oath of office on 12 December 1845. The Royal Charter of 15 July 1856 established Natal as a separate British colony. **Pietermaritzburg** was the capital, and **Durban** its port. On 31 May 1910, the Colony of Natal became a province of the Union of South Africa.

**NATAL CARBINEERS.** One of the 10 corps of **Natal Mounted Volunteers** who were called out in November 1878 for active service in the **Anglo-Zulu War**, the Natal Carbineers were formed in 1855 and had seen service in Natal in 1856, 1858, 1861, 1865, and 1873, the last being the **Langalibalele Rebellion**. The 70 Carbineers joined No. 3 **Column** at **Helpmekaar** in December 1878 and advanced with it into **Zululand**, taking part in the skirmish at **kwaSogekle** on 12 January. Half the corps was absent with Major **John George Dartnell**'s reconnaissance in force when the remainder left in the camp at **Isandlwana** suffered heavy casualties in battle. The corps retired with No. 3 Column to Helpmekaar and spent the rest of the war on the **Natal** border, engaged in patrol work, cross-border raids, escort duty, and dispatch riding. It took part in the patrol of 21 May to begin the burial of the dead at Isandlwana and mustered out in July 1879. The uniform was of dark blue cloth with white trim (and black braid for officers), with white trouser-stripes, black riding-boots, and a white helmet with spike.

**NATAL GARRISON.** The permanent presence of a British garrison in **Natal** can be dated from May 1842, when British troops took possession of Port Natal (**Durban**). The garrison established its headquarters at **Fort Napier** in **Pietermaritzburg** on 31 August 1843, and a detachment continued to be stationed at the **Durban Redoubt** until 1897. On 12 August 1914, the last British battalion in garrison departed for service on the Western Front in World War I.

In its 71 years in Natal, the garrison did much to improve the infrastructure of Pietermaritzburg and made an important contribution to the sporting, social, and cultural life of white settlers in Natal. The garrison's primary purpose, however, was to act as the local strategic reserve, ready to be deployed to maintain the colony's internal security, to defend it from attack, and to secure wider imperial interests in the region when these obligations proved beyond the capabilities of locally raised colonial units. The colonial government contributed about 10 percent of the total imperial expenditure of maintaining the garrison.

The 1st Battalion, 45th (Nottinghamshire) **Regiment**, remained in garrison from 1843 until 1859, after which it became policy to relieve the garrison of one battalion every two to three years. The experiences of the **Anglo-Zulu War** and the 1st **Boer War** proved that the colonial forces were insufficient for Natal's defense, so the establishment of the garrison was substantially increased after 1881, to make it the largest peacetime concentration of imperial troops in South Africa at that time. Until 1888, its strength consisted of a regiment of cavalry, a field battery of **Royal Artillery**, and three infantry battalions. In 1888, the three battalions of infantry were reduced to two, and in 1891 to one. The cavalry were withdrawn in 1899 and the artillery in 1898. There were also support units of **Royal Engineers** and **medical**, **commissariat**, and **ordnance** personnel. *See also* ZULULAND GARRISON.

**NATAL HORSE.** With the disbanding of the 3rd Regiment, **Natal Native Contingent** (NNC), after **Isandlwana** during the **Anglo-Zulu War** and the reorganization of the other two NNC regiments, many underutilized white noncommissioned officers volunteered to form a new unit of **irregular cavalry** consisting of three troops totaling about 150 men. They continued to wear their NNC uniforms with a hackle in their hats.

No. 1 Troop (de Burgh's Horse) joined the 1st Division, **South African Field Force**, in April and proceeded with it to **Fort Durnford**. With the breakup of the 1st Division in July, it joined **Clarke's Column** and mustered out in September.

No. 2 Troop (Cooke's Horse) joined the **Eshowe Relief Column** in March 1879 and fought at **Gingindlovu**. After the relief of **Eshowe**, it joined the 1st Division, South African Field Force, and proceeded with it to **Port Durnford**. It disbanded on the breakup of the 1st Division in July.

No. 3 Troop (Bettington's Horse) joined the 2nd Division, South African Field Force, in late April and participated in the patrolling and raiding preparatory to the 2nd Invasion of the Anglo-Zulu War. A small detachment formed the escort to **Prince Louis Napoleon Bonaparte** on the patrol during which he was ambushed and killed at **Tshotshosi**. The troop took part in the skirmish at **Zungeni** and fought at **Ulundi**. It disbanded with the breakup of the 1st Division in July.

**NATAL HUSSARS.** Initially formed in 1865 and absorbing the Greytown Mounted Rifles in 1869, the Natal Hussars was one of the 10 corps of **Natal Mounted Volunteers** who were called out in November 1878 for active service in the **Anglo-Zulu War**. In December, its 40 troopers joined the 1st Division, No. 1 **Column**, and fought at **Nyezane**. On 28 January, it returned from **Fort Eshowe** to **Natal** with the other mounted men of No. 1 Column. Until the corps was mustered out in July, it served by patrolling the border along the lines of communication between **Fort Pearson**, **Stanger**, and **Ntunjambili** (Kranskop) in **Colonial Defensive Districts** VI and VII and participating in cross-border raids. Its uniform was of dark green cloth, with green facings and black piping on the tunic and a double black stripe on the trousers. The helmet was white.

**NATAL LIGHT HORSE.** Drawn during the **Anglo-Zulu War** from the **Frontier Light Horse** and recruits originally detailed for that unit, the two troops of the Natal Light Horse (140 men) under

Captain W. Whalley took the field in May 1879, when they joined **Wood's Flying Column**. A troop took part in the skirmish at **Zungeni** and in the **White Mfolozi reconnaissance in force**, and both troops fought at **Ulundi**. After the battle, detachments garrisoned **Fort Evelyn** and **Fort Albert** until the withdrawal of the British troops from **Zululand**. Some elements might have joined the Frontier Light Horse when that unit was attached to **Baker Russell's Column**. The unit's uniform and equipment were similar to that of the Frontier Light Horse.

**NATAL MOUNTED POLICE.** The Natal Mounted Police (NMP), a permanent force of police created in 1874 to provide mobile defense for **Natal**, was organized along military lines. On 2 November 1878, on the eve of the **Anglo-Zulu War**, they were put under military command and took up position at **Helpmekaar**, where No. 3 **Column** was assembling. A detachment remained stationed at **Harding** in **Colonial Defensive District** No. IV to help the **Ixopo Mounted Rifles** defend the southern border of Natal, and another small detachment remained at **Fort Durnford**, the NMP's headquarters. The majority of the NMP crossed into **Zululand** with No. 3 Column, taking part in the skirmish at **kwaSogekle** on 12 January. The greater part of the NMP was absent with Major **John George Dartnell**'s reconnaissance in force when the remainder left in the camp at **Isandlwana** suffered heavy casualties in the battle there. Three members of the NMP took part in the defense of **Rorke's Drift**. The NMP retired with No. 3 Column to Natal, where a detachment remained at Rorke's Drift while the rest took up position at Helpmekaar.

The NMP spent the rest of the war engaged in patrol work, cross-border raids, escort duty, and dispatch riding. In June, the NMP received recruits from England and Natal. In July, a detachment escorted General **Sir Garnet Joseph Wolseley** from Rorke's Drift to the **Mahlabathini Plain**. One section then joined **Clarke's Column** in the hunt for King **Cetshwayo kaMpande**, while another joined **Baker Russell's Column**. In September, all the NMP returned to peacetime duties. Their black corduroy uniform faded on campaign to dark gray; after Isandlwana, when replacement clothing was scarce, the NMP were permitted to wear British infantry trousers.

**NATAL MOUNTED VOLUNTEERS.** At the time of the **Anglo-Zulu War**, the 11 corps of Natal Mounted Volunteers mustered 430 officers and men. On 26 November 1878, 10 of the corps, the majority of whose men had volunteered in October 1878 for active service in **Zululand**, were called out. The 11th corps, the **Ixopo Mounted Rifles**, remained in **Natal** to guard the southern border. The Volunteers mustered out in July 1879. *See also* NATAL VOLUNTEER CORPS.

**NATAL NATIVE CONTINGENT, 1ST BATTALION.** Initially mustered for the **Anglo-Zulu War** as the 1st Battalion, 1st Regiment, **Natal Native Contingent** (NNC), in the reorganization of February 1879 it became the 1st Battalion, NNC, under Commandant Alexander N. Montgomery. It was stationed at **Fort Cherry** in **Colonial Defensive District** No. VII until disbanded in October. It took part in border demonstrations and raids, but it was ineffective against the major Zulu counterraid at **Middle Drift**. In March, it built **Fort Montgomery** at Middle Drift, and detachments garrisoned the fort from late June until October.

**NATAL NATIVE CONTINGENT, 2ND BATTALION.** Initially mustered for the **Anglo-Zulu War** as the 2nd Battalion, 1st Regiment, **Natal Native Contingent** (NNC), in the reorganization of February 1879 it became the 2nd Battalion, NNC, under Major Harcourt M. Bengough. It remained at **Fort Bengough** in **Colonial Defensive District** No. I, where it was engaged in border demonstrations and raids. In May, it joined the 2nd Division, **South African Field Force**, for the 2nd Invasion of the Anglo-Zulu War. During 13–21 May, it took part in extensive raids from **Landman's Drift** to clear the countryside ahead of the advance. Detachments garrisoned **Fort Newdigate** and **Fort Evelyn**, and the battalion fought at **Ulundi**. After the breakup of the 2nd Division, it joined **Baker Russell's Column**. On the way to the Transvaal and disbandment in October, detachments garrisoned **Fort Cambridge** and **Fort George**.

**NATAL NATIVE CONTINGENT, 3RD BATTALION.** Initially mustered for the **Anglo-Zulu War** as the 3rd Battalion, 1st Regiment,

Natal Native Contingent (NNC), in the reorganization of February 1879 it became the 3rd Battalion, NNC, under Captain Charles E. Le M. Cherry and was stationed at **Fort Cherry** in **Colonial Defensive District** No. VII until disbanded in October. It took part in border demonstrations and raids, but it was ineffective against the major Zulu counterraid at **Middle Drift**.

**NATAL NATIVE CONTINGENT, 4TH BATTALION.** Initially mustered for the **Anglo-Zulu War** as the 1st Battalion, 2nd Regiment, **Natal Native Contingent** (NNC), in the reorganization of February 1879 it became the 4th Battalion, NNC, under Captain G. Barton. It joined the 1st Brigade, **Eshowe Relief Column**, and fought at **Gingindlovu**. It then formed part of the 1st Division, **South African Field Force**, in its advance to **Port Durnford**. After the breakup of the 1st Division, it served with **Clarke's Column** and was disbanded in October.

**NATAL NATIVE CONTINGENT, 5TH BATTALION.** Initially mustered for the **Anglo-Zulu War** as the 2nd Battalion, 2nd Regiment, **Natal Native Contingent** (NNC), in the reorganization of February 1879 it became the 5th Battalion, NNC, under Commandant W. Nettleton. It joined the 2nd Brigade, **Eshowe Relief Column**, and fought at **Gingindlovu**. It then formed part of the 2nd Division, **South African Field Force**, in its advance to **Port Durnford**. Detachments garrisoned **Fort Crealock** and **Fort Chelmsford** and the camp at Port Durnford until the withdrawal of all British troops from the coast. It was disbanded in October.

**NATAL NATIVE CONTINGENT (INFANTRY).** British regular infantry serving in **Zululand** during the **Anglo-Zulu War** were too valuable and scarce to be dispersed on garrison and convoy duty and were augmented by African levies (troops) intended for service in Zululand. In **Natal**, the lieutenant-governor had the right to exact *isiBhalo*, or compulsory labor and military service, from Africans. Magistrates accordingly raised Africans for military service from the chiefs in the Native Reserves, encouraging recruitment with promises of captured **cattle**. The Natal Native Contingent (NNC) assembled in December 1878. For the 1st Invasion of the Anglo-Zulu War, it was formed into three regiments of seven battalions. Each battalion consisted of 10 companies, with an initial nominal establishment of 1,100 officers and men. Three white officers and six white noncommissioned officers (NCOs) led each company, which consisted of one African officer, 10 African NCOs, and 90 men. Finding suitably qualified white officers and NCOs proved difficult. Many had to be recruited from the **Cape** or were seconded or former British officers (who were preferred for the senior command). Many knew no Zulu, and this led to great dissatisfaction among the men. In the reorganization of the NNC for the 2nd Invasion of the Anglo-Zulu War, regimental organization was abolished and the battalion became the highest military structure. Five battalions were created from the 1st and 2nd Regiments. The 3rd Regiment, disbanded after **Isandlwana**, was reassembled in April 1879 as the **Weenen Contingent**.

There was much settler resistance to Africans being issued **firearms**, so only the African officers and 10 noncommissioned officers (NCOs) in each company were issued with Enfield percussion **rifles**, and the rest of the men carried their traditional **spears** and **shields**. The white officers and NCOs were issued with **Martini-Henry** rifles. With the reorganization of the NNC for the 2nd Invasion of the Anglo-Zulu War, several hundred breech-loading Sniders and Martini-Henrys were issued to each NNC battalion in addition to the Enfields they already held. Poorly armed and ineffectually trained in unfamiliar British drill and tactics, the NNC proved of doubtful morale and effectiveness. It was primarily employed in providing border patrols, garrisons, and cattle guards. Sometimes it found itself in the front line of battle, as at Isandlwana, though in pitched engagements its primary task was to sally out of the prepared position once the Zulu were routed, as at **Gingindlovu** and **Ulundi**, and to dispatch the enemy wounded. *See also individual units.*

**NATAL NATIVE CONTINGENT, 1ST REGIMENT.** The three battalions of the 1st Regiment, Natal Native Contingent (NNC), under Brevet Colonel **Anthony William Durnford**, joined No. 2 **Column** in December 1878 at **Ntunjambili** (Kranskop) in **Colonial Defensive District** No. VII for the 1st Invasion of the **Anglo-Zulu War**. When Durnford marched on 10 January to reinforce No. 3 Column, he took two companies of the 1st Battalion with him while the 2nd Battalion followed after. After **Isandlwana**, where the detachment of the 1st Battalion was annihilated, the 2nd Battalion took up position at **Fort Bengough** in District I to defend the border from Zulu invasion. At Ntunjambili, the rest of the regiment built and garrisoned **Fort Cherry** to hold the middle border. The regiment was reorganized in February into the 1st, 2nd, and 3rd Battalions, NNC.

**NATAL NATIVE CONTINGENT, 2ND REGIMENT.** During the **Anglo-Zulu War**, the two battalions of the 2nd Regiment, Natal Native Contingent (NNC), under Major Shapland H. Graves served initially with No. 1 **Column**, and the 1st Battalion took part in the battle of **Nyezane** as part of the column's 1st Division. On 30 January, the regiment was sent back to **Natal** from **Fort Eshowe**, and in February 1879 it was reorganized into the 4th and 5th Battalions, NNC.

**NATAL NATIVE CONTINGENT, 3RD REGIMENT.** The two battalions of the 3rd Regiment, Natal Native Contingent (NNC), under Commandant Rupert La T. Lonsdale served with No. 3 **Column** in the 1st Invasion of the **Anglo-Zulu War**. The 1st Battalion took part on 12 January 1879 in the skirmish at **kwaSogekle**. Two companies from each of the battalions fought and died at **Isandlwana**; the rest of the regiment, except for a company of the 2nd Battalion stationed at **Rorke's Drift**, was absent during the battle on the reconnaissance in force. The company at Rorke's Drift deserted before the Zulu attacked, and the rest of the demoralized regiment deserted in the following days. The white noncommissioned officers subsequently formed the **Natal Horse.** In April, some of the African members of the 3rd Regiment were reassembled to form the **Weenen Contingent**.

**NATAL NATIVE HORSE.** Following **Isandlwana** in the **Anglo-Zulu War**, the three troops of **Sikali's Horse** who had taken part in the battle dispersed home, but the remaining two troops of the **Natal Native Mounted Contingent** in the battle, **Hlubi's Troop** and the **Edendale Horse**, remained at **Helpmekaar**. On 20 February 1879, they were put under the command of Lieutenant W.F.D. Cochrane and reorganized as the Natal Native Horse. Fresh recruits were attracted, and in March some 130 troopers joined No. 4 **Column**, fighting at **Hlobane** in Lieutenant-Colonel **John Cecil Russell**'s force and at **Khambula**. As part of **Wood's Flying Column** for the 2nd Invasion of the Anglo-Zulu War, they took part in the **White Mfolozi reconnaissance in force** and fought at **Ulundi**. With the breakup of Wood's Flying Column in late July, they were disbanded.

**NATAL NATIVE MOUNTED CONTINGENT.** In planning during 1878 for the **Anglo-Zulu War**, it was the British intention from the outset to raise **irregular cavalry** as well as infantry for the **Natal Native Contingent**. Keen and effective volunteers from the Natal Native Reserves and from the Christian community of Edendale outside **Pietermaritzburg** formed six troops for the 1st Invasion of the Anglo-Zulu War: three troops of **Sikali's Horse** and a troop each of the **Edendale Horse, Hlubi's Troop**, and **Jantze's Native Horse**. Maintained by the War Office and commanded by white colonial officers, they supplied their own **horses** but were armed with breech-loading **carbines** (some men also carrying traditional weapons) and were given uniforms of yellow or brown corduroy and brown broad-brimmed hats with a red puggaree. Only the Edendale Horse elected to wear the boots issued them; the rest rode barefoot, and Jantze's Native Horse refused to wear the trousers issued them. Initially, all six troops formed part of No. 2 **Column**. All except Jantze's Native Horse left Ntunjambili on 10 January 1879 to join No. 3 Column and fought at **Isandlwana**. Subsequently, the Natal Native Mounted Contingent was reorganized to form the **Natal Native Horse** and **Shepstone's Native Horse**.

**NATAL NATIVE PIONEER CORPS.** As an extension of the colonial government's right to exact *isiBhalo* (compulsory service) from Africans in **Natal**, in 1878 it raised three companies of African Pioneers, each under five white and four black officers, to repair roads and drifts and to construct earthwork fortifications during the coming **Anglo-Zulu War**.

No. 1 Company under Captain J. Nolan served initially with No. 3 **Column**, and a detachment fought at **Isandlwana**. The company was then assigned to No. 4 Column. It marched with **Wood's Flying Column** in the 2nd Invasion of the Anglo-Zulu War and was present at **Ulundi**. With the breakup of Wood's Flying Column in late July, it was assigned to **Clarke's Column** and was disbanded in October. No. 2 Company under Captain G.K.E. Beddoes served with No. 1 Column. It was present at **Nyezane** and played a significant part during the siege of **Eshowe** in helping build the fort and in undertaking scouting duties. After the relief of Eshowe, it remained on the lower Thukela border and was disbanded in October. No. 3 Company under Captain W. Allen was assigned to No. 2 Column and remained at **Ntunjambili** (Kranskop) in **Colonial Defensive District** No. VII throughout the war. It helped in the construction of **Fort Cherry** and other earthworks and participated in border raids and demonstrations.

Native Pioneers were issued uniforms consisting of an outdated red military frock with facings removed, knee-length white cotton trousers, and a blue pillbox forage cap with a yellow band. Each man carried an implement such as a shovel or pickax; **firearms** were restricted to those with rank.

**NATAL VOLUNTEER CORPS. Natal** Ordnance No. 8 of 1854 provided for the establishment of a Volunteer Corps for the protection of the colony, and the Volunteer Ordnance of 1872 better defined its organization and regulations. At the time of the **Anglo-Zulu War**, the corps mustered about 750 officers and men and consisted of one artillery, three infantry, and 11 mounted corps. Drawn predominantly from the English-speaking colonists, the men elected their own officers and provided their own uniforms and **horses**, but they were issued with weapons and maintained by the government. They were required to train 20 days a year, and the government reserved the right to disband any corps that fell below 20 members. In October 1878, the majority of men volunteered for active service outside Natal in **Zululand**. On 26 November 1878, 10 of the 11 corps of **Natal Mounted Volunteers** were called out. The Volunteers mustered out at the end of July 1879. During the **uSuthu Rebellion**, attempts in July 1888 to raise volunteers from the Natal Volunteer Corps to serve in Zululand with the **Coastal Column** met with little response and were abandoned.

**NATAL VOLUNTEER GUIDES.** In March 1879 during the **Anglo-Zulu War**, Lieutenant-General Lord **Chelmsford** raised a force of 60 **irregular cavalry** to serve with the **Eshowe Relief Column**. They were drawn from the various corps of the **Natal Mounted Volunteers** then stationed along the lower Thukela River. The contributing corps, named in order of strength of contribution, were the **Stanger Mounted Rifles**, Isipingo Mounted Rifles, **Durban Mounted Rifles**, **Victoria Mounted Rifles**, and **Alexandra Mounted Rifles**. The Natal Volunteer Guides fought at **Gingindlovu**. After the relief of **Eshowe**, they served with the 1st Division, **South African Field Force**, along the lines of communication. In early July, they withdrew to the **Natal** border and were mustered out by the end of the month.

**NATAL–ZULULAND BOUNDARY (1843).** On 5 October 1843, the British in **Natal** and King **Mpande kaSenzangakhona** in **Zululand** recognized their respective sovereignties. The British abandoned previous Boer territorial claims as far north as the Black Mfolozi River, and the boundary between Natal and Zululand was fixed from the mouth of the Thukela River to its confluence with the Mzinyathi River, and then up its course to the **Drakensberg**. *See also* BOUNDARIES AND COLONIAL CONTROL IN ZULULAND; BOUNDARY AWARD; NATALIA, REPUBLIC OF.

**NATALIA, REPUBLIC OF.** King **Dingane kaSenzangakhona**'s doubtfully authentic cession of 4 February 1838 gave the Voortrekkers Port Natal (**Durban**) together with all the lands between the **Drakensberg** and the Indian Ocean bounded by the Thukela River to the north and the Mzimvubu River to the south. The Boers set up the Republic of Natalia under an elected *volksraad* with the capital at **Pietermaritzburg**. On 25 March 1839, a new treaty between Dingane and the Boers agreed to let them live unmolested south of the Thukela. *UmNtwana* **Mpande kaSenzangakhona** struck a military alliance with the Boers on 27 October 1839 against his half-brother, Dingane. In return for making him king, he agreed to cede **St. Lucia Bay** to Natalia. Following Dingane's defeat in the 1st **Zulu Civil War**, Mpande also ceded the Boers all the land north of the Thukela up to the Black Mfolozi River. On 5 July 1842, Natalia submitted to British authority. *See also* NATAL, BRITISH COLONY OF.

**NATIVE FOOT SCOUTS (DUNN'S SCOUTS).** In December 1878 on the eve of the **Anglo-Zulu War**, **John Dunn**, King **Cetshwayo**

kaMpande's white chief in southeastern **Zululand**, defected to **Natal** with all his adherents, many of whom had worked for him as hunters. In March 1879, he raised a force of about 250 Scouts who joined the **Eshowe Relief Column** and fought at **Gingindlovu**. After the relief of **Eshowe**, the Scouts served with the 1st Division, **South African Field Force**, until the division was broken up in July.

**NAVAL BRIGADES.** On 19 November 1878, a Naval Brigade from **HMS** *Active* landed at **Durban** under the command of Acting Captain HJF. Campbell consisting of 170 sailors and **Royal Marine Light Infantry**. It joined the 1st Division, No. 1 **Column**, at the lower Thukela River for the coming **Anglo-Zulu War** and was reinforced on 6 January 1879 by a contingent of 50 sailors and Royal Marines from **HMS** *Tenedos*. The Naval Brigade helped construct **Fort Pearson** and **Fort Tenedos**, built its own Naval Redoubt overlooking the lower Thukela River, fought at **Nyezane**, and was blockaded with No. 1 Column at **Fort Eshowe**. On 6 March, **HMS** *Shah* landed a Naval Brigade in Durban of 400 men under Commander J. Brackenbury, followed on 15 March by a further Naval Brigade of 200 men under Captain T. W. Richards from **HMS** *Boadicea*. These men were joined by a contingent furnished by **HMS** *Tenedos* in addition to the men already with No. 1 Column. The Brigade joined the **Eshowe Relief Column**, the contingents from HMS *Shah* and *Tenedos* fighting with the column's 1st Brigade at **Gingindlovu**, and the contingent from HMS *Boadicea* and the detachments of Royal Marines from HMS *Boadicea* and HMS *Shah* with the 2nd Brigade. Detachments garrisoned Fort Pearson and Fort Tenedos during the Eshowe Relief Column's advance. After the relief of Eshowe, the Naval Brigade joined the 1st Division, **South African Field Force**, and advanced with it to **Port Durnford**. On 21 July, it embarked at Port Durnford for Durban, where it rejoined the ships. *See also* ROYAL MARINE ARTILLERY.

**NCOME, BATTLE OF (1838).** After months of inconclusive fighting in the **Voortrekker-Zulu War**, in late November 1838 the *Wenkommando* under **Andries Wilhelmus Jacobus Pretorius** advanced east from the Sooilaer (Sod Laager) near Loskop on the Little Thukela

River into **Zululand** to force a decisive battle with King **Dingane kaSenzangakhona**'s army. On 15 December, the **commando** (militia) formed its 64 wagons into a **laager** on a spit of land between the **Ncome River** to the east and a donga (dry watercourse) to the south. This meant that the defenders, who consisted of 472 Boers, three white traders from Port Natal (**Durban**), and 120 Port Natal African levies under **Alexander Harvey Biggar**, could concentrate when attacked along the laager's more vulnerable west and north faces. Crammed inside were some 700 **oxen,** 750 **horses,** 130 black wagon-drivers, and 200 grooms.

The Zulu army of between 12,000 and 16,000 under *inKosi* **Ndlela kaSompisi** and *inKosi* **Nzobo kaSobadli** advanced from the southeast before dawn on 16 December. The left horn of 3,000 younger *amaButho* came on in advance of the chest and right horn, crossed the Ncome south of the laager, and charged it from the west and north, attempting to envelop it. An uninterrupted rate of impenetrable fire from **muskets** and several small cannon shooting in ordered rotation repulsed the left horn, which broke and was pursued some way by Boer horsemen. The Zulu right horn then advanced on the laager, intending to cross the Ncome to the northeast of it. Fire from Boer horsemen posted along the river deflected this flanking movement, and the right horn veered to its left. Followed by the chest, it then attacked along the same route as the already defeated left horn. Despite repeated attempts, it was unable to break through the Boer zone of fire, and some Zulu units began to withdraw in disarray.

Pretorius and about 160 mounted men pursued them over several hours, scattering the Zulu in all directions. Their slaughter bloodied the waters of the Ncome, which the Boers renamed Bloedrivier, or Blood River. The Boers admitted to three wounded in the battle. Probably well over 1,000 Zulu were killed, but the Boer tally of 3,000 Zulu dead was likely exaggerated.

Their defeat at Ncome and the subsequent dispersal of their army crippled the Zulus' ability to carry on the war. They were unable to resist the forced march of the *Wenkommando* that reached **uMgungundlovu** on 20 December, while Dingane withdrew north out of its range. *See also* RECONCILIATION, DAY OF; STRATEGY, BOER; STRATEGY, ZULU; TACTICS UP TO 1879, ZULU.

**iNDABAKAWOMBE** *iBUTHO*. King **Mpande kaSenzangakhona** formed this *iButho* around 1841 of youths born about 1821. The **shield** was white. During the 2nd **Zulu Civil War**, it fought at **Ndondkusuka** on the right of the **uSuthu** chest. Most of it remained in reserve at **oNdini** during the **Anglo-Zulu War**, though local elements fought at **Nyezane**. At the time of the battle of **Ulundi**, it was guarding King **Cetshwayo kaMpande** at the **kwaMbonambi** *iKhanda*.

**kwaNDABAKAWOMBE** *iKHANDA*. This was one of the *ama-Khanda* in the **Mahlabathini Plain** burned by the British in the **Anglo-Zulu War** after the battle of **Ulundi**.

**NDABUKO kaMPANDE (c. 1843–1900).** Enrolled in the **uMbonambi** *iButho*, *umNtwana* Ndabuko was King **Cetshwayo kaMpande**'s younger brother and supported him staunchly in the 2nd **Zulu Civil War**. During the **Anglo-Zulu War**, he fought at **Isandlwana**. In the 1st Partition of **Zululand**, he was placed under *inKosi* **Zibhebhu kaMaphitha** and soon quarreled over the control of royal women and **cattle**. He assumed the guardianship of *umNtwana* **Dinuzulu kaMpande** and was prominent in leading appeals for Cetshwayo's restoration. During the 3rd Zulu Civil War, he led the **uSuthu** at **Msebe** and arrived too late with his contingent to join the battle of **oNdini**. He then joined Cetshwayo in the **Nkandla Forest**. After the king's death in 1884, he once more became Dinuzulu's guardian and effective leader of the uSuthu until Dinuzulu came of age. Ndabuko deeply resented the imposition of the British administration in the Colony of Zululand, and his recalcitrant response was instrumental in the outbreak of the **uSuthu Rebellion**. He was present at **Ceza** and **Ivuna**, then fled to the **South African Republic** with the British suppression of the rebellion. In September 1888, he surrendered to the British. With other uSuthu leaders, he was tried for high treason and public violence at **Eshowe**. Found guilty in 1889, he was sent to St. Helena to serve his sentence of 15 years. In December 1897, Ndabuko was permitted to return to Zululand with the other prisoners.

**NDEBELE KINGDOM.** In 1822, Mzilikazi kaMashobane, a Khumalo *inKosi* owing allegiance to King **Shaka kaSenzangakhona**, fled north over the **Drakensberg** to the highveld when Shaka threatened to attack him. There he established a new chiefdom in the vicinity of modern **Pretoria**, augmenting his Khumalo adherents with **Sotho** and **Pedi** people in the vicinity, and with other refugees from Shaka. He extended his kingdom and raided in all directions. In 1830 and 1832, Zulu armies sent by King **Dingane kaSenzangakhona** raided the Ndebele and this, compounded by constant Griqua and Kora mounted raids from the southwest, persuaded Mzilikazi in 1833 to move farther west to Mosega, on the Marico River, where the Ndebele displaced the Tswana chiefdoms in the area.

Mzilikazi modeled his state on the Zulu kingdom, with the *iButho system* as its central feature. He attempted to obtain **firearms** from traders and missionaries, but his armies still fought in the traditional Zulu style. The Ndebele were therefore no match for the Voortrekkers advancing into their territory in 1836. On 16 October 1836, Voortrekkers defeated the Ndebele at Vegkop. On 17 January 1837, a Boer **commando** (militia) took Mosega by surprise in a successful raid. Dingane took advantage of his old adversary's misfortune, and in June 1837 a Zulu army raided Ndebele territory, weakening Mzilikazi further. In November 1837, the Boers struck again, worsting the Ndebele in a nine-day battle at eGabeni to the north of Mosega. Mzilikazi and the remnants of his people migrated north out of range of Boer and Zulu alike. They crossed the Limpopo River and created a new state in the Matopo Hills in what is now southwestern Zimbabwe. *See also* STRATEGY, BOER; STRATEGY, ZULU; TACTICS UP TO 1879, ZULU.

**oNDINI, BATTLE OF (1883).** In July 1883 during the 3rd **Zulu Civil War**, the **uSuthu**, recovering from their crushing defeat at **Msebe** in March 1883, began preparing for an all-out assault from several directions simultaneously on their enemy, *inKosi* **Zibhebhu kaMaphitha** of the **Mandlakazi**. Threatened on all sides, Zibhebhu resolved to preempt the uSuthu. On 20 July, he concentrated about 2,400 Mandlakazi and 600 **Ngenetsheni** at his **ekuVukeni** *umuZi* along with 10 to 12 mounted white **mercenaries**. That night he led them on a march that brought them in the early morning to King **Cetshwayo kaMpande**'s **oNdini** *iKhanda* and took the uSuthu army of 3,600 men there entirely by surprise. The unprepared and disorganized uSuthu did their best to take up positions a mile east of oNdini under the command of Ntuzwa kaNhlaka. A further uSuthu force at the **kwaNodwengu** *iKhanda* three miles to the west of oNdini was too far away to join the battle in time. The left horn of Zibhebhu's force outflanked the uSuthu right that stampeded back in fear of being cut off, and the rest of the uSuthu line collapsed before Zibhebhu's men could come to grips with them. A few uSuthu tried to make a stand in oNdini, but the rest fled in complete confusion. Zibhebhu's left horn cut off their retreat to the White Mfolozi River, and the uSuthu contingent hurrying over from kwaNodwengu got caught up in the general rout. Another force of 1,500 uSuthu under *umNtwana* **Ndabuko kaMpande** that was marching toward oNdini from the north turned back about five miles short of oNdini when it saw the *amaKhanda* in the **Mahlabathini Plain** in flames.

The uSuthu cause was entirely lost in the remorseless pursuit. Among the over 500 uSuthu dead were members of Cetshwayo's family and 59 or more *amaKhosi* and men of influence from every part of the Zulu kingdom who were left defenseless when the fighting men fled. Their slaughter ended the old order in **Zululand** far more conclusively than had defeat in the **Anglo-Zulu War**. Cetshwayo and uSuthu survivors took refuge in the **Nkandla Forest** in the **Reserve Territory**, leaving Zibhebhu (who had lost only seven men in the battle) a free hand to raid and pillage in central and northern Zululand. *See also* STRATEGY, ZULU; TACTICS IN 1880s, ZULU.

**oNDINI *iKHANDA*.** In 1855, King **Mpande kaSenzangakhona** ordered the first oNdini *iKhanda* to be built for *umNtwana* **Cetshwayo kaMpande** on the southern bank of the lower Mhlathuze River in southeastern **Zululand** as a means of separating him from *umNtwana* **Mbuyazi kaMpande**, his rival for the succession. Known also as Hlalangubo, it consisted of 640 huts. At the time of his **coronation** in 1873, King Cetshwayo started building the second oNdini in the **Mahlabathini Plain** as his "great place." It contained between 1,000 and 1,400 huts. In the *isiGodlo* (private enclosure), to conduct business he erected a four-roomed, wallpapered house with glazed windows, verandahs, and a thatched roof. As the Zulu "capital," oNdini was the principal objective of the invading British columns in the **Anglo-Zulu War**. On 4 July 1879 during the 2nd Invasion of the Anglo-Zulu War, the British infantry **square** halted a mile and a half west of it. The main Zulu reserve was quartered there, but its advance at the height of the battle of **Ulundi** was broken up by British **artillery** fire. At the end of the battle, the British shelled oNdini and then set about burning it. The Zulu, having stripped it bare, had also set fire to it and the British completed the job.

After the 2nd Partition of Zululand, the restored Cetshwayo immediately set about building a third oNdini just to the east of the previous one. It was smaller in diameter but still contained 1,000 huts or more. It was not yet completed when on 21 July 1883, during the 3rd **Zulu Civil War**, *inKosi* **Zibhebhu kaMaphitha**'s forces caught the **uSuthu** forces quartered there by surprise. They formed up as best they could to the east of oNdini before being put to flight. Some of the **uThulwana** *iButho* tried to make a stand in oNdini but were cut off and killed. The victorious **Mandlakazi** and **Ngenetsheni** set oNdini and the other rebuilt *amaKhanda* in the Mahlabathini Plain ablaze.

**NDLELA kaSOMPISI (?–1840).** King **Shaka kaSenzangakhona** appointed Ndlela, who was connected through marriage to the Zulu royal house, *inKosi* of the **Ntuli people** in southern **Zululand** and raised him to high military command. When he usurped the throne in 1828, King **Dingane kaSenzangakhona** did not execute Ndlela as he did so many of Shaka's other favorites, but appointed him his commander-in-chief and chief *inDuna*. In mid-1837, Ndlela led an inconclusive campaign against the **Ndebele**. When in late 1837 the Voortrekkers invaded Zululand, Ndlela persuaded Dingane to resist rather than negotiate, and to execute **Pieter Retief** and his party when they came to **uMgungundlovu**. During the ensuing **Voortrekker-Zulu War**, Ndlela led the Zulu at **Veglaer**, and he was in joint command of the army routed at **Ncome**. He commanded Dingane's army in the 1st **Zulu Civil War** at the **Maqongqo Hills**. Ndlela escaped the rout wounded, but his defeat cost Dingane his throne, and his unforgiving master had him strangled.

**iNDLONDLO** *iBUTHO*. King **Mpande kaSenzangakhona** formed this *iButho* around 1857 of youths born about 1837 and incorporated it into the **uThulwana** *iButho*. During the 2nd **Zulu Civil War**, it fought at **Ndondakusuka** on the right horn of the **uSuthu**. In the **Anglo-Zulu War**, it formed part of the uncommitted reserve at **Isandlwana**, then went on to attack **Rorke's Drift**. It fought with the chest at **Khambula**, and at **Ulundi** it attacked the northern side of the British infantry **square**.

**iNDLUYENGWE** *iBUTHO*. King **Mpande kaSenzangakhona** formed this *iButho* around 1866 of youths born about 1846 and incorporated it into the **uThulwana** *iButho*. The **shield** was black with white spots on the lower half. In the **Anglo-Zulu War**, it formed part of the uncommitted reserve at **Isandlwana** and went on to **Rorke's Drift**, where it was first to attack. At **Khambula**, it fought with the chest. Elements stationed at the **isinPuseleni** *iKhanda* fought at **Gingindlovu**. At **Ulundi**, it attacked the southwest corner of the British infantry **square**.

**NDONDAKUSUKA, BATTLE OF (1856).** During 1856, the rivalry for the Zulu succession between *umNtwana* **Cetshwayo kaMpande** and his half-brother *umNtwana* **Mbuyazi kaMpande**, King **Mpande kaSenzangakhona**'s favorite son, reached a crisis in the 1st **Zulu Civil War**. In late November 1856, Mbuyazi and his **iziGqoza** adherents, including men, women, children, and livestock, retreated toward the drifts across the lower Thukela River to **Natal**, while Cetshwayo advanced on them with an army of between 15,000 and 20,000 **uSuthu**. Mbuyazi had only about 7,000 fighting men, but he secured the aid of 35 Natal Frontier Police and about 100 African hunters and some white hunter-traders under **John Dunn**. These **iziNqobo**, as they were known, provided the iziGqoza with much-needed firepower. On 30 December, the uSuthu army encamped close to the iziGqoza. Mbuyazi hoped to move his people to safety in Natal across the Thukela, but the river was swollen with summer rains and impassable. Five white hunter-trader families were also caught on the Zulu side of the river but managed to make it to a small island in the middle.

On 1 December, the iziGqoza began gingerly to advance against the uSuthu while their noncombatants took shelter in the wooded stream beds flowing into the Thukela. Dunn's iziNqobo fired on the uSuthu advance scouts, but it was close to dark and both sides then withdrew for the night. Early the following rainy morning of 2 December, the two sides drew up in the traditional chest and horns formation. The uSuthu plan was for their right horn to get between the iziGqoza and cut them off from escape across the river while the chest (where the most experienced fighters were placed) and the left horn would encircle them. The iziNqobo were positioned on the iziGqoza left flank to prevent the uSuthu outflanking them and successfully drove back repeated assaults. Their attack failing on the right, the uSuthu moved their best units from the chest to the left horn and turned the iziGqoza right flank. The rest of the iziGqoza then lost heart and fell back. Their orderly retreat turned into a rout when they became entangled with the panicking noncombatants to the rear. A general flight to the river began, with the remnants of the iziNqobo trying to cover them.

On Cetshwayo's orders, the uSuthu did not kill the terrified hunter-traders marooned on their island. Although Dunn escaped, most of the iziNqobo died, and the iziGqoza were massacred all along the north bank of the Thukela or perished in its crocodile-infested waters. The uSuthu showed no mercy, and Mbuyazi and five of his brothers were killed, as well as three-quarters of the noncombatants. Only about 2,000 of the iziGqoza warriors escaped to Natal. The uSuthu casualties are unknown, though their right horn suffered heavily from gunfire. The battle decided the Zulu succession in Cetshwayo's favor. *See also* TACTICS UP TO 1879, ZULU.

**NEGOTIATIONS DURING THE ANGLO-ZULU WAR.** Before the outbreak of war in 1879 and during the **Anglo-Zulu War** itself, King **Cetshwayo kaMpande** made repeated attempts to negotiate, sending emissaries to **Natal**, British forts, and the march **laagers** of the invaders in the field. But the British terms, as stated in the **ultimatum** of 11 December 1878, were emphatically not negotiable. For their part, Cetshwayo and his *iBandla* (royal council) wished for peace on terms acceptable to them, and their conditions changed in response to the course of the British invasion. Zulu peace overtures began with half-hearted fencing, followed by an attempt after **Isandlwana** to impose a settlement from strength, then increasingly desperate efforts to stem the British 2nd Invasion of the Anglo-Zulu War as *amaKhosi* scrambled to **submit**, ending with Cetshwayo's final pleas for clemency. Negotiations were further complicated by the Zulu diplomatic convention whereby the king's emissaries were dispatched merely to set up a meeting of leaders or to relay messages but had no plenipotentiary powers. Both sides, moreover, were not above using negotiations to string the other along while military preparations were being made.

Many important *amaKhosi* who were considering submitting to the British also opened up their own negotiations with them. The British were sympathetic to these overtures because it was part of their strategy to persuade the *amaKhosi* to abandon Cetshwayo's cause, and they were prepared to offer them much more favorable terms than were available to the king.

**NEW GERMANY RIFLES.** *See* PINETOWN LAAGER.

**NEW REPUBLIC.** In return for their aid in defeating *inKosi* **Zibhebhu kaMaphitha** at **Tshaneni** during the 3rd **Zulu Civil War**, King **Dinuzulu kaCetshwayo** ceded the Boers of **Dinuzulu's Volunteers** the northwestern two-thirds of **Zululand** (2,710,000 acres), which they proclaimed the New Republic. Its capital was the newly laid out village of **Vryheid**. The Boers divided the territory into 802 farms and reduced the remaining Zulu to labor tenants. Meanwhile, imperial Germany was showing interest in the Zululand coast, and the British feared they might attempt to link up with the landlocked Boers of the **South African Republic** through the New Republic. The British therefore asserted their claims to **St. Lucia Bay** on 21 December 1884 and intervened to stop the New Republic's ambitious land claims of 1885 and 1886, which thrust provocatively toward the Zululand coast at the expense of **Eastern Zululand**, the territory nominally still ruled by Dinuzulu under Boer "protection." In return for British recognition of the New Republic on 22 October 1886, the Boers agreed to limit their territorial claims and drop their attempt to impose a protectorate over Eastern Zululand. On 25 January 1887, a boundary commission completed the task of defining the New Republic's borders. The New Republic did not possess the capacity to maintain itself as an independent state and on 20 July 1888 was incorporated into the South African Republic as the Vryheid District. Following the British defeat of the South African Republic in the

**Anglo-Boer (South African) War**, on 27 January 1903 the Vryheid District was annexed to **Natal**.

**NEWCASTLE.** On 31 March 1864, Newcastle was proclaimed the seat of the magistracy for the Newcastle Division in northern **Natal**. It was only with the arrival in 1877 of a British garrison of the 80th **Regiment** (Staffordshire Volunteers) at **Fort Amiel** to monitor developments in the recently annexed Transvaal Territory that the village began to expand. By the **Anglo-Zulu War**, when it fell into **Colonial Defensive District** No. I, it had a population of about 250 white civilians. *See also* NEWCASTLE LAAGER.

**NEWCASTLE LAAGER.** In late 1877, the **Natal** government ordered that the public buildings in **Newcastle**, including the courthouse, jail, magistrate's office, and post office, be connected by a brick wall to form a **laager** for the protection of the townsfolk. During 1878, improvements were made to the fortifications, and arms and ammunition were stored for the use of the Town Guard. The laager was never remotely threatened during the **Anglo-Zulu War**, but in the panicked exodus after **Isandlwana**, few civilians were left to hold it, and its defense was in the hands of the African **Newcastle Scouts** and a few military convalescents until a small British garrison detached from **Helpmekaar** could be installed.

**NEWCASTLE MOUNTED RIFLES.** Formed in 1875, the Newcastle Mounted Rifles was one of the 10 corps of **Natal Mounted Volunteers** called out in November 1878 for active service in the **Anglo-Zulu War**. In December 1878, they joined No. 3 **Column** at **Helpmekaar** with 36 troopers. Most advanced with the column into **Zululand**, though a handful declined to do so and remained in **Natal** patrolling the border. Those still with No. 3 Column took part in the skirmish at **kwaSogekle**. Half the corps was absent with Major **John George Dartnell**'s reconnaissance in force when the remainder left behind in the camp at **Isandlwana** suffered heavy casualties in the Zulu attack. The Newcastle Mounted Rifles retired with No. 3 Column to Natal, where it garrisoned **Fort Pine** between February and July 1879. It spent the rest of the war engaged in patrol work, cross-border raids, escort duty, and dispatch riding. It took part in the patrol of 21 May that began the burial of the dead at Isandlwana. The uniform was of dark green cloth, with black facings and black trouser stripes, black riding-boots, and a white helmet.

**NEWCASTLE SCOUTS.** In the aftermath of **Isandlwana** during the **Anglo-Zulu War**, when the town of **Newcastle** had few defenders, a force of 50 mounted African levies was raised to patrol the region and was available to help defend the **Newcastle laager**. In April 1879, the Newcastle Scouts were incorporated into the **Weenen Contingent**.

**NEWDIGATE, EDWARD (1825–1902).** Commissioned in 1842, Newdigate saw service in the Crimean War (1854–1855) and the Red River Expedition (1870). In 1877, he was promoted to major-general. During the **Anglo-Zulu War**, he proceeded on special service to **Natal** in February 1879 with reinforcements. He took command of the 2nd Division, **South African Field Force**, during the 2nd Invasion of the Anglo-Zulu War and fought at **Ulundi**. Lieutenant-General Lord **Chelmsford** accompanied the 2nd Division and eclipsed Newdigate in his command. Newdigate afterward held home commands and was governor of Bermuda (1888–1892). He retired from the army in 1892 as a lieutenant-general.

**NGENETSHENI PEOPLE.** The Ngenetsheni lived in the far northwest of **Zululand** in the **Disputed Territory**. Their *inKosi* was the ambitious *umNtwana* **Hamu kaNzibe**, who opened **negotiations** with the British in late 1878 on the eve of the **Anglo-Zulu War** and who defected to them in late February 1879 with many of his adherents. The fighting men among the Ngenetsheni were drafted into **Wood's Irregulars**. King **Cetshwayo kaMpande** sent an *iMpi* (military force) after the disloyal Ngenetsheni and ravaged their district, contributing to the bitter animosities of the subsequent 3rd **Zulu Civil War**. Hamu was appointed one of the 13 chiefs in the 1st Partition of Zululand. His chiefdom incorporated Ngenetsheni territory as well as many **uSuthu** supporters, whose aspirations the Ngenetsheni were expected to suppress assiduously.

In the 3rd Zulu Civil War, the Ngenetsheni were *inKosi* **Zibhebhu kaMaphitha**'s staunchest allies. Hamu had two strongholds on either side of the Phongolo River as well as his base at **kwaMfemfe**, and between January and July 1883 the Ngenetsheni struck the uSuthu regularly from there and fought off their counterattacks. A strong contingent from kwaMfemfe reinforced the **Mandlakazi** at the battle of **oNdini** and in the aftermath worked with their allies to ravage uSuthu territory. On 29 April 1884, they defeated the **Buthelezi** in central Zululand. The tide turned once King **Dinuzulu kaCetshwayo** concluded his alliance with the Boers in May 1884. In June, the Boers blockaded the Ngenetsheni in their strongholds during their Zululand campaign. After **Tshaneni**, the Boers induced them to surrender. When in August 1884 Dinuzulu granted the Boers land for the **New Republic**, the Ngenetsheni found themselves subject to the Boers and reduced to labor tenants.

**iNGOBAMAKHOSI *iBUTHO*.** King **Cetshwayo kaMpande** formed this *iButho* in 1873 from youths born in 1850 to 1853. The **shield** was a dark mottled brown with some white patches. It was Cetshwayo's favorite *iButho* and the largest in the army. In the **Anglo-Zulu War**, it fought on the left of the Zulu chest at **Isandlwana**. Elements stationed at the old **oNdini** *iKhanda* fought at **Gingindlovu**. Elements were detached from the main Zulu army marching on **Khambula** to cut off the British retreat from **Hlobane**. At Khambula, it fought on the Zulu right, where its premature attack upset Zulu strategy. A tiny detachment was also involved in the skirmish at the **Tshotshosi** River. At **Ulundi**, it came closest to breaking through the British infantry **square** at its southwest corner. Elements fought for the **uSuthu** during the 3rd **Zulu Civil War** and at **oNdini** formed part of the uSuthu chest. In the **uSuthu Rebellion**, elements fought for King **Dinuzulu kaCetshwayo** at **Ceza** and formed the uSuthu left horn at **Ivuna**.

**emaNGWENI *iKHANDA*.** **Cetshwayo kaMpande** established this *iKhanda* on the coastal plain just north of the Mhlathuze River, and he spent many years there while still an *umNtwana*. When he became king, it was the center of royal influence in the region, and was one of the principal objectives assigned the 1st Division, **South African Field Force**, during the 2nd Invasion of the **Anglo-Zulu War.** The British patrol that burned the *iKhanda* on 4 July 1879 found it deserted.

It consisted of 310 huts. The principal hut in the *isiGodlo* was built in European fashion, like Cetshwayo's audience building at his **oNdini iKhanda**. It consisted of three rooms and had glass windows, wooden doors, whitewashed walls, and a thatched roof. On 19 July, General **Sir Garnet Joseph Wolseley** met the local Zulu *amaKhosi* near the destroyed *iKhanda* and announced the end of the **Zulu kingdom** and his intention to break it up under nominated chiefs.

**emaNGWENI PEOPLE.** The people attached to the **emaNgweni** *iKhanda* on the northern Zulu coastal plain came to dominate the surrounding region and were fiercely loyal to the Zulu royal house. In the **Anglo-Zulu War**, emaNgweni **irregulars** clashed ineffectively with the advancing 1st Division, **South African Field Force**, and surrendered on 5 July 1879. In the 1st Partition of **Zululand**, they were assigned to the chiefdom of the **Mthethwa** *inKosi* Mlandlela kaMbiya. In the 2nd Partition of Zululand, they fell into the restored King **Cetshwayo kaMpande**'s territory. During the 3rd **Zulu Civil War**, they were very active in the **uSuthu** cause under their *inDuna* (leader), **Somopho kaZikhala**, against *inKosi* **Zibhebhu kaMaphitha**'s coastal allies. During early 1884, they supported uSuthu operating from the **Nkandla Forest** by raiding the **Reserve Territory** from the north. During the **uSuthu Rebellion**, they helped cut off **Fort Andries** in June 1888 and attacked it in the battle of **Ntondotha**. Operations by the **Eshowe Column** and then by the joint **Coastal Column** and **Martin's Flying Column** finally ended their resistance by late August 1888. *See also* CIVILIANS IN WARTIME ZULULAND.

**NHLAZATSHE MOUNTAIN.** A huge, flat-topped mountain with sheer cliffs in central **Zululand** north of the White Mfolozi River, Nhlazatshe is a prominent landmark. During the **Anglo-Zulu War**, it featured repeatedly in Lieutenant-General Lord **Chelmsford**'s plans for the advance on **oNdini**, but no column actually went that way, though a patrol from **Baker Russell's Column** reached it on 16 August 1879 during pacification operations. On 31 August 1881, Major-General **Sir Evelyn Wood**, then acting high commissioner for southeast Africa, met representatives of the **uSuthu** faction and their opponents at the foot of the mountain. He made it clear that the British would uphold the 1st Partition of Zululand and back the 13 appointed chiefs against the royalists. The uSuthu understood that they could expect no redress from the British, and many subsequently claimed that the 3rd **Zulu Civil War** effectively began that day.

**eNHLWENI** *umuZI.* When in July 1883 King **Cetshwayo kaMpande** took refuge in the **Nkandla Forest** after his defeat at **oNdini** in the 3rd **Zulu Civil War**, Luhungu of the Shezi people built him this *umuZi* close to secret caves where he could hide. In August, he was joined there by a number of his brothers and other supporters. The British resident magistrate in **Zululand**, **Henry Francis Fynn Jr.**, visited him there on 13 October and persuaded him that to evade capture by *inKosi* **Zibhebhu kaMaphitha**, he must put himself under British protection in **Eshowe**. After Cetshwayo's death near Eshowe, his followers buried him on 10 April 1884 near eNhlweni, below the rolling slopes of Bhobhe Ridge in the Nkandla Forest. Luhungu became the guardian of the grave, and his descendants after him.

**NKANDLA FOREST.** With its deep gorges and steep ridges, the rainy Nkandla Forest between the middle Thukela and Mhlathuze rivers was always a place of mystery and legend for the Zulu, and a final refuge. The Cube people who lived there resisted King **Shaka kaSenzangakhona**'s direct conquest and were famed as workers of iron. During the **Anglo-Zulu War**, the fighting largely passed this impassable region by except for some patrols by **Clarke's Column**. In the 1st Partition of **Zululand**, it fell into **John Dunn**'s chiefdom, and then into the **Reserve Territory** with the 2nd Partition of Zululand. During the 3rd **Zulu Civil War**, the defeated King **Cetshwayo kaMpande** took refuge there in late 1883. After his death and burial there, near the **eNhlweni** *umuZi*, the Nkandla Forest became the focus of **uSuthu** resistance to the British officials in the Reserve Territory. Reinforcements from the **Natal garrison** had to be called in to subdue them, and it was not until early September 1884 that the uSuthu finally gave up hostilities. During the **Zulu Uprising of 1906** (Bhambatha Rebellion), the forest provided the main base for the rebels. *See also* NKANDLA FOREST, BATTLE OF (1884).

**NKANDLA FOREST, BATTLE OF (1884).** During the 3rd **Civil War, uSuthu** forces took refuge in the **Nkandla Forest** after their defeat at the battle of **oNdini** in July 1883 and came into conflict with the colonial authorities in the **Reserve Territory**. After the burial of King **Cetshwayo kaMpande** in the Nkandla Forest in April 1884, the uSuthu became increasingly defiant, and **Melmoth Osborn**, the resident commissioner, decided he must bring them to heel. On 5 May 1884, Osborn encamped six miles east of the Nkandla Forest with a combined force of 3,000 African levies and 50 men of the **Reserve Territory Carbineers** (RTCs) under Commandant **George Mansel**. After some minor skirmishing with the uSuthu, a third of the levies deserted. Then, on the afternoon of 10 May, 1,000 uSuthu under *umNtwana* **Dabulamanzi kaMpande** attacked Osborn's camp. The RTCs formed a firing line 300 yards in front of the camp and repulsed the uSuthu, killing about 100. Two of Mansel's men were also killed. Believing erroneously that another force of uSuthu under **Bhejana kaNomageje** had outflanked him and was about to cut him off from his base at **Eshowe**, Osborn fell back with all his forces on **Fort Chater** and requested British reinforcements to subdue the uSuthu.

*i***NKATHA.** The symbol of Zulu national unity and strength was the *iNkatha*, a circular grass coil about a yard in diameter and the thickness of a man's calf, wrapped in a python skin and bound with grass rope by the leading men of the Zulu nation. The Zulu believed it to have the mystical power of binding together, rejuvenating, and protecting the king and the nation. The *iNkatha* consisted of stalks of grass brushed by the people and **cattle** as they passed; the body dirt (*inSila*) of the king, his ancestors, and his relations; bits of the captured *izinKatha* of defeated *amaKhosi*; the litter from the ground where the *iBandla* met to discuss the nation's affairs; grass from the pits into which the *amaButho* vomited when they were being **ritually** purified, parts of powerful wild animals, and occult medicines. The powerful properties of the *iNkatha* were transferred by the king to the people with the aid of the *amaDlozi* (ancestral spirits). When the king squatted on the *iNkatha*, a mystical force was supposed to emanate from him that boosted the courage of the army in battle and prevented the *amaDlozi* of hostile groups from aiding the enemy. The *iNkatha* was handed down from king to king, growing in size as it was added to. It was entrusted to one of the elder queens and carefully guarded. King **Dingane kaSenzangakhona** placed it in the **esiKlebheni** *iKhanda* in the **emaKhosini valley** presided over by Langazana, *inKosi* Senzangakhona kaJama's fourth wife. It remained there until 26 June 1879, when during a British raid in the **Anglo-Zulu War**, esiKlebheni went up in flames. The Zulu keenly felt the *iNkatha's* destruction and saw it as a portent of the kingdom's ruin.

**NKONJENI.** In August 1887, British troops of the **Zululand garrison** of the Colony of **Zululand** moved forward from **Eshowe** to a camp at Nkonjeni, close to the disaffected **uSuthu** in Ndwandwe District, and were reinforced in October. During the **uSuthu Rebellion**, cavalry operated against the uSuthu from this base in May and June 1888, and loyalist Zulu and white traders raided by the uSuthu sought protection there. Additional troops from the **Natal garrison** moved up to Nkonjeni in June, and Colonel **Henry Sparke Stabb** made it his headquarters. Nkonjeni provided the base for the successful British assault on **Hlophekhulu Mountain**. On 1 August, Lieutenant-General **Henry Augustus Smyth** made Nkonjeni his headquarters for his pacification of northern Zululand. When the Zululand garrison was reduced to its normal level in September 1888, two-thirds of it remained stationed at Nkonjeni.

**NKUNKWINI** *umuZI.* This was one of *inKosi* **Zibhebhu ka-Maphitha**'s *imiZi* (homesteads) in northeastern **Zululand**. On 30 March 1883 during the 3rd **Zulu Civil War**, the **uSuthu** army advancing on **Bangonomo** torched the *umuZi*. Mounted **Mandlakazi** fired on them and drew them into the ambush set by Zibhebhu in the **Msebe** valley. On 14 August 1883, Zibhebhu mustered his forces, including white **mercenaries**, at the rebuilt *umuZi* for a successful two-pronged attack against the uSuthu on the northern coastal plain and in central Zululand.

**kwaNOBAMBA** *iKHANDA.* Originally an *umuZi* (homestead) built by *inKosi* Jama kaNdaba, it became the home of his successor, *inKosi* Senzangakona kaJama, who built his own new **esiKlebheni** *iKhanda* close by. The sacred site was rebuilt as an *iKhanda* by royal successors and was one of the nine *amaKhanda* in the **emaKhosini valley** burned on 26 June 1879 by **Wood's Flying Column** during the 2nd Invasion of the **Anglo-Zulu War**.

**kwaNODWENGU** *iKHANDA*. King **Mpande kaSenzangakhona** built the first *iKhanda* of this name in the **Mahlabathini Plain**. It contained about 500 huts. After 1843, it became his principal residence, and he died and was buried there in October 1872. He was succeeded as king by his son, **Cetshwayo kaMpande**, who built a second kwaNodwengu just south of his father's abandoned *iKhanda*. On 17 January 1879, after their **ritual** preparations for war, the Zulu army marched out of kwaNodwengu for the opening campaign of the **Anglo-Zulu War**. The *iKhanda* also featured in the war's climax. The Zulu know the battle of **Ulundi** as the battle of kwaNodwengu because that is the *iKhanda* closest to which the British infantry **square** halted. During the battle, the **iNgobamakhosi** and **uVe** *amaButho* made good use of the shelter it provided to advance to within 30 yards of the square. It also served as a rallying point for other Zulu units, and they kept up firing from its stockade. After the battle, the British burned it along with all the other *amaKhanda* in the plain.

Once Cetshwayo was restored to central **Zululand** by the 2nd Partition of Zululand, he rebuilt kwaNodwengu, though on a much smaller scale. When *inKosi* **Zibhebhu kaMaphitha** surprised the **uSuthu** at the battle of **oNdini** in the 3rd **Zulu Civil War**, elements of several *amaButho* were quartered there, but they were too far away to join in the battle in time and got caught up in the general rout. After their victory, the **Mandlakazi** and **Ngenetsheni** forces burned kwaNodwengu and all the other rebuilt *amaKhanda* in the Mahlabathini Plain.

**uNOKHENKE** *iBUTHO*. King **Mpande kaSenzangakhona** formed this *iButho* around 1865 of youths born about 1845. The **shield** was black, sometimes with white spots. In the **Anglo-Zulu War**, it fought on the Zulu right horn at **Isandlwana** and as part of the chest at **Khambula** and **Gingindlovu**, where elements had been barracked at the old **oNdini** *iKhanda*. A tiny detachment was also involved in the skirmish at the **Tshotshosi** River where **Prince Louis Napoleon Bonaparte** was killed. At **Ulundi**, it attacked the northern side of the British infantry **square**. Elements fought for the **uSuthu** during the 3rd **Zulu Civil War** and at **oNdini** formed part of the uSuthu chest.

**NONGALAZA kaNONDELA (b. c. 1805).** Enrolled in the isiPhezi *iButho*, Nongalaza was a favorite of *umNtwana* **Mpande ka-Senzangakhona**, *inKosi* of the Nyandwini people and *inDuna* of the uHlomendlini *iButho*. During the **Voortrekker-Zulu War**, Nongalaza was commander of the Zulu army under Mpande's nominal leadership that destroyed the Grand Army of Natal at the battle of the **Thukela**. During the 1st **Zulu Civil War,** he led Mpande's army into **Zululand** and defeated King **Dingane kaSenzangakhona**'s forces at the **Maqongqo Hills**. Mpande confirmed Nongalaza as his commander-in-chief and greatly enriched him. In the 2nd Zulu Civil War, Nongalaza, now an old man, loyally joined his master's favorite son, *umNtwana* **Mbuyazi kaMpande**, and barely survived the **iziGqoza** rout at **Ndondakusuka** by swimming the flooded Thukela River.

**NONGQAYI.** *See* RESERVE TERRITORY CARBINEERS; ZULU-LAND POLICE.

**NONGQAYI FORT.** In April 1883, following the 2nd Partition of **Zululand**, the paramilitary **Reserve Territory Carbineers** (or Nongqayi) were created to maintain order in the **Reserve Territory**. Construction of Fort Nongqayi was begun to the west of the incipient village of **Eshowe** to serve as their headquarters. With the annexation of the British Colony of Zululand in May 1887, the Nongqayi were officially renamed the **Zululand Police** and the fort remained their headquarters. It was strongly built of masonry with high, loopholed walls enclosing a parade ground and barracks. Square, crenellated towers were built at the four corners.

**NONKWENKWEZIYEZULU STRONGHOLD.** On 4 July 1888 during the **uSuthu Rebellion**, *umNtwana* **Shingana kaMpande** began assembling a force of about 1,000 **uSuthu** on **Hlophekhulu Mountain** in support of the uSuthu forces on **Ceza Mountain** and began raiding the country roundabout. Shingana's stronghold on Hlophekhulu, known as Nonkenkweziyezulu, was on the rocky, wooded, southeastern side of the mountain overlooking a narrow strip of land between it and the White Mfolozi River that was densely covered in bush, and where his **cattle**, women, and children were collected.

**NORTHAMPTONSHIRE REGIMENT, 2ND BATTALION.** Formerly the 58th (Rutlandshire) **Regiment** until renamed in 1881 by the **Childers Reforms**, the battalion formed part of the **Natal garrison** between 1880 and 1884. During 1880–1881, it made up part of the Natal Field Force throughout the 1st **Boer War**. In June 1884 during the 3rd **Zulu Civil War**, two companies built **Fort Northampton** in the **Reserve Territory** and garrisoned it until late 1884. During the same period, the battalion also provided a company of **mounted infantry**.

**iziNQOBO.** In late November 1856 during the 2nd **Zulu Civil War**, *umNtwana* **Mbuyazi kaMpande** requested the **Natal** border agent, Captain Joshua Walmsley, stationed just south of the Thukela River mouth, to support his **iziGqoza** forces against the advancing **uSuthu** army. Walmsley had no authority to do so, but he permitted his administrative assistant, **John Dunn**, to cross the Thukela on 28 November with 35 black frontier police trained in the use of **horses** and **firearms**, along with 100 of his African hunters. Dunn was joined by some white hunter-traders and their African assistants, and the whole force was called the iziNqobo, or "Crushers," because of their firepower. On 2 December in the battle of **Ndondakusuka**, the iziNqobo were stationed on the iziGqoza left flank to prevent the uSuthu outflanking them. The iziNqobo repulsed the uSuthu right horn, but the battle was lost for the iziGqoza on the opposite flank. The iziNgobo tried to cover the iziGqoza retreat but became caught up in the rout and almost all were killed. Dunn was almost alone in escaping across the river.

**iNSUKAMNGENI *iBUTHO*.** King **Mpande kaSenzangakhona** formed this *iButho* around 1862 from youths born about 1842, and it was possibly incorporated into the **iQwa** *iButho*. The **shield** was black with white markings lower down. During the **Anglo-Zulu War**, some elements fought at **Nyezane**, and at **Ulundi** it attacked the northeastern corner of the British infantry **square**.

**NSUKAZI FORT.** With the establishment of this fort on 9 August 1888 during the **uSuthu Rebellion**, the British increased their hold on the territory between **Ceza** and **Ivuna** previously dominated by the **uSuthu** rebels. When the **Coastal Column** and **Martin's Flying Column** left Ivuna on 18 August for the coast, the fort was abandoned in favor of the **Ceza Camp** farther north.

**NSUKAZI LAAGER.** On 1 June 1888 during the **uSuthu Rebellion**, troops from the British base at **Nkonjeni**, acting in support of the **Zululand** civil authorities attempting to arrest the **uSuthu** leaders on **Ceza Mountain**, formed a small **laager** of seven wagons close to *inKosi* **Mnyamana kaNgqengelele**'s eNsukazi *umuZi* just south of the Black Mfolozi River. When the uSuthu repulsed the British the next day, the retreating British regrouped at the Nsukazi laager, which was held by Lieutenant R. B. Briscoe and 13 men, before retiring to Nkonjeni.

**NTOMBE, ACTION AT (1879).** During the **Anglo-Zulu War**, supplies for the British garrison stationed at **Luneburg** were forwarded from Derby in the Transvaal. On 7 March 1879, Captain **David Barry Moriarty** and a company-strength detachment were sent north to escort a convoy of 18 wagons carrying ammunition and supplies. By 9 March, the straggling convoy had closed up on the north bank of the swollen Ntombe River at Myer's Drift. Two wagons got across, and Moriarty formed the rest into a sloppily arranged V-shaped **laager** on the north bank. He and 71 men remained to guard the laager while Lieutenant Henry Hollingworth Harward commanded 35 men on the south bank.

    **Mbilini waMswati**, the leader of Zulu **irregulars** in the vicinity, discerned a soft target. He concentrated about 800 men on Tafelberg, one of his fastnesses three miles northeast of Myer's Drift, and on the evening of 11 March personally reconnoitered the British laager. Under cover of mist, his men attacked the sleeping laager on 12 March, firing a volley at 70 yards and then rushing in and overwhelming the defenders. On the south bank, the British detachment fired volleys to cover about a dozen fugitives crossing the river while Harward galloped to Luneburg for help. Sergeant Anthony Clarke Booth took command in his absence. To avoid being surrounded by the Zulu now crossing the river, Booth fell back in good order on Luneburg, halting once at Myer's mission station and then at Rahbe's farmhouse to send volleys into the Zulu, driving them off. When Harward reached Luneburg, the garrison moved out to bring in Booth's men and the fugitives they were escorting. For lack of mounted men, it was not possible to pursue Mbilini's men, who retired to Tafelberg with 250 **cattle** and most of the contents of the wagons. The British lost an officer and 60 men, a civil surgeon, two white wagon conductors, and 15 black drivers, while 30 Zulu dead were found on the banks of the Ntombe. Mbilini's successful blow demonstrated that the British had not yet effectively subdued northwestern **Zululand**, and that their lines of supply remained vulnerable to attack.

Sergeant Booth was awarded the Victoria Cross. Lieutenant Harward was court-martialed in February 1880 for deserting his men and resigned his commission. *See also* TACTICS, BRITISH INFANTRY; TACTICS UP TO 1879, ZULU.

**NTONDOTHA, BATTLE OF (1888).** During the **uSuthu Rebellion**, Andries Pretorius, the resident magistrate of the Lower Umfolosi District in British **Zululand**, held his fortified post at the Ntondotha Hills (called **Fort Andries**) with a garrison of 40 **Zululand Police**. Two **emaNgweni** *izinDuna*, **Somopho kaZikhala** and **Bhejana kaNomageje**, who supported the **uSuthu**, cut off the fort's communications with **Eshowe** to the south, and Pretorius secured the assistance of a local collaborator, *inKosi* **Sokwetshatha kaMlandela** of the **Mthethwa**, to help protect it with 300 of his men.

On 30 June 1888, the uSuthu *inKosi* **Somkhele kaMalanda** attacked the fort with 1,500–2,000 of his **Mphukunyoni**, supported by a few hundred of Somopho's and Bhejana's emaNgweni, mainly with the intention of getting at their Mthethwa enemies stationed there. Their assault was easily driven off by fire from the Zululand Police. The defenders suffered no casualties; the uSuthu losses are unknown but probably small. Nevertheless, the coastal uSuthu continued to interrupt Pretorius's communications with Eshowe until the **Eshowe Column** relieved the fort on 9 July. *See also* STRATEGY, ZULU; TACTICS IN 1880s, ZULU.

**NTSHINGWAYO kaMAHOLE (c. 1823–1883).** Enrolled in the **uDlambedlu** *iButho*, Ntshingwayo was *inKosi* of the Khoza people and senior *inDuna* of the **kwaGqikazi** *iKhanda*. He was a great friend of *inKosi* **Mnyamana kaNgqengelele** and second only to him in King **Cetshwayo kaMpande**'s *iBandla* (royal council). Nevertheless, Cetshwayo always held him in some suspicion for having favored the **iziGqoza** during the 2nd **Zulu Civil War**. During the **Anglo-Zulu War**, Ntshingwayo fought as the senior commander at **Isandlwana** and surrendered to the British in mid-August 1879. In the 1st Partition of **Zululand**, he was appointed one of the 13 chiefs. He was ambivalent about Cetshwayo's restoration in the 2nd Partition of Zululand. Early in the 3rd Zulu Civil War, he was attacked by the **Buthelezi**, who believed he had stolen many royal **cattle**. Ntshingwayo eventually decided to throw in his lot with the **uSuthu**. He was killed in the rout at **oNdini**.

**NTULI PEOPLE.** The Ntuli lived along the northern bank of the Thukela River. At the time of the **Anglo-Zulu War**, most were under the rule of **Godide kaNdlela** and **Mavumengwana kaNdlela**, two sons of *inKosi* **Ndlela kaSompisi**, who had been King **Dingane kaSenzangakhona**'s chief *inDuna*. Both were initially absent from home commanding Zulu armies but were back by April when the Ntuli were holding the middle Thukela against raids from **Natal**. Mavumengwana's section of the Ntuli played a part in the successful Zulu counterraid at **Middle Drift** in June 1879. Theirs was a sector the British had never penetrated in any depth during the Anglo-Zulu War, and the younger *amaButho* in particular were loath to **submit**. It was not until **Clarke's Column** marched through the region in September 1879 that the Ntuli finally all surrendered. By the 1st Partition of **Zululand**, the Ntuli were placed in **John Dunn**'s chiefdom. They strongly supported the **uSuthu**, and they resented being consigned to the **Reserve Territory** by the 2nd Partition of Zululand. After many uSuthu took refuge in the **Nkandla Forest** after their defeat at **oNdini** during the 3rd **Zulu Civil War**, the Ntuli joined the fray but were swiftly defeated by the **Mounted Basutos**. They took no part in the **uSuthu Rebellion**, though they could not avoid disastrous involvement in the **Zulu Uprising of 1906** (Bhambatha Rebellion). *See also* CIVILIANS IN WARTIME ZULULAND.

**NTUNJAMBILI.** This huge, rocky spur of the **Drakensberg** ends precipitously on the southern side of the Thukela River, overlooking the river valley at **Middle Drift**. It was known to Natal settlers and the British as Kranskop.

**NTUNJAMBILI, RAID AT (1838).** In March 1838 during the **Voortrekker-Zulu War**, the Voortrekkers who were **laagered** in western **Zululand** joined with the settlers of Port Natal (**Durban**) to mount a joint campaign against King **Dingane kaSenzangakhona**. The intervention of the Port Natal settlers in the conflict was not necessary but opportunistic, although revenge for their compatriots in **Pieter Retief**'s party whom Dingane had executed in February 1838 was a motive. On 13 March 1838, **John Cane** advanced with a force of 2,100 colored retainers and African adherents from Port Natal to mount a raid into Zululand across the middle Thukela River in the vicinity of **Ntunjambili**, or Kranskop. They destroyed several large *imiZi* belonging to *inKosi* Sothobe kaMpangalala and *inKosi* Nombanga kaNgidli, then returned to Port Natal on 2 April with nearly 6,000 **cattle** and a few hundred women and children captured for the benefit of their labor and the *iLobolo* they would attract when married off. Cane's force had met little opposition because the Zulu cattle guards had been summoned away by Dingane to repel the anticipated Voortrekker offensive. The ease of their success fatally induced the Port Natal settlers into the rash campaign that culminated in the disastrous battle of the **Thukela** the following month. *See also* CIVILIANS IN WARTIME ZULULAND.

*umNTWANA. See* POLITICAL ORGANIZATION, ZULU.

*umNUMZANE. See* POLITICAL ORGANIZATION, ZULU.

**NUNN, HERBERT.** Nunn moved into *umNtwana* **Hamu kaNzibe**'s chiefdom in the 1860s as his resident white trader and adviser, supplying him with **firearms** and trade goods. During the **Anglo-Zulu War**, he helped Hamu defect to the British in March 1879. During the 3rd **Zulu Civil War**, he was a newspaper correspondent in **Zululand**.

**NURSES, BRITISH.** Along with the reinforcements sent out to the **Anglo-Zulu War** after **Isandlwana** were seven nurses under Superintendent of Nurses Jane Deeble. All had trained at the Royal Victoria Hospital at Netley. They were accompanied to **Durban** by a doctor and another seven nurses from the privately funded Stafford House South African Aid Society. In addition, the Bishop of Natal, **William Colenso**, provided six nuns to act as nurses. These nurses, including any other civilian volunteers, worked in the base **hospitals** in **Natal** and not in the field hospitals. *See also* MEDICAL ATTENTION, BRITISH.

**NYATHI HILL LAAGER.** On 21 May 1884, Boers of the **mercenary** force known as **Dinuzulu's Volunteers** crowned **Dinuzulu kaCetshwayo** at their Nyathi Hill **laager** and promised him military aid in the 3rd **Zulu Civil War** in return for vast land concessions. *See also* NEW REPUBLIC.

**NYEZANE, BATTLE OF (1879).** On 22 January 1879, on the same day as the battle of **Isandlwana** in the **Anglo-Zulu War**, the British No. 1 **Column** under Colonel **Charles Knight Pearson**, advancing along the coastal road to **Eshowe** from the lower Thukela River, fought its way through an ambush laid by close to 6,000 Zulu under *inKosi* **Godide kaNdlela** who had marched from **oNdini** on 17 January and been reinforced along the way by smaller local contingents. No. 1 Column was in two divisions, with the leading division escorting a straggling convoy of 50 wagons. As it began to ascend the track along a long spur running up a range of hills north of the Nyezane River, the Zulu attacked. Godide's plan was to engage the front of the column while the two horns enveloped it. When the British observed Zulu moving on Wombane, the eastern of the two hills flanking the track (the Zulu would call this the battle of Wombane), African levies were sent forward to disperse them. This movement dislocated Zulu plans, for the left horn was provoked into a premature attack before the chest and right horn were ready to commit themselves.

The Zulu left horn rushed down Wombane and engaged the British column in extended order while the British deployed to repel them in a skirmishing line. Pearson sent forward the troops at the head of the column with the **artillery** to take up position on a knoll higher up the spur and rake the Zulu position with fire. Meanwhile, the convoy closed up and stopped. The Zulu left horn made an orderly withdrawal before the British skirmishing line. Those attempting to retire across the Nyezane were intercepted by elements of the British 2nd Division now coming up, bringing the total British forces engaged to 73 officers and 2,047 men, 860 of whom were African levies. After the retreat of their left horn, the Zulu right horn began a tentative advance supported by the chest but was pinned down by British fire. The British then counterattacked, seizing the heights before them and taking the dominating crest of Wombane. With the loss of the key to their position, the Zulu dispersed in fairly good order under British artillery fire to a hill four miles to the north. They, and the Zulu non-combatants who had been watching the battle from the surrounding hills, dispersed when the British resumed their advance on Eshowe. The British lost two British officers and three soldiers, and five white officers and five black troops of the African levies. The Zulu dead numbered 300 or more. *See also* TACTICS, AFRICAN INFANTRY LEVIES; TACTICS, BRITISH INFANTRY; TACTICS UP TO 1879, ZULU.

**iNYONEMHLOPE *iBUTHO*.** *InKosi* **Zibhebhu kaMaphitha** raised this *iButho* in his chiefdom after the 1st Partition of **Zululand** in resumption of the prerogative of the great *amaKhosi* who preceded **Shaka**. Its members wore distinctive black feathers in their headdress. It fought throughout the 3rd **Zulu Civil War**; in the **uSuthu Rebellion**, it formed the chest of the **Mandlakazi** at **Ivuna**.

**iziNYOSI *iBUTHO*.** Originally called the uJubingqwanga, this *iButho* was formed by King **Shaka kaSenzangakhona** around 1828 from youths born about 1808. King **Dingane kaSenzangakhona** renamed it the iziNyosi. The **shield** was a speckled gray. In the **Voortrekker-Zulu War**, it formed part of the chest at **Ncome**.

**NZOBO kaSOBADLI (?–1840).** Along with *inKosi* **Ndlela kaSompi-si**, Nzobo was one of King **Dingane kaSenzangakhona**'s two most prominent *izinDuna*. He was influential in persuading Dingane not to negotiate with the Voortrekkers, and to execute **Pieter Retief** and his party at **uMgungundlovu**. During the **Voortrekker-Zulu War**, Nzobo led the Zulu army that defeated the *Vlugkommando* at **eThaleni**, but he jointly commanded much less successfully at **Ncome**. To shore up the tottering **Zulu kingdom**, he urged Dingane to execute *umNtwana* **Mpande kaSenzangakhona** as a rival to the throne. When the Boer ***Beeskommando*** and Mpande's army jointly invaded **Zululand** in the 1st **Zulu Civil War**, Dingane sent Nzobo to the Boers to make terms. The Boers, hating him for his part in Retief's execution, threw him into chains, and Mpande, who was with the *Beeskommando*, urged them to show him no mercy. On 31 January 1840, the Boers convened a court-martial and sentenced him (and his fellow envoy) to death by firing squad.

## – O –

**OFTEBRO, OMMUND CHRISTIANSEN (1820–1893).** In 1851, Oftebro joined Bishop **Hans Paludin Smith Schreuder** at the Norwegian Missionary Society station at Empangeni in **Zululand**. He was initially friendly with King **Cetshwayo kaMpande**, but by the late 1870s he believed the king was hindering the conversion of the Zulu. Consequently, Oftebro acted as a British agent, reporting adversely on Cetshwayo from his mission station at **Eshowe**. He abandoned Eshowe in 1878. After the **Anglo-Zulu War**, he established a mission station in the hills overlooking the **Mahlabathini Plain** from the north. During the 3rd **Zulu Civil War**, he tried to mediate between the parties. After the battle of **oNdini**, he gave refuge to members of Cetshwayo's family at his mission.

**OLIVIERSHOEK LAAGER.** The **Natal** government made plans in mid-1878 to create a **laager** at Oliviershoek in the foothills of the **Drakensberg** (in what was later designated **Colonial Defensive District** No. II) by connecting the magistrate's office and jail by an earthwork. The plans were not put into effect during the **Anglo-Zulu War** until March 1879 because it was believed that if threatened by a **Sotho** incursion over the Drakensberg from **Basutoland** (which never materialized), most settlers would prefer to take refuge at the **Strydpoort laager** closer to **Estcourt**.

**ORANGE FREE STATE.** During the **Great Trek**, Voortrekkers entered the region between the Orange and Vaal rivers in 1836 and attempted to set up an independent state. However, in 1848, the British defeated the Boers at Boomplaats and annexed the territory as the Orange River Sovereignty. The British government then went through a period of imperial retrenchment and, by the Bloemfontein Convention signed on 23 February 1854, granted independence to the 13,000 white inhabitants of what became the Republic of the Orange Free State, or Oranje-Vrijstaat, with its capital at Bloemfontein. The Orange Free State went to war with Britain in 1899, and after its defeat in the **Anglo-Boer (South African) War**, it became a province of the Union of South Africa in 1910.

**ORDNANCE STORE DEPARTMENT.** The department was formed in 1875 when the former Control Department, created in 1870, was broken up during the **Cardwell Reforms**. At the outset of the **Anglo-Zulu War**, the small number of staff available proved unequal to the task of supplying the British forces in the field with the equipment and stores that passed through the main depots in **Durban, Pietermaritzburg**, and (from May 1879) **Dundee**. Additional personnel including officers, clerks, storeholders, artificers, and military laborers were sent out in March and July from Britain. During the 2nd Invasion of the Anglo-Zulu War, detachments were distributed along the lines of communication and at every military post and depot. By the end of the campaign, the department was operating efficiently, and once the troops withdrew, it had to collect and dispose of the surplus stores and equipment. The blue tunic had dark blue facings and scarlet edgings.

**OSBORN, MELMOTH (1834–1899).** Osborn came to **Natal** from England in 1849 and in 1854 entered the Natal Government Service, becoming resident magistrate of **Newcastle** from 1867 to 1876. He accompanied **Sir Theophilus Shepstone** to the Transvaal in 1877 as secretary for native affairs. After the 1st Partition of **Zululand**, he was appointed British resident in Zululand from March 1880 to December 1882. In April 1883, he became resident commissioner of the **Reserve Territory**, and in June 1887 the resident commissioner and chief magistrate of the Colony of Zululand. From his first appointment to Zululand, Osborn showed himself a disciple of Shepstone's school of colonial administration in his determination to limit the pretensions of the Zulu royal house and to establish indirect rule through British magistrates. His extreme bias against the **uSuthu** and his inefficiency and deleteriousness as an administrator were detrimental to the situation in the Reserve Territory during the 3rd **Zulu Civil War**, and later led directly to the **uSuthu Rebellion**. He escaped censure because that would have been an admission of the culpability of the Zululand officials, something that the governor, **Sir Arthur Elibank Havelock**, and the Colonial Office were anxious to avoid. As a result, Osborn was permitted to carry on as resident commissioner until he retired in 1893 with a knighthood.

**OSBORN'S LEVIES.** During the 3rd **Zulu Civil War**, **Melmoth Osborn** raised 3,000 African levies (troops) against the threat the **uSuthu** posed to the **Reserve Territory**. Between February and June 1884, small bodies of levies were stationed along its northern border, from the coast to opposite the **Nkandla Forest**. **John Dunn** commanded the coastal levies, and Lieutenant **Richard Hallowes Addison** commanded those farther inland. A further 1,600 levies under Martin Oftebro (son of the missionary **Ommund Christiansen Oftebro**) were concentrated east of the Nkandla Forest, and 1,500 more under F. Galloway, the superintendent of roads, were to the southwest of them, to protect the **Natal** border. On 5 May 1884, Osborn concentrated a force east of the Nkandla that included 3,000 levies. After some minor skirmishing with the uSuthu, a third of the levies deserted. On 10 May, the remainder repelled an uSuthu attack on their camp in the battle of the Nkandla Forest but then fell back on **Fort Chater**. Dunn's coastal levies failed to reinforce them for fear of the uSuthu forces concentrating near the mouth of the Mhlathuze River. Galloway's levies made up part of the force that established the strategic **Fort Yolland** to the east of the Nkandla Forest. The last of the levies were disbanded in October with the **submission** of the uSuthu in the Reserve Territory.

The levies wore the usual Zulu dress of the time; to distinguish them from their foes, they wore (as levies had in the **Anglo-Zulu War**) a red cloth tied around the head. They were armed with their traditional **spears** and **shields**, though a few carried obsolete muzzle-loading **firearms**.

**OX WAGON.** From the late 17th century, a wagon drawn by oxen harnessed in pairs (*ossewa*) was the preferred form of transport in southern Africa for traders, hunters, missionaries, and explorers who used it as a mobile home. The Voortrekkers of the 1830s employed a sturdily constructed wooden wagon long in proportion to its breadth. From its shape, it was known as a *kakabeenwa*, or jaw-bone wagon. The four spoked, wooden wheels had iron rims, and the two at the back were considerably larger than those in front. Most of the load-carrying and living area was covered in a canvas canopy supported by wooden hoops. The driver sat in front, in the open, on a wooden chest (*wakis*) and drove the span of 8–16 oxen (normally of the "Africander" strain of the "Sanga" breed) by calling to each by name or urging them on with a whip. The two most powerful oxen were yoked either side of the *disselboom*, or shaft, and the rest were yoked in pairs to a *trektou*, a long chain or leather rope, attached to the *disselboom*. A young African boy (*voorloper*) led the front pair of oxen by a thong attached to their yoke, and the rest followed.

The *kakabeenwa* carried some 3,960 lbs, and this was not sufficient for later transport riders who earned a living bringing heavy goods up from the coast to the interior. In 1860, a bigger, flat ox wagon was devised, with back wheels only slightly bigger than those in front, which could carry up to 9,900 lbs. The living quarters were beneath a half-tent at the rear of the wagon. It was drawn by a span of 10–16 oxen yoked as for the *kakabeenwa*. Rather than sitting on the wagon, the conductor, or driver, walked beside the oxen, urging them on with calls and a whip.

Oxen had to be regularly rested and given time to graze. In the most favorable conditions, a wagon could not travel more than 12 miles a day. During the **Anglo-Zulu War**, they often covered no more than three. *See also* LAAGER, BOER WAGON; TRANSPORT CONVOYS, BRITISH.

– **P** –

**PADDAFONTEIN LAAGER.** *See* PIETERS LAAGER.

**PEARSON, CHARLES KNIGHT (1834–1909).** Commissioned in 1852, Pearson saw service in the Crimean War (1854–1855). He was promoted to colonel in 1872 and in 1876 sailed in command of the 3rd **Regiment** (East Kent, The Buffs) to form the **Natal garrison**. During the **Anglo-Zulu War**, he surrendered his regimental command to lead No. 1 **Column** from January to April 1879, when he commanded at **Nyezane** and at the blockade of **Eshowe**. After the relief of Eshowe, he was placed in command of the 1st Brigade, 1st Division, **South African Field Force**, until invalided home in May. He was knighted and promoted to major-general. He was later governor of the Royal Victoria Hospital at Netley (1880–1884) and commanded troops in the West Indies (1885–1890). He was promoted to lieutenant-general in 1891 and retired from the army in 1895.

**PEDI PEOPLE.** In the late 1820s, Sekwati woaThulare consolidated a kingdom dominated by the northern Sotho-speaking Pedi people in the mountainous territory of what would later be the northeastern **South African Republic** (SAR). In 1851, King **Mpande kaSenzangakhona** conducted an inconclusive campaign against the Pedi, who retired to their fastnesses. In May 1876, war broke out between the Pedi, ruled since 1861 by Sekhukhune woaSekwati (c. 1814–1882), and the SAR. The Boer campaign came to an ignominious halt in February 1877 and was a major excuse for the British annexation of the Transvaal in April 1877. The British opened a fresh campaign against the Pedi in April 1877, but that too proved inconclusive, and operations ceased in October 1878. The British believed that the Pedi only dared resist them because Sekhukhune and King **Cetshwayo kaMpande** were in alliance. The two rulers did maintain regular diplomatic contact, but no military agreement was ever formed between them, and Cetshwayo did not receive the active Pedi support he hoped for during the **Anglo-Zulu War**. At the conclusion of that campaign, General **Sir Garnet Joseph Wolseley** renewed operations against the Pedi and defeated them by December 1879.

**PENNEFATHER, EDWARD GRAHAM (1850–?).** Commissioned in 1873, Pennefather was on special service in the **Anglo-Zulu War** with the **Cavalry Brigade** attached to the 2nd Division, **South African**

**Field Force**, and fought in the skirmish at **Zungeni**. He joined **Baker Russell's Column** and took part in the mounted search for the fugitive King **Cetshwayo kaMpande**. He fought in the 1st **Boer War** (1881) and was promoted to captain in 1881 and major in 1885. In 1884–1885, he served with the Bechuanaland Expedition. Stationed in 1887 in the Colony of **Zululand** with the cavalry of the **Zululand garrison** based at **Nkonjeni**, in early 1888 he made frequent patrols of the uSuthu *imiZi* near **Ivuna** in support of the civil authorities. On the outbreak of the **uSuthu Rebellion**, he was in command of the British forces supporting the civil authorities on **Ceza** and ably covered their retreat. He was in command of the cavalry at **Hlophekhulu** that supported the assault. Pennefather was promoted to brevet lieutenant-colonel in 1888. He retired from the army in 1895 and was appointed inspector general of police for the Straits Settlement.

**PERCUSSION CAPS.** In 1807, the Rev. Alexander Forsyth (1769–1843) patented the use of fulminates of mercury, which ignites when struck, as a primer for **firearms** in place of gunpowder, which requires external fire for detonation. His percussion cap, coated with fulminates of mercury and placed over the fire hole, replaced the flintlock mechanism and produced a much more reliable, all-weather ignition system that greatly speeded up the process of fire because the priming charge and main charge exploded nearly simultaneously.

Initially developed for sportsmen, percussion caps were mass produced from 1822 and were slowly introduced into European armies. In the late 1830s, the flintlock mechanism of **muskets** began to be replaced by the percussion lock. In the early 1850s, percussion-lock **rifles** replaced muskets until they in turn were superseded in the 1860s by breech-loading rifles.

**isiPHEZI *iKHANDA*.** The main Zulu army marching against the British No. 3 **Column** at the outset of the **Anglo-Zulu War** encamped for the night of 18 January 1879 at isiPhezi, an *iKhanda* in the Mphembheni valley to the southwest of **oNdini**.

**PHOTOGRAPHY.** Photography was still in its early stages during the Zulu wars. The breakthrough came only in 1888 with celluloid-roll film. Until then, cameras were neither efficient nor easily portable.

By the 1870s, a dry plate or gelatin emulsion process enabled plates to be stored ready for many months, and it did away with the need for special vans in which to develop the glass plates before the sensitizing chemicals dried. Even so, only laboriously posed pictures were possible because of the slow exposure time, and those photographers who risked their fragile and bulky equipment on campaign had to be content with static shots of people and landscapes. After the end of the **Anglo-Zulu War**, professional photographers from **Natal** compiled commercially successful commemorative albums of the campaign, notably James C. Lloyd of **Durban**, J. W. Buchanan and George T. Ferneyhough of **Pietermaritzburg**, and Benjamin Kisch with studios in both towns.

**PIETERMARITZBURG.** The **Pieter Retief** party of Voortrekkers identified the site of the future city of Pietermaritzburg in January 1838. Named after the Voortrekker leaders Retief and **Gerrit Maritz**, it was being laid out by October 1839 in the typical grid pattern adopted by the Boers in emulation of their towns in the **Cape**. Long, straight streets were connected by cross streets, and the blocks were divided into rectangular plots (*erven*) irrigated by water furrows. Plots were laid aside for a market square, church, and public buildings. Pietermaritzburg was the seat of the short-lived Boer Republic of **Natalia**, and it continued after 1842 as the capital of British **Natal**, with **Fort Napier**, cathedral, government house, and administrative precinct. It was also the commercial hub of the Natal midlands. Its population in the early 1880s was about 6,000 white settlers, 750 Indians, and over 3,000 Africans.

**PIETERMARITZBURG JAIL.** In the panic after **Isandlwana** during the **Anglo-Zulu War**, the substantial jail in Pietermaritzburg, which had been built in 1861 with high brick walls, but which was outside the perimeter of the **Pietermaritzburg Laager**, was prepared for defense. Officials from the nearby government house were to have taken refuge there in an emergency that never arose.

**PIETERMARITZBURG LAAGER.** When during the **Anglo-Zulu War** news of **Isandlwana** reached **Pietermaritzburg** on 24 January 1879, the white citizens hastily improvised a **laager** for their protection, to be defended primarily by the **City Guard** and Natal **Rifle Association**. When completed in mid-February, the laager consisted of a number of substantial buildings, such as the government building of 1871 that housed the supreme court and the legislative council, and the Presbyterian church of 1852. They were made defensible with loopholes in the walls and with the fitting of reinforced and loopholed doors and shutters. These buildings anchored connecting barricades of sandbags and boxes filled with earth that formed the perimeter. The people of Pietermaritzburg never resorted to the laager, and it was dismantled in July 1879.

**PIETERS LAAGER (PADDAFONTEIN LAAGER).** When Boer farmers in northern **Natal** close to the Mzinyathi River (in what would later be **Colonial Defensive District** No. I) became dissatisfied in late 1877 with the Natal government's plans for their defense in case of a Zulu attack, they built this small, stone-walled **laager** with two opposing bastions. It was understood that this laager was for the Boer settlers and **Fort Pine** for the British. At the outbreak of the **Anglo-Zulu War**, a few Boers did take refuge at the laager for a short time, but most of them went to Fort Pine, and Pieters Laager was soon abandoned.

**PINETOWN DEFENSE GUARD.** *See* PINETOWN LAAGER.

**PINETOWN LAAGER.** In the panic following **Isandlwana** during the **Anglo-Zulu War**, a **laager** was built around Murray's Hotel in the village of Pinetown in the hills northwest of **Durban** in the Colonial Defensive Subdistrict of Durban. It was constructed by the Natal Railway Department of 200 railway lengths set into the ground with 4,000 timbers dropped in between, and it was properly loopholed, with two flanking bastions. The Pinetown Defense Guard and New Germany Rifles were to have manned it, but both of these volunteer groups were disbanded in mid-March 1879, and the laager (which was never remotely threatened by the Zulu) was abandoned.

**PIVAAN LAAGER.** This stone **laager** on Potgieter's farm in the **Disputed Territory** antedated the **Anglo-Zulu War**. In late 1877 and again in 1878, Boer families took refuge here when conflict with the Zulu seemed to be brewing. In May 1879, during the Anglo-Zulu

War, a small force of Dutch burghers was encamped nearby. In June, they left it for the proximity of **Fort Lawrence**.

**POINT LAAGER.** In the panic after **Isandlwana** during the **Anglo-Zulu War**, there was concern in **Durban** that the designated places of refuge in the **Durban Town Laager** were not sufficient for the number of settler women and children, Indians, and Africans who had flocked into the town. In mid-February 1879, it was decided to erect barricades across the Point beyond the harbor works and railway line to create a defensible **laager** large enough to accommodate them and to provide a last line of defense should it became necessary to evacuate the town and take to the ships. The **Durban Volunteer Artillery** took up position with two field guns behind the palisade. By April, all fear of a Zulu attack had dissipated and the barricade was dismantled.

**POLITICAL ORGANIZATION, ZULU.** Colonial commentators regularly characterized the **Zulu kingdom** as despotic and arbitrary, but the king was constrained by traditional law and custom as well as by difficulties of communication and control over the kingdom's large distances. The basis of the king's power was the *iButho* system (age-grade regiments), through which he harnessed the productive and military potential of his subjects, but there was always the danger that *amaButho* would give their first loyalty to local hierarchies, and in the absence of anything approaching a developed bureaucracy, the king had to delegate regional potentates some powers.

In practice, authority ran from the king through chiefs, or *amaKhosi*, of decreasing degree down to the individual homestead (*umuZi*) heads, or *abaNumzane*. At the top of the political pyramid below the king were the *iziKhulu*, the great ones, who were royal princes, or *abaNtwana*, senior members of the royal house who could function as *amaKhosi*, and major hereditary *amaKhosi* incorporated into the kingdom but still maintaining their regional power bases. More tightly under the king's control than the *iziKhulu* were the *izinDuna*, state officials he appointed to command the *amaButho*, preside over *amaKhanda* (royal military and administrative centers), or rule like *amaKhosi* over districts where there were no strong claims of hereditary authority. The king rewarded these men well, and they remained amenable to royal will, as they knew that their power and wealth depended on the king's favor. The king also relied upon *iziNceku*, confidential royal attendants and advisers who exercised much influence. The king could only make policy by consulting an inner core of prominent advisers, the *umKhandlu*. The king chose one among them as his chief *iNduna*, or prime minister and commander in chief. Once the *umKhandlu* reached a policy decision, it would be aired at a fuller meeting of councilors, the *iBandla*, and then made known to the people at the ***umKhosi*** (first-fruits ceremony). The king did retain the ultimate decisions over life and death and in this regard could overrule his advisers. Punishment of miscreants took the form of execution or **cattle** fine, as there was no such thing as prison in **Zululand**. Much depended on the personality of each individual monarch when it came to the actual exercise of power. Some, like King **Dingane kaSenzangakhona**, had much their own way. Others, like King **Mpande kaSenzangakhona**, were more amenable in the hands of their councilors.

**PORT DURNFORD.** On 23 June 1879 during the **Anglo-Zulu War**, patrols from the 1st Division, **South African Field Force**, confirmed that Port Durnford just north of the mouth of the Mlalazi River was an open sandy beach where the surf broke with less violence than elsewhere along the coast. It was thus considered practicable for the landing of supplies from decked surf boats, and the 1st Division moved forward to encamp there on 28 June. Between 2 and 4 July, General **Sir Garnet Joseph Wolseley** made several attempts to land there to take personal command in **Zululand**, but he was unsuccessful on account of the heavy surf and had to return to **Durban**. Stores continued to be landed when weather permitted and supplied **Baker Russell's Column** and **Clarke's Column** between July and September. After his capture, King **Cetshwayo kaMpande** was embarked on 4 September 1879 at Port Durnford to be taken to captivity in **Cape Town**. On 10 January 1883, Cetshwayo landed at Port Durnford on his restoration following the 2nd Partition of Zululand.

**PORT NATAL.** *See* DURBAN.

**PORT ST. JOHN'S.** On 4 September 1878, the Mpondo chiefs ceded this potential port at the mouth of the Mzimvubu River to Britain. A British garrison was established here, and Port St. John's was annexed to the **Cape** in 1884.

**POST CART.** The post cart service, with its posting houses, instituted in 1860, was the most rapid means of transport in **Natal**. The two-wheeled cart, drawn by two or three pairs of **horses**, carried not only mailbags but five passengers and a driver. During the **Anglo-Zulu War**, officers made much use of it, despite its extreme discomfort. *See also* TRANSPORT, BRITISH.

**POSTAL RUNNERS.** African postal runners were employed during the **Anglo-Zulu War**, 3rd **Zulu Civil War**, and **uSuthu Rebellion** to carry letters and parcels between British camps in bags or little boxes. Official dispatches or express letters (such as those sent by **special correspondents**) were fixed into a cleft stick and held high to indicate their importance. Magistrates in the colony of **Zululand** in the 1880s used relays of runners to send reports to **Eshowe**. The average speed of a runner was four miles per hour.

**POTGIETER, ANDRIES HENDRIK (1792–1852).** A farmer from the **Eastern Cape**, Potgieter led a party of Voortrekkers north into the interior at the end of 1835. At Vegkop in October 1836, his **laagered** party repulsed a **Ndebele** attack. In January 1837, he and **Gerrit Maritz** led a successful retaliatory commando (militia) against the Ndebele at Mosega. Between 4 and 12 November, Potgieter and **Petrus Lafras Uys** attacked the Ndebele again at eGabeni and drove them north into what is now Zimbabwe. A powerful personality and natural leader, Potgieter could not cooperate easily with the leaders of other Voortrekker parties, and he particularly resented **Pieter Retief**'s popularity. He favored settling in the lands north across the Vaal River and developing trade with **Delagoa Bay**; those who supported Retief preferred the lands of the **Zulu kingdom** and Port Natal (**Durban**) as their outlet to the sea. Nevertheless, in March 1838, Potgieter came to the aid of the Voortrekker parties after the

**Bloukrans Massacre** in the **Voortrekker-Zulu War**. Because he would not subordinate himself to Uys, who had also brought a commando down from the highveld, he agreed in April to joint command of the *Vlugkommando*, which was ambushed at **eThaleni**. Accused of cowardice in the battle, the indignant Potgieter and his followers withdrew to the highveld, where he became involved in setting up fractious and short-lived communities that were all subsumed in 1852 into the independent **South African Republic**.

**POTGIETER'S FARM LAAGER.** During the **Anglo-Zulu War**, a small detachment of No. 4 **Column** moved from the camp at **Khambula** on 21 April 1879 to the Widow Potgieter's farm in the **Disputed Territory** to mine coal from an exposed seam. They built a circular stone **laager** for their 28 wagons. They rejoined No. 4 Column in early May 1879.

**POTSPRUIT CAMP.** This camp was established in **Colonial Defensive District** No. VII during the **Anglo-Zulu War** as the assembly point between December 1878 and early January 1879 for No. 2 **Column** and for the four corps of **Natal Mounted Volunteers** joining No. 1 Column. In April 1879, these Natal Mounted Volunteers moved back to Potspruit after the relief of **Eshowe**, before being relocated on 15 May to the **Doornhoek Camp**.

**PRETORIA.** Founded in 1855 and named after the Voortrekker leader **Andries Wilhelmus Jacobus Pretorius**, the town became the capital of the **South African Republic** on 1 May 1860.

**PRETORIA CONVENTION.** *See* BOER WAR, 1ST.

**PRETORIUS, ANDRIES WILHELMUS JACOBUS (1798–1853).** By August 1838, fortunes in the **Voortrekker-Zulu War** were at low ebb for the Voortrekkers **laagered** in the foothills of the **Drakensberg**, and they sent a deputation to seek aid from Pretorius, a gifted organizer and experienced commando (militia) leader from the Graaff-Reinet District of the **Eastern Cape**. In 1837, Pretorius had made a reconnaissance of the regions occupied by Voortrekker parties and had taken part in the fighting against the **Ndebele**. He then returned home to organize a party to trek over the Drakensberg. On 22 November 1838, Pretorius arrived ahead of his main party, and at Sooilager on the Little Thukela River, the Voortrekkers elected him chief **commandant**. Pretorius planned the punitive expedition against King **Dingane kaSenzangakhona** and led the *Wenkommando* to victory at **Ncome**, where he was wounded in the hand during the pursuit. He played a prominent part in the negotiations leading to the peace concluded with Dingane on 25 March 1839. As chief commandant, he led the *Beeskommando* in January 1840 in support of *umNtwana* **Mpande kaSenzangakhona** in the 1st **Zulu Civil War** and proclaimed Mpande king on 10 February 1840.

Pretorius found his dominant position in the Republic of **Natalia** under attack from envious colleagues in the *volksraad*, but in May 1842 they called on him to repulse the British occupation of Port Natal (**Durban**). He defeated the British at **Congella** and besieged them in **Smith's Camp**, but when the garrison was relieved, he retreated after a skirmish on 26 July 1842 and influenced the *volksraad* into submitting to British sovereignty. In August 1842, he resigned as commandant-general and retired to his farm. When many Voortrekkers left British **Natal** in 1843, Pretorius stayed on but eventually found British rule unacceptable. In February 1848, he left Natal for the interior, and he succeeded in securing British recognition of the independent **South African Republic** by the Sand River Convention of January 1852.

**PRINCE OF WALES'S NORTH STAFFORDSHIRE REGIMENT, 1ST BATTALION.** Formerly the 64th Regiment until renamed in 1881 as a result of the **Childers Reforms**, the battalion formed part of the **Natal garrison** between 1887 and 1890. In October 1887, four companies and two **Gatling guns** were stationed at **Fort Curtis** and a detachment stationed at **St. Paul's** as part of the augmented **Zululand garrison** in the new British colony of **Zululand**. In June 1888 during the **uSuthu Rebellion**, detachments were posted forward to **kwaMagwaza**, **Entonjaneni**, and **Nkonjeni**. In July, two companies joined the **Eshowe Column** relieving **Fort Andries**. In November 1888, the battalion was withdrawn from Zululand. During the uSuthu Rebellion, it provided a company of **mounted infantry**.

**PRINCE OF WALES'S VOLUNTEERS (SOUTH LANCASHIRE REGIMENT), 2ND BATTALION.** Formerly the 82nd Regiment until renamed in 1881 as a result of the **Childers Reforms**, the battalion formed part of the **Natal garrison** between 1884 and 1887. Between February and November 1884 during the 3rd **Zulu Civil War**, three companies with two **Gatling guns** reinforced the garrison at **Fort Curtis** as a precaution against **uSuthu** operations in the **Reserve Territory**.

**PRINCESS LOUISE'S ARGYLL AND SUTHERLAND HIGHLANDERS, 1ST BATTALION.** Formerly the 91st **Regiment** (Princess Louise's Argyllshire Highlanders) until renamed in 1881 as a result of the **Childers Reforms**, the battalion had been stationed in South Africa since 1879, when it fought in the **Anglo-Zulu War**. It formed part of the **Natal garrison** between 1883 and 1885. During the 3rd **Zulu Civil War**, a company formed part of the **Etshowe Column** in September 1883 and was reinforced by another company to garrison **Fort Curtis**. In May 1884, they built **Fort Chater**, where they remained to stiffen **Osborn's levies** defending the **Reserve Territory** against the **uSuthu** in the **Nkandla Forest**. In July, they erected **Fort Yolland** nearer to the Nkandla Forest and remained in garrison in the Reserve Territory until November 1884.

**PROVISO B.** On 22 October 1886, the **New Republic**, in return for British recognition, ceded control over a block of territory in central **Zululand**, known as Proviso B. Boers who had already laid out farms there were allowed to retain ownership of them. When Proviso B was annexed by the British on 19 May 1887 as part of the Colony of Zululand, the Boer farmers were permitted to stay in possession even though the rest of Zululand was not thrown open to white settlement.

**PULLEINE, HENRY BURMEISTER (1839–1879).** Commissioned in 1855, Pulleine was posted to stations in England, Mauritius, Burma, India, Malta, and Gibraltar. In 1875, he was stationed at the **Cape** and promoted to brevet lieutenant-colonel in 1877. He saw service in the 9th **Cape Frontier War** (1877–1878), when he raised and commanded two units of mounted **irregulars**. In September 1878, he was appointed commandant of **Durban**, then of **Pietermaritzburg**, and in January 1879 president of the Remount Depot. During the **Anglo-Zulu War**, he was with No. 3 **Column**, and Lieutenant-General Lord **Chelmsford** left him in command of the camp at **Isandlwana** on 22 January 1879. Pulleine was killed in the battle, probably in its final stage when the British were attempting to conduct a fighting retreat toward the Mzinyathi River.

**isinPUSELENI** *iKHANDA*. In late March 1879 during the **Anglo-Zulu War**, noting the preparations for an advance being made by the **Eshowe Relief Column**, the Zulu began to reinforce the forces blockading **Eshowe** to contest its advance. Some 1,500 of the **iNdluyengwe** *iButho* were quartered at isinPuseleni, an *iKhanda* close to **oNdini** in southeastern **Zululand**, where other *amaButho* were stationed.

## – Q –

**oQEKETHENI** *iKHANDA*. This was one of the *amaKhanda* in the **emaKhosini valley** burned on 26 June 1879 by **Wood's Flying Column** during the 2nd Invasion of the **Anglo-Zulu War**.

*iziQU*. These carved, strung, interlocking wooden beads were worn by Zulu men around the neck or upper body. They were made of wood from the willow tree, which was associated with the *amaDlozi* (ancestral spirits) and thus treated with reverence. *IziQu* were worn as **ritual** protection against *uMnyama* (evil influence) by men who had killed in battle or had participated in the *hlomula* ritual, particularly in the period of great vulnerability before the full ritual that followed combat. Wearing *iziQu* was seen as an indication of a man's bravery and military prowess.

**QUARTER IN BATTLE.** The Zulu never gave quarter in battle, and they killed the wounded afterward. Women generally were not allowed to escape alive, on the grounds that they bore fighting men. **Cattle** fared better than did the enemy, for they were the prized booty of war. The Zulu, most of whom could not ride, also tended to kill their enemies' **horses**, reducing their dangerous mobility. The Voortrekkers were no more predisposed than the Zulu to take prisoners, and they were merciless when making mounted sorties from their **laagers**. The British in the **Anglo-Zulu War** took a small handful of prisoners in battle for the purposes of **military intelligence** but generally gave no quarter when in hot pursuit. The **Natal Native Contingent** regularly killed all the wounded they could find on the battlefield, and British regulars and colonials usually did so too. The British usually did not kill noncombatants, although they did not spare belongings or dwellings.

**abaQULUSI *iBUTHO*.** *See abaQULUSI* PEOPLE.

**abaQULUSI PEOPLE.** The people attached to the **ebaQulusini** *iKhanda* established by King **Shaka kaSenzangakhona** came to dominate the surrounding region of northwestern **Zululand**. They fell under the direct rule of the royal house and regarded themselves as a separate group. The men formed a distinct *iButho* drawn only from the specific locality. Their special connection to the royal house made them its most loyal adherents. In the 2nd **Zulu Civil War**, the abaQulusi *iButho* fought in the very center of the **uSuthu** chest at **Ndondakusuka**. During the **Anglo-Zulu War**, King **Cetshwayo kaMpande** entrusted the abaQulusi with the defense of northwestern Zululand, where they faced Brevet Colonel **Henry Evelyn Wood**'s forces. On 20 January 1879, they repulsed Lieutenant-Colonel **Redvers Henry Buller** at **Zungwini Mountain**, though Wood retaliated successfully in subsequent days. During February, British raids from **Khambula** Camp discomforted the abaQulusi, who retired deeper into Zululand, though not without successful retaliatory raids into the **Ntombe** valley. On 12 March, they participated in the successful overwhelming of a British convoy from No. 5 **Column** at Ntombe Drift. AbaQulusi **irregulars** were prominent in routing the British at **Hlobane**, and many of them and elements of the abaQulusi *iButho* fought at Khambula, where the irregulars suffered particularly heavily in the rout. Once **Wood's Flying Column** began its advance in June during the 2nd Invasion of the Anglo-Zulu War, abaQulusi irregulars became active again in the northwest. After the battle of **Ulundi**, General **Sir Garnet Joseph Wolseley** feared the abaQulusi might attempt a last-ditch resistance, and **Baker Russell's Column** was dispatched to pacify them. However, they only surrendered between 30 August and 3 September on receiving the captive Cetshwayo's secret orders to do so.

In the 1st Partition of Zululand, Wolseley deliberately placed the abaQulusi under the collaborationist *umNtwana* **Hamu kaNzibe** to suppress their royalist loyalties. With Cetshwayo's restoration following the 2nd Partition of Zululand, the abaQulusi swiftly struck at their **Ngenetsheni** oppressors and at other local enemies during the 3rd Zulu Civil War. A contingent fought at **Msebe** and continued to skirmish with the Ngenetsheni from April to July 1883. A contingent was with *umNtwana* **Ndabuko kaMpande**'s forces that retreated at **oNdini** before becoming engaged in the battle. They continued to resist the anti-uSuthu forces in the broken fighting after oNdini and in 1884 played an important part at **Tshaneni** in cutting off the **Mandlakazi** flight. As a result of the 3rd Partition of Zululand, the abaQulusi found themselves within the **New Republic** and under Boer rule, but during the **uSuthu Rebellion** they nevertheless rallied to King **Dinuzulu kaCetshwayo** on **Ceza Mountain**, and their irregulars took part in the repulse of the British. At **Ivuna**, they formed the uSuthu right horn when they came under fire from the Ivuna Fort. Their support for Dinuzulu dwindled away during July and August 1888 as the British reasserted their control of northwestern Zululand, though they were the last of the uSuthu to disperse from Ceza. *See also* KUBHEKA PEOPLE; MBILINI waMSWATI.

**ebaQULUSINI** *iKHANDA*. King **Shaka kaSenzangakhona** established the ebaQulusini *iKhanda* for the abaQulusi *iButho* on the northern flank of Mashongololo Mountain just east of **Hlobane Mountain** in northwestern **Zululand** to guard the frontier against the Ndwandwe, Khumalo, and **Swazi** people and to serve as a focus for royal authority in the region. He placed it under the command of his influential sister Mnkabayi. On 1 February 1879, Lieutenant-Colonel **Redvers Henry Buller** led a raid from **Khambula** Camp and burned it. *See also* abaQULUSI PEOPLE.

**QUNGEBE PEOPLE.** On the eve of the **Anglo-Zulu War**, King **Cetshwayo kaMpande** ordered the fighting men of the **Qungebe**

people who lived opposite Rorke's Drift to assemble at **kwaSogekle**, the stronghold of their *inKosi* **Sihayo kaXongo**, to resist the British invaders. On 12 January, men of No. 3 **Column** stormed kwaSogekle, and for the rest of the war the Qungebe kept to their places of refuge, staying away from the border and the danger of British raids. In August, they began drifting back to their homes. In terms of the 1st Partition of **Zululand**, they were placed in **Hlubi kaMota Molife**'s chiefdom. As a result of the 2nd Partition of Zululand, they found themselves in the **Reserve Territory**. During the 3rd **Zulu Civil War**, they rallied under **Mehlokazulu kaSihayo** to the **uSuthu** cause in the **Nkandla Forest**, and they reinforced the uSuthu army in central Zululand that went on to defeat the **Mandlakazi** at **Tshaneni**. In June 1888, during the **uSuthu Rebellion**, when it seemed the Qungebe might again rally to the uSuthu cause and begin operations in the Nkandla Forest, the British took their leaders into preventive custody.

**iQWA** *iBUTHO*. King **Mpande kaSenzangakhona** formed this *iButho* around 1860 from youths born about 1840. It was possibly incorporated into the **uDududu** *iButho*. The **shield** was black or red and white. During the **Anglo-Zulu War**, elements fought at **Nyezane**. At **Ulundi**, it attacked the northern side of the British infantry **square**.

## – R –

**RAAFF'S TRANSVAAL RANGERS.** The unit was originally raised in 1878 by Commandant Pieter Edward Raaff (a veteran of earlier frontier wars against the **Sotho** and **Pedi**) for the unsuccessful British campaign against the Pedi. In November 1878, Raaff went to the **Kimberley diamond fields** to raise recruits for the coming **Anglo-Zulu War** from tough diggers, both white and colored. He raised further recruits in **Pretoria** and then joined No. 5 **Column**. During February 1879, the Rangers (who numbered about 130 men) took part in the patrols mounted against the Zulu in northwestern **Zululand**, notably the raid against the **abaQulusi** on Talaku Mountain on 15 February. When in late February No. 5 Column was placed under Brevet Colonel **Henry Evelyn Wood**'s command, the Rangers joined his forces at **Khambula**. A squadron formed part of Lieutenant-Colonel **Redvers Henry Buller**'s force at **Hlobane** and fought the next day at Khambula. During the 2nd Invasion of the Anglo-Zulu War, the Rangers advanced with **Wood's Flying Column**, and a squadron took part in the **White Mfolozi reconnaissance in force** and in the battle of **Ulundi**. After the breakup of Wood's Flying Column in late July, the Rangers joined **Baker Russell's Column** in its march to the Transvaal, a detachment garrisoning **Fort George**. They were disbanded in September. Uniform was erratic, made of yellow, brown, or black corduroy, often mixed with civilian items of clothing.

**RAILWAY, NATAL.** Railway building began in a very small way in **Natal** in 1860, and in 1875 a narrow, flexible 3 foot, 6 inch gauge was adopted as suitable in the hilly terrain. In 1879, the only railway toward the **Zulu** border ran the short distance north from **Durban** to Saccharine Station (Mount Edgecombe) on the sugar-producing north coast. The extension did not reach the Thukela River until 1898. Inland, the railway from Durban had reached Botha's Hill by 1879 but would not extend to **Pietermaritzburg** until 1880 or **Ladysmith** until 1886. Consequently, during the Zulu wars, the railway was of little use in bringing up troops or supplies to the front.

**RECONCILIATION, DAY OF.** The Voortrekkers attributed their crushing victory over the Zulu at **Ncome** during the **Voortrekker-Zulu War** to divine intervention in response to a covenant made with God on 9 December 1838, which they repeated every evening until the battle was won on 16 December. They vowed that if they defeated the Zulu, they and their descendants would keep the anniversary of the battle as a day of thanksgiving to God. The covenant and victory at Ncome became cornerstones of Afrikaner nationalism. With the Union of South Africa in 1910, 16 December was proclaimed a public holiday. It was called Dingaan's Day until 1952, when the Afrikaner-dominated National Party government renamed it the Day of the Covenant, changing it in 1979 to the Day of the Vow. At the Ncome site, a large stone monument of a wagon was erected on 16 December 1947 to the Voortrekker victory, followed on the anniversary in 1971 by an impressive **laager** of bronze-plated, life-size wagons. For the Zulu people, the battle became a symbol of Afrikaner domination and racial ideology. After 1994, the new democratic government decided to redress the imbalance. The public holiday was renamed the Day of Reconciliation, and on 16 December 1998 a new monument, shaped like the horns of a Zulu battle formation, was opened across the river from the laager of bronze wagons. It is dedicated to the brave Zulu who fell in the battle defending their independence, and it incorporates a museum exhibiting Zulu material culture.

**REGIMENT, 3rd (EAST KENT, THE BUFFS), 2ND BATTALION.** During late 1878, the battalion (which had formed part of the **Natal garrison** since 1876) was concentrated on the lower Thukela River at **Fort Williamson** and **Thring's Post** from previous scattered postings around **Natal**. It was under the command of Lieutenant-Colonel H. Parnell and was brought up to full strength with the arrival of three companies from Mauritius. During November, it built and garrisoned **Fort Pearson**. In the 1st Invasion of the **Anglo-Zulu War**, a few detached personnel took part in the battle of **Rorke's Drift**. As part of No. 1 **Column**, eight companies fought in the battle of **Nyezane**. Six companies formed part of the garrison of **Fort Eshowe**, and the remaining two that had escorted a convoy back from Eshowe to the lower Thukela garrisoned **Fort Tenedos**. These two companies joined the 1st Brigade, **Eshowe Relief Column**, and fought at **Gingindlovu**. The battalion subsequently took part in the coastal operations of the 1st Brigade, 1st Division, **South African Field Force**, and on the breakup of the 1st Division on 23 July 1879 returned to Natal. In November, the battalion embarked for the Straits Settlement. Tunic facings were buff.

**REGIMENT, 4TH (KING'S OWN ROYAL), 2ND BATTALION.** The battalion under the command of Colonel Edward William Bray arrived in the field soon after **Isandlwana** and spent the **Anglo-Zulu War** in reserve as supply troops and in garrison duties along the lines of communication. Detachments served for periods at **Fort Amiel**, **Balte Spruit**, **Fort Clery**, **Conference Hill**, **Helpmekaar**, **Fort Lawrence**, the **Luneburg laager**, **Fort Moore**, and **Potgieter's Farm laager**. On 8 September, the Luneburg garrison snuffed out

Zulu resistance on Mbilini's mountain. Passing through the Transvaal, the battalion embarked in February 1880 for India. Tunic facings were blue.

**REGIMENT, 13TH (1ST SOMERSETSHIRE) PRINCE ALBERT'S LIGHT INFANTRY, 1ST BATTALION.** During the 1st Invasion of the **Anglo-Zulu War**, the battalion under the command of Lieutenant-Colonel P.E.V. Gilbert, which previously had been engaged in operations against the **Pedi** in the Transvaal, formed part of No. 4 **Column** and fought at **Khambula**. Detachments periodically garrisoned the **Balte Spruit laager**, **Luneburg laager**, **Potgieter's Farm laager**, and **Fort Tinta**. Under the command of Brevet Lieutenant-Colonel E. L. England, it formed part of **Wood's Flying Column** in the 2nd Invasion of the Anglo-Zulu War and fought at **Ulundi**. It retired with Wood's Flying Column to **St. Paul's**, then proceeded directly to **Natal** and embarked in August for England. Tunic facings were blue.

**REGIMENT, 21ST (ROYAL SCOTS FUSILIERS), 2ND BATTALION.** Sent out from Ireland as reinforcements for the 2nd Invasion of the **Anglo-Zulu War**, and made up to strength with 300 volunteers from other units, the battalion under the command of Colonel William P. Collingwood arrived in **Natal** in March 1879. Leaving two companies to garrison **Fort Napier**, it made up part of the 1st Brigade, 2nd Division, **South African Field Force**, and fought at **Ulundi**. During the advance, detachments garrisoned **Fort Marshall** and **Fort Newdigate** and built **Fort Ulundi**. On the breakup of the 2nd Division in late July, the battalion proceeded to service in the Transvaal, where it formed the **Pretoria** garrison and saw action in the 1st **Boer War**. Tunic facings were blue.

**REGIMENT, 24TH (SECOND WARWICKSHIRE), 1ST BATTALION.** The battalion under Colonel **Richard Thomas Glyn**, stationed at the **Cape** since January 1875, had most recently seen action in the 9th **Cape Frontier War**. In the 1st Invasion of the **Anglo-Zulu War**, the battalion formed part of No. 3 **Column** and garrisoned the **Helpmekaar Fort**. Five companies were annihilated at **Isandlwana**. Detached personnel were present at the defense of

**Rorke's Drift**. During the 2nd Invasion of the war, the reinforced battalion was incorporated into the 2nd Brigade, 2nd Division, **South African Field Force**, and detachments garrisoned the **Balte Spruit laager**, **Fort Newdigate**, and the **Mthonjaneni laager**. It participated in the **White Mfolozi reconnaissance in force**. During the battle of **Ulundi**, it was kept in reserve and garrisoned the White Mfolozi Camp. With the breakup of the 2nd Division in late July, the battalion returned to **Natal** and embarked in late August 1879 for England. Tunic facings were grass green.

**REGIMENT, 24TH (SECOND WARWICKSHIRE), 2ND BATTALION.** The 2nd Battalion under Lieutenant-Colonel Henry James Degacher arrived at the **Cape** in March 1878 and saw action in the 9th **Cape Frontier War**. In the 1st Invasion of the **Anglo-Zulu War**, it formed part of No. 3 **Column**. One company was annihilated at **Isandlwana**, while six more companies were absent on reconnaissance. A further company defended **Rorke's Drift**. Detachments garrisoned the rebuilt fort at Rorke's Drift and **Fort Melvill**. During the 2nd Invasion of the war, the battalion formed part of the 1st Brigade, 2nd Division, **South African Field Force**, and detachments garrisoned **Fort Jones**, **Landman's Drift**, and **Fort Whitehead** along the line of communications. The scattered battalion had reassembled in **Natal** by September 1879, and it embarked for Gibraltar in January 1880. Tunic facings were grass green.

**REGIMENT, 25TH (KING'S OWN BORDERERS).** The regiment was stationed at the **Cape** between 1840 and 1842. Five companies were sent by sea in June 1842 to relieve the **Durban** garrison being besieged by the Boers of the Republic of **Natalia**.

**REGIMENT, 27TH (INNISKILLING), 1ST BATTALION.** The battalion formed part of the **Cape** garrison and fought in the 6th and 7th **Cape Frontier Wars** of 1835 and 1846–1847. In May 1842, a detachment occupied **Durban** and was defeated at **Congella**. It was besieged in Smith's Camp by the Boers of the Republic of **Natalia** until relieved in June by the 25th **Regiment** (King's Own Borderers).

**REGIMENT, 45TH (NOTTINGHAMSHIRE), 1ST BATTALION.** In July 1843, a detachment of the battalion reinforced the British garrison in **Durban**. It then marched to **Pietermaritzburg** in August 1843 and commenced the construction of **Fort Napier**, the new headquarters of the **Natal garrison**. The battalion remained in garrison at Fort Napier until 1859.

**REGIMENT, 57TH (WEST MIDDLESEX).** Sent out from Ceylon as reinforcements for the 2nd Invasion of the **Anglo-Zulu War**, the regiment under the command of Lieutenant-Colonel **Charles Mansfield Clarke** joined the 2nd Brigade, **Eshowe Relief Column**, and fought at **Gingindlovu**. Its men suffered much from sickness. After the relief of **Eshowe**, it formed part of the 2nd Brigade, 1st Division, **South African Field Force**, and helped construct **Fort Chelmsford**. Advancing as far as **Port Durnford**, on 23 July it became part of **Clarke's Column** and reoccupied the **Mahlabathini Plain**. Detachments were involved in the pursuit and capture of King **Cetshwayo kaMpande**. The regiment marched with Clarke's Column for **Natal** in September and embarked in November for England. Tunic facings were yellow.

**REGIMENT, 58TH (RUTLANDSHIRE).** Sent out from England as reinforcements for the 2nd Invasion of the **Anglo-Zulu War**, in early May 1879 the regiment under Colonel R. C. Whitehead joined the 1st Brigade of the 2nd Division**, South African Field Force**, concentrating at **Landman's Drift**, leaving a detachment at the **Durban Redoubt**. During the advance, it built **Fort Whitehead** and **Fort Evelyn**, which it garrisoned, and it fought at **Ulundi**. On the breakup of the 2nd Division in late July, the regiment built and garrisoned **Fort Victoria** for **Clarke's Column**. From mid-August, it sent detachments to garrison **Fort Marshall** and **Landman's Drift**. The regiment evacuated **Zululand** in early September. It remained in South Africa and formed part of the **Natal garrison** from 1880 to 1884. It fought in the 1st **Boer War** as part of the Natal Field Force. As a consequence of the **Childers Reforms**, on 1 July 1881 it was renamed the 2nd Battalion, **Northamptonshire Regiment**. Tunic facings were black until 1881, when they became white.

**REGIMENT, 60TH (KING'S ROYAL RIFLE CORPS), 3RD BATTALION.** Sent out as reinforcements for the 2nd Invasion of the **Anglo-Zulu War**, the regiment under Colonel W. L. Pemberton joined the 2nd Brigade, **Eshowe Relief Column**, and fought at **Gingindlovu**. After the relief of **Eshowe**, it formed part of the 2nd Brigade, 1st Division, **South African Field Force**, under Brevet Colonel A. Tufnell and was initially occupied in constructing **Fort Chelmsford** and in convoy duties, during which time it suffered much from sickness. Advancing as far as **Port Durnford** with the 2nd Division, on 23 July it became part of **Clarke's Column** and reoccupied the **Mahlabathini Plain**. Detachments were involved in the pursuit of King **Cetshwayo kaMpande**. It marched with Clarke's Column for **Natal** in September and reached **Pietermaritzburg** in October, where it formed part of the **Natal garrison** at **Fort Napier** until 1880. It then joined the Natal Field Force and saw action in the 1st **Boer War**. The dark rifle-green tunic had scarlet facings.

**REGIMENT, 72ND (DUKE OF ALBANY'S OWN HIGHLANDERS).** The regiment was stationed at the **Cape** between 1828 and 1840 and fought in the 6th **Cape Frontier War** of 1835. In 1838–1839, it temporarily occupied **Durban**.

**REGIMENT, 80TH (STAFFORDSHIRE VOLUNTEERS).** The regiment took part in the annexation of the Transvaal in April 1877 and built the **Utrecht Fort** and **Fort Amiel** as bases for operations there. During 1878, the regiment under the command of Lieutenant-Colonel C. Tucker was engaged in operations against the **Pedi** in the Transvaal. By the end of the year, it was scattered in small detachments over the Transvaal and **Natal**. In early January 1879, it concentrated at Derby in the Transvaal, where during the 1st Invasion of the **Anglo-Zulu War** it formed the sole regular infantry component in No. 5 **Column**. In mid-February, the regiment marched with No. 5 Column to **Luneburg**, where the column was attached to Brevet Colonel **Henry Evelyn Wood**'s command on 26 February. The five companies of the regiment garrisoned **Fort Clery** and the **Luneburg laager** and were engaged in escorting convoys from Derby. On 12 March, **Mbilini waMswati** overwhelmed a detachment at the **Ntombe** River. On 9 April, the regiment was relieved and joined

Wood's Flying Column at Khambula for the 2nd Invasion of the war. Between late April and late May, a detachment was stationed at the Doornberg to cut wood for fuel, where it also built Fort Ayr. The regiment fought at Ulundi. When Wood's Flying Column was broken up in late July, detachments of the regiment were again scattered, only reuniting in February 1880 for embarkation to England. Tunic facings were yellow.

REGIMENT, 88TH (CONNAUGHT RANGERS). The regiment under the command of Lieutenant-Colonel W. Lambert landed at the Cape in July 1877 and took part in the 9th Cape Frontier War. Detachments were then posted at King William's Town on the Cape's eastern frontier, Cape Town, St. Helena, and Mauritius. Following Isandlwana during the Anglo-Zulu War, the four companies at the Cape were concentrated in Natal, with a detachment garrisoning the Durban Redoubt. They remained in reserve during the relief of Eshowe, while a further company was brought from St. Helena and another from Mauritius. At the beginning of May, the six companies joined the 1st Brigade, 1st Division, South African Field Force, for the 2nd Invasion of the Anglo-Zulu War. They were initially engaged in escorting convoys and loading provisions, then took part in the advance to Port Durnford, detaching garrisons at Fort Chelmsford and Fort Napoleon. When General Sir Garnet Joseph Wolseley redistributed the British forces in late July, he broke the regiment up into detachments at Fort Eshowe, Fort Chelmsford, and Fort Crealock to supply the units of Wood's Flying Column retiring to Natal. The regiment was ordered back to Natal in early August and embarked for India in October. Tunic facings were yellow.

REGIMENT, 90TH (PERTHSHIRE VOLUNTEERS LIGHT IN-FANTRY). The regiment under the command of Brevet Colonel R. M. Rogers landed at the Cape in January 1878. After service in the 9th Cape Frontier War, it was concentrated by late 1878 in Utrecht, where it formed part of No. 4 Column. During the 1st Invasion of the Anglo-Zulu War, it took part in the skirmishes at Zungwini Mountain and fought prominently in the battle of Khambula. During the 2nd Invasion of the war, the regiment formed part of Wood's Flying Column and fought at Ulundi. When General Sir

**Garnet Joseph Wolseley** redistributed the British forces in **Zululand**, the regiment was stationed at **St. Paul's** from 15 July until the end of September. It embarked in October for India. Tunic facings were buff.

**REGIMENT, 91ST (PRINCESS LOUISE'S ARGYLLSHIRE HIGHLANDERS).** Sent out as reinforcements for the 2nd Invasion of the **Anglo-Zulu War**, the regiment under the command of Lieutenant-Colonel A. C. Bruce was made up to active strength with 400 volunteers from other units. It joined the 1st Brigade, **Eshowe Relief Column**, and fought at **Gingindlovu**. It then formed part of the 2nd Brigade, 1st Division, **South African Field Force**. Until mid-June, it was employed on convoy duty. It then took part in the advance, leaving detachments at **Fort Napoleon** and **Port Durnford**. It built **Fort Argyll**, which it garrisoned until mid-September, when it returned to **Natal** for embarkation to **Cape Town** and Mauritius. The scarlet serge doublet had yellow facings.

**REGIMENT, 94TH.** Sent out as reinforcements for the 2nd Invasion of the **Anglo-Zulu War**, the regiment under the command of Lieutenant-Colonel Sydenham Malthus was made up to active strength with 350 volunteers from other units. It joined the 2nd Brigade, 2nd Division, **South African Field Force**, at **Dundee** and built fortifications at **Conference Hill** while two detached companies built and garrisoned **Fort Froom**. The regiment then took part in the advance and fought at **Ulundi**. When in late July General **Sir Garnet Joseph Wolseley** redistributed the forces in **Zululand**, the regiment was assigned to **Baker Russell's Column**. On its march to **Luneburg**, it helped build **Fort Cambridge**, **Fort George**, and **Fort Piet Uys**. On 5 September, it took part in the attack on the **Kubheka** in the caves in the Ntombe valley before proceeding to the Transvaal to join in renewed operations against the **Pedi**. Thereafter it formed part of the Transvaal garrison and fought throughout the 1st **Boer War**. Tunic facings were grass green.

**REGIMENT, 99TH (DUKE OF EDINBURGH'S LANARKSHIRE).** During the 1st Invasion of the **Anglo-Zulu War**, the regiment under the command of Lieutenant-Colonel W.H.D.R. Welman joined the 2nd Division, No. 1 **Column**. It fought at **Nyezane**, and three companies were among the garrison blockaded at **Fort Eshowe**. Three companies that had been left behind in **Natal** to garrison **Durban, Stanger**, and **Fort Tenedos**, including two that were sent back from Eshowe in January 1879 with a convoy of wagons, formed part of the 1st Brigade, **Eshowe Relief Column**, and fought at **Gingindlovu**. After the relief of Fort Eshowe, the regiment was stationed at the lower Thukela and formed part of the 1st Brigade, 1st Division, **South African Field Force**. Convoy duties occupied the regiment until the end of July, and detachments garrisoned **Fort Crealock** and **Fort Chelmsford**. With the breakup the 1st Division in late July, detachments were stationed at **Fort Napier**, the **Durban Redoubt, Fort Froom, Fort Melvill, Fort Pearson**, and **Port St. John's** until the regiment embarked in December for Bermuda. Tunic facings were grass green.

**REPUBLIEK NATALIA.** *See* NATALIA, REPUBLIC OF.

**RESERVE TERRITORY.** On 11 December 1882 by the 2nd Partition of **Zululand**, the British government agreed to the restoration of King **Cetshwayo kaMpande** to the central portion of his former kingdom. The southern portion of Zululand between the Thukela and Mhlathuze rivers, formerly **John Dunn**'s and **Hlubi kaMota Molife**'s chiefdoms in terms of the 1st Partition of Zululand, was excluded from his control. Known as the Reserve Territory, it was put under British protection and administered by a resident commissioner assisted by white officials recruited from **Natal** ruling through Zulu *amaKhosi*. Order was enforced through a small Zulu paramilitary force, the **Reserve Territory Carbineers**. The Reserve Territory was intended as a military buffer for Natal against independent Zululand and as a sanctuary for those Zulu who wished to avoid Cetshwayo's rule. On 19 May 1887, the Reserve Territory became part of the British Colony of Zululand.

**RESERVE TERRITORY CARBINEERS.** In 1883, with the establishment of the **Reserve Territory** under colonial administration after the 2nd Partition of **Zululand**, Commandant **George Mansel** raised the Reserve Territory Carbineers (RTC), a paramilitary police force recruited from the Zulu to maintain law and order under white officers. About a third of its complement was **mounted**, and its head-quarters were outside **Eshowe** at **Fort Nongqayi**. They wore khaki frocks and white trousers with khaki puttees above bare feet; those who were mounted wore boots. They carried either a **carbine** or **rifle**. During the 3rd **Zulu Civil War**, 50 were among **Melmoth Osborn**'s forces that engaged the **uSuthu** on 10 May 1884 in the battle of the **Nkandla Forest**. With the **submission** of the uSuthu in the Reserve Territory, in November 1884, the RTC replaced the British garrison at **Fort Yolland**. In May 1887, when the Reserve Territory became part of the Colony of Zululand, the RTC was reconstituted as the **Zululand Police**.

**RETIEF, PIETER (c. 1780–1838).** Retief was a farmer in the Gra-hamstown District of the **Eastern Cape**, where despite constant financial troubles brought on through gambling and land specula-tion, he gained a considerable reputation as a **commandant** in the 6th **Cape Frontier War**. He led a party of Voortrekkers onto the highveld in February 1837. At the Vet River on 17 April, various Voortrekker parties voted Retief governor of the United Laagers, angering **Andries Hendrik Potgieter**, whom he supplanted as chief commandant. While Potgieter continued into the interior, Retief led other parties to the **Drakensberg** passes in early October 1837 and encamped at Kerkenberg. Retief then visited Port Natal (**Durban**) to gain the traders' support and proceeded on 5 November to visit King **Dingane kaSenzangakhona** at uMgungundlovu. Retief agreed to recover Zulu **cattle** raided by Sekonyela, chief of the Mokotleng Tlokwa in the Caledon River valley, in return for a vague promise of land on which to settle. Retief sent word to the Voortrekkers at Kerkenberg to come over the mountains and camp in Zulu terri-tory while he led a **commando** (militia) to recover the cattle. Retief returned to his Doornkop **laager** on 11 January 1838 before bring-ing the cattle to Dingane for his reward. Other Voortrekker leaders, especially **Gerrit Maritz**, warned him against falling into a trap. Retief was confident of success, and on 3 February he arrived with his commando at uMgungundlovu. Dingane assented to a document ceding the Voortrekkers territory on 4 February, but on 6 February he ordered the execution of Retief and his party just as they were about to depart. They were dragged off to **kwaMatiwane**, and Retief had to witness his comrades being clubbed to death before his turn came. On 21 December 1838, the members of the **Wenkommando** found their remains and buried them in a mass grave at the base of kwaMatiwane.

**REVOLVERS.** British officers on campaign in **Zululand** in the 1870s and 1880s carried privately owned double-action revolvers, usually either the Mark II Adams model of 1872 or the Webley Royal Irish Constabulary model of 1867, using .450-caliber, center-fire ammunition. They were not accurate at more than 25 yards. It was not until 1900 that the British army insisted that officers carry .455 Webley revolvers. The troopers of the **Natal Volunteer Corps** carried the Webley Royal Irish Constabulary pattern revolver, as did the officers of the **irregular cavalry** units raised in South Africa.

**RICHMOND LAAGER.** In February 1878, the **Natal** government ordered the erection of a stone **laager** in the village of Richmond in what would be designated **Colonial Defensive District** No. IV. It was well supplied with arms before the outbreak of the **Anglo-Zulu War**, but it was never manned.

**RIETVLEI LAAGER.** This stone-walled **laager** with flanking bastions was begun in June 1878 on the initiative of local farmers at Riet Vlei in what would be designated **Colonial Defensive District** No. VII, the only post on the British line of communications between **Greytown** and **Estcourt**. It was not fully completed at the outbreak of the **Anglo-Zulu War**, and after **Isandlwana** most of its potential defenders abandoned it and fled the district.

**RIFLE ASSOCIATIONS, NATAL.** In 1862, in the wake of the Invasion Scare of 1861, Rifle Associations were formed by settlers in some areas of **Natal** for the purpose of defense. They attempted to train with some regularity and were encouraged to purchase **rifles** and ammunition from the government at a nominal cost. During the **Anglo-Zulu War**, the Klip River, Natal Coast, Natal, Umvoti, and Weenen County Rifle Associations mobilized to help defend, respectively, the **Ladysmith**, **Durban**, **Pietermaritzburg**, **Greytown**, and **Estcourt** town **laagers**.

**RIFLES, BREECH-LOADING.** Breech-loading rifles had a long genesis, but it was not until the 1860s that technology overcame problems such as the escape of gas at the breech, bolt-actions that tended to jam, and brittle firing pins. Improved breech-loading rifles made it possible not only to fire more rapidly and accurately, but to do so while kneeling or lying down. This encouraged open-order skirmishing tactics. Firing while standing was confined to old-fashioned, close-order formations in defense, like the infantry **square**, and was adopted only against enemies with inferior armaments, such as the Zulu in the **Anglo-Zulu War**. *See also* MARTINI-HENRY MARK II RIFLE; TACTICS, BRITISH INFANTRY.

**RIFLES, PERCUSSION-LOCK.** In 1853, the British War Department approved the Enfield rifled **musket** for use in the army. It remained in service until 1867, when many were decommissioned and bought up by arms dealers, who then sold them. Thousands entered **Zululand** and the Boer republics in the decade before the **Anglo-Zulu War**. These rifles used a .577 ball in a paper cartridge with a charge of black powder. The cartridge was forced down the 39-inch barrel, with its three grooves of rifling, and was fired by a percussion-lock mechanism. The rifle had adjustable ladder rear sights and an effective range of no more than 300 yards. The rate of fire was about three rounds a minute. *See also* PERCUSSION CAPS.

**RIFLES, VOLLEY FIRE.** At medium to long range (300–1,400 yards), the British in the **Anglo-Zulu War** favored rifle volley fire over independent fire because, at that distance, the enemy appeared as a dense mass with no individual targets, and it was easier to control the rate of fire and prevent wastage of ammunition. The unceasing volleys carried out by each section in turn, up and down the line, also had a distinct psychological effect on the enemy. Volley firing set up a thick pall of smoke, so another reason for firing by section was to allow time for the obscuring smoke to clear. *See also* MARTINI-HENRY MARK II RIFLE; TACTICS, BRITISH INFANTRY.

**RITUAL DURING BATTLE, ZULU.** In battle, a ritual the Zulu followed was to *hlomula*, or for many *amaButho* to stab an enemy who had already died courageously. This practice was connected with the hunt, where it was performed only when a fierce and dangerous animal like a lion had been overcome. Killing a foe in battle, as well as participating in the *hlomula* ritual, severely contaminated the *amaButho* with ***uMnyama*** (dark or evil force). It was thus necessary to undertake many ceremonies to achieve ritual purification. One was to slit open the belly of a slain foe so that *uMnyama* would not affect the killer and make him swell up like the dead. The killer would also put on items of the dead man's apparel in place of his own—which would have been contaminated by the harmful influences of the victim's blood—in order that he might *zila*, or observe the customary abstentions after a death until ritually cleansed. He would also put on a string of ***iziQu*** to guard against *uMnyama* until purification. *See also* RITUAL PREPARATION FOR WAR, ZULU; RITUAL ON RETURN FROM WAR, ZULU.

**RITUAL PREPARATION FOR WAR, ZULU.** *AmaButho*, when about to go to war, needed to be ritually purified of ***uMnyama*** (dark or evil force) and strengthened against it. They caught and killed bare-handed a black bull from the royal herds upon which all the evil influences in the land had been ritually cast. Diviners known as *izAngoma* cut strips of meat from the bull, and treated them with black symbolic medicines to strengthen the *amaButho* and bind them together in loyalty to their king. The strips of meat were then roasted on a fire of wood collected by the *amaButho* the previous day. The *izAngoma* threw the strips up into the air and the *amaButho*, who were drawn up in a great circle, caught and sucked them. Meanwhile the *izAngoma* burned more medicines and the *amaButho* breathed in the smoke and were sprinkled with the cinders. Then, in order finally to expel all evil influences, each *iButho* drank a pot of medicine, and a few at a time took turns to vomit into a great pit. The ritual vomiting was also intended to bind the *amaButho* in their loyalty to their king. Some of the vomit was added to the great ***iNkatha*** (sacred coil) of the Zulu nation. The following day, the *amaButho* went down to any running stream to wash, but not to rub off the medicines with which they had been sprinkled. With the completion of these rituals, the *amaButho* (who had undergone a symbolic death) could no longer sleep at home nor have anything to do with girls or women, since they had now taken on a dangerous state of *uMnyama*. While the *amaButho* were thus setting themselves apart from ordinary life and dedicating themselves to war, the king called pairs of favored *amaButho* into the royal cattle enclosure to boast of their courage and to issue ritual challenges to outdo one another in the coming campaign. *See also* RITUAL ON RETURN FROM WAR, ZULU.

**RITUAL ON RETURN FROM WAR, ZULU.** After returning from war, *amaButho* could not immediately report to the king nor resume normal domestic life because they were highly contagious with *uMnyama* (dark or evil force). They were separated for four days from their companions in special *imiZi* and fed on **cattle** captured in battle. Daily, they washed ritually in a river and returned to *ncinda*, which is to suck symbolic medicine from the fingertips and spit it in the direction of enemies in order to gain occult ascendancy over the vengeful spirits (*amaDlozi*) of war victims, the blood from whose fatal wounds formed a dangerous bridge between the living and the spirit world. On the final day, the *izAngoma* completed the ritual purification by sprinkling the *amaButho* with medicines before they presented themselves in the royal *isiBaya* before the king. There they exchanged accounts of the fighting and repeated the ritual challenges made before setting out to war. The king duly praised some individuals for bravery, humiliated others for cowardice, and honored and rewarded the *iButho* that had most distinguished itself. *See also* RITUAL DURING BATTLE, ZULU; RITUAL PREPARATION FOR WAR, ZULU.

**RIVER GUARDS.** *See* BORDER GUARD, NATAL.

**ROADS IN ZULULAND.** Roads, where they existed in **Zululand**, were no more than rudimentary unsurfaced wagon tracks made by traders and hunters that frequently crossed unbridged dongas (dry watercourses), rivers, and streams. Drifts across these were usually adequate except when the rivers were in spate during the rainy season from September to March, or when the cuttings became churned up with heavy traffic. On campaign in Zululand between 1879 and 1888, the British installed ponts (ferries operated by ropes) where a river was wide and usually full, or crossed it with a trestle and pontoon bridge. At the lower Thukela River below **Fort Pearson**, both systems were in operation during the **Anglo-Zulu War**. *See also* LOGISTICS, BRITISH.

**ROBERTSON, ROBERT (1830–1897).** An Anglican missionary in **Natal** since 1854, in 1860 Robertson began building a mission at **kwaMagwaza** in south-central **Zululand** once King **Mpande ka-Senzangakhona** opened Zululand to missionary endeavors. He made few converts, however. Disillusioned by the traditionalist King **Cetshwayo kaMpande**'s growing antagonism to missionaries, he began actively to canvass for British intervention in the kingdom. Sir **Bartle Frere**, anxious to find justifications for his planned war against Zululand to further the cause of **confederation**, seized on Robertson's letters for his propaganda machine. Robertson fled Zululand in August 1877. During the **Anglo-Zulu War**, he served as Anglican chaplain with No. 1 **Column**, being present at **Nyezane** and throughout the siege of **Eshowe**. After the war, he returned to kwaMagwaza and in the late 1880s and early 1890s established two further Anglican missions in Zululand.

**ROCKETS.** The British employed rockets with explosive heads in the **Anglo-Zulu War** primarily for their supposed demoralizing effect on the enemy. In flight, the rockets made a hideous shrieking sound, and their passage was marked by a thick trail of white smoke and yellow sparks. Hale's rocket, approved in 1867, came in both 24-pounder and 9-pounder versions. Instead of a stick for stability, it had three flanges at the vent, which caused it to spin in flight. It was fired by a hand-lit fuse from a V-shaped trough on a stand, though in 1879 the **Naval Brigade** continued to use the pre-1868 rocket tube, which was more suitable for shipboard service. The effective range was no more than 1,300 yards and the accuracy was very poor.

**RORKE'S DRIFT, BATTLE OF (1879).** The small British garrison holding No. 3 **Column**'s depot at Rorke's Drift defended the post against a heavy Zulu attack following the defeat of the British at **Isandlwana** on 22 January 1879 in the opening stages of the **Anglo-Zulu War**. The Zulu referred to the engagement as the battle of kwaJimu after James Rorke, who had originally established his trading store at the drift across the Mzinyathi River before it became a Swedish mission station in January 1878.

On 22 January, mounted fugitives from Isandlwana brought word to Rorke's Drift that 3,000–4,000 Zulu of the reserve under *umNtwana* **Dabulamanzi kaMpande** that had not been engaged with the rest of the Zulu army at Isandlwana were crossing the Mzinyathi in two columns. Their objectives were to ravage the plain between the river and the **Helpmekaar** Heights to the south, snatch the depot full of tempting supplies, and generally prove their prowess. Upon their advance, the **irregular** horse watching the river crossings and the 200 African levies at the depot fled toward Helpmekaar. Left to defend the post were eight British officers and 131 men, 35 of whom were sick in the mission house that had been converted into a **hospital**. Lieutenant **John Rouse Merriott Chard** of the Royal Engineers, the senior officer present, realized that the defensive perimeter he had hastily thrown up connecting the hospital, commissariat store (formerly the church), and stone-walled cattle kraal was too large to hold. He ordered it halved by building a barricade of biscuit boxes across the enclosure, but the barricade was not completed when the Zulu attacked, nor were the sick yet evacuated from the hospital outside the reduced perimeter, so the entire perimeter had to be thinly manned.

The Zulu assault was poorly coordinated, thus allowing the defenders to concentrate their forces where necessary. A Zulu detachment came around the southern side of Shiyane Mountain (the Oskarsberg) and attacked the southern and western sides of the post. Repulsed by cross-fire and in hand-to-hand fighting, they took cover. They were followed by the main Zulu force, which launched a series of assaults on the hospital and northwestern perimeter. The British drove them back in intense hand-to-hand fighting. Some Zulu sharpshooters took up position on the rocky ledges of Shiyane overlooking the post, and kept up a harassing fire. As dusk fell, the Zulu began to extend along the northern perimeter beyond the cover of the bush where they had regrouped after each failed assault. Chard decided he must withdraw to the shorter perimeter behind the line of biscuit boxes. As the British fell back, the Zulu occupied the hospital while its garrison retired room by room in desperate fighting, and it was set alight. Encouraged by this success, the Zulu attacked the stone cattle kraal on the eastern side of the perimeter. Believing that their defenses would soon be breached, the British built a redoubt out of two heaps of mealie-bags as a final defense overlooking the kraal. The Zulu, unsettled by their heavy losses and unfamiliar night fighting, held back from further full-scale assaults but maintained their positions. They kept up a heavy fire until around midnight, after which it eventually died away.

At daybreak on 23 January, the Zulu began withdrawing because they were aware that the remnants of No. 3 Column were approaching from Isandlwana. The members of this relieving force killed all the Zulu wounded or exhausted they found in the vicinity. Probably about 600 Zulu died, as well as 17 members of the British garrison.

The gallant defense of Rorke's Drift did much to compensate for the British disaster at Isandlwana, and awards were generously handed out. Those winning the Victoria Cross were Lieutenant Chard; Lieutenant **Gonville Bromhead**, 1st Battalion, 24th (2nd Warwick-shire) **Regiment**; Surgeon James Henry Reynolds, **Army Medical Department**; Acting Assistant Commissary James Langley Dalton, **Commissariat and Transport Department**; Corporal William Wilson Allan, 2nd Battalion, 24th (2nd Warwickshire) Regiment; Corporal Christian Ferdinand Schiess, **Natal Native Contingent**; and Privates Frederick Hitch, Alfred Henry Hook, Robert Jones, William Jones, and John Williams, all of the 2nd Battalion, 24th Regiment. Those awarded the Distinguished Conduct Medal were Color Sergeant Frank Bourne, 2nd Battalion, 24th Regiment; Corporal M. McMahon, **Army Hospital Corps**; 2nd Corporal F. Attwood, **Army Service Corps**; Wheeler J. Cantwell, **Royal Artillery**; and Private W. Roy, 1st Battalion, 24th Regiment. *See also* RORKE'S DRIFT FORT; TACTICS, BRITISH INFANTRY; TACTICS UP TO 1879, ZULU; STRATEGY, ZULU.

**RORKE'S DRIFT FORT.** In early January 1879 during the 1st Invasion of the **Anglo-Zulu War**, No. 3 **Column** established a depot at Rorke's Drift, a Swedish mission station on the **Natal** bank of the Mzinyathi River. The church was turned into a commissariat store and the missionary's house into a hospital. A pont (ferry operated by hauling on ropes) was established at the drift. When No. 3 Column advanced into **Zululand** on 11 January, it left a small garrison to guard the depot. On the afternoon of 22 January, being warned of the Zulu advance on the post after the battle of **Isandlwana**, the garrison improvised a defensive perimeter consisting of a breast-high barricade of mealie bags connecting the loopholed store and hospital, two wagons, and the stone-walled cattle kraal. When part of the garrison fled at the Zulu approach, this perimeter became too large to defend; it was halved by building a barricade of biscuit boxes across the enclosure. At the height of the battle the defenders turned two heaps of mealie bags into a redoubt for final defense.

On the morning of 23 January, the remnants of No. 3 Column returned to Rorke's Drift from Zululand and immediately enlarged and improved the improvised fortifications, pulling the thatch off the roof of the storehouse and clearing the perimeter for a clear field of fire. On 29 January, the enlarged garrison at the post began to fortify it properly. They replaced the barricades with strong, loopholed stone walls eight feet high that connected the kraal and storehouse in a rectangular enclosure. The troops were crammed inside the perimeter and suffered much sickness. In early March, they were permitted to pitch their tents outside the fort, although they still came in to sleep. In April, the troops abandoned the fort for the newly built **Fort Melvill** nearby. *See also* RORKE'S DRIFT, BATTLE OF.

**ROWLANDS, HUGH (1829–1909).** Commissioned in 1849, Rowlands served in the Crimean War (1854–1855), where he won the Victoria Cross at Inkerman. He then served in the West Indies and India until he became commandant of the Transvaal in 1878 and commanded during the unsuccessful campaign against the **Pedi** in late 1878. On special service during the **Anglo-Zulu War**, Colonel Rowlands commanded No. 5 **Column** until 26 February 1879, when he left for **Pretoria** to take defensive measures against a possible Boer uprising. In May, he succeeded Colonel **Charles Knight Pearson** as commander of the 1st Brigade, 1st Division, **South African Field Force**, in charge of the line of communications. He retired in 1896 as full general after holding commands in England, India, and Scotland. He was knighted in 1898.

**ROYAL ARTILLERY, H BATTERY, 4TH BRIGADE.** The battery of field artillery was ordered out to South Africa in 1884 and formed part of the **Natal garrison** until 1893. During the 3rd **Zulu Civil War**, a division with two 9-pounder guns and a **Gatling gun** formed part of the **Etshowe Column** that was stationed at **Fort Curtis** in the **Reserve Territory** between September 1883 and November 1884. When the garrison was reduced with the **submission** of the **uSuthu** in the **Nkandla Forest**, two Gatling guns remained at **Fort Northampton**. During the **uSuthu Rebellion**, a detachment of two 7-pounder mountain guns was sent forward in June 1888 from **Natal** to **Nkonjeni**, and during the assault on **Hlophekhulu** it made up part of the supporting force on **Lumbe Mountain**. Between 23 July and 30 August, the detachment formed part of the **Coastal Column**. When in November 1888 the **Zululand garrison** was reduced to its normal level, the detachment was stationed at Fort Curtis. *See also* ARTILLERY, BRITISH.

**ROYAL ARTILLERY, M BATTERY, 6TH BRIGADE.** Sent out from England as reinforcements for the 2nd Invasion of the **Anglo-Zulu War**, the field battery of six 7-pounder guns under the command of Major W. H. Sandham joined the 1st Division, **South African Field Force**, and advanced to **Port Durnford**. It took part in the patrol that burned the **oNdini** *iKhanda* on 6 July. On the breakup of the 1st Division at the end of July, the battery returned to **Natal**. *See also* ARTILLERY, BRITISH.

**ROYAL ARTILLERY, N BATTERY, 5TH BRIGADE.** After service in the 9th **Cape Frontier War**, the field battery of six 7-pounder guns under the command of Brevet Colonel Arthur Harness joined No. 3 **Column** for the 1st Invasion of the **Anglo-Zulu War**. Two of its guns were lost at **Isandlwana**; the remaining four, which had been out with the reconnaissance in force on 22 January, retired to **Rorke's Drift** and then to **Helpmekaar**, where they remained until 17 April. The battery, now reinforced to full strength, joined the 2nd Division, **South African Field Force**, in the 2nd Invasion of the war. A section took part in the patrol to **Isandlwana** to bury the British dead. Two guns were detached to garrison **Fort Newdigate** and **Fort Evelyn**, and the remaining two gave covering fire to the **White Mfolozi reconnaissance in force** and fought at **Ulundi**. The battery joined **Baker Russell's Column** on 5 August and halted at

**Fort George**. When the column was broken up on 10 September, the battery proceeded to the Transvaal, where it formed part of the Transvaal garrison and fought throughout the 1st **Boer War**. *See also* ARTILLERY, BRITISH.

**ROYAL ARTILLERY, N BATTERY, 6TH BRIGADE**. Sent out from England as reinforcements for the 2nd Invasion of the **Anglo-Zulu War**, the field battery of six 9-pounder guns under the command of Brevet Lieutenant-Colonel F. T. Le Grice joined the 2nd Division, **South African Field Force**, at **Landman's Drift**. During the advance, two guns formed part of the patrol by **Wood's Flying Column** that burned the *amaKhanda* in the **emaKhosini valley**. The battery gave support to the **White Mfolozi reconnaissance in force** and fought at **Ulundi**. When the 2nd Division was broken up in late July, two guns joined **Clarke's Column** after temporarily forming part of the garrison of **Fort Albert**. In September, they marched with the column to **Natal**; the remaining four guns returned to Natal through the Transvaal. The battery embarked in October for India. *See also* ARTILLERY, BRITISH.

**ROYAL ARTILLERY, O BATTERY, 6TH BRIGADE**. Sent out from England as reinforcements for the 2nd Invasion of the **Anglo-Zulu War**, the field battery (without guns) under the command of Brevet Lieutenant-Colonel A. W. Duncan joined the 1st Division, **South African Field Force**, and was based at **Fort Chelmsford** to supply advancing troops with ammunition, later advancing to **Port Durnford**. When the 1st Division was broken up at the end of July, the battery accompanied **Clarke's Column** and retired with it to **Natal** in September.

**ROYAL ARTILLERY, NO. 8 BATTERY, 7TH BRIGADE**. Sent out from England as reinforcements for the 2nd Invasion of the **Anglo-Zulu War**, the division of two 7-pounder guns of garrison artillery under the command of Major H. L. Ellaby served with the 1st Division, **South African Field Force**, between April and August 1879. It was stationed in succession at **Fort Pearson**, **Fort Tenedos**, and **Fort Crealock**, undertaking convoy duties. *See also* ARTIL-LERY, BRITISH.

**ROYAL ARTILLERY, NO. 10 BATTERY, 7TH BRIGADE.** Sent out from Mauritius as reinforcements for the 2nd Invasion of the **Anglo-Zulu War**, the half-battery of garrison artillery with three 7-pounder guns under Brevet Lieutenant-Colonel J. F. Owen was reorganized on arrival as a Mounted Gatling Field Battery (the first of its kind in the British army) with two **Gatling guns**. The battery joined **Wood's Flying Column** at **Munhla Hill** on 26 May 1879. It was temporarily stationed at **Fort Newdigate** but was back with the column to help cover the retreat of the **White Mfolozi reconnaissance in force** and to fight at **Ulundi**. When General **Sir Garnet Joseph Wolseley** reorganized the forces in **Zululand** at the end of July, the battery was assigned to **Clarke's Column** and returned with it to **Natal** in September. At the end of October, it embarked for Mauritius, and it later served with the Natal Field Force in the 1st **Boer War**. *See also* ARTILLERY, BRITISH.

**ROYAL ARTILLERY, NO. 11 BATTERY, 7TH BRIGADE.** The battery of garrison artillery under the command of Brevet Lieutenant-Colonel E. G. Tremlett served in several detachments throughout the **Anglo-Zulu War**. During the 1st Invasion of the war, a **rocket** detachment of three 9-pounder rocket-troughs under Brevet Major F. B. Russell served with No. 2 **Column** and was overrun at **Isandlwana**. A division of two 7-pounder guns under Lieutenant W. N. Lloyd served with No. 1 Column, fought at **Nyezane**, and was blockaded in **Fort Eshowe**. During the 2nd Invasion of the Anglo-Zulu War, the same division served with the 1st Division, **South African Field Force**. During the 1st Invasion, two divisions of four 7-pounders under Tremlett served with No. 4 **Column**, skirmishing at **Zungwini** in January 1879 and fighting at **Khambula** in March. At **Hlobane**, half a rocket battery under Tremlett was deployed with Lieutenant-Colonel **Redvers Henry Buller**'s force, and the other half under Captain A. J. Bigge with Lieutenant-Colonel **John Cecil Russell**'s force. Tremlett's two divisions then served with **Wood's Flying Column** in the 2nd Invasion and fought at **Ulundi**. When the forces in **Zululand** were reorganized at the end of July, the battery returned to **Natal**. *See also* ARTILLERY, BRITISH.

**ROYAL DURBAN RIFLES.** One of the three infantry corps in the **Natal Volunteer Corps**, the Royal Durban Rifles was not initially called up for service in the **Anglo-Zulu War**. In the panic after **Isandlwana**, its 30 men were first stationed at the Mngeni River on the northern approaches to **Durban** and then from the end of January were at the Eastern Vlei near the **Durban Redoubt** until they stood down in early March.

**ROYAL ENGINEERS.** Detachments served throughout the **Anglo-Zulu War**. No. 2 Company arrived in **Natal** from England in late 1878, served with No. 1 **Column**, fought at **Nyezane**, and served throughout the blockade of **Eshowe**. After the relief of Eshowe, it joined the 2nd Division, **South African Field Force**, in May and constructed the twin redoubts at **Conference Hill**. On the march to **oNdini**, it helped construct **Fort Evelyn**. During the battle of **Ulundi**, it formed part of the garrison holding the camp at the **White Mfolozi**. After the breakup of the 2nd Division in late July 1879, it joined **Baker Russell's Column** on its march to the Transvaal and built **Fort Cambridge** on the way.

No. 5 Company under Captain W. Parke Jones arrived in Natal from England in late 1878 and was part of No. 3 Column, but it had got no farther than **Helpmekaar** when the battles of **Isandlwana** and **Rorke's Drift** (where detached Royal Engineers were present) were fought. The company then built and helped garrison the fort at Helpmekaar until in May it joined **Wood's Flying Column** for the 2nd Invasion of the Anglo-Zulu War and was present at Ulundi. In late July, it built **St. Paul's** Redoubt.

Detached Royal Engineers with No. 4 Column built fortifications at **Balte Spruit** and fought at **Khambula**. The 30th Company joined the 1st Division, South African Field Force, built the trestle bridge and pontoon across the lower Thukela in May, and advanced with the division to **Port Durnford**. On the breakup of the division, it joined **Clarke's Column** in its march back to Natal. *See also* FORTIFICATIONS IN NATAL AND ZULULAND; ROADS IN ZULULAND.

**ROYAL INNISKILLING FUSILIERS, 1ST BATTALION.** Formerly the 27th (Inniskilling) **Regiment** until renamed in 1881 as a result of the **Childers Reforms**, the battalion formed part of the **Na-**

tal garrison between 1886 and 1888. During the **uSuthu Rebellion**, it provided a company of **mounted infantry**.

**ROYAL MARINE ARTILLERY.** The section of the **Royal Marine Light Infantry** of the **Naval Brigade** that marched with No. 1 **Column** in the **Anglo-Zulu War** and fought at **Nyezane** served two 7-pounder guns, a **Gatling gun**, and a 24-pounder **rocket** tube. The marines of the Naval Brigade with the **Eshowe Relief Column** served two 9-pounder guns, four 24-pounder rocket tubes, and a Gatling gun under the command of Captain A.L.S. Burrowes and fought at **Gingindlovu**. The guns then joined the 1st Division, **South African Field Force**, in its advance to **Port Durnford**. *See also* ARTILLERY, BRITISH.

**ROYAL MARINE LIGHT INFANTRY.** A section of marines under Captain T. W. Dowding landed in **Durban** on the eve of the **Anglo-Zulu War** as part of the **Naval Brigade** drawn from **HMS** *Active* and **HMS** *Tenedos*. The marines joined the 1st Division, No. 1 **Column**, fought at **Nyezane**, and were blockaded in **Fort Eshowe**. A further contingent of marines from **HMS** *Boadicea* and **HMS** *Shah* under Major J. Phillips marched with the 2nd Brigade, **Eshowe Relief Column**, and fought at **Gingindlovu**. After the relief of Eshowe, they joined the 1st Division, **South African Field Force**, in its march to **Port Durnford** and returned to their ships on 21 July.

**ROYAL SCOTS (LOTHIAN REGIMENT), 1ST BATTALION.** Formerly the 1st Regiment until renamed in 1881 as a result of the **Childers Reforms**, the battalion formed part of the **Natal garrison** between 1888 and 1891. In July 1888, during the final stages of the **uSuthu Rebellion**, six companies of the battalion were stationed in British **Zululand** at **Fort Curtis**. In August, three companies garrisoned the **Nsukazi Fort**, and in September all the companies in Zululand were consolidated at **Entonjaneni**. In November, the infantry companies were withdrawn from Zululand. The battalion also provided two companies of **mounted infantry**.

**RUSSELL, BAKER CREED (1837–1911).** Commissioned in 1855, Russell saw service in the Indian Mutiny (1857–1859) and the 2nd

Asante War (1873–1874), when he became a brevet lieutenant-colonel. He was a member of General **Sir Garnet Joseph Wolseley**'s Ashanti Ring and was Wolseley's assistant military secretary on Cyprus in 1878 before accompanying him on special service to South Africa in the last stages of the **Anglo-Zulu War** as a member of his staff. Between July and September 1879, he was in command of **Baker Russell's Column** and pacified central and northwestern **Zululand**. The column then proceeded to the Transvaal and concluded the campaign against the **Pedi** in November 1879. Russell was promoted to brevet colonel and knighted. He next served in the Egyptian campaign of 1882. A series of home commands followed, and he retired in 1904 as a lieutenant-general.

**RUSSELL, JOHN CECIL (1839–1909).** Commissioned in 1860, Russell served in the 2nd Asante War (1873–1874). In 1878, he was on special service in the Transvaal with the local rank of lieutenant-colonel and took part in the unsuccessful operations against the **Pedi**. During the **Anglo-Zulu War**, he served as commander of No. 1 Squadron, **Mounted Infantry**, in No. 3 **Column**. He was away skirmishing during the battle of **Isandlwana**. In March 1879, he transferred to No. 4 Column and overcautiously led one of the forces assaulting **Hlobane**. He fought at **Khambula** the next day. Brevet Colonel **Henry Evelyn Wood** attempted to shift the blame for the Hlobane debacle onto Russell, and he was ignominiously transferred to **Pietermaritzburg** as commandant of the Remount Establishment. He subsequently held commands in India and England, and he retired in 1898 as a major-general.

– S –

**SAAILAER.** *See* MARITZ, GERRIT.

**SAND RIVER CONVENTION.** *See* SOUTH AFRICAN REPUBLIC.

**iSANGQU *iBUTHO*.** King **Mpande kaSenzangakhona** formed this *iButho* around 1852 from youths born about 1832. The **shield** was black. In the 2nd **Zulu Civil War**, it formed part of the **uSuthu** right horn at **Ndondakusuka**. In the **Anglo-Zulu War**, it was part of the right horn at **Isandlwana** and of the chest at **Khambula**. At **Ulundi**, it attacked the southeastern corner of the British infantry **square**. In the 3rd Zulu Civil War, elements fought on the uSuthu side. At **oNdini**, they were stationed nearby at the **kwaNodwengu** *iKhanda* and were caught up in the uSuthu rout before they could come into action.

**SCHERBRUCKER'S HORSE.** *See* KAFFRARIAN RIFLES.

**SCHREUDER, HANS PALUDAN SMITH (1817–1882).** A Norwegian Lutheran missionary in **Zululand** from 1851, Schreuder was consecrated bishop in the Church of Norway in 1866, but he broke with the Norwegian Missionary Service in 1872 and launched an independent mission in Zululand, centered at Ntumeni. When the missionaries withdrew from Zululand in 1877, he took up position at his **Natal** station, kwaNtunjambili, near **Ntunjambili** (Kranskop), overlooking the middle Thukela River. During the **Anglo-Zulu War**, he served the British as an important source of intelligence through continuing contacts with King **Cetshwayo kaMpande** and through information furnished by his Christian converts still in Zululand. Schreuder, who prided himself on his knowledge of Zulu affairs, took great umbrage when General **Sir Garnet Joseph Wolseley** would not heed his counsel concerning the 1st Partition of Zululand.

**SEKETHWAYO kaNHLAKA (c. 1814–1883).** Enrolled in the imVokwe *iButho*, Sekethwayo was *inKosi* of the **Mdlalose** people and an *isiKhulu* (hereditary chief). He was a member of King **Cetshwayo kaSenzangakhona**'s *iBandla* (council) and was a leading advocate in 1878 of negotiating with the British to avoid war. During the **Anglo-Zulu War**, he made it known to Brevet Colonel **Henry Evelyn Wood** that he wished to **submit**, but Cetshwayo sent a force into his territory in mid-January 1879 to ensure he did not. Sekethwayo and the Mdlalose remained uncommitted to the war, and he surrendered in August to **Baker Russell's Column**. In the 1st Partition of **Zululand**, he was appointed one of the 13 chiefs but remained loyal to Cetshwayo and was active in appealing for his restoration. During the 3rd **Zulu Civil War**, his Mdlalose rallied to the **uSuthu** cause. His brother Ntuzwa kaNhlaka was in command at **oNdini**, where Sekethwayo was caught up in the rout and killed.

**SEKHUKHUNE woaSEKWATI.** *See* PEDI PEOPLE.

**SEKONYELA.** *See* RETIEF, PIETER.

**SHAKA kaSENZANGAKHONA (c. 1787–1828).** King Shaka is still revered today as the founder of the Zulu nation. His father was Senzangakhona kaJama, *inKosi* of the Zulu people who owed allegiance to the **Mthethwa**, one of the major chiefdoms then fighting to dominate the region of southeastern Africa that would later become the **Zulu kingdom**. About 1794, Shaka was driven into exile and eventually entered the service of Dingiswayo kaJobe, the Mthethwa *inKosi*. In 1816, with Dingiswayo's support, Shaka seized the Zulu chieftainship from his brother. In 1817, the Ndwandwe chiefdom defeated the Mthethwa and attacked the Zulu. Shaka responded by improving his military capability and fully institutionalizing the *iButho* **system**. He finally defeated the Ndwandwe in 1819 and incorporated their territory. He consolidated his hold over other neighboring chiefdoms through diplomacy when he could, or through conquest if they resisted. His armies levied tribute from the subordinate chiefdoms along the uncertain borders of the Zulu kingdom proper, and they regularly raided more distant peoples for booty. In 1824, white traders and hunters established a settlement at Port Natal (**Durban**) with Shaka's permission. They had **firearms**, and Shaka increasingly relied on them as **mercenaries**. Shaka faced opposition from rivals within the royal house and from dissident members of chiefdoms incorporated into the Zulu state. Even his *amaButho*, exhausted by incessant campaigns, began to turn against him. As part of a wider conspiracy, his half-brothers *abaNtwana* Mhlangana kaSenzangakhona and **Dingane kaSenzangakhona** assassinated him on 24 September 1828 at **kwaDukuza**, his principal *iKhanda*.

**SHEPSTONE, JOHN WESLEY (1827–1916).** A resident magistrate in **Natal** from 1864, Shepstone was appointed acting secretary for native affairs in 1877 (replacing his elder brother, **Sir Theophilus**

**Shepstone**, who had become administrator of the Transvaal). He delivered the British **ultimatum** to the Zulu emissaries on 11 December 1878. After the **Anglo-Zulu War**, he advised General **Sir Garnet Joseph Wolseley** on the 1st Partition of **Zululand**. He became resident commissioner of the **Reserve Territory** in January 1883, but his blatant antagonism toward the **uSuthu** led to disorders, and in April 1883 he resumed his position as acting secretary for native affairs in Natal.

**SHEPSTONE, SIR THEOPHILUS (1817–1893).** Shepstone was the **Natal** diplomatic agent to the native tribes (1845–1855) and then secretary for native affairs in Natal (1856–1876). He was knighted in 1876. On 18 April 1877, he annexed the **South African Republic** in the drive toward the British **confederation** of South Africa and was appointed administrator of the Transvaal Territory. In March 1879, he resigned the post. He left public service in 1880. Shepstone was a fervent promoter of British paramountcy in southern Africa, and he intervened directly in Zulu affairs to that end, most notably when he imposed the **coronation laws** on King **Cetshwayo kaMpande** in 1873 and broke with him at the **Conference Hill** meeting in 1877. In 1878, he advised **Sir Bartle Frere** on framing the **ultimatum** prior to the **Anglo-Zulu War**, and General **Sir Garnet Joseph Wolseley** later consulted him on the 1st Partition of **Zululand**. He was a determined advocate of indirect rule whereby real power was transferred from traditional chiefs to white, "civilizing" officials. A loyal school of Natal administrators emerged under him that wished to extend the "Shepstone system" to Zululand and that saw the Zulu monarchy as an inimical institution that should be suppressed. Although retired, Shepstone retained considerable influence over British policy toward Zululand during the 1880s. He was consulted over the 2nd Partition of Zululand and came briefly out of retirement in January 1883 to supervise Cetshwayo's restoration. With the annexation of the colony of Zululand, the new governor, **Sir Arthur Elibank Havelock**, relied heavily on him to frame its regulations and select its officials.

**SHEPSTONE'S NATIVE HORSE.** The three troops of **Sikali's Horse** that had failed to reassemble in February 1879 after their losses at **Isandlwana** during the **Anglo-Zulu War** re-formed in April under the command of Captain Theophilus Shepstone Jr., formerly the commander of the **Natal Carbineers**. The Ngwane people made up the bulk of the unit, but they were joined by new recruits from the Christian Edendale community and by a further contingent from the Christian community at Driefontein near **Ladysmith** who had been unhappy serving with **Carbutt's Border Rangers**. In May, about 120 Shepstone's Horse joined the 2nd Division, **South African Field Force**, and took part in the patrolling and raiding ahead of the advance in the 2nd Invasion of the Anglo-Zulu War. They participated in the skirmish at **Zungeni**, and a detachment helped garrison the **laager** on the **Mthonjaneni** Heights while the rest fought at **Ulundi**. After the breakup of the 2nd Division in late July, they served with **Baker Russell's Column** and disbanded in September.

**SHEZI PEOPLE.** *See* eNHLWENI *umuZI*.

**SHIELD, ZULU.** Zulu men used a small shield (*uMgabelomunye*) for dancing, a slightly larger one (*iGqoka*) for courting, and a sturdier one (*iHawu*) for everyday protection. The war shield (*isiHlangu*) belonged to the king and was a valuable item, since only two could be cut from the hide of a single cow. They were stored in an *iKhanda* and issued to the *amaButho* when they served the king. In King **Shaka kaSenzangakhona**'s time, the shield reached from foot to chin, but a wieldier version measuring some 40 by 20 inches, the *uMbumbuluzo*, came increasingly into use after the 1850s and continued to be carried during the wars of the 1880s. During the **Anglo-Zulu War**, full-sized shields were carried by *amaKhosi* as a sign of distinction, and by some veteran *amaButho*. The shields carried by members of an *iButho* were originally of identical color and patterning to distinguish one *iButho* from another. By the 1870s, the Zulu kingdom no longer had the **cattle** resources to maintain this practice fully, though the convention was generally maintained of white shields for married *amaButho* and black or red ones for unmarried *amaButho*. The shield was effective against bladed weapons but offered little protection against **firearms**.

**SHINGANA kaMPANDE (c. 1838–1909).** Enrolled in the **uDloko** *iButho*, *umNtwana* Shingana was King **Cetshwayo kaMpande**'s half-brother and supported him in the 2nd **Zulu Civil War**. After the 1st Partition of **Zululand**, Shingana was prominent among the **uSuthu** in petitioning for Cetshwayo's restoration. In the 3rd Zulu Civil War, he was a commander at both **Msebe** and **oNdini**. After Cetshwayo fled to the **Nkandla Forest**, Shingana kept up uSuthu resistance from central Zululand. During the **uSuthu Rebellion**, he defied the British from **Hlophekhulu Mountain**, from which they drove him in July 1888. He surrendered on 6 November, and the **Special Court of Commission for Zululand** sentenced him to 12 years' imprisonment on St. Helena. He was allowed to return to Zululand in December 1897.

*imiSHOKOBEZI*. These white cow-tail decorations that Zulu *amaButho* tied below the knee or above the elbow came in the 1880s to symbolize the conditions of civil strife that prevailed. *Shokobeza* meant to rebel and referred originally to those **uSuthu** who after the 2nd Partition of **Zululand** crossed out of the **Reserve Territory** and white man's rule in 1883 to serve King **Cetshwayo kaMpande** in his restored territory. The *imiShokobezi* became the emblem of the uSuthu in the 3rd **Zulu Civil War** and the **uSuthu Rebellion** and was worn in battle to distinguish them from other factions whose dress was otherwise very similar.

**ekuSHUMAYELENI** *umuZI*. This was **Mnyamana Ngqengelele**'s principal *umuZi*, located on the Sikhwebezi River in north-central **Zululand**. At the end of the **Anglo-Zulu War**, King **Cetshwayo kaMpande** took shelter there for a month in July 1879 while he tried fruitlessly to **negotiate** with the British. Throughout the 3rd **Zulu Civil War**, it was the chief rallying point of Mnyamana's **Buthelezi** people, who supported the **uSuthu**. In March 1883, the uSuthu army mustered there before the disastrous **Msebe** campaign, and again in December for an abortive offensive against *inKosi* **Zibhebhu kaMaphitha**, which he forestalled with a preemptive strike. In June 1884, the uSuthu army gathered there for the campaign in conjunction with the Boers that culminated in the victory at **Tshaneni**. On 25 August, the Boers joined the uSuthu at ekuShumayeleni for a renewed offensive against Zibhebhu, but he and his people took refuge in the **Reserve Territory**. During the **uSuthu Rebellion**, Mnyamana remained loyal to the British administration. In late May 1888, the uSuthu on **Ceza** raided his *imiZi* along the Sikhwebezi River, including ekuShumayeleni. The Buthelezi abandoned their *imiZi* and took refuge with the British at **Nkonjeni** until they regained control of the area in August.

**SIHAYO kaXONGO (c. 1824–1883).** Sihayo was *inKosi* of the **Qungebe** people and an *inDuna* of the **iNdabakawombe** *iButho*. He was a special favorite of King **Cetshwayo kaMpande** and a member of his *iBandla* (council). But when several of **Sihayo's sons** crossed the border into **Natal** in one of the incidents leading up to the **Anglo-Zulu War**, the other *iBandla* members excoriated him. The British No. 3 **Column** destroyed his **kwaSogekle** *umuZi* in the first action of the Anglo-Zulu War. In August 1879, *inKosi* **Mnyamana kaNgqengelele**, who blamed Sihayo's family for provoking the war, confiscated all his **cattle** and impoverished him. Sihayo was evicted from his chiefdom in the 1st Partition of **Zululand** and placed under **Hlubi kaMota Molife**. He supported **uSuthu** appeals for Cetshwayo's restoration. As a result of the 2nd Partition of Zululand, he came under colonial rule in the **Reserve Territory**, and the Qungebe came into conflict with Hlubi's Tlokwa people during the 3rd **Zulu Civil War**. Sihayo joined Cetshwayo in his territory and was killed in the rout at the battle of **oNdini**.

**SIHAYO'S SONS' BORDER INCIDENT.** In July 1878, at a crucial moment when **Bartle Frere** was pondering how best to deal with what he conceived of as the Zulu threat to his planned **confederation** of South Africa, an incident on the border between **Natal** and **Zululand** gave him the leverage he needed to put pressure on King **Cetshwayo kaMpande** and justify punitive action. Two adulterous wives of *inKosi* **Sihayo kaXongo** of the **Qungebe** fled over the Mzinyathi River near **Rorke's Drift** into Natal. When **Mehlokazulu kaSihayo**, his senior son, learned they were living close to the border, he crossed over twice on 28 July 1878 with two of his brothers and an armed party, abducted the wives, and shot them dead. Natal settler opinion was outraged, and the Natal government demanded that the ringleaders be surrendered for trial in Natal. Sihayo was one of Cetshwayo's favorites, and he was very loath to comply. By November, as war increasingly threatened, the Zulu leadership came erroneously to believe that the issue of the surrender of Sihayo's sons was at the root of their deteriorating relations with the British. Leading members of Cetshwayo's *iBandla* (council) consequently urged him to give up Sihayo's sons, but Cetshwayo would not, fearing that to do so would be to forfeit his authority to his great *amaKhosi*. Instead, he encouraged Mehlokazulu and his brothers to flee to **Mbilini waMswati** in the **Disputed Territory** for sanctuary. After the delivery of the British **ultimatum** on 11 December 1878, Cetshwayo's *iBandla* continued to believe that if Sihayo's sons were surrendered, as the ultimatum required, the British would drop their other demands. In the end, the *iBandla* did not take action to hand them over because of the strong feeling in Zululand, especially among the younger *amaButho*, that Cetshwayo should not appease the British in any way. *See also* DEIGHTON AND SMITH, BORDER INCIDENT.

**SIKALI'S (ZIKHALI'S) HORSE.** The Ngwane people in the foothills of the **Drakensberg** had suffered defeat and expulsion by the Zulu kings and so in December 1878 enthusiastically raised three troops of **irregular** horse for the **Natal Native Mounted Contingent** in the coming **Anglo-Zulu War**. They formed part of No. 2 **Column** and fought at **Isandlwana**, dispersing after the battle. They failed to reassemble in February when the Mounted Contingent was being reorganized because they believed the government had not recompensed them adequately for their losses, and because they insisted on being led by a white officer they trusted. The government met their concerns and they were re-formed as **Shepstone's Native Horse** for the 2nd Invasion of the Anglo-Zulu War.

**eSIQWAKENI *iKHANDA*.** *UmNtwana* **Dabulamanzi kaMpande**, who was directing the blockade of **Fort Eshowe** during the **Anglo-Zulu War**, was also the *inDuna* (commander) of the eSiqwakeni *iKhanda* near eNtumeni Hill to the west of the British fort. It consisted of 50 huts and provided the base for the Zulu raiding the British garrison's **cattle**. On 1 March 1879, Colonel **Charles Knight Pearson** decided to attack it with 450 men. As the British approached, the Zulu abandoned the *iKhanda*. The British burned it but were expertly harassed by 500 Zulu under Dabulamanzi when they withdrew to their fort.

**kwaSISHWILI CAMP.** On 10 August 1879, General **Sir Garnet Joseph Wolseley** formed camp at kwaSishwili, close to **oNdini**, which the British had burned after the battle of **Ulundi** at the climax of the **Anglo-Zulu War**. His purpose was to obtain the **submission** of the great *amaKhosi* (chiefs) of **Zululand**, organize the capture of the fugitive King **Cetshwayo kaMpande**, and impose a final peace settlement. Between 14 and 26 August, most of the *amaKhosi* of central and northern Zululand who had not already submitted came into camp to do so. The captive Cetshwayo passed through the camp on 31 August on his way to exile. On 1 September, the Zulu *amaKhosi* accepted Wolseley's term for the 1st Partition of Zululand in a ceremony there, and on 4 September 1879 Wolseley and his staff left for **Utrecht**.

**SITHOLE PEOPLE.** *See* MATSHANA kaMONDISA.

**SMALL WARS.** As early as the North American campaigns of the 18th century, the British had learned that in fighting highly mobile enemies over broken terrain, they could no longer rely on their dense columns and line formations but had to be prepared to deploy into skirmishing order. This lesson tended to be forgotten in subsequent years and had to be relearned in the colonial campaigns conducted in the late Victorian period. The requirements of these "small wars" waged by professional soldiers against "savage" **irregulars** were certainly very different from those demanded in contemporary, full-scale operations such as the Franco-Prussian War (1870–1871).

Initiative, improvisation, and flair were required in the small wars waged in inhospitable terrain against diverse kinds of enemy with differing levels of military expertise and employing a wide variety of **tactics**. Experience in these small wars served to confirm the general shift in the British army away from the dense formations employed as late as the Crimean War (1854–1856) toward a greater emphasis on open-order tactics and flexibility necessary for patrols, ambushes, and skirmishes. What made this possible was the extensive rearmament of the British army during the last three decades of the 19th century. The introduction of breech-loading **rifles** increased the rate of fire and allowed soldiers to fire from a kneeling or prone position, so they could make the most of the terrain and natural cover. Early forms of machine guns and improved **ordnance** significantly enhanced the weight of firepower available. And regular colonial campaigns provided the opportunity for testing and improving this weaponry.

Success in operations depended on maintaining the initiative by adopting a vigorous offensive **strategy** that sought out the enemy and brought him to battle. Carefully planned **logistics** and good intelligence were essential (though in operations in **Zululand** the reality fell far short of the ideal). The objective was to deliver a decisive blow to the enemy and to prevent the campaign degenerating into debilitating guerrilla operations. Unfortunately for **civilians**, it was also standard practice in small wars of conquest to destroy crops and dwellings and to run off livestock in order to induce **submissions** and to deny supplies to the enemy forces.

**SMITH'S CAMP.** On 4 May 1842, Captain Thomas Smith, in command of 263 British troops from the **Cape**, encamped in Port Natal (**Durban**) on the flat land between the Eastern Vlei and the Berea Ridge and immediately began constructing a roughly triangular entrenched wagon **laager**, called Smith's Camp. Smith's mission was to occupy **Natal**, currently held by the Boers as the Republic of **Natalia**. Once the Boers repulsed his advance at **Congella** on 23 May, Smith fell back and further improved the defenses of Smith's Camp with two batteries at opposite angles. The tents were inside the laager and the livestock in a kraal outside. The men took shelter in a trench inside the camp behind the wagons. The Boers laid siege to the camp from 31 May until its relief on 25 June 1842. Four Boers were killed in the siege and 31 British died, mainly of disease. Today Smith's Camp is often confused with the subsequent **Durban Redoubt** built on the site.

**SMOUSE.** Most Boers who trekked into the interior of southern Africa in the 1830s and 1840s had the skills necessary to maintain their wagons and **firearms**, but they depended on *smouse*, traveling traders, to supply commodities they could not produce themselves, such as gunpowder, **percussion caps**, clothing materials, tea, coffee, and sugar.

**SMYTH, HENRY AUGUSTUS (1825–1906).** Commissioned in the **Royal Artillery** in 1843, Smyth saw service in the Crimean War (1855–1856). He served in Bermuda, Nova Scotia, Corfu, India, and Britain, where he commanded the Woolwich Garrison and Military District from 1882 to 1886. He was promoted to lieutenant-general in 1886. On 23 January 1888, he was appointed the general officer commanding in South Africa, and on 28 June he took personal command of the British forces operating in **Zululand** during the **uSuthu Rebellion**. He regained control of central Zululand with the capture of **Hlophekhulu**, and of the southern coastal area by sending in the **Eshowe Column** to relieve **Fort Andries**. He next moved forward from **Nkonjeni** into northwestern Zululand, compelling the **uSuthu** to abandon **Ceza**, while the **Coastal Column** advanced to **Ivuna**. Smyth accompanied **Martin's Flying Column** in its joint march back to **Eshowe** with the Coastal Column. Satisfied that the rebellion was suppressed, on 7 September Smyth and his staff sailed for **Cape Town**. During the course of the campaign, he came into conflict with the governor of Zululand, **Arthur Elibank Havelock**, over the parameters of civil and military authority. He later acted as governor of the **Cape** (1888–1889) and was appointed governor of Malta (1890–1893). He was knighted in 1890 and promoted to general in 1891. *See also* CIVIL–MILITARY RELATIONS.

**kwaSOGEKLE *umuZI*.** This was *inKosi* **Sihayo kaXongo**'s principal *umuZi*, nestled under cliffs on the eastern side of the Batshe River valley. British detachments of No. 3 **Column** burned it on 12 January 1879 during the **Anglo-Zulu War** after worsting the **Qungebe** in a sharp skirmish.

**SOMHLOLO kaMKHOSANA.** *See* BIYELA PEOPLE.

**SOMKHELE kaMALANDA (c. 1840–?).** Somkhele was *inKosi* of the **Mphukunyoni** people and a first cousin of King **Cetshwayo kaMpande**. He dominated the Zulu north coast and lived in semi-royal style in his own huge *umuZi*. He was also an *isiKhulu* (hereditary chief) and an *inDuna* (officer) of the **uThulwana *iButho***. Somkhele was averse to fighting the **Anglo-Zulu War** and was among the coastal leaders who surrendered on 4 July 1879 to the 1st

Division, **South African Field Force**. In the 1st Partition of **Zulu-land**, he was appointed one of the 13 chiefs, but in the 2nd Partition his chiefdom fell into Cetshwayo's restored territory. In the 3rd **Zulu Civil War**, he rallied firmly to the **uSuthu** cause. Suffering reverses, he took refuge in his stronghold in the **Dukuduku** Forest. During the **uSuthu Rebellion**, his followers attacked **Fort Andries** in June 1888 in the battle of **Ntondotha**, but in July he swiftly surrendered to the **Eshowe Column** and was fined 1,800 **cattle**. In 1889, the **Special Court of Commission for Zululand** sentenced him to five years' imprisonment. He was released in 1890 and his cattle fine reduced by 799 head.

**SOMOPHO kaZIKHALA.** A Mthembu *inKosi* (hereditary chief) and senior *inDuna* (headman) of the **emaNgweni** people, Somopho was personally close to King **Cetshwayo kaMpande** and his was head gunpowder manufacturer and chief armorer. During the **Anglo-Zulu War**, Somopho was one of the Zulu commanders blockading the British in **Fort Eshowe**, and he was the senior commander at **Gingindlovu**. He surrendered to the 1st Division, **South African Field Force**, on 4 July 1879. In the 1st Partition of **Zululand**, he was placed reluctantly under *inKosi* Mlandlela kaMbiya of the **Mthethwa** people, but after the 2nd Partition of Zululand he found himself in the restored Cetshwayo's territory and joined the **uSuthu** cause in the 3rd **Zulu Civil War**, operating especially against the Mthethwa. During the **uSuthu Rebellion**, he joined with **Bhejana kaNomageje**, another *inDuna* of the emaNgweni, in operating against Andries Pretorius, the resident magistrate of the Lower Umfolosi District, and attacked **Fort Andries**. The **Eshowe Column** ravaged his territory in July 1888, and Somopho took refuge in the Nhlati Hills in the northern coastal district, where he was attacked in late August by **Martin's Flying Column** and fled to the **Dukuduku** fastness. He did not surrender until 1890, when the High Court of Zululand sentenced him to two years' imprisonment.

**SOOILAER.** *See* MARITZ, GERRIT.

**SOTHO BORDER WITH NATAL IN 1879.** In late 1878, there were concerns that the Sotho chiefdoms in **Basutoland** abutting **Colonial**

**Defensive District** No. II might take advantage of the coming **Anglo-Zulu War** to raid **Natal** in conjunction with the Zulu. In October 1878, messengers from King **Cetshwayo kaMpande** to the Sotho chiefs Letsie, Masopha, and Molapo were detained in Natal, and in December Cetshwayo sent mounted messengers to Molapo. In late January 1879, after the war had broken out, rumors were rife in Natal that Zulu messengers were making their way along the **Drakensberg** to the Sotho chiefs as well as to Mpondo chiefs south of Natal. From March 1879, the district authorities ran regular patrols along the foot of the Drakensberg. There was some alarm in late March that some of the Phuti people of Moorosi, who were in rebellion against the **Cape**'s administration in Basutoland (imposed in 1871), might come over the passes into Natal, but the threat did not materialize. *See also* GRIQUA AND MPONDO BORDERS WITH NATAL IN 1879.

**SOTHONDOSE'S DRIFT.** This drift across the Mzinyathi River was where the British survivors of the battle of **Isandlwana** in the **Anglo-Zulu War** tried to cross the swollen river on the afternoon of 22 January 1879, and it has been known to the British ever afterward as Fugitives' Drift. The Zulu named it after Sothondose kaMalusi, the Nxumalo *inKosi*, who in June 1843 crossed the Mzinyathi there to find refuge in **Natal** with many other Zulu notables and up to 3,000 adherents. They were all malcontents who had fallen out with King **Mpande kaSenzangakhona** and had thrown their support behind his ambitious and last surviving half-brother *umNtwana* Gqugqu kaSenzangakhona. Gqugqu's execution on Mpande's orders was the signal for their flight, which is commonly known as the "Crossing of Mawa" after Mpande's influential aunt Mawa, who joined the fugitives.

**SOUTH AFRICA MEDAL.** *See* AWARDS.

**SOUTH AFRICAN FIELD FORCE, 1ST DIVISION.** On 13 April 1879 during the 2nd Invasion of the **Anglo-Zulu War**, the No. 1 **Column** at **Fort Pearson** and the **Eshowe Relief Column** at the **Gingindlovu** Camp were restyled the 1st and 2nd Brigades respectively of the 1st Division, South African Field Force of 7,500 men under Major-General **Henry Hope Crealock**. April was spent methodically bringing up supplies, bridging the lower Thukela River, strengthening Fort Pearson and **Fort Tenedos**, building **Fort Crealock** and **Fort Chelmsford** as advanced posts, and identifying **Port Durnford** as a landing place for supplies. By 20 June, the 1st Division was concentrated at Fort Chelmsford and advanced across the Mlalazi River, where it started **Fort Napoleon** on 25 June. By 1 July, it was encamped at Port Durnford and was sending out patrols to raid the countryside and induce Zulu **submissions**. Its slow progress allowed the Zulu to ignore its presence and concentrate on facing Lieutenant-General Lord **Chelmsford**'s advance from the northwest with the 2nd Division, South African Field Force. On 4 July, a patrol burned the **emaNgweni** *iKhanda* across the Mhlathuze River, and another destroyed the old **oNdini** *iKhanda* on 6 July. On 5 June, most of the local *amaKhosi* submitted to Crealock at his camp at the lower drift of the Mhlathuze. On 19 July, General **Sir Garnet Joseph Wolseley** received the formal surrender of the coastal *amaKhosi* near emaNgweni. Wolseley broke up the 1st Division on 23 July and formed **Clarke's Column** out of those units he did not send back to **Natal**.

**SOUTH AFRICAN FIELD FORCE, 2ND DIVISION.** On 13 April 1879 during the 2nd Invasion of the **Anglo-Zulu War**, the command of the 2nd Division (to which the **Cavalry Brigade** was attached on 8 April) was given to Major-General **Edward Newdigate**. The 2nd Division of 5,000 men was made up of the troops already stationed in the **Utrecht District** of the Transvaal Territory and of the reinforcements recently landed in **Durban**. It concentrated at **Dundee**, which Lieutenant-General Lord **Chelmsford** selected over **Helpmekaar** as its main depot because it offered better access to supplies and superior communications, and because it avoided the road by way of **Isandlwana** and the still unburied dead. On 2 May, the 2nd Division moved forward to **Landman's Drift** accompanied by Chelmsford and his staff. Between 13 and 21 May, it sent forward many patrols to reconnoiter a suitable route to the **oNdini** *iKhanda* and mounted extensive raids to clear the countryside of Zulu before it resumed the advance. A reconnaissance in force to Isandlwana on 21 May in cooperation with the **Rorke's Drift** garrison began the burial of the dead. On 31 May, the 2nd Division advanced to **Koppie Alleen** and built **Fort Whitehead** as its forward base. The following day, while on patrol, **Prince Louis Napoleon Bonaparte** of France was killed in a skirmish at the **Tshotshosi River**.

The 2nd Division resumed its advance on 3 June and effected its junction with **Wood's Flying Column** advancing from **Khambula**. The mounted men from the joint column had an unsuccessful encounter with Zulu irregulars on 5 June at **Zungeni Mountain**. The joint column continued the advance up the Ntinini valley before halting from 7 to 17 June to escort convoys of supplies and to raid the countryside to clear it of Zulu. The joint column resumed its advance on 18 June. It moved slowly and methodically, reconnoitering ahead, **laagering** every night, and building fortified depots (**Fort Newdigate**, **Fort Marshall**, and **Fort Evelyn**). On 27 June, the joint column reached the **Mthonjaneni** Heights, where it laagered on 29 June. The following day, it marched down toward the **Mahlabathini Plain** and on 2 July constructed a fortified camp on the banks of the White Mfolozi. **White Mfolozi Reconnaissance in Force** on 3 July barely escaped a Zulu ambush. On 4 July, the joint column fought as an infantry **square** at **Ulundi** and routed the Zulu.

Short of supplies and confident that Zulu resistance was over, Chelmsford decided to withdraw rather than advance to consolidate his victory. On 5 July, the 2nd Division returned to Mthonjaneni, followed by Wood's Flying Column the next day. Rain between 6 and 8 July prevented further movement until 9 July, when Wood's Flying Column withdrew toward **St. Paul's**. On 10 July, the 2nd Division began its march back to **Natal** by the way it had come and was formally broken up on 26 July near **Fort Marshall**. Some units remained in garrison at various posts in **Zululand** until convoys could bring out all unconsumed supplies, and the rest returned to **Durban** for embarkation.

**SOUTH AFRICAN REPUBLIC.** On 17 January 1852, by the Sand River Convention, the British recognized the independence of the 15,000 Voortrekkers who had settled north of the Vaal River, and who in September 1853 adopted the title of the South African Republic, or Zuid-Afrikaansche Republiek (SAR) for their new state with its capital at **Pretoria**. The British hoped thereby to reduce their strained financial and military commitments in southern Africa while setting up a buffer state to cushion their coastal colonies against the unrest in the interior. For its part, the SAR set about parceling out the land into large farms, building up Afrikaner identity, and creating a society based on white racial supremacy in which Africans were reduced to labor tenants and servants. The fledgling republic continued to be troubled by internal divisions and to be involved in a constant struggle for survival against hostile African neighbors. Cut off from direct access to the sea by British **Natal** and the Portuguese at **Delagoa Bay**, the SAR also failed to push through the **Disputed Territory** to a potential port on the **Zululand** coast. The SAR's undiversified economy remained based primarily on stock farming and it stagnated, while the Boers' isolation led to cultural and intellectual impoverishment.

In the late 1870s, British policy toward southern Africa changed, and a drive began to force the **confederation** of the region's white-ruled states. On 12 April 1877, Britain annexed the bankrupt SAR as the British Transvaal Territory, but in December 1880, the Boers rose in rebellion. In the 1st **Boer War**, the British failed to defeat the Boers. By the Pretoria Convention of 3 August 1881, the Transvaal gained independence under nebulous British "suzerainty." After defeat in the **Anglo-Boer (South African) War**, the SAR again lost its independence. In 1910, it was incorporated into the Union of South Africa as the Transvaal Province.

**SPEAR, ZULU.** The principal Zulu weapon was the spear or *umKhonto* (still popularly called the "assegai" after the Arab term for the weapon), of which there were some 10 varieties. The deadliest was the short-handled, long-bladed stabbing spear, the *iKlwa*, introduced by King **Shaka kaSenzangakhona**, probably a refinement on a weapon already familiar in the region. It was wielded at close quarters, and an underarm stab aimed at the abdomen was followed by ripped withdrawal. This operation required considerable skill and practice. In addition to the *iKlwa*, an *iButho* usually carried two or three throwing spears with long shafts (*iziJula*). These were also used for hunting and could find their target at up to 30 yards. The making of spears was a specialized task that was concentrated among blacksmiths in the regions of the **Nkandla Forest** and Black Mfolozi River. The spears, as a national asset, belonged to the king, who distributed them to his *amaButho*.

**SPECIAL ARTISTS.** With photography in its infancy, "special artists" (a term first used of artists commissioned by the *Illustrated London News* to cover the Crimean War) were required by the British illustrated papers to supply pictures of wars to boost their circulation. Experienced artists could capture action and movement that the camera could not, and in order to scoop their rivals in the field, the special artists vied with each other to send their sketches back as quickly as possible for completion by staff artists in Great Britain. In the process, the original sketch was often transformed to conform to the conventions of contemporary war illustrations, and images might be subtly distorted by staff artists unfamiliar with the foreign places and people depicted. The illustration was then traced in reverse onto a wood block, engraved, and a facsimile in copper made for printing, a process that might further alter the work of the artist in the field. In the **Anglo-Zulu War**, 3rd **Zulu Civil War**, and **uSuthu Rebellion**, newspapers often made use of skilled soldiers or colonists to supplement the drawings of the professional journalists. *See also* SPECIAL CORRESPONDENTS.

**SPECIAL BORDER POLICE, NATAL.** In November 1878, the **Natal** government raised a small force of about 100 Special Border Police consisting of local Africans under appointed white border agents and positioned them along the Thukela and Mzinyathi rivers in **Colonial Defensive Districts** I, VI, and VII. Their function during the **Anglo-Zulu War** was to gather intelligence and monitor the movement of individuals to and from **Zululand**, rather than to deter a Zulu incursion into Natal. They were disbanded in October 1879.

**SPECIAL CORRESPONDENTS.** War correspondents, a self-consciously glamorous elite among journalists who sometimes became public celebrities, were known as "special correspondents" and were always in hectic competition to bring the news to their own newspapers ahead of their rivals. Only the national papers could afford the costs of supporting them and their expensive telegraphed reports, and provincial newspapers made do with reprinting their lengthy dispatches appearing in the major papers. Special correspondents identified with the British army and its ethos and enjoyed an ill-defined, quasi-officer status on campaign. They often took the stereotypical line about savage foes and the justice of the British cause, and although the free press in Britain and the colonies meant that their reports were uncensored, they exercised some self-censorship to preserve the army's honor and the public's faith in it. Relations between special correspondents and military commanders usually depended on the extent to which the journalists' reporting of the conduct of a campaign was favorable, and canny commanders cultivated them to ensure a positive press. Special correspondents could act as stringers for a number of newspapers, and newspapers looked beyond full-time correspondents to draw on reports from British officers, colonial officials, and ordinary settlers affected by the war. In 1879, after the battle of **Isandlwana** turned the **Anglo-Zulu War** into international news, the number of special correspondents increased. The **Natal** newspapers covered the 3rd **Zulu Civil War** and the **uSuthu Rebellion**, but these conflicts elicited little interest in the British press and no special correspondents were sent out to **Zululand**. *See also* FORBES, ARCHIBALD (1838–1900); SPECIAL ARTISTS.

**SPECIAL COURT OF COMMISSION FOR ZULULAND.** With the collapse of the **uSuthu Rebellion**, the British put the arrested rebels on trial. The Colonial Office and the **Natal** judiciary agreed that **Zululand** officials, who would normally have tried them, could not be regarded as impartial. Consequently, the trial that commenced in **Eshowe** on 15 November 1888 was convened as a Special Court of Commission for Zululand under the presidency of Walter Wragg, senior judge of the Supreme Court of Natal, and two other members. The trial of the ringleaders for high treason and public violence began on 13 February 1889 and ended on 27 April. **Dinuzulu kaCetshwayo**, **Ndabuko kaMpande**, and **Shingana kaMpande** were all found guilty. In the belief that it might prove inflammatory if they served their sentences (confirmed on 18 December) in British Zululand or Natal, they were held instead on the remote Atlantic island of St. Helena.

**SPIES.** *See* MILITARY INTELLIGENCE, BRITISH; MILITARY INTELLIGENCE, ZULU.

**SQUARE, INFANTRY.** By the late 19th century, the infantry square, which was originally developed as a means of all-round defense against cavalry, was obsolete on the battlefields of Europe and North America. However, it retained its value in **small wars** as a defensive formation against overwhelming numbers of enemy attempting to envelop the troops prior to engaging in hand-to-hand combat. Squares were difficult to maneuver on the march, especially when the ground was uneven, and were very vulnerable to enemy fire, although poor Zulu marksmanship made this a small risk in the **Anglo-Zulu War**. The corners of a square were vulnerable because of a loss of fire from the ranks of infantry forming the sides, and they were normally reinforced with **artillery**. If a square was penetrated by the enemy, it was liable to be thrown into complete confusion, so the objective was to hold the enemy at bay at some distance by laying down an impenetrable barrier of volley-fire. During the Anglo-Zulu War, the British successfully deployed an infantry square at **Ulundi**. *See also* TACTICS, BRITISH; TACTICS UP TO 1879, ZULU.

**ST. LUCIA BAY.** A large, shallow, enclosed bay on the north coast of **Zululand** into which the Mkhuze River drains, St. Lucia Bay provided a reasonable holding ground for anchoring, provided the wind was not blowing a gale from the south. On 27 October 1839, *umNtwana* **Mpande kaSenzangakhona** struck an alliance with the Boers for a combined attack on King **Dingane kaSenzangakhona**. In return for their making him king, Mpande undertook to cede them St. Lucia Bay and much **cattle**. This cession fell away when the British and Mpande agreed on the **Natal-Zululand** border on 5 October 1843. When Germany later showed an interest in the Zululand coast, the British feared they might attempt to link up with the landlocked **South African Republic** through the newly established **New Republic**. The British therefore asserted their claims to St. Lucia Bay on 21 December 1884. When the British annexed the Colony of Zululand in May 1887, St. Lucia Bay became part of the Lower Umfolosi District. *See also* LANDING PLACES, ZULULAND.

**ST. PAUL'S.** St. Paul's Anglican mission station, situated on the great Nkwenkwe spur overlooking the coastal plains to the south, was a strategic point on the winding track between **Eshowe** and the heart of

**Zululand**. During the **Anglo-Zulu War, Baker Russell's Column** began a small earthwork redoubt there on 28 July 1879 to guard its depot when it was drawing supplies from **Port Durnford**. It was garrisoned until the column reached the Transvaal in early September 1879. In October 1887, the post was again garrisoned by a detachment of the **Zululand garrison** of the Colony of Zululand to secure the main route from Eshowe to the Ndwandwe District. During the **uSuthu Rebellion**, it provided a camp for troops moving forward to central and northern Zululand. With the suppression of the uSuthu Rebellion, the small garrison was withdrawn in September 1888.

**STABB, HENRY SPARKE (1835–1888).** Stabb fought in the Indian Mutiny (1857), served as a major on special service in the **Anglo-Zulu War** with the 2nd Division, **South African Field Force**, and was present at **Ulundi**. He was subsequently president of a board for the investigation and settlement of claims made by colonists for losses suffered during the Anglo-Zulu War. In March 1880, he was in command of the party that, on Queen Victoria's wishes, erected a memorial cross at the site of the death of **Prince Louis Napoleon Bonaparte**. In September 1886, Stabb was appointed a colonel on the staff in **Natal**, and in May 1887 he commanded troops in Natal and **Zululand**. He was in command during the **uSuthu Rebellion** until Lieutenant-General **Henry August Smyth**, the general officer commanding in South Africa, took personal command of operations in June 1888. Under Smyth's orders, Stabb successfully stormed **Hlophekhulu** and regained control of central Zululand. Stabb died in **Pietermaritzburg** in October 1888 of a heart attack.

**STANGER LAAGER.** In mid-1878, the **Natal** government sanctioned the construction of a loopholed, stone-walled **laager** at the little village of Stanger (in what was later designated **Colonial Defensive District** No. VI) as a place of security for the local settler population. A small existing post begun in early 1878 was included in the enclosure as an armory. The laager was adjacent to the jail, which likely formed part of the perimeter. In December 1878, a detachment of No. 1 **Column** garrisoned the laager to secure its line of communication between the lower Thukela River and **Durban**. In the panic after **Isandlwana** during the **Anglo-Zulu War**, the settlers crowded into the laager, but confidence was soon restored and they returned home.

**STANGER MOUNTED RIFLES.** Formed in 1875, the Stanger Mounted Rifles was one of the 10 corps of **Natal Mounted Volunteers** who were called out in November 1878 for active service in the **Anglo-Zulu War**. It mobilized in December 1878 and joined No. 1 **Column** at **Fort Pearson**, leaving a few men behind at the **Stanger laager** for defense duties. It fought at **Nyezane** as part of the 1st Division. On 28 January, it returned from **Fort Eshowe** to **Natal** with the other mounted men of No. 1 Column. Until the corps of about 50 men was mustered out in July, it continued to serve by patrolling the border along the lines of communication between Fort Pearson, Stanger, and **Ntunjambili** (Kranskop) in **Colonial Defensive Districts** VI and VII. In March, nearly half its men volunteered for active service in the **Natal Volunteer Guides**. The uniform was of dark blue cloth with an edging of black braid and yellow piping. The helmet was white.

**STRATEGY, BOER.** By the 18th century, Boer **commandos** (militia) on the **Cape** frontier had institutionalized an effective strategy for attacking African foes. The Boers took this strategy with them on the **Great Trek** into the interior of South Africa in the 1830s and consistently applied it in **Zululand** from 1838 onward. The very first encounters in the **Voortrekker-Zulu War** confirmed for the Voortrekkers that if they drew together in their wagon **laagers** for protection, they could withstand even the heaviest Zulu assaults. Based on their experience in the **Cape Frontier Wars**, the strategy was then to send out a retaliatory mounted commando to engage the Zulu, destroy their property, and capture or recover livestock. The disaster that befell the *Vlugkommando* at **eThaleni** demonstrated that it was too dangerous to seek out the Zulu on their own ground with only a mounted commando, and that a commando should advance with supply wagons that could be drawn up to form a defensive laager. The laager would also form a secure base deep in enemy territory for punitive raiding expeditions.

In late 1838, this strategy allowed the *Wenkommando* to defeat the Zulu army, destroy their principal *amaKhanda*, drive King

**Dingane kaSenzangakhona** away to the north of his kingdom, and capture huge numbers of **cattle**. This punitive strategy was limited, for it stopped short of conquest and was content with forcing the Zulu king to permit the Voortrekkers to settle in part of his kingdom. In the 1st **Zulu Civil War**, the *Beeskommando* that advanced in support of *umNtwana* **Mpande kaSenzangakhona** applied the same methods to secure a political outcome. In promoting their claims to the **Disputed Territory** in 1861, the Boers set up their laagers and threatened to send out commando raids. In the 3rd Zulu Civil War, the Boers who supported the **uSuthu** in their Zululand campaign of 1884 once again operated as commandos from laagers in Zulu territory, and they bartered their military aid for captured livestock and the territory that formed the **New Republic**.

**STRATEGY, BRITISH.** During the **Anglo-Zulu War**, the British essentially followed the principles behind the conduct of **small wars**. Lieutenant-General Lord **Chelmsford** wished at all costs to avoid debilitating guerrilla operations and hoped to end the campaign swiftly with a series of pitched battles. In dividing his invading army into several columns converging on the **oNdini** *iKhanda*, he correctly calculated that the Zulu would be enticed into confronting them in the open field, where British tactical superiority would prove overwhelming. His related strategy was to induce the Zulu people to **submit** through the systematic destruction of their means of subsistence, coupled with reasonable terms if they abandoned resistance. While the main British striking force was engaged in **Zululand**, the **Natal** border region was left vulnerable to Zulu counterattack, but Chelmsford calculated that it could be defended sufficiently while the war was won in Zululand itself. The British debacle at **Isandlwana** only temporarily unhinged this strategy, and it was resumed once the British were sufficiently reinforced for the 2nd Invasion of the Anglo-Zulu War.

During the 3rd **Zulu Civil War** and the **uSuthu Rebellion**, the prime objective of British forces in Zululand was to establish fortified bases that could be held against any attack and from which offensives could be mounted. It was equally important to secure the vulnerable lines of communication over the large territory with its broken terrain. The soundness of this limited strategy was underscored during the uSuthu Rebellion when, despite some initial local setbacks, the British remained in a strong position to counterattack effectively from their bases. As in the later stages of the Anglo-Zulu War, flying columns were efficacious in inducing submissions through punitive measures against **civilians** combined with **negotiations**, and they were also used to break up lingering concentrations of resistance. *See also* FORTIFICATIONS IN NATAL AND ZULULAND; TACTICS, BRITISH INFANTRY; TACTICS, BRITISH MOUNTED TROOPS.

**STRATEGY, ZULU.** Zulu strategy from the time of King **Shaka kaSenzangakhona** was to concentrate the *amaButho* at a major *iKhanda* and then to march into the enemy's territory, living off the countryside as they advanced. The primary objectives were to capture the enemy's **cattle** and drive the enemy from the territory he occupied. The preferred way of doing so was to crush enemy forces in battle. If the enemy would not be drawn into battle, the Zulu would compel him to evacuate his lands by destroying his means of survival. The Zulu would burn his *imiZi* and fields, plunder his grain stores, and drive off his livestock. If, like the **Swazi**, the enemy avoided battle and took refuge with families and livestock in impregnable strongholds, then the invaders might have to be content with plunder before withdrawing. Although considerable hardship attended those sheltering in a stronghold, it was even more difficult for an army to maintain itself in a countryside it had ravaged. Stalemate was the consequence of this sort of campaign, and minor skirmishing between full-scale operations also fell short of the primary objective of driving the enemy out. Only a pitched battle could deliver conclusive results.

In the **Voortrekker-Zulu War** and in the 1st and 2nd **Zulu Civil Wars**, Zulu armies sought the decisive encounter of pitched battle. What made these campaigns different from earlier ones was that they were conducted on Zulu soil instead of in the territory of the enemy. In all three cases, the issue was decided in battle. The situation was somewhat different for the Zulu in the **Anglo-Zulu War**, for the kingdom was invaded by a number of **columns** simultaneously deploying unprecedented armed might. While Zulu **irregulars** in northwestern **Zululand** resorted to their strongholds and conducted a war or raid and counterraid, the *amaButho* pursued the conventional strategy of seeking out the enemy and forcing a pitched battle. It seems

King **Cetshwayo kaMpande**'s plan was to win enough victories to stall the British invasion and force a **negotiated** peace. However, the British were not to be budged from their objective of dismantling the kingdom. The Zulu, who found it difficult for **logistical** and **ritual** reasons to sustain a campaign over many months, played into British hands by insisting on conventional set-piece battles. A more effective defense would have been to use guerrilla **tactics** on a wider scale than merely in the northwest. But this was not the way the *amaButho* were honor-bound to fight, and they sought conclusions on the open battlefield.

The 3rd **Zulu Civil War**, fought between Zulu forces aided by white **mercenaries** or Boer allies, saw much raiding, ravaging, and taking refuge in strongholds. Nevertheless, in traditional fashion, pitched battles ultimately decided the issue, causing the collapse of the enemy's forces. The leaders then took flight, and great tracts of territory were abandoned to the victors.

While a traditional strategy proved effective against other Zulu in the 3rd Civil War, the **uSuthu** lacked coherent or viable strategic objectives in the **uSuthu Rebellion**. The Anglo-Zulu War had taught them the futility of taking on the British in the open field or of attacking prepared defenses. In 1888, they might raid British collaborators and the British lines of communication from the strongholds where they had concentrated, but the British soon isolated them there and then evicted them. Any guerrilla resistance was scotched by the rapid movement of British flying columns. The uSuthu fighters were able to operate out of neighboring Boer territory because the **South African Republic** turned a blind eye on their activities, but since no concrete aid was forthcoming, this was of limited benefit. The uSuthu uprising was too limited in scale and scattered in action to ever cohere sufficiently for a viable strategy to evolve.

**STRYDPOORT LAAGER.** This square, stone-walled **laager** with opposing bastions was built in 1878 in **Colonial Defensive District No. II** by local farmers. It served throughout the **Anglo-Zulu War** as the base for the **Upper Tugela Defense Corps** and was where they stored their arms and ammunition.

**SUBMISSIONS, ZULU.** During the **Anglo-Zulu War**, several *amaKhosi* who were not in favor of fighting entered into negotiation with the British to submit, but their intentions were thwarted by the intervention of King **Cetshwayo kaMpande** or local loyalists. In the west and southeast of **Zululand**, where the British military presence was most heavily felt on **civilians** in accordance with the ruthless practices of **small wars**, negotiation and submission followed an accelerating pattern during the course of the war. The far northwest maintained a die-hard resistance until **Baker Russell's Column** enforced surrender. The southern border region, which the fighting had largely bypassed, submitted with the passage of **Clarke's Column**. Great districts of east, central, and northern Zululand, although never entered by the British, submitted soon after the battle of **Ulundi,** when the war was clearly lost. This variegated pattern of submission can be explained by the pragmatic efforts of the *amaKhosi* to salvage what they could of their local power from national defeat. Indeed, some saw opportunities for personal aggrandizement in the collapse of centralized royal authority. Since it was British **strategy** to detach them from the king's cause, they offered the *amaKhosi* indulgent peace terms that left their local prerogatives intact and exploited their ambitions to impose the 1st Partition of Zululand.

During the period of the 3rd **Zulu Civil War**, military defeat and deteriorating conditions for civilians in the endemic conflict induced the warring parties to submit to Boer rule in the **New Republic**, or to British rule in the **Reserve Territory** and subsequently the British Colony of Zululand. With the outbreak of the **uSuthu Rebellion,** most *amaKhosi* stayed loyal to the British because continued submission meant security. In contrast to the easy terms that accompanied submission in the Anglo-Zulu War, those who rebelled were subjected to severe penalties once they surrendered. This time the British were not looking for collaborators in a political solution, but for obedient subjects in their new colony.

**SURRENDER, ZULU.** *See* SUBMISSIONS, ZULU.

**uSUTHU.** Originally, uSuthu was the war cry and collective name for *umNtwana* **Cetshwayo kaMpande**'s followers in the 2nd **Zulu Civil War**. The name was derived from the large Sotho-type **cattle** his supporters in the Zulu army had captured from the **Pedi** in the campaign of 1851. It became the national cry when he became king in 1872, and it was uttered by the *amaButho* at the great festivals and in battle. After Cetshwayo's defeat in the **Anglo-Zulu War** and his subsequent exile, the term came to denote all those who still adhered to the royalist cause. In the 3rd Zulu Civil War, his faction in the relentless struggle against the **Mandlakazi** was called the uSuthu, as were those who joined King **Dinuzulu kaCetshwayo** in the **uSuthu Rebellion** against British rule.

**uSUTHU REBELLION (1888).** In 1887, King **Dinuzulu kaCetshwayo** and the **uSuthu** found it humiliating and irksome to cooperate with the colonial administration of freshly annexed British **Zululand**. To curb the uSuthu, in November 1887 the Zululand officials (in a disastrous policy decision) restored their remorseless enemy *inKosi* **Zibhebhu kaMaphitha** and his **Mandlakazi** adherents to his former chiefdom in the Ndwandwe District, from which he had fled at the end of the 3rd **Zulu Civil War**. The size of his territory was increased so that it encompassed many uSuthu *imiZi*, and this inevitably sparked unrest. By April 1888, the uSuthu were in open rebellion, defying the paramilitary **Zululand Police**, the regular troops of the **Zululand garrison**, their Mandlakazi allies, and other African auxiliaries. The scale of operations was small, with the uSuthu never raising an army of more than 4,000 and the Mandlakazi no more than 800. British troops in Zululand finally numbered just under 1,000, with about 2,000 African auxiliaries.

On 2 June, the uSuthu repulsed a British force at **Ceza Mountain**. On 23 June, they routed the Mandlakazi at **Ivuna**. The British withdrew south of the Black Mfolozi River to regroup under Lieutenant-General **Henry Augustus Smyth**. They also lost control of the coastal region, where on 30 June the coastal uSuthu attacked **Fort Andries** in the battle of **Ntondotha** and then blockaded it.

Rapidly reinforced, the British went on the offensive. On 2 July, a force under Colonel **Henry Sparke Stabb** drove the uSuthu under Dinuzulu's uncle *umNtwana* **Shingana kaMpande** from **Hlophekhulu Mountain** and regained control of central Zululand. On 9 July, the **Eshowe Column** under Major **Alexander Chalmers McKean** relieved Fort Andries and then returned to **Eshowe**, burning uSuthu *imiZi* on the march. In late July, a new **Coastal Column** under Major McKean marched up the coast again, enforcing **submissions**, while

**Martin's Flying Column** from **Nkonjeni** reestablished civil authority in northwestern Zululand. On the night of 6 August, Dinuzulu disbanded the uSuthu still on Ceza Mountain and sought refuge in the **South African Republic**. The two flying columns then rendezvoused at Ivuna and between 18 and 30 August marched together back to Eshowe, subduing the last pockets of uSuthu resistance. During August and September, some fighting continued in northeastern Zululand between the uSuthu and Mandlakazi, but by the end of September, General Smyth considered the rebellion over. On 2 November, the Zululand garrison was reduced to its normal levels.

**oSUTHU *umuZI*.** In 1884, King **Dinuzulu kaCetshwayo** built oSuthu, his chief *umuZi*, in the Vuna valley, where his adherents were concentrated. On 26 April 1888, 1,000 **uSuthu** *amaButho* gathered there under *umNtwana* **Ndabuko kaMpande** and intimidated a force of 80 **Zululand Police** into failing to execute warrants of arrest issued by **Richard Hallowes Addison**, the resident magistrate of Ndwandwe District, against four uSuthu taking refuge there. The standoff signaled the beginning of the **uSuthu Rebellion**. The oSuthu *umuZi* was plundered between 6 and 9 June 1888 by *inKosi* **Zibhebhu kaMaphitha**'s **Mandlakazi**. On his return to **Zululand** in 1898 after imprisonment on St. Helena, Dinuzulu rebuilt oSuthu in a mixture of traditional *izinDlu* and European-style dwellings.

**SWAZI KINGDOM AND THE ANGLO-ZULU WAR.** During the **Anglo-Zulu War**, the Zulu were concerned that their antagonist Swazi neighbors to the north might use the opportunity to intervene on the side of the British. In fact, the Swazi were determined not to do so until they were certain of British victory. In late 1878, King Mbandzeni waMswati brushed off the overtures repeatedly made by **Norman Magnus MacLeod**, the Swazi border commissioner, to persuade the Swazi to invade northern **Zululand** to protect the flanks of Nos. 4 and 5 **Columns**. Following the Zulu victory at **Isandlwana**, the Swazi became even charier of making a firm commitment to the British cause and remained on the defensive behind their own borders. After **Ulundi** and King **Cetshwayo kaMpande**'s flight, the Swazi were at last prepared to cross the Phongolo and to operate with Lieutenant-Colonel **the Hon. George Patrick Hyde Villiers**, who was advancing on **Luneburg** with troops from the Transvaal and with *umNtwana* **Hamu kaNzibe**'s **Ngenetsheni**. Reluctant to commit their army too deeply in Zululand, the Swazi were content to raid Zulu *imiZi* along the Phongolo before being recalled on 24 August 1879.

**SWAZI KINGDOM, ZULU INVASIONS OF.** Like the **Zulu kingdom**, the Swazi kingdom to its north across the Phongolo River was a conquest state that arose in the 1830s. It was in chronic conflict with its powerful southern neighbor. When threatened by a Zulu raid, the Swazi took to the natural defenses of their mountainous kingdom. In this way, they thwarted Zulu raids dispatched by King **Shaka kaSenzangakhona** in 1827 and 1828, and by King **Dingane kaSenzangakhona** in 1836. In 1837, Dingane recruited 30 white **mercenaries** under **John Cane** from Port Natal (**Durban**) in a further raid against the Swazi, and this time the hunters' guns led to greater success. After the Boer victory at **Ncome** in the **Voortrekker-Zulu War**, Dingane attempted to carve out a new kingdom north across the Phongolo to put space between him and the Voortrekkers. In the winter of 1839, he made a serious attempt to conquer the southern half of the Swazi kingdom, but the Swazi defeated him at the battle of **Lubuye** and forced him to abandon the project.

A dynastic dispute in Swaziland in the 1840s gave King **Mpande kaSenzangakhona** a fresh opportunity for Zulu intervention. One claimant, Mswati waSobhuza, secured the military assistance on 27 July 1846 of the Ohrigstad Boers (in what would later be part of the **South African Republic**) in return for ceding them a massive stretch of territory in northwestern Swaziland. They defeated Malambule waSobhuza, the claimant supported by Mpande, and pursued him into northwestern **Zululand**. This gave Mpande his casus belli, and his *amaButho* invaded Swaziland in early 1847. Baffled by Swazi irregular warfare and Boer firepower, the Zulu withdrew in July 1847. In 1848, Mpande invaded again. This time, Mswati had no Boer support because they had switched it to another royal claimant, Somcuba waSobhuza. Mswati therefore submitted to the Zulu king and paid tribute for a while, but Mpande had to stop short of outright conquest because the British in **Natal** were concerned at the growth of Zulu power and threatened military intervention.

In 1852, Mswati rose up against Zulu control, and Mpande responded with a major raid that swept the country clean of **cattle**. Fearing a massive influx of Swazi refugees, the Natal government put pressure on Mpande to withdraw, and Mswati was able to start consolidating his hold over his kingdom. Mpande contemplated new raids in 1858 and 1862, but internal conflicts in Zululand and British disapproval prevented him.

On his accession in 1872, King **Cetshwayo kaMpande** was ardent for a fresh Swazi campaign to blood his younger *amaButho* and to acquire booty. But Swazi power had grown in the 20 years since the last Zulu invasion, and many of his councilors advised against a new attempt. Most importantly, they were concerned that the British were consistently opposed to wars that might destabilize the region, and they hoped to secure British support in the long standoff over the **Disputed Territory** with the Boers. Consequently, when Cetshwayo planned Swazi campaigns in 1874, 1875, and 1876, he was dissuaded on every occasion.

**SWORD, BRITISH CAVALRY.** Cavalry troopers carried the 1864-pattern sword, with a single-edged, slightly curved, 35-inch blade in a steel scabbard, and a sheet steel guard. In 1882, there were modifications to the guard and scabbard design, and a stronger blade was introduced in 1885. Between 1856 and 1912, heavy cavalry officers carried the 1856-pattern sword, with its three-quarter basket guard, in steel. Light cavalry officers carried the 1822-pattern sword, with its three-bar hilt, until they adopted the heavy cavalry pattern in 1896.

**SWORD, BRITISH INFANTRY OFFICERS.** British officers in **Zululand** carried the 1822-pattern infantry sword, with a gilt half-basket guard and with a "Wilkinson" blade in a steel scabbard introduced in 1866. This sword remained in service until 1892. Officers in Highland regiments carried the 1865-pattern broadsword.

**SWORD, COLONIAL MOUNTED TROOPS.** Colonial mounted officers carried the 1822-pattern, light British cavalry officer's sword.

**SWORD, NAVAL OFFICERS.** The 1856-pattern naval sword was similar to that worn by British infantry officers, but the gilt hilt was solid, with a lion's head on the pommel, and the scabbard was of black leather.

**SWORD, ROYAL ARTILLERY OFFICERS.** The sword, prescribed in 1855, was of the same pattern as the 1822 light cavalry sword, except for a difference in the pommel.

**SWORD, ROYAL ENGINEERS OFFICERS.** The sword was identical with that of the heavy cavalry officer's sword of 1856, except the hilt was of gunmetal instead of steel.

## – T –

**TACTICS, AFRICAN INFANTRY LEVIES.** The prime task of African infantry levies (troops) in the **Anglo-Zulu War** was to support other troops, undertake patrol and garrison duties, and guard **cattle**. In battle, they were to pursue the flying enemy, unofficially dispatch the wounded, and round up abandoned livestock. During the **uSuthu Rebellion**, they were sometimes given a more active role in combat: outflanking the **uSuthu** and cutting off their retreat as the British troops attacked.

**TACTICS, BOER.** *See* COMMANDO SYSTEM, BOER.

**TACTICS, BRITISH INFANTRY.** In countering highly mobile enemies in **small wars**, it was necessary for the British army to be able to work in loose skirmishing order, making the most of terrain and natural cover. By the late 1870s, emphasis was placed on attacking in depth, with a battalion deploying two companies as skirmishers, two further companies in line some distance behind in support, and the remaining four companies in line behind them. During the 9th **Cape Frontier War**, the British employed the extended skirmishing line with supports against the Ngqika and Gcaleka Xhosa in running fire-fights over broken terrain. However, it was equally essential on occasion to concentrate firepower and present a solid line to a rapidly advancing enemy.

At **Isandlwana** in the **Anglo-Zulu War**, the dispersed firing line with no adequate supports could not put up enough firepower to stem the enveloping Zulu mass attack over open ground. After Isandlwana, the British opted for concentration over dispersal, and troops were placed in close order in prepared, all-around defensive positions (whether **forts**, **laagers**, or infantry **squares**) in order to give maximum effect to the concentrated fire of **rifles**, **artillery**, and **Gatling guns**.

During the 3rd **Zulu Civil War** and the **uSuthu Rebellion**, the British realized that they were no longer confronted by mass Zulu attacks. Rather, encounters took the form of running skirmishes in which the British attempted to dislodge the Zulu from their mountain strongholds without being outflanked. In these circumstances, the trend toward even more flexible attack formations proved appropriate. While the first line dominated the enemy with its firepower, the second advanced in support, charging through the first at the enemy with the bayonet. The third line either pursued the broken enemy or covered the retreat of the first two if repulsed. The battle of **Hlophekhulu** was a classic demonstration of these tactics.

**TACTICS, BRITISH MOUNTED TROOPS.** Mounted troops in the **Anglo-Zulu War** were required for long-range reconnaissance and vedette (sentry) duties, patrolling the lines of communications, and drawing the enemy into range of prepared infantry positions. They were also deployed to strike unexpectedly against Zulu concentrations, destroy their *imiZi* and provisions, and capture their livestock. **Irregular cavalry**, operating as **mounted infantry**, were particularly effective in these duties, but regular cavalry were most useful for shock action with sword and lance when they issued from the prepared infantry position and turned the Zulu withdrawal into a rout. During the 3rd **Zulu Civil War** and the **uSuthu Rebellion**, all mounted troops, whether regular cavalry, mounted **Zululand Police**, or irregular cavalry, operated as mounted infantry, scouting and skirmishing and dismounting in action to make more effective use of their firearms. The single instance of cavalry shock action took place at **Ceza** in June 1888.

**TACTICS UP TO 1879, ZULU.** The tactical unit of the Zulu army was the *iButho*. Zulu battle tactics formalized under King **Shaka kaSenzangakhona** persisted with little modification up to the **Anglo-Zulu War**. Once a Zulu army neared the enemy, the single column in which it had been marching normally split into two divisions that continued to advance parallel to and in sight of each other. Bodies of scouts, about 500 strong, preceded each division in extended order by about 10 miles. These small advance guards moved provocatively in the open, sometimes even driving **cattle**, with the intention of drawing the enemy onto the main army. Once the enemy was located, the Zulu commander, who had been appointed by the king, consulted with his officers. When the decision was taken to engage, the army was drawn up into a circle, or *umKhumbi*, and **rituals** were performed to prepare for combat. The commander and his staff then took up position on high ground some distance from the battlefield, which allowed them to escape if the battle was lost, and they directed operations from there by runner.

The Zulu conventional tactic dating back to Shaka or before was to outflank and enclose the enemy in hand-to-hand fighting with stabbing **spear** or clubbed stick. This tactic had been successful against other African armies in the wars of Shaka's reign, and it continued to be so in the internal strife of the 1st and 2nd **Zulu Civil Wars**. In the **Voortrekker-Zulu War**, the Zulu were repeatedly repulsed at the Boer wagon **laagers**, but they twice defeated the invading whites in the open field. Thus when the British invaded 41 years later in the Anglo-Zulu War, the Zulu believed they could win against whites carrying firearms if they could force them to give battle in the open field outside their defenses. Besides, their tradition as an aggressive, conquering people demanded honorable frontal assault and hand-to-hand combat. Night attacks and ambushes might be resorted to, but the desired battle was by daylight, in the open field.

In executing their standard tactical maneuver, the army was divided into four divisions in a formation likened to an ox. The *isiFuba*, or chest, which consisted of veteran married *amaButho*, advanced slowly, while the flanking *izimPondo*, or horns, of younger *amaButho* were rapidly sent out. One horn made a feint, while the other, trying to remain concealed by the terrain, moved with greater speed to join the less advanced horn. The chest then charged the surrounded enemy and destroyed him in close combat. The *umuVa*, or loins, kept seated in reserve, with their backs to the enemy, in order not to be provoked into precipitate action. They supported an engaged *iButho* in difficulties, or they pursued the fleeing enemy. A reserve of youths, or a very young, untried *iButho*, might be held back to be sent in later for support, pursuit, or rounding up captured cattle.

The Zulu did not advance in a solid mass but came on rapidly in lines of skirmishers several ranks deep, advancing in short rushes and making good use of cover. They only concentrated when about to engage in close combat, hurling their throwing spears or discharging their firearms to distract the foe as they charged. Imbued with their heroic military ethic, each man vied to be first among the enemy, and rival *amaButho*, spurred on by the ritual challenges exchanged earlier before the king, contended to gain the honors. *See also* LOGISTICS, ZULU.

**TACTICS IN 1880s, ZULU.** In the decade following the **Anglo-Zulu War**, the traditional Zulu tactics of envelopment and close combat seemed unaffected by the disasters of 1879 and were resolutely pursued in the 3rd **Zulu Civil War** and the **uSuthu Rebellion**. Nevertheless, some familiar elements in the Zulu tactical repertoire began to be given more prominence, particularly by *inKosi* **Zibhebhu kaMaphitha**, the most innovative Zulu commander of the time. He repeatedly made good use of ambush and surprise, including night marches. He also fielded mounted riflemen (including white **mercenaries**) to devastating effect against the **uSuthu** flanks in battle. The uSuthu tried to emulate his tactics, but with less flair and effect. Perhaps because the heroic ethos of the *iButho* system had faded by the 1880s, all Zulu forces were more prepared than previously to adopt flexible skirmishing tactics, making better use of cover and mobility. A regular feature of operations in the 1880s (as it had been in northwestern **Zululand** in the Anglo-Zulu War) was the repeated use of natural fastnesses, not only as strongholds to be defended against attack but as secure bases for small parties raiding for **cattle** and supplies from the surrounding countryside. In the 1880s, the previous tactical unit of the *iButho* that numbered up to several thousand strong was replaced by the *iViyo* of no more than 60 men, underlining the real change in the scale of warfare in Zululand since the end of the Anglo-Zulu War.

**TELEGRAPH.** The telegraph line was essential for communication between London and colonial officials, military commanders, and special correspondents in South Africa. In 1878, the nearest points to South Africa of the international telegraph system were in the Cape Verde Islands or Madeira, where the transatlantic cable, which had been laid from Brazil to Europe in 1874, touched land. The weekly mail steamer took at best 16 days between **Cape Town** and Madeira. Cape Town was linked overland to **Durban** by telegraph cable in April 1878, and Durban had been connected to **Pietermaritzburg** since 1864. Telegrams to the **Zululand** front during the **Anglo-Zulu War** had to be carried by dispatch rider. In 1879, a cable already existed from London to Bombay via Aden; a few months after the end of the Anglo-Zulu War, a new link was established down the east coast of Africa from Aden via Zanzibar and **Delagoa Bay** to Durban, thus directly connecting South Africa with London. During the 3rd **Zulu Civil War** and the **uSuthu Rebellion**, Pietermaritzburg was connected to **Eshowe** by telegraph, and from there temporary telegraph lines kept military headquarters in communication. *See also* MILITARY INTELLIGENCE, BRITISH; ROADS IN ZULULAND.

**TETELEKU'S MOUNTED NATIVES.** During the **Anglo-Zulu War**, Chief Teteleku of the Phumuza people in **Colonial Defensive District** No. III raised and led a unit of **irregular** mounted horse that from April 1879 periodically garrisoned various posts in Colonial Defensive District No. I, including the magistracy at Umsinga, the **Helpmekaar Fort**, and **Fort Melvill**. It participated in patrols and raids across the border, also in May assisting in the burial of the dead at **Isandlwana**. A detachment accompanied the 2nd Division, **South African Field Force**, in the 2nd Invasion of the Anglo-Zulu War and then joined **Baker Russell's Column**. On 4 September, they were involved in an operation to clear the **Kubheka** out of their caves in the Ntombe valley and disgraced themselves by butchering the prisoners.

**eTHALENI, BATTLE OF (1838).** After the **Bloukrans Massacre** in February 1838 at the outset of the **Voortrekker-Zulu War**, the Voortrekkers in western **Zululand** (numbering about 640 men, 3,200 women and children, and 1,260 colored servants) drew together in **laagers** for protection. In March, they agreed with the settlers at Port Natal (**Durban**) to take joint retaliatory action against the Zulu, and on 6 April the Voortrekkers sent a **commando** (militia) toward **uMgungundlovu**, King **Dingane kaSenzangakhona**'s principal *iKhanda*.

The commando soon divided into two sections because rivalry between the leaders made a single command unacceptable. **Andries Hendrik Potgieter** commanded 200 men and **Petrus (Piet) Lafras Uys** 147. They took no wagons, intending to move fast and surprise the Zulu as they had the **Ndebele** in the 1837 campaign. But the Zulu were fully aware of the commando's advance and set an ambush on the far side of the Mzinyathi River near the source of the Mhlathuze River and the eThaleni Hill. On 10 April, the commando sighted a herd of **cattle** being driven as a decoy between two hills leading to a rocky basin seamed with deep dongas, and they imprudently gave pursuit. The Zulu force, under the command of **Nzobo kaSobadli**, was several thousand strong, with a division posted on each of the two hills. A third remained at some distance to cut off the commando's retreat. Uys's force dismounted and attacked the Zulu division sitting among the rocks on the northernmost of the two hills. The Zulu then deliberately fell back, drawing Uys's men, who had remounted, into the rocky basin. In their reckless pursuit, the Boers broke into small groups and were attacked on all sides by the Zulu. Meanwhile, Potgieter's force had moved halfway up the broken terrain of the southern hill and then prudently withdrawn. The Zulu charged down, and Potgieter and his men fled. The third Zulu division tried to cut them off, but Potgieter's men evaded them. Uys's force, left in the lurch and surrounded, conducted a fighting retreat for nearly two hours over the broken country, alternately dismounting, firing, and retiring until they eventually joined up with Potgieter's force.

Uys and his son Dirkie, age 14, died fighting, as did seven other Boers in his party. Only one of Potgieter's men was killed. The Boers also lost 60 pack **horses** and most of their baggage. Zulu casualties are unknown, but they must have been fairly high, as they were confronting organized Boer fire. The defeat of the *Vlugkommando*, or Flight Commando as it was derisively dubbed, caused fresh consternation among the Voortrekkers. It also exacerbated dissension in the Boer camp. Potgieter, openly accused of cowardice, withdrew across the **Drakensberg** with his followers to the highveld. *See also* COMMANDO SYSTEM, BOER; TACTICS UP TO 1879, ZULU.

**THRING'S POST FORT.** In May 1879 during the **Anglo-Zulu War**, Captain George Lucas, commander of **Colonial Defensive District** No. VI, built this earthwork fort as a stronghold for his **Border Guard**.

**THUKELA, BATTLE OF (1838).** The Port Natal (**Durban**) settlers, hoping to repeat the success of their raid of March 1838 at **Ntunjambili** in support of the Voortrekkers also sending in punitive expeditions against the Zulu during the **Voortrekker-Zulu War**, mounted a large expedition in April. **Robert Biggar**, **John Cane**, and John Stubbs led out 16 white settlers, 30 colored retainers, and 400 African retainers all armed with **muskets**, as well as several thousand African auxiliaries carrying **spears** and **shields** in support. The strategic objectives of this "Grand Army of Natal" were hazy. On reaching the southern banks of the lower Thukela, they decided after rancorous debate to make a sudden foray across the river, even though little intelligence of the situation on the Zulu bank was available. In fact, several *amaButho* were waiting for them, under the nominal command of umNtwana **Mpande kaSenzangakhona** and actual leadership of **Nongalaza kaNondela** and Madlebe kaMgedeza.

The "Grand Army" crossed the Thukela lower drift early on the morning of 17 April and overran and burned **Ndondakusuka**, a large *umuZi*. The Zulu army then advanced rapidly from the north in two columns either side of the hill overlooking Ndondakusuka. They surrounded Biggar's force and cut it off from retreat to the Thukela. Those Port Natalians with muskets made a stand near the *umuZi* with some success, but when the African auxiliaries found themselves cut off from the musketeers by the Zulu advance, they panicked. To save themselves, they threw off the white calico that distinguished them from the Zulu, who otherwise were similarly dressed and armed. The musketeers could no longer make out who was the enemy, and this added to the confusion of the fierce hand-to-hand fighting. Biggar, Cane, and all except four of the settlers, two or three coloreds, and a handful of African auxiliaries died where they stood or were herded down to the river to be speared or drowned as they attempted to cross. Zulu losses are unknown, although the musketeers seem at first to have done much execution among the Zulu who charged them.

Several survivors brought word of the disaster to Port Natal, and the settlers were able to take refuge on the *Comet*, anchored in the bay, before the Zulu army swept down on the settlement on 24 April and sacked it. *See also* TACTICS, AFRICAN INFANTRY LEVIES; TACTICS UP TO 1879, ZULU.

**uTHULWANA *iBUTHO*.** King **Mpande kaSenzangakhona** formed this *iButho* around 1854 of youths born about 1834. The **shield** was white with small red spots. In the 2nd **Zulu Civil War**, it formed part of the **uSuthu** right horn at **Ndondakusuka**. In the **Anglo-Zulu War**, it formed part of the uncommitted reserve at **Isandlwana** and went on to attack **Rorke's Drift**. It fought with the chest at **Khambula** and attacked the southern side of the British infantry **square** at **Ulundi**. Elements fought with the **uSuthu** in the 3rd Zulu Civil War and were part of the uSuthu chest at **oNdini**.

**TLOKWA PEOPLE.** *See* HLUBI'S TROOP (MOUNTED BASUTOS); MOUNTED BASUTOS.

**TOLLBOSCHE LAAGER (INGAGANE LAAGER).** In early 1878, local settlers began work on a stone **laager** on Crown Land in what was later designated **Colonial Defensive District** No. I. But they could not come to an agreement with the **Natal** government over terms for tenure and financing. Indignant as a result of the dispute, the settlers abandoned work in late 1878 on the nearly completed laager. The only purpose the laager filled during the **Anglo-Zulu War** was as a rendezvous in January 1879 for settlers trekking out of the district for the safety of the Transvaal or **Orange Free State**.

**TOWN GUARD, DURBAN.** In November 1878, a Town Guard with elected officers was organized in **Durban** for the defense of the town in case of Zulu attack in the coming **Anglo-Zulu War**. The possibility was not taken seriously by the people of Durban until after **Isandlwana**, when the Town Guard was assigned to defend specified buildings that constituted part of the **Durban Town laager**. The perceived Zulu threat soon receded, and by early March 1879 the Town Guard stood down, though as a reserve unit it retained its arms until early September.

**TOWN GUARD, LADYSMITH.** In early January 1879, a Town Guard was organized for the defense of the **Ladysmith laager** during the **Anglo-Zulu War**. Its complement included townsfolk and members of the **Klip River rifle association**. The Town Guard and **Carbutt's Rangers** who were stationed in **Ladysmith** were too few to hold the laager, so William James Dunbar Moodie, the resident magistrate, raised a native contingent to supplement the defenders. However, the settlers were suspicious of them and insisted they stay in reserve outside the laager. With the buildup in May of the 2nd Division, **South African Field Force**, for the 2nd Invasion of the Anglo-Zulu War, military units entered Ladysmith and the Town Guard became irrelevant, finally standing down in July.

**TOWN GUARD, NEWCASTLE.** In early January 1879 during the **Anglo-Zulu War**, the citizens of Newcastle formed a Town Guard, but it was not large enough to defend the **Newcastle laager**. **Fort Amiel**, on the hill above the town, was initially held only by a few military convalescents, so until February when reinforcements arrived, the Town Guard presented no potential deterrent to the Zulu. All danger of a Zulu incursion had passed by April, when the Town Guard stood down.

**TRANSPORT, BRITISH.** For lack of **railways**, proper **roads**, and navigable rivers, the only feasible form of transport for the British in **Zululand** during the **Anglo-Zulu War**, 3rd **Zulu Civil War**, and **uSuthu Rebellion** was animal drawn. The **ox wagon** was the preferred type, but it was very slow because oxen required eight hours a day to graze and a further eight to rest. Nevertheless, oxen could carry heavy loads over poor roads more efficiently than other draught animals, though mules were also extensively used, as were **horses**. In 1879, the British employed as many as 15 different varieties of wagons and carts. The draught animals and vehicles were obtained from **Natal**, the **Cape**, and the Boer republics or as far afield as North Africa and South America. The disadvantage of herding together so many beasts was the spread of contagious diseases that carried off great numbers. Local wagon owners made enormous profits in 1879 selling or leasing them to the military, and wagon drivers and team leaders demanded rates far above the normal for their services. During the Anglo-Zulu War, the British ultimately required a transport establishment of 748 horses, 4,635 mules, 27,125 oxen, 641 horse or mule carriages, 1,770 ox wagons, 796 ox carts, and 4,080 conductors and *voorlopers* (team leaders).

**TRANSPORT CONVOYS, BRITISH.** Battalion transport during the British campaigns in **Zululand** consisted of eight wagons carrying officers' personal baggage, the men's accoutrements, reserve ammunition, tents, camping equipment, and rations. Transport was also required for **artillery** and **rocket** batteries, engineering and signaling equipment, medical stores, camp kitchens, shoeing smithies, and fodder for cavalry chargers. Transport convoys moved very slowly over the difficult terrain (often no more than three miles a day) and had to halt at regular intervals to establish forward depots for reserve supplies, and to allow wagons to move back and forth between depots and rear supply bases until they were filled. After **Isandlwana** during the **Anglo-Zulu War**, wagon trains **laagered** at every halt, reducing the time on the march by at least an hour a day. Convoys required protection on the march, particularly on the flanks, and forward mounted patrols to give warning of enemy movements. Because a single wagon in full span extended 60 yards, trains of several hundred wagons stretched out dangerously, especially where tracks up steep hills or across rivers and dongas caused bottlenecks. In open country, wagons could moved eight abreast, making them easier to escort effectively. *See also* TRANSPORT, BRITISH.

**TRANSVAAL.** *See* SOUTH AFRICAN REPUBLIC.

**TRANSVAAL BURGHER FORCE.** On the eve of the **Anglo-Zulu War**, the British tried to recruit Transvaal Boers, but most of them resented the recent British annexation of the Transvaal and did not come forward. Brevet Colonel **Henry Evelyn Wood** had some success in the **Utrecht** and **Wakkerstroom Districts** along the Zulu border where **Pieter Lafras Uys** Jr. joined No. 4 **Column** with a force of some 45 local farmers experienced in **commando** (militia) operations. They played a significant part in patrolling and raiding northwestern **Zululand**, including the raid of 15 February against the **Kubheka** in the Ntombe valley. Fighting at **Hlobane** with Lieutenant-Colonel **Redvers Henry Buller**'s force, Uys was among the many casualties. Most of the survivors did not remain at **Khambula** to defend the camp next day but returned after the battle. On 5 April, they elected Adriaan Rudolph as their new commandant, and when **Wood's Flying Column** commenced its advance in the 2nd Invasion of the Anglo-Zulu War, they remained behind, based at **Fort Lawrence** to patrol the border area between **Balte Spruit** and **Luneburg**. They disbanded in September. In commando fashion, they wore civilian clothes and rode their own **horses**, though the British military provided **firearms** and ammunition.

**TRANSVAAL TERRITORY.** See SOUTH AFRICAN REPUBLIC.

**TSHANENI, BATTLE OF (1884).** In May 1884, in the last stages of the 3rd **Zulu Civil War**, the uSuthu under King **Dinuzulu ka-Mpande** entered into an agreement with the Boers infiltrating northeastern **Zululand** whereby the Boers were promised land in return for aid against the **Mandlakazi** and **Ngenetsheni**. In early June, the uSuthu gathered an army of more than 6,000 near the **ekuShumaye-leni** *umuZi* under Dinuzulu's command. They were joined there by a **commando** (militia) of 100–120 Boers under Commandant **Lukas Johannes Meyer**, and by about 20 mounted volunteers from **Luneburg** under Adolf Schiel, Dinuzulu's secretary and political adviser.

To avoid falling into an ambush like the uSuthu army had at **Msebe** in 1883, the joint force scouted ahead as they pushed eastward through Mandlakazi territory. On the afternoon of 5 June, they reached its furthest extremity, where the Mkhuze River flows through a poort (narrow pass) in the Lubombo Mountains. *InKosi* **Zibhebhu kaMaphitha** had fallen back there with all his women and children and **cattle**. To defend them, he had only about 3,000 men and three or four white **mercenaries**. He placed all the noncombatants and livestock on a spur north of the Mkhuze River and positioned the bulk of his fighting men on the slopes of Tshaneni Mountain, believing the dense thorn bush would impede the Boer horsemen. The rest of his men he drew up in a deep donga in advance of the Mandlakazi right.

The uSuthu advanced in traditional chest and horns formation, with Schiel's volunteers supporting the left horn and Meyer's commando supporting the chest and right horn. While the uSuthu left successfully engaged the Mandlakazi at the donga, the charging Mandlakazi rolled up the uSuthu right horn and forced it back on the chest. The Boers fired fusillades from the saddle over the heads of the wavering uSuthu and drove the Mandlakazi back. The Mandlakazi then gave way, making for the river and their families on the other side, but the uSuthu cut them off, pinned them against the river, and slaughtered them there. Zibhebhu and some of his men made their escape across the river and were joined by those noncombatants who could outpace their pursuers. The Boers suffered no casualties, and the uSuthu losses are unknown. Mandlakazi losses must have been significant, with six of Zibhebhu's brothers dying in the rout. The victorious uSuthu and Boers captured as many as 60,000 head of cattle. Their victory ensured that their defeated foes could not reestablish themselves in their old territory, and in September Zibhebhu was left with no option but to find sanctuary in the **Reserve Territory** with 6,000 Mandlakazi. *See also* BOERS AND THE ZULULAND CAMPAIGN OF 1884; CIVILIANS IN WARTIME ZULULAND; TACTICS IN 1880s, ZULU.

**TSHOTSHOSI SKIRMISH (1879).** The death while on patrol during the **Anglo-Zulu War** of **Prince Louis Napoleon Bonaparte**, the prince imperial of France, caused considerable consternation. The prince was attached as an additional aide-de-camp to Lieutenant-General Lord **Chelmsford**'s staff during the 2nd invasion of the war. On 1 June 1879, he joined a patrol of six mounted **irregulars** and a guide under Lieutenant **Jahleel Brenton Carey** who were to select a suitable camping ground for the 2nd Division, **South African Field Force**, along the banks of the Tshotshosi River. The area was believed free of Zulu combatants, and the patrol off-saddled at a deserted *umuZi* (Zulu homestead) on the riverbank. Meanwhile a Zulu patrol of 30–60 men spotted the British party from Mhlungwane Hill to the southeast and, moving along a deep donga (dry watercourse) opening into the Tshotshosi, came undetected to within 15 yards of the *umuZi*. When the guide with the British patrol detected enemy movement, Bonaparte, who was exercising effective command of the patrol, gave the order to move out. The Zulu fired two ragged volleys and charged. The British panicked, threw themselves as best they could into their saddles, and galloped for their lives. Carey made it back to Chelmsford's camp at Thelezi Hill and reported on the incident. Two troopers, the guide, and Bonaparte were killed by the Zulu. The British found the prince's body the next day, and his embalmed corpse was returned to England for burial. In March 1880, Major **Henry Sparke Stabb** erected a memorial stone cross, paid for by Queen Victoria, to mark the spot where Bonaparte had fallen. His death further tarnished Chelmsford's already sullied military reputation. Carey was court-martialed for his discreditable part in the affair.

**TSONGA PEOPLE.** To the south and west of the **Mabhudu-Tsonga chiefdom**, and north of the Hluhluwe and Mkhuze rivers, were various small Tsonga chiefdoms that had a strong cultural and tributary relationship with the Zulu state. The more southerly of these chiefdoms were expected to assist the Zulu in war as **irregulars**, since they were not part of the *iButho* system. As war approached in 1878, the Tsonga, who supplied labor to **Natal** and were allowed safe passage through **Zululand** in return for a payment to the king, began leaving Natal for home, though many stayed on in southeastern Zululand to fight for King **Cetshwayo kaMpande** during the **Anglo-Zulu War**. Nearly 3,000 Tsonga irregulars fought at **Gingindlovu**, and some were present at **Ulundi**.

## – U –

**ULTIMATUM CRISIS.** **Sir Bartle Frere**, the British high commissioner for South Africa, believed that in order to bring about the **confederation** of the subcontinent, it was necessary to break the military power of the **Zulu kingdom**. During the course of 1878, he seized on minor border incidents in July and October along the Mzinyathi and Thukela rivers and in the **Disputed Territory** to provide the necessary justification for punitive action. By September, Frere's naval and military commanders were preparing for war against **Zululand**. The alternative of taming Zulu power through diplomatic means was never seriously explored because Frere doubted if any verbal Zulu undertaking would be binding unless a British force was maintained on the border to ensure compliance.

Consequently, Frere's ultimatum to King **Cetshwayo kaMpande**, which he drafted with the advice of **Sir Theophilus Shepstone** and **Sir Henry Ernest Gascoyne Bulwer**, required (among other stipulations) that the Zulu *iButho* **system** be abolished and the king **submit** himself to the authority of a British resident. Since such requirements would have subverted the social, economic, and political structure of the Zulu kingdom, it was never supposed that Cetshwayo would comply without a fight. **Sir Michael Edward Hicks Beach**, the British colonial secretary, faced with a fresh war in Afghanistan and strained relations with Russia, tried to put on the brakes. But Frere kept his superiors in the dark while he hurried on his plans without their prior sanction. He took this risk because he believed the war would be swift and decisive and that the results would exonerate him.

The Zulu, who previously had tried to maintain good relations with the British as a counterweight to Boer ambitions, could not fathom the change in British policy and the reasons behind their menacing military buildup in the last months of 1878. Cetshwayo made frequent attempts to resolve the crisis, but Frere brushed these aside. On 11 December 1878, Cetshwayo's representatives were summoned to the **Natal** side of the Thukela River at the Lower Drift to hear **John Wesley Shepstone**, the acting secretary for native affairs in Natal, deliver the long-delayed **boundary award** that was followed and negated by the impossible terms of the ultimatum. Though given 30 days in which to comply, Cetshwayo had no alternative but armed resistance if he were to maintain Zulu independence. He therefore mobilized his armies for the coming **Anglo-Zulu War** and allowed the ultimatum to expire unanswered.

**ULUNDI, BATTLE OF (1879).** The British called it the battle of Ulundi, after **oNdini**, King **Cetshwayo kaMpande**'s principal *iKhanda*, and celebrated it as the engagement that terminated the **Anglo-Zulu War**. The Zulu referred to it as the battle of **kwaNodwengu**, after the *iKhanda* nearest which it was fought, or as oCwecweni, the battle of the corrugated-iron sheets, because the flash of weapons in the tight British formation gave the impression they were fighting from behind iron shields.

On 29 June 1879, Lieutenant-General Lord **Chelmsford**'s combined force of the 2nd Division, **South African Field Force**, and **Wood's Flying Column** formed a triple **laager** on the **Mthonjaneni Heights** overlooking oNdini and the other *amaKhanda* clustered in the **Mahlabathini Plain** below. The Zulu *amaButho* had been slowly concentrating there over the past month for a last-ditch defense of their kingdom. With only a minimum of baggage, Chelmsford marched down to the south bank of the **White Mfolozi**, where on 2 July he formed a double laager commanded by **Fort Ulundi**. Before dawn on 4 July, Chelmsford marched his force of 5,170 men (1,005 of them African) to a favorable position facing the oNdini *iKhanda* that the **White Mfolozi Reconnaissance in Force** had identified the previous day.

The British formed an infantry **square** four ranks deep interspersed with **artillery**. The Zulu *amaButho*, 15,000–20,000 men under *umNtwana* **Ziwedu kaMpande**, loosely surrounded the square and were drawn onto it by the British **irregular** horse. Meanwhile, a force of 5,000 Zulu moved toward **Fort Ulundi** across the White Mfolozi held by 622 troops under the command of Colonel William Bellairs, but they melted away without attacking it, in order to join in the general battle. Unable to break through the concentrated fire to come to grips with the British, and with their reserve advancing out of oNdini in a dense column broken up by artillery fire, the Zulu began to withdraw. The British then unleashed a mounted counterattack conducted by the cavalry, **mounted infantry**, and irregular horse that, supported by **artillery** fire, turned the Zulu retreat into a rout. While the **Natal Native Contingent** killed the Zulu wounded, the British systematically burned all the *amaKhanda* in the plain before withdrawing to their camp. The Zulu *amaButho*, acknowledging that they had been decisively defeated in the open field, dispersed, never to re-form. Cetshwayo fled north, his power irrevocably broken. The British lost 13 killed, the Zulu an estimated 1,500. Distinguished

Conduct Medals went to Color Sergeant J. Phillips, 58th (Rutland-shire) **Regiment**, and Gunner W. Moorhead, **Royal Artillery**. *See also* TACTICS, AFRICAN INFANTRY LEVIES; TACTICS, BRITISH INFANTRY; TACTICS, BRITISH MOUNTED TROOPS; TACTICS UP TO 1879, ZULU.

**UMLALAZI CAMP.** On 23 July 1888 during the **uSuthu Rebellion**, Major **Alexander Chalmers McKean** formed the **Coastal Column** at this camp close to the **Zululand** coast, preparatory to marching north to enforce the **submissions** of the **uSuthu**.

**UMVOTI LAAGER (FORT MIZPAH).** Local Boer farmers of **Colonial Defensive District** No. VII built this square, stone-walled **laager** with two opposing bastions in late 1878, without receiving any **Natal** government support. During the **Anglo-Zulu War**, it was briefly occupied in late January 1879 after **Isandlwana**, but it was abandoned on 12 February for lack of defenders. It was used again during the **Zulu Uprising of 1906** (Bhambatha Rebellion).

**UMZINTO LAAGER.** This stone-walled **laager**, commenced in February 1878 on the orders of the **Natal** government, abutted the magistrate's office at the village of Umzinto in what was subsequently designated **Colonial Defensive District** No. V. It was completed by the outbreak of the **Anglo-Zulu War** and stocked with **rifles** and ammunition, but it was never occupied.

**UPPER TUGELA DEFENCE CORPS.** In December 1878, Boer farmers in **Colonial Defensive District** No. II close to the **Drakensberg** formed a local defense corps under elected leaders, with their base at the **Strydpoort laager**. In late February 1879 during the **Anglo-Zulu War**, they were put on the alert for fear of action by the Phuti, who were in rebellion in **Basutoland** against the **Cape** authorities, and they patrolled the border with the **Weenen Yeomanry**. By April, all fears of Zulu or **Sotho** attack had dissipated and they stood down.

**UTRECHT DISTRICT.** In the 1820s, the **Zulu kingdom** extended its sway up the valleys of the Mzinyathi and Ncome rivers, dislodging the Hlubi and Ngwane chiefdoms. Thereafter, the Zulu were the dominant power in the region and extracted tribute from the people who remained, but Zulu control was never complete over this territory on the periphery of the kingdom. Thus in September 1854, King **Mpande kaSenzangakhona** was prepared to cede the wedge of land between the Mzinyathi and Ncome rivers to Boer settlers, who set up their insecure Utrecht Republic. On 6 November 1859, the Utrecht Republic submerged itself into the **South African Republic** as the Utrecht District. As the Utrecht settlement grew, so the Boers sought to extend their land claims east into **Zululand**, and this was the genesis of the **Disputed Territory**. At the time of the **Anglo-Zulu War**, there were 248 whites in the little village of Utrecht and 1,352 in the district as a whole, of whom 375 were men of military age. On 27 January 1903, following the British defeat of the South African Republic in the **Anglo-Boer (South African) War**, the Utrecht District was annexed to the Colony of **Natal**.

**UTRECHT FORT.** In December 1877, preparatory to operations against the **Pedi** in the northeastern Transvaal Territory, men of the 80th **Regiment** (Staffordshire Volunteers) built a military earthwork fort in the village of **Utrecht** next to the existing **Utrecht laager**. Its perimeter protected a number of **commissariat** sheds. Throughout the **Anglo-Zulu War**, the fort protected the main depot from which No. 4 **Column** and subsequently **Wood's Flying Column** drew their supplies.

**UTRECHT LAAGER.** A decrepit, stone-walled settlers' **laager** existed in the village of **Utrecht** on the eve of the **Anglo-Zulu War**, adjoining the **Utrecht Fort**. In December 1878, the local settlers made clear that they were not prepared to defend it should the Zulu make a raid.

**UTRECHT, VILLAGE OF.** *See* UTRECHT DISTRICT.

**UYS, PETRUS (PIET) LAFRAS, JR. (1827–1879).** Uys was a son of the Voortrekker leader **Petrus Lafras Uys Sr**. The Uys family acquired farms in the Republic of **Natalia**, but after the British annexation of **Natal**, Piet Uys was among those who in 1847 settled in what became the **Utrecht District** of the **South African Republic**. On the eve of the **Anglo-Zulu War**, Brevet Colonel **Henry Evelyn**

**Wood**, whose No. 4 **Column** was based at Utrecht, tried to raise a burgher force from the Boers of the district. Most remained resentful of the British annexation of the Transvaal in 1877, and only Uys, his family, and associates came forward. He was motivated by the vulnerability of his border farms, his desire for revenge against the Zulu for the death of his father and brother Dirkie Uys at **eThaleni** in the **Voortrekker-Zulu War**, and his desire to acquire land in the **Disputed Territory**. He and his **Transvaal Burgher Force** proved very effective in scouting and raiding. They formed part of Lieutenant-Colonel **Redvers Henry Buller**'s force raiding **Hlobane Mountain** on 28 March 1879. During the rout, Uys was killed at the bottom of Devil's Pass. Dismayed, his men abandoned the British camp at **Khambula** before the Zulu assault the following day.

**UYS, PETRUS (PIET) LAFRAS, SR. (1797–1838).** A prosperous farmer from the Uitenhage District of the **Eastern Cape**, Uys gained a military reputation on the volatile **Cape frontier** and was chosen in 1834 to lead a *kommissietrek*, or scouting mission, to Port Natal (**Durban**) to ascertain whether the region was suitable for farming. His favorable report persuaded many of his neighbors to join his party of Voortrekkers, which set out for the interior in April 1836. In November 1837, Uys responded to a request by **Andries Hendrik Potgieter** to aid him with a **commando** (militia) in defeating the **Ndebele**. Uys was jealous of **Pieter Retief** and skeptical of his judgment in negotiating with King **Dingane kaSenzangakhona**, so he did not move his party over the **Drakensberg** to join him. However, after the **Bloukrans Massacre** in the **Voortrekker-Zulu War**, Uys brought a commando to the survivors' aid. Because he would not subordinate himself to Potgieter, who had also brought a commando down from the highveld, Uys agreed in April to joint command of the *Vlugkommando*, which was ambushed at **eThaleni**. When Uys was mortally wounded, his 14-year-old son, Dirkie Uys, rode back to save him and was killed at his side.

– V –

**uVE** *iBUTHO*. King **Cetshwayo kaMpande** formed this *iButho* around 1875 from youths born about 1854–1855. The **shield** was either black or brown. On the eve of the **Anglo-Zulu War**, it was incorporated into the **iNgobamakhosi** *iButho*. During the war, it fought on the left of the Zulu center at **Isandlwana**. Elements were detached from the main Zulu army marching on **Khambula** to intervene at **Hlobane**. At Khambula, it fought on the Zulu right horn with the iNgobamakhosi, where their premature attack upset Zulu strategy. At **Ulundi**, it came closest to breaking through the British infantry **square** at its southwest corner.

**VEGLAER (VECHTLAAGER), BATTLE OF (1838).** During the **Voortrekker-Zulu War**, the Zulu were encouraged by their victories in April 1838 at **eThaleni** and **Thukela**. They took the offensive in August 1838 in a campaign designed to destroy the Voortrekker invaders once and for all. Under the command of **Ndlela kaSompisi**, about 10,000 of the more experienced *amaButho* marched from **uMgu-ngundlovu** toward the Boer **laager**, the Gatslaer, on a low ridge called the Gatsrand in the valley of the Bushman's River. There a number of Boer parties had come together for mutual protection under **Johan Hendrik (Hans Dons) de Lange**. The Gatslaer was shaped in a rough triangle and consisted of a double line of 290 wagons, lashed together, with small cannon at the apex. It enjoyed a generally good field of fire, but dongas (dry watercourses) to the east and west offered cover to assailants. Because the Boers had dug *trous-de-loup* (pits) to entrap an enemy crossing the river on the southeastern side of the laager, the Zulu would call the battle emaGebeni, or Place of the Pits.

The Zulu hoped to take the laager by surprise, but on 13 August, herd boys caught sight of the Zulu scouts and there was time for the Boers to prepare. The noncombatants took cover in a spear-proof shelter made of wagons and boards in the middle of the laager. One division of the Zulu forded the Bushman's River below the laager; the rest advanced directly from the east and swung around to the west, encircling the laager. The Zulu attacked in waves, probing one point of the defenses after another. A few Zulu carried **firearms** captured in previous engagements and kept up a constant fire. The Boers, who numbered only about 75 fighting men, with some women dealing out powder and bullets, had to move repeatedly to reinforce the sectors of the perimeter under attack, but they managed to maintain an impenetrable wall of fire. The Zulu attack faltered at midday, and de Lange led out a mounted sortie. The Zulu withdrew downstream and encamped for the night.

Early on 14 August, de Lange made a mounted sortie and drew the Zulu into the laager's zone of fire. The Zulu retreated, having failed to set the laager alight with burning grass plaited around hurled **spears**. But they rounded up all the Boers' **cattle** and other livestock and drove them east into **Zululand**. That night, the Boers again stood to arms, but the Zulu did not attack. On 15 August, the Zulu decided to withdraw without renewing the assault. The Boers attempted to harry their retreat, but their **horses** were too weak for lack of fodder inside the laager to carry up the pursuit for long. Not a single defender of the laager was killed, and Zulu losses are unknown.

The battle of Veglaer or Vechtlaager (fight laager), as the Boers called it, confirmed that the all-around defensive position was the key to success over the Zulu. As for the Zulu, the laager's successful defense had baffled their every effort and they fell back on the defensive, awaiting the next move by the Boers. *See also* COMMANDO SYSTEM, BOER; TACTICS UP TO 1879, ZULU.

**VERULAM LAAGER.** In September 1878, this brick-walled **laager** encompassing the jail and courthouse in the village of Verulam in what would be designated **Colonial Defensive District** No. VI was commenced on the orders of the **Natal** government. It was to be defended by the Verulam Defence Guard. Despite some alarms after **Isandlwana**, the laager was never manned during the **Anglo-Zulu War**.

**VICTORIA CROSS.** *See* AWARDS.

**VICTORIA MOUNTED RIFLES.** Formed in 1862, the Victoria Mounted Rifles was one of the 10 corps of **Natal Mounted Volunteers** called out in November 1878 for active service in the **Anglo-Zulu War**. It was mobilized in December 1878 and joined No. 1 **Column** at **Fort Pearson**. It advanced into **Zululand** with the column and fought at **Nyezane** as part of the 1st Division. On 28 January, it returned from **Fort Eshowe** to **Natal** with the other mounted forces of the column. Until the corps of 50 men was mustered out in

July, it served by patrolling the border along the lines of communication. The uniform was of dark blue cloth, with scarlet braid edging and piping and with broad scarlet trouser stripes. The helmet was white with a white metal spike.

**VILLIERS, THE HON. GEORGE PATRICK HYDE (1847–1892).** Commissioned into the Grenadier Guards in 1867, Villiers performed staff duties in England and India and served in the 2nd Afghan War (1878) before arriving in South Africa in May 1879 as a lieutenant-colonel on special service to serve in the **Anglo-Zulu War** with the 2nd Division, **South African Field Force**. In August 1879, General **Sir Garnet Joseph Wolseley** appointed him special commissioner to *inKosi* **Hamu kaNzibe** with orders to cooperate with **Baker Russell's Column** in the pacification of northwestern **Zululand**. **Villiers's Column** advanced from Derby to **Luneburg** and was broken up on 8 September. The following day, Wolseley appointed Villiers to chair a boundary commission to demarcate the 13 chiefdoms created in the 1st Partition of Zululand. Villiers submitted his final report in December 1879 and left Zululand to become military attaché successively in St. Petersburg, Berlin, and Paris. In 1889, he was given the command of the 1st Battalion, Grenadier Guards.

**VILLIERS' COLUMN.** While **Baker Russell's Column** was at **Fort George** during late August 1879 in the final stage of the **Anglo-Zulu War**, General **Sir Garnet Joseph Wolseley** ordered Lieutenant-Colonel **George Patrick Hyde Villiers** to advance from Derby with a motley force of 300 Mounted Burghers and 700 **Ngenetsheni** and **Swazi** allies to catch the Zulu of northwestern **Zululand** between the two columns and enforce their **submission**. Villiers's African troops had little stomach for military action and fortunately met no resistance before they reached **Luneburg** on 25 August. They were keen for loot and comprehensively devastated the countryside between the Phongolo and Bivane rivers. On 8 September, Wolseley broke up the ill-disciplined force, whose pillaging had played some part in convincing the **Kubheka** of the Ntombe valley finally to submit.

*iVIYO. See iBUTHO,* STRUCTURE AND SIZE OF.

**VLUGKOMMANDO.** The *Vlugkommando*, or Flight Commando, was the derisive name given to the Boer **commando** (militia) under **Andries Hendrik Potgieter** and **Petrus (Piet) Lafras Uys Sr.** that the Zulu ambushed and routed on 10 April 1838 at **eThaleni** during the **Voortrekker-Zulu War**.

**VOORTREKKER.** *See* GREAT TREK.

**VOORTREKKER-ZULU WAR (1838–1839).** On 3 February 1838, **Pieter Retief** and his **commando** (militia) arrived at the **uMgungundlovu** *iKhanda* to negotiate a treaty with King **Dingane kaSenzangakhona** to permit his party of Voortrekkers to settle in his kingdom. Dingane greatly feared the intruders with their **firearms** and **horses** and was persuaded by his advisers that he must destroy them while he still could. So on 6 February, he ordered the execution of Retief and his men, an act that the Boers never forgave. In the **Bloukrans Massacre** on 16–17 February, the Zulu army overran many Voortrekker encampments in the foothills of the **Drakensberg** (the region later known as *Weenen*, or Weeping) before being driven off. In March, the Voortrekkers and Port Natal (**Durban**) settlers agreed on a joint offensive against Dingane. A commando (later known as the *Vlugkommando*) led by **Petrus Lafras Uys Sr.** and **Andries Hendrik Potgieter** advanced toward uMgungundlovu, but the Zulu under **Nzobo kaSobadli** ambushed and defeated them on 10 April at **eThaleni** in central **Zululand**. Seven days later, the Zulu under *umNtwana* **Mpande kaSenzangakhona** routed the "Grand Army of Natal" under **Robert Biggar** at the **Thukela**, and the Zulu army went on to sack Port Natal between 24 April and 3 May, while the settlers took refuge on the *Clyde* in the bay. Determined to finish off the white invaders, between 13 and 15 August the main Zulu army under *inKosi* **Ndlela kaSompisi** repeatedly attacked the Voortrekkers in the Gatslaer under **Johan Hendrik (Hans Dons) de Lange.** They finally retired defeated in what came to be known as the battle of **Veglaer**, unable to storm a prepared position defended by gunfire.

The Boers now counterattacked, and on 27 November the *Wenkommando* under **Andries Wilhelmus Jacobus Pretorius** (whom the Boers had elected their chief commandant) began its advance toward uMgungundlovu from the Sooilaer **laager** near Loskop on the Little Thukela River. It was joined on 3 December by the Port Natal contingent. On 9 December, the Voortrekkers made a covenant with God at Danskraal on the Wasbankspruit in return for victory over the Zulu. The laagered *Wenkommando* routed the main Zulu army under Ndlela and Nzobo at **Ncome** on 16 December. Continuing its advance into Zululand, on 26 December the *Wenkommando* encamped on the **Mthonjaneni Heights** above the valley of the White Mfolozi River. The next day, a commando under **Karel Pieter Landman** and Port Natal forces under **Alexander Biggar** raided the valley and were ambushed and routed by the Zulu. On 28 December, the commando burned three *amaKhanda* in the **emaKhosini valley**. On 1 January 1839, they captured 5,000 **cattle**. The following day, the *Wenkommando* withdrew to the Sooilaer laager, which it reached on 8 January, and the campaign ended. On 25 March, the Voortrekkers concluded a peace with Dingane and began settling south of the Thukela River in the Republic of **Natalia**, while the Zulu king tried to restore his kingdom's fortunes to the north at the expense of the **Swazi kingdom**. *See also* RECONCILIATION, DAY OF.

**VOS'S NATIVES.** This small force of African levies (troops) raised in the Transvaal during the **Anglo-Zulu War** served with No. 5 **Column**. They took part in the raid of 15 February against the **abaQulusi** on Talaku Mountain. When No. 5 Column was attached in late February to Brevet Colonel **Henry Evelyn Wood**'s command, Vos's Natives apparently were incorporated into **Wood's Irregulars**.

**VRYHEID.** On 13 August, the *volksraad* (legislature) of the **New Republic** resolved to establish a capital for their new state. On 23 September, the name Vryheid, or Freedom, was adopted, reflecting the Boers' aspiration for self-government. The tiny village was laid out southwest of **Zungwini Mountain** in the typical grid pattern adopted by the Boers wherever they settled. *See also* PIETER-MARITZBURG.

**ekuVUKENI *iBUTHO*.** *InKosi* **Zibhebhu kaMaphitha** raised this *iButho* of **Mandlakazi** in his chiefdom after the 1st Partition of **Zululand**, in resumption of the prerogative of the great *amaKhosi* who preceded **Shaka**. Zibhebhu named it after one of his principal *imiZi*.

It participated in the victories at **Msebe** and **oNdini** during the 3rd **Zulu Civil War** but was defeated at **Tshaneni**. During the **uSuthu Rebellion**, it formed the Mandlakazi left horn at **Ivuna** and was routed. *See also* ekuVUKENI *umuZI*.

**ekuVUKENI** *umuZI*. On 20 July 1883, threatened by **uSuthu** advances on all sides during the 3rd **Zulu Civil War**, *inKosi* **Zibhebhu kaMaphitha** mustered his forces at ekuVukeni, his *umuZI* on the eastern slope of the Nongoma ridge in the southwest of his chiefdom, for his successful preemptive strike at **oNdini**. On 14 December 1883, the uSuthu concentrated at **ekuShumayeleni** for an attack on ekuVukeni, but Zibhebhu forestalled them with another preemptive strike.

**VUMANDABA kaNTATI (c. 1818–1883).** Enrolled in the uMkhulutshane *iButho*, Vumandaba likely took part in the **Voortrekker-Zulu War**. During the reign of King **Mpande kaSenzangakhona**, he became a trusted *iNceku* (personal attendant) of the king. He stayed aloof in the 2nd **Zulu Civil War**, and King **Cetshwayo kaMpande** confirmed him as *iNceku* on his accession in 1873. Vumandaba was prominent in the Zulu delegation that heard the British **ultimatum** on 11 December 1878. As the senior *inDuna* (officer) of the **uMcijo** *iButho* he fought at **Isandlwana**. After the 2nd Partition of **Zululand**, he rallied to the **uSuthu** cause. In the 3rd Zulu Civil War, he was killed in the rout at **oNdini**.

## – W –

**WAAIHOEK, TREATY OF.** *See* DISPUTED TERRITORY.

**WAGON.** *See* OX WAGON.

**WAKKERSTROOM DISTRICT.** The Wakkerstroom District of the **South African Republic** lay north of the **Utrecht District**, abutting the **Zulu kingdom** and the **Swazi kingdom**. It was first settled by whites in 1853, and only by 1859 did it have enough settlers to be proclaimed a district. Thereafter it steadily attracted immigrants because it was the healthiest district for **horses** and was excellent for wool farming.

**WEATHERLEY'S BORDER HORSE.** In late 1878, Lieutenant-Colonel Frederick Augustus Weatherley (1830–1879) began recruiting volunteers in the Transvaal for a unit of 60 mounted **irregulars** (initially called Weatherley's Border Lances) to fight in the **Anglo-Zulu War**. In early February 1879, a troop joined No. 5 **Column**. When No. 5 Column fell under Brevet Colonel **Henry Evelyn Wood**'s command later that month, Weatherley's troop joined No. 4 Column at **Khambula**. They fought at **Hlobane** with Lieutenant-Colonel **Redvers Henry Buller**'s force, and Weatherley (along with his 14-year-old son Rupert) was among the killed. The survivors fought at **Khambula** next day, but shortly afterward they left the camp for **Pretoria** and disbanded. The uniform seems to have been of corduroy with a red sash and a white hat.

**WEENEN CONTINGENT.** In April 1879, during the **Anglo-Zulu War**, the **Border Guard** in **Colonial Defensive District** No. I was reinforced by the Weenen Contingent from District II. The contingent was made up of reassembled members of the 3rd Regiment, **Natal Native Contingent** (NNC), which had been disbanded after **Isandlwana**, and of the reassigned **Newcastle Scouts**. It was mustered in traditional African fashion and no longer organized along standard British military lines as the NNC had been, but its morale remained poor.

**WEENEN MASSACRE.** *See* BLOUKRANS MASSACRE.

**WEENEN YEOMANRY.** A small **Natal Mounted Volunteer** unit formed in 1876 from among English-speaking settlers in Weenen County (later **Colonial Defensive District** No. II), the Weenen Yeomanry had its headquarters at **Weston**. In February 1879 during the **Anglo-Zulu War**, it was called upon to patrol the border with **Basutoland** in conjunction with the **Upper Tugela Defense Corps**. It mustered out in July 1879 and ceased to exist.

**WELSH REGIMENT, 1ST BATTALION.** Formerly the 41st Regiment until renamed in 1881 as a result of the **Childers Reforms**, the battalion was ordered out to South Africa in 1881 to reinforce the Natal Field Force in the last stages of the 1st **Boer War**. It then formed part of the **Natal garrison** until 1886. During the 3rd **Zulu Civil War**, five companies (one of which was mustered as **mounted infantry**) formed part of the **Etshowe Column** in September 1883 and were stationed at **Fort Curtis**. By September 1884, this force was reduced to two companies that remained as part of the garrison of the **Reserve Territory** until May 1886.

***WENKOMMANDO.*** The *Wenkommando*, or Winning Commando, was the name given to the Boer **commando** (militia) led by **Andries Wilhelmus Jacobus Pretorius** that defeated the Zulu at the battle of **Ncome** on 16 December 1838 during the **Voortrekker-Zulu War**. It withdrew after its setback in the battle of the **White Mfolozi** on 27 December.

**WESTERN VLEI REDOUBT.** In the panic after **Isandlwana**, the **Durban laager** was fortified against possible Zulu attack during the **Anglo-Zulu War**. The northern approaches to the town were guarded by the **Durban Redoubt**, and the eastern and southern approaches were protected by the sea, but there was no fortification to defend the western approaches. Accordingly, on 5 February 1879, a gang of convicts built a redoubt on rising ground overlooking the Western Vlei, where guns or troops could be positioned if the need arose. It never did.

**WESTON.** In February 1879 during the **Anglo-Zulu War**, St. John's Church at Weston in **Colonial Defensive District** No. II was designated a defense post for local settlers. Plans were made to loophole the walls and erect a sod enclosure if an emergency arose, and arms and ammunition were stored there. It never became necessary to erect the planned defenses.

**WHITE MFOLOZI, BATTLE OF (1838).** After its victory at **Ncome** in the **Voortrekker-Zulu War**, the *Wenkommando* pushed deeper into **Zululand**, one of the objectives of its punitive expedition being to recover the livestock previously captured from the Boers by the Zulu. On Christmas Day 1838, the Boers seized an apparent Zulu spy, Bhongoza kaMefu, near their **laager** at **uMgungundlovu**. He was in fact a decoy and persuaded the Boers that all of King **Dingane kaSenzangakhona**'s **cattle** were in the valley of the White Mfolozi River to the north. Accordingly, on 26 December the Boers moved their camp to the **Mthonjaneni Heights** overlooking the river and the **Mahlabathini Plain**. On 27 December, Bhongoza guided about 300 mounted Boers under **Karel Pieter Landman**, as well as about 70 Port Natal (**Durban**) Africans on foot under **Alexander Biggar**, down into the valley close to where the uPhathe stream flows into the White Mfolozi through a rocky kloof (ravine). The Boers mistook Zulu creeping among the rocks and bushes with shields on their backs for cattle, and they were taken by surprise when on a signal the Zulu attacked them from all sides. Landman wanted to make a stand, but **Johan Hendrik (Hans Dons) de Lange** persuaded him that the only feasible course was to break out onto the open ground across the river. The Zulu did not press home their attack, and the mounted Boers fell back west across the Mahlabathini Plain, alternately firing and retiring, followed by the straggling Port Natal contingent.

When the Boers reached the White Mfolozi again, where the Mkhumbane stream flows into it from the south, they tried to cross but were ambushed by an *iButho* lying in wait for them. Four Boers were killed, as were Alexander Biggar and almost the entire Port Natal contingent. The mounted Boers broke through and were closely pursued until they regained their camp 14 miles away. Zulu losses are unknown, but the Boers quite unrealistically claimed they had killed 1,000.

Their setback persuaded the Boers that they had achieved all they could on their punitive expedition, and the *Wenkommando* withdrew early in the new year. The Zulu gained some consolation from their success, but they realized only a stalemate had been achieved and that it was necessary to negotiate a peace with the Voortrekkers. *See also* COMMANDO SYSTEM, BOER; TACTICS, AFRICAN INFANTRY LEVIES; TACTICS UP TO 1879, ZULU.

**WHITE MFOLOZI CAMP.** *See* FORT ULUNDI.

**WHITE MFOLOZI RECONNAISSANCE IN FORCE (1879).** During the 2nd Invasion of the **Anglo-Zulu War**, about 500 mounted troops of **Wood's Flying Column** under Lieutenant-Colonel **Redvers Henry Buller** crossed the White Mfolozi River on 3 July 1879 to reconnoiter a suitable position to fight the subsequent battle of **Ulundi** in the **Mahlabathini Plain**. They were lured forward by mounted Zulu scouts and fell into an ambush of several thousand Zulu that *inKosi* **Zibhebhu kaMaphitha** had skillfully laid between the **kwaNodwengu** and **oNdini** *amaKhanda*. Buller's men only narrowly extricated themselves with support from covering artillery and infantry fire from **Fort Ulundi** and the British double **laager** on the south side of the river. Three British troopers were killed, and there were many considerable acts of bravery in rescuing men who were unhorsed or wounded. The Victoria Cross was awarded to Captain Lord William Leslie de la Poer Beresford, 9th Lancers, and Commandant Henry Cecil Dudgeon D'Arcy and Sergeant Edmund O'Toole of the **Frontier Light Horse**. The Distinguished Conduct Medal went to Sergeant-Major Simeon Kambule, **Edendale Horse**. *See also* TACTICS, BRITISH MOUNTED TROOPS; TACTICS UP TO 1879, ZULU.

**WILLIAMSTOWN LAAGER.** On the eve of the **Anglo-Zulu War**, the jail in the little settlement of Williamstown in **Colonial Defensive District** No. VI began to be fortified on the orders of the **Natal** government as a place of refuge for local settlers. A **laager** was completed by March 1879. A small number of arms and ammunition were stored there, but the post was never occupied.

**WOLF HILL.** When advancing from **Khambula** during the 2nd Invasion of the **Anglo-Zulu War**, to effect a junction with the 2nd Division, **South African Field Force**, **Wood's Flying Column** threw up entrenchments when it encamped at Wolf Hill between 12 and 25 May 1879.

**WOLF TRAP FORT.** In March 1879 during the **Anglo-Zulu War**, the **Ixopo Native Contingent** from **Colonial Defensive District** No. IV in the south of **Natal** arrived in District VII to reinforce the troops guarding the Natal border with **Zululand**. In May, to defend their camp, they built the stone-walled Wolf Trap Fort (in local parlance, a "wolf" is actually a hyena). They occupied the fort until 26 August, when they returned home.

**WOLSELEY, SIR GARNET JOSEPH (1833–1913).** Wolseley entered the army in 1852 and saw service in the 2nd Anglo-Burmese War (1852–1853), Crimean War (1855–1856), Indian Mutiny (1857–1858), and 2nd China (Opium) War (1860–1861). He suffered many wounds, but his military reputation was secured. He led the Red River Expedition in Canada (1870) and was knighted. He commanded in the 2nd Asante War (1873–1874) that was regarded as a model campaign, and he was promoted to major-general. His handpicked staff officers, known as the Ashanti Ring or Wolseley Ring, formed a group in the British army that supported him over issues of **army reform**. In 1875, he was appointed administrator of Natal to forward the cause of **confederation** in South Africa. In 1878, he was promoted to lieutenant-general and appointed high commissioner and governor-general of Cyprus. During the **Anglo-Zulu War**, Wolseley was sent out in May 1879 on special service as high commissioner in southeastern Africa, governor of Natal and the Transvaal, and commander-in-chief of the forces in South Africa with the local rank of general. He arrived too late for the battle of **Ulundi** but sent in columns to pacify **Zululand** in July–September. His expedient 1st Partition of Zululand proved a recipe for civil war.

In December 1879, Wolseley brought the war against the **Pedi** in the Transvaal to a successful conclusion. He commanded in the Egyptian campaign of 1882, was promoted to full general, and was created Baron Wolseley of Cairo. He next commanded the Gordon Relief Expedition (1884–1885), in which he did not enjoy the success of his previous campaigns. He was elevated to Viscount Wolseley in 1885. Throughout his career, and in his many staff appointments, Wolseley pursued the reform of the British army. In 1894, he was created field marshal, and he was appointed commander-in-chief of the British army the following year, but his health was in sad decline and he retired in 1900.

**WOLSELEY'S ZULULAND SETTLEMENT.** *See* ZULULAND, 1ST PARTITION OF.

**WOMEN, BOER.** *See* BLOUKRANS MASSACRE; DRESS, BOER WOMEN; LAAGER, BOER WAGON; MEDICAL ATTENTION, BOER; eTHALENI, BATTLE OF; VEGLAER, BATTLE OF.

**WOMEN, NATAL SETTLER.** *See* FORT NAPIER; POINT LAAGER.

**WOMEN, ZULU.** *See* *iBUTHO* SYSTEM DURING THE ZULU KINGDOM; CIVILIANS IN WARTIME ZULULAND; *inDLU*; DRESS, ZULU WOMEN; *inGXOTHA*; *iKHANDA*; LOGISTICS, ZULU; MAQONGQO HIILS, BATTLE OF; NDABUKO ka-MPANDE; NDONDAKUSUKA, BATTLE OF; NONKWENK-WEZIYEZULU STRONGHOLD; NTUNJAMBILI, RAID AT; POLITICAL ORGANIZATION, ZULU; QUARTER IN BATTLE; RITUAL PREPARATION FOR WAR, ZULU; TSHANENI, BAT-TLE OF; *umuZI*.

**WOOD, SIR HENRY EVELYN (1838–1919).** Commissioned in 1852 into the Royal Navy, Wood saw service in the Crimean War (1854–1856) before transferring into the army in 1855. He fought in the Indian Mutiny (1858–1860) and in 1859 was awarded the Victoria Cross. He attended Staff College in 1863. He served next in the 2nd Asante War (1873–1874), was made brevet colonel, and became a member of the Ashanti Ring, a group of officers supporting General **Sir Garnet Joseph Wolseley**. In 1878, Wood commanded a column in the 9th **Cape Frontier War**. He was on special service as a brevet colonel in command of No. 4 **Column** during the 1st Invasion of the **Anglo-Zulu War** when his forces skirmished actively with the Zulu in northwestern **Zululand**. His crucial victory over the main Zulu army at **Khambula** effaced his significant defeat at **Hlobane** the previous day. During the 2nd Invasion of the war, he commanded **Wood's Flying Column** with the local rank of brigadier-general and was present at **Ulundi**. He was knighted at the end of the war. In February 1881, he took command in the last stages of the 1st **Boer War** with the local rank of major-general and reluctantly concluded a peace in March on the instructions of the Liberal government. While acting high commissioner for South Africa in 1881, he presided over the meeting at **Nhlazatshe Mountain** that upheld the 1st Partition of Zululand. He was confirmed as major-general in 1881. In 1882, he served in the Egyptian campaign and was appointed sirdar of the Egyptian army, resigning in 1885. He then held home commands and was promoted to general in 1895. He was adjutant-general at the Horse Guards from 1897 until his retirement in 1901. He was created field marshal in 1903.

**WOOD'S FLYING COLUMN.** On 13 April 1879, Brigadier-General **Henry Evelyn Wood**'s forces at **Khambula** (3,200) were restyled Wood's Flying Column, which was to cooperate with the 2nd Division, **South African Field Force**, in its advance on the **oNdini** *iKhanda* from the northwest. Wood began his movement on 5 May by way of **Wolf Hill** and **Munhla Hill** and effected his junction with the 2nd Division on 3 June at the **Tshotshosi** River. On 5 June, mounted men of the Flying Column and the 2nd Division encountered the Zulu in a skirmish at **Zungeni Mountain**. The joint column halted from 7 to 17 June at the Ntinini River to bring up supplies and sent out extensive patrols to clear the area of Zulu. The joint advance resumed on 18 June. On 20 and 24 June, the Flying Column sent out mounted patrols to skirmish with the Zulu. On 26 June, Wood led a strong patrol into the **emaKhosini valley** and destroyed nine *amaKhanda*. On 2 July, the joint column formed a double **laager** and built **Fort Ulundi** on the south bank of the White Mfolozi. The next day, Lieutenant-Colonel **Redvers Henry Buller** led the **White Mfolozi Reconnaissance in Force** into the **Mahlabathini Plain**. The force, consisting of mounted men of Wood's Flying Column, narrowly escaped from a Zulu ambush.

The Flying Column formed the advance portion of the infantry **square** at the battle of **Ulundi** on 4 July, and its mounted men charged out of the front of the square during the pursuit. After the battle, the Flying Column remained on Mthonjaneni between 6 and 8 July while Buller raided south to **kwaMagwaza**. On 9 July, it started retiring to **St. Paul's**, where General **Sir Garnet Joseph Wolseley** broke it up on 31 July. Those units required for the final pacification of Zululand became **Baker Russell's Column**.

**WOOD'S IRREGULARS.** In late 1878, Lieutenant-General Lord **Chelmsford** authorized the raising of African levies (troops) in the

Transvaal for No. 4 **Column** and for them to be maintained like other imperial troops. For the most part, the levies, many of them of **Swazi** origin, were labor tenants on white farms pressed into service by the *landdroste* (magistrates) of the **Wakkerstroom** and **Utrecht Districts**. Two battalions of about 700 men under white officers were formed and were organized along less formal lines than was the **Natal Native Contingent**. The 1st Battalion served with Lieutenant-Colonel **Redvers Henry Buller**'s force at **Hlobane**, and the 2nd Battalion with Lieutenant-Colonel **John Cecil Russell**'s, both suffering heavy casualties. The contingent of *umNtwana* **Hamu kaNzibe**'s **Ngenetsheni**, who had defected to the British in March and joined Wood's Irregulars, was also with Russell's force. Wood's Irregulars were indignant at the way in which the white troops had abandoned them during the rout, and most defected, leaving only a handful to fight at **Khambula**. Brevet Colonel **Henry Evelyn Wood** succeeded in reassembling some of the unit and it marched with **Wood's Flying Column** during the 2nd Invasion of the **Anglo-Zulu War**, fighting at **Ulundi**. The Irregulars then dispersed.

Many of Wood's Irregulars wore full Swazi war panoply and retained their elaborate headdresses in battle. They carried **shields** and **spears**, and 10 men per company received **percussion firearms**. All wore a strip of colored cloth around the head or upper arm to differentiate them from the Zulu. The Wakkerstroom men's cloth was red and white, the Utrecht men's blue and white, and the Ngenetsheni's red or yellow. *See also* FAIRLIE'S SWAZI.

**WOOD'S SCOUTS.** In November 1878, Brevet Colonel **Henry Evelyn Wood** recruited African scouts from the **Luneburg** district and allocated six men to each company of the 90th **Regiment** (Perthshire Volunteers Light Infantry) to perform outpost duties. They served with the regiment until the end of the **Anglo-Zulu War**, first in No. 4 **Column**, and then in **Wood's Flying Column**.

– X –

**ekuXEDINI** *umuZI.* This *umuZi* of *inKosi* **Zibhebhu kaMaphitha** was strategically placed 10 miles east of his **ekuVukeni** *umuZi* in the southwest of this chiefdom. He regularly mustered his forces here during the 3rd **Zulu Civil War** for operations against the **uSuthu.**

**XHOSA PEOPLE.** *See* CAPE FRONTIER WARS.

## – Z –

*imiZI. See umuZI.*

*umuZI.* Tens of thousands of scattered *imiZi*, or homesteads, each looking like a tiny village, dotted the Zulu countryside. Self-sufficient and supported by its own grazing and agricultural land, each *umuZi* was the home of an *umNumzane*, or married headman, and his wives and their children. A headman usually had two or three wives, but a man of wealth and status might have as many as a dozen. Every *umuZi* was circular and built on sloping ground for drainage, with the main entrance at the bottom of the incline. The *izinDlu*, or huts, which should be seen as separate rooms in a single home, were arranged hierarchically in a crescent, with the *inDlu* of the chief wife at the top and the others dropping progressively in status, so those of retainers or dependents were nearest the entrance.

The *izinDlu* surrounded the *isiBaya*, a kraal or cattle-fold, with its protective palisade, where the **amaDlozi**, or ancestral shades, were believed to dwell and where sacrifice was made to them. Deep pits with funnel-shaped mouths were dug in the *isiBaya* to store grain and seed-corn during winter, and to conceal them from raiders. The storage huts for beer, vegetables, and grain were usually built between the *izinDlu* and the outer palisade surrounding the entire *umuZi*.

On the death of an *umNumzane*, his *umuZi* would break up, or segment, and each of his sons would have the right to establish his own *umuZi*. In practice, though, during the time of the **Zulu kingdom**, the *iButho* system regulated the creation of new *imiZi* through the control of the process of marriage. These *imiZi* were the basis of Zulu social and economic life, and the basic objective of the *iButho* system was to extract male and female labor from them, as well as food, for the benefit of the Zulu state. In time of war, these *imiZi*, constructed of combustible materials, were very vulnerable to the looting of their grain stores and livestock, and they were easily burned by armies intending to defeat their inhabitants or drive them away. *See also* CATTLE, ZULU; CIVILIANS IN WARTIME ZULULAND.

**ZIBHEBHU kaMAPHITHA (c. 1841–1904).** Enrolled in the **uMxhapho** *iButho*, Zibhebhu succeeded in 1872 as the *inKosi* of the **Mandlakazi** people. He supported his cousin, *umNtwana* **Cetshwayo kaMpande**, in the 2nd **Zulu Civil War** but subsequently exerted his regional authority to flout royal control and forged strong trading contacts with the colonial world. He advised against war with Britain but nevertheless fought throughout the **Anglo-Zulu War**. The senior *inDuna* (officer) of the **uDloko** *iButho*, he was wounded at **Isandlwana** and was one of the junior commanders at **Khambula**. He commanded the mounted scouts who drew the British **White Mfolozi reconnaissance in force** into an ambush.

Zibhebhu **submitted** to the British on 26 August 1879 and was appointed one of the 13 chiefs in the 1st Partition of **Zululand**. Thereafter he collaborated with the British to suppress the aspirations of the deposed royal house. In the 2nd Partition, he received an enlarged territory in northeastern Zululand as a counterweight to King **Cetshwayo kaMpande**'s restored territory in central Zululand. During the 3rd Zulu Civil War, Zibhebhu used his innovative military skills to defeat the **uSuthu** at **Msebe** and finally crush them at **oNdini**. Following these victories, Zibhebhu ravaged uSuthu territory. In 1884, King **Dinuzulu kaCetshwayo**, in alliance with the Boers, defeated Zibhebhu at **Tshaneni** and forced him to take refuge with his people in the **Reserve Territory**.

Following their annexation of the Colony of Zululand, in November 1887 the British restored Zibhebhu to his chiefdom. In January 1888, the resident magistrate of the Ndwandwe District of the British Colony of Zululand, **Richard Hallowes Addison**, assigned Zibhebhu and his Mandlakazi a greatly enlarged location to cow the neighboring uSuthu. Addison assisted Zibhebhu in evicting 5,000 uSuthu living within the new boundaries, and despite a reduction of the size of the location in April 1888, this action greatly embittered the uSuthu and contributed materially to the outbreak of the **uSuthu Rebellion**. Zibhebhu supported the British forces, but Dinuzulu surprised and routed him at **Ivuna**. With the suppression of the rebellion, the British finally accepted that their ally Zibhebhu was a threat to the future peace of Zululand. In 1889, he and his followers were resettled in southern Zululand. In 1898, the colonial authorities allowed Zibhebhu to return to his old chiefdom as part of a general settlement of the warring Zulu factions. *See also* BOERS AND THE ZULULAND CAMPAIGN OF 1884; BOUNDARIES AND COLONIAL CONTROL IN ZULULAND.

**ZIWEDU kaMPANDE (c. 1834–?).** Enrolled in the **uThulwana** *iButho*, *umNtwana* Ziwedu was King **Cetshwayo kaMpande**'s favorite half-brother and second in status among the *abaNtwana* only to **Hamu kaNzibe**. During the **Anglo-Zulu War**, Ziwedu was the senior Zulu commander at **Ulundi** and surrendered to the British on 16 August 1879. He was placed under *inKosi* **Zibhebhu kaMaphitha** in the 1st Partition of **Zululand** and was active in promoting Cetshwayo's restoration. During the 3rd **Zulu Civil War**, he joined in the **uSuthu** offensive against Hamu. After the uSuthu defeat at **oNdini**, he continued the struggle against the **Mandlakazi** and **Ngenetsheni** from the **Nkandla Forest** until 1884. During the **uSuthu Rebellion**, he remained loyal to the British administration and was raided in retaliation by the uSuthu under King **Dinuzulu kaCetshwayo**. He took refuge with his adherents at the **Ivuna** magistracy and suffered heavy losses of **cattle** during the battle there. He and his people were evacuated to **Nkonjeni** and left British protection in August 1888 with the final suppression of the rebellion.

**ZUID-AFRIKAANSCHE REPUBLIEK.** *See* SOUTH AFRICAN REPUBLIC.

**eZULANENI.** On 4 June 1879 during the 2nd Invasion of the **Anglo-Zulu War**, a patrol of **Baker's Horse** from **Wood's Flying Column** had a slight skirmish with a force of Zulu quartered in this cluster of four *imiZi* belonging to *inKosi* **Sihayo kaXongo**, about 400 yards to the west of Zungeni Mountain. Three wagons and an ammunition cart, captured from the British at **Isandlwana**, were parked outside one of the *imiZi*. The following day, **irregular** horse under Lieutenant-Colonel **Redvers Henry Buller** put eZulaneni to the torch but were forced to withdraw under effective Zulu fire. *See also* ZUNGENI MOUNTAIN SKIRMISH.

**ZULU BORDER WITH NATAL IN 1879.** The British offensive into **Zululand** during the **Anglo-Zulu War** left British territory vulnerable to Zulu counterthrusts, especially in the broken terrain of the **Natal** frontier, where a Zulu raid would be less easily detected and countered than in the open country of the Transvaal. Settlers were additionally in dread of a Zulu raid because they feared it might spark off an uprising among colonial Africans. All the colonial authorities could do for defense was to hold the **laagers** in the towns and countryside and raise a force that eventually numbered over 8,000 African part-time levies and border guards in the border districts (in Natal, these were **Colonial Defensive Districts** I, VI, and VII) to dissuade the Zulu from raiding the farmlands between the fortified points. Otherwise, it was hoped that the frontier rivers, which would be unfordable in the rainy season between January and March (except at the drifts, which could be guarded), would act as a deterrent.

The panic after **Isandlwana** exposed the vulnerability of the border region with Zululand, which is why the lieutenant-governor of Natal, **Sir Henry Gascoyne Bulwer**, so vehemently opposed Lieutenant-General Lord **Chelmsford**'s decision in March 1879 to adopt the "active defense" along the border. Chelmsford ordered the Natal forces to create a diversion in favor of the **Eshowe Relief Column** by demonstrating along the border line and raiding into Zululand itself, thereby (in theory) forcing the Zulu to abandon the border zone and securing Natal from invasion. Accordingly, the colonial forces in District VII demonstrated on 24 March and raided on 2 and 3 April, and those in District VI demonstrated on 27 March. To divert the Zulu from his developing 2nd Invasion of the Anglo-Zulu War, Chelmsford ordered more raids. On 20 May, a substantial raid was launched from District VII, and another on 28 May from District VI. Bulwer's fears that these raids would achieve little and only provoke retaliation was borne out by the successful Zulu counterraid at **Middle Drift** on 25 June, which proved the frontier defenses sadly wanting. It was fortunate for the colonial border region that the war came to an end before the Zulu attempted further raids. *See also* BORDER GUARD, NATAL; CIVIL–MILITARY RELATIONS.

**ZULU CIVIL WAR, 1ST (1840).** In September 1839, *umNtwana* **Mpande kaSenzangakhona** fled with his adherents to the Republic of **Natalia** in fear that his half-brother King **Dingane kaSenzanga-khona** was intending to order his death. On 27 October 1839, Mpande struck an alliance with the Boers to mount a joint campaign against Dingane. In return for their making him king, he agreed to cede them the lands south of the Thukela River as well as **St. Lucia Bay**. On 14 January 1840, Mpande's army under **Nongalaza kaNondela** and the Boer *Beeskommando* under **Andries Wilhelmus Jacobus Pretorius** invaded **Zululand**. The Boers had not advanced farther than the Ncome River when on 29 January Mpande's forces engaged and destroyed Dingane's army under *inKosi* **Ndlela kaSompisi** at the battle of the **Maqongqo Hills** in northern Zululand. Dingane fled, and on 10 February the Boers recognized Mpande as Zulu king.

**ZULU CIVIL WAR, 2ND (1856).** In 1839, King **Mpande kaSenzan-gakhona** had acknowledged his son *umNtwana* **Cetshwayo ka-Mpande** as his heir. Yet Mpande increasingly feared Cetshwayo's growing power and popularity and from 1852 began to foster the claim of his favorite son, *umNtwana* **Mbuyazi kaMpande**, to succeed him. Mpande tried to separate the rival *abaNtwana* by placing Mbuyazi and his followers, the **iziGqoza**, in northern **Zululand** and Cetshwayo and his **uSuthu** following in southern Zululand. In a bid to settle the issue by force of arms, the two *abaNtwana* challenged each other to a mock hunt at the confluence of the Black and White Mfolozi rivers, but at the last moment the iziGqoza lost their nerve and withdrew. To help Mbuyazi, in November 1856 Mpande allocated him a tract of land in southeastern Zululand where the king's personal influence was greatest, and which was close to **Natal**, where Mbuyazi could flee for sanctuary, or from where he might secure military support. Mbuyazi did gain the assistance of **John Dunn** and his force of gunmen known as the **iziNqobo**, but Cetshwayo pursued Mbuyazi with an uSuthu army much larger than that of the iziGqoza and forced it and its **civilian** dependents against the swollen Thukela River. On 2 December 1856, the uSuthu utterly destroyed the iziGqoza and their iziNqobo allies at the battle of **Ndondakusuka**, killing Mbuyazi and five of his brothers. Mpande was left with no choice but to accept Cetshwayo as his successor, and Cetshwayo subsequently secured his position by purging further potential rivals.

**ZULU CIVIL WAR, 3RD (1883–1884).** In terms of the 2nd Partition of **Zululand**, the British returned the exiled King **Cetshwayo ka-Mpande** to the central portion of his former kingdom in January 1883. Fighting immediately broke out between his **uSuthu** adherents and their principal opponents in northern Zululand, *umNtwana* **Zibhebhu kaMaphitha**'s **Mandlakazi** and *umNtwana* **Hamu kaNzibe**'s **Ngenetsheni**. On 20 March, Zibhebhu, supported by white **mercenaries**, routed the uSuthu army at **Msebe**. After more inconclusive fighting, on 21 July Zibhebhu routed the uSuthu army at **oNdini**. Cetshwayo took refuge in the **Nkandla Forest** in the **Reserve Territory** and was followed there by many uSuthu. During August and September, Zibhebhu and Hamu ravaged central and coastal Zululand while Boers from the **South African Republic** began to occupy northwestern Zululand. In late September, the **Etshowe Column**, drawn from the **Natal garrison**, moved into the Reserve Territory to support the African levies, raised by **Melmoth Osborn**, the resident commissioner, to maintain order. On 15 October, Cetshwayo took refuge with the British in **Eshowe** while chaotic fighting continued across Zululand with the Mandlakazi and Ngenetsheni still in the ascendant.

Cetshwayo died on 8 February 1884 and was succeeded by his minor son **Dinuzulu kaCetshwayo** under the guardianship of his uncles. On 2 May, Dinuzulu met the Boers at **Hlobane Mountain** to negotiate an alliance, and on 21 May a committee of the Boer mercenaries known as **Dinuzulu's Volunteers** proclaimed him king of the Zulu and promised him military assistance against Zibhebhu in return for land. On 5 June, the Boers and uSuthu routed Zibhebhu at **Tshaneni Mountain** in northeastern Zululand and went on to ravage Mandlakazi and Ngenetsheni territory. Zibhebhu and his adherents took refuge in the Reserve Territory. On 16 August, the Boers proclaimed the **New Republic**, incorporating the land ceded them by Dinuzulu, and made claim to a "protectorate" over the rest of Zululand outside the Reserve Territory (**Eastern Zululand**). Meanwhile, in the Nkandla Forest in the Reserve Territory, where many uSuthu were concentrated under *umNtwana* **Dabulamanzi kaMpande** and were resisting British authority, Osborn and his levies, supported by British troops, conducted military operations until the uSuthu **submitted** in late August. The fighting ended for the time being, but the bitter animosities that divided the uSuthu and their foes remained deeply seated and resurfaced during the **uSuthu Rebellion** of 1888.

The scale of military operations in the 3rd Zulu Civil War was much smaller than in the **Anglo-Zulu War**, when the Zulu had fielded armies of over 20,000. In no battle of the civil war did the combined forces of both uSuthu and Mandlakazi exceed 9,000 combatants. The British deployed no more than about 600 regular troops and 300 mounted African auxiliaries, as well as several thousand untrained levies. *See also* NHLAZATSHE MOUNTAIN.

**ZULU INVASION SCARE (1861).** The Invasion Scare that so galvanized settler society in **Natal** in 1861 was inextricably linked with the issues of the Zulu succession and the **Disputed Territory**. In June 1861, *umNtwana* **Cetshwayo kaMpande** repudiated his cession of March 1861 of land east of the Ncome River to the Boers of the **Utrecht District** in return for handing over some rivals to the Zulu throne. The Boers moved into the territory anyway, took up defensive positions in their **laagers**, and called on the **South African Republic** for military assistance. Cetshwayo began mobilizing his *amaButho* (regiments) to prevent the Boers' making good their claim. The Natal colonists, who were suspicious of his intentions after Cetshwayo's destruction of rival claimants to the throne in the 2nd **Zulu Civil War**, jumped to the conclusion that he was planning to invade Natal to seize *umNtwana* Mkhungo kaMpande, another rival to the throne, who in 1857 had taken refuge in the colony under the protection of Bishop **John William Colenso**. The British troops of the **Natal garrison** rushed to the border and built fortified bases, while the frontier farmers trekked away to the security of the towns. Cetshwayo misunderstood this military activity as preparation for a British invasion of **Zululand** in favor of his rival. So in July 1861, he withdrew his *amaButho* from the Disputed Territory and concentrated them along the Natal border. Since neither side wanted a confrontation, the crisis subsided by August 1861. But the Invasion Scare caused Cetshwayo to lose the crucial opportunity to deal immediately and decisively with the Boers settling in the Disputed Territory, and the issue would continue to destabilize relations in the region until the **Anglo-Zulu War**.

**ZULU KINGDOM.** The Zulu kingdom lasted only a little over six decades in the 19th century before being overthrown in war, broken into pieces, consigned to civil war, and eventually annexed piecemeal by its rapacious colonial neighbors. It was founded in the second decade of the 19th century by King **Shaka kaSenzangakhona,** who brought it to its greatest extent by the late 1820s through conquest and diplomacy. He was assassinated by his half-brother and successor Dingane kaMpande, who was defeated in the **Voortrekker-Zulu War** and then overthrown in the 1st **Zulu Civil War** by his half-brother **Mpande kaSenzangakhona.** Mpande managed with some success to balance his reduced kingdom between the competing ambitions of his colonial neighbors in **Natal** and the **South African Republic,** but when these coalesced in the reign of his son **Cetshwayo kaMpande,** who had secured his succession in the 2nd Zulu Civil War, the kingdom fell to invasion during the **Anglo-Zulu War.** The 1st Partition of **Zululand** effectively marked the demise of the kingdom, although it pursued a diminishing half-life in the 1880s during the 2nd and 3rd Partitions and the 3rd Zulu Civil War, until Cetshwayo's son and successor **Dinuzulu kaMpande** was deposed by the British with the failure of the **uSuthu Rebellion.** The region generally comprising the historic Zulu kingdom is also referred to loosely as "Zululand."

**ZULU UPRISING OF 1906 (BHAMBATHA REBELLION).** The economy of **Natal** went into recession after the **Anglo-Boer (South African) War,** and the imposition of a poll tax on an African peasantry already deeply resentful of colonial rule led to armed resistance in February 1906. The uprising in the Natal midlands was no sooner put down by the Natal militia when Bhambatha kaMancinza, a Zondi *inKosi* in the southern part of the province of **Zululand,** began guerrilla operations with support from other local chiefdoms from a base in the **Nkandla Forest.** Their forces were finally defeated with heavy losses on 10 June 1906 at Mome Gorge. Bhambatha was killed, as was *inKosi* **Mehlokazulu kaSihayo.** The Natal troops then withdrew from Zululand. Further outbreaks followed in Maphumulo in northeastern Natal, and operations continued until August. King **Dinuzulu kaCetshwayo** was subsequently imprisoned for harboring rebels.

The Natal militia put down the uprising ruthlessly. As many as 4,000 Africans were killed in the struggle, as were about 24 whites.

**ZULULAND.** It is difficult to say what territory precisely comprises Zululand, for its boundaries have changed substantially over the years through treaty, partition, and administrative reorganization. At is furthest extent, when in the second decade of the 19th century the power of King **Shaka kaSenzangakhona** was at its height, Zulu dominance extended over all the lands from the **Drakensberg** in the west to the Indian Ocean in the east, in the north from the southern reaches of what are now the states of Swaziland and Mozambique, across the present-day Province of KwaZulu-Natal in the Republic of South Africa, to the borderlands of the Province of the Eastern Cape in the south. Yet Zululand does have a historic heartland in the northern part of KwaZulu-Natal between the Phongolo River to the north, the Thukela River to the south, and the Mzinyathi River to the west. This was the area generally referred to as "Zululand" from the early 1840s onward. *See also* BOUNDARY AWARD; DISPUTED TERRITORY; KLIP RIVER REPUBLIC; NATAL–ZULULAND BOUNDARY; NEW REPUBLIC; PROVISO B; RESERVE TERRITORY; UTRECHT DISTRICT; ZULU KINGDOM; ZULULAND, BRITISH COLONY OF; ZULULAND, 1ST PARTITION OF; ZULULAND, 2ND PARTITION OF; ZULULAND, 3RD PARTITION OF.

**ZULULAND, 1ST PARTITION OF (1879).** Following defeat in the **Anglo-Zulu War** and the capture of King **Cetshwayo kaMpande**, on 1 September 1879 the Zulu *amaKhosi* (chiefs) assembled at General **Sir Garnet Joseph Wolseley**'s camp at **kwaSishwili** accepted the peace terms he laid down. The Zulu monarchy was suppressed, and the former kingdom was fragmented into 13 chiefdoms, each under a chief appointed by Wolseley. Although formally independent, these chiefs accepted the arbitration of a British resident official.

In devising the partition, Wolseley was following the instructions of the British government to avoid the expense and responsibility of direct annexation but to ensure the security of Zululand's British-ruled neighbors. Wolseley knew that by abolishing the Zulu monarchy he was also fatally emasculating the centralized **iButho** system on which it rested. None of the appointed chiefs would command anything approaching the military power previously deployed by the Zulu kings and so would no longer pose a military threat. These appointed chiefs would also be insecure in their authority and fear a resurgent Zulu royal house. They could thus be counted on to collaborate with the British to stifle royalist ambitions, and **Zululand** would be kept as weak and divided as desired.

With this in mind, Wolseley apportioned the two strategic chiefdoms along the southern border of Zululand with **Natal** to chiefs considered reliable. Both **Hlubi kaMota Molife** and **John Dunn** had fought on the British side in the **Anglo-Zulu War**, both were aliens in Zululand, and their chiefdoms would act as a buffer between Natal and possibly less amenable appointed chiefs to the north of them. In northern Zululand, where royalist supporters, or the **uSuthu**, were particularly strong, Wolseley appointed two powerful and ambitious Zulu magnates as chiefs to suppress them: *umNtwana* **Hamu kaNzibe** of the **Ngenetsheni** and *inKosi* **Zibhebhu kaMaphitha** of the **Mandlakazi**. In central Zululand, sandwiched between these four chiefs, Wolseley appointed nine others on account of their record of collaboration with the British, or their early **submission**. Many had no hereditary status in their new chiefdoms and would find it hard to assert any authority.

Wolseley's pragmatic scheme to neutralize Zululand by dividing it against itself rapidly and inevitably provided a recipe for disastrous internecine conflict. *See also* BOUNDARIES AND COLONIAL CONTROL IN ZULULAND; ZULULAND, 2ND PARTITION OF; ZULU CIVIL WAR, 3RD.

**ZULULAND, 2ND PARTITION OF (1882).** The **uSuthu** and other victims of the 1st Partition of **Zululand** soon began to draw together to resist their oppressors, particularly *umNtwana* **Hamu kaNzibe** and *inKosi* **Zibhebhu kaMaphitha**. They first took the route of negotiations. In May 1880, and again in April 1882, the uSuthu sent deputations to **Pietermaritzburg** to petition for the restoration of the monarchy. At a meeting at **Nhlazatshe** on 31 August 1881, Major-General **Evelyn Wood**, the acting high commissioner for southeast Africa, confirmed that the British intended to uphold the settlement.

Sporadic fighting broke out in late 1881 between the uSuthu and the enemies, but both sides drew back from a major clash.

Meanwhile, the exiled King **Cetshwayo kaMpande** petitioned the Colonial Office repeatedly to be restored to Zululand, and his pleas bore fruit when officials began to admit that the 1st Partition was breaking down. In August 1882, they permitted Cetshwayo to travel to London to plead his cause. The colonial secretary, the Earl of Kimberley, was under pressure from **Natal** officials who feared a reunited Zululand, and he believed he had an obligation to the 13 appointed chiefs. Accordingly, Cetshwayo was pressured to assent on 11 December 1882 to terms for his restoration that he found deeply disappointing. His authority was confined to the central portion of his former kingdom, including Hamu's and eight other former chiefs' territories, under the supervision of the British. He was hemmed in to the northeast by Zibhebhu, who was awarded an enlarged chiefdom that included the uSuthu heartland. To the south, as a further check against Cetshwayo's ambitions, a **Reserve Territory** was created out of **John Dunn**'s and **Hlubi kaMota Molife**'s chiefdoms as a military buffer for Natal and as a sanctuary for those Zulu who wished to avoid living under Cetshwayo's authority. It was to be administered by officials recruited from Natal.

The 2nd Partition proved even more disastrous than the 1st, for Cetshwayo's return to Zululand in January 1883 only intensified the simmering conflict between the uSuthu and their foes, and the 3rd **Zulu Civil War** immediately broke out. *See also* BOUNDARIES AND COLONIAL CONTROL IN ZULULAND.

**ZULULAND, 3RD PARTITION OF (1884).** In return for their aid in defeating the **Mandlakazi** and **Ngenetsheni** in the climax to the 3rd **Zulu Civil War**, on 16 August 1884 King **Dinuzulu kaMpande** ceded to the Boers of **Dinuzulu's Volunteers** all of northwestern **Zululand** (2,710,000 acres), which they proclaimed the **New Republic**. *See also* BOUNDARIES AND COLONIAL CONTROL IN ZULULAND.

**ZULULAND BOUNDARY COMMISSION.** *See* BOUNDARY AWARD.

**ZULULAND, BRITISH COLONY OF.** Alarmed by growing turbulence in the **New Republic** and in **Eastern Zululand**, **Melmoth Osborn,** the resident commissioner of the **Reserve Territory**, took the initiative and on 5 February 1887 informed King **Dinuzulu ka-Mpande** that British protection had been extended over Eastern Zululand. The British government, faced by the accomplished fact, annexed Eastern Zululand, the Reserve Territory, and **Proviso B** on 19 May 1887 as the British Colony of Zululand. For reasons of economy, the governor of **Natal** also became the governor of Zululand and was represented in **Eshowe** by the resident commissioner. Administratively, Zululand was divided into six magisterial districts under white magistrates. Order was kept through the locally recruited **Zululand Police**. The skeleton administrative machinery was financed by a hut tax. The British District of Ingwavuma was incorporated into the Colony of Zululand on 15 July 1895, and the British protectorate of Tongaland (Amaputaland) followed on 24 December 1897. *See also* ZULULAND, PROVINCE OF.

**ZULULAND GARRISON.** **Zululand** was in the sphere of responsibility for the **Natal garrison**, and it deployed a part of its strength to garrison military posts in the **Reserve Territory** between September 1883 and May 1887 or to undertake military operations during the 3rd **Zulu Civil War**. With the annexation of the British Colony of Zululand in May 1887, small detachments from the Natal garrison constituted the Zululand garrison and were concentrated at **Fort Curtis**. During the **uSuthu Rebellion**, the Zululand garrison was reinforced by the Natal garrison and moved forward to **Entonjaneni**, **Nkonjeni**, and other bases. On 2 November 1888, the Zululand garrison was reduced to its "normal" level of a squadron of cavalry and two companies of **mounted infantry** at Fort Curtis and Entonjaneni. A small garrison continued to be stationed at Fort Curtis until 1899.

**ZULULAND POLICE.** On the annexation of the British Colony of Zululand in May 1887, the paramilitary **Reserve Territory Carbineers** (RTC) were restyled the Zululand Police (ZP), or Nongqayi, and were maintained by the Zululand administration. Retaining the same uniforms and weapons as the RTC and their headquarters at **Nongqayi Fort**, their numbers were increased to 250 men under commandant **George Mansel** and white subinspectors. The ZP were posted to the six new magisterial posts in British Zululand to protect the white magistrates and enforce their authority. However, by late 1887 it was clear that they required the support of British troops from the **Zululand garrison** to keep the **uSuthu** in check. On 26 April 1888, a menacing gathering deterred a force of 80 ZP from effecting the arrest of contumacious uSuthu leaders at **oSuthu**, and this failure hastened open hostilities. During the **uSuthu Rebellion**, a force of 50 ZP was repulsed when trying to arrest the uSuthu leaders on **Ceza**. Fifty of them stationed at **Ivuna** fired on the uSuthu when they bypassed the fort to defeat the **Mandlakazi**, and they were evacuated to **Nkonjeni**. A small contingent stationed at **Fort Andries** fought off an uSuthu attack in the battle of **Ntondotha**, while those stationed at **Nkonjeni** took part in the successful assault of **Hlophekhulu**. The ZP remained concentrated at Nkonjeni during the pacification operations of later July and August, and once the Zululand garrison was reduced to its normal level, they were redistributed by December 1888 to six posts around the colony.

**ZULULAND, PROVINCE OF.** On 30 December 1897, the Colony of **Zululand** was annexed to the colony of **Natal** and administered as Natal's Province of Zululand until all of Natal became a province of the Union of South Africa on 31 May 1910.

**eZULUWINI** *umuZI.* On 4 April 1879, the day after the relief of **Eshowe** during the **Anglo-Zulu War**, and while Colonel **Charles Knight Pearson** was supervising the evacuation of **Fort Eshowe**, Lieutenant-General Lord **Chelmsford** and 225 men from the **Eshowe Relief Column** destroyed *umNtwana* **Dabulamanzi kaMpande**'s eZuluwini *umuZi* (homestead) at eNtumeni, which had escaped burning in Pearson's earlier, inconclusive raid of 1 March. Dabulamanzi and 40 Zulu kept up ineffective fire from a neighboring hill while the British completed their mission.

**ZUNGENI MOUNTAIN SKIRMISH (1879).** On 5 June 1879, during the joint advance in the **Anglo-Zulu War** of the British 2nd Division, **South African Field Force**, and **Wood's Flying Column** on the **oNdini** *iKhanda*, some 300 **irregular** horse from Wood's Flying

Column under Lieutenant-Colonel **Redvers Henry Buller** made a reconnaissance toward Zungeni Mountain. Coming into contact with a Zulu force of about 300 men stationed at **eZulaneni**, a cluster of four large *imiZi* on the side of the mountain to the east of the Ntinini stream, they charged and scattered them, put eZulaneni to the torch, and then withdrew under fire from the Zulu, who were shooting at them from under cover and trying to outflank them. Some 500 regular cavalry of the **Cavalry Brigade** attached to the 2nd Division, who were in support under Major-General **Frederick Marshall**, were eager for action and unnecessarily charged toward eZulaneni. The cavalry became caught up in the difficult terrain and fell back under brisk fire from the Zulu working around their flanks. The cavalry were finally extricated under the covering fire of the irregular horse. One British officer was killed, and a later British reconnaissance found 25 Zulu corpses. *See also* TACTICS, BRITISH MOUNTED TROOPS; TACTICS UP TO 1879, ZULU.

**ZUNGWINI MOUNTAIN SKIRMISHES (1879).** At the outset of the **Anglo-Zulu War**, King **Cetshwayo kaMpande** ordered the **abaQulusi** people of northwestern **Zululand** to make a stand against No. 4 **Column**, and Brevet Colonel **Henry Evelyn Wood** realized he would have to defeat them to secure his lines of supply. On 20 January 1879, Lieutenant-Colonel **Redvers Henry Buller** led 104 **irregular cavalry** out from **Fort Tinta** to reconnoiter Zungwini Mountain, seven miles to the west of **Hlobane Mountain**, where **Mbilini waMswati** had reinforced the abaQulusi under their senior *inDuna*, Msebe kaMadaka. Buller captured an *umuZi* on the southeastern spur, but the 1,000 defenders on the summit, most of whom had **firearms**, then advanced in traditional formation in disciplined skirmishing order. The two horns threatened to outflank Buller, who had to retreat across the White Mfolozi River, where he made a stand, driving the abaQulusi back. On 22 January, Wood led out a strong patrol of infantry and irregular horse and captured much livestock on Zungwini without encountering resistance. However, on seeing several thousand Zulu near Ntendeka Mountain, four miles to the east, he rapidly retired. On 24 January, Wood advanced again with a strong patrol and **artillery**, surprising the abaQulusi and Mbilini's forces still between Zungwini and Ntendeka, scattering and killing about 50. Wood was unable to pursue his advantage because on receiving news of **Isandlwana**, he withdrew to **Khambula**. *See also* TACTICS, BRITISH INFANTRY; TACTICS, BRITISH MOUNTED TROOPS; TACTICS UP TO 1879, ZULU.

# Glossary

In accordance with current practice, Zulu words, which appear in *italics* in the text, are alphabetized under the root word rather than under the prefix.

**agterryer.** black "after-rider" or servant who accompanies his Boer master on horseback on a journey or to war

**isAngoma (pl. izAngoma).** diviner inspired by ancestral spirits

**assegai.** spear

**iBandla (pl. amaBandla).** royal council of state

**isiBaya (pl. iziBaya).** enclosure for livestock where ceremonies are performed

**isiBhalo.** compulsory labor and military service required of Africans living in the Colony of Natal

**Boer.** Dutch- (later Afrikaans-speaking) white settler

**iButho (pl. amaButho).** Zulu age-grade regiment of men or women; member of age-group; warrior

**commando.** Boer militia

**conductor.** driver of team of oxen pulling a wagon

**uDibi (pl. izinDibi).** youth who serves as a carrier or cattle handler with the army

**iDlozi (pl. amaDlozi).** ancestral spirit

**inDlu (pl. izinDlu).** hut

**donga.** dry, eroded watercourse, running only in times of heavy rain

**drift.** shallow, fordable point in a river

**inDuna (pl. izinDuna).** officer appointed by *inKosi* or king to a position of command in the state or army; headman; councilor; military officer

**isiFuba (pl. iziFuba).** "chest" or center of army

**isiGodlo (pl. iziGodlo).** king's or *inKosi*'s private enclosure at upper end of his *iKhanda* or *umuZi*; women of king's establishment

**inGxotha (pl. izinGxotha).** heavy brass armlet conferred as mark of distinction by king

**herneutermes.** large hunting-knife

**uHlangothi (pl. izinHlangothi).** wing of *iButho* or section of *iKhanda* where it is quartered

**isiHlangu (pl. iziHlangu).** war shield

**isiJula (pl. iziJula).** throwing spear

**kappie.** large sunbonnet worn by Boer women

**iKhanda (pl. amaKhanda).** royal military and administrative center and where *amaButho* are stationed to serve the king

**umKhoka (pl. imiKhoka).** ritual defilement

**umKhosi (pl. imiKhosi).** annual "first-fruits" ceremony

**isiKhulu (pl. iziKhulu).** chief of high hereditary status in the political hierarchy of the kingdom

**umKhumbi (pl. imiKhumbi).** circular assembly of men, especially *amaButho*

**kisklere.** Sunday-best clothes

**klapbroek.** trousers with a front flap

**kloof.** a deep ravine or valley, usually wooded, or a gorge between mountains

**iKlwa (pl. amaKlwa).** stabbing spear

**knobkerrie.** knobbed stick carried by a Zulu man

**kop or koppie.** prominent hill or peak

**inKosi (pl. amaKhosi).** king; hereditary chief

**kraal.** enclosure for livestock

**laager.** defensive formation of parked wagons, but also any defensive enclosure, whether of barricades, masonry, bricks, or turf

**landdros.** magistrate

**iLobolo.** cattle handed over by man's family to formalize a marriage transaction

**loopers.** small leather cartridges of buckshot

**mealie.** maize; Indian corn

**uMnyama.** spiritual force of darkness or evil influence

**iMpi (pl. iziMpi).** military force; army; battle

**iNceku (pl. iziNceku).** king's or *inKosi*'s personal attendant and adviser

**nek.** mountain pass

**iNkatha (pl. iziNkatha).** sacred grass coil, symbol of the Zulu nation

**umNtwana (pl. abaNtwana).** prince of the royal house; child of the king

**umNumzane (pl. abaNumzane).** married headman of an *umuZi*

**iNyanga (pl. iziNyanga).** traditional healer; herbalist

**uPondo (pl. izimPondo).** horn or wing of army

**pont.** large, flat-bottomed ferryboat, worked by ropes attached to both banks of the river

**poort.** narrow pass between mountains

**puggaree.** scarf worn around the hat and sometimes falling down behind to keep off the sun

**sanna.** general name given by Boers of the 1830s to the large variety of muzzle-loading firearms they carried

**umShokobezi (pl. imiShokobezi).** cow-tail decorations worn by *ama-Butho*; in the 1880s, the insignia of the uSuthu, or royalist faction

**snaphaan.** flintlock

**span.** team of draught animals

**spruit.** a tributary watercourse

**trek.** to make an arduous journey overland, often in permanent migration

**umuVa (pl. imiVa).** reserve force of army

**veld.** open, uncultivated grasslands

**iViyo (pl. amaViyo).** section or company of an *iButho*

**vlei.** marsh

**volksraad.** legislative assembly of a Boer republic

**voorlaaier.** muzzle-loader

**voorloper.** leader on foot of a team of oxen pulling a wagon

**Voortrekkers.** Boer pioneers who, dissatisfied with British rule, left the Cape Colony in the late 1830s for the interior of South Africa

**iWisa (pl. amaWisa).** knobbed stick

**umuZi (pl. imiZi).** family homestead of huts under an *umNumzane*

**ukuZila.** to observe ritual abstinence

# Bibliography

## CONTENTS

## INTRODUCTION

The sources for the Zulu Wars of 1838–1888 are very unevenly weighted. By far the greatest number relates to the Anglo-Zulu War of 1879. As befitted a major colonial war at the height of the Victorian era, a stream of published contemporary eyewitness accounts, reminiscences, and critiques followed hard on its heels, lending human interest and controversy to the official published documents. After this initial outpouring, the torrent of publications rapidly dwindled and by the end of the 19th century had pretty well dried up as new colonial wars captured the public's attention. Interest resurfaced in the mid-20th century and has maintained a gathering momentum in the 21st century, presenting the reader with both scholarly works pioneering new directions of research and with more derivative (if not repetitive) works of popular history. The Voortrekker-Zulu War of 1838–1840 has not spawned nearly so large a literature as has the Anglo-Zulu War, and much of it is necessarily in Dutch or Afrikaans, thus closing it to most English readers. This literature generally betrays a strong ideological coloring because the Boers saw their victory over the Zulu as God's unmistakable sanction that provided the justification for racial domination and, in due course, for apartheid. Zulu historians today, who strongly reject this reading, are currently forging an Afrocentric interpretation of the events of 1838–1840. In contrast to the two wars already mentioned, the 3rd Zulu Civil War and the uSuthu Rebellion of 1883–1888 have only gained the attention of a handful of historians. Both conflicts, perhaps, were too small in scale, local in scope, and complicated in detail to find a wide audience. Nevertheless, the consequences of the wars of the 1880s were extremely far-reaching for the Zulu themselves, and at the time they elicited a limited, if strong, polemical literature by perceptive commentators.

The archival records essential for researching the history of the Zulu Wars are scattered among repositories in South Africa and the United Kingdom. The major South African collections of private papers and unpublished official papers are housed in the KwaZulu-Natal Archives, Pietermaritzburg Repository; the National Archives of South Africa: Pretoria Depot; the Killie Campbell Africana Library and the Local History Museum in Durban; the Africana Library, Brenthurst Library, and William Cullen Library in Johannesburg; and the Cape Town Archives. In the United Kingdom, the official papers are to be found in the National Archives at Kew. The widest collection of private military papers (including the Chelmsford Papers) is held in the National Army Museum, Chelsea, though there are also significant collections in the Royal Archives, Windsor Castle; the National Maritime Museum, Greenwich; Rhodes House, Oxford; and the Regimental Museum of the Royal Welsh (formerly South Wales Borderers), Brecon. The latter museum also holds large collections of artifacts relating to the British army in Zululand, as does the National Army Museum. In South Africa, the KwaZulu Cultural Museum, Ulundi; the Voortrekker Museum and Natal Museum in Pietermaritzburg; the Killie Campbell Collections and the Old Court House Museum in Durban; the Talana Museum, Dundee; and the Fort Nongqayi and Zululand Historical Museum, Eshowe, are essential for viewing Zulu, Boer, and British material culture. The sites of two royal Zulu *amaKhanda* (royal military homesteads) have been excavated by archeologists and partially restored. Both have small museums attached: namely, the Mgungundlovu and oNdini Open Air and Site Museums. Three battlefields are also served by small museums: the Blood River Heritage Site and Ncome Museum and Monument Complex; the Isandlwana Museum and Battle Site; and the Shiyane/Rorke's Drift Interpretative Center.

Fortunately for those studying the Zulu Wars, a considerable quantity of the primary archival material is available in printed form. For the 1838–1840 period, there is John Bird's invaluable compilation *The Annals of Natal 1495–1845*, 2 vols. (1885); Basil Leverton's *Records of Natal*, 3 vols. (1989, 1990, and 1992); and H. S. Pretorius and D. W. Kruger's *Voortrekker Argiefstukke 1829–1849* (1937). The extensive published British Parliamentary Papers relating to South Africa cover the entire period 1838 to 1888 and are an invaluable resource for official dispatches and reports. Those Parliamentary Papers relating to the Anglo-Zulu War have been reprinted in an archival collection edited by John Laband and Ian Knight, *Archives of Zululand: The Anglo-Zulu War 1879*, 6 vols. (2000). This collection also includes official publications such as Major J. S. Rothwell's account of the Zululand campaign, *Narrative of Field Operations Connected with the Zulu War of 1879* (1881), which was prepared in the War Office primarily from the diaries of operations kept by the various British columns, as well as a range of contemporary parliamentary debates, articles, pamphlets, and books. Many contemporary private manuscript sources, such as diaries and collections of letters, have been printed in edited or annotated editions, such as George Cory, ed., *The Diary of the Rev. Francis Owen, M.A., Missionary with Dingaan in 1837–38* (1926); Sonia Clarke, ed., *Zululand at War 1879: The Conduct of the Anglo-Zulu War* (1984); and John Laband, ed., *Lord Chelmsford's Zululand Campaign 1878–1879* (1994).

Many significant contemporary printed memoirs, books, and pamphlets, such as Major Walter Ashe and Captain E. V. Wyatt Edgell's *The Story of the Zulu Campaign* (1880), have been reissued in recent years, making them readily available to informed readers. Colonial newspapers of the time, notably the *Natal Colonist, Natal Mercury, Natal Witness*, and *Times of Natal*, as well as metropolitan newspapers such as *The Times* and periodicals like the *Illustrated London News* and *Graphic*, are a crucial and detailed resource. Some of these have been made available through modern reprints, such as Ron Lock and Peter Quantrill, comp., *The Red Book. Natal Press Reports: Anglo-Zulu War 1879* (2000), which groups together the reports from the *Natal Mercury*. Moreover, soldiers' letters to the newspaper have been collected and printed with a connecting commentary, as in Frank Emery's classic *The Red Soldier: Letters from the Zulu War* (1977). There have been similar treatments of war correspondents' reports, as in John Laband and Ian Knight, *The War Correspondents: The Anglo-Zulu War* (1996).

Recent serious studies of the Zulu Wars have pioneered new avenues of investigation. Much previously neglected evidence is available for investigating white colonists and African levies (troops) in time of war, as in John Laband and Paul Thompson's *Kingdom and Colony at War* (1990). Even more significantly, historians have shifted their gaze from the Boers and British to focus on the Zulu. A scarcity of evidence makes it challenging for historians readily to grasp Zulu society, religion, political structure, diplomacy, military organization, strategic planning, and tactical objectives. Yet sources do exist in the testimonies of Zulu envoys, war captives, spies, political prisoners, and others, which have been preserved in depositions, court proceedings, magisterial reports, and missionaries' accounts. Such evidence has been problematically filtered through colonial pens, but sensitively recorded Zulu oral evidence, most notably *The James Stuart Archive of Recorded Oral Evidence Relating to the History of the Zulu and Neighbouring Peoples*, edited by Colin Webb and John Wright in five volumes between 1976 and 2001, opens an unparalleled window onto the Zulu view of their own world. As a result, it has been possible to write histories that take the Zulu perspective much more fully into account, such as Jeff Guy's *The Destruction of the Zulu Kingdom: The Civil War in Zululand, 1879–1884*, 3rd ed. (1998), or John Laband's *The Rise and Fall of the Zulu Nation* (1997).

Even in the more traditional arena of the British Army in South Africa, considerable advances have been made with works like Edward Spiers's *The*

*Late Victorian Army, 1868–1902* (1992) in explaining the way the British campaigned in South Africa. Masterful interpretations such as Spiers's are supported by a large and burgeoning corpus of technical works on everything from tactical training to transport and supply, weaponry, fortifications, uniforms, signaling, and medical care. There has been much more emphasis by historians on active fieldwork outside the archives, and they have worked increasingly in cooperation with archeologists. Battlefields have been carefully traversed and excavated to establish military dispositions, and over a hundred forts and laagers, as well as some two dozen Zulu *amaKhanda*, have been identified and charted. The results can be seen in works like John Laband and Paul Thompson's *The Illustrated Guide to the Anglo-Zulu War* (2000) and David Rattray's *The David Rattray Guide to the Zulu War* (2003).

The number of registers and related publications being brought out is also growing and usefully augments the more standard dictionaries of biography to provide career details of most of the participants in the Zulu Wars. One of the most recent and comprehensive of these is Adrian Greaves and Ian Knight, *Who's Who in the Anglo-Zulu War 1879*, 2 vols. (2006).

Studies such as these, informed by the latest developments in research, mean that the Zulu Wars are better understood than ever before. For the earlier period, Norman Etherington has opened up wider perspectives on the Voortrekker-Zulu War of 1838–1840 with *The Great Treks: The Transformation of Southern Africa, 1815–1854* (2001). Zulu-centric interpretations of the conflict are evident in collections like K. Malefane's *The Re-Interpretation of the Battle of Blood River/Ncome* (1998). The comparatively less familiar period of the civil war and rebellion in Zululand between 1879 and 1888 has been illuminated by Jeff Guy in works such as *View Across the River: Harriette Colenso and the Zulu Struggle Against Imperialism* (2001). John Laband, in *The Atlas of the Later Zulu Wars 1883–1888* (2002), has provided the first full military analysis and campaign history of the period.

It is the Anglo-Zulu War of 1879, however, that continues to stimulate the greatest interest in scholars and public alike. Donald Morris's *Washing of the Spears* (1966) effectively engaged the modern public's imagination and has meshed with films like Stanley Baker and Cy Enfield's *Zulu* (1964) to create a cult following for the Anglo-Zulu War. On the other hand, recent television documentaries like *The Zulu Wars* (2003) enjoy the benefit of decades of subsequent scholarly research to present a far more accurate (if less immediately enthralling) analysis of the war. Many recently published books and articles are also still pushing the boundaries of our understanding of 1879. For example, Richard Cope's *Ploughshare of War: The Origins of the Anglo-Zulu War, 1879* (1999) is the masterly and persuasive culmination of a long-running debate on the causes of the war. Ian Castle and Ian Knight's *Fearful Hard Times: The Siege and Relief of Eshowe, 1879* (1994) analyzes the coastal campaign as never attempted before. Ron Lock's *Blood on the Painted Mountain: Zulu Victory and Defeat, Hlobane and Kambula, 1879* (1995) has opened up a fruitful debate on the campaign in northwestern Zululand that has elicited Huw Jones's masterly critiques in various articles and in his *The Boiling Cauldron: Utrecht District and the Anglo-Zulu War* (2006). Inevitably, the Zulu defeat of the British at the battle of Isandlwana in January 1879 has continued to attract the most controversy. Contemporary critiques of deficient British generalship have been refurbished and greater credit given to Zulu military expertise in a broad sweep of publications, ranging from David Jackson's painstakingly researched *Hill of the Sphinx: The Battle of Isandlwana* (2004) to Ron Lock and Peter Quantrill's more controversial *Zulu Victory: The Epic of Isandlwana and the Cover-Up* (2002). The biannual *Journal of the Anglo Zulu War Historical Society*, which first appeared in 1997, continues to play an invaluable role as the main forum for debates about the war and as a vehicle for presenting new research. Not every article published there could be cited in this bibliography, but the most trenchant have been selected for inclusion.

The bibliography has been arranged so as to follow the broad sweep of history over the period of the Zulu Wars. An essentially chronological approach has accordingly been adopted, with the sequence of campaign topics being prefaced and interspersed with sections devoted to reference, interpretative, and technical matters. The intention throughout has been to identify published source materials and the secondary articles and books that best characterize the established historiography of the Zulu Wars and the more recent avenues of exploration. A number of essential academic theses have consequently been included, even though this vital research is unpublished and not readily available. The sources are overwhelmingly in English, as this was the language of British colonists, missionaries, officials, and soldiers in Natal and Zululand in the 19th century, and that of the great majority of subsequent historians of the region. The exceptions to the rule involve the period of the Great Trek (which was until recently a major focus of research and writing in Afrikaans) and the disputed Transvaal-Zululand border lands. There is a substantial literature in Afrikaans on these subjects, and the relevant books (but not articles) have been included in the bibliography, with the titles translated within square brackets. Zulu historians today write almost entirely in English in order to make their work accessible to the international community of scholars and informed general readers. Consequently, all the works by Zulu mother-tongue authors cited in this bibliography are in English. When facsimile reprints of books are cited, the original date of publication is indicated within square brackets.

## WORKS OF REFERENCE

### Encyclopedias and Dictionaries

Austin, Ronald J. *The Australian Illustrated Encyclopedia of the Zulu and Boer Wars*. McCrae, Australia: Slouch Hat, 1999.

Branford, Jean, and William Branford. *A Dictionary of South African English*. Cape Town: Oxford University Press, 1991.

Jaques, Tony. *Dictionary of Battles and Sieges: A Guide to 8,500 Battles from Antiquity Through to the Twenty-First Century*. 3 vols. Westport, Conn.: Greenwood Press, 2007.

Lugg, Harry, comp. Revised by A. Trevor Cope. *Zulu Place Names in Natal*. Durban: Daily News, 1968.

Saunders, Christopher, and Nicholas Southey. *Historical Dictionary of South Africa*. 2nd ed. Lanham, Md: Scarecrow Press, 2000.

### Biographical Registers

Bancroft, James W. *The Zulu War VCs*. Manchester: J. W. Bancroft, 1992.

Beyers, C. J., ed. *Dictionary of South African Biography*. Vol. 4. Cape Town: Human Sciences Research Council, 1981.

Davis, Henry William Carless, and John Reginald Homer Weaver. *The Dictionary of National Biography, 1912–1921*. London: Oxford University Press, 1927.

*Dictionary of South African Biography*. 3 vols. Cape Town: Human Sciences Research Council, 1968, 1972, 1977.

Greaves, Adrian, and Ian Knight. *A Review of "The South African Campaign of 1879."* Tenterden, U.K.: Debinair, 2000.

———. *Who's Who in the Anglo-Zulu War 1879*. Vol. 1, *The British*; vol. 2, *Colonials and Zulus*. Barnsley, U.K.: Pen and Sword, 2006.

Holme, Norman. *The Noble 24th. Biographical Records of the 24th Regiment in the Zulu War and the South African Campaigns 1877–1879*. London: Savannah, 1999.

Jones, Huw M. *A Biographical Register of Swaziland to 1902*. Pietermaritzburg: University of Natal Press, 1993.

Lee, Sidney, ed. *Dictionary of National Biography: Supplement, January 1901–December 1911*. London: Oxford University Press, 1920.

Mackinnon, John Price, and S. Shadbolt, comps., with a new index by John Young. *The South African Campaign, 1879* [1880]. London: Greenhill Books, 1995.

*The Monthly Army List.* January to December 1878, 1879, 1883, 1884, 1887, 1888. London: Her Majesty's Stationery Office, 1878, 1879, 1883, 1884, 1887, 1888.

*The Natal Who's Who, 1906.* Durban: Natal Who's Who, 1906.

*Oxford Dictionary of National Biography.* Oxford: Oxford University Press, online edition. www.oxforddnb.com.

Robinson, Charles N., ed. *Celebrities of the Army.* London: George Newnes, 1900.

Rosenthal, Eric, comp. *Southern African Dictionary of National Biography.* London: Frederick Warne, 1966.

Spencer, Shelagh O'Byrne. *British Settlers in Natal, 1824–1857: A Biographical Register.* 6 vols. Pietermaritzburg: University of Natal Press, 1981, 1983, 1985, 1987, 1989, 1992.

Stephen, Leslie, and Sidney Lee, eds. *The Dictionary of National Biography.* 21 vols. London: Oxford University Press, reprinted 1937–1938.

Tabler, Edward C. *Pioneers of Natal and South-Eastern Africa 1552–1878.* Cape Town: A. A. Balkema, 1977.

Townsend, Peter, ed. *Burke's Genealogical and Heraldic History of the Peerage, Baronetage, and Knightage.* London: Burke's Peerage, 1963.

## Guides to Historic Sites in Natal and Zululand

Dlamini, Nsizwa. "Monuments of Division: Apartheid and Post-Apartheid Struggles over Zulu Nationalist Heritage Sites." In *Zulu Identities: Being Zulu Past and Present*, ed. Ben Carton, John Laband, and Jabulani Sithole. New York: Columbia University Press, 2009.

Lugg, Harry C. *Historic Natal and Zululand.* Pietermaritzburg: Shuter and Shooter, 1949.

Oberholster, J. J. *The Historical Monuments of South Africa.* Stellenbosch, South Africa: Rembrandt van Rijn Foundation for the National Monuments Council, 1972.

Smail, J. L. *With Shield and Assegai: Historical Monuments and Battlefields in Natal and Zululand.* Cape Town: Howard Timmins, 1965.

———. *Monuments and Trails of the Voortrekkers.* Cape Town: Howard Timmins, 1968.

———. *Those Restless Years: Dealing with the Boer Wars and the Bambata Rebellion.* Cape Town: Howard Timmins, 1971.

———. *From the Land of the Zulu Kings: An Historical Guide for Those Restless Years in Natal and Zululand 1497 to 1879.* Durban: A. J. Pope, 1979.

## Source Guides

Haythornthwaite, Philip J. *The Colonial Wars Source Book*. London: Caxton Editions, 2000.

Verbeek, Jennifer, Mary Nathanson, and Elaine Peel, comps. *Webb's Guide to the Official Records of the Colony of Natal. An Expanded and Revised Edition Together with Indexes*. Pietermaritzburg: University of Natal Press, 1984.

## GENERAL HISTORIES RELATING TO NATAL AND ZULULAND

## Select General Histories

Davenport, T.R.H., and Christopher Saunders. *South Africa: A Modern History*. 5th ed. New York: St. Martin's Press, 2000.

Hamilton, Carolyn, ed. *The Mfecane Debate: Reconstructive Debates in Southern African History*. Johannesburg: Witwatersrand University Press; Pietermaritzburg: University of Natal Press, 2001.

Iliffe, John. *Honour in African History*. Cambridge: Cambridge University Press, 2005.

MacKinnon, Aran S. *The Making of South Africa: Culture and Politics*. Upper Saddle River, N.J.: Pearson Prentice Hall, 2004.

Maylam, Paul. *A History of the African People of South Africa: From the Early Iron Age to the 1970s*. Cape Town: David Philip, 1986.

Saunders, Christopher C., ed. *Black Leaders in Southern African History*. London: Heinemann, 1979.

——, ed. *Reader's Digest History of South Africa: The Real Story*. 3rd ed. Cape Town: Reader's Digest Association, 1994.

Saunders, Christopher, and Iain Smith. "Southern Africa 1795–1910." In *The Oxford History of the British Empire*. Vol. 3, *The Nineteenth Century*. Ed. Andrew Porter and Alaine Low. Oxford: Oxford University Press, 1999.

Thompson, Leonard. "The Subjection of the African Chiefdoms, 1870–1898." In *The Oxford History of South Africa*. Vol. 2, *South Africa 1870–1966*. Ed. Monica Wilson and Leonard Thompson. Oxford: At the Clarendon Press, 1971.

Van Lingen, Gail, and Geoffrey Allan Chadwick. *Battlefields of South Africa*. Johannesburg: Times Media with Jonathan Ball, 1991.

## General Histories of Natal and Zululand

Brookes, Edgar Harry, and Colin de B. Webb. *A History of Natal*. Pietermaritzburg: University of Natal Press, 1965.

Bryant, Alfred Thomas. *A History of the Zulu and Neighbouring Tribes*. Cape Town: C. Struik, 1964.

Bulpin, Thomas Victor. *To the Shores of Natal*. Cape Town: H. B. Timmins, 1953.

——. *Shaka's Country: A Book of Zululand*. 3rd ed. Cape Town: H. B. Timmins, 1956.

——. *Natal and the Zulu Country*. Cape Town: Books of Africa, 1966.

Colenbrander, Peter. "The Zulu Kingdom, 1828–79." In *Natal and Zululand from Earliest Times to 1910: A New History*, ed. Andrew Duminy and Bill Guest. Pietermaritzburg: University of Natal Press and Shuter and Shooter, 1989.

Dodds, Glen Lyndon. *The Zulus and Matabele: Warrior Nations*. London: Arms and Armour, 1998.

Duminy, Andrew, and Bill Guest, eds. *Natal and Zululand from Earliest Times to 1910: A New History*. Pietermaritzburg: University of Natal Press and Shuter and Shooter, 1989.

Gibson, James Young. *The Story of the Zulus*. London: Longmans, Green, 1911.

Gillings, Ken, and John Hone. *Battles of KwaZulu-Natal*. Durban: Art Publishers, 2003.

Gluckman, Max. "The Kingdom of the Zulu of South Africa." In *African Political Systems*, ed. Meyer Fortes and Edward E. Evans-Pritchard. London: Oxford University Press and H. Milton, 1940.

Hattersley, Alan F. *More Annals of Natal with Historical Introductions and Notes*. Pietermaritzburg: Shuter and Shooter, 1936.

——. *Later Annals of Natal*. London: Longmans, Green, 1938.

Holden, William Clifford. *History of the Colony of Natal*. London: Alexander Heylin, 1855.

Ingram, J. F. *A Condensed History of the Exploration and Colonization of Natal and Zululand*. London: Harvey Greenacre, 1897.

Intelligence Branch of the Quartermaster-General's Department, Horse Guards, War Office. *Précis of Information Concerning the Zulu Country, with a Map. Corrected to January 1879*. London: Her Majesty's Stationery Office, 1879.

Knight, Ian. *The Zulus*. London: Osprey, 1989.

Laband, John. *The Rise and Fall of the Zulu Nation*. London: Arms and Armour, 1997.

——. "The Rise and Fall of the Zulu Kingdom." In *Zulu Identities: Being Zulu Past and Present*, ed. Ben Carton, John Laband, and Jabulani Sithole. New York: Columbia University Press, 2009.

Leitch, Barry, Sue Derwent, and Roger De la Harpe. *Zulu*. Cape Town: C. Struik, 1998.

Moodie, Duncan Campbell Francis, ed. *The History of the Battles and Adventures of the British, the Boers, and the Zulus in Southern Africa, from 1495 to 1879, Including Every Particular of the Zulu War of 1879, with a Chronology.* Sidney: George Robertson, 1879.

Morris, Donald R. *The Washing of the Spears: A History of the Rise of the Zulu Nation Under Shaka and Its Fall in the Zulu War of 1879.* London: Jonathan Cape, 1966.

Mountain, Alan. *The Rise and Fall of the Zulu Empire.* Constantia, South Africa: KwaNtaba, 1999.

Peires, J. B., ed. *Before and After Shaka: Papers in Nguni History.* Grahamstown, South Africa: Institute of Social and Economic Research, Rhodes University, 1981.

Selby, J. *Shaka's Heirs.* London: George Allen and Unwin, 1971.

Sutherland, Jonathan, and Diane Canwell. *Zulu Kings and Their Armies.* Barnsley, U.K.: Pen and Sword, 2004.

Taylor, Stephen. *Shaka's Children: A History of the Zulu People.* London: HarperCollins, 1994.

## FILMS AND DOCUMENTARIES ON ZULU HISTORY

Hale, Frederick. "The Defeat of History in the Film *Zulu*." *Military History Journal* 10, no. 4 (1996). http://rapidttp.com/milhist/vol04fm.html.

Hamilton, Carolyn, and Litheko Modisane. "The Public Lives of Historical Films: The Case of *Zulu* and *Zulu Dawn*." In *Black and White in Colour: African History on Screen*, ed. Vivian Bickford-Smith and Richard Mendelsohn. Oxford: James Currey, 2007.

*The History of Warfare: Zulu Wars 1879.* Cromwell Productions. 55 minutes. Allegro DVD, 2007.

*Shaka Zulu.* Produced by William C. Faure. 500 minutes. South African Broadcasting Corporation; A&E DVD, 1986.

*The Symbol of Sacrifice.* Produced by I. W. Schlesinger. African Film Productions, 1918.

*De Voortrekkers.* Produced by I. W. Schlesinger. African Film Productions, 1916.

*"Wet with Yesterday's Blood." A History of the Anglo-Zulu War.* Produced by Geoff Dickson. 90 minutes. 1997.

*Zulu.* Produced by Stanley Baker and Cy Endfield. 138 minutes. MGM DVD, 1964.

*Zulu Dawn.* Produced by Nate Kohn and James Faulkner. 115 minutes. America Cinema Releasing, 1979. Tango Entertainment DVD, 2005.

*The Zulu Wars.* Produced by Steve Gilham and Ian Knight. 164 minutes. Cromwell Films, 2002; Eagle Media Productions DVD, 2003.

## ZULU KINGDOM

### Zulu Histories of Zululand and Recorded Zulu Oral History

Cope, Trevor, ed. *Izibongo: Zulu Praise-Poems Collected by James Stuart.* Trans. Daniel Malcolm. Oxford: Clarendon Press, 1968.

Fuze, Magema M. *The Black People and Whence They Came: A Zulu View* [1922]. Trans. Harry C. Lugg; ed. A. Trevor Cope. Pietermaritzburg: University of Natal Press, 1979.

Rycroft, David K., and A. Bhekabantu Nbcobo, eds. *The Praises of Dingana (Izibongo zikaDingana).* Pietermaritzburg: University of Natal Press, 1988.

Webb, Colin de B., and John B. Wright, eds. *The James Stuart Archive of Recorded Oral Evidence Relating to the History of the Zulu and Neighbouring Peoples.* 5 vols. Pietermaritzburg: University of Natal Press, 1976, 1979, 1982, 1986, and 2001.

### Zulu Kings

Ballard, Charles. "The Historical Image of King Cetshwayo of Zululand: A Centennial Comment." *Natalia* 13 (December 1983): 29–42.

——. *The House of Shaka: The Zulu Monarchy Illustrated.* Durban: Emoyi Books, 1988.

Becker, Peter. *Rule of Fear: The Life and Times of Dingane, King of the Zulu.* London: Longmans, 1964.

Binns, Charles Theodore. *The Last Zulu King: The Life and Death of Cetshwayo.* London: Longmans, 1963.

——. *Dinuzulu: The Death of the House of Shaka.* London: Longmans, 1968.

Dhlomo, R.R.R. *uDingane* [Dingane]. Pietermaritzburg: Shuter and Shooter, 1947.

Gon, Philip, Rosemary Mulholland, and Catherine Kraetschner. *The First Zulu Kings: Shaka and Dingane.* Craighall, South Africa: A. D. Donker, 1985.

Guy, Jeff. "Cetshwayo kaMpande, c. 1832–1884." In *Black Leaders in Southern African History*, ed. Christopher Saunders. London: Heinemann, 1979.

Kennedy, Philip A. "Mpande and the Zulu Kingship." *Journal of Natal and Zulu History* 4 (1981): 21–38.

Laband, John, and John B. Wright. *King Cetshwayo kaMpande (c. 1832–1884)*. Pietermaritzburg: Shuter and Shooter, 1980.

Ndlovu, Sifiso. "Zulu Nationalist Representations of King Dingane." In *Zulu Identities: Being Zulu Past and Present*, ed. Ben Carton, John Laband, and Jabulani Sithole. New York: Columbia University Press, 2009.

Nzimande, Themba. *King Mpande's Children: The Blood-Royal Zulu Princes and Princesses*. Durban: KwaZulu Monuments Council, 1997.

Okoye, Felix. "Dingane: A Reappraisal." *Journal of African History* 10, no. 2 (1969): 221–35.

Ritter, E. A. *Shaka Zulu*. London: Longmans, 1955.

Roberts, Brian. *The Zulu Kings*. London: Hamilton, 1974.

Shamase, M. Z. *Zulu Potentates from Earliest to Zwelithini KaBhekuzulu*. Durban: S. M. Publications, 1996.

Wright, John, and Ruth Edgecombe. "Mpande ka Senzangakhona, c. 1798–1872." In *Black Leaders in Southern African History*, ed. Christopher Saunders. London: Heinemann, 1979.

Wylie, Dan. *Myth of Iron: Shaka in History*. Pietermaritzburg: University of KwaZulu-Natal Press, 2006.

## Formation of the Zulu Kingdom

Bryant, Alfred Thomas. *Olden Times in Zululand and Natal: Containing Earlier Political History of the Eastern-Nguni Clans*. London: Longmans, Green, 1929.

Gump, James Oliver. *The Formation of the Zulu Kingdom in South Africa, 1750–1840*. San Francisco: Em Texts, 1990.

Hamilton, Carolyn. *Terrific Majesty: The Powers of Shaka Zulu and the Limits of Historical Invention*. Cape Town: David Philip, 1998.

Raum, Johannes W. "Historical Concepts and the Evolutionary Interpretation of the Emergence of States: The Case of the Zulu Reconsidered Yet Again." *Zeitschrift für Ethnologie* 114 (1989): 125–38.

Wright, John. "Political Transformations in the Thukela-Mzimkhulu Region in the Late Eighteenth and Early Nineteenth Centuries." In *The Mfecane Debate: Reconstructive Debates in Southern African History*, ed. Carolyn Hamilton. Johannesburg: Witwatersrand University Press, 2001.

Wright, John, and Carolyn Hamilton. "Traditions and Transformations. The Phongolo-Mzimkhulu Region in the Late Eighteenth and Early Nineteenth Centuries." In *Natal and Zululand from Earliest Times to 1910: A New History*, ed. Andrew Duminy and Bill Guest. Pietermaritzburg: University of Natal Press and Shuter and Shooter, 1989.

## Zulu Society, Economy, and Political Structure

Barter, Catherine. *Alone Among the Zulus: The Narrative of a Journey Through the Zulu Country, South Africa* [1886]. Ed. Patricia L. Merrett. Pietermaritzburg: University of Natal Press, 1995.

Bryant, Alfred Thomas. *The Zulu People as They Were Before the White Man Came.* Pietermaritzburg: Shuter and Shooter, 1949.

Carton, Ben, John Laband, and Jabulani Sithole, eds. *Zulu Identities: Being Zulu Past and Present.* New York: Columbia University Press, 2009.

Colenbrander, Peter. "External Exchange and the Zulu Kingdom: Towards a Reassessment." In *Aspects of the Economic and Social History of Colonial Natal*, ed. Bill Guest and John Sellers. Pietermaritzburg: University of Natal Press, 1995.

Delegorgue, Adulphe. *Travels in Southern Africa* [1847]. Trans. Fleur Webb. Intro. Stephanie J. Alexander and Colin de B. Webb. Vol. 1. Pietermaritzburg: University of Natal Press, 1990.

Fynn, Henry Francis. *The Diary of Henry Francis Fynn* [1863]. Ed. James Stuart and Daniel McK. Malcolm. Pietermaritzburg: Shuter and Shooter, 1969.

Grout, L. *Zulu-land, or, Life Among the Zulu-Kafirs of Natal and Zulu-land, South Africa.* London: African Publication Society, 1861.

Guy, Jeff. "The Political Structure of the Zulu Kingdom During the Reign of Cetshwayo kaMpande." In *Before and After Shaka: Papers in Nguni History*, ed. J. B. Peires. Grahamstown, South Africa: Institute of Social and Economic Research, Rhodes University, 1981.

———. "Production and Exchange in the Zulu Kingdom." In *Before and After Shaka: Papers in Nguni History*, ed. J. B. Peires. Grahamstown, South Africa: Institute of Social and Economic Research, Rhodes University, 1981.

Hammond-Tooke, William David. *The Roots of Black South Africa.* Johannesburg: Jonathan Ball, 1993.

Humphreys, William Clayton. *The Journal of William Clayton Humphreys. Being a Personal Narrative of the Adventures and Experiences of a Trader and Hunter in the Zulu Country During the Months July–October 1851.* Intro. Julie Pridmore. Pietermaritzburg: University of Natal Press, 1993.

Isaacs, Nathaniel. *Travels and Adventures in Eastern Africa Descriptive of the Zoolus, Their Manners, Customs with a Sketch of Natal* [1836]. Ed. Louis Herman and Percival R. Kirby. Cape Town: C. Struik, 1970.

Jenkinson, Thomas B. *Amazulu: The Zulus, Their Past History, Manners, Customs and Language with Observations on the Country and Its Productions, Climate, etc., the Zulu War and Zululand Since the War* [1882]. Pretoria: State Library, facsimile reprint 1968.

Junod, Henri Alexandre. *The Life of a South African Tribe.* Vol. 1. Neuchâtel: Attinger Frères, 1912.

Krige, Eileen Jensen. *The Social System of the Zulus*. Pietermaritzburg: Shuter and Shooter, 1974.

Maclean, Charles Rawden. *The Natal Papers of "John Ross." Loss of the Brig Mary at Natal with Early Recollections of That Settlement and Among the Caffres* [1853–1855]. Ed. Stephen Grey. Pietermaritzburg: University of Natal Press, 1992.

Poland, Marguerite, David Hammond-Took, and Leigh Voight. *The Abundant Herds: A Celebration of the Nguni Cattle of the Zulu People*. Vlaeberg, South Africa: Fernwood Press, 2003.

Samuelson, Robert Charles Azariah. *Long, Long Ago*. Durban: Knox, 1929.

———. (Nomeleti). *Some Zulu Customs and Folk-Law*. London: Church, n.d.

Shooter, Joseph. *The Kaffirs of the Natal and Zulu Country* [1857]. Wolverhampton, U.K.: Advance Micrographics, facsimile reprint 1983.

Tyler, J. *Forty Years Among the Zulus* [1891]. Cape Town: C. Struik, facsimile reprint 1971.

Wilson, Monica. "The Nguni People." In *The Oxford History of South Africa*. Vol. 1, *South Africa to 1870*. Ed. Monica Wilson and Leonard Thompson. Oxford: At the Clarendon Press, 1969.

Wood, Marilee, coord. *Zulu Treasures: Of Kings and Commoners. A Celebration of the Material Culture of the Zulu People*. Durban: Local History Museums, 1996.

Wright, John. "Control of Women's Labour in the Zulu Kingdom." In *Before and After Shaka: Papers in Nguni History*, ed. J. B. Peires. Grahamstown, South Africa: Institute of Social and Economic Research, Rhodes University, 1981.

## Zulu Religion

Berglund, Axel-Ivar. *Zulu Thought-Patterns and Symbolism*. Uppsala: Swedish Institute of Missionary Research, 1976.

Bryant, Alfred Thomas. *Zulu Medicine and Medicine-Men*. Cape Town: C. Struik, 1966.

Callaway, M. D. *The Religious System of the Amazulu* [1877, 1884]. Cape Town: C. Struik, facsimile reprint 1970.

Hale, Frederick, ed. *Norwegian Missionaries in Natal and Zululand. Selected Correspondence 1844–1900*. Cape Town: Van Riebeeck Society, Second Series No. 27, 1997 for 1996.

Lambert, Michael. "Ancient Greek and Zulu Sacrificial Ritual: A Comparative Analysis." *Numen* 40 (1993): 293–318.

Ngubane, Harriet. *Body and Mind in Zulu Medicine: An Ethnography of Health and Disease in Nynswa-Zulu Thought and Practice.* London: Academic Press, 1977.

## Zulu Military System

Anon. [Fynney, Frederick Bernard.] *The Zulu Army, and Zulu Headmen. Compiled from Information Obtained from the Most Reliable Sources, and Published by Direction of the Lieut.-General Commanding, for the Information of Those Under His Command.* 2nd ed., revised. Pietermaritzburg, April 1879.

Bourquin, S. B. "The Zulu Military Organization and Challenge of 1879." *Military History Journal* 4, no. 4 (1979): 138–51.

Greaves, Adrian. "The Origin and Development of Age-Sets." *Journal of the Anglo Zulu War Historical Society* 12 (December 2002): 24–39.

Guy, Jeff. "A Note on Firearms in the Zulu Kingdom with Special Reference to the Anglo-Zulu War, 1879." *Journal of African History* 12, no. 4 (1971): 557–70.

Knight, Ian. "The Zulu Army, 1879." In *There Will Be an Awful Row at Home About This*, ed. Ian Knight. Shoreham-by-Sea, U.K.: Zulu Study Group, Victorian Military Society, 1987.

——. *The Anatomy of the Zulu Army from Shaka to Cetshwayo 1818–1879.* London: Greenhill Books, 1995.

——. *Zulu Warrior 1816–1906.* London: Osprey, 1995.

——. *Warrior Chiefs of Southern Africa: Shaka of the Zulu, Moshoeshoe of the Basotho, Mzilikazi of the Matabele, Maqoma of the Xhosa.* New York: Sterling, 1995.

——. *Great Zulu Battles 1838–1906.* London: Arms and Armour, 1998.

——. *Great Zulu Commanders.* London: Arms and Armour, 1999.

Laband, John. "The Zulu Army in the War of 1879: Some Cautionary Notes." *Journal of Natal and Zulu History* 2 (1979): 27–35.

——. "'Bloodstained Grandeur': Colonial and Imperial Stereotypes of Zulu Warriors and Zulu Warfare." In *Zulu Identities: Being Zulu Past and Present*, ed. Ben Carton, John Laband, and Jabulani Sithole. New York: Columbia University Press, 2009.

Lugg, Harry C. *Life Under a Zulu Shield.* Pietermaritzburg: Shuter and Shooter, 1975.

Thompson, Paul S. "Isandlwana to Mome: Zulu Experience in Overt Resistance to Colonial Rule." *Soldiers of the Queen* 77 (June 1994): 11–15.

Uzoigwe, G. N. "The Warrior and the State in Precolonial Africa: Comparative Perspectives." In *The Warrior Tradition in Modern Africa*, ed. Ali A. Mazrui. Leiden: E. J. Brill, 1977.

Wright, John B. "Pre-Shakan Age-Group Formations Among the Northern Nguni." *Natalia* 8 (December 1878): 22–30.

## Transfrontiersmen

Ballard, Charles. *John Dunn: The White Chief of Zululand.* Craighall, South Africa: A. D. Donker, 1985.
Laband, John. "Longcast in Zululand: The Paradoxical Life of a Transfrontiersman, 1850–1909." *Journal of Natal and Zulu History* 15 (1994/1995): 17–39.


# VOORTREKKER-ZULU WAR

## Printed Collections of Archival Materials

Bird, John, comp. *The Annals of Natal 1495–1845* [1885]. 2 vols. Cape Town: C. Struik, facsimile reprint 1965.
Chase, John Centlivres. *The Natal Papers: A Reprint of All Notices and Public Documents Connected with That Territory Including a Description of the Country and a History of Events from 1498 to 1843* [1843]. Cape Town: C. Struik, facsimile reprint 1968.
Leverton, Basil J. T., ed. *Records of Natal.* Vol. 2, *September 1828–July 1835.* South African Archival Records: Important Cape Documents Vol. 5. Pretoria: Government Printer, 1989.
———, ed. *Records of Natal.* Vol. 3, *August 1835–June 1838.* South African Archival Records: Important Cape Documents Vol. 6. Pretoria: Government Printer, 1990.
———, ed. *Records of Natal.* Vol. 4, *July 1838–September 1839.* South African Archival Records: Important Cape Documents Vol. 7. Pretoria: Government Printer, 1992.
Preller, G. S. *Voortrekkermense* [Voortrekker People]. 6 vols. Cape Town: Nasionale Pers, 1918, 1920, 1922, 1925, 1938.
Pretorius, H. S., and D. W. Kruger, eds. *Voortrekker Argiefstukke 1829–1849* [Voortrekker Archival Documents 1829–1849]. Pretoria: Staatsdrukker, 1937.

## Boers and the Great Trek

Becker, Peter. *Path of Blood: The Rise and Conquests of Mzilakazi, Founder of the Matabele Tribe of Southern Africa.* London: Longman, 1962.

Bulpin, T. V. *The Great Trek*. Cape Town: Books of Africa, 1969.

Cloete, Henry. *The History of the Great Boer Trek and the Origins of the South African Republics*. London: John Murray, 1899.

Crais, Clifton. *White Supremacy and Black Resistance in Pre-Industrial South Africa: The Making of the Colonial Order in the Eastern Cape, 1770–1865*. Cambridge: Cambridge University Press, 1992.

Du Bruyn, Johannes T. "The Great Trek." In *An Illustrated History of South Africa*, ed. Trewhella Cameron and Burridge Spies. Johannesburg: Jonathan Ball, 1986.

Etherington, Norman, "The Great Trek in Relation to the Mfecane: A Reassessment." *South African Historical Journal* 25 (1991): 3–21.

——. *The Great Treks. The Transformation of Southern Africa, 1815–1854*. Great Britain: Longman Pearson Education, 2001.

——. "Old Wine in New Bottles: The Persistence of Narrative Structures in the Historiography of the Mfecane and the Great Trek." In *The Mfecane Debate: Reconstructive Debates in Southern African History*, ed. Carolyn Hamilton. Johannesburg: Witwatersrand University Press, 2001.

Leach, Graham. *The Afrikaners*. London: Mandarin, 1989.

Le May, G.H.L. *The Afrikaners. An Historical Interpretation*. Oxford: Blackwell, 1995.

Meintjes, Johannes. *The Voortrekkers: The Story of the Great Trek and the Making of South Africa*. London: Cassell, 1973.

Muller, C.F.J. *Die Britse Owerheid en die Groot Trek* [The British Government and the Great Trek]. Cape Town: Juta, 1948.

——. *Die Oorsprong van die Groot Trek* [The Origin of the Great Trek]. Cape Town: Tafelberg, 1974.

——. "The Period of the Great Trek, 1834–1854." In *500 Years: A History of South Africa*, ed. C.F.J. Muller. 2nd ed. Pretoria: Academica, 1977.

——. *A Pictorial History of the Great Trek: Visual Documents Illustrating the Great Trek*. Pretoria: Tafelberg, 1978.

Nathan, Manfred. *The Voortrekkers of South Africa from Earliest Times to the Foundation of the Republics*. London: Gordon and Gotch, 1937.

Ransford, Oliver. *The Great Trek*. London: John Murray, 1972.

Theal, George. *History of the Boers in South Africa* [1887]. Cape Town: C. Struik, facsimile reprint 1973.

Thompson, Leonard. "Co-Operation and Conflict: The High Veld." In *The Oxford History of South Africa*. Vol. 1, *South Africa to 1870*. Ed. Monica Wilson and Leonard Thompson. Oxford: At the Clarendon Press, 1969.

Van der Merwe, Petrus J. *Die Matabeles en die Voortrekkers* (The Matabele and the Voortrekkers]. Pretoria: Staatsdrukker, 1986.

Van Jaarsveld, F. A. *Die Tydgenootlike Beoordeling van die Groot Trek* [The Contemporary Critique of the Great Trek]. Pretoria: UNISA, 1962.

———. *Die Beeld van die Groot Trek* [The Image of the Great Trek]. Pretoria: UNISA, 1963.

Walker, Eric A. *The Great Trek*. London: A. and C. Black, 1934.

———. "The Formation of New States, 1835–1854." In *The Cambridge History of the British Empire*. Vol. 8, *South Africa*. Ed. Eric A. Walker, 2nd ed. Cambridge: At the University Press, 1963.

## War of 1838–1840

Ballard, Charles. "Natal 1824–44: The Frontier Interregnum." *Journal of Natal and Zulu History* 5 (1982): 49–64.

———. "Traders, Trekkers, and Colonists." In *Natal and Zululand from Earliest Times to 1910: A New History*, ed. Andrew Duminy and Bill Guest. Pietermaritzburg: University of Natal Press and Shuter and Shooter, 1989.

Bantjes, J. G. *Journal der Ekspeditie van die Uitgewekene Boeren, onder hunnen Hoofd-Kommandant Andreas Wilhelmus Jacobus Pretorius (voormals van Graaff-Reinet), tegen Dingaan, Koning der Zulus, in de Maand November en December 1838.* [Journal of the Expedition of the Emigrant Farmers, under Commandant-General Andreas Wilhelmus Jacobus Pretorius (formerly of Graaff-Reinet), against Dingaan, King of the Zulus, in the Month November and December 1838]. In *Voortrekkermense*, vol. 6, ed. G. S. Preller. Cape Town: Nasionale Pers, 1938.

Cloete, Henry. *Five Lectures on the Emigration of the Dutch Farmers from the Colony of the Cape of Good Hope, and Their Present Settlement in the District of Natal, Until Their Formal Submission to Her Majesty's Authority, in the Year 1843.* Pietermaritzburg: Natal Society, 1856.

Cory, George E., ed. *The Diary of the Rev. Francis Owen, M.A., Missionary with Dingaan in 1837–38. Together with Extracts from the Writings of the Interpreters in Zulu, Messrs. Hully and Kirkman.* Cape Town: Van Riebeeck Society, 1926.

D'Assonville, V. E. *Blood River*. Weltevreden Park, South Africa: Marnix, 2000.

Du Buisson, Louis. *The White Man Cometh*. Johannesburg: Jonathan Ball, 1987.

Du Toit, A. C. *Offisiere en Manskappe Wat Deelgeneem Het aan die Slag van Bloed Rivier, 16 Desember 1838* [Officers and Men Who Took Part in the Battle of Blood River, 16 December 1838]. Pretoria: Genealogiese Genootskap van Suid-Afrika, 1995.

Duvenage, G.D.J. *Die Groot Trek: Die Eerste Drie Jare* [The Great Trek: The First Three Years]. Pretoria: Afrikanervolkswag, 1988.

Forman, Lionel. *Why Did Dingane Kill Retief? And Other Extracts from His History Notebooks*. Cape Town: S. Forman, 1964.

Gardiner, Allen Francis. *Narrative of a Journey to the Zoolu Country in South Africa, Undertaken in 1835* [1836]. Cape Town: C. Struik, facsimile reprint 1966.

Gie, S.F.N., ed. *Die Retief-Dingaan Ooreenkoms* [The Retief-Dingane Treaty]. Cape Town: Nasionale Pers, 1923.

Hugo, M. *Piet Retief* [Piet Retief]. Johannesburg: Voortrekkerpers, 1961.

Jansen, E. G. *Die Voortrekkers in Natal* [The Voortrekkers in Natal]. Cape Town: Nasionale Pers, 1938.

Kenny, R. V. *Piet Retief* [Piet Retief]. Cape Town: Human and Rousseau, 1976.

Kirby, Percival R., ed. *Andrew Smith and Natal. Documents Relating to the Early History of the Province*. Cape Town: Van Riebeeck Society, 1955.

Knight, Ian, and Gerry Embleton. *Boer Wars (1) 1836–1898*. London: Osprey Military, 1996.

Liebenberg, Barend Jacobus. *Andries Pretorius in Natal* [Andries Pretorius in Natal]. Pretoria: Academia, 1977.

Mackeurtan, Graham. *The Cradle Days of Natal, 1497–1845* [1930]. Durban: T. W. Griggs, facsimile reprint 1972.

Malefane, K., ed. *The Re-Interpretation of the Battle of Blood River/Ncome*. Pretoria: Department of Arts, Culture, Science, and Technology, 1998.

Opperman, A.J.P. *The Battle of Blood River*. Roodepoort, South Africa: CUM Books, 1982.

Preller, G. S. *Piet Retief* [Piet Retief]. Cape Town: Nasionale Pers, 1920.

———. *Andries Pretorius: Lewensgeskiedenis van die Voortrekker Kommandant-Generaal* [Andries Pretorius: Life History of the Voortrekker Commandant-General]. Johannesburg: Die Afrikaanse Pers, 1940.

Raum, Otto Friedrich. "Aspects of Zulu Diplomacy in the Nineteenth Century." *Afrika und Übersee* 66 (1983): 25–42.

Richards, Maureen. "The Battle of Blood River." *Journal of the Anglo Zulu War Historical Society* 1 (June 1999): 28–35.

Schoon, H. F., ed. *The Diary of Erasmus Smit, Minister to the Voortrekkers*. Trans. W.G.A. Mears. Cape Town: C. Struik, 1972.

Sithole, Jabulani. "Changing Meanings of the Battle of Ncome and Images of King Dingane in Twentieth-Century South Africa." In *Zulu Identities: Being Zulu Past and Present*, ed. Ben Carton, John Laband, and Jabulani Sithole. New York: Columbia University Press, 2009.

Theal, George. *The Republic of Natal*. Cape Town: Saul Solomon, 1886.

Thom, H. B. *Die Lewe van Gert Maritz* [The Life of Gert Maritz]. Cape Town: Nasionale Pers, 1947.

Thompson, Leonard. "Co-Operation and Conflict: The Zulu Kingdom and Natal." In *The Oxford History of South Africa.* Vol. 1, *South Africa to 1870.* Ed. Monica Wilson and Leonard Thompson. Oxford: At the Clarendon Press, 1969.


## BRITISH ARMY AND THE CONDUCT OF SMALL WARS

### Late Victorian Army and Society

Barnett, Correlli. *Britain and Her Army 1509–1970: A Military, Political, and Social Survey.* London: Allen Lane, 1970.

Bond, Brian. "The Late Victorian Army." *History Today* 11 (1961): 616–24.

Clayton, Anthony. *The British Officer: Leading the Army from 1660 to the Present.* Harlow, U.K.: Pearson Longman, 2006.

French, David. *Military Identities: The Regimental System, the British Army, and the British People c. 1870–2000.* Oxford: Oxford University Press, 2005.

Harries-Jenkins, Gwyn. *The Army in Victorian Society.* London: Routledge and Kegan Paul, 1977.

Spiers, Edward M. *The Army and Society 1815–1914.* London: Longman, 1980.

———. *The Late Victorian Army, 1868–1902.* Manchester: Manchester University Press, 1992.

———. "The Late Victorian Army 1868–1914." In *The Oxford Illustrated History of the British Army*, ed. David Chandler and Ian Beckett. Oxford: Oxford University Press, 1994.


### British Army and the Cardwell Reforms

Bond, Brian. "Edward Cardwell's Army Reforms, 1868–74." *Army Quarterly and Defence Journal* 84 (1962): 108–17.

Erickson, Arvel B. "Abolition of Purchase in the British Army." *Military Affairs* 23 (1959): 65–76.

Harries-Jenkins, Gwyn. "The Development of Professionalism in the Victorian Army." *Armed Forces and Society* 1, no. 4 (1975): 472–89.

Monick, S. "An Army in Transition." *Military History Journal* 4, no. 6 (1879). http://rapidttp.com/milhist/vol046sm.html.

Strachan, Hew. "Military Modernization 1789–1918." In *The Oxford Illustrated History of Modern Europe*, ed. T.C.W. Blanning. Oxford: Oxford University Press, 1996.

Tucker, Albert V. "Army and Society in England, 1870–1900: A Reassessment of the Cardwell Reforms." *Journal of British Studies* 2 (1963): 110–41.


## British Military Doctrine

Callwell, Charles Edward. *Small Wars: Their Principles and Practice*. 3rd ed. London: Her Majesty's Stationery Office, 1906.

Preston, A. W. "British Military Thought, 1856–90." *Army Quarterly and Defence Journal* 89 (1964): 57–74.

Strachan, Hew. "The British Way in Warfare." In *The Oxford Illustrated History of the British Army*, ed. David Chandler and Ian Beckett. Oxford: Oxford University Press, 1994.


## British Campaigning in Africa During the Victorian Era

Bailes, Howard. "Technology and Imperialism: A Case Study of the Victorian Army in Africa." *Victorian Studies* 24, no. 1 (1980): 83–104.

Barthorp, Michael. *The British Army on Campaign 1816–1900*. London: Osprey, 1987.

Beckett, Ian F. W. *The Victorians at War*. London: Hambledon and London, 2003.

Boyden, Peter B., Alan J. Guy, and Marion Harding, eds. *"Ashes and Blood." The British Army in South Africa, 1795–1914*. London: National Army Museum, 1999.

Burroughs, Peter. "Imperial Defence and the Victorian Army." *Journal of Imperial and Commonwealth History* 15, no. 1 (1986): 55–72.

Castle, Ian. *British Army: Zulus to Boers*. Washington, D.C.: Brassey's, 2000.

Emery, Frank. *Marching over Africa: Letters from Victorian Soldiers*. London: Hodder and Stoughton, 1986.

Farewell, Byron. *Queen Victoria's Little Wars*. New York: Norton, 1972.

Headrick, Daniel R. *The Tools of Empire: Technology and European Imperialism in the Nineteenth Century*. New York: Oxford University Press, 1981.

James, Lawrence. *The Savage Wars: British Campaigns in Africa, 1870–1920*. New York: St. Martin's Press, 1985.

Knight, Ian. *Go to Your God Like a Soldier: The British Soldier Fighting for Empire, 1837–1902*. London: Greenhill Books, 1996.

Laband, John. "The British Way of War in South Africa, 1837–1902: New Approaches." *Society for Army Historical Research*, Special Publication No. 16 (2007): 10–22.

Lieven, Michael. "Heroism, Heroics, and the Making of Heroes: The Anglo-Zulu War of 1879." *Albion* 30, no. 3 (1998): 419–38.

———. "The British Soldiery and the Ideology of Empire: Letters from Zululand." *Journal of the Anglo Zulu War Historical Society* 12 (December 2002): 8–15.

MacKenzie, John M., ed. *Popular Imperialism and the Military, 1850–1950.* Manchester: Manchester University Press, 1992.

Pakenham, Thomas. *The Scramble for Africa: White Man's Conquest of the Dark Continent.* New York: Avon Books, 1992.

Porch, Douglas. "Imperial Wars: From the Seven Years War to the First World War." In *The Oxford History of Modern War*, ed. Charles Townshend. Oxford: Oxford University Press, 2000.

———. *Wars of Empire.* London: Cassell, 2000.

Spiers, Edward. *The Victorian Soldier in Africa.* Vancouver: University of British Columbia Press, 2004.

Strachan, Hew. *European Armies and the Conduct of War.* London: Routledge, 2001.

Vandervort, Bruce. *Wars of Imperial Conquest in Africa 1830–1914.* Bloomington: Indiana University Press, 1998.

Whitehouse, Howard, and Peter Dennis. *Battle in Africa, 1879–1914.* Mansfield, U.K.: Fieldbooks, 1987.

## HISTORIES OF THE ANGLO-ZULU WAR

### Printed Collection of Archival Materials

Laband, John, series ed., and Ian Knight, volume ed. *Archives of Zululand: The Anglo-Zulu War 1879.* 6 vols. London: Archival Publications International, 2000.

### Official History

Intelligence Branch of the Quartermaster-General's Department, Horse Guards, War Office. *Narrative of the Field Operations Connected with the Zulu War of 1879.* London: Her Majesty's Stationery Office, 1881.

Laband, John. *Companion to Narrative of the Field Operations Connected with the Zulu War of 1879.* Constantia, South Africa: N and S Press, 1989.

## General Histories of the Anglo-Zulu War

Barthorp, Michael. *The Zulu War: A Pictorial History*. Poole, U.K.: Blandford, 1980.

——. *The Zulu War: Rorke's Drift to Ulundi*. London: Cassell, 2002.

Clammer, David. *The Zulu War*. New York: St. Martin's Press, 1973.

Coan, Stephen. "Sir H. Rider Haggard and the Anglo-Zulu War in Fact and Fiction." *Journal of the Anglo Zulu War Historical Society* 10 (December 2001): 45–56.

Creswicke, Louis. *The Zulu War*. Edinburgh: E. C. Jack, 1900.

David, Saul. *Zulu: The Heroism and Tragedy of the Zulu War of 1879*. New York: Penguin, 2005.

Diamond, Michael. "Popular Entertainment and the Zulu War." *Journal of the Anglo Zulu War Historical Society* 4 (December 1998): 40–47.

Duminy, Andrew, and Charles Ballard, eds. *The Anglo-Zulu War: New Perspectives*. Pietermaritzburg: University of Natal Press, 1981.

Edgerton, Robert B. *Like Lions They Fought: The Zulu War and the Last Black Empire in South Africa*. London: Collier Macmillan, 1988.

Greaves, Adrian. *Redcoats and Zulus: Myths, Legends, and Explanations of the Anglo-Zulu War 1879*. Barnsley, U.K.: Pen and Sword, 2004.

——. *Crossing the Buffalo: The Zulu War of 1879*. London: Weidenfeld and Nicolson, 2005.

Greaves, Adrian, and Ian Knight. *A Review of the South African Campaign of 1879*. Tenterden, U.K.: Debinair, 2000.

Gump, James Oliver. *The Dust Rose Like Smoke: The Subjugation of the Zulu and the Sioux*. Lincoln: University of Nebraska Press, 1996.

Guy, Jeff. "The British Invasion of Zululand: Some Thoughts for the Centenary Year." *Reality* 11, no. 1 (1979): 8–14.

Knight, Ian. *Brave Men's Blood: The Epic of the Zulu War, 1879*. London: Greenhill Books, 1990.

——. *The Zulu War 1879*. London: Osprey, 2003.

——. *The National Army Museum Book of the Zulu War*. London: Sidgwick and Jackson, 2004.

——. *A Companion to the Anglo-Zulu War*. Barnsley, U.K.: Pen and Sword, 2008.

Knight, Ian, ed. *There Will Be an Awful Row at Home About This*. Shoreham-by-Sea, U.K.: Zulu Study Group, Victorian Military Society, 1987.

Knight, Ian, and Ian Castle. *The Zulu War: Then and Now*. London: After the Battle, 1993.

——. *The Zulu War: Twilight of a Warrior Nation*. London: Osprey, 1994.

Laband, John. Zulu Strategic and Tactical Options in the Face of the British Invasion of 1879." *Scientia Militaria: South Africa Journal of Military Studies* 28, no. 1 (1998): 1–15.

——. "Anglo-Zulu War Studies: Where to from Here?" *Journal of the Anglo Zulu War Historical Society* 12 (December 2002): 44–47.

——. *Kingdom in Crisis: The Zulu Response to the British Invasion of 1879.* Barnsley, U.K.: Pen and Sword, 2007.

Laband, John, and Paul Thompson. *Kingdom and Colony at War: Sixteen Studies on the Anglo-Zulu War of 1879.* Pietermaritzburg: University of Natal Press, 1990.

——. *The Illustrated Guide to the Anglo-Zulu War.* Pietermaritzburg: University of Natal Press, 2000.

Lloyd, Alan. *The Zulu War.* London: Hart-Davis, MacGibbon, 1973.

McBride, Angus. *The Zulu War.* London: Osprey Men-at-Arms, 1976.

Pollard, Tony. "The Mountain Is Their Monument: An Archaeological Approach to the Landscape of the Anglo-Zulu War." In *Fields of Battle: Terrain in Military History,* ed. Peter Doyle and Matthew R. Bennett. Dordrecht: Kluwer Academic, 2002.

Rattray, David. *The David Rattray Guide to the Zulu War.* Barnsley, U.K.: Pen and Sword, 2003.

Wilmot, Alexander. *History of the Zulu War.* London: Richardson and Best, 1880.

## Firsthand Narratives of the Zulu Campaign

Ashe, Walter, and Edmund Verney Wyatt Edgell. *The Story of the Zulu Campaign* [1880]. Intro. John Laband. Cape Town: N and S Press, 1989.

Ashwood, Rodney, ed. *For Queen and Country: The Zulu War Diary of Lieutenant Wilfred Heaton 24th Regiment of Foot 1879.* Darlington, U.K.: Serendipity, 2005.

Bennett, Ian H. W., ed. *Eyewitness in Zululand: The Campaign Reminiscences of Colonel W. A. Dunne, CB: South Africa, 1877–1881.* London: Greenhill Books, 1989.

Butterfield, Paul Henry, ed. *War and Peace in South Africa 1879–1881: The Writings of Philip Anstruther and Edward Essex.* Johannesburg: Scripta Africana, 1987.

Child, Daphne, ed. *The Zulu War Journal of Colonel Henry Harford, C. B.* Pietermaritzburg: Shuter and Shooter, 1978.

Clarke, Sonia, ed. *Invasion of Zululand 1879: Anglo-Zulu War Experiences of Arthur Harness; John Jervis, 4th Viscount St Vincent; and Sir Henry Bulwer.* Johannesburg: Brenthurst Press, 1979.

Emery, Frank. *The Red Soldier: Letters from the Zulu War, 1879.* London: Hodder and Stoughton, 1977.

Hart-Synnot, Beatrice M., ed. *Letters of Major General Fitzroy Hart-Synnot C. B., C.M.G.* London: E. Arnold, 1912.

Jones, Leonie Twentyman, ed. *Reminiscences of the Zulu War by John Maxwell.* Cape Town: University of Cape Town Libraries, 1979.

Knight, Ian. *"By the Orders of the Great White Queen": Campaigning in Zululand Through the Eyes of the British Soldier, 1879.* London: Greenhill Books, 1992.

Ludlow, Walter Robert. *Zululand and Cetywayo.* London: Simpkin, Marshall, 1882.

Mitford, Bertram. *Through the Zulu Country: Its Battlefields and Its People* [1883]. Intro. Ian Knight. London: Greenhill Books, 1992.

Molyneux, William Charles Francis. *Campaigning in South Africa and Egypt.* London: Macmillan, 1896.

Smith-Dorrien, Horace Lockwood. *Memories of Forty-Eight Years Service.* London: J. Murray, 1925.

## War Correspondents and Newspaper Reports

Bourquin, S. B., comp. *The First Six Months of the Zulu War of 1879 as Reported in "The Graphic" January–June 1879.* Durban: Department of Bantu Administration, 1963.

——, comp. *The Concluding Stages of the Zulu War of 1879 as Reported in "The Graphic" July–December 1879.* Durban: Department of Bantu Administration, 1965.

Bourquin, S. B., and Tania M. Johnston, comps. *The Zulu War of 1879 as Reported in "The Illustrated London News" During January–December 1879.* Durban: Department of Bantu Administration, 1971.

Deléage, Paul. *End of a Dynasty: The Last Days of the Prince Imperial, Zululand 1879.* [*Trois Mois chez les Zoulous et les Derniers Jours de Prince Impérial* (1879).] Trans. Fleur Webb. Intro. Bill Guest. Pietermaritzburg: University of KwaZulu-Natal Press, 2008.

Fripp, Charles E. "Reminiscences of the Zulu War, 1879." *Pall Mall Magazine* 20 (1900): 547–62.

Laband, John, and Ian Knight. *The War Correspondents: The Anglo-Zulu War.* Stroud, U.K.: Alan Sutton, 1996.

Lock, Ron, and Peter Quantrill, comps. *The Red Book. Natal Press Reports: Anglo-Zulu War 1879.* London: *Anglo Zulu War Historical Society*, 2000.

Moodie, D.C.F. *Moodie's Zulu War* [1879]. Intro. John Laband. Cape Town: N and S Press, 1988.

Norris-Newman, Charles L. *In Zululand with the British Throughout the War of 1879* [1880]. London: Greenhill Books, facsimile reprint 1998.

Prior, Melton. *Campaigns of a War Correspondent*. London: Edward Arnold, 1912.

Wilkinson-Latham, Robert. *From Our Special Correspondent: Victorian War Correspondents and Their Campaigns*. London: Hodder and Stoughton, 1979.


## Collections of Campaign Paintings and Drawings

Brown, Ronald Arden, ed. *The Road to Ulundi: The Water-Colour Drawings of John North Crealock (the Zulu War of 1879)*. Pietermaritzburg: University of Natal Press, 1969.

Rattray, David. *A Soldier Artist in Zululand: William Whitelocke Lloyd and the Anglo-Zulu War of 1879*. KwaZulu-Natal, South Africa: Rattray, 2007.


## Eyewitness Accounts from Within the Zulu Kingdom

"Cetywayo's Story of the Zulu Nation and the War." *Macmillan's Magazine* (February 1880): 273–95.

Filter, H., comp. *Paulina Dlamini: Servant of Two Kings*. Ed. and trans. S. B. Bourquin. Pietermaritzburg: University of Natal Press, 1986.

Knight, Ian, ed. "'Kill Me in the Shadows': The Bowden Collection of Anglo-Zulu War Oral History." *Soldiers of the Queen* 74 (September 1993): 9–18.

Laband, John. *Fight Us in the Open: The Anglo-Zulu War Through Zulu Eyes*. Pietermaritzburg: Shuter and Shooter, 1985.

Moodie, D.C.F., ed. *John Dunn, Cetywayo, and the Three Generals*. Pietermaritzburg: Natal Printing and Publishing, 1886.

"Statement of Two Zulu Prisoners." *The Aborigines' Friend: A Journal of the Transactions of the Aborigines' Protection Society*, new series, 5 (June 1879): 147–49.

Vijn, Cornelius. *Cetshwayo's Dutchman: Being the Private Journal of a White Trader in Zululand During the British Invasion*. Trans. from the Dutch and edited with preface and notes by J. W. Colenso, Bishop of Natal [1880]. London: Greenhill Books, facsimile reprint 1988.

Webb, C. de B., and John B. Wright, eds. *A Zulu King Speaks: Statements Made by Cetshwayo kaMpande on the History and Customs of His People*. Pietermaritzburg: University of Natal Press, 1978.

Webb, Colin de B., ed. "A Zulu Boy's Recollections of the Zulu War." *Natalia* 8 (December 1978): 8–21.

# ORIGINS OF THE ANGLO-ZULU WAR

## General Analysis

Bird, John. *An Inquiry into the Causes of the Zulu War*. Pietermaritzburg: Vause, Slatter, 1880.

Cope, Richard. *Ploughshare of War: The Origins of the Anglo-Zulu War, 1879*. Pietermaritzburg: University of Natal Press, 1999.

Holden, W. Clifford. *British Rule in South Africa: Illustrated in the Rule of Kama and His Tribe, and of the War in Zululand*. London: Wesleyan Conference Office, 1879.

Webb, C. de B. "The Origins of the War: Problems of Interpretation." In *The Anglo-Zulu War: New Perspectives*, ed. Andrew Duminy and Charles Ballard. Pietermaritzburg: University of Natal Press, 1981.

## Confederation

Benyon, John A. *Proconsul and Paramountcy in South Africa: The High Commission, British Supremacy, and the Sub-Continent, 1806–1910*. Pietermaritzburg: University of Natal Press, 1980.

Etherington, Norman. "Labour Supply and the Genesis of South African Confederation in the 1870s." *Journal of African History* 20, no. 3 (1979): 235–53.

Goodfellow, Clement Francis. *Great Britain and South African Confederation, 1870–1881*. Cape Town: Oxford University Press, 1966.

Guest, Bill. "The War, Natal, and Confederation." In *The Anglo-Zulu War: New Perspectives*, ed. Andrew Duminy and Charles Ballard. Pietermaritzburg: University of Natal Press, 1981.

Headlam, Cecil. "The Failure of Confederation, 1871–1881." In *The Cambridge History of the British Empire*. Vol. 8, *South Africa*. Ed. Eric A. Walker, 2nd ed. Cambridge: Cambridge University Press, 1963.

## Relations Between the Zulu Kingdom and Its Neighbors

Colenbrander, Peter. "The Zulu Political Economy on the Eve of the War." In *The Anglo-Zulu War: New Perspectives*, ed. Andrew Duminy and Charles Ballard. Pietermaritzburg: University of Natal Press, 1981.

Etherington, Norman. "Anglo-Zulu Relations 1856–1878." In *The Anglo-Zulu War: New Perspectives*, ed. Andrew Duminy and Charles Ballard. Pietermaritzburg: University of Natal Press, 1981.

Kennedy, Paul A. "Fatal Diplomacy: Sir Theophilus Shepstone and the Zulu Kings, 1839–1879." Doctoral thesis, University of California, 1976.

Lucas, Thomas J. *The Zulus and the British Frontiers*. London: Chapman and Hall, 1879.

Mann, Robert James. *The Zulus and Boers of South Africa: A Fragment of Recent History*. London: Edward Stanford, 1879.

Monteith, Mary A. "Cetshwayo and Sekhukhune 1875–1879." Master's thesis, University of the Witwatersrand, 1978.

Reynecke, S. J. "Utrecht in die Geskiedenis van die Transvaal tot 1877" [Utrecht in the History of the Transvaal Until 1877]. *Archives Year Book for South African History*, 1958 (2). Pretoria: Publications Branch of the Office of the Director of Archives, 1958.

Van Rooyen, T. S. "Die Verhouding tussen die Boere, Engelse, en Naturelle in die Geskiedenis van die Oos Transvaal tot 1882" [Relations Between the Boers, English, and Natives in the History of the Eastern Transvaal Until 1882]. *Archives Year Book for South African History*, 1951 (1). Cape Town: Publications Branch of the Office of the Director of Archives, 1951.

## Britain and the Transvaal

Fisher, W. E. Garrett. *The Transvaal and the Boers*. London: Chapman and Hall, 1900.

Haggard, H. Rider. *The Days of My Life: An Autobiography*. Vol. 1. London: Longmans, Green, 1926.

Intelligence Branch of the Quartermaster-General's Department, Horse Guards, War Office. *Précis of Information Concerning South Africa: The Transvaal Territory*. London: Her Majesty's Stationery Office, 1878.

Smith, Kenneth Wyndham. "The Campaigns Against the Bapedi of Sekhukhune, 1877–1879." *Archives Year Book for South African History*, 1967 (2). Johannesburg: Publications Branch of the Office of the Director of Archives, 1967.

Thompson, Leonard. "Great Britain and the Africana Republics." In *The Oxford History of South Africa*. Vol. 2, *South Africa 1870–1966*. Ed. Monica Wilson and Leonard Thompson. Oxford: At the Clarendon Press, 1971.

## Sir Bartle Frere and the Making of a War

Benyon, John. "Isandhlwana and the Passing of a Proconsul." *Natalia* 8 (December 1978): 38–45.

Emery, Frank. "Geography and Imperialism: The Role of Sir Bartle Frere (1815–84)." *Geographical Journal* 150, no. 3 (1984): 342–50.

Frere, Bartle. *Afghanistan and South Africa: Letters.* London: J. Murray, 1881.

Hallam Parr, Henry. *A Sketch of the Kafir and Zulu Wars.* London: C. Kegan Paul, 1880.

Martineau, John. *The Life and Correspondence of the Right Hon. Sir Bartle Frere, Bart., G.C.B., ER.S., Etc.* Vol. 2. London: John Murray, 1895.

O'Connor, Clare. "Sir Michael Hicks Beach." *Journal of the Anglo Zulu War Historical Society* 11 (June 2002): 12–19.

O'Connor, Damian. *The Zulu and the Raj: The Life of Sir Bartle Frere.* Knebworth, U.K.: Able, 2002.

Webb, Colin de B. "Lines of Power: The High Commissioner, the Telegraph, and the War of 1879." *Natalia* 8 (December 1978): 31–37.

Worsfold, W. Basil. *Sir Bartle Frere.* London: T. Butterworth, 1923.

## Colenso Critique of the War

"The Bishop of Natal on the Zulu War." *The Aborigines' Friend: A Journal of the Transactions of the Aborigines' Protection Society*, new series, 6 (December 1879): 165–78.

Chesson, Frederick William. *The War in Zululand: Brief Review of Sir Bartle Frere's Policy, Drawn from Official Documents.* London: P. S. King, 1879.

Colenso, Frances E., assisted by Edward Durnford. *History of the Zulu War and Its Origin.* London: Chapman and Hall, 1881.

Colenso, John William, and Harriette Emily Colenso. *Digest of Zulu Affairs Compiled by Bishop Colenso and Continued After His Death by His Daughter Harriette Emily Colenso.* Series no. 1 (December 1878–April 1881). Bishopstowe, Natal: privately printed, 1878–1888.

Cox, George W. *The Life of John William Colenso.* London: W. Ridgway, 1888.

Edgecombe, Ruth. "Bishop Colenso and the Zulu Nation." *Journal of Natal and Zulu History* 3 (1980): 15–29.

Greaves, Adrian, ed. "Bishop Colenso's Sermon, March 12th 1879." *Journal of the Anglo Zulu War Historical Society* 6 (December 1999): 47–51.

Guy, Jeff. *The Heretic: A Study of the Life of John William Colenso 1814–1883.* Johannesburg: Ravan Press; Pietermaritzburg: University of Natal Press, 1983.

Henfrey, Anthony W. "What Doth the Lord Require of Us? Bishop John William Colenso and the Isandlwana Sermon Preached in the Cathedral Church of St. Peter. Pietermaritzburg March 12th, 1879." *Journal of the Anglo Zulu War Historical Society* 5 (June 1999): 41–51.

*The Zulu War: Correspondence Between His Excellency the High Commissioner and the Bishop of Natal, Referring to the Present Invasion of Zululand, with Extracts from the Blue Books and Additional Information from Other Sources.* Durban: n.p., 1879.

## ZULULAND CAMPAIGN OF 1879

### Critique of Chelmsford's Conduct of the Campaign

Anon. "The Zulu War." *Blackwood's Edinburgh Magazine* (March 1879): 376–94.

Clarke, Sonia, ed. *Zululand at War 1879: The Conduct of the Anglo-Zulu War.* Johannesburg: Brenthurst Press, 1984.

Durnford, Edward. *Isandhlwana, Lord Chelmsford's Statements Compared with Evidence.* London: P. S. King, 1880.

Forbes, Archibald. "Lord Chelmsford and the Zulu War." *Nineteenth Century* 7 (February 1880): 216–34.

French, Gerald. *Lord Chelmsford and the Zulu War.* London: John Lane, 1939.

Harness, Arthur. "The Zulu Campaign from a Military Point of View." *Fraser's Magazine* (April 1880): 477–88.

Laband, John, ed. *Lord Chelmsford's Zululand Campaign 1878–1879.* Stroud, U.K.: Alan Sutton for the Army Records Society, 1994.

———. "'The Danger of Divided Command': British Civil and Military Disputes over the Conduct of the Zululand Campaigns of 1879 and 1888." *Journal of the Society for Army Historical Research* 81, no. 328 (2003): 339–55.

———. "Lord Chelmsford." In *Victoria's Generals*, ed. Steven J. Corvi and Ian F. W. Beckett. Barnsley, U.K.: Pen and Sword, 2009.

Mathews, Jeffrey. "Lord Chelmsford: British General in Southern Africa 1878–1879." Doctoral thesis, University of South Africa, 1986.

O'Connor, Damian P. "Running for Cover: Parliament and the Anglo-Zulu War January–March 1879." *Journal of the Anglo Zulu War Historical Society* 10 (December 2001): 37–44.

### 1st Invasion (No. 2 Column and No. 3 Column)

*General*

Atkinson, Christopher Thomas. *The South Wales Borderers 24th Foot 1689–1937.* Cambridge: Printed for the Regimental History Committee at the University Press, 1937.

Chadwick, G. A. "The Anglo-Zulu War of 1879: Isandlwana and Rorke's Drift." *Military History Journal* 4, no. 4 (1979): 115–32.

Drooglever, Robin W. E. *The Road to Isandhlwana: Colonel Anthony Durnford in Natal and Zululand*. London: Greenhill Books, 1992.

Durnford, Edward. *A Soldier's Life and Work in South Africa, 1872–1879: A Memory of the Late Colonel A. W. Durnford, Royal Engineers*. London: Sampson Low, Marston, Searle and Rivington, 1882.

Elliott, W. J. *The Victoria Cross in Zululand and South Africa*. Vol. 1, *Isandhlwana and Rorke's Drift*. London: Dean and Son, n.d. [late 1880s].

Furneaux, Rupert. *The Zulu War: Isandhlwana and Rorke's Drift*. London: Weidenfeld and Nicolson, 1963.

Gon, Philip. *The Road to Isandlwana: The Years of an Imperial Battalion*. Johannesburg: A. D. Donker, 1979.

Hamilton-Browne, George. *A Lost Legionary in South Africa*. London: T. W. Laurie, 1912.

*Historical Records of the 2nd Battalion, 24th Regiment, for the Campaign in South Africa, 1877–78–79: Embracing the Kaffir and Zulu Wars*. Confidential. Published for the use of the officers, non-commissioned officers, and men of the 24th Regiment only. Secunderabad, Deccan: Press, 2nd Battalion, "The South Wales Borderers," January 1882.

Holme, Norman, comp. *The Silver Wreath: Being the 24th Regiment at Isandhlwana and Rorke's Drift*. London: Samson Books, 1979.

Knight, Ian. *Zulu: The Battles of Isandlwana and Rorke's Drift 22nd–23rd January 1879*. London: Windrow and Greene, 1992.

———. "Charlatan of Empire: Did a Colourful Victorian Adventurer Invent His Military Career?" *Journal of the Anglo Zulu War Historical Society* 20 (December 2006). www.azwhsmembers.org.

Lock, Ron, and Peter Quantrill. *Zulu Vanquished: Isandlwana and the Early Months of the Zulu War*. London: Greenhill Books, 2006.

Paton, George, Farquar Glennie, and William Penn Symons, eds. *Historical Records of the 24th Regiment from Its Formation in 1689*. London: A. H. Swiss, 1892.

## Isandlwana

Alexander, Graham. "Lucky Essex." *Journal of the Anglo Zulu War Historical Society* 14 (December 2003): 1–14.

Ashwood, Rodney. "Lieutenant Heaton's Dairy: Fresh Evidence Concerning Events on 22 January 1879." *Journal of the Anglo Zulu War Historical Society* 15 (June 2004): 11–16.

Beckett, Ian. *Isandlwana 1879*. London: Brassey's, 2003.

Clements, William H. *The Glamour and Tragedy of the Zulu War*. London: John Lane, 1936.

Coghill, Patrick. *Whom the Gods Love: A Memoir of Lieutenant Neville Josiah Aylmer Coghill, VC*. Gloucestershire: private publication, 1966.

Coupland, Reginald. *Zulu Battlepiece: Isandhlwana*. London: Collins, 1948.

Durnford, Edward. *Isandhlwana, 22nd January, 1879. A Narrative, Compiled from Official and Reliable Sources*. London: P. S. King, 1879.

Greaves, Adrian. "Lt. Col. Durnford RE and the Isandlwana Court of Enquiry." *Journal of the Anglo Zulu War Historical Society* 4 (December 1998): 1–7.

———. *Isandlwana*. London: Cassell, 2001.

Greaves, Adrian, and Brian Best, eds. *The Curling Letters of the Zulu War: "There Was Awful Slaughter."* Barnsley, U.K.: Pen and Sword, 2001.

Jackson, F. W. David. "Isandhlwana, 1879: The Sources Re-Examined." *Journal of the Society for Army Historical Research* 49, nos. 173, 175, 176 (1965): 39–43, 113–32, 169–83.

———. "Isandhlwana Revisited: A Letter to the Editor." *Soldiers of the Queen* 33 (July 1983): 9–20.

———. "The First Battalion, Twenty-Fourth Regiment, Marches to Isandhlwana." In *There Will Be an Awful Row at Home About This*, ed. Ian Knight. Shoreham-by-Sea, U.K.: Zulu Study Group, Victorian Military Society, 1987.

———. *Hill of the Sphinx: The Battle of Isandlwana*. London: Westerners, 2004.

Knight, Ian. "Ammunition at Isandlwana: A Reply." *Journal of the Society for Army Historical Research* 73, no. 296 (1995): 237–50.

———. *The Sun Turned Black*. Johannesburg: Watermans, 1995.

———. "'A Scene of Utter Confusion Seems to Have Occurred . . . ': An Explanation of Some of the Controversies Which Still Surround the Battle of Isandlwana." *Journal of the Anglo Zulu War Historical Society* 2 (December 1997): 37–49.

———. "'The Sun Turned Black.' The Isandlwana Eclipse Debate." *Journal of the Anglo Zulu War Historical Society* 7 (June 2000): 21–22.

———. *Isandlwana 1879*. Oxford: Osprey, 2002.

———. *Isandlwana 1879: The Great Zulu Victory*. Westport, Conn.: Praeger Illustrated Military History, 2005.

Knight, Ian, and Ian Castle. *Isandlwana*. Barnsley, U.K.: Pen and Sword, 2000.

Laband, John, and Jeff Mathews. *Isandlwana*. Pietermaritzburg: Centaur, 1992.

Lock, Ron. "Isandlwana: New Clues to the Reason Why." *Journal of the Anglo Zulu War Historical Society* 3 (June 1998): 12–19.

———. "Captain Alan Gardner." *Journal of the Anglo Zulu War Historical Society* 5 (June 1999): 16–22.

Lock, Ron, and Peter Quantrill. *Zulu Victory: The Epic of Isandlwana and the Cover-Up*. London: Greenhill Books, 2002.

———. "The Encounter with the Zulu Army." *Journal of the Society for Army Historical Research* 83, no. 334 (2005): 158–64.

Morris, Donald. "Isandhlwana." *Soldiers of the Queen* 29/30 (Summer 1982): 3–22.

Smith, Keith I. "Isandlwana: The Zulu Bivouac." *Journal of the Anglo Zulu War Historical Society* 15 (June 2004): 39–42.

———. "Isandlwana: A Timetable." *Journal of the Anglo Zulu War Historical Society* 18 (December 2005). www.azwhsmembers.org.

Snook, Mike. *How Can Man Die Better: The Secret of Isandlwana Revealed*. London: Greenhill Books, 2006.

Verbeek, Jennifer. "Saving the Queen's Colour." *Natalia* 8 (December 1978): 46–53.

Wagner, Captain Erich. "A Lion Dishevelled: The Response of the British Press to the Battle of Isandlwana." *Journal of the Anglo Zulu War Historical Society* 7 (June 2000): 29–39.

Whybra, Julian. "Contemporary Sources and the Composition of the Main Zulu Impi, January 1879." *Soldiers of the Queen* 53 (June 1988): 13–16.


## Rorke's Drift

Anon. *Defence of Rorke's Drift January 22, 1879. By an Eye-Witness*. Durban: Natal Mercury Press, n.d.

Bancroft, J. W. *Rorke's Drift*. Tunbridge Wells, U.K.: Spellmount, 1991.

Bayham-Jones, Alan, and Lee Stevenson. *Rorke's Drift, by Those Who Were There*. Brighton: Lee Stevenson Publishing, 2003.

Glover, Michael. *Rorke's Drift*. London: Wordsworth Military Library, 1997.

Greaves, Adrian. *Rorke's Drift*. London: Cassell, 2002.

Johnson, Barry C. *Hook of Rorke's Drift: The Life of Henry Hook VC*. Birmingham: Johnson-Taunton Military Press, 2004.

Knight, Ian. *Nothing Remains but To Fight: The Defence of Rorke's Drift, 1879*. London: Greenhill Books, 1993.

———. *Rorke's Drift 1879. "Pinned Like Rats in a Hole."* London: Osprey Military, 1996.

———. "'Cruel Slaughter and Bloodshed.' Some Reflections on the Battle of Rorke's Drift." *Journal of the Anglo Zulu War Historical Society* 3 (June 1998): 47–54.

——. "The Mysterious Lieutenant Adendorff of Rorke's Drift: Hero or Coward?" *Journal of the Anglo Zulu War Historical Society* 5 (June 1999): 23–28.

Knight, Ian, and Ian Castle. *Rorke's Drift.* Barnsley, U.K.: Pen and Sword, 2000.

Laband, John. "'O! Let's Go and Have a Fight at Jim's!' The Zulu at the Battle of Rorke's Drift." In *Kingdom and Colony at War: Sixteen Studies on the Anglo-Zulu War of 1879,* ed. John Laband and Paul Thompson. Pietermaritzburg: University of Natal Press,1990.

Lloyd, William Glyn. *John Williams V.C.* Cwmbran, Wales: W. G. Lloyd, 1993.

Lummis, William M. *Padre George Smith of Rorke's Drift.* Norwich, U.K.: Wensome Books, 1978.

Holme, Norman. "The Roll of Rorke's Drift Defenders: The Sources Investigated." *Journal of the Anglo Zulu War Historical Society* 3 (June 1998): 29–34.

Snook, Mike. *Like Wolves on the Fold: The Defence of Rorke's Drift.* London: Greenhill Books, 2006.

Thompson, P. S. "The Natal Native Contingent at Rorke's Drift, January 22, 1879." In *There Will Be an Awful Row at Home About This,* ed. Ian Knight. Shoreham-by-Sea, U.K.: Zulu Study Group, Victorian Military Society, 1987.

Yorke, Edmund. *Rorke's Drift: Anatomy of an Epic Zulu War Siege.* Stroud, U.K.: Tempus, 2001.

## Coastal Campaign (No. 1 Column, the Eshowe Relief Column, and the 1st Division, South African Field Force)

Anon. "The Zulu War: With Colonel Pearson at Eshowe. By One Who Was There." *Blackwood's Edinburgh Magazine* (July 1879): 1–29.

Blood, Bindon. *Four Score Years and Ten: Bindon Blood's Reminiscences.* London: G. Bell, 1933.

Castle, Ian, and Ian Knight. *Fearful Hard Times: The Siege and Relief of Eshowe, 1879.* London: Greenhill Books, 1994.

Dawnay, Guy C. *Private Journal of Guy C. Dawnay. Campaigns: Zulu 1879; Egypt 1882; Suakim 1885* [1886]. Cambridge: Ken Trotman, facsimile reprint 1989.

Gillings, Ken. "Inyezane, Gingindlovu, and the Relief of Eshowe." *Military History Journal* 4, no. 4 (1979): 162–66.

Lloyd, W. N. "The Defence of Ekowe" [1881]. Reprint. *Natalia* 5 (December 1975): 15–28.

Mynors, Arthur Clynton Baskerville. *Letters and Diary of the Late Arthur C. B. Mynors, Lieut. 3rd. Batt., 60th Rifles, Who Died at Fort Pearson, Natal the 25th of April, 1879.* Margate, U.K.: H. Keble, 1879.

Norbury, Henry F. *The Naval Brigade in South Africa During the Years 1877–78–79.* London: S. Low, Marston, Searle, and Rivington, 1880.

Tucker, Gordon. "The Diaries of Private George William Tucker No. 2126: 'Our Voyage to South Africa and Doings in Zululand from February 1879 to October 1879.'" *Journal of the Anglo Zulu War Historical Society* 14 (December 2003): 45–64.

Whitehouse, Howard, ed. *"A Widow-Making War": The Life and Death of a British Officer in Zululand, 1879. The Letters and Diaries of Major Warren Wynne, RE.* Nuneaton, U.K.: Paddy Griffith, 1995.

## Campaign in the Northwest (No. 4 Column, No. 5 Column, and Wood's Flying Column)

Booth, Ron. "Anthony Booth VC. Hero of Intombi Drift." *Journal of the Anglo Zulu War Historical Society* 22 (December 2007). www.azwhsmembers.org.

Edgecombe, Ruth. "Appendix: The Battle of Hlobane." In *The Constancy of Change: A History of Hlobane Colliery 1898–1998.* Vryheid, South Africa: Railway, Coal and Iron Company, 1998.

Hope, Robert. *The Zulu War and the 80th Regiment of Foot.* Leek, U.K.: Churnet Valley Books, 1997.

Jones, Huw M. "Why Khambula?" *Soldiers of the Queen* 74 (September 1993): 18–22.

———. "*Blood on the Painted Mountain: Zulu Victory and Defeat, Hlobane and Kambula, 1879*: A Review Article." *Soldiers of the Queen* 84 (March 1996): 20–29.

———. "Hlobane: A New Perspective." *Natalia* 27 (1997): 42–68.

Knight, Ian. "'Captured!' The Strange Story and Thrilling Adventures of Trooper Grandier." *Soldiers of the Queen* 84 (March 1996): 3–9.

Laband, John. "The Battle of Khambula, 29 March 1879: A Re-Examination from the Zulu Perspective." In *Kingdom and Colony at War: Sixteen Studies on the Anglo-Zulu War of 1879*, ed. John Laband and Paul Thompson. Pietermaritzburg: University of Natal Press, 1990.

Lock, Ron. *Blood on the Painted Mountain: Zulu Victory and Defeat, Hlobane and Kambula, 1879.* London: Greenhill Books, 1995.

———. "The Battle of Hlobane: New Evidence and Difficult Conclusions." *Journal of the Anglo Zulu War Historical Society* 6 (December 1999): 41–46.

Manning, Stephen. "Press Confusion over the Battles of Hlobane and Kambula in the London and Devon Newspapers." *Journal of the Anglo Zulu War Historical Society* 19 (June 2006). www.azwhsmembers.org.

———. *Evelyn Wood: Pillar of Empire.* Barnsley, U.K.: Pen and Sword Military, 2007.

McToy, Edward D. *A Brief History of the 13th Regiment (PA.L.L) in South Africa During the Transvaal and Zulu Difficulties.* London: A. H. Swiss, 1880.

Mossop, George. *Running the Gauntlet.* London: T. Nelson, 1937.

Reyburn, Lindsay. "The 1879 Zulu War Diary of RSM F.W. Cheffins." *Journal of the Anglo Zulu War Historical Society* 13 (June 2003): 1–16.

Schermbrucker, Frederick. "Zhlobane and Kambula." *South African Catholic Magazine* 3, nos. 30 and 31 (1893): 335–48; 378–81.

Tomasson, William Hugh. *With the Irregulars in the Transvaal and Zululand.* London: Remington, 1881.

Williams, W. Alister. *Commandant of the Transvaal: The Life and Career of General Sir Hugh Rowlands VC KCB.* Wrexham, Wales: Bridge Books, 2001.

Wood, Evelyn. *From Midshipman to Field Marshal.* 2nd ed. Vol. 2. London: Methuen, 1906.

## 2nd Invasion (2nd Division, South African Field Force, and Wood's Flying Column)

Beckett, Ian W. F. "'Such Generals As They Have Sent Out!' Chelmsford's Major Generals." *Soldiers of the Queen* 84 (March 1996): 16–19.

Clarke, Sonia. "Ulundi: Two Views of the Battle." In *There Will Be an Awful Row at Home About This,* ed. Ian Knight. Shoreham-by-Sea, U.K.: Zulu Study Group, Victorian Military Society, 1987.

Emery, Frank. "At War with the Zulus 1879: The Letters of Lieutenant C.E. Commeline R.E." *Royal Engineers Journal* 96, no. 1 (1982): 33–39.

Harrison, Richard. *Recollections of a Life in the British Army.* London: J. Murray, 1908.

Laband, John. *The Battle of Ulundi.* Pietermaritzburg: Shuter and Shooter, 1988.

———. "'Chopping Wood with a Razor': The Skirmish at eZungeni Mountain and the Unnecessary Death of Lieutenant Frith, 5 June 1879." *Soldiers of the Queen* 74 (September 1993): 5–9.

Malet, T. St. Lo. *Extracts from a Diary in Zululand.* Upper Norwood: Imperial, 1880.

Montague, William Edward. *Campaigning in South Africa: Reminiscences of an Officer in 1879.* Edinburgh: W. Blackwood, 1880.

## Death of Prince Louis Napoleon Bonaparte

Featherstone, Donald. *Captain Carey's Blunder: The Death of the Prince Imperial.* London: Leo Cooper, 1974.

Knight, Ian. *With His Face to the Foe: The Life and Death of Louis Napoleon, the Prince Imperial, Zululand 1879.* Staplehurst, U.K.: Spellmount, 2002.

Laband, John. "'He Fought Like a Lion': An Assessment of Zulu Accounts of the Death of the Prince Imperial of France During the Anglo-Zulu War of 1879." *Journal of the Society for Army Historical Research* 86 (Autumn 1998): 194–201.

——. "An Empress in Zululand: The Pilgrimage in 1880 by the Empress Eugénie to the Site of the Death of Her Son, the Prince Imperial of France." *Natalia* 30 (2000): 45–57.

Rubin, G. R. "The Non-Confirmation of Captain Carey's Court Martial, 1879." *Journal of the Anglo Zulu War Historical Society* 11 (June 2002): 24–31.

## Zulu Peace Overtures

Colenso, John William. "Cetywayo's Overtures of Peace." *The Aborigines' Friend: A Journal of the Transactions of the Aborigines' Protection Society,* new series, 5 (June 1879): 149–54.

Laband, John. "Humbugging the General? King Cetshwayo's Peace Overtures During the Anglo-Zulu War." *Theoria* 67 (October 1986): 1–20.

## War on the Borders

Alexander, Graham. "The Defence of Helpmekaar." *Journal of the Anglo Zulu War Historical Society* 19 (June 2006): www.azwhsmembers.org.

Bonner, Phillip L. *Kings, Commoners, and Concessionaires: The Evolution and Dissolution of the Nineteenth-Century Swazi State.* Cambridge: Cambridge University Press, 1983.

Chadwick, G. A., and E. G. Hobson, eds. *The Zulu War and the Colony of Natal.* Mandini, South Africa: Qualitas, 1979.

Delius, Peter. *The Land Belongs to Us: The Pedi Polity, the Boers, and the British in the Nineteenth Century Transvaal.* Johannesburg: Ravan Press, 1983.

Fannin, Natalie, ed. *The Fannin Papers: Pioneer Days in South Africa.* Durban: Robinson, 1932.

Harries, Patrick. "History, Ethnicity, and the Ingwavuma Land Deal: The Zulu Northern Frontier in the Nineteenth Century." *Journal of Natal and Zulu History* 6 (1983): 1–27.

Jones, Huw M. *The Boiling Cauldron: Utrecht District and the Anglo-Zulu War.* Bisley, U.K.: Shermershill Press, 2006.

Laband, John. "Bulwer, Chelmsford, and the Border Levies: The Dispute over the Defence of Natal 1879." *Natalia* 57 (October 1981): 1–15.

———. "Mbilini, Manyonyoba, and the Phongolo River Frontier: A Neglected Sector of the Anglo-Zulu War of 1879." *Journal of Natal and Zulu History* 10 (1987): 1–31.

Laband, John, and Paul Thompson. *War Comes to Umvoti: The Natal-Zululand Border, 1878–9.* Research Monograph No. 5. Durban: Department of History, University of Natal, 1980.

———, with Sheila Henderson. *The Buffalo Border 1879: The Anglo-Zulu War in Northern Natal.* Research Monograph No. 6. Durban: Department of History, University of Natal, 1983.

Thompson, Paul S. "'The Zulus Are Coming!' The Defence of Pietermaritzburg, 1879." *Journal of Natal and Zulu History* 6 (1983): 28–47.

———. "The Active Defence After Isandlwana: British Raids Across the Buffalo, March–May 1879." In *Kingdom and Colony at War: Sixteen Studies on the Anglo-Zulu War of 1879,* ed. John Laband and Paul Thompson. Pietermaritzburg: University of Natal Press, 1990.

———. "Captain Lucas and the Border Guard: The War on the Lower Thukela, 1879." In *Kingdom and Colony at War: Sixteen Studies on the Anglo-Zulu War of 1879,* ed. John Laband and Paul Thompson. Pietermaritzburg: University of Natal Press, 1990.

———. "The Defence of Durban, 1879." In *Kingdom and Colony at War: Sixteen Studies on the Anglo-Zulu War of 1879,* ed. John Laband and Paul Thompson. Pietermaritzburg: University of Natal Press, 1990.

———. "The Griqua and Mpondo Marches: Natal's Southern Border During the Anglo-Zulu War." In *Kingdom and Colony at War: Sixteen Studies on the Anglo-Zulu War of 1879,* ed. John Laband and Paul Thompson. Pietermaritzburg: University of Natal Press, 1990.

———. "Town and Country and the Zulu Threat, 1878–9: The Natal Government's Arrangements for the Protection of Settlers." In *Kingdom and Colony at War: Sixteen Studies on the Anglo-Zulu War of 1879,* ed. John Laband and Paul Thompson. Pietermaritzburg: University of Natal Press, 1990.

———. "Weenen County and the War, 1879." In *Kingdom and Colony at War: Sixteen Studies on the Anglo-Zulu War of 1879,* ed. John Laband and Paul Thompson. Pietermaritzurg: University of Natal Press, 1990.

Unterhalter, Elaine. "Confronting Imperialism: The People of Nquthu and the Invasion of Zululand." In *The Anglo-Zulu War: New Perspectives*, ed. Andrew Duminy and Charles Ballard. Pietermaritzburg: University of Natal Press and Shuter and Shooter, 1981.

Van Zyl, Deborah. "Boom and Bust: The Economic Consequences of the Anglo-Zulu War." *Journal of Natal and Zulu History* 9 (1986): 26–54.

## Capture of Cetshwayo, the 1st Partition of Zululand, and Pacification

Ballard, Charles. "Sir Garnet Wolseley and John Dunn: The Architects and Agents of the Ulundi Settlement." In *The Anglo-Zulu War: New Perspectives*, ed. Andrew Duminy and Charles Ballard. Pietermaritzburg: University of Natal Press, 1981.

Lehmann, Joseph H. *All Sir Garnet: A Life of Field-Marshal Lord Wolseley.* London: Jonathan Cape, 1964.

Marter, R. J. C. *The Capture of Cetywayo, King of the Zulus.* London: Army and Navy Co-Operative Society, 1880.

Maurice, Frederick, and George Arthur. *The Life of Lord Wolseley.* London: W. Heinemann, 1924.

Maxwell, Leigh. *The Ashanti Ring: Sir Garnet Wolseley's Campaigns 1870–1882.* London: L. Cooper in association with Secker and Warburg, 1985.

[Murray, R. W.] Special Reporter of the "Cape Times." *Cetywayo, from the Battle of Ulundi to the Cape of Good Hope.* Cape Town: Murray and St. Leger, 16 September 1879.

Preston, Adrian W., ed. *Sir Garnet Wolseley's South African Journal, 1879–1880.* Cape Town: A. A. Balkema, 1973.

## IMPACT ON THE ZULU OF THE ANGLO-ZULU WAR

Anon. "Alleged Cruelties in Zululand." *The Aborigines' Friend: A Journal of the Transactions of the Aborigines' Protection Society*, new series, 6 (December 1879): 335–38.

Knight, Ian. "'What Do You Red-Jackets Want in Our Country?' The Zulu Response to the British Invasion of 1879." In *Zulu Identities: Being Zulu Past and Present*, ed. Ben Carton, John Laband, and Jabulani Sithole. New York: Columbia University Press, 2009.

Laband, John."The Cohesion of the Zulu Polity Under the Impact of the Anglo-Zulu War: A Reassessment." *Journal of Natal and Zulu History* 8 (1985): 33–62.

———. "'War Can't Be Made with Kid Gloves': The Impact of the Anglo-Zulu War of 1879 on the Fabric of Zulu Society." *South African Historical Journal* 43 (November 2000): 179–96.

———. "Zulu Civilians During the Rise and Fall of the Zulu Kingdom, c. 1817–1879." In *Daily Lives of Civilians in Wartime Africa from Slavery Days to Rwandan Genocide*, ed. John Laband. Westport, Conn.: Greenwood Press, 2007.

Lieven, Michael. "'Butchering the Brutes All over the Place': Total War and Massacre in Zululand." *History* 84 (October 1999): 614–32.

## BRITISH MILITARY SYSTEM DURING THE ZULULAND CAMPAIGN

## Army Organization, Regulations, Tactical Training, and Intelligence

Best, Brian. "Campaign Life in the British Army During the Zulu War." *Journal of the Anglo Zulu War Historical Society* 1 (1997): 1–5.

Colley, G. Pomeroy. "Army." In *Encyclopaedia Britannica*, 9th ed. Edinburgh: National Library of Scotland, 1875.

Fergusson, Thomas G. *British Military Intelligence, 1870–1914: The Development of a Modern Intelligence Organization*. London: Arms and Armour, 1984.

Hall, D. D. "Squares in the Zulu War." *Military History Journal* 4, no. 5 (1979). http://rapidttp.com/milhist/vol045dh.html.

*Infantry, Field Exercises and Evolutions of*. Pocket edition. London: Her Majesty's Stationery Office, 1877.

Knight, Ian. *British Forces in Zululand*. London: Osprey, 1989.

Langley, D. E. "The Organisation of the British Imperial Army." In *There Will Be an Awful Row at Home About This*, ed. Ian Knight. Shoreham-by-Sea, U.K.: Zulu Study Group, Victorian Military Society, 1987.

Maplesden, Mark. "A Consideration of the Adequacy of British Military Tactics During the Battles of the Anglo-Zulu War." *Journal of the Anglo Zulu War Historical Society* 21 (June 2007). www.azwhsmembers.org.

Monick, S. "Profile of an Army: The Colonial and Imperial Forces of the Zulu War of 1879." *Military History Journal* 4, no. 5 (1879). http://rapidttp.com/milhist/vol045sm.html.

O'Connor, Damian. "Dragoons and Commandos: The Development of Mounted Infantry in Southern Africa 1654–1899." *RUSI Journal* 153, no. 1 (2008): 90–94.

*Regulations: Field Forces, South Africa, 1878.* General Order by Command of Lieutenant-General Lord Chelmsford. Pietermaritzburg: November 1878.

Richards, Walter. *Her Majesty's Army: A Descriptive Account of the Various Regiments Now Comprising the Queen's Forces, from Their First Establishment.* 2 vols. London: J. S. Virtue, n.d. [1887?].

*Rifle and Field Exercises and Musketry Instructions 1877.* Doncaster, U.K.: D. P. and G. Military Publishers, 2005.

## Weapons, Uniforms, and Decorations

*General*

Barnes, R. M. *A History of the Regiments and Uniforms of the British Army.* London: Sphere Books, 1972.

Featherstone, Donald F. *Weapons and Equipment of the Victorian Soldier.* Poole, U.K.: Blandford, 1978.

Wilkinson-Latham, Christopher. *Uniforms and Weapons of the Zulu War.* London: Batsford, 1978.

*Weapons*

Best, Brian M. "The Martini-Henry Rifle." *Journal of the Anglo Zulu War Historical Society* 3 (June 1998): 1–4.

Hall, D. D. "Artillery in the Zulu War, 1879." *Military History Journal* 4, no. 4 (1979): 152–61.

Knight, Ian. "'Old Steady Shots.' The Martini-Henry Rifle, Rates of Fire and Effectiveness in the Anglo-Zulu War." *Journal of the Anglo Zulu War Historical Society* 11 (June 2002): 1–5.

Machanik, Felix. "Firepower and Firearms in the Zulu War of 1879." *Military History Journal* 4, no. 6 (1979). http://rapidttp.com/milhist/vol046fm.html.

Rogers, Hugh C. B. *Weapons of the British Soldier.* London: Sphere Books, 1972.

*Treatise on the Construction and Manufacture of Ordnance in the British Service 1877, Extracts from.* Doncaster, U.K.: D. P. and G. Military Publishers, 2005.

*Uniforms and Accoutrements*

*Dress Regulations for Officers of the British Army 1874.* Doncaster, U.K.: D. P. and G. Military Publishers, 2005.

Turner, Pierre. *Soldiers' Accoutrements of the British Army, 1750–1900.* Marlborough, U.K.: Crowood Press, 2006.

Wilkinson-Latham, Robert, and Christopher Wilkinson-Latham. *Cavalry Uniforms of Britain and the Commonwealth Including Other Mounted Troops.* London: Blandford, 1969.

——. *Infantry Uniforms Including Artillery and Other Supporting Corps of Britain and the Commonwealth.* London: Blandford, 1970.

*Awards, Honors, and Memorials*

Best, Brian. "Zulu War Medals." *Journal of the Anglo Zulu War Historical Society* 3 (June 1998): 35–38.

——. "Zulu War Victoria Cross Holders." *Journal of the Anglo Zulu War Historical Society* 1 (June 1999): 36–48.

——. "Colonial VCs of the Zulu War." *Journal of the Anglo Zulu War Historical Society* 17 (June 2005). www.azwhsmembers.org.

Coghlan, Mark. "The Last Casualty of the Anglo-Zulu War: Damage to the Anglo-Zulu War Memorial, Pietermaritzburg." *Journal of the Anglo Zulu War Historical Society* 22 (December 2007). http://rapidttp.com/milhist/vol101mc.html.

Hope, Robert. "British Battle Honours in the Zulu War." *Journal of the Anglo Zulu War Historical Society* 9 (June 2001): 31–32.

Kinsey, H. W. "The Lonely Graves of Zululand." *Military History Journal* 5, no. 1 (1980). http://rapidttp.com/milhist/vol051hk.html.

Knight. "A Tale of Two Letters." *Journal of the Anglo Zulu War Historical Society* 22 (December 2007). www.azwhsmembers.org.

Michell, F. K. "The Medals of the Zulu War, 11th January to 1st September, 1879." *Military History Journal* 4, no. 4 (1979). http://rapidttp.com/milhist/vol04fm.html.

## Signaling and Telegraph

Mullineaux, David. "Signalling in the Anglo-Zulu War, 1879. Part 1." *Journal of the Anglo Zulu War Historical Society* 14 (December 2004): 15–28.

——. "Signalling in the Anglo-Zulu War, 1879. Part 2." *Journal of the Anglo Zulu War Historical Society* 16 (December 2004): 14–25.

————. "The Natal Colonial Telegraph." *Journal of the Anglo Zulu War Historical Society* 17 (June 2005). www.azwhsmembers.org.

## Transport and Supply

Burman, Jose. *Towards the Far Horizon: The Story of the Ox-Wagon in South Africa.* Cape Town: Human and Rousseau, 1988.

Hall, H. I. "With Assegai and Rifle: Reminiscences of a Transport Conductor in the Zulu War." *Military History Journal* 4, no. 5 (1979): Appendix 8.

His Excellency the Lieutenant-General Commanding [Lord Chelmsford]. *Special Instructions Regarding the Management of Ox Transport on the Line of March, and for Conducting the Line of March When Troops March with Ox Wagon Transport, and for Forming Wagon Laagers.* Durban: Mercury Press, n.d. [1879].

Kemmis, William. *Treatise on Military Carriages and Other Manufactures of the Royal Carriage Dept. 1876.* Doncaster, U.K.: D. P. and G. Military Publishers, 2005.

Mathews, Jeff. "Lord Chelmsford and the Problems of Transport and Supply During the Anglo-Zulu War of 1879." Master's thesis, University of Natal, 1979.

## British and Colonial Fortifications

Kinsey, H. W. "Fort Amiel." *Military History Journal* 3, no. 2 (1974). http://rapidttp.com/milhist/vol032hk.html.

Knight, Ian, and Adam Hook. *British Fortifications in Zululand.* London: Osprey Fortress, 2005.

Laband, John. "British Fieldworks of the Zulu Campaign of 1879, with Special Reference to Fort Eshowe." *Military History Journal* 6, no. 1 (1983): 1–5.

Molyneux, William Charles Francis. "Notes on Hasty Defences as Practised in South Africa." *Journal of the Royal United Service Institution* 24 (1881): 806–14.

Plé, J. *Les Laagers dans La Guerre des Zoulous.* Paris: Librairie Militaire de J. Dumaine, 1882.

Portlock, J. E., and Charles Nugent. "Fortification." In *The Encyclopaedia Britannica*, 9th ed. Edinburgh: National Library of Scotland, 1879.

Tylden, Geoffrey. "The Waggon Laager." *Journal of the Society for Army Historical Research* 41, no. 168 (1963): 200–205.

## COLONIAL DEFENSE

### General Accounts

Castle, Ian, and Raffaele Ruggeri. *Zulu War: Volunteers, Irregulars, and Auxiliaries.* London: Osprey Men-at-Arms, 2003.
Paterson, Hamish. "The Military Organisation of the Colony of Natal, 1881–1910." Master's thesis, University of Natal, 1985.

### Imperial Garrison

Crossley, R. G. "The Imperial Garrison of Natal." *Military History Journal* 2, no. 5 (1973). http://rapidttp.com/milhist/vol025rc.html.
Dominy, Graham. "Women and the Garrison in Colonial Pietermaritzburg: Aspects and Ambiguities of the Domestic Life of the Military." *Journal of Natal and Zulu History* 13 (1990–1991): 33–50.
——. "'An Emblem of Peace and Security': The Construction of Fort Napier and Its Impact on Pietermaritzburg, 1843–1848." *Natal Museum Journal of the Humanities* 4 (October 1992): 89–106.
——. "The Imperial Garrison in Natal with Special Reference to Fort Napier 1843–1914: Its Social, Cultural, and Economic Impact." Doctoral thesis, University of London, 1995.

### Colonial Volunteers and Police

Coghlan, Mark. *Pro Patria: Another 50 Natal Carbineer Years 1945 to 1995.* Pietermaritzburg: Natal Carbineers Trust, 2000.
Goetzsche, Eric. *"Rough but Ready": An Official History of the Natal Mounted Rifles and Its Antecedent and Associated Units.* Durban: Natal Mounted Rifles, 1973.
Holt, H. P. *The Mounted Police of Natal.* London: J. Murray, 1913.
Hurst, Godfrey Thomas. *Short History of the Volunteer Regiments of Natal and East Griqualand: Past and Present.* Durban: Knox, 1945.
Stalker, John. *The Natal Carbineers.* Pietermaritzburg: P. Davis, 1912.

### African Levies

Bourquin, S. B. "The N.N.C. and Associated Units During the Zulu War of 1879." In *The Zulu War and the Colony of Natal*, ed. G. A. Chadwick and E. G. Hobson. Mandini, South Africa: Qualitas, 1979.

Laband, John, and Paul Thompson. "African Levies in Zululand, 1838–1906." In *Soldiers and Settlers in Africa 1850–1918*, ed. Stephen M. Miller. Leiden: Brill, 2009.

Machin, Ingrid. "The Levying of Forced African Labour and Military Service by the Colonial State of Natal." Doctoral thesis, University of Natal, 1996.

Mitchell, F. K. "Troop Sergeant Major Simeon Kambula, DCM Natal Native Horse." *Military History Journal* 7, no. 6 (1988). http://rapidttp.com/milhist/vol076fm.html.

Thompson, Paul. *Black Soldiers of the Queen: The Natal Native Contingent in the Anglo-Zulu War*. Tuscaloosa: Alabama University Press, 2006.

Watkins, O. "They Fought for the Great White Queen, Edendale." In *The Zulu War and the Colony of Natal*, ed. G. A. Chadwick and E. G. Hobson. Mandini, South Africa: Qualitas, 1979.

## BRITISH MEDICAL CARE AND CASUALTIES IN THE ANGLO-ZULU WAR

Best, Brian, and Katie Stossel. *Sister Janet: Nurse and Heroine of the Anglo-Zulu War 1879*. Barnsley, U.K.: Pen and Sword, 2006.

Blair Brown, D. "Surgical Notes on the Zulu War." *Lancet* (5 July 1879): 5–7.

Greaves, Adrian, comp. "Medical Matters: Observations from *The Lancet* During 1879." *Journal of the Anglo Zulu War Historical Society* 6 (December 1999): 23–25.

———. "Zulu War Nurse: Sister Janet Wells." *Journal of the Anglo Zulu War Historical Society* 17 (June 2005). www.azwhsmembers.org.

Greaves, Adrian, and Alan Spicer. "Disease and Illness Prevalent During the Anglo-Zulu War." *Journal of the Anglo Zulu War Historical Society* 2 (December 1998). www.azwhsmembers.org.

Stevenson, Lee. *The Rorke's Drift Doctor: James Henry Reynolds and the Defence of Rorke's Drift*. Brighton: Lee Stevenson, 2001.

Sutherland, Duke of. *Report of the Stafford House South African Aid Committee: Zulu War, 1879*. London: Spottiswoode, 1880.

Young, John. *They Fell Like Stones: Battles and Casualties of the Zulu War, 1879*. London: Greenhill Books, 1991.

## PARTITION, CIVIL WAR, AND REBELLION
## IN ZULULAND, 1879–1888

### General Accounts

Colenso, John William, and Harriette Emily Colenso. *Digest of Zulu Affairs Compiled by Bishop Colenso and Continued After His Death by His Daughter Harriette Emily Colenso.* Series no. 1 (December 1878–April 1881); series no. 2 (October 1881–June 1883); series no. 3 (1884); series no. 5 (November–June 1887); series 6–9 (1887–1888). Bishopstowe, Natal: privately printed, 1878–1888.

Davenport, T. R. H. "The Fragmentation of Zululand 1879–1918." *Reality* 11, no. 5 (1979): 13–15.

Guy, Jeff. "The Role of Colonial Officials in the Destruction of the Zulu Kingdom." In *The Anglo-Zulu War: New Perspectives*, ed. Andrew Duminy and Charles Ballard. Pietermaritzburg: University of Natal Press, 1981.

——. *The Destruction of the Zulu Kingdom: The Civil War in Zululand, 1879–1884.* Pietermaritzburg: University of Natal Press, 1998.

——. *View Across the River: Harriette Colenso and the Zulu Struggle Against Imperialism.* Oxford: James Currey, 2001.

Haggard, H. Rider. *Cetywayo and His White Neighbours; or, Remarks on Recent Events in Zululand, Natal, and the Transvaal.* London: Trübner, 1888.

Intelligence Branch of the Quartermaster-General's Department, Horse Guards, War Office. *Précis of Information Concerning Zululand. Corrected to December, 1894.* London: Her Majesty's Stationery Office, 1895.

Laband, John. "British Boundary Adjustments and the uSuthu-Mandlakazi Conflict in Zululand, 1879–1904." *South African Historical Journal* 30 (May 1994): 33–60.

——. *The Atlas of the Later Zulu Wars 1883–1888.* Pietermaritzburg: University of Natal Press, 2002.

Laband, John, and Paul Thompson. "The Reduction of Zululand, 1878–1904." In *Natal and Zululand from Earliest Times to 1910: A New History*, ed. Andrew Duminy and Bill Guest. Pietermaritzburg: University of Natal Press and Shuter and Shooter, 1989.

Nicholls, Brenda M. "The Colenso Endeavour in Its Context, 1887–1897." Doctoral thesis, University of Natal, 1997.

Van Zyl, Mathys Christoffel. "Die Uitbreiding van Britse Gesag oor die Natalse Noordgrensgebiede 1879–1897" [The Expansion of British Rule over the Northern Border Districts of Natal 1879–1897]. *Archives Year Book for South African History*, 1966 (1). Cape Town: Publications Branch of the Office of the Director of Archives, 1966.

## 3rd Zulu Civil War, the New Republic, and British Annexation

Campbell, W. Y. *With Cetywayo in the Inkandhla and the Present State of the Zulu Question.* Durban: P. Davis, 1883.

Colenso, Frances E. *The Ruin of Zululand: An Account of British Doings in Zululand Since the Invasion of 1879.* 2 vols. London: W. Ridgway, 1884–1885.

Dixie, Florence. *In the Land of Misfortune.* London: R. Bentley, 1882.

Dominy, Graham. "The New Republicans: A Centennial Reappraisal of the 'Nieuwe Republiek' (1884–1888)." *Natalia* 14 (December 1984): 87–97.

———. "In the Aftermath of the Anglo-Zulu War: The Battle of Etshaneni 5 June 1884." *Soldiers of the Queen* 74 (September 1993): 25–32.

Montgomery, A. N. *Cetywayo, Natal, Zululand.* n.p.: August 1882.

O'Connor, Damian. "Who Killed King Cetshwayo? A Case Study of Ethical Foreign Policy." *Journal of the Anglo Zulu War Historical Society* 19 (June 2006). www.azwhsmembers.org.

Pridmore, Julie. "The Diary of Henry Francis Fynn, Junior, 1883." Master's thesis, University of Natal, 1987.

Webb, Colin de B. "Great Britain and the Zulu People, 1879–1887." In *African Societies in Southern Africa: Historical Studies*, ed. L. M. Thompson. London: Heinemann, 1969.

## uSuthu Rebellion

Colenso, Harriette Emily. *The Zulu Impeachment of British Officials 1887–8 Confirmed by Official Records in 1892.* London: P. S. King, 1892.

———. *Mr. Commissioner Osborn as One Cause of the Confusion in Zulu Affairs.* London: P. S. King, 1892.

———. *Cases of 6 Usutu (Other than the Exiles at St Helena) Punished for Having Taken Part in the Disturbances of 1888.* London: Arthur Bonner, 1893.

Escombe, Harry, and Frank Campbell Dumat. *A Remonstrance on Behalf of the Zulu Chiefs 1889.* London: P. S. King, 1889.

Laband, John. "The Battle of Ivuna (or Ndunu Hill)." *Natalia* 10 (1980): 16–22.

———. "The Establishment of the Zululand Administration in 1887: A Study of the Criteria Behind the Selection of British Colonial Officials." *Journal of Natal and Zulu History* 4 (1981): 62–73.

Nicholls, Brenda M. "Zululand 1887–1889: The Court of the Special Commissioners for Zululand and the Rule of Law." *Journal of Natal and Zulu History* 15 (1994/1995): 41–63.

Van Wyk, Johannes. *Dinuzulu en die Usutu-Opstand van 1888* [Dinuzulu and the Usutu Rebellion of 1888]. Pretoria: Staatsdrukker, 1983.

Van Zyl, Mathys Christoffel. "Dinuzulu se Vlug na did Suid-Afrikaanse Republiek in 1888" [Dinuzulu's Flight to the South African Republic in 1888]. *Communication of the University of South Africa, C30.* Pretoria: UNISA, 1961.

## CONSEQUENCES OF THE ZULU
## WARS FOR THE ZULU PEOPLE

Braatvedt, H. P. *Roaming Zululand with a Native Commissioner.* Pietermaritzburg: Shuter and Shooter, 1949.

Carton, Benedict. *Blood from Your Children: The Colonial Origins of Generational Conflict in South Africa.* Charlottesville: University Press of Virginia, 2000.

Cloete, D. "From Warriors to Wage Slaves: The Fate of the Zulu People Since 1879." *Reality* 11, no. 1 (1979): 20–23.

Cope, Nicholas. *To Bind the Nation: Solomon kaDinuzulu and Zulu Nationalism 1913–1933.* Pietermaritzburg: University of Natal Press, 1993.

Guy, Jeff. "The Destruction and Reconstruction of Zulu Society." In *Industrialization and Social Change in South Africa: African Class Formation, Culture, and Consciousness 1870–1930*, ed. Shula Marks and Richard Rathbone. London: Longman, 1982.

Plant, Robert. *The Zulu in Three Tenses: Being a Forecast of the Zulu's Future in the Light of His Past and Present.* Pietermaritzburg: P. Davis, 1905.

# About the Author

John Laband is a graduate of Sidney Sussex College, University of Cambridge, in England, and of the University of Natal in South Africa. He is currently a professor of history at Wilfrid Laurier University, Waterloo, Ontario, Canada, and an associate of the Laurier Centre for Military, Strategic and Disarmament Studies. His books include *Kingdom in Crisis: The Zulu Response to the British Invasion of 1879* (1992 and 2007); *Lord Chelmsford's Zululand Campaign 1878–1879* (1994); and *Rope of Sand: The Rise and Fall of the Zulu Kingdom in the Nineteenth Century* (1995); with Ian Knight, *The War Correspondents: The Anglo-Zulu War* (1996); with Paul Thompson, *The Illustrated Guide to the Anglo-Zulu War* (2000); *The Atlas of the Later Zulu Wars 1883–1888* (2001); and *The Transvaal Rebellion: The First Anglo-Boer War 1880–1881* (2005). He is the editor of *Daily Lives of Civilians in Wartime Africa from Slavery Days to Rwandan Genocide* (2007) and co-editor of *Zulu Identities: Being Zulu, Past and Present* (2009).